The Dynamics of Christian Mission

of

History through a Missiological Perspective

Also by Paul E. Pierson:

A Younger Church in Search of Maturity:
Presbyterianism in Brazil, 1910-1959

Themes from Acts

Emerging Streams of Church and Mission

The Good News of the Kingdom (co-editor)

The Dynamics of Christian Mission

of

Christian Mission

History through a
Missiological Perspective

PAUL E. PIERSON

2009

Published by

©2009 WILLIAM CAREY INTERNATIONAL UNIVERSITY PRESS
1539 E. Howard St.
Pasadena, CA 91104
(626) 398-2106
wciupress_orders@wciu.edu

Printed in the United States of America

Pierson, Paul E.
The Dynamics of Christian Mission: History through a Missiological Perspective / Paul E. Pierson.

ISBN: 978-0-86585-006-4

Library of Congress Control Number: 2008930382

This book is composed of edited transcriptions from lectures and study materials prepared by Paul E. Pierson, Ph.D., at Fuller Theological Seminary, School of World Mission, 1990.

This book is for Rosemary,
with profound gratitude
for fifty-eight years of blessing.

Contents

The "Great Centuries"

The New Era

The Dynamics of Christian Mission

The material in this book is based on a course I taught for over twenty-five years at the School of World Mission (now the School of Intercultural Studies) at Fuller Theological Seminary. It is a comprehensive history neither of the Church nor of the missionary movement.

Traditional "church history" examines the development of the institution we call "the Church." It also seeks to understand the Church's theological struggles and divisions. Early church history focuses on the Middle East and North Africa. Church historians then typically turn almost all of their attention to the advance of the Church in western Europe and the United States. Church historians routinely ignore the extraordinary growth of the Church in Asia, Africa, and Latin America during the last two centuries, and the movements that brought such growth.

However, the questions we ask of the historical data on the Church will largely determine what we learn from our study. We need to ask different questions than have been asked previously as we look back over two thousand years of Christianity, beginning with the apostolic age. This book, then, will study the history of the Church, the People of God, from a missiological perspective; that is, it will seek to discover the dynamics of missionary movements. What motivated those unique men and women who took the Good News of Jesus Christ across geographical and cultural barriers, usually at great risk? What were some of the obstacles they faced? What kinds of movements gave birth to mission? What structures were used as they engaged in mission? What were the characteristics of the mission movements' leaders? How did these leaders interact within their own churches and societies?

We will find that in general, mission has been the result of personal and/or corporate renewal, and that such mission movements always appear to have arisen on the periphery of the broader Church. Those who responded to the missionary call have always been a minority, often perceived with disdain or rejection by their societies and even their churches. Yet they persevered and, despite their apparent failures, God did "exceedingly abundantly" above all they had hoped. Often, like their Lord, these missionaries were grains of wheat that fell into the ground and died in order that fruit could come later. Among the leaders of Christian missionary movements throughout history, we will find men and women who enjoyed a profound life with God. Moreover, as they moved deeper in their life with God, they began to feel His heartbeat for the world. As in Isaiah 6:1–8, they overheard the voice of God. They were then able to communicate their vision to others.

Thus, the purpose of this work is as follows:

> To study church history in a way that will encourage you to appreciate the importance of the dynamic principles underlying the expansion of the Christian movement.

To help you recognize the dynamic principles involved in the past, current, and future expansion of the Christian faith.

To challenge you to apply these underlying principles to present strategies of mission, assuming these principles are transferable.

To challenge you in your commitment to God's purposes for our world by exposing you to many people who have served the will of God in their generation, and by reminding you of God's desire to use their examples in your own life. (See Hebrews 13:7–8.)

As I have studied this material over the years, a number of theses have jumped out at me. Not all of them fit every movement we will examine. However, they provide a grid, or tools of analysis, that I believe will be helpful to you.

Movements of renewal and mission always seem to arise on the periphery of the churchly structures. This is not to denigrate those structures; they are often helpful and even essential. Nevertheless, this thesis does remind us to be always open to the surprises of the Holy Spirit, who has worked through unexpected people in unexpected ways so often throughout history.

Typically, two kinds of structures have been equally important in the history of the Church.

The first is the local church congregation and a network of such groups. Ralph Winter uses a broader term, "modality," which includes everything from families to cities. I focus on "congregational structures." These structures are local and inclusive of fervent as well as nominal believers, youth and the elderly, new Christians, and mature disciples.

The other structure, equally important, is called a "sodality" by Winter, who includes both military forces as well as private enterprises in his definition. Within that category I focus on "mission structures." They are small, mobile, focused groups of men and/or women who know that God has called them to a specific missionary task in a different place or culture. It might be a group of InterVarsity Christian Fellowship workers on a university campus, or a team going to an unreached people on another continent. Obviously, there is a great variety of form in the basic mission structure.

My thesis is that both congregational structures and mission structures are essential to the completion of the mission of the Church to the end of history, and that both are equally the Church, the People of God. (I reject the term "parachurch" to describe mission structures, because this implies that such structures are something less than the Church.)

A key leader has triggered most mission movements. This leader has typically experienced a profound life with God, felt God's heartbeat for the world, and been able to communicate his or her vision to others. New methods in selecting and training leadership have often been a characteristic of renewal and mission movements. These new methods have recognized the gifts of all believers and have moved from elitist, institutionalized modes to a more grassroots approach. This has made it possible to recruit and train a much greater number of leaders, which is necessary for the growth of movements. This grassroots approach has also produced evangelists and pastors having more in common with the people to whom they minister.

Mission has normally come out of renewal. As men and women go deeper in their life with God and receive a new touch of His grace, they are motivated to follow the Lord in radical obedience.

Movements of renewal and mission have often involved theological breakthroughs: a discovery or rediscovery of a previously unrealized or forgotten aspect of biblical faith. The first example comes in Acts 15, when the Spirit led the infant Church to realize that Gentiles were saved by faith and heart obedience alone, without first becoming Jews and accepting circumcision and the law. A second example, seen often in renewal movements, is the recognition that every believer has unique gifts of the Spirit and that these gifts are for use in ministry.

The historical context of mission movements is important. The mission does not change, but the context in which God calls us to carry out our mission changes constantly. This opens up new and creative possibilities for sharing the Gospel. One example is the way in which the Koine Greek language and the Pax Romana aided the early Church as it evangelized the Greco-Roman world. A second example is the way the fall of Communism in 1989 has facilitated the spread of the Good News in much of Eastern Europe, Russia, and the post-Soviet states.

New, more contextualized forms of spirituality are often a characteristic of the movements we will study. Small, face-to-face groups in which believers encourage each other to deeper faith and discipleship have been characteristic of the movements we will study. Such groups have existed together with corporate worship.

Finally, the distribution of information has often been important. News of new initiatives in mission or renewal has often stimulated similar movements in other places. The interaction between the Great Awakening in early eighteenth century North America and the evangelical revivals in England is an example. The influence of William Carey on the students in the Haystack Prayer Meeting is another.

There can be no doubt that we are living in the most widespread and creative period in the history of Christian mission. A greater number of men and women of more races, cultures, and nationalities are now communicating the Good News of Jesus than ever before. Certainly, defeats and failures will come. Despite these, the mission of Jesus Christ will continue through the power of the Holy Spirit until every knee bows and every tongue confesses that he is Lord, to the glory of God the Father!

My greatest wish is that as you study this material, you will be motivated to discover how and where God is calling you to participate in his mission today. I believe this is the greatest privilege of the Christian life.

~Paul E. Pierson

Chapter One

Introduction

Devotional

> In the fifteenth year of the reign of Tiberius Caesar—when Pontius Pilate was governor of Judea, Herod tetrarch of Galilee, his brother Philip tetrarch of Iturea and Traconitis, and Lysanias tetrarch of Abilene—during the high priesthood of Annas and Caiaphas, the word of God came to John son of Zechariah in the desert. He went into all the country around the Jordan, preaching a baptism of repentance for the forgiveness of sins. (Luke 3:1–2 NIV.)

Why does Luke go into so much historical detail (Caesar, Pilate, Herod, Annas, Caiaphas) when describing the beginning of the ministry of John the Baptist and our Lord Jesus Christ? I think the reason is a simple. Luke is the primary historian of the New Testament. His use of detail is one way of showing that God does not work in a vacuum. God comes to us in the midst of our own real, human lives, in specific historical contexts. It is His will to save us and to call out a people for himself to serve him, not in some vaguely spiritual world somewhere, but in the real-life situations in which we live.

Is God interested in the real world? Or is he interested in some imaginary, make-believe spiritual world? How we answer that question will have a powerful effect on us. If we believe God is only interested in some kind of make-believe, spiritual, churchy world, that is where we will spend our lives and ministries. But then we will often fail to touch the real world that Jesus Christ came to save.

If we do not learn anything else in this course, I hope we will discover that God calls his people to serve in real historical contexts that change all the time, in places where people are hurting in every way—spiritually, psychologically, physically. Therefore, Luke's words are a reminder to us that God is not interested in a make-believe world or an imaginary universe. God sent his son to a very specific world in first century Palestine, where an emperor who claimed divine power was on the throne, a despotic and bumbling governor was ruling, and an immoral, brutal tetrarch was seeking power. Even the religious leaders, Annas and Caiaphas, were more concerned with protecting their own positions of influence than they were in being God's people.

That is the kind of world to which God calls us also. So with that, let us pray.

> Lord, we thank you that you have called us to know you, to serve you, and to love you in the world in which we live, and not in some other world, real or imaginary. We pray that as we study and learn together and discuss new questions during these weeks, you will stretch us and enlarge our perspective on this world in which we live. Help us to discern how you are working today in ways we have not seen and, above all, deepen our commitment and strengthen our obedience to your will in this world. We ask this in Christ's name. Amen.

Composition of the Course

In this course, we will not cover two thousand years of mission history exhaustively. We will examine significant movements that we believe illustrate dynamics and factors that teach us more about how God may be working today As we look at history we will raise certain questions and encourage you to form the lifelong habit of doing the same. For example, ask, "Why did the Church or the Gospel move into one particular people and territory, but not another?" "What were the factors involved?" "What people groups were not reached?" Were they resistant or simply bypassed?" In other words, we want you to begin to ask the missiological questions of church history.

Why Study History?

Many people have a bad image of the study of history and consider it boring. At the beginning of my academic career, I was interested in chemistry, physics, and math; I went to the University of California and graduated as a chemical engineer. I did not think that history and the social sciences were very practical. Then God turned my life in another direction. I studied theology and enjoyed church history. Nevertheless, I still did not plan to go further in that field. Then I went to Brazil. After some years on the Brazil-Bolivian border as a church-planting missionary, I was asked to teach church history in a seminary. So on my first study leave, I entered a doctoral program in church history at Princeton.

Now I have come to believe that history teaches us lessons and brings us perspectives that we cannot get in any other way.

Henry Ford, one of the early automobile manufacturers in the United States, was a very pragmatic, practical person. He asserted, "History is bunk." On the other hand, Santana, a Harvard philosopher, said, "He who does not learn from the errors of history is condemned to repeat them." But there is more to the study of history than simply learning to avoid its errors. There is much more.

Identity

Our study of history helps us understand our identity—who we are, how we understand the Gospel, how we read the Scriptures. History teaches us that we are spiritual descendents of Israel. We are children of the prophets and the New Testament Church. Whether we recognize it or not, we are spiritual children of the medieval church, the Protestant Reformation, and the evangelical awakenings of the 17th and 18th centuries. In addition we are sons and daughters of our various denominational traditions and the movements that brought them to birth. So we are all children of various movements. The study of our roots helps us discover that before we are Presbyterians, Anglicans, Baptists, Pentecostals, or Methodists, we are sons and daughters of Augustine, Luther, Calvin, and Wesley. Whether we realize it or not, the thought and action of those men and many others have influenced our understanding of what it means to be a follower of Jesus Christ. Furthermore, the movements that gave birth to modern Protestant missions, with their strengths and weaknesses, have influenced us profoundly. Their understanding of the Christian Faith has powerfully shaped our own understanding of the Gospel and our mission.

Therefore, the study of history is critical. For example, what did your particular movement react against? Almost all of us are the fruit of a movement that reacted against something. I am a Presbyterian, and that Reformed tradition has made a great contribution to the world church. Sixteenth century Calvinism reacted against a corrupt medieval church with its excessive credulity and superstition about miracles and healings. Its strong focus on Scripture led to an insistence that pastors be trained in universities. Thus Calvinism has made a great contribution to education. However one result is that often Christians in that tradition have not been very open to the unusual work, the surprises, of the Holy Spirit. A second result has been suspicion of grassroots movements led by men and women with little formal education.

From another perspective, we look at our Pentecostal brothers and sisters. Their movement was born in 1906, primarily in the United States, and soon spread around the world. Because the Pentecostal movement enjoyed a rediscovery of the power and activity of the Holy Spirit, often expressed in an exaggerated manner, the older 'respectable,' mainline churches rejected and criticized it. So in reaction against the disdain by those with higher education and because the movement grew especially among the poor and uneducated (in the formal sense), early Pentecostalism often rejected formal education for its leaders. That tendency has now been reversed by a number of fine institutions and scholars, including a number at Fuller.

Calvinism and Pentecostalism are only two illustrations of the fact that most movements began in an attempt to recover forgotten or neglected biblical values in reaction to some distortion or failure of the Church in its time. But we can never simply live in reaction. We need to discover the positive values that motivated our movements. Such discoveries will help us rediscover who we are, and can become a trigger to renewal.

For example, the early Methodist movement arose primarily among the poor. Among its greatest values were the advocacy of the ministry of laymen and women, and the fact that they went to the streets and fields where they communicated the Good News to people who were alienated from the Church. The formation of 'classes' for discipleship was another essential element. Could the recognition of these early strengths become a path to renewal for the Methodist Church today?

Perspective

History gives us perspective. We want to look at the current activity of God in the Church and the world in the light of His overall activity throughout history. It is too easy to be limited to our own particular church or our ministry, and think they are the only things that are important. However, as we examine history, we see how God has been working in many places, peoples, and church traditions for two thousand years. This gives us a broader perspective on what He is doing today. It may give us a much greater vision for our own

ministry. It will certainly help us avoid becoming narrow and parochial in our outlook.

The Old Testament prophets constantly called on the people to "remember." It is one of the great biblical words. What were they asking Israel to remember? Usually, they were referring to the Exodus, when God had delivered them from Egypt and done an apparently impossible thing. Later prophets were referring to the restoration from Exile. We Christians working in the twentieth century are also called to remember the great things that God has done in the past, through our own traditions and many others. Remembering gives us perspective on the past, confidence in the present, and hope for the future. The same God who worked in the Old Testament is working with, in, and around us today.

Discernment

At times we feel overwhelmed with problems, change, and apparent chaos. But when we look at history we see how God has often worked in the midst of great difficulties among the most seemingly resistant people. Today there is greater movement of people than ever before. It is said that in the last twenty-five years over 450 million people have flocked to the cities of the world. There are more refugees, driven from their traditional homes, than ever before. Many see such movements as threats because we have grown up with a small town or suburban model of the Church in a relatively stable society. We realize that these new movements will require new forms of the Church. History shows us the need to be open to new methods of communicating the Gospel, structuring the Church, and selecting and preparing leadership. In North America our traditional churches are usually weak in the great urban centers. But in some cities of the world the opposite is the case. That is probably true in Singapore, Seoul, and Lagos. However, in most cases churches there look quite different from traditional American congregations. That is also true of growing churches among minority peoples in New York City.

History shows us that often people are more open to the Gospel when they have been forced from their homes into exile. We do not say that God causes such tragedies but we know He uses even the wrath of men and women to praise Him. Think of Afghanistan. We devoutly hope that order can be restored to that country because of the terrible suffering and heartache that have come on the Afghan people. Yet we recognize that while God does not cause such tragedies, more Afghans have become believers in Jesus Christ during this period of turmoil and exile than ever before. None of us can fully understand this, but we can observe the phenomenon. Migrations, exiles, persecution, urban problems—a study of history will give us perspectives on such issues and help us discover how God may be working in such circumstances.

Tools

History also gives us tools for understanding issues in our own ministry as well as new developments in the mission movement as a whole. For example, many non-Western churches are now establishing their own mission organizations. I believe that is the most important development in mission since Carey sailed to India. But these new mission structures have something to learn from the older Western missions. They certainly should not copy them but there are lessons, positive and negative, to be learned from their experience. There is also a constant stream of new Western mission organizations. Often those from the more established older churches tend to look with disdain at such groups. They usually arise on the periphery and are often led by men or women with little or no official status. But history show that such was the case with many of the older structures that are now widely recognized. The Haystack Prayer Meeting, which led to the formation of the first North American mission board, the Anglican Church Missionary Society, and the China Inland Mission are examples. One was led by students, the second by a group of laymen and clergy, the third by a physician.

The Christian and Missionary Alliance began as two peripheral groups, one seeking renewal, the other focused on mission. They were initiated by A. B. Simpson, a Presbyterian pastor. That evolved into a new denomination with a strong mission program, especially in Southeast Asia. Twenty-five years ago, few had heard of Youth With a Mission (YWAM), with its innovative methods of recruiting and training its personnel. Established by Loren Cunningham of the Assemblies of God, it was interdenominational from the beginning. Today it has workers from many countries and is one of the largest and most creative mission organizations in the world.

Arthur Glasser, formerly the Home Director of the China Inland Mission, (now known as the Overseas Missionary Fellowship) said that in 1934 the president of the mission asserted, "We already have enough mission structures. We don't need any more to get the job done." Three weeks later, William Cameron Townsend started selling Spanish Bibles in Guatemala. However, missionaries already at work on the indigenous languages explained to him that more than half of the people in that nation could not read Spanish. Because of that experience, Wycliffe Bible Translators, which has filled an essential niche in the whole mission movement, was born.

History teaches us never to dismiss too quickly those new strange movements out on the periphery. There the Holy Spirit may be expressing his greatest creativity. History is full of such examples.

Issues

History does not repeat itself, but many of the same issues arise repeatedly. One is the relationship between culture and Christian faith: How should a Christian dress in Kenya? Must he or she put on Western clothing? Does he or she have to accept a European name to be an authentic Christian? The early Scottish and English missionaries seemed to think so. They were wrong.

We need to address the issue of how much of your own culture needs to accompany the communication of the Gospel. We also need to ask how the receptor culture should structure the church. These questions, which come up repeatedly, arose first in Acts 15 in the Council of Jerusalem. Paul and Barnabas had returned, excited because Gentiles were accepting the Gospel. But some in Jerusalem insisted, "If Gentiles accept the Gospel, they must also accept Jewish culture and law in order to be authentic followers of Jesus, who after all, was the Jewish Messiah. They must be circumcised."

That was the first theological crisis in the history of the Church. It was not only a theological question; it was also a missiological issue. Were Gentiles saved by faith, plus the works of the law, or by faith alone? Furthermore, did these Gentile believers have to accept Jewish culture in order to be part of the Church? The Council, led by the Holy Spirit, decided, first of all, that gentiles were saved by faith in Jesus Christ alone. Nor should they be forced to reject their own cultures and become Jewish. They could retain the essential elements of their non-Jewish cultures and still be authentic followers of the Jewish Messiah. However, not everything in pagan Greek culture should be accepted. There were ethical issues. They were to reject the rampant sexual immorality so common in their culture. And in order to avoid needless offense to their Jewish brothers and sisters, gentile believers were to avoid blood and meat offered to idols. The Council of Jerusalem dealt with several issues relevant to us today.

Should Christians in northwest Burma be required to worship in the same way that North American or Korean Christians do in order to be authentic followers of Jesus? Should churches in Sumatra, resulting from the Lutheran mission there, be required to follow the Augsburg Confession, written in sixteenth century Germany, or should they be encouraged to write a new confession dealing with issues in their own culture? These issues arise repeatedly especially as we move into new cultures.

Openness

Finally, a study of history will help us remain open to new things that God is doing. Obviously the creativity of the Holy Spirit has yet been exhausted. To use a colloquial expression, He still has a few things up his sleeve. Our natural, human tendency is to think that we are the last in a chain of innovation. We tend to think that when our organization came into being, that ended the chain. No one would ever say that openly, but we often seem to think so implicitly. However, I believe that until the end of history, we will see new kinds of mission structures emerging, normally on the edge of the older movements, usually led by a person or group without much status. But God constantly does new things through such groups. Similarly, some mission structures need to die a natural death. Maybe it is harder for mission structures and churches to die than it is for new ones to be born.

What Is History?

Reporting of Events

Have you heard the statement "This is a historic event," or "We are making history today"? What does it mean? It is a way of saying the event will be remembered because of its uniqueness or more likely, because it will have far reaching consequences. It also implies that similar events that are not reported are not as important.

Selection of Events

Historians report events they deem important and leave out others they believe are unimportant. Obviously much depends on the point of view of the reporter. For example, if I broke my leg today it would not be reported in the local newspaper. But if the President of the United States broke his leg it would probably be a story on the front pages of every paper in the country. That indicates that most people (except my family) think he is more important than I am.

Therefore, while history is, first of all, the reporting of event, it is much more than that. It also involves a selection of which events to report. By selecting some events and leaving out others, we are already doing some interpretation, indicating our conviction that some events are important while others are not, at least for our purposes.

Interpretation of Events

Interpretation is much more than simply deciding which events to report. It involves the attempt to show the relationship of that event to others, and to a broader network of results.

Why report something that happened to the President? It would be important because the President is at the center of a vast network of influence and power in the world, for good or ill. His illness could have worldwide consequences.

William Carey sailed to India in 1793. He was not the first Western missionary to Asia. Why did the missionary movement grow so rapidly in the nineteenth century and not earlier? Carey's going to India was a powerful factor in launching the Protestant missionary movement. It has grown to become world-wide and we are his heirs. We see Carey as a towering figure in history and try to discover the factors and influences that led him to take that step. And we recognize that most events will be interpreted quite differently, depending on those who observe them. Carey, whom we revere today as the "Father of the Protestant Missionary Movement," was denounced on the floor of the British Parliament! He and his colleagues were called "a nest of consecrated cobblers."

Let me give you another example. Here is an imaginary clipping from the Memphis, Egypt newspaper on June 6, 1300 B.C.: "Flash floods in the Red Sea area yesterday caused a death by drowning of many of Pharaoh's crack armored troops. Pharaoh Rameses II sent the military units to capture the illegal aliens who were attempting to flee. Earlier they had crossed the Palestinian border and taken brick-making jobs in the Goshen area. A palace spokesman denied that the sudden flooding was in any way connected with the recently experienced natural catastrophes in the Nile River Valley."

That is the way a local newspaper might have reported the event.

We would report it quite differently. We believe God was working through these events, natural and supernatural, in a unique way, for a special purpose. We know this to be true because we believe that Scripture is not only an inspired, accurate recording of events, it also gives us an inspired, accurate understanding of their meaning and significance.

There is always more than one way to look at an event. Was the fall of Judah important on the world scene? By the time Judah fell, Jerusalem was a minor city, caught between two great powers in the Mesopotamian and Nile Valleys. When that little group of Jews was restored to Jerusalem under Nehemiah and Ezra, it would not have seemed very important to a secular historian of the day in Cairo or Alexandria.

Would the newspapers or television in Rome have reported a man dying on a cross outside Jerusalem early in the first century, condemned by a Roman court and by the Jewish religious leaders? I doubt it. Would they have reported a man writing some letters from a Roman prison? Yet we know in these unique events, God was working out his redemptive purpose. We discover this when we read the inspired record and the inspired interpretation of these same events in Scripture.

While we have both inspired reporting and interpretation in Scripture, in church history we have neither. What do we have? After the Apostolic age we have oral traditions for the most part, passed down for two or three centuries before being written. We have the writings of both friends and enemies of the Faith. Celsus wrote against the Church in the second century. He said, "Only the author of a farce would send his spirit to be born in Palestine." He was a Roman, and Palestine (especially Nazareth) was the end of the world to him. He could not imagine that a god of any significance would have anything to do with Palestine. If a god was going to do something important he would do it in Rome.

In church history we have letters and records, apologetic and polemical literature. We have a few secular references to the early Christian movement. We also have 'hagiography,' which comes from the Greek word for "saint." These were stories written usually much later than the events they described, about great early church figures. They were normally so embellished with miracles and perfection of character that we suspect some exaggeration. That makes it hard to discern what really happened during the two centuries after the Apostolic age.

From A.D. 325 to 340, we have Eusebius, the first post-apostolic church historian. He was a great admirer of the Emperor Constantine, so he tended to minimize the Emperor's many faults. Nevertheless, Eusebius was a great historian, and gave us the first organized history of the Church in that period. Later, as the Church grew and was established in the Roman Empire, there were many learned men who left written records.

We must remember that until very recently, men did almost all of the writing about the history of the Church. Because men were in control and usually wrote only about men, it is difficult to discover the contributions of women. But we know that beginning in the New Testament period, women played an important role in the Church. At times we can read between the lines and discover more about the role of women. In many cases Christian wives exerted strong influence on their husbands. We also have to realize that whenever there was a controversy, the winning side usually wrote the history. Think about the significance of that. Very often, we cannot really tell what the losing sides believed, because we are seeing them through prejudiced eyes. History is not an exact science, but it is a fascinating one.

Our Church History Is Mostly from a Western Perspective

Most church history has been written from a very ethnocentric perspective until recently. After the first few centuries the focus was on Europe and North America. If an event took place there, it was 'church history.' If it happened in Asia, Africa, or Latin America, it was 'mission history.' Usually that was not a required course. If you studied in a seminary or Bible school overseas, your history courses probably focused mostly on Europe and North America. It is possible that you did not spend much time on the history of your own church and nation, to say nothing of the Church in continents other than your own. For example, I suspect that if you studied in Brazil, you probably did not study very much about the history of the Church in Asia or Africa ex-

cept in the early years of North Africa. And you probably did not study much about denominational groups other than you own, even in your own country. We want to overcome such a narrow, ethnocentric perspective.

A second issue is that most teaching of church history, except that of Latourette, focuses on the development of the institution called "the Church," its struggles and its theological controversies. The study of church history very rarely asks missiological questions of the data. It seldom asks, "Why and where did the Church expand across geographical and cultural barriers? Where did it not expand?" These are the missiological questions, and they are our primary interest.

Recurring Themes: Questions to Ask

The questions we bring to history will largely determine what we learn from our study. The questions we ask of history will determine what we learn from it. Memorizing a few facts for the final exam is not very profitable. However, if you develop the habit of constantly asking questions, the habit will stay with you. It will enhance your learning throughout your life.

Where Is the Church Growing?

It is clear that today the most exciting developments in the growth of the Church are taking place in Asia, Africa, and Latin America, not in Europe or North America. (There are some exciting things happening in Eastern Europe, however.) In 1900, for example, Kenya had a few thousand professing Christians—a tiny percent of the population. Now there are somewhere around eight to ten million professing Christians there, although not all of them are vital in their faith. Some suggest that about sixty-six percent of the population of Kenya profess the Christian faith. That is incredible church growth, and we see similar growth across much of Sub-Saharan Africa.

In China, when Mao Zedong's revolution triumphed in 1949, there were approximately 750 thousand Protestant Christians and three million

Roman Catholics in the nation.. Since then we have seen extraordinary growth among Roman Catholics, and even more among Protestants. It is estimated that there are around fifteen million Catholics today. Among Protestants, the government-sanctioned 'Three Self Church' numbers at least sixteen million and the 'house churches,' some registered, some underground, may count as many as seventy million or more. While our statistics cannot be exact, there is no doubt that the Holy Spirit has worked in an extraordinary manner in China during the last fifty years. And most of that growth came after Western observers believed the Church had disappeared in China! There are also growing 'insider movements' among Muslims who go to the mosque and pray in the name of 'Isa the Messiah,' and movements among Dalits (untouchables) in India, who see Jesus as the God who became one of them. Many of these groups do not look like our traditional churches but they are clearly part of the Body of Christ.

Thus if we define "the Church" not in terms of our Western ecclesiastical structures but as the 'People of God' existing in many forms throughout the world, our understanding of church history will be greatly expanded.

What Are Our Own Biases?

We must recognize that every writer comes to his or her subject with a particular bias, which will largely determine how the events will be reported and interpreted.

Let me give you two examples. You will remember that 1979 was the year of the Iranian revolution, and the taking of the American hostages in Teheran, and the Soviet invasion of Afghanistan. If you were writing that history as a Soviet government official, you would have one point of view. If you were an Iranian student, you would interpret events very differently. Imagine how differently an Afghan tribesman or an American government official would explain the events of that year.

Or think of the Protestant Reformation of the sixteenth century. If you were a secular humanist, you would interpret the movement in terms of the social sciences. If you were a convinced

Protestant, you would evaluate it primarily in theological terms. If you were a pre-Vatican II Roman Catholic, you would see it as a rebellion against the true Church. How would you evaluate it if you were a Muslim, or a scholar in China, to whom Europe was a distant place inhabited by barbarians? China saw itself as the Middle Kingdom, and believed that what happened outside China was unimportant. It is important to see how differently we look at history depending on who we are and where we come from religiously, ideologically, nationally, and culturally.

Every historian writes out of certain convictions. None of us views history from a standpoint of neutrality. It is important that we recognize our own convictions. My first conviction in viewing history is that the biblical narrative and theological doctrines of the Christian faith are true. God is working in history to call out a people to serve Him in history. He sent his son who died on a cross and rose from the dead, who ascended into heaven, and who called out a people to himself. These are the basic contours of the Christian faith.

There is a second basic conviction I believe we all share. It is that the essence of the Church is to be missionary in nature. I believe that the mission to all the people groups on earth is the core of the Church's task. I can still hear the words of one of my own professors, Dr. John MacKay, a Scot and a great missionary to Latin America before he worked in theological education. He often said, "The Church that is not missionary is not truly the Church!" We recognize that, because so often the institutional church has forgotten this, mission movements have arisen on the periphery of the institution. We must insist that mission is at the center of the Church's task. This is basic to our point of view in this course.

Two Assumptions

To conclude, there are two basic assumptions in this course.

First, God is sovereign. We can never explain completely how or why God works in a particular circumstance.

Secondly, this sovereign God chooses to work in concrete, historical situation, not in a vacuum. The study of the contexts in which God has worked in the past can often help us understand more adequately how God wants to work today in our own circumstances.

Some questions will arise as we study. One question will be "What is the definition of 'a Christian'?" At some times, being a Christian has been defined in very simple, creedal terms: "Jesus is Lord" was the first New Testament confession. When you said, "Jesus is Lord, my Lord," you became a part of the group. You were a Christian. At other times, being a Christian has been defined primarily by being a member of a particular ecclesiastical institution called "the church." At times, being a Christian has been defined culturally. If one was a member of a group that called itself "Christian," then he or she was a Christian, whether or not one had much personal knowledge of, or commitment to, the faith.

We will not deal with this question explicitly. However, it is one you will want to keep in mind, because definitions of "Christian" will differ. We might not consider all to be valid. Clovis, the King of the Franks, was baptized in 496 with three thousand of his soldiers. His wife was a Christian. He felt that by becoming a Christian, he would be more acceptable politically, to Rome. So he and his soldiers were baptized. We cannot judge to what extent Clovis and his soldiers were actually Christian in the personal sense of the word. Their understanding of and commitment to the New Testament faith was probably minimal. Nevertheless, that event did open up the opportunity for the Church to teach and nurture the people. It was through such circumstances that most of Europe became Christian.

I hope that as we study and reflect together, we will come to a new appreciation of the many ways God has worked in the last two thousand years to take the Good News of Jesus Christ to the nations. I believe that will stimulate and challenge us as we continue to take part in that same mission.

Chapter Two

Biblical Background:
Expansion in the Apostolic Period

Introduction

It is important that we learn to read the Bible with missiological eyes. We are all normally selective in our use of scripture. We probably have favorite passages from which we preach or teach while leaving out many others. That is not all wrong. But often we are conditioned to see that which we already know as we read Scripture. Recently I discovered something I had never seen before in Romans 16. We think of all the theological meat in that letter. There St. Paul expounds the meaning of the coming of Christ more completely than anywhere else. Then we come to the final chapter. First we find greetings to several people. This does not seem very exciting until we note that many are women, and Paul recognizes the importance of their ministries. But we find a great missionary text in the conclusion of chapter 16. In a few words Paul sums up the purpose of all the great theological doctrines he has been expounding in this letter. Listen to the ascription of praise with which he ends the letter. He stands in awe of all that God is doing.

> Now to him who is able to establish you by my gospel and the proclamation of Jesus Christ, according to the revelation of the mystery hidden for long ages past, but now revealed and made known through the prophetic writings by the command of the eternal God, so that all nations might believe and obey him—to the only wise God be glory forever through Jesus Christ! Amen. (Rom. 16:25–27 NIV)

In the NIV, we read "all nations" in verse 26. However, the Greek reads *panta ta ethne*. The phrase means every cultural, racial, language group. The words "might come to believe" denote evangelism, and "obey" implies discipleship. So we see here God's desire that men and women of every cultural, racial, and language group be evangelized, believe, and begin to live in obedience. Is there any other passage that sums up more powerfully and succinctly God's purpose as expressed in the Bible? Yet very often, we miss it.

Thus as we go back and look at the Bible with missiological eyes, we will see things we have not discovered before. Today we will look primarily at the book of Acts to illustrate how to do so. But first we will look at a few Old and New Testament passages.

The Old Testament through Missiological Eyes

In the Old Testament, the concept that the mission of God must go to all peoples on earth is implied in the Creation story. One God created all peoples. Logically then, He must be concerned about all of his creation. Thus, the first missionary text in the Bible is the creation passage.

We move to the story of the Tower of Babel and the scattering of the nations in Genesis 11. The first step in God's strategy follows the Babel story. God called Abraham (Gen. 12:1–3) and promised that he and Sarai would become parents of a great nation. But that was only to be the means to accomplish God's purpose. The purpose was that through their descendents all the families on earth would be blessed.

The word "blessed" in Hebrew has a much more profound meaning than we give it in English. It meant being incorporated into a family. Jacob was blessed but Esau was not. The word conveyed authority, responsibility, reconciliation, and meant opposition to evil and to satanic darkness. Rescuing people out of evil meant opposing that darkness. Blessing in the Bible is something that unites men and women with God and each other and brings them into a permanent fellowship.

This stands in contrast to the scattering of the nations (Gen. 11:8) and the confounding of the tongues (Gen. 11:9). God's strategy of reconciliation and redemption, began in Genesis 12. "Through you all of the families"—we might say all of the *ethne*, all the people groups; all the racial, cultural, linguistic groups on earth—"will be blessed" through the descendents of Abraham and Sarai.

Therefore, at the very beginning of God's redemptive action in history, we find this great mission text. I was raised in a very fundamentalist Baptist church and heard the story of Abraham from childhood. Yet nobody ever pointed out the reason for the call of Abraham, which was to bless all the families on earth. This is probably the clearest missionary text in the Old Testament.

In the Old Testament, we find outsiders who become part of the People of God and became symbols of God's intention to reach beyond Israel. Rahab, a prostitute, became an ancestress of our Lord. Ruth, a Moabitess, was another. The testimony of a slave girl and an act of God brought Naaman, a Syrian general and conquering imperialist, into the family of faith. These, and other Old Testament stories demonstrate God's concern with all the people groups on earth.

There are several poems or songs of the suffering servant in the book of Isaiah: chapters 42, 49, 50, 52, and 53. Isaiah 53 is the best known. These are certainly the deepest Old Testament portrayals of the coming Messiah. In Isaiah 42:6 and 49:6, God says it is not enough that his servant would restore Israel. He says, "I will keep you and will make you to be a covenant for the people and a light for the Gentiles" (Isa. 42:6 NIV), and "I will also make you a light for the Gentiles, that you may bring my salvation to the ends of the earth" (Isa. 49:6 NIV). The prophecy of the mission of the suffering servant is as important as the prophecy of his death in chapter 53. We have often missed it.

The Son of Man passage in Daniel 7:13 is another verse that we often miss. I am sure you all remember that the favorite term Jesus used in referring to himself was "Son of Man." What did he mean by it?

Psalm 8:4 reads, "What is man that you are mindful of him, the son of man that you visit him?" Obviously, "Son of Man" here is a synonym for "man" or "person." In Ezekiel 2:1, God addressed Ezekiel, "Son of man, stand on your feet." Here, too, "Son of Man" is a synonym for a person.

But read Matthew 26:63. Jesus appeared before the High Priest, who asked, "Are you the Messiah?" Jesus replied, "You will see the Son of Man coming on the clouds of heaven." Both Jesus and the High Priest knew that Jesus' reply was an echo, a paraphrase, of Daniel 7:13, 14 (NIV):

> In my vision at night I looked, and there before me was one like a son of man, coming with the clouds of heaven. He approached the Ancient of Days and was led into his presence. He was given authority, glory and sovereign power; all peoples, nations and men of every language worshiped him. His dominion is an everlasting dominion that will not pass away, and his kingdom is one that will never be destroyed.

We understand why the high priest tore his robes and cried 'blasphemy.' He recognized the dimensions of the claims Jesus was making. We can easily see the missionary implications also.

The New Testament through Missiological Eyes

Now we move to the New Testament. Luke, the primary historian in the New Testament, proclaims, "all flesh shall see the glory of God." As a gentile he was concerned with all humanity, thus mission is at the heart of his understanding of the Gospel. Dr. Glasser gave us a brilliant insight into the words of the risen Christ to the disciples in Luke 24: "Then he opened their minds so they could understand the Scriptures. He told them, 'This is what is written.'" Now I interrupt to ask: what are the essential aspects of the Good News? We will agree that the incarnation, the death, and the resurrection are the central events of the Gospel. The call to repent and believe, and the call to discipleship, are to be our response to these central event. Now listen to the entire passage:

> Then he opened their minds so they could understand the Scriptures. He told them, "This is what is written: The Christ will suffer and rise from the dead on the third day, and repentance and forgiveness of sins will be preached in his name to all nations, beginning at Jerusalem" (Luke 24:45–47 NIV).

The Christ (the incarnation) will suffer (the cross) and rise from the dead on the third day (the resurrection). Here are the three essentials. But there is a fourth. We have the following words, on the same grammatical level with the incarnation, death, and resurrection: "And repentance and forgiveness of sins will be preached in his name to all the *ethne*, beginning at Jerusalem."

Thus, the Good News is not only about the incarnation, the death, and the resurrection of Jesus Christ. An equally essential part of the Good News is that in this fragmented, divided, and hostile world, the message of forgiveness and reconciliation is to be preached to every racial, linguistic, and cultural group on earth.

This says powerfully that we cannot separate mission from the rest of the business of the Church. Mission is what the Church is about; it is fundamental to our identity.

Now we will examine Acts. I was asked to write a little commentary on Acts for lay persons a few years ago. I read a number of commentaries by some fine scholars. However, as far as I could discover, none of them looked at Acts from a missiological perspective. I attempted to do so, and will share some of my insights with you.

First, we will examine Acts 1:6-8. The disciples had walked with Jesus for three years. He had taught them for another forty days after the resurrection, and now He was preparing for the ascension. However, the disciples had not yet understood the scope of His mission. They were still very ethnocentric. Their question, "Lord, are you at this time going to restore the kingdom to Israel at this time," showed that they had not yet understood the universal scope of the Kingdom of God and its inauguration with the coming of Jesus. They still thought of the Kingdom as belonging only to Israel. They had missed the point of Jesus' mission.

Jesus answered the question of time directly. He said, "It is not for you to know the times or dates the Father has set by his own authority."

He replied to their other question by gently pushing it aside. The disciples were looking inward, at themselves and their own people. Jesus turned their attention outward and said, "You will receive power when the Holy Spirit comes on you, and you will be my witnesses." Where? Jerusalem, Judea, Samaria, and to the ends of the earth. It is as though Jesus drew an almost infinite series of concentric circles in the dirt to show the disciples how far the Good News would travel, beginning with their own ministries in Jerusalem. It would go to the ends of the earth. He was telling them, "Instead of focusing inward on what God is going to do for you and your people, begin to focus outward on what God wants to do through you in the world."

We can see how the book of Acts depicts the working out of Jesus' statement to the disciples. First, we will look at it geographically. The narrative in Acts moved from Jerusalem, a Jewish center and provincial capital at one end of the Mediterranean, to Rome, the center of the empire and a gentile city. Rome was the geographical center of the Mediterranean world—the powerful cultural, political, and commercial center of their world. In addition, we know from the book of

Romans that as Paul traveled to Rome, his goal was ultimately to go to Spain. Spain represented, for him, the end of the earth.

In 1971, I began to teach in a small theological seminary in Lisbon, Portugal. My family and I arrived on a Thursday. On Sunday, we went to a little Presbyterian church in the city. Afterward we wandered down to the old lower section of the city, called 'the Baixa,' and came to an elevator built by Eiffel, the same man who built the tower in Paris. We went up four or five levels, went to the observation platform, looked across the city, and saw our first castle. I rushed over to a Portuguese man standing there and asked, "What castle is that?" He said, " The St. George castle." (That indicated the British connection with Portugal dating back to the Crusades.) I said, "When was this built?" He replied, "I don't know."

Nobody seemed to know when it had been built. But I found out the castle had been a fortified point since Phoenicians sailors had arrived a century before Christ. Then the Romans came, then the Visigoths, then the Moors. Finally, the British crusaders came in the thirteenth century and expelled the Moors, and Portugal became Catholic again.

It is interesting to note that to get to Lisbon from the Mediterranean, you sail through the Straits of Gibraltar, then north up the Portuguese coast to the estuary of the Taugus River. A few miles inland, on the estuary, lies the city of Lisbon that grew up around that castle. We know that Phoenician sailors from Palestine had colonized Carthage in North Africa. This tells us that they also sailed outside the Mediterranean, up the European coast, and probably down the African coast.

Thus, I believe that Paul knew there was more world out there beyond the Mediterranean. For him, Spain symbolized not only the end of one world, but also the beginning of another. I doubt if Paul knew how much more world there was, but he knew there was more, and was thinking strategically. I believe we see that kind of thinking in the geographical schematic of Acts.

Secondly, we see how Acts moves from one cultural and linguistic group to another. Thus we see that Acts is primarily the history of the Gospel moving across both cultural and geographical barriers in obedience to Christ.

First we will examine the Pentecost event (Acts 2). It is often called the birthday of the Church. Because of the giving of the Holy Spirit in power, Pentecost was the confirmation of the apostolic message. I believe it was, above all, a missiological event, the reversal of Babel. Where there had been fragmentation, hostility, division, and scattering, God began to bring humankind together.

Pentecost celebrated the first fruits of the harvest, in which part of the earliest harvest was presented to the Lord with thanksgiving, recognizing the promise of the full harvest to come. The three thousand who were converted on that day represented that promise of the infinitely greater harvest to come.

The basic elements in the Pentecost event were these. As the infant church prayed, the Holy Spirit was given in power. Men and women were present from every corner of the Empire, and some from outside its borders. As Peter preached on the mighty act of God in Jesus, they all heard the message in their native languages. Why?

I once heard a seminary professor say there was no need for the miracle in which everyone understood Peter's sermon in his or her own language. Everyone there understood Greek, Aramaic, or both. The Jews of the Diaspora who were present certainly knew Greek. It was probably the first language for most of them. Of course, the Palestinians there understood Aramaic, it was the language of Jesus and the apostles. Some of them must have spoken Greek also. So what was the point of the miracle?

There are at least three fundamental missiological principles we see at Pentecost.

First, God wanted all who were there to hear of his mighty works in their heart language, the language in which they were born. I think you agree with me that the deepest things of life are best communicated in the language you learned at your mother's knee. I am fluent in Portuguese. Before I came back to the States in 1973, I had taught, preached, and functioned in Portuguese for many years. But English, my first language, speaks more deeply to my heart.

That God desires to speak to people in their own language and culture is a basic missiological principle. Pentecost says that God wants to speak to each person in his or her heart language where communication takes place at the deepest level.

Secondly, the whole world was represented symbolically at Pentecost. It is a clear sign to the Church on its birthday that its task is to communicate the Good News of the mighty acts of God in Christ, to every people in their heart language and culture.

Thirdly, Peter proclaimed that Pentecost was the fulfillment of the prophecy of Joel (Joel 2:28–29) in which the Holy Spirit was poured out on all flesh—old, young, men, women, even slaves. I believe this indicates that the gifts of the Spirit are for all believers and that the primary function of those gifts is to equip us to fulfill God's mission. Pentecost, then, is a very powerful missiological event with clear implications for its future direction.

The Process of Growth

Geographical Growth

We can see first that the Gospel was spread from Jerusalem to Rome, and we know that at some point, Spain was in the mind of Paul. We do not know if he got there, but it was certainly in his mind.

Cultural and Racial Growth

But it is important to note that a number of cultural and racial barriers were crossed as the Gospel moved across the Empire. The first people group to become followers of the Messiah were Aramaic-speaking Jews who lived in Judea. The second group consisted of Hellenists, Greek-speaking Jews who had been born and raised in the Diaspora, around the Mediterranean world, outside of Palestine. These Hellenistic Jews were bicultural and would play a crucial role in the

early missionary movement. Among them was Stephen, who began to make the first great theological breakthrough of the early Church. Along with Barnabas he had a great impact on Saul of Tarsus. Could this indicate that a bicultural person is often more open to other cultures and can more easily relate to them?

Those two groups were both reached on the Day of Pentecost. As far as we know, there were no Hellenistic Jews in the original band of disciples, but beginning with the Day of Pentecost, we see rapid growth in believers in both groups.

The third people group to be reached were the Samaritans in chapter 8. There was great hostility between Jews and Samaritans. In 722 B.C., Assyria had conquered Israel, the northern kingdom. Assyria's policy was to mix up its conquered peoples. They took some Israelites and moved them to other areas and brought other conquered people and settled them in northern Palestine. The purpose was to mix the groups religiously and racially and thus eliminate or minimize nationalistic sentiment. So the Jews considered the Samaritans inferior. During the restoration under Nehemiah, the Samaritans attempted to prevent the rebuilding of Jerusalem, adding to the enmity between the two groups.

However, the Samaritans still observed the Law, albeit in a corrupted form. They were circumcised, and they had the same religious orientation as the Jews, but were perceived by the Jews as impure. Thus, for a Jewish believer in Jerusalem, it was not as great a scandal to see a Samaritan come into the kingdom of God as it would be later on when uncircumcised Gentiles entered the Church. Nevertheless, it was still hard to accept Samaritans as believers.

I believe that is why the Holy Spirit was not given before John and Peter went to Samaria. The Holy Spirit had to confirm the entrance of the Samaritans into the new Israel in the presence of the two apostles if the Jerusalem church was to accept them. But we note that it was Philip, a Hellenistic Jewish believer, who evangelized the Samaritans (Acts 8:5). (Could it be that as a bicultural person himself, Philip was more open to other groups?) However, because of the enmity and suspicion between Jews and Samaritans, it was still important for the Holy Spirit to confirm Philip's ministry through the presence of Peter and John.

The Ethiopian represented another barrier, geographical and racial (Acts 8:27–39). Scholars differ on this, but I believe the Ethiopian was a proselyte who had accepted the Jewish faith including circumcision. There were such proselytes all around the Mediterranean world who had done so. If the Ethiopian had not been a proselyte, there certainly would have been a great scandal over the baptism of an uncircumcised person.

Now we come to the conversion of Saul of Tarsus (Acts 9). At first, it appears to be a parenthesis in the story of progression from one people group to another, but it it is an essential part of the story. Saul/Paul will become the primary apostle to the Gentiles. Luke shows the importance of Saul's conversion by recounting it three times.

The first account, in Acts 9, tells of Saul's conversion to Jesus as Messiah and Lord. The second account, in Acts 22, speaks of his conversion to mission to the world. The third account, in Acts 26, focuses specifically on his call to the Gentiles. Read the three accounts and you will see how the mission to the Gentiles becomes the primary focus of his conversion. God called Saul/Paul especially to take the Gospel to the Gentiles.

The development of Saul's thought regarding the Gentiles must have involved a terrible spiritual/theological struggle. Remember, he was a Pharisee. To a Pharisee, even half-hearted Jews were outside the Kingdom. For Pharisees, it was unthinkable that an uncircumcised Gentile who did not observe the law could even begin to approach the Kingdom of God. I believe it was as hard for Saul to recognize that God loved Gentiles and called them into his kingdom as it was for him to accept the crucified carpenter as Messiah. Saul needed a double conversion. What began to change his thinking?

I believe the process began as Saul listened to Stephen's speech. The speech is inconclusive, but very important. Have you ever wondered why Luke devoted three times as much space to Stephen's speech as he did to any of the sermons of Peter or Paul? Remember, Luke had to write down his whole story on a papyrus scroll with limited space. Yet he chose to devote a great deal of space to the speech of Stephen. That indicates that Luke considered it extremely important.

So let us analyze Stephen's speech. He seems to be saying that God is not as limited or predictable as the Jews believed. God was not limited to one place, and by implication, to one people. He works when and where he chooses, according to his grace. Stephen was moving beyond the theology of the Jerusalem church, which still thought of Jesus as the Messiah only for the Jews. In that theology, anyone who wanted to follow Jesus and become a part of the new Israel had to become a Jew first. Stephen was beginning to build a theological bridge from that position to the theology that Paul would espouse. That theology would proclaim that the Kingdom is open to all and that we enter it by faith alone, that God's greatest desire is that all peoples enter that Kingdom. Stephen was beginning to move from an extremely ethnocentric theology to a missionary view of history. Stephen did not get all the way there, but he began to move down that road.

I can imagine Saul, the Jewish Pharisee, was enraged as he listened to Stephen. He knew Stephen was correct in his analysis of Israel's history. However, as he realized where Stephen's speech was heading, Saul could see that it contradicted his pharisaic theology. He must have hated Stephen even more, and resisted Stephen's thought with all his power. Yet he could not forget Stephen's argument. The risen Lord would soon say to him, "It is hard for you to kick against the goads." I believe Saul the Pharisee was kicking against two goads. One was the concept that the crucified carpenter was the Messiah. The other was the idea that God's kingdom was open to Gentiles. The two ideas must have been equally difficult for the Pharisee to accept. Thus, Saul experienced a double conversion, the first, to Jesus as Lord, the second, to the mission to the Gentiles. We cannot say whether the second took place all at once or over a period of time and reflection. Perhaps, after Saul affirmed Jesus as Lord, he began to study the Jewish Scripture again and discover God's concern for all peoples there. He must have reread passages such as Genesis 12:3, Isaiah 42:6 and 49:6, and Daniel 7:13. His ethnocentric theological paradigm changed. That might have taken place when he went into the Arabian Desert for a time of reflection. We do know that when we meet Paul later on, he knows that the Kingdom of God is for all peoples. He becomes the missionary to the Gentiles and shapes his theology around that mission.

Many of our church people, and many of our churches, still need that second conversion. How many Christians have experienced the first conversion—they know that Jesus is Lord and Savior—but have never had the second, the recognition that God cares as much about people in Zambia or Gambia as he does about people in Pasadena, California?

The next great missionary event is the conversion of Cornelius (Acts 10). This is almost a humorous story. Peter had already progressed in his thinking, because he was staying in the house of Simon the tanner, who was ritually unclean by Jewish law. While Peter prayed, he saw a vision repeated three times (Acts 10:10–16). This repetition served to emphasize God's message, "Don't call anything unclean that I have cleansed." Peter understood that God is doing something new, but did not know what it was. He must have wondered what was to happen when he descended from the rooftop and found the men from Cornelius, a Gentile, awaiting him.

Meantime, Cornelius had also had a word from God. There are only two situations in the Bible that I can remember where God worked both sides of the street at the same time. One is the story of Peter and Cornelius. He spoke to both of them to bring them together. The other is the account of Saul and Ananias. Both of these events

have to do with bringing the Gospel to the Gentiles. Isn't that interesting?

When Peter entered the house of Cornelius, he must have been the second most reluctant evangelist in the Bible (Jonah was even more reluctant.) Peter entered the house and said, in effect, "You know, I really shouldn't be here. Why did you send for me?" Cornelius gave him an invitation that no preacher can resist: "Tell us about the Gospel."

As Peter spoke, the Holy Spirit descended on the hearers (Acts 10:44). Peter did not even have a chance to give an altar call. His response was, "What can we do? We must baptize them because the Holy Spirit has clearly called them into His Kingdom."

This was his defense when he returned to Jerusalem. Even though he was the leader of the Church, he knew he would have to defend his action in baptizing a household of uncircumcised Gentiles. He was the evangelist through whom many Jerusalem believers had become followers of Jesus, yet he still had to defend himself for taking such a radical step. With foresight he had taken six witnesses with him to the house of Cornelius and then to Jerusalem. In effect, his defense was "Don't blame me, blame God. God did it." It is really a rather humorous story.

Perhaps the Jerusalem church thought that since Cornelius was a "God-fearer," who worshipped in the synagogue, prayed to the God of Israel, and gave generously, he would be acceptable even though he did not accept the Jewish law completely. Perhaps because he was such an important and good man, the believers in Jerusalem considered him an exception to their understanding that only a circumcised Jew could become an authentic follower of the Jewish Messiah.

However, the next event was even more extraordinary. Beginning in Acts 11:19, Luke related that some of the believers who were scattered after the persecution of Stephen went here and there preaching the Gospel to Jews only. But in Antioch, they preached to Gentiles also, and many were converted. Men, Hellenistic Jews, whose names we do not even know, made this amazing breakthrough. They were what we would call today ordinary laymen. This was only the first example of a major new step in Christian mission led by men and or women whose names are not in the history books. Now, when the Antioch church, the first predominately Gentile church, was born, the focus of Acts shifted to the Gentile world. From there the Gospel was taken across Asia Minor and on to Europe.

The First Specific Missionary Structure

In Acts 13, three theses of this course are illustrated. As the leaders of the Antioch church were praying, the Holy Spirit said "Separate Barnabas and Saul for the task to which I am sending them (Acts 13:2)." The first mission structure of the Church was born in a small meeting of prayer and fasting. The development of a key leader is begun. While the whole Church is indeed called to mission, it needs to carry out its mission through focused, committed groups of people in structures of one kind or another. It has normally happened that way throughout history.

The Special Action of the Holy Spirit

As we read Acts, we note the special activity of the Holy Spirit at breakthrough points. Whenever the Gospel spreads from one people group to another or from one place to another, we seem to witness special activity of the Spirit.

The Holy Spirit's main business is not to make us feel good. His gifts are for ministry and mission. Those of us who are not from charismatic groups need to recognize that. In addition, those from charismatic traditions need to be careful not to trivialize the work of the Spirit and turn his work into an experience to make us feel good or spiritually superior. We all have something to learn here.

We noted that Pentecost and the pouring out of the Holy Spirit was a missiological event. The Spirit specifically guided Philip to the Samaritans, and then to the Ethiopian. The Spirit led Peter and Cornelius to each other. The Spirit clearly created the first mission structure: "Separate Barnabas and Saul for the work to which I have called them (Acts 13:2)."

In Acts 16, Paul, Silas, and Timothy were wondering where to go as they journeyed across Asia Minor. They had not accomplished their first plan or the alternative. The doors they had hoped to enter had been closed. Then they had a vision: a man of Macedonia asking, "Come over to Macedonia and help us" (Acts 16:9).

So the mission to Europe began through a specific act of the Holy Spirit. Later, during his voyage to Rome, in the storm before the shipwreck, Paul told his companions, "The God whom I serve has appeared to me and said, 'You will get to Rome'" (Acts 27:24).

There is an important lesson here. When we are in breakthrough situations, running great risks, moving out beyond where the Church has been, we will often see the Holy Spirit work in new ways. We should expect it. We should seek it. While we can never dictate what the Spirit of God will do, we can seek and expect his special activity as we move out in response to His guidance. Perhaps one reason many of us do not see very much activity of the Holy Spirit is that we always play it safe. To be honest, we really do not need a lot of the power of the Spirit to run most church machinery, or even mission machinery at times. This suggests to us the importance of moving out and taking risks with confidence in the Spirit as we follow his leading.

Finally, in Acts and elsewhere, several of the basic theses of this course are illustrated. I am only going to note a few at this point. First, mission always comes out of renewal movements—new activity of the Holy Spirit. Of course, Pentecost was unique. A colleague of mine said that the Church in Acts was not renewed; it was "newed." It lived in the first love of the Gospel, the power of the Spirit. However, I have yet to find any significant mission movement in history that was not the result of a movement of renewal or awakening. If we are interested in mission, we must seek renewal.

A second thesis is the importance of theological breakthroughs; that is, the discovery of some aspect of the Gospel that we have either not yet seen, or have forgotten. Often such breakthroughs or rediscoveries make mission possible. For example, the mission to Gentile Europe could not have taken place if the Church had not been led, reluctantly, to discover that God called Gentiles into His Kingdom without their first becoming Jews (Acts 15).

Third, we often see the role of key leaders, both women and men, who have sought God deeply and have listened to Him profoundly. The result has been new vision that reflected the heartbeat of God for the world. Such leaders have followed that vision, often at great risk. They have communicated their vision to others who have followed them. They have been the kind of people whom God has used to take the Gospel to new places and peoples. We will meet a number of them: Peter Waldo, St. Francis of Assisi, William Carey, Hudson Taylor, Cameron Townsend, and others.

We also see the importance of mission structures and the importance of understanding the historical context in which mission is carried out. The first century world was unique, with Roman roads, the Koine Greek language, Roman peace and order, the synagogues of the diaspora, and growing trade. These factors all facilitated the spread of the Gospel. Think of our context today. Do you realize that now in the twenty-first century, it is easier for a Christian to travel and live in almost any country in the world than ever before in history? I do not mean necessarily to live as a professional missionary, but as a Christian. Think about this—the modern equivalent of the Roman roads.

Chapter Three

The Two Structures of the Church

Introduction

Let us read John 4:34–37, a very familiar passage. It occurred after Jesus had met the Samaritan woman and his disciples had urged Him to eat.

> "My food," said Jesus, "is to do the will of him who sent me and to finish his work. Do you not say, 'Four months more and then the harvest'? I tell you, open your eyes and look at the fields! They are ripe for harvest. Even now the reaper draws his wages, even now he harvests the crop for eternal life, so that the sower and the reaper may be glad together. Thus the saying 'One sows and another reaps' is true." (John 4:34–37 NIV)

Throughout history we have seen many church leaders and ordinary believers say, "The harvest isn't ripe yet; maybe some day, but not now," or perhaps, "Those people (usually of a different race or culture) could never become faithful disciples of Jesus; they are not our kind of people." That was the implicit attitude of most of the European Church in the seventeenth and eighteenth centuries. Fortunately, there have been some who listened to the Holy Spirit and realized that people who seemed far away and closed to the Gospel were receptive if sympathetic messengers presented the Good News to them in terms they could understand. As Jesus noted in John 4, there was a harvest among the Samaritans, and we see in Acts 8 that shortly after Pentecost, the harvest came. No doubt that was a surprise to the Jewish believers.

Do not ever think we are immune to the tendency to dismiss certain people groups just because we are missionaries or teachers. We can fall into the same temptation and say, "Oh no, God couldn't possibly have any harvest there." All the while, the Holy Spirit is probably saying, "Yet God does have a harvest there." Maybe it is not immediate. Perhaps it will come in five, ten, or one hundred years.

One of the most moving incidents in the history of Christian mission came at the Madras (Chennai) Conference of the International Missionary Council in 1938. At that conference, Dr. Paul Harrison spoke. Harrison, an MD, had gone to Arabia with Samuel Zwemer years earlier to initiate work among Muslims. At that conference, where churches from all over the world were represented, Dr. Harrison stated that after fifty years of missionary work in Arabia, there were five believers. Then he said, "The Church in Arabia salutes you." It was not a very big church—five believers, or an average of one believer for every ten years of missionary work. Yet we believe that someday, there will be a great harvest there. But these growing communities of followers of Jesus will not necessarily look like our traditional western churches.

Some of us are in fields where the harvests are very clearly ripe: Sub-Saharan Africa, Indonesia, Singapore, and much of Latin America are among them. Some of us are in countries where the harvest is still far off. The point is, the Holy Spirit calls us. We are to have our eyes open. Conventional wisdom says, "Oh no, it's a long way off," or "It couldn't possibly ever come." Yet we are to be sensitive to the calling of the Holy Spirit, whose wisdom is never conventional, it is often the opposite, telling us that God is at work there even when we cannot see it.

The Means of World Evangelization

The Means or Structures God Uses

In this chapter we will look at the 'means' of world evangelization. We begin with William Carey who is rightly called the "father of the modern Protestant missionary movement," even though German Pietists from Halle had gone to India three-quarters of a century earlier.

Carey was a Baptist preacher, a part-time cobbler and part-time schoolteacher, who became one of the most brilliant linguists of all time. Carey's story teaches us never to despise the person who does not have formal credentials. That will be a recurring theme in this course.

In 1792, Carey published a little book called *An Enquiry into the Obligations of Christians to Use Means for the Conversion of the Heathen.* "Heathen" was a word used in those days for non-Christians. We do not consider it a very good word today, but we must understand it in its historical context.

Carey came from the Particular Baptist Church, which was not even a part of the larger Baptist denomination of England at the time. It was hyper-Calvinist. Some took Calvinism to its extreme and said, "If God wants to bring the people of other nations and lands to himself, he will do it in his own time and in his own way." Of course, that rationalization relieved the Church of all responsibility to evangelize or engage in mission beyond its shores. It left mission totally up to God with no human responsibility.

Later on, when Hudson Taylor was back from his first term in China and struggling with what God wanted him do, he heard a hymn with this line in an English church: "Waft, waft ye winds the story." Taylor said, "The winds are never going to take the story. People are." Carey believed the

same thing, so he wrote his book on the necessity of taking specific steps to take the Gospel to the rest of the world. Specifically, Carey proposed the formation of a mission structure.

In our study of history, we will look at the "means," or the structures, God has created and used to take the Gospel across significant cultural, racial, and geographical barriers. Become a life-long student of the various 'means' God has used in cross-cultural mission. Look for the different structures He has used to take the Gospel to new places, and be open to new methods the Holy Spirit is constantly creating for this purpose.

Thirty years ago, Youth With A Mission (YWAM) did not exist. Last year, 116 thousand people served in a short-term or long-term capacity in eighty-four different countries through that organization. Although it began in the United States, now over half of its workers are from Asia, Africa, and Latin America. It is one of many examples of a movement that began on the periphery of a denomination, in that case, the Assemblies of God. We now live in the most creative period in the history of the Church since the first centuries. That is especially true of the missionary movement. Never in all of history have so many new mission structures (means to take the Gospel where it has not yet been heard) been created as in the last twenty or thirty years. I believe this is clearly the action of the Holy Spirit. And of course, now many of those structures are from non-Western churches.

Structure in Personal Experience

What structures has God used to evangelize across significant geographical and cultural barriers, historically and in your own experience? One thesis of this course is that alongside the local church or denominational structures, God has often used alternative structures to fulfill his mission. Sometimes they are called "parachurch organizations." I do not like the term because it implies that they are alongside, and less than, the Church, and thus, inferior. I do not agree with that point of view. I believe they are an integral part of the People of God, working in different structures. In this understanding, our local and denominational church structures do not comprise the totality of the Church, the People of God. It is clear that followers of Jesus have lived and worshipped in a variety of structures throughout history. These might include a group of monks in the Egyptian desert in the third century, a Korean megachurch in the twentieth, a Christian group ministering in a poor urban community today, or a house church in Cuba. We could add many other examples. Sociologically, structurally, culturally, even theologically, they will be very different. The one thing they have in common is that they worship God through Jesus Christ and seek to be His disciples. Isn't that the only thing that is essential?

We see many examples of focused mission structures through history. I believe that such structures constitute an essential part of the Church, the People of God. I often ask my students how many of them have come to Christ or received their call to ministry or mission in a structure other than a local church. By that I mean an organization such as InterVarsity Christian Fellowship (IVCF), The Navigators, Campus Crusade for Christ, or a similar organization. Usually half or more respond. The local churchly structure is a part of God's plan. But God often uses such mission structures as well. We affirm the importance and validity of both. That is a fundamental thesis of this course.

The Whole Church Is Called to Mission

We agree with the theological principle that the whole Church is called to mission. But some draw the false conclusion that, because the whole Church is called to mission, separate mission structures have no place. They assert that the existence of mission societies separate from the denominationally organized churches is a sign of a defective church. Latourette says the opposite: a healthy church is constantly spinning off new mission structures for specific tasks. Often, churchly bureaucracies are too cumbersome to be creative. They also find it difficult to take risks—they need to preserve the institution.

The entire Antioch church did not travel with Barnabas and Saul across Asia Minor. Certainly the whole Antioch church was called to mission, but most of the community stayed in Antioch and sent out the missionary team. I believe that implied a high degree of autonomy and the ability to respond to the Spirit as he led them, both geographically and theologically. As we look at history, we see that repeated, as small, focused, committed communities of men and women who knew that God was calling them to a specific place or people or task, often all three, have carried the Gospel across significant cultural and geographical barriers.

The majority of Christians from the non-Western world, and indeed many of us from the Western world, will recognize that either we or our ancestors came to faith in Christ through people working in such focused, committed communities. Indeed, many of you are members of such groups. Ralph Winter calls them "second-decision people." That is a good term. After we were called to Christ, at some point in our lives we knew that God was speaking to us and calling us, very specifically, not just to Christian faith, but also to mission. Almost all missionaries can identify two different conversions in that sense: first a conversion to Christ, then a conversion to mission. The context of that second calling will be different: a local church, a conference, a retreat, or maybe short-term involvement with a group like Operation Mobilization or YWAM. So we want to be students of the means that God uses to motivate people into mission, and then to enable them to carry out their mission.

Such movements always involve minorities in the Church, and that is not bad. While the whole Church is called to be involved in mission, not everyone is called to be a cross-cultural missionary. Not everyone has the gift or call to take the Gospel to another geographical area or culture. However, a healthy local church will always encourage and support those of its members who hear that call.

Sometimes God leads a person in a direction different from his or her first intention. When I was a pastor, we had a young couple in our church who believed they were called to agricultural mission. We sent them on a short term to Guatemala one summer to work with a missionary in that field. They returned knowing that their call was in a different direction. Shortly after that, they were invited to work with IVCF in California. Now, for thirty years, they have had a very effective and expanding ministry with that ministry, first in a number of universities in the San Diego area, and now in New England. The role of the local church was to help them discover their call, encourage them to pursue it, and support them.

What Structures Should the Church Use?

Historically, we have to recognize that most mission movements have not originated at the center of the institutional Church. Most, if not all, have originated on its periphery. We will see this illustrated repeatedly. The first North American missionary movement started in a student prayer meeting under a haystack. Often a layman or woman had a vision that the Church as a whole did not share: Wycliffe Bible Translators, YWAM, Operation Mobilization, Frontiers, the China Inland Mission (OMF as it is now known) and a host of others originated in that way. Often a pastor or a layperson had deep heartfelt vision that the Church as a whole did not share. There are many such examples.

It is always good to go back, look at the origins of our own particular movement, and see what that has to teach us. We do not ignore the contributions of the larger churchly structures, but as we recognize how God has worked through unexpected, peripheral groups in the past it will help us remain open to the new things God is doing now.

We need to consider our definition of the Church. I come from a tradition that talks a lot about the Church and defines it as the denominational structure and entities connected to it; I respect that and am a loyal part of it. I have served my denomination as a church planter, seminary professor, and pastor in Brazil, Portugal, and the United States. However, as an historian, I have to recognize that God has worked both through denominational structures and outside of them.

The American Board of Commissioners for Foreign Missions (ABCFM) was established in 1810 at the insistence of a group of Congrega-

tional students in New England. It sent out missionaries from the Congregational, Presbyterian, and Reformed Churches. But in 1837, the Presbyterian Church separated from the ABCFM and said, "We will have our own denominational board, asserting, "The Presbyterian Church is a mission society." That signaled a rejection of voluntary interdenominational groups that originated outside of the official churchly structure. Denominational control was important.

That was a great mission board. I went to Brazil under it in 1956. Yet its greatest number of missionary candidates and its greatest mission leader came from the Student Volunteer Movement, which began in Northfield, Massachusetts, in 1886. Who led that conference? D. L. Moody, a ninth grade dropout and a shoe salesman; Luther Wishard, a secretary of the Young Men's Christian Association (YMCA); Robert Wilder, a student who had just graduated from Princeton College; and a Presbyterian pastor, Arthur T. Pierson. (Unfortunately, I am not related to him).

There a group of 251 students initiated a movement that eventually sent over twenty thousand men and women from Europe and the United States to mission fields around the world. It provided the greatest mission leaders in the United States for half a century. But it was initiated primarily by a layman and some students. It did not start at the center of the Church. In John 3, our Lord said, referring to the Holy Spirit, "The wind blows wherever it pleases (John 3:8 NIV)." That is certainly true in mission history.

My basic thesis in this chapter, then, is that the People of God need to exist in its two structures, even though we see a great variety among them. One is the congregational, or nurture, structure. Winter includes this structure as a part of a term of wider meaning, a modality. The other is a mission structure, or sodality. Both are a legitimate and essential part of the Church, the Body of Christ. We should not fall into the fallacy of thinking that a worshipping group in a local congregation is the Church, while a mission structure ministering on a campus or in another country is somehow less than the Church. I believe they are simply different manifestations of the Church, the People of God.

Mission Structures

As we have seen, a fundamental thesis of this course is that normally mission structures or sodalities have been used to take the Gospel to new cultures and places. Charles Mellis calls them "committed communities"; that is, communities of men and women (sometimes one gender only) who know that God has called them to a specific task, culture group, or place of ministry. As we examine history, we see that such communities have nearly always carried out the missionary task which we believe to be essential to the life of the Church. And as we have noted, they have usually arisen on the periphery of the institutional church.

Mission Structures: The Manifestation of a Healthy Church

Some say that if the Church were completely healthy it would not need such mission structures. That is clearly wrong. A healthy church will constantly form teams that are called to specific mission projects, whether at the local level, focusing on special groups in its own area; or at the international level, focusing on a distant culture. In the latter case, it will probably need to cooperate with other congregations of the same heritage in a denominational mission board, or with a multi-denominational mission structure. Both are legitimate. However, we must recognize that with rare exceptions, the most creative and effective mission societies today are multi-denominational. Thus, I believe that a healthy church will engage in mission both through its denominational board and through some of the creative new mission structures that are constantly emerging in unexpected places through the initiative of little-known visionaries. We also must recognize that a theology which asserts that only the organized Church should be involved in mission has a very serious quarrel with history.

It is important to note that in many cases, even the denominational mission boards were formed only after an individual or group from that church had taken the initiative and gone to a distant mission field. The Presbyterian Church in the United States formed its own board in 1837 out of a desire to exert greater influence over the Presbyterian missionaries already serving under the ABCFM. The American Baptists formed their foreign mission board after Adoniram and Ann Judson and Luther Rice, who had gone to Asia under the ABCFM, had become Baptists. Rice returned to suggest to the American Baptists that because they now had a missionary couple in Asia, they should form a mission board to support them! So the Baptist board was established in 1814. That should not surprise us. We see this pattern beginning in the book of Acts. The Spirit led Philip, who was not one of the apostles, to the Samaritans, a suspect group. Unnamed believers who were not part of the leadership of the Jerusalem church went to Antioch where they proclaimed the Gospel to uncircumcised gentiles. It was from that Antioch church, not Jerusalem, that the first intentional mission to Gentiles was launched. I have often wondered how the Jerusalem church would have responded if Barnabas, Saul and the other leaders in Antioch had asked its permission before beginning the mission to the gentiles! In light of the later controversies, the Jerusalem church would have been very reluctant to endorse the mission!

I do not want to denigrate the institutional churches. We need them. They often provide stability, continuity, and a system of checks and balances needed in every enterprise. However, even while we recognize their importance, we must also be open to the creativity of the Holy Spirit, as He surprises us and works outside these structures.

Many of us are from churches that came out of the Protestant Reformation of the sixteenth century. Some have accused Luther and Calvin of refusing to engage in mission beyond their own borders. That is not correct. A number of Luther's students took the Reformation to Denmark, Norway, Sweden, and Finland. Calvin prepared over 160 pastors and sent them as missionaries to France, Hungary, Poland, and the Netherlands. However, no mission structures were established to continue these efforts, and their definition of "the Church" was inadequate. Thus nearly two centuries passed before Lutherans again engaged in cross-cultural mission, and that began through a peripheral group, the pietists. The Reformers, struggling for survival in Europe, said the true Church exists "where the Word is rightly preached and the sacraments properly observed." It was a good definition as far as it went, but it lacked any missionary dimension. It was a definition of the Church for a static Christendom, but not for mission.

It is interesting to note that the Roman Catholic Church began to engage more fully in mission after the Protestant Reformation, primarily through the Jesuits, Franciscans, and Dominicans. One of the accusations hurled by Roman Catholic leaders against the Protestants was that their lack of missionary work proved that they were not true churches. They had a valid point.

An early definition spoke of "one holy, apostolic, catholic church." At least three of these words are missionary terms. "Holy" means "set apart": not only for an ethical life, but for the purpose of God. "Apostolic" does not only refer to the apostolic message; apostle from Greek is the same word as the Latin-based term, "missionary." The true Church is a church "sent" out into the world. Apostolic is a missionary word. "Catholic" simply means" universal," and the Church cannot be universal unless first it is missionary. Therefore, mission is embedded in that second-century definition of the Church.

Thus, if we are to be theologically correct in our understanding of the Church, we see that we are called to be one, seeking to manifest that unity to the world. (We must be honest and recognize that we do not do that very well.) We are called to be holy, called out for a special purpose and living in ways that reflect and seek to fulfill that purpose. We are called to be apostolic, both in being faithful to the apostolic teaching and to the "sent" nature of the Church. We are called to be catholic, meaning "universal" (not "Roman Catholic"), and eventually including all the families on earth.

Difference in Composition and Character

Both Adolph von Harnack, the German historian, and the *Didache*, a second-century document reflecting the life of the Church, show that there were two kinds of leadership in the second-century Church.

As churches grew, they had local leaders, usually called bishops or administrators; the word *episcopos* refers to those leaders the New Testament. It appears that at first, each local church had a group of bishops, but by the middle of the second century, most churches seem to have had a single bishop who acted as a supervising pastor over the Church in a city. Apparently, he also had presbyters, or elders, working with him. Their pastoral activities extended to the countryside around the city. Thus, the Church had local leadership, which it always needs.

We also find mobile leadership in the second century. These men traveled from place to place to preach the Gospel and plant the Church where it did not yet exist.

So in the first and second centuries, and indeed, all through history, we see two types of leaders in the Church. But often the local leadership structures have tended to overcome and swallow up the missionary leadership, and the itinerant leadership has not always been responsible. Usually we find some tension between the two. We can see it even in the New Testament. Many of us who have been missionaries have experienced this tension between leaders concerned with maintaining the institution, and those oriented toward mission. That tension arose early with negative results. David Bosch observed,

> There can be no doubt that as early as the late first century a shift in the understanding of the Church had set in. In fact, some of the New Testament texts already reflect a situation where the mobile ministry of apostles, prophets, and evangelists was beginning to give way to the settled ministry of bishops (elders) and deacons. The creative tension between these two dynamics of the Church's ministry gradually collapsed in favor of the second. (Bosch, David. *Transforming Mission: Paradigm Shifts*

in Theology of Mission. Maryknoll, N.Y.: Orbis Books, 1991, p. 201)

That process became almost complete with the establishment of the Church in the Roman Empire. As Wilbert Shenk has noted, in the fourth century, "as the Church became established it lost its sense of missionary purpose. Increasingly the claim was made that lands governed by Christian kings were Christianized. The Church was seen as an institution responsible for the pastoral care of the citizenry and to help maintain public order. (Shenk, Wilbert, "Emerging Church Streams in the Twenty-First Century," in Bush, et al, *Evangelizing Our World Inquiry, Preliminary Findings*. Seoul, World Inquiry International Coalition. 2003.1-20) That pushed new mission efforts even more to the periphery.

My basic thesis is that both kinds of structures and leaders are a permanent necessity for the Church until the end of history. Mission structures are not simply a temporary expedient. One of the older illustrations of mission work was that the mission was to go to a country to plant and build up the Church. The mission structure was like the scaffolding used to construct a building. When the building was finished, the scaffolding was to be taken down. That is not a perfect illustration and we recognize its defects. But in the last half of the twentieth century, some mainline denominations began to decrease or even dismantle their mission structures, with the rationale that the Church had now been planted in many countries. Ralph Winter, who served under the same mission board that I did, had a great reply. He said, "When you construct the building, you take down the scaffolding, but you do not disband the construction company!" The point is, there are still many places and peoples not yet reached with the Gospel, to say nothing of many other aspects of mission to be carried out in partnership with the newer churches.

What are some of the differences between the two types of structures? Mission structures are normally mobile: they move from place to place. They tend to be elitist in the sense that they ex-pect their people to have a high commitment to their goals and a lifestyle of simplicity. They are task-oriented, outreach-oriented, and often innovative. We recognize that at times they can become institutionalized and fall into routine just as much as any other structure. However, they are usually innovative, especially in their early stages.

Think of the early years of the China Inland Mission. They went to places in China where no westerner had ever gone. They adopted Chinese dress and a Chinese lifestyle when most other European missionaries considered that scandalous. Hudson Taylor was bitterly criticized in those years. Yet we know he was right. When the China Inland Mission had to leave China in the early fifties, it reinvented itself and became the Overseas Missionary Fellowship, and now works in a number of Asian countries. But today the Mission has over 150 Christian professionals working and witnessing back in China. Operation Mobilization (OM) is another example. Not since early mission efforts in the South Pacific has a mission structure used ships, but now OM has begun to do so. So mission structures at their best are innovative. Today we westerners need to learn from many emerging mission structures coming out of churches in Asia, Africa, and Latin America.

Mission structures tend to have charismatic (gifted, attractive, visionary) leadership, especially at their beginning. We think of people like John Wesley, William Carey, Hudson Taylor, Loren Cunningham, and many others. However, often after the second or third generation, there is danger that the quality of leadership will decline, and managers, whose purpose is simply to maintain the organization, succeed the original, visionary leaders. This often creates a crisis.

As we have observed earlier, a characteristic of creative leaders is that they have listened to God more profoundly than their contemporaries, have felt God's heartbeat for the world, caught a vision from the Holy Spirit, and communicated that vision and attracted others to join them. That is how new mission movements have started.

A related observation is that the more culturally and geographically distant a group is, the higher the degree of intentionality necessary to reach it. That is, it takes a certain degree of purpose to reach your neighbor across the street, assuming he or she speaks the same language and is part of your culture. It takes a more focused intention to reach someone in your neighborhood of a different race, language, or culture. However, if a people group lives a great distance away in Nepal, and has a different language and culture it requires a far greater degree of focus and commitment to reach them. It is highly unlikely that mission would have begun in Nepal without a mission structure from India, the United States, or elsewhere participating.

We have emphasized the need of mission structures. We must recognize that congregational structures are equally necessary. If I have put special emphasis on the need for mission structures, it is because so often the congregational or denominational structures do not recognize their legitimacy. However, we cannot fail to see the importance of the local group of men and women who come together to worship God through Jesus Christ and seek to follow Him. The major focus of mission is always to proclaim the Gospel, call men and women to repent and believe in Jesus, and form them into the worshipping, nurturing communities we call "churches." These communities, in turn, are to witness in their own contexts, engage in ministries of compassion in their own societies, and engage in mission beyond their own geographical and cultural boundaries in cooperation with mission structures. The cycle continues.

The definition of a congregational structure is simple; it is what we call a local church and that church's extension to a network of local churches or a denominational structure. For most Protestants, with the exception of some Anglicans, no particular denominational structure is mandated. It is simply a way in which local churches cooperate for certain purposes. Historically, those purposes were to define their understanding of the faith, train and certify ministers, and engage cooperatively in mission. As time has passed, Protestant denominations in the United States have added many other functions, sometimes blurring their focus.

The local church will include old, young, and new believers, some mature, some committed, others seemingly nominal in their faith. It will include long-time members confined to their homes or beds, as well as children and youth who we hope are moving toward professing their faith and growing in discipleship. In short, it includes all kinds of people. Every pastor knows that. This structure leads people in worship each week, seeks to teach people the Scriptures, and encourages them to grow in their understanding of the Christian life and in their service to Christ wherever he calls them. A healthy local church will send some of its own members to engage in mission elsewhere, working with mission agencies.

Maintenance is another aspect of the local church. The maintenance of buildings, programs, and consensus among its members assumes importance. The danger is that maintenance can become the goal, and the other more important functions of the Church can be forgotten. For this reason every congregation needs positive, active relationships with mission structures. Such relationships serve as a constant reminder to the local congregation that the whole Church is called, not primarily to maintenance, but to mission. Thus, when mission structures live in healthy relationships with congregational structures, they can become a means of renewal for the broader Church. I believe the best situation exists where we have various mission structures in healthy, mutually affirming relationships with the local church. I am thankful for the church in which I was raised. However, when I became involved in a Presbyterian church in Berkeley as a university student, we were in constant contact with missionaries and mission structures. Then my vision for the world began to expand. That contact stimulated many in that church not only to support missions, but also to go to various parts of the world. Mission structures exist as a constant reminder to the larger Church that it is called to turn itself inside out; that it exists for the world, not simply for itself.

Independence and Interdependence

If the local church is vital, it is good at E–0 evangelism (evangelizing people within the Church, children of the Church and nominal believers who are not yet committed to Christ), and E–1 evangelism (of people of the same culture who live in the same area). However, the local church will not evangelize anyone in Nepal all by itself. Incidentally E-2 refers to people considerably different in culture, while E-3 refers to those who are even more culturally distant.

When my predominately white, middle-class Presbyterian church in Fresno wanted to get involved in with black and Hispanic youth in the inner city, we found no easy way to do so. I was a part of a group of five men—two doctors, a lawyer, a Buick dealer and myself, struggling and praying about it. Finally, we got in touch with a mission structure that works in inner cities and believes that you do not minister in there unless you live there. We got other churches involved with us, and together were able to help the team structure move into that inner city.

Through the work of that group, a significant number of youth meet in Bible clubs and classes every week in the inner city. We could not have been able to do that as a local church working alone. That same local church helps sponsor the ministry of IVCF at the local university. My point is that there are ministries that a local church cannot do by itself, or even in cooperation with other local churches. Mission structures are necessary for many ministries.

Certainly, there are other models. Now the only other Protestant church downtown in that city, an Assemblies of God congregation, has a highly contextualized ministry that is also reaching out to youth. That might be a still better model.

My thesis is that those in each kind of structure need to understand and appreciate the validity and functions of the other. That is true whether the mission structure is denominational or multi-denominational. Each needs to have a degree of independence from the other, but at the same time, recognize their interdependence. I have seen two destructive tendencies. In the first case, some denominational bureaucracies have swallowed up the older "mainline" mission boards, resulting in a severely diminished focus in mission by those

churches. In 1900, seventy-five percent of North American missionaries came from those churches. Today it is only five percent. The growth in North American missionaries during the twentieth century has come from the newer evangelical groups, the Southern Baptists, multi-denominational boards, and the Pentecostal/Charismatic movement. For example, the board under which I served had around two thousand missionaries in 1956. Today the number is less than two hundred.

Ronald Fung of the Commission on World Mission and Evangelism of the World Council of Churches (WCC) reminded the older churches,

> In the WCC scheme of things, the answer to unfaithful churches lies with Christian communities that engage in mission but are not necessarily part of the organizational structures of the churches. These communities, missionary societies, renewal movements, small ecclesiastical cells, evangelistic teams, mission study centers, action groups for justice, etc., in their very action proclaim Christ, and challenge and encourage the established churches to renewal and faithfulness. Of these communities, probably the most immediately relevant to our concern for world evangelism are the mission boards and mission societies…The missionary, with his or her sojourner's eyes, sees wonders and surprises, miseries and lostness, which might well have been hidden from the eyes of the established setters. Thus, the Kingdom is spread. (R. Fung, Newsletter of the CWME of the WCC, October 1989)

Some mission groups have a very low opinion of the Church, seeing it only as a source of support, but failing to appreciate its other important functions. On the mission field, such groups may show an inadequate understanding of the importance of the local church and little accountability. Someone has spoken of the danger of "missionless churches" and "churchless missions." We need to avoid both dangers. A positive relationship between the two types of structures is essential.

An additional problem is the notion in some national churches that missionaries who come from outside are to reach out in mission, while the national church is to maintain what others have started. One of our Brazilian students is now a missionary in Mozambique. He told me that when his colleague, the senior pastor of a Presbyterian church in Brasilia, suggested that they contribute a percentage of their income to support missions to indigenous groups in Brazil or abroad, the reaction was negative. The response was, "That is the task of the missionaries; it is not our job."

Fortunately, that attitude is changing in many places. The lesson is that whenever churches are planted, they should be taught to have a mission focus from the very beginning.

I have served on a number of multi-denominational mission boards. All have affirmed the validity and importance of the churches in the areas where they work. The mission boards' goals are to work with these national churches—to aid them in leadership development, ministries of compassion, and church planting. The mission boards do not attempt to plant churches that will belong to the mission. Rather they become servants of the existing churches, in hope of becoming factors of renewal, evangelism, and growth in discipleship within them. Obviously, in areas where there are no believers, the goal is to evangelize and plant the Church.

Some groups began as a combination of both structures, church and mission. The early Moravians are probably the best example. The early Methodists were similar in some ways. As time passed, both groups evolved into more traditional churches with their own denominational mission boards.

Tragically, the mission focus of both groups has declined dramatically.

Tensions between the Two Structures

Often there are tensions between the two structures. Tension is not necessarily bad. It can be creative and good. Have you ever stopped to think that you cannot move your body without tension? One can only move an arm or a leg when two muscles work in tension with each other. If there were no tension, the arm would hang limply at the side and would be useless.

Therefore, tension is not necessarily destructive. Too much tension can be destructive, but too little can cause lifelessness. At times, those in a congregational structure or church say regarding mission groups, "Those people are taking our resources and our best young people. We want them here!" But at times, people in mission structures have said, " The Church is dead. It has no life!" Such attitudes demonstrate arrogance and shortsightedness on both sides.

In the early days, when Dawson Trotman was founding the Navigators, he would not have anything to do with the local church. He considered it dead, even though two women who worked with youth in a local church had encouraged him to memorize the Scripture that eventually led to his conversion. (One of these women was my high school English teacher.) Today, of course, the Navigators have grown to affirm the importance of the local manifestation of the Body of Christ.

The New Testament does not tell us simply to disciple individual believers; it speaks of the Church, the Body of Christ. It does not depict solitary Christianity, it shows us the Christian community. If we focus only on individual conversions and do not attempt to build up the Body of Christ, we will not be effective. None of us can live a healthy Christian life alone. We need the support, input, and sometimes criticism or even confrontation of our brothers and sisters in the faith. We need to learn from them and be supported by them. We are all called to be a part of a Christian community even though we recognize that it will take different forms in different contexts.

Often a cause of tension is a combination of superiority and inferiority complexes on both sides. The churchly groups may glory in their size, finances, and traditions, and look down on groups like YWAM, OM, or Wycliffe, which have arrived on the scene recently. Yet the churches may secretly envy the zeal and commitment of the mission groups. On the other hand, the mission structures may be both thankful and a bit proud of the zeal and vision they have been given, and may feel spiritually superior. At the same time, they may envy the resources and traditions of the older churches. Thus, there is danger of a love-hate relationship between the two structures, each with a superiority and inferiority complex. We need to get beyond that, but first we must recognize its reality.

Max Warren served as Secretary of the Anglican Church Missionary Society (CMS) for several decades in the twentieth century. A local rector, John Venn, and a group of laymen who had been influenced by the Wesleyan revival, established that society in 1799. Fifty years passed before the Anglican bishops would recognize it as legitimate. CMS missionaries and some of their converts were responsible, under God, for the East African revival that had a powerful impact on Uganda, Kenya, Tanzania, and other areas for three decades or more. Speaking of the tension that often exists between the Church and mission structures, Warren wrote, "If a society is to be dynamic, it must accept the inevitability of tension. Too much tension makes administration impossible. We need both coordination and decentralization of power. We need to give people space and enough independence to act. At the same time, they need to be accountable." This summarizes it very well.

The "Go On" and the "Go" Structures
Charles Mellis served as President of Mission Aviation Fellowship and wrote the excellent book, *Committed Communities: Fresh Streams for World Missions* (Pasadena: William Carey Library, 1976). He used the terms "Go on" and "Go" structures. These two terms do not correlate to the two structures we are discussing, they relate to the relationship between renewal and mission. Mellis suggests that renewal movements begin in a desire to go deeper into the faith, to "go on" in Christian discipleship. Puritanism originated that way; so did Pietism and the Pentecostal movement. None of these began as missionary movements, yet very soon, as they sought a more authentic Christian life, they became missionary in nature. These are the "go on" structures.

Mellis also speaks of "go" structures that had a missionary vision from the very beginning. However, I believe that if we examine the lives of the founders of such movements, we will always discover some special touch of the Holy Spirit in the individual or group before the missionary vision came.

At any rate, it is clear that throughout history, mission has been the result of renewal. Rarely has mission happened without a fresh experience of God's grace.

The Dominicans and Franciscans, the great Roman Catholic orders of the thirteenth century, and the Jesuits in the sixteenth century, had a missionary vision from the beginning. However, each of their leaders had gone through a process of spiritual discipline and discovery. The movements of William Carey and Hudson Taylor had a missionary vision from the beginning, but both came after periods of revival in England. So I am not sure Mellis' distinction is completely valid. My point is that we never see significant mission breakthroughs, new mission movements, without renewal.

By renewal, I am speaking of movements in which people are convicted of the lukewarm nature of their Christian life, their sin, and their lack of commitment. This brings a fresh touch from the Spirit of God in an individual or group, which leads them to seek God's face and His will in their lives. The result is serious discipleship—a desire to see God's will done in one's own society and in the world beyond. The logical consequence is mission. Any renewal movement that does not result in mission will soon turn inward, focus on itself, and stagnate.

The Institutionalization and/or Absorption of Mission Structures
Let me make it clear that mission structures as well as churchly structures can become institutionalized and lose their original vision. There is nothing wrong with becoming an institution. We need structures, and that means that institutions will develop. The churches of which we are members are institutions. YWAM is an institution, even though its leaders might not like the term. To speak of an "institution" simply means that the group has a structure. We cannot really live without some kind of structure. We cannot pass on tradition or carry on a task without some structure. We cannot take water from one place to another without a structure—a bucket, or a pipe.

However, "institutionalization" happens when the maintenance of the institution becomes more important than the original vision for which it was created. At that point, the group has lost sight of its original vision and goals, and simply lives to maintain itself. That can happen to mission structures as well as churches.

Again, I quote Max Warren:

> Mission, understood as world evangelization, calls for almost infinite flexibility, because no two situations are alike. And flexibility demands, in practice, specialist organs for action and…a readiness to take initiatives which may be mistaken. Official bodies have an inbuilt hesitation about ever taking risks…This is where, as I see it, the voluntary principle becomes important. (Harvey Hoekstra, *Evangelism in Eclipse: World Mission and the World Council of Churches* [Exeter, Paternoster Press, 1949], 44)

Warren was an Anglican from a very high-church tradition, with an appreciation for the whole Church, and in particular his own church with its system of bishops. He did not reject that system, but he said, "That kind of a churchly tradition can only be vital if within it and alongside it you've got dedicated bands of volunteers who know that God has called them, not out of the Church, but as a part of the Church, to take the Gospel somewhere else." The importance of holding these two things in balance is the basic thesis of this chapter.

General Observations

In conclusion, I will make some general observations that I believe are valid. However, your own observations may differ from mine as you continue your study.

- Cross-cultural mission is rarely done without focused mission structures. I do not say never, but rarely. I define "mission" as crossing a significant cultural or linguistic barrier to take the gospel to a people where there is no well-established church as yet. This has rarely been done in history without the creation of some specifically focused mission structure.

- Mission structures seldom, if ever, originate at the ecclesiastical center. They always seem to arise on the periphery. Keep that in mind. It will enable you to be more open to the creative new initiatives of the Holy Spirit.

- Such movements are usually, if not always, the result of renewal movements.

- Unrecognized groups of laymen and laywomen with little or no status in the Church have started at least half of the mission movements in the history of the Church, and perhaps more. That may shock you. It should revolutionize our theology of the gifts in the Body of Christ. Laymen started Wycliffe Bible Translators, The China Inland Mission, and YWAM, to name a few. The three greatest missionary orders in the Roman Catholic Church are the Franciscans, the Jesuits, and the Dominicans. Francis and Loyola were laymen when they established their orders. (The Papacy recognized the respective orders of St. Francis and Loyola with some reluctance.) And we remember Mother Teresa and her Sisters of Charity. We can see parallels in Protestantism. The Student Volunteer Movement sent out over twenty thousand missionaries from North America and Europe. Its early leaders were all laymen.

These observations all have enormous implications for our theology of the Body of Christ, the diversity of the Body, and the gifts of the Spirit. It also expands our understanding of the sovereignty of God. The Spirit works where he will. He is rarely predictable. This should make us open to any new thing God always wants to do in our lives and in our time.

The historian John T. McNeill wrote about the Celtic missionaries. "These Irish saints poured from Ireland across to Scotland, down through England, onto the Continent, and then into what we now call Germany." He said they largely evangelized and tutored the Germanic world. "They came to pagan tribes almost as squatters, without ecclesiastical credentials, in unquestioned obedience to the heavenly vision. They found a way to approach the minds and spirits of their hearers."

We have talked about structure and its importance, but McNeill concludes that without question vitality was essential and organization secondary. The Celtic missionaries had some organization. However, remember that organization or structure is never a substitute for vitality.

Chapter Four

The Early Church:
Apostolic and Post-Apostolic

Geography

Johannas Blauw, the Dutch theologian, wrote an excellent book on the missionary nature of the Church. His thesis, perhaps overly simplistic, was that during the Old Testament period, mission was "centripetal, That is, it invited people to come to Jerusalem, to Mt. Zion, to the mountain of the Lord. It was a "come" mission. People came, and of course, many were there on Pentecost. In a sense, Pentecost was the fulfillment of the centripetal understanding of mission.

After Pentecost, the mission became "centrifugal." The Church was sent out. People were not invited to come to Zion; they went out from Zion to the ends of the earth.

Today we are seeing a new centripetal mission, as multitudes from many nations are coming to Western cities. This does not substitute for sending out missionaries to other areas of the world, but it tells us to see the many people groups around us. It is said that at least 150 languages are now spoken in greater Los Angeles. There is also true of London and probably all world-class cities in the West and elsewhere. Almost every major city in the world can count several score of languages among its people.

Now let us look at Jerusalem and Palestine as centers of the world of that era. We are not used to looking at the map in that perspective, but of course viewing the globe from any angle is legitimate. Celsus, an early critic of the Church, said, "Why would God send his Spirit to one corner of the world? Only the author of a farce could imagine the Son of God being sent to Jerusalem!" (John Foster, *Beginning from Jerusalem* [New York: Association Press, 1956], 9–10). Obviously, Celsus was a Roman. But Palestine, at that time, was not a "corner." In the providence of God, during the Old Testament period Israel was in a corridor that linked the two great power centers of the world—the Nile Valley in Egypt, and Mesopotamia, where Babylon and Assyria were located. They frequently fought each other, and Israel was often the battleground. Then the situation changed.

First, Alexander the Great came on the scene, spreading his empire from Greece to the borders of India, which of course included Israel. After Alexander's empire broke up, the Romans appeared on the scene, and in A.D. 64, the Roman general, Pompey, conquered much of the Middle East, including Israel and Judah. Therefore, by the time our Lord was born, the historical context of Jerusalem and Palestine had changed.

(We want to become students of our own historical context. The historical context of the twenty-first century is very different from that of two decades earlier. Globalization and the end of the Cold War have changed our world in ways we are just beginning to see. This changes the ways in which God will call us to fulfill our mission.)

Other Factors

By the end of the fourth century, Christianity had moved from a stable in Bethlehem to the Lateran

Palace in Rome. This palace had once been the residence of Constantine, who gave it to the bishop of Rome, in an office that would eventually evolve into the Papacy. How did that happen? Here we look both at the actions of the sovereign God, and the historical circumstances in which He works.

Destruction of Jerusalem

The destruction of Jerusalem and the Temple in A.D. 70, and then again in A.D. 134, led both to the scattering of the Jewish church and its growing animosity toward Christianity. Earlier Jews who believed Jesus to be the Messiah but continued to observe the law, were considered a sect within Judaism. But by the end of the century any Jew who confessed Jesus as Messiah was considered cursed or anathematized. These factors, in addition to the growth of Gentile Christianity, meant that the Christian Church would not continue to be tied to Jewish culture. Instead, it became a gentile church for all practical purposes, and rejected most Jewish traditions. The issue in Acts 15 of whether or not Gentile converts should observe Jewish law now became completely irrelevant. If Jewish Christianity had dominated the Church with controversy over the role of Jewish law, it would have been much more difficult for the Faith to spread in the Gentile world. It appears that it was necessary for the early Church to be freed from Jewish culture if it was to spread widely.

Today, in a sense, we are in a parallel situation. For two centuries, since the beginning of the modern Protestant missionary movement, many have perceived the Christian faith as a "Western" or "white man's" religion. In Indonesia, for example, Christianity was called the "Dutch religion." The Dutch took the faith to Indonesia, and for some time if Indonesians wished to worship as Christians, they had to do so in the Dutch language. Obviously, theirs was a very westernized form of the faith. That is ironic in view of the fact that the Dutch Reformed Church came out of the Reformation of Calvin, which had encouraged the translation of the Bible and liturgy into various languages. The Dutch in Indonesia forgot their own history!

We need to remind people that Jesus did not wear a three-piece suit and tie when he entered the Synagogue on the Sabbath. He never visited Europe or North America. He was born at the crossroads of Asia, Africa, and Europe. Today, primarily because of the growth of missionary movements and the Church in Asia, Africa, and Latin America, the Church is being freed from its Western constructs and will take many new, more indigenous forms. This is healthy, and mirrors the earlier release of the Church from its initial Jewish forms. And today there are movements led by Messianic Jews who are recontextualizing the faith back into Jewish culture.

Today God seems to be reshaping the Church just as he did in the first century. The People of God are being released from some of the traditional institutional forms and discovering new ways of worshipping and structuring its life.

The Roman Empire

Now we will look at the Roman Empire. There were unique factors that made the first century Mediterranean world relatively hospitable to the spread of the Faith.

First, there was the *Pax Romana* (Roman peace). Never before had peace existed over such a wide area as under the Roman Empire. You could travel across a wide area with relative security. Pirates would probably not attack you if you sailed across the Mediterranean.

Secondly, there were Roman roads made for relative ease of travel. The Romans built 135 thousand miles of roads so durable that many of them are still in use. Travel conditions would seldom be as good in southern Europe, and never would they be better in Europe until the invention of the steam locomotive in the nineteenth century. A chariot could travel 70 to 100 miles (100 to 150 kilometers) a day over Roman roads.

I can remember how astonished I was when we visited Spain and found out that I was driving a twentieth century automobile over a bridge built by the Romans! That indicates the quality of Roman roads; they were good engineers and builders.

Thirdly, there was a great increase in trade. Ships sailed down the Red Sea across to India. We do not know if St. Thomas got to India, but some of our Indian friends believe he did. We know that it was possible for him to have gone there because of the trade routes. Xian in China, for example, was one end of the silk route. Traders in Roman times were going clear across Central Asia. It was possible for early missionaries not only to go west, but also to go east and south because of the trade routes that had been opened up at that time.

Finally, Roman administration was relatively fair and uniform, until the Empire began to persecute the Church. We know that Paul appealed to Roman law and Roman justice.

Koine Greek

Then there was the legacy of Alexander the Great. He considered himself a missionary of Greek culture. He and his soldiers spread that culture and the Koine Greek language across their vast empire. Koine was not classical or literary Greek. It was the common language of soldiers and traders. The great Greek philosophers did not write in Koine Greek, but the common people and their associates spoke it clear to the borders of India and all around the Mediterranean basin. Paul could preach in Greek and have a hearing in any city in the Roman Empire. The New Testament was written not in a classical language for the elites, but in the common vernacular of the people. It was a universal language in most of the Roman Empire. There are modern parallels to this today.

It is significant that in regard to the Old Testament, it was not for a thousand years that the Jewish people came up with anything comparable, and when they did, they chose all the same books. In other words, the so-called translators of the Septuagint were as much "selectors" as they were translators. They created the Greek Old Testament and added books called the Apocrypha. They left out some of the additions to Daniel and other books, but they chose the same books, even though they put them in a different order. Protestants have often thought there was a Hebrew Bi-

ble and it was simply translated into Greek. But there was no Jewish canon in 160 BC. However, the formation of the Septuagint a century before Christ made it possible for Hellenistic Jews and now gentiles to read the Jewish Bible, the "Old Testament," in Greek. And we note that Paul, in his letters, often quoted from the Septuagint.

The Synagogue and the Diaspora

The Synagogue was another important factor in the life of the early Church. As far as we know, it was formed during the Exile in Babylon, probably as an informal structure. The Jews could no longer go to the Temple in Jerusalem to worship. Those Jews who wanted to maintain their heritage apparently formed small groups to study their Scriptures, and the Synagogue evolved as a result.

As Jews were scattered around the empire in the Diaspora, they formed synagogues in nearly all the important cities. Ten pious men were required to form a local synagogue. If there were not ten such men, a group of Jews might simply have a place of prayer, such as Paul found in Philippi. A large synagogue was established in Alexandria, Egypt, and there the Septuagint was translated during the first century before Christ. Eighty per cent of the quotations in the New Testament come from the Septuagint.

Synagogues were found in most of the cities mentioned in the book of Acts. That indicates the wide dispersion of the Jewish community. They constituted a natural bridge over which the Good News traveled. Three kinds of people worshipped there.

There were devout Jews who read their Scriptures and waited for the coming of the Messiah. Paul and his colleagues went to them to proclaim that the Messiah had come. Some believed; most did not. The second group were the proselytes—those who had been raised as gentiles and completely accepted the Jewish faith, including circumcision, and observance of the Law. Some proselytes believed the Gospel.

The third group proved the most strategic for the spread of the Faith. They were called "God-fearers." This is a technical term found in Acts:

those who "feared God" (Acts 10:2) were non-Jews who accepted the Jewish faith enough that they believed in the one God, the Jewish God, and were thus monotheists rather than pagans or polytheists. They worshipped at the Synagogue and followed Jewish ethical standards, but did not accept the Law to the point of circumcision. Thus they were not full members of the Jewish community. Cornelius was the first "god fearer' encountered in Acts.

They formed the nucleus of the churches in most of the cities where Paul went. But for theological as well as strategic reasons Paul always went to the Jew first and then to the gentile. He went to the Synagogue and proclaimed the coming of the Messiah. Usually some accepted the Gospel while others rejected it. Division resulted and a church was then formed separate from the synagogue. Paul's hope, of course, was that each synagogue as a whole, would accept Jesus as Messiah, and he agonized over the fact that most Jews did not do so. But we must recognize that if the entire Jewish community had accepted the Gospel, it no doubt would have been more difficult for the Faith to spread from Jewish to Gentile culture.

I suggest we look at the cultures in which we work and see if we can discover something in them that might be analogous to the synagogue. Studies have been done on the *bhakti* within Hinduism. They are people who fear God. We cannot agree with much of their ideas, yet they are people seeking to know and love God. Can Christians in India explore positive approaches in presenting the Gospel to those in the that movement?

There are growing "insider movements" elsewhere in which people affirm Jesus Christ as their only Lord without leaving their traditional religious groups or associating with the westernized churches. Could this point to a new work of the Holy Spirit in the future?

Roman Civilization in Decline, Searching
Roman civilization was in decline. (There are some analogies to our own civilization today with its secularism and disillusionment.) It was troubled and unsettled. Sexual promiscuity was rampant. Rome was a sick society because one-third of the people were slaves. A slave was a living tool, with no power. The master had the authority of life and death over his slave. He could kill the slave in a fit of anger with impunity.

Most emperors were notorious for their sexual promiscuity. Many of the nobles traded wives or husbands each year. If parents did not want their infants (especially girls), the children were exposed in the town square, and there met one of two fates: either the wild animals would get them, or they would be raised to become prostitutes. That was Roman society.

Most leaders did not believe in the old Roman gods, but had to practice the proper rituals as a civic duty. Temple prostitution, as we see in Corinth and elsewhere, was common: using a prostitute was part of the worship of the gods and goddesses of fertility.

The "mystery religions," new religious movements from the East, used rituals of rebirth. They were only for the wealthy, since for some of them "rebirth" required taking a bath in the blood of a bull. That, of course, was expensive.

Greek philosophy was in decline. Plato's Republic was a great work in many ways, but was built on a foundation of slavery. Even Plato said that society had three kinds of women: a wife whom you married, a mistress with whom you had pleasure and prostitutes on the street. The wife was protected, but was not considered a companion. The whole idea of marital fidelity was simply not meaningful in Roman society.

What Did Christianity Bring?
What did the Church bring to Roman society? First, it brought a new quality of life in community. New believers not only found personal salvation, they discovered a loving community that cared especially for the poor. It was not perfect. We see this from Paul's letter to Philemon and the Corinthians. Nevertheless, in the Church, a slave was a person. That is the significance of Paul's letter to Philemon. The slave and the free person were equal, and the community was open to all.

Secondly, there was the quality of individual Christian life and witness. One of the loveliest stories is that of the conversion of Justin Martyr, an early Christian theologian. He was a philosopher seeking the truth and met an ignorant fisherman as he walked on the beach. Certainly the fisherman was the very opposite of the sophisticated philosopher, yet this ignorant fisherman shared his faith, and Justin became a Christian, a theologian, and later, a martyr.

Let me read a quote here again from Celsus, who despised Christians. We will not agree with his male chauvinism, but we see how, in his desire to insult Christians, he paid them a great compliment. He also gave us insight into how the faith was spread. Listen to his complaint:

> We see in private houses weavers, cobblers, washermen, and persons of the most uneducated and rustic kind. They would not venture to open their mouths in the presence of their elders or their wise masters. But they get hold of children privately and any women who are as ignorant as themselves. When a teacher or master approaches, they say, 'With him here we can't explain...but you can come with the women and your playmates to the women's quarters, the cobbler's shop or the laundry, that you may get all there is. With words like this, they win them over. (Foster, *Jerusalem*, 18).

In this diatribe, we see a marvelous picture of common people sharing their faith in their daily lives.

A third factor Christians brought was their belief in Jesus' resurrection, and the certainty of their own eternal life. That made them willing to die for their faith. There are many stories of martyrs who, before death, won to the faith their persecutors or those who watched them die.

Christianity also brought power encounters and miracles to Roman culture. In his book, *Christianizing the Roman Empire, A.D. 100–400,* Ramsay McMullen, the professor of classics at Yale, (Yale University Press, 1984), attributes the Church's growth mainly to power encounters and miracles. When we look at history, we see many stories of miraculous events, healings, exorcisms, nature miracles, and visions. No doubt many of these are ex-

aggerations and have been embellished throughout history. However, I believe many are true and have their basis in fact. The problem is that a secular historian or even a liberal churchman looks at those stories with the presupposition that they could not have happened; therefore, the conclusion is that they did not happen.

We come with a different worldview. We believe God can and does work miraculously, in extraordinary ways, and has done so all through history, including today. That does not mean we accept every story. We recognize that often there has been exaggeration and excessive credulity. For example, during the Middle Ages churches were said to contain enough pieces of the "true cross" (venerated as relics) to build at least ten crosses. When that was noted, the pope said, "It's very simple. The Lord has miraculously multiplied the wood of the true cross."

We should not let our reaction to such excessive credulity and superstition blind us to the fact that throughout history, especially in breakthrough points, the Lord has indeed acted in ways beyond the ordinary, which we call miraculous. Therefore, I am convinced that such activity was a very important factor in the history and growth of the early Church.

Christianity also brought intellectual satisfaction for people who were seeking answers to the ultimate questions of life, people like Justin Martyr, Augustine, and others. Not only the poor and those impressed by miracles came to faith; Christianity attracted those who were trying to make sense out of life. They discovered in the Christian faith the God who was active in history to redeem lost humanity. Christianity brought to them a worldview by which they could orient their lives.

The message and hope of the Resurrection brought the only ultimate answer to questions about suffering, meaning, and purpose in life. More than simply the hope of resurrection for the believer, this message proclaimed that history is moving toward its consummation, the restoration of creation. Paul said that if this is the only life we have, then we are of all people most miserable, because we are living an illusion. The early Church was bold in proclaiming the hope of the Resurrection; we must do the same.

When I was a pastor, I liked to startle the people every now and then in the selection of hymns. I liked to sing two hymns, especially, on Sundays when you would not expect them. One was "Joy to the World," which we sang at times other than Christmas; the other was "Jesus Christ is Risen Today," which we sang at times other than Easter. I did so to remind the people that we celebrate the coming of Christ and the Resurrection every Sunday. It is often good to do the unexpected. Communication is more powerful when it is not predictable.

Finally, the Church brought to Roman society a message that combined high ethical standards with the assurance of grace and forgiveness. We need both. All of us live in the tension between law and grace. Law says that God has certain standards for our lives. Grace says that God forgives us when we fail. If we go too far in one direction, we fall into legalism—the idea that one must conform to the standard or be expelled. On the other hand, we see the common tendency in much of the Church today to present "cheap grace"—the belief that forgiveness is easy and that God does not require us to take our discipleship seriously. This viewpoint tells us that we are not to be too concerned about our moral lapses because God will forgive us. It brings a failure to take repentance and restoration seriously. We must live in constant tension between the two, and the early Church seems to have maintained that tension.

In summary, the Christian message proclaimed the Good News that God had acted decisively in history to save all who came to Christ in repentance and faith. It addressed the deepest questions people were asking in Roman society. This calls us to discover what questions people are asking in our own society. So often, we talk too soon, giving answers to questions people are not asking. The early Church brought hope to the hopeless, and acceptance and love to the unlovable.

Today where Muslims are coming to Christ, they are coming primarily through power encounter.

However, I have a Muslim friend who came to Christ and he told me that a man loved him into the Kingdom. He said, "I just couldn't get over the love of this man." Our polemics and our arguments are not nearly as important as the love and power of the Holy Spirit.

Methods of Expansion
Formal Mission Bands
One of the most important methods of expansion was the formation of missionary bands. Paul and Barnabas, Barnabas and Mark, Peter and Mark, Paul, Silas, Timothy and Luke were just probably a few of the missionary bands sent out. They were the earliest mission structures.

Post-Apostolic Structures
According to Michael Green's *Evangelism in the Early Church,* there were itinerant evangelists in the second century.

Eusebius wrote:

> Many of the disciples of that age...divided their goods among the needy. Then they set out on long journeys, doing the work of evangelists, eagerly striving to preach Christ to those who had never heard the word of faith...In foreign lands they simply laid the foundations of faith. That done, they appointed others as shepherds, entrusting them with the care of the new growth, while they themselves proceeded with the grace and cooperation of God to other countries and peoples. (Michael Green, *Evangelism in the Early Church* [Grand Rapids, MI: Eerdmans, 1970], 169).

Others mention such bands also. It is clear that in the post-apostolic Church, there were two kinds of ministry.

We see a settled local ministry—a local church, or group of them—with a growing system of governance by presbyters (or pastors) and bishops, or administrators. There were also itinerant bands of evangelists and missionaries. Some were quite spontaneous and probably disorganized at times.

While throughout history these two kinds of structures have not always worked without some tension between them, we still need both.

Non-Professional, "Lay" Witness

It is important to recognize that in the early Church and at other times of renewal, there were the non-professional, unrecognized "lay" witnesses. This is not a good distinction to make, because "lay" comes from the word *laos*, which simply means "people," the People of God. We have made a false distinction between clergy and laity. We are all laity: laymen and women, because we are all part of the people of God. I am not sure our modern concept of ordination is biblically valid, but I will not discuss that here.

The greatest of the early churches were Antioch, Rome, Alexandria, and Jerusalem. No one knows who founded the Church in Antioch. Acts simply tells us that it was established by "some believers." (Acts 11:20). We do not know who founded the Church in Rome, either. We know it was not Peter or Paul. Paul wrote his letter to the Church in Rome before he got there. There is a tradition that Mark established the church in Alexandria but we are not sure of its validity.

Thus we see people whose names we do not know, who went everywhere planting the Church, witnessing to their faith. They worked alongside the more formalized missionary bands. They were ordinary believers who held no office in the Church, but who shared their faith when they went to new places. Andrew Walls wrote of Nigerian Christians who went to new areas of their country and attracted others to the faith through their worship and life style. The house churches in China grew explosively in that manner. So did the East African and Korean revivals. It is clear that God has used "lay" people very effectively throughout history.

Urban Strategy

The early Church followed an urban strategy. Roland Allen in his book *Missionary Methods: St. Paul's or Ours?* noted that Paul went from city to city. He did not go to the countryside; he went to the centers of population, power, and influence. There he planted the Church, and from there the Church radiated out to the surrounding areas.

We have an interesting example in Brazil. I was a Presbyterian missionary there and did my doctoral work on the history of Presbyterianism in Brazil.

In the early years in the United States, as the population moved west, too many Presbyterian ministers stayed in the east. Presbyterians did not move west nearly as rapidly as did the Methodists and Baptists.

Therefore, in reaction to this problem in the U.S., when Presbyterian missionaries went to Brazil, they moved west. However, in Brazil, moving west meant moving away from the coastal cities, where most of the people lived. For example, the Presbyterian missionaries moved to the state of Mato Grosso, which is over twice as big as Texas, yet had fewer people than the city of São Paulo. When given a choice, they put one of their best missionaries in Mato Grosso instead of São Paulo. As the Presbyterian missionaries moved west, the people were moving east. Presbyterians forgot to study their demographics in Brazil. Consequently they were not as effective in planting churches in the growing cities as they should have been.

On the other hand, the Pentecostals established the Assemblies of God in Brazil starting in Belém, at the mouth of the Amazon River. Two Swedish Baptist charismatics, who had heard a prophecy, went to Belém, and there the Assemblies of God was born in a Baptist church. They moved down to the other coastal cities where, until very recently, all the major population centers existed. From those centers, they moved west into the interior.

That was not the only reason for Pentecostal effectiveness, but it was important in Brazil. We are called to an urban strategy of mission. Many of us were raised in small town or rural environments, where we feel more comfortable. The growing cities of the world constitute one of the greatest missiological challenges for the future.

The Powerless and the Powerful

I am going to read a familiar passage in 1 Corinthians:

> Now remember what you were, my brothers and sisters, when God called you. From the human

point of view, few of you were wise or powerful or of high social standing. God purposely chose what the world considers nonsense in order to shame the wise, and he chose what the world considers weak in order to shame the powerful. He chose what the world looks down on and despises and thinks is nothing in order to destroy what the world thinks is important. (1 Cor. 1:26–28 GNB.)

I could continue, but you know the rest of the passage. I want to note something important but often overlooked in the history of the Church, and especially in the history of the Christian mission.

I believe it has great relevance for our day, for the way in which the Gospel is communicated, and for those whom it is communicated.

In the first three centuries of the history of the Church, roughly to the time of Constantine, people who were perceived as powerless took the Gospel to those considered powerful. That is, it was taken from Jerusalem to Rome—from Paul to Caesar. There is logic in this, since the Gospel is the Good News of the all-powerful and sovereign God, who made himself powerless in Jesus Christ—powerless in the human sense. We are called as followers of Jesus to go to the world cloaked only in his power, not that of our nation or culture.

A shift came with Constantine. While those who took the Gospel to others were not powerful people in their own cultures, they went out from cultures and nations perceived as powerful, and often went to those seen as powerless or less powerful. This continued, with some exceptions, through the centuries. The modern missionary movement was caught in a serious dilemma, because its message often accompanied colonialism.

When we look at the modern Protestant and Catholic missionary movements (Catholics beginning in the sixteenth century and Protestants in the eighteenth), we see the Gospel was almost always taken from cultures and nations that were powerful economically, politically, and militarily, to nations and peoples that generally lacked that kind of power. The question that arises in my mind is,

"What kind of distortion of the Christian message did this cause, both in those who brought the message and those who received it?" I do not think we have dealt with that issue adequately.

Today, we are beginning to see a change in this dynamic. Western Christians are no longer the only, or even the primary, carriers of the Gospel across cultural and geographical barriers today. Increasingly, our brothers and sisters from Asia, Africa, and Latin America are leading the cross-cultural missionary movement. This is a very positive development. I believe this shift has more implications for evangelism and how the Gospel will be perceived than any of us realize.

We also need to grapple with the fact that in the earliest centuries and other periods of history, the powerless have heard the Gospel most gladly. Yet, perhaps because of our Western middle-class mindset and other reasons, the great mass of poor people in the world, especially the urban poor, are being bypassed and neglected. This is another critical issue in mission today.

Means of Evangelism
Going to the Synagogue

This section is taken primarily from Green's Evangelism in the Early Church, cited earlier. He talks about the means of early evangelism. We see one method clearly in the book of Acts: Paul and his colleagues went to the synagogue. It was their primary point of contact, and, as we know, there were three kinds of people there: Jews, proselytes, and God-fearers.

I suggest you reflect on this question: In the cultures in which you work, are there any analogies to the synagogue that might serve as bridges to the Gospel? Is it possible that a temple in Thailand, a Hindu temple of the *bhakti* group, or a mosque in Central Africa, where people are genuinely seeking God, might be analogous to the synagogue? We do not want to rule out, à priori, any potential bridge. Paul obviously had a special reason for going to the synagogue, but there may be analogous institutions where we work.

Focusing on What God Has Done

Green notes that the basic message of the early Church rejoiced in the activity of God. I still hear many preachers attempting to communicate the Gospel, yet talking primarily about what we should do. It took me many years (perhaps I was in seminary) before I realized this crucial difference. The apostolic message always begins with what God has done, and invites us to respond in faith. Remember, the Christian life is, above all, a joyful response to that which God has done in Christ. Too often in the Church, we turn it around and begin to speak first of what we should do.

Household Evangelism

Green mentions household evangelism; it is important to understand the sociological significance of the household in Greco-Roman culture. It was an extended family, and the head of the household was very important. Some evangelism took place without reaching the head of the household, but frequently a whole household was won. We note that the entire households of Cornelius and the Philippian jailor were baptized. When the word *ecclesia* is used in the New Testament, it usually refers to worship in a household like that of Cornelius or Lydia. That should lead us to pay more attention to the social structures where we work: the key leaders, heads of households, heads of groups, or what some sociologists call "the gatekeepers." These are the people who allow a person to enter the cultural matrix, or who perhaps prevent a newcomer from being accepted. This calls us to be more sophisticated about the cultures in which we work and the key people to whom we witness.

Chapter Five

Expansion in the Roman World

Devotional

Now we will examine the expansion of the Christian faith in the Roman world. First, let us pray:

Father, we thank you that you have come to us as one who laid aside all of your prerogatives in Jesus Christ, who first of all became a man, born to a peasant woman in a manger, lived with us as a servant, laid aside your power and went to a cross to die the death of a criminal in order to reconcile us, to bring us forgiveness, salvation, and life. We pray, Lord, that you will help us to discover increasingly what it means to live as followers of this Christ, who bids us take up our own crosses and follow. We ask this in His name. Amen.

Asia

Palestine and the Fall of Jerusalem

Jerusalem fell first in A.D. 70 and then again in 134, when it was destroyed completely. Some of you may have been in Rome and visited the Arch of Titus, which is near the Coliseum. Roman generals and emperors often built arches to commemorate their great deeds. Titus was the general who conquered Jerusalem in the year 70, and later became emperor. Carved in his arch is a bas-relief sculpture that shows Roman soldiers carrying off the menorah, seven-pronged brass candlesticks from the Temple, symbolizing his conquest of Jerusalem. This event had great significance for the Christian Church.

It meant, among other things, that the Church would never be tied primarily to Jewish culture. That had positive and negative aspects.

Positively, it released the Church to move into Gentile culture without the problems of the Judaizers, whom Paul opposed so strongly. The tragedy was that Jewish followers of Jesus became more and more isolated from the gentile church. It also exaggerated and deepened the division between Jewish believers in the Messiah and those who rejected that faith. The Jewish church eventually seems to have lapsed into legalism in the East and seems to have disappeared by the third or fourth century.

Think about what happened from a missiological perspective. The Gentile church, which had fought to avoid being tied exclusively to Jewish culture (the issue of Acts 15), now had freedom to be fully gentile. It is ironic that when Jews became believers in subsequent years, they were not free to continue to affirm their Jewish culture. The issue in Acts 15 was reversed. It is only in our time in history that some Christians recognize that Jews should continue to affirm their ancient culture and still be authentic followers of Jesus as Messiah." I am referring of course, to the Messianic Jewish movement.

Syrian Antioch

We move on to Syrian Antioch, where the first Gentile church was established after the martyrdom of Stephen (Acts 11:19). By the fourth century, Antioch had a population of 500,000, and half were professing Christians. The faith apparently spread primarily among the Greek-speaking city people. Likely factors in this expansion were the ease of communication in the Greek language, and the fact that the city people were probably less tied to traditional forms and more open to the new. Apparently, the faith did not spread as much among the country people, who did not speak Greek. Could there be a missiological pattern here?

Some research has indicated that in Brazil, when people first come from the interior to the city, they are more open to the evangelical faith than when they lived in the tightly knit social fabrics of their rural communities. They also seem to be more open than they will be a generation later, after they have been in the city for some years.

In other words, times of movement and transition seem to provide greater openness to new ideas. Could this be a general principle worth further investigation? It has implications for our understanding of ministry in cities today. One thing it suggests is that we should be in contact with immigrant groups as they arrive in new places.

It is reported that over half the Koreans in the United States (perhaps even seventy-five percent) are now professing Christians. That compares with only twenty-five to thirty percent of those in Korea. This indicates that as Koreans move into a new nation and culture, there is greater openness to the Christian message. It also indicates that the Korean churches have become an entry point, a place of community and support, for Koreans coming into this new society. As part of their process of adjustment, many Koreans new to the U.S. are hearing Korean churches communicate the gospel. Could that have lessons for the rest of us?

Edessa, Northern Mesopotamia

Another place of special interest in Asia Minor is Edessa, located in northern Mesopotamia, between the Tigris and Euphrates rivers. According to a legend, Abgar, the king of Edessa, had invited Jesus to visit him. While we do not believe this legend is true, it does indicate that quite early, the Christian faith arrived in there. We can guess how it arrived there. Scholars believe that the Jewish synagogue originated in Babylon during the exile. The synagogue, which was a highly

structured institution by the time of our Lord, probably started like a cell group among believing Jews who wanted to maintain their faith during the exile. It is logical to believe that the synagogues among the Jews of the Diaspora in the Tigris-Euphrates Valley, which dated back four to five centuries before Christ, were the bridges over which the faith arrived and began to penetrate that community.

We find that later, Edessa became the principal training and sending point for the Nestorian missionaries. They went across Asia Minor and central Asia to China, India, and elsewhere. That mission movement was almost completely destroyed by Islam and other forces. Dr. Samuel Moffett of Princeton has written the first two volumes of a projected three-volume work on the history of Christianity in Asia. It is the most complete source we have on the history of that movement.

India

Although some scholars would disagree, the Christian faith probably moved to South India from Edessa. The ancient Church of St. Thomas in South India goes back at least to the third century. However some scholars believe there is evidence to show that it was established by the Apostle Thomas in the first century. According to tradition, he arrived in south India in 52 AD. There was heavy maritime traffic between Asia Minor, North Africa, Egypt, Arabia, and South India at the time. Thomas could have gone to India on one of the many ships that sailed across the Indian Ocean during the first century.

We also know that the Church in South India used Syriac, the language of Edessa and much of the Middle East. Syriac is related to Hebrew and Aramaic. Aramaic, of course, was the language Jesus spoke. Hebrew was the older language of the Old Testament, but by Jesus' time, the Jewish people spoke Aramaic. That could indicate the Church in South India was started directly by the Apostle Thomas, or more likely, that it came from the Syriac-speaking missionary center in Edessa.

We do know that in the fourth century, another Thomas came with a large group from Edessa to plant a missionary colony in South India. It is from one of these two attempts, or a combination of them, that the ancient Church, now a family of churches in South India grew.

Later the Mar Thoma Church broke off from the older Church in South India after a renewal movement sparked by Anglican missionaries. Others became Roman Catholics, so now a family of churches has descended from the original. The Church of South India represents a unification of several different denominational traditions that came from the West.

Armenia: The First State Church

Armenia is a most interesting case study in early evangelization. There are many legends involved in the arrival of Christianity in the nation, and it is not easy to separate legend from fact. The key man was Gregory, called "the Illuminator." He lived from about 240 to 332, and was of royal blood.

Armenia is located between northern Turkey and southern Russia. It has not been a separate nation in modern times until recently. When Persia conquered Armenia, Gregory went into exile and became a Christian in Cappadocia, (now part of central Turkey) which was strongly Christian. When Armenia achieved independence from Persia early in the fourth century, Gregory returned.

It was a time of transition. The Armenian people and the aristocracy wanted to re-establish their ancient traditions and religion, and reorganize their national life. Gregory, as one related to the royal family, was expected to participate and give leadership in traditional religious practices. At a worship service, he refused to lay a garland on the altar of the goddess Anahit. That was the point at which Gregory asserted his Christian faith.

He was imprisoned and tortured, but persevered. There are stories of power encounter, although we do not know the details. Eventually, Gregory's relative, the king, became a Christian through his witness and perseverance. Then the king and Gregory worked together to persuade the aristocracy to accept the Christian faith, and it became the national religion.

As modern evangelicals, we ask, "What does a 'national religion' mean? What does a group decision for Christ mean?" While it may not mean personal faith and understanding on the part of every person, it can mean a changing of allegiance—as people recognize the God and Father of Jesus Christ, as their God, and seek to follow and serve him. There may be a low level of understanding and morality at the beginning. Nevertheless, it brought an opportunity to begin to disciple the Armenian people. That seems to have happened to a significant extent. Gregory preached in the vernacular language. Then, in 406, according to tradition, Mesob, a monk, encouraged the creation of an alphabet and a written language in order to translate the New Testament. The translation was finished in 410. We believe it was the second time in history that a language was reduced to writing in order to translate the Bible.

This affirmation of Armenian culture and nationality, and its identification with the Scriptures and the Christian faith, gave an amazing power of resiliency and perseverance to Armenian society. Armenians have often been denied their own homeland and persecuted through the centuries much like the Jews. We remember the Armenian genocide early in the twentieth century. Yet we find Armenians everywhere in positions of influence and power.

However, a problem arises when a culture and the Christian faith are so closely united. It often becomes difficult to distinguish between the two. For many, to be an Armenian is to be an Armenian Orthodox Christian. That has been the tradition. Religion can become simply a cultural overlay, like being a Lutheran in Sweden, or a Roman Catholic in Spain or Brazil, a Presbyterian in Scotland, or a Southern Baptist in Texas. That can become a problem for any church or Christian tradition.

There are both positive and negative sides to this identification between culture and faith. It can overcome some barriers to faith. However it can restrict the Faith only to a certain cultural group. For example, many of the Christians of South India have become a Christian caste, and that severely limits their outreach. Of course, that also happens to middle-class American Baptists or Presbyterians. A renewing movement of the Holy Spirit is normally needed to overcome the tendency to identify one's faith too closely with one's culture, especially as most societies are multi-cultural today.

I had a young man in my church in Fresno whose parents were Armenians. He had a profound conversion while in college, and began working, not in the Presbyterian Church in which he was raised, but in the Armenian Orthodox Church in Fresno. As we talked, he said, "I found that I could use good evangelical jargon, I could say,' Praise the Lord', or I could talk about 'accepting Christ' and 'following Christ' if I spoke Armenian. If I did so in English, I would be considered an evangelical American and an outsider. If I did it in Armenian, I was an insider. You can do all sorts of things if you use the Armenian language that you can't do with these bilingual people if you use English."

There are important missiological issues here. One is the importance of being sensitive to the culture and being perceived as an insider, not an outsider. Later on, for example, we will see the alliance between the Christian faith and nationalism in the Reformation. Luther was a German nationalist as well as a reformer. Knox was a Scottish nationalist as well as a reformer.

Nationalism was an important factor in the rapid growth of the Christian faith in Korea. The missionary history of Korea is quite different from that of China. In China, the missionaries came on the heels of Western imperialism, the Opium Wars, and unequal treaties forced on the nation. The missionaries, sometimes exhibiting a lack of wisdom, were able to go into China because of the unjust treaties forced on that nation by England and other Western powers. Thus, the missionaries were inevitably identified with Western imperialism. That was one reason for the virulent anti-Christian attitude of the Communist movement in China.

In Korea, the situation was different. American missionaries arrived in Korea just as Japan was beginning to dominate the nation. The first Protestant missionaries arrived in 1884 and 1885, and in 1910, Japan annexed Korea. In 1919, many Korean Christians took the leadership in the movement that demanded independence. There was no conflict between being a Korean nationalist and a Christian. In fact, there was an alliance between the two. Dr. Shin Kim has just finished a fine D. Miss dissertation on the positive role of nationalism in the early Korean church.

This teaches us always to be sensitive to the best aspirations of every people. Each person should be encouraged to be a patriot, advocating a healthy nationalism. Positive nationalism involves affirming one's culture and seeking the best for one's people and their development. As Christians, we identify with that kind of nationalism.

Nationalism becomes non-Christian when it attempts to assert one's own culture and power against others. I can still remember how puzzled I was with some North American missionaries in Brazil who were very nationalistic when it came to the United States, but thought Brazilian nationalism was bad. That was a terrible contradiction. There are certainly some dangers in North American nationalism and some positive aspects to Brazilian nationalism. We as Christians believe that God wants the best for every people, and that includes the best for their political, economic, and social lives.

We see the issue of nationalism arise throughout the history of the Church. For example, how are Christians to participate in nation building in Indonesia? One of the problems there was that Dutch colonists were "Christians." In order to achieve its independence and build the nation, Indonesia had to get rid of the Dutch. The number of Christians in Indonesia, the largest Muslim nation in the world, has probably reached around fifteen percent now. Thus, the role of Christians in nation building and Indonesian development in a predominantly Muslim nation is complicated. Nevertheless, a Christian in this situation cannot and should not turn his or her back on the issue of nation building. Quite the contrary! Followers of Jesus should find positive ways to be involved, because that too is an expression of the love of God. On the other hand, we cannot make nation building and nationalism a god that becomes lord above Jesus Christ. It is an issue of priorities.

These are missiological issues. Missionaries can never fail to be concerned about politics and economics. Obviously, I do not suggest that missionaries are to become personally involved in politics, but we must move beyond a missionary mentality that says, "God is only interested in saving souls, not in politics or economics, because that is outside the realm of heaven." Our theology of mission, focused on the Kingdom of God, certainly puts the priority on communicating the Good News of Jesus and inviting men and women to become His disciples. However, it also teaches us to seek the welfare of those among whom we live as an expression of the compassion of Christ.

Europe
Rome
Now we move to Europe. Rome soon became a center of Western Christianity. The Roman Church did not claim that to be dominant until late in the fourth century. The Council of Nicæa, in 325 was the first great ecumenical council. Held in Asia Minor, it brought bishops from as far away as Spain and North Africa. Constantine called the Council to settle a doctrinal issue, not because he understood the theological issue involved, but because he wanted a unified church.

The Bishop of Rome had no position of prominence in the Council, but by the end of the fourth century the Roman Church began to claim that it, along with its bishop, was the first among equals. There were some natural reasons for this. Constantine moved the seat of his empire to Constantinople, now Istanbul. When he moved out of Rome he left a weak subordinate in Italy to rule. The civil rulers in the West, called *ethnarcs*, eventually moved from Rome to Ravenna, isolated from the rest of Italy. That left the Bishop of Rome as the most prominent and strongest leader, not only in Rome, but also in the western Empire.

Barbarian invasions threatened, and the Roman Empire began to deteriorate. In this context, the bishops of Rome, many of whom were very able and godly men, filled the vacuum and naturally assumed leadership. Many became civic as well as religious leaders. Rome was now the most significant city in the western part of the Roman Empire and the Bishop of Rome its most prominent leader.

Stephen Neill notes that the first Christians in Rome typically spoke Greek, not Latin. That suggests they were mostly from the lower classes. The aristocratic class spoke Latin, the slaves, the poor, and the common people usually spoke Greek. This does not mean there were not some aristocrats in the early Church in Rome, but its primary growth took place among the poor.

Gaul
The key leader in Gaul (now France) was Irenaeus. He was born in Smyrna, in Asia Minor, and lived from about 130 until 200. Shortly after mid-century, he went to what is now southern France, and eventually became bishop of Lyon. Later we will hear about another remarkable leader from Lyon, Peter Waldo, in the twelfth century.

In that historical context, the bishop was the pastor of a city, and as the Church grew, he became the primary pastor of the city. The concept was that of one church with many congregations. This is certainly a more biblical concept that what we have today with many churches of different denominations existing in a city. The word "bishop" simply means "administrator," and did not imply then what it would come to mean later. Iraneaus, as the head pastor of the city, would have had other pastors or priests working under his leadership in the various congregations in the city and surrounding rural areas. He ministered in two languages. One was Latin. Naturally, the Romans and those who had been assimilated into their culture spoke that language. Julius Caesar had conquered Gaul, and made it part of the Roman Empire. Therefore, Latin was the language used to minister to the Romans and those who had accepted their culture.

Irenaeus is of special interest because he also ministered to the Celts in their own language. Even though we usually associate the Celts with Ireland and Scotland, in fact they were scattered all over Europe. They were also found in what is now Turkey. Paul's Letter to the Galatians—note "G-L-T" and "C-L-T"—may well have been written to a Celtic group. The fact that Irenaeus ministered in Celtic as well as Latin indicates several things. He probably learned the Celtic language when he was in Asia Minor, where there were Celts. It also indicates that he ministered, not only to the dominant people—the Romans and Romanized people—but also to the tribal people who had not adopted that culture. Thus, he understood an important missiological principle: the differences between various people groups and the importance of including all in his ministry.

Britain

Soldiers, traders, and government officials probably took the Christian faith there by the third, perhaps even the second century. Apparently, the Church was limited primarily to the Romans and those who had adopted their culture and lived in the towns they built. Apparently it had not spread to the so-called "barbarians": the rough, unruly, unconquered, undisciplined tribes. That would come later with the Celtic movement.

Hadrian's Wall was built in the second century across the island, near what is now the English-Scottish border. Its purpose was to prevent the northern "barbarians," the Picts and the Scots, from invading. But in the sixth century, Celtic Christian missionaries came from Ireland to Scotland and then down into England on their mission of evangelization. There is an interesting parable here. Sometimes we build walls to keep people out, but then they come in and bless us. Could that be happening as Christian believers come to the West from the majority world?

Africa

Alexandria

As we move to Africa, we look first at Alexandria, at the mouth of the Nile. The city had the largest Jewish community outside of Palestine before the time of Christ. Philo of Alexandria lived there. He was the great Jewish philosopher who tried to build bridges between Jewish theology and Greek philosophy, using the *logos* concept. The Septuagint was produced there a century before Christ. Later on, two of the great early theologians, Clement of Alexandria and Origen, would be found there. In the third century, the Scriptures were translated into Coptic, the language of Egypt before the Arab Muslim conquest. The Coptic Church in Egypt, that numbers at least six million people today, is the largest church to remain in any North African or Middle Eastern country after the Muslim conquest.

Tunis & Algeria

We know the faith spread further west to what are now Tunisia and Algeria, but we do not know how. We find three primary people groups in that part of North Africa. The first group, of course, was the Romans and those who had adopted their culture. The second group was composed of the Punic people, descendents of Phoenician sailors who had arrived before the Romans and built their capital city, Carthage. The two groups were bitter enemies. Carthage was so strong militarily that Hannibal, the Punic general, took elephants across the Mediterranean, up through Spain and over the Alps in the war against Rome. That was an amazing feat! Carthage was eventually destroyed by Rome, but the Punic people remained and constituted the second major people group there.

The third group was the Berbers, desert tribes, with a lower level of civilization, as we normally define the word. They were the indigenous people.

In the Church in North Africa we find well-known Christian leaders among the Romanized population. The greatest Christian thinker between St. Paul and Martin Luther was St. Augustine, a North African who wrote in Latin. Earlier there were others, including Cyprian and Tertullian. The first theologians who wrote in Latin lived, not in Italy or Rome, but in North Africa. Before them Greek had been the language of theology, the gentile Church having come first out of Asia Minor and Greek culture.

We know that there were Christians among in the Punic people. We do not know much about the progress of the faith among the Berbers, but we suspect there were not many Christians among them. If there were Berber Christians, we wonder if any were in leadership in the Church.

One of the great, unanswered questions of church history has been why these strong churches in Asia Minor and North Africa succumbed so quickly to the onslaught of Islam. How did Islam sweep so rapidly across North Africa and obliterate the Church that had furnished some of the greatest Christian leaders in the first few centuries? The reason may very well be that North Africa had a relatively elitist church within one segment of the population, and had not encompassed the Carthaginian and Berber peoples. One scholar has asserted that Augustine insisted that the Berbers worship in Latin, not in their own languages. That, of course, was a violation of the Pentecost principle that each person should hear the Good News in his or her own language. It is probable that many Christians by that time were quite nominal in their faith and accepted Islam under pressure.

After the Islamic conquest, many of the Romanized Christians returned to Europe. Others stayed, but the Church eventually died because of persecution and the pressures of Islam. It is worth noting that only at the end of the twentieth century was the New Testament translated into one of the Berber languages. It is encouraging to note that recently there has been a growing church, primarily among Berbers, in Algeria.

Constantine and Toleration

Persecutions

By the end of the third century, it is estimated that ten percent of the people of the Roman Empire were Christians. The level of Christian faith and life must have been quite high because of the constant wave of persecutions but there were now some third, fourth, and fifth generation Christians. Most of the persecutions were not Empire-wide, nor were they continuous. They were usually sporadic events in various areas of the Empire. But in the middle of the third century under the Emperor Valerian, and at the beginning of the fourth century under Diocletian, there were attempts to exterminate the Christian faith completely within ten years.

Constantine

At the same time, there were rivalries between the leaders. The Empire was large and unwieldy. Think about the difficulties of communication when someone in Britain attempted to communicate with a leader in Asia Minor. Eventually there were four key leaders in a power struggle to rule the entire Empire.

Constantine, who had marched south from Britain, was more sympathetic to Christianity than the other three rulers. His father had been somewhat sympathetic to Christianity, and his mother was a Greek-speaking Christian from the East. In the year 312, Constantine faced a crucial battle in Italy. The winner would dominate the western empire. Before the battle, he believed he had a vision in which he saw the Christos symbol, with the words: "In This Sign Conquer." He quickly had the symbol put on his helmet and the shields of his soldiers. The next day he went into battle as a Christian in some sense at least, and defeated his enemy. He now confessed the Christian God as his God, and soon began to favor the Church.

Constantine's life was far from a model of Christian discipleship. He was brutal. He was not baptized until he was on his deathbed. Nevertheless, the battle in Italy marked a great shift in the history of the Church and Western culture. In the following year of 313, in the Edict of Milan, Constantine and his eastern rival gave freedom of conscience to the Christians. That put Christianity on a full legal basis with other religions. Christian organizations could now hold property for the first time. In 323, Constantine became the sole ruler of the Roman Empire.

The New Situation: Christendom

Now the Church entered what is called the Constantinian era. That meant that among other things, it was no longer a despised, persecuted minority. Rapidly, it became a powerful majority. In 370, the Emperor declared that all people in the Empire must be Christian. That had both positive and negative effects. We face one set of temptations when we are part of a persecuted, despised minority, but we face different, more subtle temptations when we are a powerful majority. The latter set of temptations may be more dangerous. Then the temptation will be to take and abuse power, to use it for the wrong reasons. There is always the temptation to identify our own culture or political party with the Christian faith and, motivated by our own self-interest, but in the name of the faith, to oppress other people. We must confess that it has happened frequently throughout history.

As evangelical churches in certain parts of the world—in Latin America, Korea, and areas of Africa—grow to become respectable and powerful, they face certain temptations that the American church constantly faces. We must always deal with the issue of the relationship of the Christian faith to culture.

The book by H. Richard Neibuhr, *Christ and Culture*, examined the question "What should the relationship of the Christian Church be to its surrounding culture?" One view says the gathered community is to turn its back on the culture. That was both the monastic and early Anabaptist ideal. The Amish in Pennsylvania are an extreme example of that view, as are some of the monastic groups.

Others say the Church should dominate the culture. This was the view of the medieval Catholic Church. The Church taught that the state and culture should be subservient to the Church. The goal was to build a Christian culture. But too often, Christians have been absorbed into the culture and baptized its values as Christian, even when those values included slavery and racism. The Calvinist ideal has been to attempt to work alongside culture and transform it. I personally believe that should be the goal of all of us, even though we always do so imperfectly.

Many have come from church traditions with a view of history that went something like this: the Holy Spirit was alive, well, and active during the first three centuries. Churches were vital, they were growing, and God was doing great things. Then the Constantinian era began and nothing of significance happened until the sixteenth century. (Perhaps with your group, it was the seventeenth, eighteenth, nineteenth, or even twentieth century.) *Halley's Bible Handbook* expresses this view.

What this view really implies is that the Holy Spirit was alive and well for the first three centuries, then died, and rose from the dead in whatever century your group happened to have begun.

I was raised with that implicit view of history. I hope we will all come out of this course with a realization that through many different people, movements, and traditions different from our own, the Holy Spirit has been alive and active through all of the centuries. We want to learn from them.

The most significant aspect of the Constantinian era was the establishment of Christendom. This term indicates the support of the Church by the state, and the assumption that all citizens were, in some sense, Christians, and members of the Church. For example, it may have referred to the Roman Catholic Church in Spain or Italy, the Anglican Church in England, the Presbyterian Church in Scotland, or the Lutheran Church in areas of Germany. While most would agree that the system brought some advantages, many believe that it brought serious distortions to the life of the Church and the Christian faith. I believe it did so, and will add that even though we have not had a legally established church in the United States, in many ways we have had a de facto Christendom. By that, I mean that for many years the underlying assumption was that the United States was a Christian (mainly Protestant) nation. The President of the United States, along with a former and future President, spoke at a Protestant missionary conference in New York in 1900. During the Second World War, both Winston Churchill and Franklin Roosevelt spoke of 'saving Christian civilization.' That would not happen today. That era has clearly ended. The de facto

Christendom in the United States and the legally established Christendom in most other nations is ending. While that may have its negative aspects, I believe that overall, it is a positive development. It forces all of us to recognize that wherever it exists, the Church of Jesus Christ always lives in a missionary situation.

Other Areas

The word "barbarian" was a term given by the Romans to the waves of peoples who came from Central Asia and poured into Central and Southern Europe as the Roman Empire began to weaken. It was obviously a derogatory term.

We find a most interesting figure at this time. His name was Ulfilas. Born about 311, he went up north of the Danube River and began to evangelize the Goths. For forty years, from 341 until he died in 381, he was perhaps the only missionary beyond the frontiers of the Roman Empire. He went to an area where he would have no status or protection. In that sense, he represents the best of the missionary tradition. And yet, his theology was heretical in that he was an Arian, rather than a Trinitarian.

We know that some of the Goths, in raids on Roman territory, had captured Christian women and made them slaves or wives, so there was some Christian influence among them. The Christian faith often spread in those early years in that way. Women who were captured in raids and taken as wives, mistresses, or slaves, shared their Christian faith. At times, the men accepted that faith or at least became favorably disposed toward it.

Ulfilas reduced the Gothic language to writing in order to translate the Bible. As far as we know, this was the first time that any language of Northern Europe was reduced to writing, and it was for the purpose of Bible translation. I have often wondered if he should not be the patron saint of Wycliffe Bible Translators.

You will read in Latourette's *A History of Christianity* that Persia and Rome showed great hostility toward each other at this time. When Rome became nominally Christian, the Persians perceived Christians as their enemies and persecuted them. In one week, fifty bishops were slaughtered in Persia and more Christians were killed in a very short time than had been killed in all the years of Christianity under Roman occupation. Very often, the friend of my enemy is seen as my enemy. There are modern analogies to this syllogism.

We can see several issues affecting the spread of the Gospel among Muslims in general and Arabs in particular. Because Muslims see no separation between religion and culture, church and state, they automatically assume Christians advocate the things they see in America and other Western nations: war, materialism, and all manner of immorality. Another hindrance to leading our Arab Muslim friends to trust and respect Christians is the unequivocal support the United States and the American church give to Israel as a political entity. Our Arab friends do not understand how we can seem to ignore some of the injustices that their children, neighbors, and cousins, the Palestinians, are facing in Israel. These issues must be dealt with thoughtfully by those who would see Muslims and Arabs follow Jesus.

Chapter Six

Early Monasticism

Issues of the Post-Apostolic Era

There is always the danger of nominalism in a third or fourth generation church. By that term I mean those who formally profess the Christian faith and perhaps participate in some Church activities, but show little or no understand of, or commitment to, Christ. It will exist in a relatively new church on a mission field, in a movement that began as renewal in Europe or North America, and even more so in older, more traditional churches. It is an issue we must always face, no matter how our particular movement began.

It appears that the Church must always grapple with three issues. The first is the constant necessity of renewal, a return to its first love for Jesus. The second is the need to define the essentials of the Faith. The third is the understanding of the Christian life, how is a follower of Jesus to live? New movements focus especially on the latter two.

Renewal (Montanism)

Montanism arose in the middle of the second century. It was a movement we would call "charismatic" today. The Church had been in existence for over a century. Despite persecution, there must have been some loss of ardor by many believers. The early hope that Christ would soon return had not been fulfilled. Perhaps the ministry of women, quite prominent in the early Church (see Romans 16), was no longer encouraged. The Church was taking on a more formal structure, with bishops leading in most places. Montanism was a response to those second-century circumstances. It focused on the gifts of the Spirit, prophecies by both men and women, and the early return of Christ. Women were prominent in leadership. The movement even predicted where Christ would return. In a sense, it sought to return to the vitality and freedom of action of the earliest Christian communities. But it rejected the broader Church and became schismatic. Thus, although it apparently had some very positive aspects, it was eventually condemned by the Church and considered heretical.

But the Church always needs renewal. One of the critical questions we must always ask, no matter where we are, is how the Holy Spirit works to renew the Church. While renewal has taken different forms throughout history, essentially it has meant calling the Church back to its first love; bringing Christians back to an ardent desire to seek God, to know Him, to live for Him, and to share the Faith. This needs to happen repeatedly. Let none of us think our movements are immune to the need for renewal. An issue that the Church faces over and over again is how to encourage such movements and keep them within the broader church, where they are most needed. Often the Church has rejected renewal movements, or the movements have rejected the broader Church, leaving both groups impoverished.

Defining the Faith, Contextualization (Gnosticism, Arianism)

The Church needed to define the Faith, especially in the first three centuries. The earliest Christian creed, found in the New Testament, is simply this: "Jesus is Lord." That meant that Jesus was God— the Greek word *kurios* used in the Septuagint to translate one of the Hebrew terms for God in the Old Testament. It also meant a personal affirmation of Jesus as Lord. Furthermore, for Christians in the Roman Empire, it affirmed Jesus Christ as the ultimate authority over the state. This affirmation, of course, would lead to the persecution of Christians. Thus, the confession "Jesus is Lord" had profound theological, personal, and political meaning.

A related issue was the contextualization of the faith. As a missionary, Paul took the Christian faith from Hebrew to Greek culture. That meant he had to communicate the Gospel in categories that made sense to the Greeks. John did this same thing in the prologue to his Gospel, particularly with his use of the term, *logos*, an important concept in Greek philosophy. Paul did not speak primarily about the Kingdom of God, a phrase constantly on the lips of Jesus. The phrase would not have had the same meaning for Greeks that it did for Jews. So he spoke, instead, of the Lordship of Christ. We believe he was inspired by the Holy Spirit in doing so.

However, in the second and third centuries, a movement arose called Gnosticism, from the word *gnosis* (knowledge). The movement took different forms, but essentially taught that a group of especially spiritual persons possessed a secret saving knowledge that was denied to common believers. Furthermore, Gnosticism was constructed on a philosophical base that said, "Spirit is good; matter is evil." That fundamental premise, had two implications: first, that the god of the Old Testament, the Creator of this world, was an evil god; and secondly, that the Incarnation was a hoax. The Spirit of God could not have become incarnate in a real person because matter, including the body, was evil. That made Jesus into a ghostly figure who left no footprints in the sand. He was not tempted like we are. He did not die on the cross, but rather watched while Simon of Cyrene was crucified.

Obviously, then, since there was no death on the cross and no resurrection, our human condition was left unredeemed. People were to be saved by a special knowledge, a gnosis, imparted only to a few.

The Church struggled against Gnosticism in different forms for centuries. Recently, the book *The Da Vinci Code* and other works, have seriously distorted history and suggested that the Gnostic interpretation of the Christian faith could be a valid alternative. But its worldview is completely contrary to that of the Bible, which begins by saying that creation is good. The issue raised by Gnosticism and other heresies is contextualization. What constitutes legitimate contextualization as we take the Gospel from one culture to another? If we are to be faithful, we will need to understand both Scripture and the history of the Church as they have dealt with this and similar issues.

In the third and fourth centuries, the Church began to define more completely what it meant to say, "Jesus is Lord." This could happen in your own ministry, especially in a newly evangelized group. A serious controversy arose early in the fourth century over this issue. Arius, a presbyter of great learning and good reputation, taught that Christ was a created being, more than human, but less than God. His opponent, Athanasius, insisted that Christ was both fully God and fully man. The first ecumenical council, held at Nicæa in 325, rejected Arianism and affirmed the view of Athanasius, but the struggle continued for over a century. Nevertheless, that council, followed by others, affirmed the basic Christology of the Church universal (Roman Catholic, Orthodox, and Protestant), that Jesus Christ is fully God and fully human.

The Definition of Christian life

How do we define the Christian life? How are we to live as followers of Jesus? In first century Antioch, to be a Christian meant to confess Jesus as Lord, be baptized, become part of the Christian community, and seek to live according to the norms of that community. However, in the fourth century, as the Empire became Christian, almost everyone, many with little or no understanding of the Christian life, entered the Church. Soon, within a century, everyone was nominally Christian.

With this, the definition of "Christian" also changed. It came to mean being a member of the right institution—the Church. One was baptized as an infant, grew up in the Church, took part in its rituals, and hopefully lived a reasonably moral life. Earlier, to be a follower of Jesus involved going against much of the surrounding culture, often at great danger. Now, to be a Christian was to follow the norms of society, it was the easy thing to do. Yet the society was still corrupt; there were still gladiatorial combats and slavery. The age of persecution and martyrdom was over, but especially with the growth of nominalism and the disappearance of martyrdom in the Roman Empire, some sought a living 'martyrdom,' a return to a more rigorous Christian lifestyle.

Monasticism began in the third and fourth centuries. A few men, first in Asia Minor and Egypt, went into the desert to pray and live a very simple, ascetic lifestyle. They lived on as little food and drink as possible. They were celibate and lived lives of prayer and devotion. Usually, their disciples brought them just enough food and water to sustain life. Often they attracted people who came to them asking for their prayers and teaching. They were believed to work miracles.

So monasticism raised the question, "Who is the model for the Christian life: John the Baptist, or Jesus, or both?" John the Baptist, in a sense, is the forerunner of the monks.

How to Deal with an Imperfect Church

Another question arises: How do we deal with a less-than-perfect church? Many Christians come from a church that at some point in its history broke off from a parent body to form a purer church. That is probably true unless we are Roman Catholic, Coptic, or Eastern Orthodox Christians. Most of our churches have broken off from some parent body because our spiritual ancestors were seeking a more pure form of the Church and the faith, at least in theory. I am not suggesting that as the ideal, but historically we observe that one way people have dealt with a

less-than-perfect church has been to leave and form a new one. Of course the new Church will not be perfect either, and as generations pass, will often forget its original values.

Sometimes new churches form involuntarily. The Methodists are an example. Wesley did not want to leave the Anglican Church, but he and his followers found they had to do so if they were to care for their new converts. Wesley maintained the fiction that he was still a loyal Anglican, but in reality, he created a new church structure that was necessary to care for his converts and to choose and train leaders for his movement. The rigid Anglican structure could not contain the new wine of Wesley's movement. Some of the early Pentecostals were forced out of their churches in the United States, Chile, and Brazil. We see that sometimes the division has been the fault of the parent body, because it was unwilling to recognize the new wind of the Spirit or allow the creation of new wineskins.

Another way to deal with a less-than-perfect church is to remain a part of it but form small groups within it for discipleship, nurture, and fellowship for those seeking a deeper life. This is the classical pattern of monasticism in the Roman Catholic and the Eastern Orthodox churches, and for some in the Anglican and Lutheran traditions. Similarly, small groups have been significant in Pietism and Puritanism, and in many evangelical movements today. People have remained within the larger Church, while forming small groups to encourage deeper discipleship. This pattern has been a characteristic of renewal movements throughout history and in turn has often led to new mission.

God has often called many of us to be a part of small covenant groups seeking a deeper and more obedient Christian life. We trust that will lead to greater responsiveness to the mission to which God calls us. However, we believe such groups should remain within the context of the existing churches wherever possible, and seek to stimulate renewal within them. We do not want to be schismatic.

Roman Catholic monasticism has exhibited negative features at time, but repeatedly we see how peripheral groups of monks, friars, and nuns have been the source of mission and renewal. Similar groups have brought renewal and mission to Protestant bodies.

For some, the alternative to separation or seeking renewal through small groups within the broader Church, has been to conform, give up, and stop trying for change.

Monasticism: General Observations

Positive

First, we will make some general observations about the positive aspects of the monastic movement. It sought deeper discipleship, renewal, and spiritual depth. It was often a reaction against the formalism, institutionalism, and nominalism of the broader Church. Interestingly enough, laymen and laywomen started most monastic movements. Mother Theresa was a laywoman. Francis of Assisi was a layman when he began his movement. So was Ignatius Loyola when he established the Jesuits. There is an interesting parallel here because so many Protestant missionary movements were initiated by lay persons. This should encourage us to remain open to the sovereign and often surprising work of the Holy Spirit.

The monks sought a lifestyle consistent with the Gospel as they understood it, leading to a much simpler way of life. St. Francis of Assisi said, "I wed Lady Poverty." He believed that anything he possessed would constitute a barrier between him and his neighbor, and between him and God, because he would be tempted to love his possessions more than his neighbor or God. That has the ring of truth to it. I suspect we all struggle with that.

So the early monks sought a lifestyle more consistent with the Kingdom of God as they understood it. The oft-quoted, golden text of monasticism was Jesus' words to the rich young ruler: "Sell everything you have and give to the poor, and you will have treasure in heaven. Then come, follow me" (Luke 18:22 NIV).

In addition, the early monastic movement functioned as a type of rough democracy. Some were probably the most democratic institutions in exis-

tence during the Middle Ages. They elected their own leaders, who had to be obeyed, but who also had to consult the monks on important matters.

Finally, even though it was not part of their original purpose, at times monasticism became ardently missionary. We will see that the majority of missionaries during most of Church history came from the monasteries.

Negative

Lest we idealize the monastic movement too much, we must see some of its negative factors. Gnosticism, expelled from the Church through the front door, seemed to enter the monastic movement through the back door. There was a tendency in monasticism to despise the flesh and teach that the married state was spiritually inferior to the celibate state. This led to some very unhealthy tendencies in the Roman Catholic Church. With Gnosticism came the concept that one was more spiritual if he or she made the body suffer. This led to a tendency toward salvation by works, the belief that we are saved not only by our faith and God's gracious acceptance of us in Jesus Christ, but by beating the body, living a simple lifestyle, and spending hours in prayer.

There was also a focus on withdrawal from the world, not primarily in order to worship God, but to seek one's own salvation. When Martin Luther was on his way to law school, a bolt of lightning nearly killed him. He fell to the ground, and when he awoke, his first words were, "St. Anne, I'll be a monk." (St. Anne was believed to be the mother of the Virgin Mary.) Luther had been struggling over the issue of his salvation. His medieval culture taught that the only way to be relatively sure of your salvation was to go to the monastery and spend an ascetic life of prayer, fasting, meditation, and good works. That conviction that Luther to the monastery. As he struggled theologically and biblically with the issue of how one received salvation, he was brought to another conclusion, which led to the Protestant Reformation. We will look at that later.

St. Bernard of Clairvaux was the primary leader of the Cistercian order, a monastic renewal movement. He was probably the most influential churchman in twelfth century Europe. He wrote and traveled widely. In his papers, we find correspondence with a priest who had served a parish in Germany. After some years of service as a parish priest, he entered a monastery to seek a deeper relationship with God. After a period in the monastery, he decided to return to the parish and serve his people. But Bernard wrote him and asserted that if he left the monastery and returned to the parish, he would surely be in danger of losing his salvation. Bernard was a great man in many ways, but clearly had a serious flaw in his theology. The concept that the focus on ministry instead of one's own salvation could lead to the loss of salvation, is obviously unbiblical.

In addition, monasticism tended to divide Christians into two categories using external criteria. There were the spiritual athletes (the monks), and there were the ordinary believers.

Monasticism also gave great impetus to the veneration of the Virgin Mary in the Roman Catholic Church that for many has made her the primary focus of worship and devotion. One does not have to be a Freudian psychologist to understand how that could happen. Bernard himself wrote over thirty sermons on the Virgin Mary, based on the Song of Solomon. Thus, monasticism, with its emphasis on celibacy, encouraged some unhealthy attitudes towards sexuality and exalted the role of the Virgin Mary in the medieval church. This issue is still with us today.

The paradox is that even though most of the monks wished to withdraw from society and normal life, they often became missionaries. Not all the monastic groups continued their original emphasis on withdrawal from the world. Some later movements, especially the Celts and the friars (Franciscans and Dominicans), and later, the Jesuits, had a powerful missionary orientation. These men used withdrawal for a time of prayer and preparation to prepare them to go back out in the world with their message. Theirs was a much healthier model.

The History of Monasticism

As we begin to study the history of monasticism, we recognize that most missionaries from the fourth to the eighteenth centuries, two-thirds of the history of the Christian Church, were monks and nuns. There were a few exceptions: the Waldensians, starting in the twelfth century, the Lollards in fifteenth century England, and some Lutherans, Calvinists, and Anabaptists in the sixteenth century. However, the great majority of missionaries of both the Eastern and Western churches during those fourteen centuries were monks.

The Hermits

Monasticism is believed to have begun with Anthony, a hermit, who adopted a very severe ascetic lifestyle. Late in the third century, he went into the desert to live in total solitude. Some came to him and, seeing his piety, were converted to the faith. The movement grew gradually as others followed his example. At first, the monks lived alone, some in caves. One, Simeon Stylites, became well known because he lived for twenty-five years on top of a pillar in the desert. His disciples brought him food and drink. He was considered an example of a holy person. There are other examples that seem bizarre to us.

Early Monastic Communities

Eventually, communities of men and then women were established, many in the Egyptian desert. Worship was their primary focus. They had a strong emphasis on spiritual warfare. They saw life as combat against the world, the flesh, and the devil. They prayed for themselves and the world around them. Sexual temptation was often a great concern and at times the monks did not allow any female, not even their mothers or sisters to come near them. Some would not allow female animals to approach. There are still monasteries in Greece where no women can enter—not even tourists!

Late in the fourth century, there was further evolution of community life. Some began to work, worship, and in some cases, study together. The next step was to elect a head of each community. There were not yet monastic orders in which various monasteries were related to each other and followed the same rules. They were still all quite independent of each other. Their focus was on fellowship within the group, worship, and spiritual combat through prayer.

I have a friend and former student, Bishop Markos Antonios, of the Coptic Church of Egypt. He has been a missionary bishop in Kenya for many years. He served many years as a doctor in Ethiopia, and as a professor in a medical school in Addis Ababa. Markos had a large Bible study group for university students, with up to eight hundred students present, and he started Sunday schools. He prepared Sunday school material for the ancient Ethiopian church, seeking to renew it. When the Marxist government would not allow him to continue his Christian ministry, he left. He said, "I went to a monastery and took my vows as a monk, which I had always wanted to do. I went out in the desert for a year and I prayed. It was wonderful!"

Those of us with a Western mentality find it difficult to think about going to the desert to pray for a year, but Markos said he hated to leave that life. There is a kind of spirituality we Protestants need to know more about and learn from, even though we might not be called to that lifestyle.

I am convinced that marriage is wonderful! Being a husband and a parent has been the most marvelous experience of my life. However, God calls us to different life styles, and it has been refreshing for me to see this dear brother who loves Christ and who has had experiences very different from mine.

Lynn T. White, a former UCLA professor, in his article "The Significance of Medieval Christianity" (Thomas, George, ed. *The Vitality of the Christian Tradition*, Harper & Brothers, 1944) made the point that the early monks were the first to bring manual and intellectual labor together. Some of us have worked in cultures where it is still assumed that if you have degrees after your name and put on a necktie when you go to work, you do not get your hands dirty. That was true of the Greco-Roman world. Slaves did manual labor, gentlemen did intellectual work, and women did not work if they were of the nobility. White

wrote that the monks were the first intellectuals to get dirt under their fingernails. That was a great gain for Western culture.

There is a delightful story about St. Bonaventure, one of the early Franciscan theologians, who wrote a fine book on the journey of the soul toward God. The pope honored him by making him a cardinal. When the emissary of the pope came to the house where St. Bonaventure was living to award him his red cardinal's hat, he found him in the backyard washing dishes. The story says that the new cardinal took his red hat, hung it on a tree, and continued washing dishes. That is a beautiful picture of monasticism at its best.

Benedict of Nursia

The story continued with Benedict of Nursia. In 529, monasticism had already existed in the West for three centuries, but was in decline. Some monasteries had become decadent and immoral. St. Benedict, who had a gift for organization, founded a monastery on Monte Casino in central Italy and created a rule to guide community life. One writer has called them "a permanent, self-contained, self-supporting garrison of Christ's soldiers" (Williston Walker, *A History of the Christian Church* [New York: Scribner, 1959 Revised Edition], 127). However, they should be called "soldiers," because they were not supposed to leave the monastery. They were designed to be a self-supporting community. The abbot or head of the house was to be obeyed, but he had to consult the brothers on some matters. The word "abbot" comes from the Aramaic word *Abba*, meaning "father."

Worship was the monks' primary duty. They spent four hours in worship each day, divided into seven different periods. They also spent several hours each day at work. That included both manual work in the fields, and intellectual work in the library. Both made a great contribution to Western culture. As they planted and cultivated their fields, they often developed new methods of agriculture. Their work in the library included the copying of ancient manuscripts, consequently many works of the ancient world came to us through the monasteries. Normally they established schools only for their members. However, Charlemagne brought three thousand Celtic monks to establish schools in his realm. Eventually the movement contributed to the formation of the universities.

The monks' food and dress were very simple. They wore the plain garb of the common people of their day. While a monk's robe may appear exotic to us today, in that context it was the garment of the common people.

Reasons for Decline
Wealth
As we examine the reasons for a decline in monasticism, McGavran's phrase "redemption and lift" applies here. As time passed, many monasteries became wealthy. They often went to new areas, cleared the land, planted crops, and prospered. I once visited the little town of Alcobaça, where the largest church in Portugal is located. It was founded by Cistercian monks who came from France in the thirteenth century. The monks introduced the cultivation of apples and pears and the finest fruit in Portugal is raised in there. The Cistercians were also responsible for the growth of the wool industry in England.

In addition to their work, there was a second reason for their wealth. Members of the nobility often donated land and other property to the monasteries with the stipulation that the monks pray for their souls after death. This reflected the medieval teaching that the soul went to purgatory after death and that the prayers of the monks would aid in the journey to heaven. Thus, many nobles donated land and other goods to the monasteries, making them very rich. Wealth often brought corruption.

Another example is the monastery at Melk, in Austria. Overlooking the Danube River, its buildings are constructed of the finest marble—a far cry from the simplicity and austere life of the early monks.

Feudalism
Monasteries often became centers of political power. With the evolution of feudalism, monasteries came to possess more and more land, and their abbots often became power brokers. Members of the nobility who were attempting to construct political coalitions had to make alliances with many of the abbots. Some because feudal lords themselves. Such coalitions were necessary to establish some kind of order in society, but the process seriously compromised the role of many monasteries. Power, not piety, became the goal.

In Salzburg, Austria, you may visit the palace of the Prince-Archbishop on the mountain that overlooks the city. It includes a medieval torture chamber. The palace built for his mistress is located in front of the cathedral in the city below. Thus, the Prince-Archbishop was similar to any other medieval ruler, imposing his will through torture and power. This was not unusual in the medieval church during the feudalism. While the Prince-Archbishop was not the abbot of a monastery, he stands as an example of many medieval church leaders, including some abbots.

The Younger Sons of the Nobles
The monasteries also became places for the younger sons of the nobility. The oldest son by law and custom inherited the property, and the next son might become a soldier, but the youngest son had difficulty in finding his place. Noble families often sent these sons to monasteries even though they did not have any inclination toward the monastic life. That of course led to a serious decline in the quality of their spiritual life, and often to debauchery and immorality.

Self-Centered Theology
In addition, the self-centered theology that focused on one's own salvation was an unhealthy aspect of monastic life. Earlier, I mentioned Luther as an example. But the monastic movement, that began with people seeking renewal and an authentic Christian lifestyle (as they understood it) made a positive impact on medieval culture. We are all in their debt. However, for the reasons discussed above, they often declined.

Means of Renewal
The normal means of renewal in monasticism were to create new communities with more rigorous rules. At times, men left an older monastery, went to a deserted area, and built a new commu-

nity. Sometimes, in order to maintain their original vision, these new communities joined with others and attempted to avoid the interference of the nobility and local bishops. In some cases, such movements had a positive effect.

Some monasteries became missionary as they went out and formed new Christian communities in areas where there was little Christian influence. The lifestyle of the monasteries, their spiritual power, and their authority often attracted the surrounding peoples. In that way some monasteries became missionary communities.

A Missionary Movement?

To what extent was monasticism a missionary movement? Ralph Winter has praised the missionary aspect of monasticism. We Protestants need to hear that praise; we have much to learn from monasticism. However, I am a bit critical of it as a missionary movement when we look at it as a whole. The first goal of the monks was not to go out into the world and share the Gospel. Their first goal was to withdraw from the world and cultivate their own spiritual lives. To use Mellis's terms, these were "go on" or "go deeper" rather than "go out" communities.

The by-product was often the formation of communities that modeled the Christian life for the pagan or semi-Christian societies around them. Thus they often became centers that depicted a more Christian life style, encouraged education and what we call 'civilization,' as well as evangelization and Christian nurture. Most priests during the Middle Ages were illiterate and could barely say the Lord's Prayer, the Mass, and the Ave Maria in Latin. Almost none of them could preach. The monks were usually the best-educated men of their day, and some left the monasteries to preach and teach the people. The very fact that they withdrew from society to seek a deeper Christian life led some of them to go back out into the world to share the Gospel as they understood it.

At times they became a mobile missionary force. When the church leaders wanted to send missionaries to a new place to evangelize, who was available? Only the monks. In 596, Gregory the Great decided to send missionaries to England, partly to counteract the Celtic influence coming down from Scotland, and partly to reassert authority over the English Church. He sent a group of monks to England, led by Augustine, who landed near Canterbury. As far as we know that was the first formal missionary venture of the Roman bishop. And it was undertaken by a group of reluctant monks!

Lessons for Renewal Movements

Institutionalization

Every renewal movement, including those in which we are involved, faces the danger of institutionalization. This happens when the maintenance of the institution becomes more important than the original vision of the founders. Every movement lives with this temptation, and it is important to guard against it.

Power

Movements also face the danger of becoming powerful both materially and politically. We know that serious new temptations come with power. That is true even of mission societies. At times they have used their political and financial power unwisely.

Popularity

Movements face dangers when they become popular. We are reminded that men and women who enter a new movement are going against the grain of their society, rejecting some of its values and direction, affirming new loyalties, and, in effect, making a 180-degree turn. They often do so with great sacrifice and danger. However, the experience of their children is very different. They are born into the movement without necessarily undergoing the kind of crisis that led the parents to make such a radical decision. They may continue to be loyal, but their experience is very different, and not nearly as radical. This continues with each following generation of the movement. While inherited faith can be a good beginning, without the constant renewing work of the Holy Spirit, vitality and commitment will inevitably decline. This is the dilemma of every new work of the Holy Spirit, and is a problem all through church history.

Chapter Seven

The Celtic Church

Devotional

I will read now a passage very familiar to some, and perhaps not as familiar to others. It is quoted often in some circles, and ignored in others. These are words from our Lord's prayer before his crucifixion. It is often called his "high priestly prayer." In it, he prayed for his disciples and for us.

> My prayer is not for them alone. I pray also for those who will believe in me through their message, that all of them may be one, Father, just as you are in me and I in you. May they also be in us so that the world may believe that you have sent me. I have given them the glory that you gave me, that they may be one as we are one—I in them and you in me—so that they may be brought to complete unity. (John 17:20-23 NIV)

These powerful words came from our Lord just before he went to the cross. That should give this prayer great authority for us.

It represents one of the great dilemmas of the Christian Church throughout all of its history, and we cannot fail to recognize it. I am not suggesting how we choose to express our unity, but the Lord's Prayer affirms that we are already one in Jesus Christ. That is true whether we recognize it or not.

The fact is, that as men and women who confess Jesus Christ as Lord, we are one—brothers and sisters in Christ—whether we come from older so-called "mainline" Protestant churches, Pentecostal groups, some of the newer "post-denomi-national" churches, or the more ancient churches of the East or West. We are one in Jesus Christ if we confess him as our Lord and Savior.

I suggest that we take that gift of unity back to our ministries, wherever we are called to serve. I cannot say how Christian unity is to be manifested in our lives and ministries. I am not advocating some kind of structural unity. But I am suggesting all of us are called to a life-long struggle to discover how to express our oneness in Christ. Remember, that unity is not something we achieve; it has already been forged on the cross of Christ and in his resurrection. It is his gift to us. To return to the words of our Lord, we look again at the purpose of that unity. Jesus prayed that his followers would be one "that the world may believe." Therefore, our task is to live and act in such a way that the world will eventually believe in Jesus Christ and become his disciples.

Throughout this course, we will discover that mission and unity have often been separated. Frequently, people have had to turn their backs on the larger body of the Church in order to pursue mission. That may include some of us as we have sought to pursue the mission to which God has called us. Yet I am convinced that the Church as a whole, the entire Body of Christ in all its manifestations throughout the world, is strongest when our recognition of our unity and our call to mission are held together. However, that has rarely, if ever, happened. That is our dilemma and our challenge.

Let us pray together.

> Father, we thank you that you have called us, first, to know you as Lord and Savior, and to be your disciples. We thank you that you have called us also into the Body of Jesus Christ, and into a particular manifestation of that Body. We thank you that just as we were called into a particular part of that Body, we were also called into the totality of the Body, which includes brothers and sisters from every race and language and culture and nation in a variety of denominational traditions. Lord, we thank you for this gift of unity, which we do not know how to express adequately. We pray that you will draw us closer to you, and in that process, draw us closer to each other. Lead us to express the love that you have given us for each other as well as for yourself, in ways that will draw others into your Kingdom. We ask in Jesus' name, Amen.

Introduction

We will examine one of the most interesting missionaries in history and the movement he initiated. I refer to St. Patrick and the Celtic movement. Even though we normally associate Celts with Scotland and Ireland, we know they were much more widespread. There were Celtic blacksmiths in Austria seven hundred years before Christ. The salt mines outside Salzburg, Austria were opened up by Celts centuries before Christ.

In 500 B.C., we find Celts in the south of France and northern Spain. They lived in areas of what are now Germany, Switzerland, and Austria. They plundered Rome in 390 B.C. The churches of Galatia may well have been Celtic: note the similarity in the consonants "C,L,T" and "G,L,T." Ankara, now the capital of Turkey, was originally a Celtic city. An area of northern Spain called "Galicia" must have been originally Celtic.

Irenaeus, (died, 212) came from Asia Minor (now Turkey) to southern France in the middle of the second century. He spoke a Celtic language and engaged in mission to Celts in southern Gaul as well as to the Romanized invaders. However, the Church in Gaul was incorporated into the Roman system.

The Christian faith reached Roman-occupied areas of Britain by the third century, and perhaps as early as the second. Hadrian's Wall was built in 142 to prevent the Celtic tribes in Scotland from raiding the south. It is ironic that later on, those same people, now Christians, came across the wall into the southern part of the island as effective evangelists.

Apparently, during those first centuries, the Christian faith was limited to the Romanized Britons. There was a strong church among them, but it did not spread to the tribal peoples around them. By "Romanized Britons," I mean those who had come from Rome, or been assimilated into the Roman culture. They were the dominant group and their language was Latin.

Patrick

One of the most interesting people in the history of the Church is Patrick. He is known as a great Roman Catholic saint. He was great and saintly, but his connection with the Roman Church was tenuous at best. He showed more influence of the Eastern Church than Rome. This is indicated primarily in two ways: the date of the celebration of Easter, and the manner in which the monks cut their hair. On both of those matters, Patrick followed the practices of the Eastern Church.

We want to study Patrick's life and the movement that came from his work, because in many ways he stands as a model for us. An important thesis in this course is that key leaders often play an essential role in starting movements. I refer to men and women who have gone deeper in life with God and then begun to feel his heartbeat for the world. Patrick is such a leader. As we look at his life, we ask these questions: How did God shape him? How did God call him and use him so uniquely? There are lessons to be learned from his life, just as there are from other great men and women who have been uniquely used in mission.

Birth and Early Life

Patrick was born around 390, the son of a deacon and grandson of a priest. Church leaders in Britain were married at the time. He was from a well-to-do family. We do not know much about the level of Christian commitment in his family but his own personal faith was not strong. When Patrick was sixteen, he was captured and taken as a slave to Ireland. Here was the son of an aristocrat, raised a Christian but apparently quite nominal in his faith, now a slave in a foreign country. He had to learn a new language and live among people of a different culture. For six years he tended sheep in solitude. He probably felt like his life was over. It is not uncommon for men and women who later become significant leaders, to go through a desert experience, just as Moses did. This happened to Patrick. Before he became a slave, he said, he paid no attention to the teachings of his faith, did not believe in God, and found priests foolish. But now he turned to the God of his parents.

"Tending flocks was my daily work and I would pray constantly during the daylight hours. The love of God and the fear of Him surrounded me more and more—and faith grew and the Spirit was roused so that in one day I said as many as a hundred prayers and after dark nearly as many again…I would wake and pray before daylight— through snow, frost and rain…because then the Spirit in me was ardent." (Thomas Cahill, *How the Irish Saved Civilization* [New York: Doubleday, 1995], 102). Like many others, Patrick discovered that after the desert, God opened new doors of ministry— much wider doors.

Eventually he escaped. Our historical data is vague on the next period of his life. But because Patrick adhered to the practices of the Eastern Church on the matter of the date of Easter and the tonsure of the monks, it seems probable that he studied with someone on the continent who was still in touch with the Eastern Church. Could it have been the continuing influence of Irenaeus? Around 430, after having served as a priest in England, he saw a man in a dream, pleading with him to return to Ireland. It reminds us of Paul's vision of the man asking him to go to Macedonia. (Acts 16:9)

We are finding new openness in the Western church today in the fact that God still calls people,

or otherwise reveals himself, through dreams and visions. We western Christians, with our more rationalistic view of life and the faith, have often disregarded such accounts. However, we are learning to become more open to the various ways in which God continues to reveal himself to humans. We are learning from the Charismatic movement; from our brothers and sisters in Asia, Africa, and Latin America; and, even more, from the Scriptures. Dr. Woodberry's study of 700 conversions from Islam to Christ indicates that frequently a dream or vision has been a major cause.

His Return to Ireland and Ministry

Apparently, Patrick was not highly regarded by his contemporaries. We do not know if they thought he was poorly prepared, or if there was something in his background that reflected negatively on him. We do know that he considered himself very unworthy. Despite the opposition of family and friends, he went to Ireland and lived there another thirty years until he died, never returning to his homeland. There was some Christian presence in the country, but as far as we know, Ireland was primarily pagan. Celtic religion was polytheistic and often focused on fertility. Fertility cults often involved some kind of temple prostitution—that is, a worshiper used a male or female prostitute as part of the act of worship. At times, Celtic religion involved infant sacrifice, also a practice of fertility cults. Parents sometimes sacrificed their firstborn son to insure the favor of the gods or goddesses. Patrick faced the very heart of a brutal form of paganism. The Celts were also headhunters and used the skulls of their enemies as drinking cups.

Patrick's ministry lasted from about 431 to 460. His method of operation was to approach the local king or chief to communicate the faith. This frequently involved power encounter or confrontation with priests and magicians of the pagan religion. "Power encounter" may be a new term to some. Biblical examples are Elijah on Mount Carmel and Paul's confrontation of the demonized girl in Philippi. Power encounter is not primarily an encounter between human forces, it is an encounter between God (the God of the Bible) and false gods—demons and devils.

Today the worldwide Church is learning to take power encounter more seriously. It was eliminated as a theological category during the Reformation. This was partly in reaction to the excessive credulity and superstition of the medieval church. However, we have often fallen into the opposite danger of excessive rationalism in our faith.

A Unique Monastic Pattern

A second aspect of Patrick's ministry was also important. He formed monasteries, but they were quite different in emphasis from the Benedictines. He brought his most zealous converts into monastic communities where they were discipled and trained to go back out as evangelists. They adopted very rigorous spiritual disciplines, and were imbued with missionary passion. In addition, they put great emphasis on Bible study and learning. The system multiplied itself as Patrick's disciples established other monasteries that became new centers of mission. Houses for women were also established. Because they had played a prominent role in pre-Christian Celtic culture, women had an important role in the life of the Church. In some cases, the abbesses of convents exerted authority over men.

Patrick and his disciples planted monasteries all over Ireland. Then, as we will see, his successors eventually came across to Scotland, then down into England, and back to the continent, into what is now Germany.

During those first centuries, the monasteries and their abbots were the center of the Irish church, rather than the bishops in the diocesan structure. Because Celtic monasticism was oriented toward mission, it grew rapidly by planting new communities. It seems to have been a very healthy model that combined the modality/sodality pattern. As we have seen, it was a highly evangelistic kind of monasticism, and the churches drew their leadership from the monasteries. Later, in the seventh century, as Rome asserted its authority over the English and Irish church, the bishops began to rule through the diocesan system.

Note that Patrick, like other leaders of rapidly growing movements such as the Methodists or early Pentecostals, had to devise new methods of selecting and training leaders. Apparently, he did so very effectively.

The Faith of Patrick

We must think geographically to understand the call of Patrick. To Patrick as an Englishman, Ireland was the end of the world. That was one reason he wanted to go there. Beyond Ireland, as far as he knew, there was nothing but ocean. Just as Paul looked at Spain, Patrick looked at Ireland. In other words, they both had a strategy for evangelization, and a sense of history; they did not know as much about geography as we do, but they knew a lot about history and strategy.

While today we think of Patrick as a Roman Catholic saint, he apparently had little or no contact with Rome. He was an extremely evangelical person in his faith and theology.

First, in his writing and in his preaching, he exhibited a strong sense of God's grace and mercy. He could never get over the fact that he was a sinner saved by grace. Even though he had been through all kinds of hardships, the heart of his message was always the joyful acknowledgement of what God had done in Christ. In other words, his was a very Christ-centered message, focusing on what God had done in Christ. His deepest desire was to proclaim God's mercy revealed in Christ, which he had experienced personally. Along with this was the strong conviction that his own life had been ordered not by his plans, but by the power and providence of God.

That is significant for someone who had been kidnapped as a sixteen-year-old boy and spent years in slavery. He looked back at all he had suffered and saw in it the hand of God, preparing him for his mission. Can we doubt that he was right?

Dr. Clinton's course at Fuller Theological Seminary on Leadership Emergence Patterns examines the ways in which God has called and shaped key people throughout history. It helps us to examine how God has worked in our own lives, to shape us into servants of the Gospel.

Many of the elements in Patrick's life are common to some of the great figures we will study. Patrick, a nominal Christian, had a deep encounter with God through hardship and struggle when everyone else had apparently abandoned him. He went through a long, desert period. Then he had a period of undistinguished ministry in England, probably for eighteen years.

We remember other great men and women of God who have shown promise or had a deep experience early in their lives and then gone through a period in which apparently nothing of significance happened. They wondered if God had forgotten them. At times many years passed before their ministries began to flourish. That was the case with Saul of Tarsus and Hudson Taylor.

Patrick was not the last person to be ridiculed by others when he heard a call from God to go to a distant place. When William Carey proposed to his Baptist minister colleagues that they form a mission society and send him out, an older pastor is reputed to have said, "Young man, sit down. When God chooses to convert the heathen, he'll do it without the likes of you or me." We see this pattern repeatedly. The pioneers and visionaries have usually been rejected by the majority.

Patrick also had great confidence in the power of the Gospel. He faced paganism at its heart. He knew the Scriptures and quoted them frequently. His favorite book of the Bible was Romans! It is interesting to note how often Romans or a passage from that letter has become the trigger of renewal in the Church. We think of Luther and his rediscovery of the Gospel in Romans 1 as an example.

Speaking of Patrick, one author wrote, "He certainly knew the Latin Bible, which was used by the British church. He constantly quotes it in season and out of season. Its phrases seem to have impregnated his mind and dominated his thought." (R.P.C. Hanson, *The Life and Writings of the Historical St. Patrick* [Oxford: Oxford University Press, 1983], 45). Hanson continued, "Its words were household words to him. His biblical interpretation is remarkably sound and sensible. He goes straight to the heart of the biblical message to the promises of God in the Old Testament; to the redemption bought by Christ in the New; God's self-giving and love, God's demand of holiness and faith; God's trustworthiness and providence; the presence of the Holy Spirit in the hearts of believers." (ibid., 49). Clearly, Patrick was a very evangelical person.

I remember thinking about Scripture impregnating one's mind and thoughts. When I was a seminarian, I was at a retreat with a few students interested in mission. It was led by Dr. J. Christy Wilson. Dr. Samuel Zwemer, an old friend of Dr. Wilson's, was also at the retreat. It was only a few months before Zwemer's death. It was an incredible privilege to be with him for a weekend.

Dr. Wilson roomed with Dr. Zwemer, and afterwards told us, "Dr. Zwemer was ill; he was coughing throughout the night and could hardly sleep." However, Dr. Wilson added, "When I woke up in the middle of the night because Zwemer was so restless, I heard him reciting the Psalms over and over again to himself."

Zwemer was one of the greatest missionary figures of the 20th century. When he was awake in the middle of the night and could not sleep, his mind was so impregnated with the Psalms that he said them repeatedly as prayers to God, and as words of comfort to himself. That is what comes of a lifetime of living with the Scripture. Patrick was that kind of person.

The historical Patrick was utterly different from the mythological picture of him. The historical Patrick was very human, distrustful of himself, full of a delightful humility, and by no means successful in everything that he undertook.

That is encouraging. The stories of people who are successful in everything they do make us feel terribly inferior and unworthy. More importantly, such stories are simply not true. A great blessing for those who serve Christ is the assurance that God uses flawed, imperfect people. Continuing Hansen's comments, Patrick was "a holy man, a man of integrity, no fool in his episcopal office, courageous when circumstances required courage, concerned about slaughtered and kidnapped converts, compassionate toward the struggling slave-girl Christians, full of an admirable faith. We leave him as an old bishop, by his own wish forever separated from his native land, devoted entirely to his task of converting the Irish in spite of opposition and misunderstanding. (Hanson, *Historical St. Patrick,* 49.) A great man! And a model missionary!

Patrick's final words are consistent with the spirit that pervades his confession:

> I pray those who believe and fear God, whosoever shall have deigned to look upon or receive this writing which Patrick, a sinner, an unlearned man as everyone knows, composed in Ireland. Let no one ever say it was my ignorance that did whatever small matter I did or proved in accordance with God's good pleasure. But judge ye and let it be most truly believed that it was the gift of God. And this is my confession before I die (Saint Patrick: *Confession et Lettre à Coroticus,* R.P.C. Hanson, translator, [Paris: Editions du Cerf, 1978], 133).

Here was one of the great missionaries of all history. His final words were that whatever he did, it was God who did it.

We conclude this sketch of his life by reciting one of his prayers:

> Christ to shield me today against poison, against burning, against drowning, against wounding, so that there may come to me an abundance of reward. Christ with me, Christ before me, Christ behind me Christ in me, Christ beneath me, Christ above me, Christ on my right, Christ on my left, Christ when I lie down, Christ when I sit down, Christ when I rise up,...I arise today through a mighty strength, the invocation of the Trinity (Cahill, *How the Irish Saved Civilization,* 118).

One way Irish monks expressed their love for God and the Word was by copying manuscripts of the Bible using beautiful illuminated script. Many illuminated manuscripts came out of the Irish monasteries. However, do not look at it simply as art; look at it as one of their ways of honoring the Word of God and showing their love and concern for that Word.

Columba of Iona

By the time of Patrick's death, Ireland was basically Christian. Many of the people had a profound personal faith; for others, it was no doubt more superficial. Nevertheless, it was a magnificent achievement. Then one of Patrick's spiritual descendents, Columba, became the leader of the movement in Scotland.

Columba went to Scotland at age forty-two. There is evidence that he had some failure or grievous sin in his background. But in 563, with twelve disciples, he embarked in a small boat and went across from Ireland to Scotland. It seems some of the Irish monks—I am not recommending this as a missionary strategy—embarked in their small boats and put out to sea without any oars, to see where the Lord took them. They had a great sense of adventure, calling themselves pilgrims, *peregrini,* for Christ's sake. They believed that God would take them where he wanted them to go. There is evidence that some of them got to North America.

Columba went to the island of Iona, off the northwest coast of Scotland. There he and his colleagues built a monastery on that bleak, cold island, only about five square miles in area.

Lindisfarne and a Chain of Monasteries

From the base in Iona, the Celtic missionaries established a chain of monasteries across the island, ending at Lindisfarne off the northeast English coast. They were missionary centers, and from them the monks went north into the mountain tribes of Scotland, and south into England. While there are many gaps in our knowledge of his work, apparently Columba and his colleagues used the same techniques Patrick had used.

Thus, the Faith went from Romanized Britain across to Ireland and then after more than a century, the Celtic monks took it to Scotland and into England. That fresh burst of vitality began to reach the tribal, indigenous people who had not adhered to Roman culture.

The Mission of Augustine to England

Gregory the Great was bishop of Rome from 590 to 605. Historians have called him the last of the church fathers and the first of the popes. He was a great leader of the Roman Church.

Legend is that he saw slave boys from England for sale in a Roman marketplace. When he asked who they were, the response was, "They are Angles." Gregory said, "Not Angles, but angels." According to tradition, this experience motivated Gregory to send missionaries to the British Isles.

Gregory recruited the missionaries from a local monastery and Augustine was designated to be the leader of the group. But they went only went part way before they returned! Gregory insisted that they go. The reluctant missionaries arrived in England in 596. Augustine established his see, or bishopric, at Canterbury and that location has served as the center of the English, or Anglican Church to the present.

Some have suggested that Gregory sent missionaries to England primarily to counteract the work of the Celts and to bring their churches under the leadership of Rome.

Some might disagree, but when Augustine and his fellow monks arrived in England, they spent their first night in a church! They did not go to engage in frontier missions. They went to England where churches already existed, primarily to bring greater organization and leadership to those churches.

Ecclesiological Issues

While there were cultural differences, the primary issue seems to have been whether the Celtic movement would come under the authority of Rome or remain independent. The British bishops and monks who were already in England came from both the ancient Roman and Celtic traditions. When the Celtic leaders came to see Augustine, he refused to rise to his feet and pay them respect as equals. There was clearly a power struggle between the Church in Rome and the Church in England.

Augustine's goal, to bring the Celtic church under Rome and unify Christianity in Britain, no doubt had its positive sides. Certainly, the Christian Church should be unified. However, it appears that the Celts had far more to do with the evangelization of the tribal groups of England than did the Roman missionaries.

Besides the issue of the authority of Rome, there were three main differences between the Celtic and Roman missionaries: how the date of Easter was determined, how the monks cut their hair, and how the Church was governed. These differences may seem trivial to us, but they were important to the missionaries.

The Celtic church calculated the date of Easter following the practice of the Church in the East. The Celtic monks tonsured their heads in the manner used in the East.

So clearly, there was a connection between the Church in Asia Minor and the Celtic church in Ireland and Scotland. Those two practices, different from those of the Church in the West, also symbolized a more fundamental issue: authority.

Rome insisted on the diocesan system of church government, with bishops loyal to Rome, while the monasteries played a greater role in Celtic Christianity. As we have noted, the monastery was its primary center of church life and authority. But the diocese with its bishop was the central authority for Rome. The Roman system had monasteries, but the diocese was the center of ecclesiastical authority.

Thus one cause of the differences between the two groups was the eastern influence among the Celts. Another was the isolation of the Celtic movement from Rome. Rome was distant, and quite possibly not seen as relevant by the Celts.

Another factor probably involved the basic cultural differences, (Celts and Anglo-Saxons still do not get along very well today) and the rugged independence of the Celts.

I believe a fourth factor was involved. At this point in history, the two Christian groups that showed the deepest devotion to missionary endeavor and a life of piety and dedication to Christ were the Celts in northwestern Europe and the Nestorians in Asia Minor, who had been able to move across Central Asia.

I suspect the Celtic Christians were analogous to a group of newly converted young people, perhaps charismatics, who looked at the older, more "respectable" church with great impatience. They wanted to engage in much more radical discipleship.

The Conversion of England Delayed

The unity and conversion of the Church in England was delayed in good part because of the Roman insistence on its authority. The rivalries between the Irish and the English, which have lasted through the centuries, no doubt complicated things. Finally, in 664, at the Synod of Whitby, near York, the majority of the Celtic leaders, under duress, accepted the authority of Rome. The Church in the British Isles was eventually unified. But as Cahill pointed out, it is clear that for several centuries the most serious biblical and theological study in Europe was done in the Celtic centers in Ireland and York.

Columbanus

The Church Among the Franks

A third great Celtic missionary was Columbanus. His name was originally Columba, he is called Columbanus to distinguish him from Columba of Iona. He went to the European continent at the age of forty in the year 590. The continent was supposedly largely Christian. The Franks, who were the predecessors of the French, had been nominally Christian since 496 when Clovis, their king, was baptized along with his soldiers. Clovis had married a Christian wife. But while the Franks were nominally Christian, theirs was a very low, corrupt form of the Faith.

Columbanus and his colleagues began to establish monasteries that became centers both of evangelism for the barbarians arriving from the East, and spiritual renewal for some of the nominal Christians already there. Something similar is beginning to happen in the Europe and North America as brothers and sisters from the Majority World come to those areas and exhibit a vital faith that challenges both the traditional churches and the secularized culture.

Picture a diocese on the European continent, with a bishop as its leader. The diocese primarily served the Romanized people, along with the barbarians who had come across from Central Europe and been assimilated into that culture. Christianity, then, was identified with a particular culture. However, other tribal groups were arriving.

The Romanized people and the tribal people looked on each other with suspicion and hostility. We see that dynamic nearly everywhere in the world today where there is significant migration. The reasons why some people cannot hear and accept the Gospel are often as much cultural as they are spiritual or theological. We can voice the feeling in the minds of many like this: "I don't want to hear your religious message, because you are a different cultural group, and I feel that if I hear your Gospel and accept it, I will have to leave my cultural group and become something I'm not." That is a critical missiological issue!

His Work

Even if they had a vital faith, the bishops in France could not minister well to the tribal peoples. But Columbanus and his colleagues were able to do so. Because they were not part of the dominant cultural group, and because of the high level of their spiritual lives, two things happened. They evangelized the tribal people, while nominal Christians from the dominant church came to them for spiritual counsel. A measure of renewal took place in the Frankish church through that sodality or mission structure.

That still happens today. At times a person who has been raised in a more traditional church has experienced conversion or renewal through some outside structure, such as Young Life, Campus Crusade for Christ, or IVCF. This is not to devalue the traditional church, but often God needs to get us off our familiar turf to get our attention. So Columbanus and his monks performed at least two functions: they evangelized the unreached barbarian peoples, and became a means of renewal for some of the nominal Christians in the dominant culture.

Columbanus Expelled, Went to Italy

This led to problems. The relationship with the local bishops was not very good. The bishops were tied to the royal court, which was nominally Christian but actually very pagan. When Columbanus rebuked the immorality of the rulers, he was expelled from France. He went to Switzerland and finally to northern Italy, where he started another monastery, not far from Rome.

It is fascinating to see this Celtic Christianity going back into Italy! It was a period of chaos, the old socio-political structures were falling apart. It was a time of destruction and decadence. In the midst of that situation, the monks exhibited disciplined Christian lives and a high standard of Christian conduct. They were sacrificial; they were not seeking anything for themselves. Therefore they attracted men and women, were evangelists, and brought a measure of spiritual renewal.

In summary, the Celtic movement had three important features. It exhibited deep devotion to Christ, a love of learning, and missionary passion. It can serve as a model of some of the best characteristics of any missionary movement.

Chapter Eight

The Barbarian World

Introduction

When we look at a long period of history over a vast area, we see many different tracks, but we can follow only a few. We will examine those that illustrate certain trends and the dynamics of important movements.

When cultures are in conflict, and Christianity is part of one or more of them, it raises a special set of missiological issues. Political and cultural factors are often important in peoples' decision to accept or reject the Christian faith.

Clovis, king of the Franks, was baptized in 496 with three thousand of his soldiers. This was during the Arian controversy in Europe. Arianism taught that Jesus was less than God but more than human. The Nicene Council had declared in 325 that Jesus was fully God and fully man, but many still adhered to Arianism and the Church was divided. Because his wife was a Catholic who adhered to the orthodox position, Clovis was baptized in that faith, not as an Arian. That does not say anything about the depth of his understanding or faith, but indicates his formal Christian allegiance. Thus, he and his kingdom had a closer relationship with Rome and with most of the Church in the West than would have been the case if he had been baptized an Arian.

Clovis and his soldiers were one of the bands of invaders who came across from central Asia and into what is now France. Others were coming on their heels; soon, along with the Franks, Goths, Visigoths, Lombards, Huns, and other peoples settled in different areas of western Europe. Visigoths came from Central Asia to Central Europe, and then poured down into the Iberian Peninsula.

The Lombards also came from Central Asia, into Central Europe, and then down into Italy. As a result, an area of north central Italy is called "Lombardy." There were many "barbarian" invasions for several centuries. "Barbarian" was the term the Romans gave the invaders who did not speak Latin.

Europe was changing. The Roman Empire was fading and falling into chaos. By now, the Empire identified itself as Christian. That was the nominal faith of its people. An important question arose. As the invaders came, what would be their attitudes toward Christianity? Would they see it with hostility, as a part of a culture they wanted to reject and overcome? Or would they see it as a part of the culture that they wanted to accept?

The relationship between Christianity and culture is still a critical issue with us today. We recognize that during the last century or two, some peoples have not wanted to embrace the Christian faith because the missionary movement and, hence, the Christian faith, were closely associated with Western culture. I believe we are undergoing a critical shift at this time. The early

Church had to be released from Jewish culture so that it could move into the Gentile world. It was no longer seen as a part of the Jewish community and Jewish faith, but stood on its own feet. We are now moving into a new period in which the Christian Gospel will no longer be viewed as a part of Western culture, but will be seen as a valid faith apart from the West. It will be able to move anywhere, affirming and enhancing the most valid aspects of each culture. People will not feel that they have to look and dress like a westerner in order to be a Christian. That is now taking place with the rapid growth of the Church in the 'majority world,' and the emergence of new forms of the Church, often quite different from traditional western forms.

Missionaries have often been unduly criticized, I think, because of their identification with Western culture. Certainly, that criticism is valid. We need to recognize that.

I knew a distinguished Kenyan Christian lay leader, businessman, and chairman of the Bible Society of Kenya. He was on the board of World Vision International. When he walked into my office, he wore a three-piece suit. He is a world citizen, at home anywhere, and is a committed Christian. He told me that when his grandfather, the first Christian in their tribe, was converted through Scottish Presbyterians, he had to give up his African name and adopt a European name. He had to give up his African dress and adopt European dress. African customs were believed to be pagan, but European culture was considered Christian. That identification of the faith with Western culture often led to unnecessary barriers to evangelization and serious distortions in the understanding of the Faith, on the part of both the westerner and the new Christians. On the other hand, when those same missionaries spoke out against female 'circumcision,' a brutal cultural ritual, one missionary was killed as a result. The relationship between cultures and the Faith is complex.

There are three new factors helping to reverse the identification of Christian faith with Western culture today. One is the internationalization of the Christian missionary movement. A second is the role of the social sciences in analyzing and affirming non-Western cultures. The third is the increasing distance of Western societies from the Christian faith. All of these are helping the Church today to become more universal and increasingly freed from Western culture. This may be the most significant new step in the missionary movement today.

The house fellowships in China are a significant example. Under persecution they have developed their own forms of worship, leadership, and training. Their isolation from the Western church has permitted them to find new, more Chinese, and probably more biblical ways of worshipping and leading.

We see another example in the Andes of South America where the two great people groups were never totally conquered by the Spaniards. They are the Quechuas and the Aymaras who live in the high Andes of Ecuador, Peru, and Bolivia. For four and a half centuries, they were told that their culture was inferior, that it should die out, and that Hispanic culture (including Hispanic Catholicism) should replace it. For years, a few Protestant missionaries worked among these people, using Spanish because that was the language they knew. There was very little success. Then a few missionaries began to learn the tribal languages and cultures, and a few Quechuas and Aymaras became evangelical Christians.

Development in the last twenty or twenty-five years has been remarkable. As missionaries began to communicate the faith using not only the indigenous languages but also indigenous cultural forms (music, musical instruments, and forms of worship), church growth has taken an extraordinary leap forward!

The early Celtic missionaries affirmed the vernacular languages and cultures where they went. Because they translated the liturgy and their worship into the vernacular, they were effective in evangelization.

Another introductory issue is the relationship between unity and diversity. How do we express the unity of the faith, the fact that we are all one in the body of Christ, and still respect cultural diversity? Roman Catholics and Eastern Orthodox Christians, and some Anglicans believe a certain type of structure is essential to the Church. For a Roman Catholic, submission to the papacy is essential if one is to be part of the true Church. However, most Protestants agree that we need diversity in church structures, ways of worship, communication, and leadership styles. That is a major challenge today as we see greater, not less, diversity in the shape of the Church worldwide. The challenge is to affirm our unity even while we celebrate growing diversity of forms. This also means that as we move toward greater contextualization of the faith in different cultures, we need to think biblically and theologically to define the essentials of the Gospel. We must not mark as "essential" practices that are helpful to us but not part of the essence of the Gospel.

The Church has faced this missiological issue throughout history. But it is easier today to recognize great diversity in worshiping and communicating the Gospel, and still affirm our unity in the body of Christ, than in the past. In the past, most if not all traditional cultures assumed that religious uniformity was essential to social and political unity. That is still true in most Muslim nations and accounts for the intolerance of the Hindu party in India.

That helps us understand the religious intolerance at the time of the Reformation. Even the Reformers assumed that religious uniformity was necessary for social unity. Today, western secularized nations embrace religious, ethic, and racial diversity as an important value, but for most, that implies religious relativism. As Christians we are called to affirm the uniqueness of Jesus Christ as Lord, even as we recognize the validity of different kinds of worship that focus on that Lord.

Thus one of the great missionary tasks we face as we go to different ethnic groups is to encourage them to use their own means of communicating the Gospel, their own means of worshiping God, and not feel that they have to become copies of the churches from which we come.

That was a difficult issue for the Church in the period we will examine. There were a number of divisions in the East. The churches in Egypt and Asia Minor for the most part were divided from the Church in Constantinople over theological issues. In most cases, the divisions were caused by attempts to define the nature of the relationship between the human and divine in the person of Jesus Christ. At least that was the surface issue. We suspect there were also issues of power, authority, and personality behind the divisions.

Eventually, in the eleventh century, the Church in the East, centered in Constantinople, and the Church in the West, centered in Rome, divided and hurled anathemas at each other. The theological question was the modification of the Nicene Creed by the Roman Church, but the primary reason was the issue of authority and power. The Eastern Church refused to recognize the Roman bishop as the head of the whole Church. The Roman bishop insisted on primacy, and the final division came as a result.

Western Europe
The Celtic Church

Again we see here a basic thesis of this book—that movements of renewal and mission normally arise on the periphery of the broader Church. If we draw a large circle to represent the Church, with the bishop at the center, we find that renewal movements always seem to begin on the perimeter. At times the Church has rejected and cast off the movements; sometimes they were eventually absorbed into the institutional Church. At times they have helped to bring a measure of renewal, then been absorbed, institutionalized, eventually losing their distinctive character.

The Celtic church, which was absorbed into the larger Roman structure in the seventh century, maintained its missionary dynamic, its zeal for learning, and depth of piety for two or three more centuries. Thus, in the eighth, ninth, and tenth centuries, the most learned men in the Church in the West were not in Rome, they were in Britain, coming out of that Celtic tradition.

Later, after the Vikings had pillaged, raped and destroyed cities, churches, and monasteries in Ireland, England, and France, the missionaries who brought them to the Christian faith, came from England, again from the Celtic tradition.

It was kept alive by the monasteries and combined deep piety and the love of learning with missionary passion. This is an important lesson for us. The Celtic leaders were not a group of unlearned zealots. They were the most learned churchmen in their day in the West. They studied the Scriptures and they combined their scholarship with deep devotion, and a lifestyle that reflected their faith.

Therefore, in Western Europe, the Celts were still the primary source of vitality and mission. While it is true that three streams of Christianity met in Britain—the old Roman, the Roman Catholic, and the Celtic—the Celtic stream was the most vital.

The Celtic monks poured out of England and Scotland across to France and then into Central Europe. They met the barbarian tribes who were coming from Central Asia into what is now Germany and evangelized them.

Whereas the Latin Christians thought that the barbarian languages were useless, the Celts valued the vernacular languages. We have already asserted that Pentecost stands as the symbol that each person should hear of the mighty works of God in his or her heart language. The Celts understood that.

For example, Xhosa is one of the great languages of South Africa. If I go to my Xhosa-speaking brother and say, "We do not need to translate the Gospel into Xhosa. You can understand English," I devalue his culture, and am not fully respecting him as a human being or brother in Christ. There is profound psychological as well as spiritual truth in recognizing the importance of respecting each person's heart language.

In the Celts, we see the continuation of missionary zeal and mobility. They called themselves "pilgrims for Christ" and were ready to go anywhere. They set out knowing they would never see their family or friends again, often not knowing where they were going. They were open to go wherever God led them. Sometimes this led to some rather bizarre disciplines. However, it had great results as well.

Some of the extreme ascetic practices of the Celts leave us cold, quite literally. For example, at times the monks sat in icy water for hours at a time meditating. The purpose was to mortify the flesh. Perhaps their piety was too austere, but it attracted young men and young women who became monks and nuns, at a time when society was chaotic and many lacked purpose in life.

Recently, college students across North America were interviewed about their goals. The largest number of students wanted to go into business and become rich. The number of those who wanted to go into education has decreased; those interested in engineering, computers and science has stayed level or declined slightly. The primary goal for most students in North American society was to become affluent. The interviews must have included many Christians.

There are similarities between our period in history and that in which the Celts moved on to the European continent. It was a time of decline, decay, and chaos in society. The high standards and ideals of the Celtic monks attracted many people. A few years ago, the National Council of Churches in the United States sponsored a study that resulted in the book *Why Conservative Churches are Growing* (Dean M. Kelly, New York: Harper & Row, 1977). Although the author came with a more liberal bias, he concluded that the reason the more conservative churches were growing was that they demanded more, not less, of their members. We see that same phenomenon among the Celts. There is a lesson here for us.

Willibrord

We find two great Celtic missionaries in the late eighth and early ninth centuries. The first was Willibrord, who lived from about 658 to 739 and evangelized the Frisians in what is now part of the Netherlands. The second was Boniface, the apostle to Germany.

The monks established churches, but the monastery was still the center of authority and spiritual life. However, because they had come under the authority of the Roman Catholic Church, both Willibrord and Boniface were consecrated as missionary bishops. Thus, they were not tied to any particular area, nor were they under the authority of local bishops. To follow our earlier observation on the importance of semi-independent mission structures, that gave them greater independence in their mission than they would have had if they had been under the authority of local bishops. This appears to be an important issue throughout the missionary movement. Paul and Barnabas clearly needed some independence from the Jerusalem church if they were to pursue their mission among the Gentiles and baptize those who were uncircumcised. William Carey later discovered he had to break from his Baptist Missionary Society in order to have enough flexibility of action in India.

In this missionary model, we see the missionary bishop going with a band of monks to an area where there are no Christians, and planting churches. He assigned priests or pastors to work with them. He also created new monasteries alongside the churches, and the new pastoral leadership came from the committed communities of the monasteries. In other words, to use Ralph Winter's term, we see a sodality planting modalities, but we also see the sodality planting new sodalities. Using simpler terminology, we see a mission structure planting churches, but also a mission structure planting new mission structures.

Historically, most Protestant mission agencies have planted churches of their denomination, or, if they are multi-denominational agencies, they have created their own denominations. Examples are the Evangelical Church of West Africa, established by Serving in Mission (SIM, formerly Sudan Interior Mission), or the African Inland Church of Kenya, established by the African Inland Mission. I am not criticizing this, and it has been an effective method of evangelism. However, it has led to an often-confusing variety of churches of different denominations in many areas. One important issue it raises is how to manifest the unity of the Body of Christ that our Lord prayed for in John 17.

It also raises an important and oft-debated issue in Europe. When North American, African, or Latin American evangelicals initiate missionary work in secularized Europe, should they attempt to work with the older churches (such as Lutheran, Reformed, or even Roman Catholic), seeking renewal, or should they plant new, "free" churches outside of the traditional denominations? There are no easy answers to that question, and the debate continues.

We also see many mission agencies that work with existing churches, seeking to determine how expatriate missionaries can work alongside national and local leadership to help the churches grow in both number and depth. Groups like the Latin America Mission, OC International, and Youth with a Mission are examples.

Getting back to Willibrord, we discover he was sent to what is now part of Holland and Belgium. The pope made him an archbishop, giving him independence from the Frankish bishops who ruled the older French Church. Normally their authority would have encompassed the region of the Frisians. That gave independence to Willibrord in his mission.

Boniface

The other great figure was Boniface, who in 722 was consecrated a bishop in the Roman Church. It is important to understand the historical context. Ten years later, Charles Martel, the "hammer," defeated the Muslims at the Battle of Tours. Their powerful army appeared invincible as it plundered and penetrated from Spain into central France. Some historians have said that if the Muslims had won the Battle of Tours, Europe would be filled with minarets instead of cathedrals. Today, of course, immigration is bringing a new Muslim invasion of Europe. A major question is how secularized Europe with its weak traditional churches will meet this new challenge.

At this time of instability and chaos in southern Europe, with Islam dominating Spain, Boniface moved east into what is now central Germany and evangelized. Like Willibrord, he had the support of Rome, which gave him independence as a missionary bishop.

Like many others throughout history, Boniface had to consider which of the pre-Christian religious practices the Church could legitimately accept. When any missionary goes into a new culture to evangelize and to plant the Church, the question arises. How does the missionary and the new Christian community decide which elements in that culture can be retained in worship, and which must be rejected? This is a very critical issue, and Scripture is not always clear in its guidance.

In 601, Pope Gregory the Great gave this principle of accommodation, which the Roman Catholic Church has usually followed.

> The heathen temples of these people need not be destroyed, only the idols which are to be found in them. If the temples are well built, it is a good idea to detach them from the service of the devil and adapt them for the worship of the true God. And since the people are accustomed, when they assemble for sacrifice, to kill many oxen in sacrifice to the devils, it seems reasonable to appoint a festival for the people by way of exchange. The people must learn to slay their cattle not in honor of the devil but in honor of God and for their own food. And when they have eaten, they must render thanks to the Giver of all good things.

> If we allow them these outward joys, they are more likely to find their way to the true inner joy. It is impossible to cut off all abuses at once from rough hearts, just as the man who sets out to climb a high mountain does not advance by leaps and bounds, but goes upward step by step. (Stephen Neill, *A History of Christian Missions* [New York: Penguin Books, 1969], 68).

There is wisdom here. However many who have worked in Latin America believe the Roman Catholic Church took that principle much too far, resulting in severe syncretism and a loss of focus on the center of the Gospel. The Basilica of Our Lady of Guadalupe outside of Mexico City is built on the site of the shrine to the most important pre-Columbian goddesses for that part of Mexico. It is the most important Roman Catholic Church in the country. There Our Lady of Guadalupe, not Jesus Christ, is the focus of worship. In the Church in Chichicastenango, Guatemala, one sees the indigenous people burning candles to the traditional pagan deities on the steps of the Church, and then, as they go inside they burn the same candles to the Christian saints. One has to ask, how much of genuine, informed Christian faith is there? That is, in my judgment, far too much continuity.

But we Protestants very often have stressed discontinuity too much. In Africa, for example, some missions refused to allow the people to use drums in worship. Drums were considered pagan because they were used in pre-Christian worship. The xylophone is used a great deal in Guatemala. Harry Strachan, the co-founder of the Latin America Mission, scandalized other Protestants in Central America in the 1920's when he said, "Why shouldn't the people use xylophones in their worship? It's a good instrument." That was controversial at the time.

Which cultural forms can be retained and used to worship God and communicate the Gospel? Which ones must be cast off? It is easy to say we get our guidance from the Scriptures (and indeed, that is true); however, it often takes a great deal of wrestling with the Scripture by the indigenous Christian community to arrive at answers. I think the outsider has a role in the process of discernment, giving counsel and guidance. Ultimately, however, the indigenous Christian community, informed by the Scriptures and guided by the Holy Spirit, has to make the decisions. The outsider by himself will often make the wrong decision. We see this issue arising throughout church history.

Another issue Boniface faced was that of power encounter. The most famous incident occurred when he came to Geismar. There the people worshipped a sacred oak, believing it to be the habitation of one of their gods. They were convinced that if anyone touched it he would die. Boniface took an ax and cut it down. When he was not harmed, he told the people to take the wood and use it to build a small chapel. That was a powerful object lesson! We hear echoes of Elijah on Mount Carmel. That kind of power encounter was part of the ministry of Boniface.

Another important factor in Boniface's ministry was his use of communities of women as well as men in mission. As far as we know, he was the first to do so. We have noted that women played an important role in the Celtic church. Thus, including women in mission must have seemed natural to him. When he established monasteries with men on the frontiers, he also established convents staffed with women. These monasteries and convents modeled a Christian lifestyle, a different type of community for the surrounding peoples. This was a powerful tool of evangelization. It must have required a lot of courage for groups of single women to go into central Germany at that time.

Returning to Germany in his old age, Boniface was martyred around 754. Many of us who have ancestors from central Europe can count ourselves as Boniface's spiritual descendents.

The Nestorian Movement

Moving to the East, we will look briefly at the Nestorian Church, which took its name from Nestorius, Archbishop of Constantinople in the fifth century. In the struggles over the definition of the two natures of Christ, he was eventually called a heretic and deposed, more because of a power struggle than a theological issue. His followers eventually embraced orthodox Christology. However, the movement began long before Nestorius lived. We find it in Edessa in Mesopotamia in the first or second century.

While the Roman Empire was still persecuting Christians, Edessa, at that time under the Persian Empire, had a flourishing Christian community. There were times of persecution when tens of thousands were killed and also periods of toleration when Christians who were persecuted in the Roman Empire fled to Persia, where they had greater freedom. During the periods of toleration, the missionary zeal of these Christians built up this church in the East. It is said that the early priests and bishops often went to new places to evangelize. They worked as carpenters or in other trades, but their goal was to spread the Gospel. In other words, they were tent-making missionaries. So this Church in Persia demonstrated missionary zeal.

During the second century, various parts of the New Testament circulated among Christians. The New Testament canon was well recognized in the third century and circulated increasingly. By the fourth century, there were Christian schools in Asia Minor. Theoretically, every bishop was then supposed to have a school where the students studied Scripture, especially the Psalms. It was said that in order to graduate, one had to memorized all of the Psalms. That indicated a great focus on Scripture—perhaps more on the Old Testament than on the New. That might have caused part of the weakness later on.

Persecution arose in the fourth and fifth centuries. Perhaps one error of the Christians in the Middle East was their use of Syriac in the Church, instead of the vernacular Persian the language of their rulers.

After the Roman Empire became (nominally) Christian, Constantine asked the Persian Emperor to favor the Christians. That led to widespread, tragic persecution of Christians in Persia. The two empires were in constant conflict. Thus, when the Roman Empire persecuted Christians, the Persian Empire was quite tolerant toward them. When the Roman Empire became nominally Christian, the Persians intensified persecution.

Nestorius, the Patriarch or Archbishop of Constantinople, was condemned and deposed in 431. Personal rivalries as well as theological issues were involved. Later Nestorian leaders affirmed Chalcedonian Christology; that is, the doctrine of Christ espoused by the Church as a whole: Eastern Orthodox, Roman Catholic, and Protestant. However, the Nestorian Church remained separate and was considered schismatic by Constantinople.

For several centuries, the Syriac-speaking Nestorians, like the Celts, constituted one of the most passionately missionary arms of the Church. They established a school in Nsiblis, in Mesopotamia, with a strong focus on spiritual discipline, Bible study, and mission. It counted over one thousand students in the sixth century. The Nestorians spread their faith through merchants, bankers, and physicians as well as missionary monks and priests. In some cases, Nestorian women married chiefs of central Asian tribes and led them to faith. In the sixth century, Nestorians arrived in India. The mission to the Huns in central Asia evangelized, reduced their language to writing, and taught new methods of agriculture. There is evidence that they arrived in Arabia, Tibet, and Afghanistan.

The best-known mission was to China. A monument discovered in 1623 described the arrival of a Nestorian named Alopen, who arrived in Xian in 635. Churches and monasteries were established, Christian literature was produced, and the movement received the favor of the Emperor. A missionary might have reached the border of Korea, where tradition says he was killed. The Nestorian Church nearly died out in China in the tenth century, but experienced resurgence from the eleventh to the thirteenth, when it disappeared.

There seem to be a number of reasons for the demise of the Nestorian Church in China. Apparently there was over-contextualization to the point of religious syncretism, with inadequate focus on the cross and resurrection. The missionaries apparently accommodated their message so much to Chinese culture that they lost some essential aspects of the Christian faith. Secondly, foreign leadership continued to dominate the Church, which meant that there was inadequate focus on indigenous leadership. Thirdly, there was strong dependence on the imperial house. The movement nearly disappeared when the Tang dynasty fell in the tenth century, and it died out in the fourteenth century because of government persecution. It is also important to note the strange fact that the movement that put such stress on memorization of Scripture apparently did not translate the Bible into Chinese. Another factor was the isolation of the Nestorians from the rest of the Church. When Franciscans arrived in China in the thirteenth century, they looked on Nestorians as heretics and schismatics.

The Nestorian movement reached several central Asian tribes, including the Uighurs, whose language was reduced to writing in the eighth century. From there it was passed to the Mongols. By the thirteenth century, the Keraits were considered Christian. For some time Nestorians coexisted with Islam and served its leaders as physicians and scholars, even translating a number of Greek philosophical works into Arabic. However, the Christian faith in that part of Asia was eventually exterminated by a combination of Islamic pressure and the massacres of Tamerlane in the fourteenth century.

To sum up, we see two great movements here, and two great peoples: the Celts and the Nestorians. Both were peripheral movements. Neither came from the center of the Church, both were considered schismatic to some degree, and even heretical, in the case of the Nestorians. In both we see a great combination of spiritual discipline, missionary zeal, piety, and learning. Not a bad combination!

Chapter Nine

Major Defeats:
Islam and the Viking Invasions

Introduction

From the seventh to the ninth centuries, the Church suffered two major defeats. Christendom would never suffer such a loss of territory again until the advent of Communism and modern secularism in the twentieth century. The first, Islam, is still a powerful and growing presence in the world. Along with secularism it constitutes the greatest challenge to the Church.

Muhammad and Islam
Basic Beliefs
The most basic belief of Islam is that there is only one God, Allah, and that Muhammad is his prophet. The Old Testament prophets and Jesus are also considered prophets, but Muhammad is believed to be the last and greatest.

The will of Allah is written in the Qur'an, which Allah sent down from heaven during Ramadan and revealed to Muhammad. It is believed that the Qur'an was not created; it is the earthly expression of tablets that are with Allah, and is held to be untranslatable. (The Old and New Testaments of Christians are believed to have been corrupted.) All one needs for salvation is written in the Qur'an, and all that is necessary to organize and guide society is believed to be found in the Shari'a, law, which is based upon it. Today, in a fundamentalist reaction against secularism, there is a movement in a number of Islamic countries to introduce Shari'a. The goal is to go back to the Qur'an and regulate all of life, society, the state,

the economy, by Shari'a law. In other words, the ideal society is believed to be a theocracy with Islam as its center.

A third belief is that there will be a resurrection for all people and a final judgment. Good Muslims will go to Paradise. Bad Muslims and infidels will go to the abyss. The concept of Paradise caters especially to men, who will be served by beautiful maidens.

Basic Practices
The basic practices of Islam are to pray five times a day, facing toward Mecca, and to practice charity, which is a necessity. Another special duty is the fast during the month of Ramadan, when from sunrise to sunset the pious Muslim is to refrain from all gratification of the senses, including food and drink. One can gratify the senses at night, but not during the day. The other major duty is to make a pilgrimage to Mecca once during the lifetime, either personally or by proxy.

This brief outline of the Muslim faith shows that Muhammad was a very sincere man, willing to go to great sacrifices for the truth as he understood it. It presents a serious historical dilemma for Christians as we seek to discover why Islam spread so rapidly in so many areas where the Church had been strong, and why the Church collapsed so quickly.

Evangelical scholars, including Dudley Woodberry, Joseph Cumming, and others, are seeking points of contact between Muslims and Christians. For example, the Qur'an speaks of Jesus in positive terms. And Islam considers the New Testament to be a holy book, even though it believes our Christian version has been corrupted.

Many of the barriers between Islam and Christianity are cultural and historical: the Crusades and colonialism, for example. We do not have time to examine these issues now, but we need to be aware of them.

Today, in the midst of the growth of Islamic fundamentalism, we are also seeing significant, often highly contextualized movements to Christ. Underground fellowships of followers of Jesus are growing in a number of Muslim nations. And "insider movements," in which the adherents go to the mosque and pray in the name of Isa (the name for Jesus in the Qur'an) are growing also. At the same time there is often tragic persecution of followers of Jesus, leading to martyrdom in a number of cases.

The Conquest
Conquered Lands

The map shows that in A.D. 420, well before the Muslim conquest, the Arabs dominated a large region of the Middle East. The Islamic conquest itself was an amazing series of events. Much of the East was ripe for revolt against the Eastern Roman Empire. The Roman Empire, east and west, still dominated much of the region, even though the western Empire was becoming increasingly weakened. Various tribes were coming across from central Europe: the Franks, the Saxons, the Alemanni (Germans are still called *Alemanni* in Portuguese), the Lombards, the Visigoths, and others. The 'barbarians' were overwhelming the weakened western Empire.

At the beginning of the seventh century, the Eastern Empire was still very large and powerful. It dominated Egypt, Asia Minor, much of the Middle East, and part of North Africa. But in a few decades its territory and power were greatly reduced and it became a shadow of its former self.

The Hegira, in 622, which refers to the flight of Mohammed from Mecca to Medina, is considered to be the starting date of Islam. Ten years later, in

632, Muhammad died and his successors began a series of conquests. They took Damascus in 635 and Jerusalem two years later. A year later, Antioch, Tyre, and cities along the Mediterranean fell. In the next ten years, Islam conquered North Africa, moved into Asia Minor, and took most of that area between 673 and 678. However Constantinople was not conquered. But by then, the capital of the Eastern Empire ruled over a relatively small state. It survived until 1453, but was much weakened. By 715, the Muslim conquerors had taken most of Spain and Portugal. In 732, they were defeated and turned back in the battle of Tours in southern France. When we think of the Crusades, a tragic chapter in the history of the Church, we must see it as only one more chapter in the long history of conflict between Islam and the West. We remember that the Turks were at the gates of Vienna in the sixteenth century, and occupied much of the Balkans into the twentieth.

The Fate of Christians

What happened to the Christians in these regions? Some left. Those more connected with Rome returned to Italy. Others lived on in Muslim lands as Christians. The largest church in any Muslim country is the Coptic Church in Egypt, which numbers between six and eight million adherents. It remained in Egypt, using the ancient Coptic language in its liturgy rather than the new language, Arabic, which came with the Muslim conquerors.

Other churches continued to exist in different parts of the Middle East, especially in Lebanon and Syria. They included Nestorians and others, most were Syriac-speaking groups. The Church in North Africa, west of Egypt, seems to have died out completely in a few decades.

The Muslim conquerors did not persecute the Christians immediately, nor did they force conversion. They considered the Christians to be "people of the Book," in a different category from those of other religions. However, Christians had to pay special taxes, and were forbidden to propagate their faith. Eventually, the churches in many places simply died out as many Christians assimilated and were converted to Islam.

Reasons for the Disappearance of Much of the Church

Disunity of the Church

We should not think that the Muslims wiped out the Christians. However, the Christian churches existed under relentless pressure, were forbidden to evangelize, suffered great disadvantages in society, and were required to pay high taxes. Gradually the Church was simply squeezed to death and disappeared.

The disunity of the Church was another major reason for its demise. A number of North African and Middle Eastern churches were out of fellowship with the larger Church, for at least three reasons. They were cut off from contact with the larger Church because they were surrounded by Islamic societies. The claim that the Bishop of Rome was the head of the entire Church meant that the churches in North Africa and the Middle East felt estranged. They had never recognized Rome's claim to dominance. They did not accept the sovereignty of either the Bishop of Rome or the Archbishop or Patriarch of Constantinople, so were considered schismatic or heretical by both centers. In addition, the theological controversies in the fourth and fifth centuries had led to schisms and left those churches isolated.

This disunity and isolation left the churches in North Africa and the Middle East in a very precarious situation. Later on, when missionaries from Rome came to some of these areas, they created conflict by attempting to bring the surviving churches under papal authority. This was clearly a situation in which the divisions seriously hindered the mission and even the survival of the Church.

Superficial Evangelism and Discipleship

In some areas, the people seem to have been very superficially evangelized and discipled. Apparently there were large people movements without adequate follow-up, probably in North Africa.

Religion of Foreign Elites

It appears the Church in North Africa was identified with the more elitist Romans and Romanized population, less so with the Carthaginians, and even less with the Berbers. There were three primary people groups in North Africa. The Romans were the last colonists who had come to dominate under the Roman Empire. The Carthaginians were in the middle. They had come from Phoenicia, founded Carthage, and dominated the Berbers. The Berbers were the indigenous people, the lowest stratum of society.

Records indicate that most of the theology and liturgy of the Church was in Latin, the language of the Romans; considerably less was in Carthaginian, and almost none was in Berber. That probably indicates a class system in the Church. The great North African theologians—Tertullian, Augustine, and Cyprian—were all Latin speakers. There had been serious schism in the North African church in the fourth century, and we wonder if some of the reasons for this were the ethnic differences. After the Muslim conquest, many of the Romanized peoples fled to Italy, leaving the others behind. Consequently, the stratification of society and uneven evangelization and discipleship of the peoples were probably major factors in the disappearance of the Church in North Africa.

The first New Testament in one of the Berber languages was not completed until the 1980s, and today we are hearing of a growing movement to Christ in Algeria, primarily among Berbers.

Oppression by the Empire and Church

Another reason for the disappearance of the Church was the strong identification of church and state in the Eastern Empire. For reasons partly historical (a weak empire in the West and a strong papacy), the Bishop of Rome and the Church in the West were far more independent of the state than was the Church in the East. In these societies it was always assumed that church and state were one and reinforced each other. This is also true in tribal societies where it is believed that everyone in the tribe must practice the same religion. A major task of religion in such cases is to uphold the status quo in the tribe or state with its patterns of the leadership.

The concept of separation of church and state which has sometimes enabled the Church to speak out against the excesses of the state, is a modern, idea. It has its roots in the Old Testament prophets. We see some separation of church and state taking place in the Church in the West during the Middle Ages, but not much. It is really a modern idea.

The Eastern Church had evolved a theology that said the Emperor represented Christ the King, while the Patriarch or Archbishop represented Christ the Priest. However, if the Emperor represented Christ the King, there was no way the Church could speak out against the abuses of the Empire.

I once visited the beautiful castle at Neuschwanstein in Bavaria, built by Ludwig "the Mad." Ludwig was an ardent Roman Catholic, but the mural in his throne room depicts, not a Roman Catholic concept of the relationship between the Church and state, but a Byzantine or Eastern concept. The king in the mural is depicted as Christ the King. That accorded much better with Ludwig's idea of the proper relationship between church and state than did the Roman Catholic concept. In other words, he wanted to rule over the Church.

The close identification of the Church and the state in the Eastern empire meant that if one rebelled against the oppression of the state he or she was also rebelling against the oppression of the Church.

James Hastings Nichols, a historian of the modern European church, pointed out that in seventeenth, eighteenth, and nineteenth century England, the Anglican Church was closely identified with the state and its class systems. But there were also the dissenting churches, that came from the Puritan and Methodist movements. There, those who protested against the abuses of the state could find their spiritual home. One did not have to leave the Church in order to protest against the oppression of the state. In France, because the Calvinist Huguenots had been so greatly persecuted, it was different. There was only one Church and its hierarchy was identified with the state. Thus if one wished to protest against the excesses of the state, he or she had to leave the

Church and be both anti-church and anti-Christian. That was an important difference in the history of the two nations.

We see something similar in the Muslim conquest. For many Christians in Asia Minor, the Middle East, and North Africa, the Muslims were seen as liberators from the corrupt Christian state. The incessant wars between the Eastern Roman Empire and the Persian Empire had left both exhausted. This left a power vacuum. The new, vigorous Arabian faith rushed in with the sword and conquered. The primary surviving church in North Africa was the Coptic Church in Egypt. It is important to note that it had the Bible in its vernacular language.

Islam remains a serious problem for the Christian Church and Western culture today. But we do know of a number of Muslim cultures where growing numbers of men and women are coming to faith in Christ. Dr. Dudley Woodberry affirms that more Muslims are coming to Christ in this period of history than ever before. That does not minimize the problem, rather it calls the Church to find ways to communicate the Good News of Jesus Christ in ways that honor the many positive qualities in that culture without compromising our conviction that Jesus is "The Way, the Truth, and the Life."

The Viking Invasions and Their Results

The Holy Roman Empire

Charles the Great, or Charlemagne, was the grandson of Charles Martel, who had defeated the Muslim invasion in 732. He unified most of what is now France and Germany. On Christmas Day, 800, the Pope crowned him the "Holy Roman Emperor." Historians have speculated about this act. Many believe that Charles wanted to be crowned Holy Roman Emperor but did not want the Pope to place the crown on his head. Instead, he wanted to take the crown from the Pope's hands and place it on his own head. Later churchmen would cite the fact that the Pope had crowned Charlemagne Holy Roman Emperor as the basis for the claim that the Roman Pontiff had the power both to give and to withhold the crown. The struggle for supremacy between church and state would continue in Europe for centuries.

The concept was that this new "Holy Roman Empire," was the legitimate successor of the earlier Roman Empire. The problem, as many have pointed out, is that it was neither holy, nor Roman, nor an empire. Yet it lasted for over a thousand years in Europe in some form or another. This fictitious concept finally ended after the first World War.

Decadence in Church and Society

The Roman Empire had disappeared long before this period. To some extent, Charles brought about a Renaissance of learning in the Church in his territories. He brought Alcuin from York, England, who came from the Celtic tradition, to bring some reforms to the Church. He encouraged learning and better administration. However, after Charles died in 814, his sons inherited various parts of his empire; it fell apart with the death of one of his sons, Charles the Fat, in 888. That left a power vacuum.

Western Europe now fell into a period of chaos and darkness. But we remember that such periods are often a prelude to renewal. The great historian, Arnold Toynbee, suggested we could study all of the great civilizations of world history from the perspective of challenge and response. His thesis was very simple: when a civilization fails to respond positively to new challenges, it begins to decline. As long as it continues to respond positively to its new challenges, it survives and moves ahead. He believed that was the most important factor in the development and survival of civilizations.

God at Work

Throughout history, we often see that when the situation appears to be darkest, God is preparing to do a new thing. As you examine your own history or that of your mission or church, look at those periods when nothing of significance seemed to be happening. Perhaps there was a period of great hardship and oppression. Then ask if at that time God was preparing to do something new, about

to demonstrate a fresh outburst of his Spirit. For example, we see the oppression that the Korean church experienced under the Japanese from 1910 to 1945. Afterward came a brief period of peace, and then, starting in 1950, several years of terrible, destructive war. The Church survived through all of that tragedy, and then burst forth into a period of unparalleled growth and worldwide ministry. The rapid growth of the Church in China after the persecution of the Communist government and then the Red Guards is another example.

I once was taken to a 'dry creek' in the mountains of Montana, to fish. It seemed strange. For some distance no water appeared to be flowing. But it was there, flowing under the surface. A short distance downstream, the water was on the surface where one could fish successfully.

The history of the work of God is something like that. There are periods when we can see it openly. There are other periods when everything seems dry, as if God is distant and uncaring. However, as followers of Jesus, we know that God is still alive and active. If we go through dry periods in our own ministry, it is our task to be faithful and obedient and trust Him to bring the water of life to the surface again. Remember the 'dry creek.'

Feudalism

Europe now fell into the pattern called "feudalism." It led to a very difficult existence for the great majority of people. Society was organized into two classes; the nobility, who ruled and were landowners and soldiers, and the serfs. The serfs were semi-slaves.

They had to stay on their land. They had a certain amount of freedom, but they could not leave. In return for their protection by the nobility and the knights, the serfs gave part of their produce and owed their service to their lord.

Architecture symbolized the society. The dominant construction was the castle, a combination of fortress and living space. Nearby were the huts of the serfs. The 'middle class' would emerge later with the beginning of manufacturing, trade, and the rise of cities.

There were incessant wars. Most nobles were constantly trying to protect and, if possible, enlarge their territories. The only way to achieve political and economic stability in feudalism was to form alliances with other powerful nobles. By this time most bishops were appointed from the nobility, and often held both secular and religious authority. In addition, many monasteries now owned significant tracts of land. Consequently, many church leaders were caught up in this feudal system and functioned like secular princes.

Political alliances through marriages and other agreements were used to maintain a certain level of economic and political stability. Most bishops were chosen for their political power and ability to help maintain that stability, rather than for any spiritual qualities. They were now de facto rulers over considerable areas. When monasteries became great landholders, some abbots also exercised political power. We can imagine what this wealth and power did to the spiritual life of the Church—the societal and spiritual decline that came with feudalism.

Viking Destruction

In the ninth century, Europe suffered a tragic series of invasions by the Vikings, the Norsemen who came from Scandinavia—now the nations of Denmark, Sweden, and Norway.

They were pagans, but different from the earlier tribes that had poured into Central Europe from Asia. Those groups had adopted Roman institutions and Christianity. The Vikings, however, rejected Christian faith. They were brutal. They sacked, raped, burned, and pillaged wherever they went.

They attacked towns and castles, monasteries, and churches. They killed priests and took monks into slavery. A third of the clergy in France were killed. The Vikings sailed up the rivers of Western Europe and Russia, and into the Mediterranean where they captured Sicily.

Many of the monasteries in England and Ireland, the Celtic centers of learning, were burned and destroyed. In 789, the Vikings attacked Lindisfarne near York, on the northeast coast of England. It had been one of the key centers for the evangelism of England. The Vikings sacked Lindisfarne fourteen times. They also attacked Iona many times and ultimately destroyed it.

The school of Alcuin of York, one of the great medieval centers of learning, was destroyed in the ninth century; other Celtic centers of mission and learning met the same fate.

The Church in Decline

Things got worse. In 846 Muslims plundered Rome and burned the Church of St. Peter. If you were a visitor from Mars and came to the world at the end of the ninth century, you would never have thought that the Church of Jesus Christ would survive, let alone expand worldwide. It looked like a tiny, dying, threatened minority. Muslims were coming from the east and would continue to do so for several centuries. They also came from the south up through Sicily. Vikings came from the north. The Church was corrupt in many places.

By now, a third of Italy consisted of the Papal States, ruled by the pope. These states included the middle third of the Italian peninsula. Consequently, the Pope was no longer primarily a religious leader, now he was a civil ruler and a minor king. This continued until 1870. The Popes were no longer chosen for their spiritual qualities. They were chosen because of their connections with powerful people and their own ambitions to become rulers over the Papal States.

The spiritual tone of the papacy declined disastrously. Soon we come to a period in which historians call the papacy the "pornocracy." There was gross sexual immorality.

Some popes lasted only a month or three months before being assassinated. Terrible things were happening in the name of the Church. Rome, supposedly its center, was a center of corruption and violence.

Once more, new streams of life in the West had come from two sources: continuing strands of the old Celtic tradition, and new monasteries established by people seeking to be serious disciples of Jesus Christ.

Gleams of Light

Alfred the Great

One gleam of light came from Alfred the Great. He was a sincere Christian who ruled England from 871 to 899. He defeated the Danish Vikings and began to unify his people and reestablish the Church. He led a religious and intellectual renaissance in England. From the chaos that existed, he began to reform the organization of the Church and encouraged learning. He deserves to be considered one of the great men in history.

It is interesting to note that England became the source of the missionaries who eventually brought the Scandinavian countries to the Christian faith. They continued the vitality of the older Celtic tradition that had nearly been destroyed by the Viking invasions. Significantly, England posed no military threat to the Scandinavians. Could that be a reason why the English missionaries were far more successful than those from the old Holy Roman Empire who had gone earlier. The fact that the Holy Roman Empire was a political, economic, and military rival must have been an important reason for their rejection. That has lessons for contemporary missions.

Conversion of the Scandinavians

The conversion of the Scandinavians came about through people movements led by royal initiatives. In several cases, the rulers accepted the faith and led the people to do so, at times, by force. It was far from a perfect process, but it was the method by which the great majority of peoples in Europe had become Christians earlier.

One of the best-known cases was that of Olaf Tryggvason in Norway. He had been a slave, was released, and became a Viking leader. While he was a Viking raider, he met an English hermit, a monk who had gone out to seek God in solitude. The hermit met the Viking raider, convinced him of the faith, and baptized him. When Tryggvason was crowned king of Norway in 995, he led the nation to become nominally Christian within five years.

The process was somewhat similar to that in Armenia, where the king and another leader worked together. Olaf Haraldsson, who would later be known as St. Olaf, completed the task. He destroyed pagan temples, organized the churches into the diocesan structure, and appointed bishops.

Haraldsson was a wise missiologist, even though he did not use the term. In many cultures, folk singers and story tellers pass on the values, wisdom, and traditions from one generation to the next. Haraldsson encouraged the people to transmit the Gospel and Christian values using traditional folk songs and ballads. He placed respected men in church leadership. So it became a national church very quickly. Of course, what McGavran has called "the discipling process" needed to go on, and indeed did so. The Church was only loosely connected with Rome. That is probably one reason why the Norwegian and other Scandinavian churches quickly became Lutheran during the Protestant Reformation.

I once spoke to a group on the campus of Luther Seminary in Minneapolis, Minnesota. That seminary came out of Norwegian Lutheranism. On the campus, I saw a large Celtic cross which I usually associate with Roman Catholics and Presbyterians—with Ireland and Scotland.

Why would Lutherans have a large Celtic cross on their campus? I read the inscription. It was a replica of a similar cross in Norway. Of course! Missionaries from the Celtic tradition went from England to Norway in the tenth and eleventh centuries to take the Christian faith there. So there on a campus in Minnesota, we still see the traces of that vigorous missionary Celtic Christianity.

Today, the Norwegian Church, like most others in Europe, counts only five to eight percent of its people as active Christians. Yet, for decades, it has sent out twice as many missionaries per capita as the North American Church.

We should not think just because Norway was converted through a people movement led by a king's initiative that there was no vital Christian faith there. In spite of much nominalism, Norway still has vital churches. It certainly needs to be renewed, as does the Church elsewhere. But it is interesting that even after the Viking invasions, which destroyed so much that was good in Church and state in Europe, that stream of vital Celtic Christianity with its missionary passion and love of learning still made such an impact. As a person with Swedish Baptist background, I am personally indebted to it.

Chapter Ten

Monastic Renewal and the Crusades

Monastic Renewal

In 909 clerics in France wrote,

> The cities are depopulated, the monasteries ru-
> ined and burned, the country reduced to soli-
> tude. As the first men lived without law or fear
> of God, so now every man does what seems
> good in his own eyes, despising laws human
> and divine, and the commands of the Church.
> The strong oppress the weak, the world is full
> of violence against the poor and of the plunder
> of the goods of the Church... Men devour one
> another like the fishes of the sea.

Not a pretty picture.

That was Europe after the decline of the Holy Roman Empire and the Viking invasions. About the same year, a new monastery was established at Cluny in what is now the French region of Bourgogne. It would have a significant effect on both church and state. Within a century, we will begin to see the dawn of a new era—not a perfect time by any means, but one with considerably more stability and possibility for genuine life and faith.

First, we must see these new monasteries as renewal movements. Most Protestants are not used to seeing them that way, because their forms of piety and communal life seem so foreign. In addition, those who have lived in countries where the Roman Catholic Church has dominated for centuries, have experienced some of the negative consequences of that Church. However, it is important to realize that a genuine desire for renewal has inspired many monastic movements in history. And in some cases, they have been at least partially successful in achieving their goals in the broader Church.

The source of these monastic revivals was the desire for a genuinely authentic Christian life. Their founders believed they must withdraw from both the broader Church and society to pursue a life of devotion to Christ. At times they were concerned to renew the whole Church, and beyond that, the larger society. Once more, we see Max Warren's concept of the "diffusion of authority" illustrated. There were two foci of authority in the Church—the diocese with its bishop, and the monastery with its abbot. Most people were a part of the diocesan system with its bishops and priests. Often, both diocesan clergy and laity manifested a low level of understanding and spiritual commitment. Alongside that system was the monastery. At their best, the monks (and nuns) followed certain spiritual disciplines and demonstrated a genuine hunger for God. Thus they modeled a more authentic Christian lifestyle.

The Establishment of Cluny

The monastery at Cluny was established in 909 or 910. Until that time, there were no monastic orders. That is, the individual monasteries had no connection with each other and did not follow a general rule under an external authority. Often they followed the Benedictine rule, but because they were not connected with each other, it was easier for the bishops and the nobility to dominate them. Their agendas were normally political, economic, and military, quite different from the original aims of the monasteries. Thus it was difficult for the monks to maintain their original goals.

As we mentioned earlier, two factors often contributed to the decline and corruption of the monasteries. Often the nobles sent their younger sons, who could not inherit land and titles, to the monasteries. Their daughters who could not find suitable husbands were often sent to the convents. Many had no deep Christian faith, let alone a vocation for the monastic life. Secondly, because of their success in agriculture and donations from wealthy noble patrons, the monasteries often became wealthy. Consequently, they often declined and became as corrupt as the rest of society.

Now something new, the development of a monastic order, occurred. After the monastery was founded at Cluny, other existing monasteries as well as newly established houses came under its leadership. The abbot elected as the head of Cluny was the head of the entire order. Eventually hundreds of monasteries throughout Western Europe were tied together in this network.

Monastic houses that were part of such an order could not be so easily dominated by the local bishop or nobles. Theoretically, the order lived under the authority of the Pope. However, that centralized authority, while quite corrupt at this time, was far away. Consequently, the Cluniac order became a new force for reform in the Church and, to some degree, in the state.

Founded by the Duke of Aquitaine

The Duke of Aquitaine in central France established Cluny with a mind towards glorifying God and saving his own soul. He gave land and money to construct the buildings for the glory of God, with the stipulation that the monks would pray for the salvation of his soul. That reflected the belief in the need for prayers to release one from purgatory.

Monks Elect the Abbot

It was a period of great decadence in the papacy. When he established the monastery, the Duke stipulated that the monks were to follow the Rule of St. Benedict with no outside interference. He insisted that no secular prince, count, or bishop place an abbot over the monks against their will. In other words, the monastery was to be independent of both secular and local ecclesiastical power. The request was respected. Cluny was to be under the protection of the Pope. It is ironic that the popes were extremely corrupt at this point in history, but fortunately were far away. That gave a great degree of freedom for Cluny to order its life and pursue its goals.

Growth of the Monastic Movement

The movement grew. It was not part of the original idea to bring other monasteries into association with Cluny, and it certainly was not part of the original plan to attempt to change the Church. However, others were also searching for renewal and reform. Within a few years, six other monasteries asked to come under the control of Cluny and its abbot. By the time of the fifth abbot, who ruled from 994 to 1048, Cluny was the head of a congregation of several hundred monasteries. All of them had either been founded or reformed by Cluny and were under the control of its abbot. Their heads were appointed by the Cluniac abbot and responsible to him.

A Monastic Order

Cluny developed into an order in which a whole series of houses were linked together under one central authority. Later on in the thirteenth century, we will see two newer orders that became great missionary arms of the Roman Catholic Church: the Franciscans and the Dominicans. In the sixteenth century, another order—the Jesuits—was established. These three orders—Franciscans, Dominicans, and Jesuits—became the greatest missionary arms of the Roman Church. We see this concept of a monastic "order" beginning in Cluny.

This was also a period in which the concept of "nation" was slowly beginning to develop. Travel was difficult and dangerous during the Middle Ages. Most people never travelled more than ten miles away from their birthplaces. Most knew little or nothing about life outside their own immediate context. Consequently, it was hard for a sense of nationhood to evolve.

That was beginning to change but it would take centuries. The Crusades were an important factor in this process, as soldiers and pilgrims from different parts of France or Germany, for example, marched together and discovered some commonality. The concept of nationalism began to develop at this point, although it would become much stronger in the fifteenth and sixteenth centuries.

Theoretically, the Church saw itself as one in Europe, and that contributed to the concept of a cohesive order of monasteries scattered across a broad area. Even the original Benedictine monastery in Monte Cassino, Italy was reformed and became a part of the Cluny order. A Cluniac monastery was established in Rome itself.

Wealth and Influence

The order grew in wealth. Many people gave land to the various monasteries, as the first donor had done, and this constituted a great danger to the maintenance of a simple lifestyle. Two centuries after its founding, Cluny had seriously declined.

Reforming Church and Society

Cluny began as a place for those who wanted to pursue an authentic Christian life in a monastic context. Later came the attempt to reform both church and society. At other times in history, as followers of Christ have sought to go deeper in their life with God, it has led to renewal in the Church and some reform in society. I have not seen such renewal movements affect society unless they have first begun to affect the Church to a significant degree. When churches talk a great deal about changing society, without first seeking renewal in their own faith and devotion to Christ, their words seems to have little or no effect.

I believe the proper sequence is seen when Christians realize their own need for renewal by the Holy Spirit and the new life begins to spill over into society in ministries of compassion and even social reform.

Hildebrand

By the latter part of the eleventh century, a little over a century-and-a-half after Cluny was founded, a Cluniac monk named Hildebrand was elected as Pope Gregory VII. He ruled the Church from 1073 to 1085. His concern for reform focused on two major issues: he wanted to enforce the celibacy of the clergy and prevent the appointment of bishops by lay nobles. Hildebrand was only partially successful in his aims.

The Church had taught for centuries that priests were not to be married. But while they could not marry legally, it was common for priests either to live in de facto marriages or have a series of concubines. In a curious reversal of what we would consider "morality," the Church considered legal marriage of priests much worse than either of the other two situations. The problem in the eyes of the Church was that if a priest who was legally married acquired property, his children would be legitimate and would inherit it. If he was not legally married, his children would not be considered legitimate, and any property he acquired would revert to the Church. So in part, it was an issue of property.

However, property ownership was not the only reason Hildebrand wished to enforce celibacy and do away with clerical marriage. For him it was a moral issue. Whether we agree or not, he believed the unmarried, celibate state to be the ideal, and he tried to enforce it.

The other issue Hildebrand championed during his Papacy regarded the ceremony in which the bishop was invested with the symbols of his office. Normally the local noble—a count or a duke— gave the symbols of office to the bishop during his investiture. That implied, of course, that the secular prince had authority over the Church, and the power to both appoint and depose bishops. Hildebrand believed this practice had led to considerable corruption.

He was not completely successful in these battles. His campaigns symbolize how often a genuine movement can fail to see its own fallibility, make extravagant claims, and contribute to its demise.

In that context Hildebrand made the highest claims for the authority of the papacy in all of history. Even though we would not agree with them, we need to understand the context from which they came, and his reasons for making them. He said,

> The Roman Church alone was established by God.
>
> The Roman Pontiff alone can be called universal.
>
> He alone can depose or reinstate bishops.
>
> He is the only one whose feet princes must kiss.
>
> He can depose emperors.
>
> He may be judged by no one.
>
> The Roman church has never erred and never will err.
>
> The Pope may absolve subjects from their allegiance to wicked men.
>
> (R. Clouse, R. Pierard, and E. Yamauchi, *Two Kingdoms: the Church and Culture Through the Ages* [Chicago: Moody Press, 1993], 158).

The pope claimed the power to release subjects from their vows of allegiance to a wicked ruler and that was done at times. There were times when the Pope refused to allow any celebration of the sacraments in a ruler's territory because of Church-state conflict. What did that mean? Remember that in Roman theology, the grace of God comes almost exclusively through the sacraments of the Church. If one do not receive the sacraments of the Church and the grace that comes through them, he or she is doomed to hell. We can imagine the pressure it put on a secular ruler when the Pope interdicted all sacramental acts in his territory.

Hildebrand's goal was good. He wanted to re-establish the purity of the Church. However, his assertions led to a tragic expansion of papal claims. His statements were frequently used later in different contexts to the detriment of both Church and state. Hildebrand did not win his battles in the end. Despite this, some reform occurred in the Church. The struggles between church and state continued for centuries.

The Cistercians

Founded by Robert Champagne

By the end of the eleventh century, Cluny had declined and corruption had set in. This led to the establishment of a new order, the Cistercians, in 1098. That year that one Robert of Champagne left a Cluniac monastery because it was not rigorous enough. With twenty companions, he founded a new monastery at Citeaux, near Dijon, in southeastern France. In some ways, the Cistercians were to be a resurgence of the original Cluniacs. The monks were determined to remain poor and live an extremely austere existence.

The new order attracted few adherents, but in 1112 a young man named Bernard, who would be known in history as Bernard of Clairvaux, came with thirty companions. He was of the petty nobility, and would become the most influential churchman of his day. Because of the power of Bernard's personality and influence, the Cistercian movement, with its strict ascetic life style and mystical piety, grew.

The monks were to have a diet only of fresh or dried vegetables, a little oil, a little salt, and water. They would sleep in a common dormitory, always with a candle lit, fully dressed and ready for duty. They were to spend six hours in prayer a day.

Important in Bernard's piety was the contemplation of Christ. The hymns, "Jesus, the very thought of Thee, with sweetness fills my breast," and "O Sacred Head Now Wounded," are ascribed to Bernard. He also showed great devotion to the Virgin Mary and wrote a number of hymns to her, based on the Song of Songs. In many ways a great man, he was far from perfect. He was ruthless toward his enemies. He strongly supported the Crusades. As we previously noted, he wrote to a priest who had left the monastery to return to his parish ministry, warning that he was in danger of losing his salvation. Yet Bernard was probably the most influential man in his day in Western Europe. He certainly sought to serve God according to his own understanding.

Bernard saw one of his former monks from Clairvaux become Pope, and wrote to him, suggesting how the Church should be reformed. He was only partially successful. We recognize that it is relatively easy to tell the people at the center of things how an organization should be run and what reforms are needed. Solutions often seem clear to those who are not in authority. But those in charge find that reform is much more complicated and difficult. No doubt, that is what Bernard's former student discovered.

Bernard was intensely loyal to the Church as he knew it and was fiercely orthodox in medieval terms. When Peter Abelard, a theologian in Paris, advocated a new view of the atonement, Bernard condemned him.

Primarily because of Bernard's influence, the Cistercian movement brought a measure of reform and greater purity of life in the Church.

The monastery in Alcobaça, Portugal, is a fascinating symbol of what often happens to a monastic movement or, indeed, any movement. Connected to the monastery is the largest church in Portugal. It is located in a little town at the confluence of two small rivers, the Alco and the Baça. Some of the finest fruit in the country is raised there, a result of the Cistercian heritage.

The Church is unadorned because the Cistercians insisted on simplicity in contrast to the Cluniacs. It does not have the elaborate stone carvings we often find in Portuguese churches, except for the elaborately carved sarcophagi of a former ruler and his princes. Otherwise the church is typical of Cistercians simplicity.

Alongside the Church is a cloister where the monks lived. From there one enters the kitchen where meals were prepared. Remember that originally the order insisted on the utmost simplicity in diet: fresh or dried vegetables, a little salt, and oil. Yet two centuries after the monastery was established in the thirteenth century, the kitchen evolved to the point where it included two tables, each large enough to carve a whole beef, and a huge fireplace so large that I could easily stand inside of it. There were two towering chimneys overhead, and the monks could roast an entire beef on a spit over the fire. They had also diverted the water from one of the rivers so it ran through the kitchen, into a pond where the water still flows. There they could keep fresh fish and eels.

On one side of the kitchen is a wine cellar as large as most churches. On the other side is the refectory, with two doors. One is very wide; the other, narrow. Presumably, if the monks got too fat they were expected to attempt to enter through the narrow door to remind them to lose some weight. It is an amusing but graphic symbol of what McGavran called "redemption and lift," or the danger of affluence. We know that danger in North America. We are reminded that the Pentecostal movement began among the poor, and then remember some in the movement who insisted on gold-plated bathroom fixtures in the resort they were building for their followers. We North American evangelicals, indeed all of us, must keep on asking ourselves what an authentic Christian lifestyle should look like. I have never forgotten the great Cistercian monastery at Alcobaça.

Other Monastic Reform Groups
Canons Regular of St. Victor
At the same time, we begin to see more concern for spiritual discipline among the clergy in a number of areas. One group was called the Canons Regular of St. Victor. "Regular" meant they followed a rule or spiritual discipline as the monks did.

The canons were the clergy of a cathedral. Traditionally, the priests lived as they pleased out in the village or town. That of course made it much easier to evade the rules regarding celibacy. Now some bishops, seeking a measure of reform, began to require the priests of the cathedral to live together in a disciplined lifestyle. In time priests of different parishes followed a similar rule together as in community. That lifestyle often involved spiritual, intellectual, and moral discipline as they lived under a "rule" or "regula." That was a new trend in the Church, and reflected the influence of monasticism on some of the secular clergy.

We still hear of "regular" and "secular" clergy in the Roman Catholic Church today. "Regular" refers to one who follows a rule as a member of a monastic order, "secular" refers to a priest who is not attached to a monastic order. The secular clergy are under the discipline of a bishop, and are assigned to a church or other duties. Regular clergy live under the authority of the leaders of their communities or orders. Bishops can also assign regular clergy loaned to them from monastic orders.

Thus in the twelfth and thirteenth centuries, we begin to see concern for greater order and discipline among the clergy. It was not all that we would want, but it was improvement. When I was at Princeton, one of my teachers was Georges Barrois. A Frenchman, he had spent many years as a Dominican monk and priest. He was a leading authority on the geography of the Holy Land and had written a two-volume manual of archeology in French. He was a marvelous man.

He came to the United States to teach in Washington, D.C. and became increasingly dissatisfied with the Roman Church. He began attending a Presbyterian church and told me that one Sunday, "I took the Lord's Supper, and I knew I had passed the point of no return." He went on to Princeton and did a second doctorate, having received his first at the Vatican. He stayed on as a professor at Princeton. He was not rigidly anti-Catholic. He still maintained many friendships in the Roman Catholic Church, and appreciated much of what it had done for him. However, he felt he could no longer remain in there.

An extremely learned man, Dr. Barrois was an authority on medieval history and theology, as well as the Old Testament. He said that the great majority of priests in the medieval church did not preach. Most were illiterate or semi-literate, and could just barely recite the Lord's Prayer and the Ave Maria and get through the mass in Latin. He said this was typical of the Medieval Church. The level of learning was very low. We hear about the great universities started in the thirteenth century in Europe, and the great theologians, but they touched only a tiny portion of the Church and its people.

Thus, the medieval church was essentially an institution that administered the sacraments to the people. Even though the great majority of people believed in the Church and its teaching, the level of understanding and conduct was very low.

That was true of the clergy as well as the laity. Thus, any improvement in discipline and learning among the priests was a gain.

The Causes of the Crusades
Religious

We will now examine perhaps the most tragically distorted form of Christian mission in history. I refer to the Crusades. When examining the causes of the Crusades, we first need to understand medieval theology, and especially, how one received salvation according to that theology.

I said at the beginning that we need to ask ourselves constantly about the definition of a "Christian." The medieval definition of a true Christian was one who had been baptized into the right ecclesiastical institution in Western Europe—the Roman Church—and was relatively obedient to that Church. The Church taught that if you received the sacraments with some regularity, you would eventually go to heaven.

Naturally then, it was considered appropriate to do almost anything to lead a person to be baptized and enter the true Church. This helps us understand the Crusades, but is only one factor in their development.

Medieval theology taught there were two kinds of penalties for sins: eternal and temporal. Jesus had paid the eternal penalties, but payment of the temporal penalties was still up to each person. Either one paid through acts of penance done in this life, or he or she paid afterwards in the flames of purgatory. When sins were confessed to the priest, he was to prescribe certain acts of penance. They might include giving alms, a pilgrimage to some holy place, a certain number of prayers, or the veneration of sacred relics. If one did not do enough, the understanding was that the balance was to be paid in "purgatory."

I am not sure when the concept of purgatory emerged. But once the concept of both temporal and eternal penalties for sin was established, along with the understanding that one could never be sure if all of the temporal penalties had been paid, purgatory became necessary.

This leads us to another factor in the Crusades. Throughout the Middle Ages, people made pilgrimages to special shrines where they often venerated relics of the saints. It was believed there were enough pieces of the "true cross" scattered throughout Europe to make ten crosses. One of the popes is said to have resolved this discrepancy by saying the wood of the true cross had miraculously multiplied itself. Other relics supposedly included milk from the breast of the Virgin Mary and bones of St. Peter and other great figures of the past. The Church taught that the veneration of such relics would reduce one's time in purgatory. During the time of Martin Luther, his prince, Frederick the Elector of Saxony had collected so many relics in the castle church that if you venerated them all, it would reduce your stay in purgatory by over twenty thousand years!

Naturally, a pilgrimage to the Holy Land was the greatest of all acts of penance.

The Muslim powers had allowed Christians to make pilgrimages to the Holy Land for centuries, but in the time leading up to the Crusades, the Seljuk Turks had refused permission for them to do so. Thus, the theology that good works had to be done as an indication of penance encouraged the Crusades.

Economic Factors

There were also economic reasons. From 970 to 1040 there were forty-eight years of famine. From 1085 to 1095, things got even worse. At the end of the century, there was widespread misery and unrest. Europe was considered to be too densely populated, with no place for the surplus population. The younger sons of the nobility had special problems. They could not inherit their fathers' lands or titles. If they did not want to go to a monastery, war or a life of adventure seemed to be the only alternative. It was a time of chaos and unrest.

Church Schism

The stated motive for the Crusades was to wrest the Church in the East, centered in Constantinople, from the near control of the Muslim Turks. What eventually happened was the opposite. The attack of the fourth crusade on Constantinople weakened the Eastern Empire and eventually hastened its fall to the Turks in 1453.

In 1054, the Church in the east and west had formally separated. There was a theological issue involved: Did the Holy Spirit proceed from both the Father and the Son, or only from the Father? However, the primary issue was the claim of the Bishop of Rome to be the head of the whole Church. Constantinople had never accepted that assertion. In fact, Constantinople claimed to be the second Rome, following the logic that since Constantine had transferred the seat of the Empire to the city named for him, the Patriarch of Constantinople should rule over the whole Church. Neither side was willing to accept the claims of the other, yet even after the schism in 1054, there was still hope that they could reunite. (Later on, Moscow would call itself the third Rome.)

The Crusades began in 1096 when Alexis I, emperor of the Eastern Empire in Constantinople requested help from Pope Urban II to come to his aid in the struggle against the Turks. The Pope hoped that if the crusaders aided the Eastern Church by defeating the Turks, the Church would be reunited under his leadership.

Therefore, we see religious, economic, and ecclesiastical reasons for the Crusades.

A Series of Crusades

In response to the request from Constantinople, in a sermon at Clermont, France in 1096, Urban II proclaimed the First Crusade. He called on the people to go to the Holy Land and liberate the holy places from the Turks. He finished by saying, "God wills it," and the crowd shouted in response, "God wills it!" Urban genuinely wanted to reform the Church and society. He believed he needed to increase the Church's power to do so.

Urban offered a plenary indulgence to everyone who took part in the First Crusade. As we discussed earlier, the Church taught that there were both eternal and temporal penalties for our sins. Jesus had paid the eternal penalties, but we must pay the temporal penalties through acts of penance. If there were not enough acts of penance, the remaining penalties would be paid in the flames of purgatory. An indulgence was the forgiveness of all or part of one's time in purgatory. A plenary indulgence meant that all temporal penalties would be forgiven, and thus one would go directly from this life to heaven. Barrois said the average person the Middle Ages was much more terrified of purgatory than of hell. A reasonably obedient son or daughter of the Church would not go to hell, but purgatory was a virtual certainty for all. Thus, the promise of a full indulgence was powerful for the crusaders. Later we will see the sale of indulgences as a trigger of Luther's revolt in the sixteenth century.

The First Crusade was really an armed pilgrimage. At least as many civilians went as did soldiers. We are used to thinking of the Crusades as soldiers going with their banners flying to liberate the Holy Land. While some movies and books have glamorized the Crusades, they were actually were a sordid chapter in Western history.

There was a great deal of popular enthusiasm for the Crusades. One leader, called Peter the Hermit, was followed by mobs who attacked the Jews along the way and slaughtered thousands. Most of those who followed Peter died before they got to the Holy Land.

There were several Crusades. The first was successful in capturing Jerusalem, where the inhabitants were slaughtered. A European model of feudalism was established, and castles were built. We should note that during the five hundred years prior to that time, in which Muslims held the city, Christians were respected and given half the city as their own. That was in stark contrast to the Crusaders, who slaughtered everyone in the city whether they were Christian or Muslim. In the fourth Crusade, soldiers plundered the treasures of Constantinople, appointed a Latin patriarch for the Eastern Church, and made it subservient to Rome. That alienated the Eastern Church from the West, weakened the Eastern Empire, and made its conquest by the Turks inevitable. Eventually, as we know, the Muslims regrouped and drove out the westerners.

The Legacy of the Crusades

Several results of the Crusades are relevant to mission. They were perhaps the worst example in history of a perverted understanding of Christian mission. They illustrate how bad theology leads to distorted and ineffective mission.

The first result was the rise of the crusading spirit in the Church. That led to the practice of using the sword not only against non-Christians, but also against other Christians. Soon, the Church, allied with some political rulers, pronounced crusades against people in Europe considered unorthodox. Eventually the Inquisition developed.

Three military monastic orders—the Templars, the Hospitallers, and the Teutonic Knights, developed from the Crusades. Their members were monks—laymen who used the sword. The Teutonic Knights were involved in the conquest of East Prussia. The Templars were established in 1119 as a military monastic order and eventually became extremely powerful and wealthy. In 1307 they were brutally suppressed by the king of France who wanted their wealth.

Henry the Navigator, prince of Portugal in the fifteenth century, was grand master of the Order of Christ which had taken over the property of the Templars in Portugal. Henry's passion was the study of navigation. He established a center at Sagres on the south Portuguese coast, for the study of navigation. There, the Age of Exploration, led by the Portuguese and Spanish, began. Columbus 'discovered' the New World in 1492. Vasco da Gama sailed around Africa and arrived in India in 1498. Cabral arrived in Brazil in 1500, and soon Magellan was the first to sail around the world, even though he was killed on the way. They had all learned navigation at Sagres. Prince Henry was a monastic person in his lifestyle and goals and the explorations were really a continuation of the Crusades. They went out with crosses on their sails and priests onboard, with the hope of outflanking Islam on their way to the riches of the Indies. They went to the Americas seeking "gold and souls."

There were also positive intellectual, economic and political consequences from the Crusades. They stimulated the growth of cities and trade. A new social structure, with towns and a "commercial" or "middle class," arose in Europe. They hastened the end of a decadent feudalism and began to stimulate more trade. They broadened the outlook of many who had previously never left their home villages but now had traveled to foreign countries. Thus the Crusades contributed both to a greater sense of nationalism, and eventually internationalism. In addition, some classical literature that had been preserved by Nestorian Christians and translated into Arabic now entered Europe again, partly because of the Crusades.

Religiously, of course, the Crusades were a disaster. As we have seen, they greatly increased the hatred of the Eastern Church toward Rome. They drove an even greater wedge between Islam and Christianity.

As a strategy for mission, the Crusades were tragic. Long after the Crusades had ended in the Middle East, Catholics were fighting to drive them out Spain. In the cathedral in Granada, we find a striking painting. It portrays the last Moorish ruler of southern Spain surrendering to Ferdinand and Isabella, whose marriage had unified Spain. The year was 1492, the same year that Columbus sailed.

The Crusades continued in Portugal to a lesser degree. The cathedral in the old section of Lisbon was built to celebrate the feat of the English Crusaders who stopped there and drove out the Moor in the thirteenth century.

This crusading spirit, still alive in Spain and Portugal, was taken to the New World. The form of Christian faith introduced to Latin America in the sixteenth century was a fanatical, intolerant Catholicism, strongly identified with Spanish and Portuguese nationalism and feudalism.

Chapter Eleven

Medieval Lay Movements

Devotional

I am going to read a hymn in a free translation from Medieval Italian. The introduction reads "O Most High, Almighty, good Lord God, To Thee belong praise, glory, honor, and all blessing." Here are some of the seven verses:

Praised be my Lord God with all His creatures, and especially our brother the sun, who brings us the day and who brings us the light. Fair is he, and shines with very great splendor. O Lord, he signifies to us Thee.

Praised be my Lord for our sister the moon, and for the stars, which He hath set clear and lovely in heaven.

Praised be my Lord for our brother the wind and for air and cloud, calms and all weather, by which Thou upholdest life in all creatures.

Praised be my Lord for our sister water, who is very serviceable to us, and humble and precious and clean.

Praised be my Lord for our brother fire, through whom Thou givest us light in the darkness. He is bright and pleasant and very mighty and strong.

Praised be my Lord for our mother the earth, which doth sustain and keep us, bring forth diverse fruits and flowers of many colors, and grass.

Praised be my Lord for all those who pardon one another for His love's sake and who endure weakness and tribulation. Blessed are they who peaceably shall endure, for Thou, O Most High, shall give them a crown.

Praise ye and bless the Lord and give thanks unto Him, and serve Him with great humility.

This was written shortly before the death of the author:

Praised be my Lord for our sister, the death of the body, from which no man escapeth. Woe to him who dieth in mortal sin. Blessed are they who are found walking by Thy most holy will, for the second death shall have no power to do them harm.

As you probably guessed, St. Francis of Assisi wrote these verses. They are the expression of one of the most attractive people in history—one who consistently demonstrated his devotion and love for Christ. They also show love and appreciation for God's creation. I know that in many places in our world, people are wasting and destroying God's beautiful creation. This is a tragedy. We need to take a new look at our theology of creation.

Often in the winter, I think about a lake in the high mountains of central California. A friend has a cabin there where my wife and I have often spent a week or two. There is no telephone and no electricity, only running water. There are two lovely streams that flow into the lake, where I often catch some trout.

I enjoy being with people, but when I get away and am surrounded by the beauty of God's creation in solitude, it refreshes me in a special way. I believe we have something to learn theologically and spiritually from St. Francis in his appreciation for the beauty of God's creation. It can point us to the beauty of the Creator.

Some years ago, I visited Masai Mara, the great game park at the northern end of the Serengeti in Kenya. This was a very different experience of nature for me. The thought struck me, "What a marvelous witness to the variety and creativity of the Creator!" I suggest we listen to St. Francis, who had many things to teach us about poverty and identification with the poor, about devotion and love for Jesus Christ, about a transparent life-style, but also about his love for God's creation, which was reinforced by his love for the Creator.

Let us pray together.

> Father, thank you for men and women of the past through whom we learn so much, who inspire our spirits and lift them, who teach us to look at new aspects of your creative power, your grace, the life which you give to your creation and the new life which you give to us in Jesus Christ. So teach us, as we look at men and women from a very different period of history and a very different culture, men and women who loved you, who sought to serve you, and who shared your love with those around them. We ask this in Christ's name, Amen.

We will look at some interesting people in this chapter. One of the key theses of this book is that new mission movements are nearly always initiated by key leaders—men or women who have gone deep in their life with God and consequently felt His heartbeat for the world and then have communicated their vision to others. This is how movements begin. I hope that sometime during your Christian pilgrimage you will make a special study of key men and women whom God has used uniquely in mission history. Study their lives and try to discover the factors that shaped them. In doing so you will learn important lessons about your own lives.

We will not have time to examine the lives and spiritual formation of men we study today in detail, but we want to ask why God used them uniquely. What were the factors that shaped them in their spiritual and intellectual development?

Note that as we look at movements of renewal and mission, some of the leaders were laymen and some were priests. Some were very well educated; others were not. This tells us that God chooses whom He will; His ways are often unpredictable. We need to be open to the surprises of the Holy Spirit. How impoverished the history of the people of God, especially the missionary movement, would be without those surprises!

Introduction

During the eleventh and twelfth centuries, the medieval church was a powerful and corrupt institution. The level of Christian understanding and discipleship was very low for the great majority of people. If you were a Christian who lived at that time and you wanted to work toward renewal in the Church, what would you do?

Let me read some excerpts about the lives of priests in Normandy (northern France) in the thirteenth century.

> We just visited the deanery of St. Just. We found that the priest of Ruiville was ill famed with the wife of a certain stone-carver, and by her is said to have a child. Also, he is said to have many other children. He does not stay in his church. He plays ball; he rides around in his short garb (James Bruce Ross and Mary Martin McLaughlin, eds., *The Portable Medieval Reader* [New York: Viking Press, 1949], 78).

The archbishop wrote, in one paragraph after another, about priests living with one woman or several, and having children. Other priests were said to drink too much, go to taverns, and be involved in brawls. However, the primary failure was sexual immorality. It was a very sordid picture.

The Church in its diocesan structure was in general quite corrupt. Most of the genuine spiritual life was found in the various monastic orders and in some lay-led groups. The institutional church was very defensive about holding onto its power. Its theology said that the grace of God only came through the sacraments of the Church. It taught that outside the Roman Catholic Church, there was no possibility of salvation. Only the bishops could preach, and those to whom the bishops gave permission. Most bishops were appointed for political reasons and were incapable of preaching even if they had been so inclined. Very few priests preached; most were illiterate and ignorant. It was said that one group of priests was challenged to say just one line from the celebration of the mass in Latin, but could not do so.

Such was the state of the Church. The great majority of the people believed in the Christian faith, but their understanding and practice of the Faith were at a low level. Even so, the people were basically Christian in their religious allegiance. The Church held out a very high standard of Christian life, but the leaders of the Church with rare exceptions did not practice it. Some monasteries were exceptions.

While the level of Christian life and teaching was not high, many people, especially the more humble, were seeking more. It is clear the Church and aristocracy were threatened by these movements in which people sought a more authentic Christian life. In its sacramental system the Church taught that the very worst priest, by virtue of the sacrament of ordination, was worthy to administer the sacraments through which the grace of God came to people. But it taught that the holiest layperson could not celebrate them. It did not matter how bad the priest was; by virtue of the sacrament of ordination, the grace of God could only come through him. The only exception was baptism, where a layperson might baptize in an emergency. The incongruity in the Church's teaching was that a layman or laywoman might live a very holy, dedicated life, but still could not administer the sacraments through which saving grace was believed to come.

If you were in that church, either as a priest or a layperson, and you wanted renewal, what would you do? That was the dilemma.

As we examine history, we discover more evidence for the thesis that mission and renewal movements virtually always (I would tend to say "always") arise on the periphery of the broader Church. Often, but not always, they are led by laypersons. Laymen started two of the four movements we will examine in this chapter. If we take Acts 2:17 seriously—"I will pour out my Spirit upon all flesh" (KJV)—we should not be surprised. The Church always shows the greatest health and vitality when each believer is encouraged to use his or her gifts.

First we will examine movements rejected and cast off by the Church. One has survived until today. In the next chapter, we will look at two movements the Church accepted, perhaps reluctantly. They became the most important mission structures in the Medieval Church.

We must ask the question, if the broader Church rejects a renewal movement, does the movement retain its vitality longer and have a greater impact on church and society? On the other hand, is it more effective in the end if the broader Church embraces it? I am not sure there is strong historical evidence either way. The Franciscans and Dominicans were accepted and became a part of the Roman Catholic system. While they have gone through a process of institutionalization, decadence at times, and renewal, they have exerted a positive influence on the Church over the centuries.

The Roman Church rejected the Waldensians, but they had a powerful impact across Central Europe in the twelfth and thirteenth centuries and afterward. They were terribly persecuted and almost destroyed. Now they are a tiny denomination in Italy with a few congregations elsewhere. The early Moravians, an important catalyst in the Protestant missionary movement, included some remnants of the Waldensians.

Many of us come out of renewal movements that were rejected by their parent body and formed a new structure. This is true of most of the Pentecostal movements, the Christian and Missionary Alliance, and many other denominations including the Methodists. The historical reality is that every movement, no matter how it began, will become institutionalized and fall into the danger of losing its original vision and vitality. None is exempt from that danger.

The Cathari

The first movement we examine was not Christian, although it looked like a Christian movement from the outside. The group was called the *Cathari*, which meant "those who were cleansed." They were also referred to as the Albigensians. I mention this movement only in passing, because it was a Christian heresy. It was a dualistic movement linked to older philosophically dualistic systems such as Gnosticism and Manichaeism.

By dualism, I refer to the concept that spirit is good, and matter (and, therefore, the body) is evil. That was an underlying presupposition of Gnosticism. If you held to this belief, there could be two different ways of treating the body. One would be to deny all bodily appetites. The person who wished to be holy would eat and drink as little as possible—only enough to keep alive. He or she would be celibate; there would be no marriage.

However, there was a minority who said, "The body is not evil, but it is neutral and has no effect on one's relationship with God, so anything goes."

The Cathari chose to deny their bodily appetites, and lived rigorously moral lives.

The group included two classes. The *perfecti* were celibate. They ate no meat, no milk, and no eggs, possessed no property, and did not go to war. It is easy to see how, to the common people, the *perfecti* looked like monks.

The other class consisted of Cathari "believers." They lived normal family lives, but were expected to become *perfecti* before death in order to achieve salvation. They were upright morally and spread their faith with great zeal. They did not believe in the historic Christian faith regarding Jesus Christ and salvation, and rejected the doctrine of the Incarnation. However, because their lives seemed to reflect the teachings of the Church more authentically than many of its leaders, they were very attractive to many. They grew to include the population of a number of cities, especially in southern France. Eventually the Church and state, in a series of crusades, exterminated them. It would not be the first time that heretics seemed to live closer to the Christian ideal than many of orthodox faith.

Early Twelfth Century Movements

Western European societies were changing in the twelfth century. They were moving from a strictly barter economy to one involving more trade. The textile industry was growing, and in tradesmen we see the emergence of a middle class between serf and noble. In this context, various wandering preachers began to attack the structures of the Roman Church, including the papacy. They said its practices were not consistent with the Bible. This indicated that these preachers either read the Bible in Latin or had some vernacular translations. They attacked the wealth of the Church and rejected some of the sacraments. Some said that sacraments performed by unworthy priests were not valid. Among these wandering preachers were Tanchelm of Utrect (Holland), Henry of Lausanne (Switzerland), Arnold of Brescia (Italy) and Peter of Bruys (Belgium). Some were priests, some laymen, but they had a similar message and concerns.

Most of them were burned or hanged as heretics. We read about their ideas through their opponents, who condemned them, so there may be some distortion of their ideas. They might have been much more orthodox than their opponents declared them to be. These men all wanted both Church and society to follow the Bible. They found the Christian life and faith portrayed in the New Testament very different from that which they observed around them. These preachers showed that some, at least, wanted to find a more biblical form of Christianity.

Popular Movements within the Church

At the same time there were lay men and women who led popular movements that remained within the Church. Some were called "confraternities." These were brotherhoods or sisterhoods of laypersons who came together for special worship, mutual help, or the celebration of certain acts of devotion. (We still see confraternities in parades during Holy Week in Spain, carrying huge images of the Virgin or the crucified Jesus.) There were also guilds of men and women who came together to sing hymns of penitence and adoration. It is significant they sang in the vernacular languages rather than Latin.

These and other activities reflected impulses of the Holy Spirit that the normal churchly rituals did not satisfy. Their adherents were not heretical nor were they against the Church. However, they found that the formal church structures did not meet all their needs for praise, penitence, and adoration. I believe this is normally a healthy sign.

There were also flagellants: men and sometimes women, who, in penitence for their sins, walked through the streets punishing their bodies with whips to show their penitence. This happened especially during the plagues. While the movement included some unhealthy manifestations, it also indicated the desire to recognize sin, repent, and experience a deeper life with God.

Other groups were called Beguines. They consisted primarily of women but included men. Most were laywomen. Some were very poor, and some well-to-do. Some lived with their families and observed certain spiritual disciplines. Others formed houses where they lived together. They did not necessarily take permanent vows of poverty, but they were seeking a more authentic spiritual life. Often these groups ministered to the poor and the sick.

Most of these groups wanted a return to the Scriptures, which were becoming more available. These groups were popular with the common people and often stressed the vernacular languages when they preached in the streets and marketplaces. Naturally, they could not preach in the churches. Only the priest or bishop could preach there, and usually did not do so. Therefore, if the common people were to hear the biblical message, they often had to do so outside of the institutional Church.

So it is clear that during the Middle Ages there were many such movements of men and women.

They did not begin with the Protestant Reformation. We believe there were many underground streams of life that we cannot always discover for lack of source material.

At times such groups seem insignificant and appear to accomplish nothing. However, often God accomplishes something new through them. A movement may grow until finally the stream bursts out above ground. It is important to recognize this, because some day you may be a part of an underground group of prayer that is apparently achieving nothing. It is easy to become discouraged, and it can be hard to continue. But God has a way of using such groups during dry periods in history. We remember the tiny, persecuted groups of Christians praying in China, daring to worship secretly during the Cultural Revolution. Then suddenly that stream of life burst to the surface. We see this phenomenon at various times in history.

The Waldensians

The Waldensian movement arose as European society was changing. This reminds us of the importance of looking at the historical context. Today we are moving into a period of great economic, social, and political changes in many societies. Is this not going to lead the Holy Spirit to create new forms of the Church in various cultures? It is probable that some newer forms of the Church will be more effective than some familiar ones. We already see evidence of that in many societies. We need to be open to the new forms of the Church that the Holy Spirit will bring forth in the future.

Early History

Western Europe was in transition. It was changing from a feudal society, where the architectural symbols were the castle and the serf's hut, to a more commercial society. The bourgeoisie—the townspeople, the traders and small manufacturers, the middle class—was emerging. The term, "middle class," referred to the group between the nobility and the serf. The serf produced agricultural products, and the nobles ruled and fought.

Now manufacturing, usually of fabric or textiles, was beginning.

With manufacturing, bartering, trading, and selling occurs. That requires places where people come together to carry on such activities. First it may be only a crossroads, then a village grows up, and then a city. An important question arises: When change comes, how will the Church respond? How should it shape itself for the new era? How will it be different?

Peter Waldo was born around 1140 in Lyons, in southern France. He was a cloth merchant and had become quite wealthy. He had practiced usury; that is, he had charged interest on loans, a common practice. But the Church said it was sin. Jews were allowed to lend money at interest and that made them useful, even necessary, in medieval societies. However, Christians were not supposed to charge interest.

Tradition says that Waldo heard the legend of St. Alexis, who said that the true Christian is willing to give up all and follow nakedly a naked Christ, to be a pilgrim, and call no place on earth home. The words burned into his soul. Continuing his spiritual search, Waldo paid to have the New Testament translated into his vernacular French. He took a radical step and followed the golden text of monasticism, the word of Jesus to the rich young ruler, "Go, sell all that you have, give to the poor, and come and follow me." In 1176, Waldo took that literally. He gave away all that he had, after providing for his wife and daughters, and began to follow Christ by going out and preaching wherever he could, and begging to sustain his life.

Few were preaching at this time. Now multitudes began to follow him. As people responded and became his followers, he began to send them out two by two to preach the simple, biblical faith as he understood it. He requested permission to preach from the bishop, but that was denied in 1179. There were probably two reasons. First, Waldo was a layman, not a priest. I also suspect the authorities were uncomfortable with his message, believing it to be too radical. Without permission, Waldo continued to preach. In 1184, five years after the denial of permission to preach,

the Church condemned Waldo and his followers as heretics. Nevertheless, they began to spread across southern France and northern Italy, then across central Europe. In many respects, it was a reformation movement before Protestantism.

Beliefs and Practices

The beliefs and practices of the Waldensians were similar to many of the earlier preachers we have mentioned. They saw the Bible, primarily the New Testament, as a book of laws. They sought to be as literal as possible in their biblical interpretation. They attempted to follow the Sermon on the Mount literally. They would not take any oath or shed any blood. They did not resist persecution. They were pacifists. They went out two by two to preach to the poor, and lived from the offerings of the believers. At first, they took no money with them, but that later changed. They memorized large portions of Scripture, especially the New Testament, in the vernacular languages. They took their message to the common people of southern and central Europe.

At first they were loyal to the doctrines of the Roman Church, but that gradually changed. Eventually they said the Church and the papacy were corrupt. They criticized the use of Latin, a language that the common people did not understand. They eventually rejected all of the sacraments except those they found in the New Testament—baptism and the Lord's Supper. They also rejected the hierarchy of the Church. We have observed that often a movement of renewal or mission makes theological rediscoveries. Such was the case with the Waldensians, who rediscovered the New Testament message and its simple form of the Church. Hundreds of thousands responded to their message.

We have also noted that renewal movements are often accompanied by new patterns of leadership selection and training. The Waldensians rejected the older priestly pattern, and began to send out laymen and even laywomen to preach. They were one of the first groups after second century Montanism to permit and encourage women in ministry. These lay men and women administered the sacraments of baptism and the Lord's Supper. It is clear they had a different view of ministry as well as a different view of message and structure. Often the Waldensian evangelists traveled in disguise as cloth merchants.

Eventually, two classes or two levels of leadership evolved, reflecting our two-structure idea of sodality and modality. In some ways, they were similar to the *perfecti* and the "believers" among the Albigensians. That is, there were those who were full-time evangelists or missionaries, who wandered about preaching, living off the believers, always in danger of losing their lives. Then there were the people who remained where they were and simply believed, followed, and came together for worship.

They spread rapidly in Italy. A similar group, the *Humiliati*, had been formed in Italy. It was also condemned in 1184. Many of its adherents became Waldensians. By mid-thirteenth century Waldensians were found in Austria, Bohemia, and Moravia. In the fourteenth century they had spread to Germany, Hungary, and Poland. Even some princes and magistrates were reputed to be Waldensians. They were terribly persecuted. In 1211, eighty were burned at the stake in Strassburg. In the fifteenth to seventeenth centuries, they were driven into the mountains of northern Italy, where they formed their communities and schools. Thousands were wiped out through persecution and the movement nearly disappeared.

Today the Waldensians have a close relationship with the Reformed family of churches. The Waldensian Church in Italy, now merged with the Methodists, numbers a few thousand members. There are also Waldensian churches in Uruguay and Argentina.

Later History

We find a charming story early in the sixteenth century. Etienne de la LaForge, a Waldensian cloth merchant in Paris, was an ardent Christian. He demonstrated his compassion for the poor and concern for the Gospel by giving them cloth along with evangelical tracts. At times, students at the University of Paris lived with him.

One young man who lived with LaForge had first prepared for the priesthood and then had studied law. Now he had returned to Paris, hoping to become a humanist scholar, similar to Erasmus of Rotterdam. At that point, the young man showed no particular interest in religion. He lived with LaForge for nine months in 1533 and 1534. We do not know anything about the conversations between them, but we do know that the young man left the home of LaForge early in 1534 to live elsewhere. Shortly after that, the Waldensian was burned at the stake. He was one of the first Protestant martyrs in France. A few months later, the young man declared himself an evangelical—a Protestant—and in 1536 published his first book. It was called *The Institutes of the Christian Religion*. The young man was John Calvin.

How wonderful it would be to know more about their conversations and the influence of LaForge, but we do not. However, I suspect that if we knew more about the lives of the men and women whose names are in the history books, we would discover many unknown people who had a profound influence on them.

Wycliffe and the Lollards

Now we come to a very different person: John Wycliffe. It is interesting to note that while Peter Waldo was a businessman, a layman with very little education, Wycliffe was the most erudite man of his day in England.

Wycliffe, the greatest scholar of his day in England, was strongly influenced by Augustine of Hippo. The first years of his life and ministry at Oxford apparently were rather quiet. He received his doctorate in 1372. As he saw what was happening in society and in the Church, he began to study the Scriptures and the church fathers more profoundly. (The term "church fathers" generally refers to the theologians of the first three or four centuries of the history of the Church.)

The historical context was confused. The Pope supposedly had authority over the whole Church in virtue of his position as the bishop of Rome. However, in the year 1309, the papacy had moved from Rome to Avignon, which is now in southern France. (It was on the border in those days).

It is a commentary on the papacy and the Church that contemporary writers say the number of prostitutes in Avignon increased greatly with the arrival of the papacy. It is a sordid tale. The papacy remained in Avignon until 1377, when the Pope was finally persuaded to return to Rome. Immediately, one group elected a rival pope who remained in Avignon. Now there were two popes, each claiming to be the only Vicar of Christ on earth. For a time, there were three! Not until 1417, after a series of councils, was there general agreement to recognize only one Pope in Rome.

Emphases

The Roman Church taught that there was only one true Church, with one Pope. The Church taught that a person had to be a member of that ecclesiastical structure in order to be saved. Thus one had to be obedient to the Pope. But which one? Obviously the existence of two popes, each claiming to be the only Vicar of Christ on earth, created a terrible spiritual dilemma!

The problem was made worse by the fact that the individual had no choice in the decision. His or her ruler decided, for political reasons, which pope was to be followed. Yet theoretically, one's salvation depended on it! Obviously this eroded the authority of the Church and the papacy. An additional problem lay in the fact that now, with two papal courts, the taxes paid to the Church were doubled.

In this confused context, Wycliffe progressively became more radical in his views, and arrived at a number of interesting conclusions. He offended nearly everyone! In his attempt to return to biblical faith, he attacked many of the basic ideas of the medieval Church. He argued that the true Church is invisible, made up only of those elected by God. Since it is God's choice that determines membership, no visible church or its officer, no pope or bishop, can determine who is a true part of it. For Wycliffe, salvation does not depend on connection with a visible church or the mediation of the priesthood, but solely upon election by God. He was critical of monks and friars. Later he held that every one of the elect is a priest. In this he anticipated the Reformation concept of the priesthood

of all believers. Priests and bishops, he maintained, should be honored because of their character and should set an example to their flocks, but, he said, the New Testament recognized no distinction between them. Clergy who tried to enforce the collection of tithes were unworthy. He condemned the cult of the saints, relics, and pilgrimages. He believed in the real presence of Christ in the bread and the wine of the mass, but attacked the doctrine of transubstantiation and taught that under some circumstances a layman might officiate in the Eucharist, or mass. He did not reject the seven sacraments, but did not believe confirmation to be necessary. He repudiated indulgences and masses for the dead, but retained a belief in purgatory. He declared that intelligent sincerity in worship was of more value than the form. Indeed, he believed, formalism in elaborate services might hinder true worship (Kenneth S. Latourette, *A History of Christianity* [San Francisco: Harper San Francisco, 1975 Revised Edition], 663).

Wycliffe attacked the medieval concept of authority in Church and state. He said that God gave the dominion of grace, as he put it, not to the Pope, nor to the hierarchy, but to the people. The traditional idea was that God gave authority to the Pope in the Church and the Emperor in the state. In the Church, authority was delegated downwards: from the pope to the bishop, bishop to priest, and priest to the people, who were to obey. Authority was also delegated downwards in the State; from emperor to prince, prince to magistrate, and magistrate to the people, who again were to obey One chain of authority was the mirror image of the other, and believed to have divine sanction.

If you wish, you can put a diagram in here.

GOD

Pope	Emperor
Bishop	Prince
Priest	Magistrate
People	People

Medieval thought taught that this was a direct model of the hierarchical system in the heavens.

It was fixed, and to take any other view in either church or state was heresy.

Wycliffe was not the only one to reject this concept. There were others, including Marsilius of Padua in Paris a bit earlier. Their point was that God gave power to the people in both church and state, and they were to delegate it upward. We can imagine what a radical idea this was in the Middle Ages, and why it was considered subversive.

Wycliffe's Following Among Students

From this concept, Wycliffe drew the conclusion that an unworthy pope or bishop or priest should be removed from office. However, he did not propose a way to do this. Students responded to Wycliffe's ideas and teaching. He began to send his followers out to preach. We are not sure where the term came from, but they were called "Lollards." The first Lollard preachers were Wycliffe's students, but later many came from the poor. They wore the clothing of the common people and lived from offerings they received. Thus, they followed the New Testament pattern of ministry. They preached from portions of Scripture in their vernacular English.

Translation of the Bible

Wycliffe's greatest achievement was his translation of the Bible into English with the help of his associates.

There was a rising sense of national consciousness in this period. Accompanying it was a new focus on the vernacular language. Wycliffe did not do the first translation into English; there were others. Even before the Reformation some were beginning to translate parts of the Bible into the vernacular languages. But Latin was still the language of literature, including theology. The vernacular Bibles at this time typically had "glosses" (footnotes that interpreted the particular passage in accordance with the doctrine of the Church). The purpose of glosses, of course, was to eliminate any independent biblical interpretation.

Wycliffe and his associates made a compete translation of the whole Bible into the English vernacular with no glosses. His goal was that the common people would hear and read the Bible in their own language.

He wanted such a Bible located in every church. He said his goal was that every plowboy—that is, field laborer—should be able to read the Bible in his own language. It was a very radical idea! He encouraged lay people to memorize the Scriptures in schools and "conventicles" (non-official, non-churchly meetings of people for study and prayer). We will find them later in Puritanism, and see similar meetings adopted by various other renewal movements. Wycliffe's ideas had radical implications for changing society since the great majority of people were illiterate. The only schools that existed were for the children of the rising middle class and nobility.

Wycliffe was condemned in 1382 and died eighteen months later. Powerful members of the nobility who liked some of his political ideas protected him. They did not necessarily agree with him religiously, however. Wycliffe died in bed. Later, after his burial, his bones were dug up, burned, and thrown into the river. As one poet put it, they threw his ashes into the Severn, which flowed into the Thames, from there into the English Channel, from there into the Atlantic Ocean, and from there all over the world! It is a wonderful and true picture.

Lollard Preachers

Wycliffe's Lollards continued as an underground movement for a century and a half. We do not know how much success they had since records are scant. Some believe they won a significant number of people to their understanding of the Christian faith. Many of them were martyred. Wycliffe died at the end of the fourteenth century. A little less than a century and a half later, students at Cambridge were reading the writings of Luther. Thus we see a longing for a more authentic Christian life among some students at Cambridge as well as some of the common people.

It is believed that the Lollard influence, which continued underground, was one of several factors that contributed to the more spiritual and theological aspects of the English Reformation in 1534. We know that it was triggered first by political factors, but we know there were groups that greatly desired genuine theological, structural, and spiritual reform. Many of those concerns would lead to Puritanism.

Chapter Twelve

The Friars: Mission Accepted

Lest we think there was no spiritual life in the Middle Ages, listen to this poem, written for Pentecost in 1367.

Come down, O Love divine, seek thou this soul of mine,

And visit it with thine own ardor glowing.

O Comforter, draw near, within my heart appear,

And kindle it, thy holy flame bestowing.

O let it freely burn, till earthly passions turn to dust and ashes in its heat consuming,

And let thy glorious light shine ever on my sight

And clothe me round, the while my path illuming.

And so the yearning strong with which the soul will long,

Shall far outpass the power of human telling,

For none can guess its grace, til he become the place wherein the Holy Spirit makes his dwelling.

Introduction

The personal purity of at least three popes of the thirteenth century was seriously doubted by their contemporaries; and popes lie in Dante's hell like sheep. The papal court was then, as always until recent times, a notorious den of corruption. As one of the few good cardinals complained, it had turned the city of Lyons into one huge brothel during its few years of residence there, and the same evil reputation was enjoyed by Avignon, Constance, and Rome during other periods of papal residence. The other prelates were just as bad. Gregory X complained, in 1274, that 'they were the ruin of Christendom,' and only by exerting the whole weight of his authority at a great general council did he succeed at last in deposing Henry of Liege, whose episcopal career of nearly thirty years would be incredible but for the number of parallel instances that might be quoted. Two abbesses and a nun were among his concubines, and he boasted of having had fourteen children in twenty-two months. Yet he was bishop by the special grace of Pope Innocent IV. (G.G. Coulton, *Ten Medieval Studies* [Boston: Beacon Press, 1959], 76–77).

The inferior clergy followed suit. St. Bonaventure complained of their ignorance and immorality, in language that would be treated as bigoted in a Protestant's mouth.

Another writer said:

> A hundred times he heard the Italian parish clergy say, if not chastely, at least cautiously, to justify their immorality, "English cathedrals were partly built out of the fines of incontinent or immoral priests" (Ibid., 76).

In 1222, the priests in charge of five out of seventeen chapters or parishes in the Salzburg cathedral diocese were found on examination unable to say correctly a single sentence of the mass, which they had mumbled daily for years.

John Gerson represented the Church as crying aloud to the pope, "What priest wilt thou give me who knoweth God's law?" (ibid., 113.)

That was the tragic picture of the Church in the thirteenth century.

A century after Bernard had entered Clairvaux, the Cistercian abbot lived in wealth and traveled widely, in total contradiction of the order's ideals. The "heretic" Albigensians and Waldensians clearly lived lives much closer to the ideal of Christ than did the clergy and monks.

At the same time, Europe was moving from a feudal, agricultural society to one of rising trade, new cities, and a middle class. The new entrepreneurial middle class was often more critical, asked more questions, and was more dissatisfied with the status quo than were the serfs and the nobles.

We have already seen two key leaders—Waldo and Wycliffe—who initiated movements that the Church rejected. In this chapter, we will examine two more men—St. Francis and St. Dominic—who led movements that the Church accepted.

It is always interesting to ask what factors shaped such leaders, and to look at history in terms of the "missiological entrepreneurs." I define a "missiological entrepreneur" as one whose vision goes beyond that of the dominant Church and mission structures of the time, and who consequently creates new movements to implement the vision. We have many such entrepreneurs in history. Samuel Mills, who was responsible for the first North American foreign missionary movement, was such a person. He created several new missionary structures. Hudson Taylor and Cameron Townsend were such pioneers. So is Ralph Winter. They all spun off new ideas and structures, followed a vision, and communicated that vision to others.

Viv Grigg is another. He sees Asian cities where millions live in the worst poverty. His vision is to send out teams of committed Christian young people who will live at a subsistence level in the worst of the slums, minister to the people wholistically, and, in that context, share the Gospel and plant the Church. Mother Teresa and Loren Cunningham are others.

God may call some of us to such a role. It is always important to look through history and see the kind of people whom God has used to create new structures, to follow a new vision for ministry, and to call others to join them. So often the Church has rejected new vision and methodology. Someone has said that the seven last words of the Church are, "We never did it that way before." However, the very fact that a concept is new might be the best reason for considering it. Not every new idea is of God, but certainly, the Holy Spirit has not yet exhausted His creativity.

Now we will return to the thirteenth century. The Waldensian movement was growing and Europe was changing. The traditional monasteries were more suited to the former feudalistic society than to the new town- and city-oriented societies. The earlier monasteries were located in deserted places. The founders had often gone into the wilderness and built their first simple dwellings, cleared the land, and grown their crops. The two new monastic movements would go to the growing cities. Children of the nobility primarily inhabited the older monasteries; in the new monastic movements, we find more children of the middle and lower classes.

The Church responded to the Waldensians and Albigensians with violence. The crusade against the Albigensians in Languedoc, southern France from 1209 to 1229 resulted in the massacre of the entire populations of some towns.

Louis IX, known as St. Louis (for whom the city of St. Louis in the United States is named), was a devout, pious king and a good Catholic. He instituted military campaigns against those of his own subjects believed to be heretical. We will soon see the development of the Inquisition.

It is important to note that at times, new movements are genuine initiatives of the Holy Spirit, but at times they depart from the historic faith. It is imperative that we establish criteria that are clearly biblical, so that the Church does not reject or accept such movements for the wrong reasons.

For example, some years ago, the major Presbyterian and Baptist denominations in Brazil expelled groups that advocated all of the charismatic gifts. Those groups grew rapidly. The Assemblies of God in the United States would not allow Loren Cunningham to pursue his vision of a youth mission movement (Youth With a Mission) under its sponsorship because he insisted that it be interdenominational. In all three cases, the new movements flourished. On the other hand, there are those in the older denominations in Europe and the United States who have gone to the other extreme, advocating theological and ethical diversity that goes well beyond biblical standards. Today, as we see new movements with non-traditional forms of the Church arising in various parts of the world, it is even more important to examine the Scriptures carefully to determine how we understand the essentials of the historic faith.

In 1229, a church council declared that the laity could not possess any portion of the Bible except the Psalms. It asserted that the Bible was a source of heresy! The same council condemned vernacular translations of the Bible. But during this same period of history, God raised up two significant new movements.

The thirteenth century papacy was at the height of its political power. Never again would it be so powerful. Neither of the two movements, which brought a measure of renewal to the Church and society, was a part of the papal strategy. Both the Dominicans and the Franciscans apparently arose by coincidence. They were called the "Mendicant orders," referring to their practice of begging to sustain the monks. These peripheral movements were the response of the Holy Spirit to deep needs in both church and society.

The Poor Catholics

There were some precursors to the Mendicant orders. One was called the "Poor Catholics." It began in 1207 in the south of France. The pope initially approved the order. Their goal was to win back the Waldensians by adopting a similar lifestyle of poverty, and, simplicity, renouncing all wealth. This monastic group refused gifts of gold, silver, and land. They would take no thought for the morrow and live simply. Although they grew to number six communities by 1209, the bishops were suspicious and the knights were impatient—it was easier to use the sword on the heretics than to try to win them with holy living. In 1237, the Church ordered the Poor Catholics to live by a traditional monastic rule, and in 1247, the order was no longer allowed to preach. They could live in their monasteries, but they could not share their message outside of their communities. Thus, the Poor Catholics were crushed by the hierarchy.

The Dominicans

St. Dominic

Dominic of Guzman, born in Castille, Spain, in 1179, would be known in history as St. Dominic. He was well educated under a reforming bishop—a godly man, who wanted administrative and moral reform in his diocese. Therefore, Dominic was brought up under spiritual discipline, living as an Augustinian Canon. The canons were priests who ministered in a cathedral. In some cases, bishops who sought reform required that their clergy live in a regime of discipline similar to that of the monastic orders. Augustinian canons adopted spiritual disciplines that were believed to have come from the great theologian. Thus, Dominic came from a community of priests and was mentored by a bishop who sought spiritual discipline, moral purity, and a deeper knowledge of God.

Mission to France

In 1206, Dominic accompanied his bishop on a mission to southern France, hoping to convert 'heretics.' They established a house and formed a community, vowing to live in holiness, love, and poverty, hoping to win 'heretics' back to the Church. They rejected the use of the sword. However, two years later, the authorities proclaimed another crusade against the heretics in their area, and many were killed. The little community of Dominic and his bishop was dissolved, and they were forced to return to Spain.

The bishop died, but Dominic refused to give up their dream. He returned to southern France, and in Toulouse a rich citizen gave him a house and became his companion. Others joined them. The local bishop was favorably impressed. He was also desperate. Obviously, the violent approach of the military and ecclesiastical authorities was not effective. Dominic's approach, in addition to the lifestyle of the monks, was to share the Word of Scripture in order to win people back to the faith. What a radical idea!

The Order of Preachers

The bishop gave Dominic some support, and the pope reluctantly endorsed the new order in 1216. Their basic goal was to win people by the preaching of the Word. Thus they are known as "the Order of Preachers." If you see "OP" after a priest's name, he is a Dominican. Their preaching was to be informed by the study of theology and Scripture, along with a lifestyle of love, sympathy, and service.

Dominic only lived a few years after his order was established, but his remarkable vision and strategy continued. Immediately after the Order was established, he deployed his disciples to strategic points throughout Europe. Their purpose was to form houses in various cities, then train others and send them out to other important centers.

Mission to Europe

Dominic's first group consisted of only sixteen men. However, they came from Castille, Navarre, Languedoc, Normandy, France, England, and Germany: seven different territories of Western Europe. They were to be mobile, like an army. Dominic dispersed them to Paris, Bologna, Rome, and Spain, probably to Toledo.

Paris and Bologna were important because two of the first medieval universities were established in those cities. Spain was Dominic's own home territory, and Rome was the center of the Church.

Organization

Within four years, the order was organized in eight countries or territories and had sixty houses. The Dominicans adopted a vow of poverty in 1220. It is important to note that they did not go to the deserted rural places and retreat from soci-

ety; their strategy was to go to the emerging cities, especially those where emerging universities were located. As an order, they were bound together in one structure, and that made them more effective as they carried out their overall strategy. Each province, which consisted of several houses, had an elected head—a prior—and one supreme head, responsible only to the Pope.

As long as the pope left them alone yet gave them some support, the Dominicans had great freedom to go and minister in different places. They provided an alternative to village priests and local bishops, in a manner similar to the early Celtic monks who had carried on a ministry of evangelism and renewal in France.

The Dominicans were absolutely obedient to their prior. They were mobile soldiers of Christ. Walker suggested that the early Benedictines were like soldiers of Christ. However, for the most part, the Benedictines were soldiers who never left the garrison. The Dominicans were different; they were soldiers who saw the cloister, the monastery, as a place of study and prayer where they prepared to go back out into the world. They lived like monks in a monastery, but their field was the world. Their purpose was to teach and preach effectively in order to win people to the Church and the Christian faith as they understood it.

Subsequent History

Dominic died in 1222, but had laid such a good foundation that the Dominican order flourished. By that time, they had sixty houses. Twenty-one years later, one member of the order was a cardinal, and by 1276, a Dominican became Pope. Before the end of the century, there were 404 Dominican houses. They put a greater focus on learning and the study of theology than any other order of their time. They believed that preachers and teachers in the emerging universities needed to study, and needed to know both their theological tradition and the Scriptures. Because learning was so important to the Dominicans, every house had a doctor of theology in residence. The word "doctor" in that context meant "teacher." ("Master" also originally meant "teacher.") Each house had a teacher responsible for the education of all the new monks or priests joining the order.

The Dominicans played a key role in the universities. One of the greatest names in medieval theology was Albertus Magnus, who introduced the philosophy of Aristotle to Western Europe. The older theology was based on the philosophy of Plato, so for a time, the thought of Aristotle was considered a threat. Albertus Magnus began to synthesize Aristotelian philosophy (which was the new, more scientifically oriented philosophy) with Augustinian thought. Magnus's great pupil and disciple, Thomas Aquinas, carried his teacher's thought much further and laid the intellectual foundation for medieval theology.

The Dominicans included some great and some not-so-great men. Eckhart and Tauler were mystics who had a very deep life of prayer and exerted influence through their writing. They influenced some Protestant reformers. Savonarola was a fiery, passionate, zealous monk in Florence who succeeded for a time in bringing a degree of reformation to the city. He spoke out so strongly against the corruption of the rulers and people that eventually he was burned at the stake.

Other Dominicans were not so admirable. Thomas de Torquemada, a Dominican, was chosen to lead the Inquisition in Spain in the fifteenth century. The Dominicans were the most learned men in the Church, therefore they could determine best who was a heretic and who was not. A terrible betrayal! The Inquisition was the total reversal of St. Dominic's original ideal. Another notorious Dominicans was Johan Tetzel. In the sixteenth century, he sold indulgences in the various territories of Germany to raise money to repay the debts of Albert of Mainz and build the Basilica of St. Peter in Rome. It was against Tetzel's sale of indulgences that Luther protested. That triggered the Protestant Reformation.

Thus we see some great Dominicans, and some who were quite the opposite. We see that every movement runs the danger of betraying its original ideals. This has happened to many Protestant movements, also. For example, John Wesley would not allow a slaveholder to exercise leadership in the early Methodist movement. Nevertheless, early in the nineteenth century, we find Methodist preachers in North America who were slaveholders.

The Dominican order continues today making a significant contribution to the Roman Catholic Church. It became one of the greatest missionary orders of the Roman Catholic Church along with the Franciscans, and later, the Jesuits.

The Franciscans

St. Francis

The origins of the Franciscans were quite different, but in many ways the two orders became quite similar to each other. Certainly, the two founders were different. Giovanni Bernadone was known as "Francis," perhaps because his father spent some time in France, but we are not sure. He was a layman and was largely unlearned. Giovanni was born in 1182. He was the son of a cloth merchant who had become quite wealthy by the standards of the day. Thus in some ways his father was similar to Peter Waldo as a member of this new middle class, symbolizing a changing society. Francis loved adventure, was a romantic person, and lived a life of revelry. He took part in a battle with the common people of Assisi against a nearby noble, and was imprisoned for a year. He went on another military expedition, but then withdrew at the last minute. He was a troubled youth. If he were living today, we would say Bernadone was "trying to find himself."

Some of us have been raised in Christian homes, have never left the faith, and have never fallen into destructive lifestyles involving sex, drugs, or alcohol. We are rightfully thankful for this. Sometimes those who have never been involved in such behaviors dismiss those who have indulged in destructive lifestyles. At times we find it difficult to believe that God can take people like that, transform them, and use them magnificently. We need both kinds of people in the Church. Each has important things to learn from the other. In both we can see the marvelous power of grace, but especially in the latter. John Newton wrote the hymn "Amazing Grace" after a life as the captain of a slave ship!

We see Dominic, a sincere and godly priest, and contrast him with Francis, who was quite different. The fact that God used both men, who came to faith by different paths, is a powerful demonstration of the creativity of the Holy Spirit. An important focus of this book is to discover the creativity in men and women of very different backgrounds. How impoverished the history of the Church—especially the history of the missionary movement—would be without those surprises of the Spirit!

Now we look at Francis, son of a wealthy father, and apparently without any direction in life. We do not know what went on in his mind during his year in prison, or as he started out on the military expedition from which he withdrew. He seems to have undergone a gradual conversion that included certain crisis experiences. He was especially repelled by anyone afflicted with leprosy, probably because he had lived quite well. There were many lepers in central Italy during his day. Leprosy is not so much a disease of the tropics as we tend to think. It is a lack-of hygiene disease.

We cannot always disentangle fact from fiction, but there is a beautiful tradition about Francis. Apparently, he was on a quest to know God, and one day as he was wandering along a road he saw a leper approaching. Instead of feeling repelled, he found himself drawn to the man. He went to him and kissed him. As he continued on his way, he turned around to look for the man, but the leper was gone. He was convinced that he had kissed Jesus Christ in that encounter. The incident transformed his attitude toward lepers and toward the poor in general. It was clearly a benchmark in his Christian experience.

His Call

Francis made a pilgrimage to Rome. While he was there, he had a dream in which he believed he heard a divine command to restore the Church. In his vision, he saw the Vatican buildings falling with the foundations giving way, and saw himself

holding them up. He returned to Assisi, took some cloth from his father's business, and began selling it. He used the money to rebuild a church building that was falling down. There were many ruined churches around. Needless to say, his father objected and took him to the bishop who told him to be obedient. There, in the presence of his father and the bishop, Francis said, "Naked I came into this world, and I renounce my inheritance and everything you've given me." He took off his clothes and walked out naked. Presumably, someone gave him some clothes. This was about 1206 or 1207.

Francis was obviously a little bit strange. Nevertheless, he was in love with Jesus Christ and, as he put it, he wed 'Lady Poverty.' We cannot tell how much Francis's philosophy of poverty was developed by this time. Somehow he realized, in this context of rising classes in the midst of great poverty, that wealth could easily become a barrier between a person and God, and between a person and others. He believed that any possessions he had would create barriers between himself and God, and himself and others. That was his basic philosophy of poverty.

He wandered around for about two years helping the poor and rebuilding church buildings. In about 1208 or 1209, during the mass, he heard the words of Christ to the Apostles being read. They came to him as a personal call. He would go out and preach repentance and the Kingdom of God. He would go without money, wearing the plainest of garments. He would eat what was given him. He would imitate Christ as closely as he knew how, and would live in absolute poverty. He was not against the Church and its hierarchy; he deferred to priests as the representatives of Christ. At this point, Francis was obviously a layman. We do not know when, if ever, he was ordained.

The Beginning of the Order

Francis began to gather companions, mostly from among the poor, who were highly motivated. It did not appear to be a very promising start. They might have been compared to a group of hippies today. Their dress was a homespun garment, which was the simplest dress of the poor country people. Today the equivalent might be jeans and a T-shirt, or something similar.

The group was unstructured at first. Francis's only goal was to live the Gospel, to minister to people in need, to live in absolute poverty, to possess nothing, and to sustain the body sparsely with whatever was given them. In the early days, Francis and his companions wandered around, helping those working in the fields or meeting other needs. If the person gave them food, they took it. If not, they continued on their way. As a last resort, they begged for their food.

A delightful story is told of Francis and a young man who wanted to become one of his disciples and learn how to preach. Francis said, "Come with me!" They started out on a journey. First, they found a man working in a field harvesting his crop, and worked with him for a time. Then they found a woman struggling with a heavy load, and carried it. They found a man with a cart in the ditch and helped get it back on the road. They went from one town to another doing similar works. At the end of the day, the young man said, "Aren't you going to preach, and teach me how to do so?" Francis responded, "That's what I've been doing all day."

In other words, the philosophy of the Dominicans was to learn in order to preach. The philosophy of the early Franciscans was to live as followers of Christ, and from that lifestyle they shared their message. The two groups were not totally antithetical because both focused on a simple, loving, and compassionate lifestyle, although they started from somewhat different points.

The original Franciscan rule was simple: each member of the order was to live by the Gospel and possess absolutely nothing at all. They went out two by two, preaching repentance, singing, helping peasants, and caring for lepers and outcasts. They were all to learn a trade so they could set a good example and work. When they were not given anything to eat, they begged.

Missions

Franciscans had the greatest missionary focus of any medieval group. St. Dominic had also read the

Great Commission to his followers and the Dominicans soon sent missionaries across the Silk Road to China. Francis himself went to Egypt and preached to the Sultan during the Crusades. That showed remarkable courage! Apparently, the Sultan considered him a holy man and received him with respect, listened to him, and sent him on his way in safety. Francis sent other Franciscan monks to preach to Muslims; most of them were killed. Their missionary focus led them to go outside of Europe, beyond the bounds of Christendom. Their vision surpassed that of the Dominicans, who worked primarily within Europe. Franciscans went to the Middle East, North Africa, and China by the end of the thirteenth century—a remarkable achievement in that era.

The Order Recognized

The pope recognized the Franciscans as the "Order of Little Brothers" (OFM, or Minor Friars, in Latin) in 1216. A powerful cardinal, Ugolino, who later became Pope, was their sponsor and protector. It is possible that the Roman Church had learned a lesson from the way it had treated the Waldensians. At any rate, half a century after Peter Waldo initiated his movement, two new Roman Catholic orders arose, both showing missionary passion and a desire to renew the Church. However, they sought reform following the existing pattern of the medieval church. That is, they did not advocate theological or structural reform. They wanted better preaching and teaching, and a lifestyle of purity and simplicity. The ethos of the two groups was different. As we have seen, the Dominicans were the Order of Preachers, focusing on learning, teaching, and preaching. The Franciscans were the Order of Little Brothers, seeking to be brothers to all who were in need. Both had qualities that we should imitate today.

Francis was a visionary, not an organizer. He was a charismatic figure who drew people around him, but he was not an administrator. As the order grew, others began to take over its administration, and Francis distanced himself more and more from leadership. He died in 1226, a relatively young man in his forties.

In some kind of vision or mystical experience, Francis received the stigmata, the marks of the crucifixion, on his body, before he died. There have been other authenticated cases in history of mystics who received the stigmata. I have no way of explaining this, but there seems to be historical evidence for the fact.

As we have seen, the first rule of the Franciscan order was very simple; a second one came in 1221, and a third in 1223. The spontaneous nature of the group changed. They took permanent vows and begging became normal rather than exceptional. That changed the attitude of many toward them. However, it is hard to see how the old system could have worked well as the order expanded. A simple structure might have worked in rural Italy, but as the order grew, went to the cities, and sent missionaries to far places, a new structure was obviously needed.

Therefore, the Franciscan order changed from very simple people going around helping others and sharing the Word, to more sophisticated theologians. That was probably inevitable, especially if the monks were to make an impact on the new emerging Western European society. It was even more important if they were to go to Muslims in North Africa and the Middle East, and to China, where there were proud ancient cultures.

Perhaps we face that dilemma. Many of us have come from warm evangelical communities, alive with the first glow of Christian faith. As we have matured, we have felt the need for more study and reflection on our faith and experience, and especially on the question of how to communicate that faith to those of other cultures. However, as we do so we do not want to lose the vitality of the relationship with Christ that brought us here. We all face that tension, just as the early Franciscans did. This makes it important to maintain contact with our Lord, but also with the grassroots, the poor, and those who have not had the opportunities we have had. This will certainly help us stay in touch with the realities of the world in which we serve.

Before long, the Franciscans suffered controversy and division. Some wanted to relax the rule and allow the order to receive gifts of property and money, even though the monks themselves would still own nothing. That branch of the Franciscans became very wealthy—a great contradiction of Francis's ideal. At the other extreme were the "zealots" or "spirituals" who insisted on following the original ideal. Some were burned at the stake and called "heretics" by the more dominant group. There was also a moderate, middle group. Among the branches of the order today, the Capuchin are most faithful to Francis's ideal.

Both Franciscans and Dominicans had great popular influence. Because they were models of Christian life and piety, and communicated their faith effectively, they strengthened the faith of many. And because they provided an alternate church structure, they lessened the influence of the bishops. In this way, they were similar to the work of Columbanus in northern France in the sixth and seventh centuries. Because they were under the direct authority of the Pope and not the bishops, they strengthened papal authority. Because they traveled and could preach and hear the confessions of people anywhere, they provided a healthy alternative to the local priests, who were usually quite corrupt and ignorant. Thus, the Franciscan and Dominican orders were a renewing influence in the thirteenth century.

The Second and Third Orders

Franciscans and Dominicans were innovators in another way. As far as we know, they are the first to establish second and third orders. The first order was composed of men, priests, and lay brothers. The second order was composed of women who took permanent vows of celibacy, poverty, and obedience similar to those of the first order. Convents, or communities of nuns, had existed for centuries. They were important in the Celtic movement. However, as far as we know, they had not been part of a monastic order. A wealthy woman, Clare, became a follower of Francis and established a group called the "Poor Clares." They became the second order, the women's branch of the Franciscans.. That order had great influence in both mission and educational work. Nuns have staffed most Catholic schools through the centuries. The Dominicans had similar groups.

The third order was an even greater innovation. It was composed of lay men and women who lived a normal married life and carried on their trade or business. Nevertheless, they considered themselves part of the Franciscan or Dominican order, following prescribed spiritual disciplines, and seeing that order as the major source—under the Church—of their own spiritual life and discipline. Some of these third orders would eventually exercise political power.

Some third orders built churches. Others exerted influence beyond their own families. I have visited a church in Olinda, Brazil, built by the third order of the Franciscans in the eighteenth century. Catherine of Siena, one of the great medieval saints, was a woman of great devotion and belonged to the third order of the Dominicans. She longed to see renewal in the Church; she wrote to popes, scolding them at times, and advocated reform. She worked especially hard to have the papacy return from Avignon to Rome in the fourteenth century. She never married and was celibate, but did not live in a convent. She lived in her home with her family, and followed a disciplined, ascetic lifestyle of meditation, prayer, and letter writing.

We Protestants can learn something here. The early Protestant missionary societies were similar to third order. When Carey went to England, the concept was that his supporters back in England were a part of the mission. They did not simply contribute money; theoretically, they were to be as committed to the mission as were Carey and his colleagues.

Ralph Winter has tried to revive the idea, hoping to form a Presbyterian order of world evangelization. In such a structure, Christians in this country would live at a subsistence level in order to contribute and pray more for world evangelization. One of the goals of some student circles is to recruit people who are senders as well as goers. The idea is that each one is to be equally committed to world evangelization, whether he or she is called to stay, support, and pray, or called to go to another culture or country. This is a third order concept.

The Opus Dei group in the Roman Catholic Church has some similarities to the third orders, but its agenda seems to be different. It is extremely conservative in terms of theology, liturgy, and politics, and is not connected with a specific order like the Franciscans or Dominicans. There are also some Anglican groups similar to Roman Catholic orders. There is even an Anglican Franciscan order.

There are concepts from the Middle Ages from which we might learn and even revive, especially in our affluent, often hedonistic evangelical churches in the United States. Some churches calling themselves "evangelical" focus more on prosperity than on our call to sacrifice. This is a tragic betrayal of the Gospel.

The Sisters of Darmstatt are a group in German Lutheranism. Started after World War II, their ministry sponsors houses of prayer, and engages in service, and witness. Christians of the Reformed tradition started the movement in Taize, France. They are very ecumenical and follow spiritual disciplines, similar to the monastic life, as a witness to the larger community and church. God may call some of us to similar communities or lifestyles.

I suspect that ministries to the urban poor in the world (who probably number at least two billion) will only be effective as men and women, called by Christ, are willing to live among the poor at subsistence level. As they do so, they will minister holistically and share the Gospel. Some will be called to a single life. I do not believe that a celibate life is spiritually superior to a married life. However, it is entirely possible that God does call some people to be single for part or all of their lives for the sake of ministry. We Protestants need to recognize that fact.

Another possibility is that married couples will be called to live in these situations and forgo having children for a period, or maybe for all of their lives, as part of the their missionary vocation. We need to learn from some of the Roman Catholic orders. We will approach these issues from a different theological base, but we can learn lessons from the sense of sacrifice we see in those who remain celibate for the sake of the mission of Christ.

We find this same sense of sacrifice among the earliest Protestant missionaries to Asia and Africa. They set out knowing that many would perish within a few months, and that most would never see their homeland and families again in this life.

Mission to Central Asia and China

The missionaries of the Mendicant orders went across central Asia in the thirteenth and fourteenth centuries. The Franciscans established seventeen mission stations between Russia and the China Sea, and the Dominicans were active in Persia.

Two Venetian merchants, Nicolo and Maffeo Polo, returned to Europe from China in 1269 with a message from the Chinese emperor asking for Christian teachers to be sent there. In 1271, two Dominicans started out with them on their return journey, but soon turned back. The son of one of the two brothers, Marco Polo, accompanied them and later wrote about his adventures. Is it a judgment on the Church that in some cases merchants have been more willing to take risks than those who were called to spread the Gospel.

The most successful missionary of the era was John de Monte Corvino, a Franciscan who arrived in China in 1294. He found Nestorians there (despite their having almost died out for a time), but they worked in opposition to each other.

John de Monte Corvino was quite successful for a time. By 1305, he had built a church and had six thousand converts. He translated the New Testament and the Psalms into the language of the Tartars, who dominated northern China at that time. More Franciscans were sent, but very few arrived. The last medieval missionary to China arrived in 1342 and returned eleven years later. The dynasty that had given them protection, the Mongol Dynasty, ended in 1368. It was suc-

ceeded by the Ming Dynasty, which was antiforeign. This second attempt to plant the Church in China also seems to have failed; apparently, the Church disappeared again. The saga of the spread of the Christian faith in China is fascinating. As we will see, a great Jesuit missionary, Matteo Ricci, arrived in Beijing in the sixteenth century, and then Robert Morrison, a Protestant, arrived in 1807. Most of the world believed these attempts had also failed, and that the Chinese church had disappeared completely with the cultural revolution in the 1960s and 70s. Now we find that the Church has not only survived, but has grown in an amazing manner despite severe persecution. But that is another story.

Raymond Lull

Raymond Lull was a remarkable visionary. Born in 1232, he was a younger contemporary of Francis and Dominic. An aristocrat, he lived a dissolute life before his conversion. This experience changed the direction of his life dramatically. He left resources to take care of his wife and children, gave the rest away to the poor, and, from that point on, made his chief concern in life the winning of all peoples to the Christian faith. He urged the Church to reach the Mongols and Muslims. He traveled extensively, urging the popes to establish a school of mission—a monastic school to prepare missionaries who would study the Asian languages, including Arabic.

Lull wrote an apologetic for Christianity against other religions. It was not very contextualized, but he showed his great concern for the evangelization of non-Christian peoples. He even learned Arabic. In 1311, at the Council of Vienne, he persuaded the Church to adopt his proposal to train missionaries in Arabic and other languages. The Church adopted the proposal formally, but never fully implemented the decision. Lull himself traveled three times to North Africa where he preached to Muslims. The last time, as an elderly man, he was stoned to death.

We will find a similar man, Baron Von Welz, in the Protestant tradition. In the seventeenth century he begged the Lutheran Church in Germany to begin mission to the rest of the world. The church leaders considered him a fanatic and said he wanted to cast pearls before swine. As we have already seen, mission to the far places of the world has rarely been high on the agenda of most church leaders, whether Catholic or Protestant!

However, it is important for us to remember men like Lull and von Welz, who apparently achieved nothing. They were voices crying in the wilderness, unheard and unheeded. Nevertheless, they were faithful to God and to the biblical mandate. In many ways they were like grains of wheat that fell in the ground and died. Only later would the fruit of the vision be seen.

It is important for us to notice not only the figures who emerge as leaders of new movements, but also those who were disregarded and unheeded. Some of us may be in that latter category as well. Not everyone who speaks for God in his or her time is "successful" in terms of being heard by the people of God. However, we cannot measure their success—only God can do so. Our call, first of all, is to be faithful. There have always been major obstacles to mission. Perhaps the historical context made Christian mission difficult, perhaps mission looked impossible at the time, and perhaps church leaders were indifferent. It is important to know that despite these obstacles, there have been men and women in every period who were faithful to the missionary mandate and who called the Church to be obedient, even though it often did not respond. Lull and Von Welz are two such examples, and we must honor them.

Chapter Thirteen

Preparation for Reformation

Introduction

A century and a half before the Protestant Reformation, many in Western Europe were seeking reformation in the Church. Some wanted only administrative and moral reform. Others sought a deeper spirituality. Still others began to study the Bible anew, and discovered that its theology differed from the dominant theology of the medieval Church. We do not adopt the view of church history that says the Holy Spirit died early in the fourth century when Constantine became a Christian, and only rose from the dead in the sixteenth. We must recognize that the Spirit was alive and working all through history, often through people in churchly and theological traditions quite different from our own. There are lessons we can learn from such movements.

Often in periods of great deal of ferment, God has been preparing the world for something new. We might be in such a period in our own time. We see growing disillusionment with secularism, a New Age mentality in the West, and spiritism in much of Latin America. These may be signs of spiritual hunger. Perhaps God is preparing the world for something new in our generation.

Keep in mind the metaphor of the "underground streams" in history, when little change appeared on the surface, but powerful ideas were flowing underneath, developing among little-known people, and preparing to burst to the surface. So it was in the fourteenth and fifteenth centuries. There were streams of spiritual life flowing underground, out of sight.

The Need for Reform

The Orders and Church in Decline

A century after their establishment, the Mendicant orders (the Franciscans and Dominicans) had lost most of their early vitality and were generally in decline. The institutional church was wealthy and greedy, and sexual immorality was flagrant. Contemporary writers tell of sexual orgies in the papal court. However, it is important to note that the primary reason for the Protestant Reformation was not the moral corruption of the medieval Church. The motivation for the Reformation was theological. It came from Luther's rediscovery of the basic biblical message: salvation by grace received by faith alone. The biblical Gospel had been distorted and nearly lost in medieval theology and ritual, and the great virtue of the Reformation was the rediscovery of the Gospel of grace. Reaction against corruption and heavy papal taxation were issues, but they were not the main factors.

The Papacy

When French cardinals won a power struggle against the Italian cardinals in 1309, the papacy was moved from Rome to Avignon on the bank of the River Rhone. It remained there until 1377. This period was called the "Babylonian Captivity" of the Church. This move contradicted the concept that papal authority lay in the Pope's role as Bishop of Rome. From 1378 to 1409, there were two popes: one in Rome, and one in Avignon. To make matters worse, from 1409 to 1417 there were three! As we have seen in our study of Wycliffe, new political theories began to emerge in this context.

One of the new theories came in 1324 from Marsillius of Padua, an Italian at the University of Paris. He taught that both papal and royal powers were based on the sovereignty God had conferred on the people, and that neither the Church nor the state had the right to interfere in the sphere of the other. This was an extremely radical concept at the time, and is still considered subversive in many places today. Laws, Marsillius said, were to be made by an assembly of all-male adult citizens. Unfortunately, he did not advocate the rights of women, but it was a start. He said that instead of an empire, there should be many states, each self-governing. His ideas contradicted the teaching by the Church and the state that the hierarchical order in both reflected a similar order established by God in heaven. The hierarchical system was believed to have divine sanction.

Marsillius added that the only final authority in the Church was the New Testament, that it provided the model to be followed, and that Church should never coerce people to obey. Bishops and priests, he said, were equal, and no priest, not even the pope, should have power over another. He also said that Peter had no higher rank than any other apostle, and perhaps had never even arrived in Rome. Marsillius advocated a kind of rough democracy in church and state. He taught that only the whole body of Christian believers, represented in a general council, should have legislative authority in the Church. There were others, writing at the same time, who espoused similar ideas.

Papal Schism and Taxation

Taxation by the Church was scandalous. Now that there were two papal courts, taxation doubled. Moreover, as we have seen, from 1408 to 1417 there were three popes. Naturally, the prestige of the papacy declined greatly. A number of general councils were held, each attempting to resolve the problem and transform the papacy into something like a constitutional monarchy, but with no success. As soon as a new Pope was appointed, he ignored any restraints on papal power that the councils had attempted to impose.

John Huss

John Huss, the Czech reformer, emerged in this context. He was an ardent patriot at a time when Bohemia, now part of the Czech Republic, sought political independence from the Germans and ecclesiastical independence from Rome. He became very popular as he preached in both Latin and the vernacular language. The Bethlehem Chapel, where he preached fiery sermons in the vernacular, was built for him. He also taught at the university and was elected its rector at the age of twenty-nine.

The sister of the King of Bohemia had married the King of England and, as a result, students went from Prague to Oxford. They brought the ideas of Wycliffe back to their homeland. These ideas greatly influenced Huss. He was more conservative than Wycliffe and continued to believe in transubstantiation, the doctrine that in the Mass, the bread and wine actually become the body and blood of Christ. However, Huss opposed the use of force by the Pope, said that money could not bring forgiveness of sins, and rejected indulgences. As a result, he was excommunicated. The Council of Constance met in 1415, attempting to resolve the papal impasse and other problems in the Church. When Huss was summoned to go and defend his ideas, the Holy Roman Emperor, Sigismund, guaranteed his safe conduct. Yet when Huss arrived, he was imprisoned. The Council soon condemned the ideas of Wycliffe and ordered his body exhumed and burned. Sigismund now withdrew his promise of safe conduct, and when Huss refused to recant, he was burned at the stake. The Council declared, "We do not need to keep our word to a heretic."

The Council was attempting to exert its own authority against a corrupt papacy and believed it needed to protect that authority. Its goal was good, but the great irony is that a council that hoped to reform the Church burned the genuine reformer. He obviously wanted to go much further in reformation than did the council.

The Continuing Movement

The followers of Huss divided into two groups. One was more aristocratic and conservative; the other grew primarily among the poor and was more radical. Some Waldensians merged with them, and in 1453, they organized themselves as the Unitas Fratrum (the Unity of the Brethren). They continued to exist as a heroic, persecuted underground church during the following centuries. Finally, in 1722, a small group of them made their way to the estate of Count Nicholas Ludwig von Zinzendorf and there formed the nucleus of the Moravian movement. As we will see, that group became the primary catalyst of the Protestant missionary movement.

Signs of Life

The Renaissance

As we move into the fifteenth century, we enter the era called the Renaissance (rebirth). The goal was to seek a rebirth of Western European culture.

The art and architecture of the Renaissance, found especially in Rome and Florence, are marvelous! We wish that the theology of the period were as good as its art! St. Peter's basilica in Rome is magnificent. The sculptures of Michelangelo are amazing: the Moses, located in a church behind the Coliseum; the David, in Florence; the Sistine Chapel; and his other works. Certainly, no artist in history has ever depicted both the works of God and the human body in greater majesty and glory.

In many ways, the Renaissance was a magnificent achievement. Perhaps we find a greater concentration of artistic genius in this period than at any other time in history. It also represented a philosophical shift. As you go through the great art galleries of Europe, especially the Prado in Madrid and the Louvre in Paris, you note that in the earlier period the human body was depicted in an ethereal, shadowy, heavenly manner. This reflects Platonism, where the real was believed to exist in heaven, not here on earth.

A shift came with the Renaissance. Aristotle became the most important philosopher, and art now became much more concerned with this life and sensory data. The human form has never been depicted as beautifully and powerfully as it was at that time, with the possible exception of the Greek classical period. One can sit down in front of Michelangelo's Moses and marvel at the powerful way in which he showed the human body. There was certainly artistic greatness in the Renaissance.

The Renaissance was an attempt to rediscover the roots of western European culture. For some, those roots lay in classical pagan (Greek and Roman) antiquity. For others, the roots lay in the Bible, especially the New Testament. South of the Alps, especially in Italy, the primary focus was on the pagan sources of culture. North of the Alps, in Germany and elsewhere, a number of scholars began to study the Scriptures more profoundly. However, the papacy was not a center of biblical study or concern. The popes of the period were primarily Italian princes who came from the most powerful families.

Christian Humanism

In the desire to go back to biblical sources, we find Christian humanists beginning to study the New Testament in Greek and the Old Testament in Hebrew. At the same time, there were monks in Spain, called *Iluministas* (illuminated ones) who sought a deeper spirituality. Oratories, places of prayer, were established in Italy. Thus, in the midst of the paganism of the papal court and much of the hierarchy, there were glimmers of light here and there. They came from those who wanted a more authentic spiritual life as they sought to return to biblical sources.

The term "humanist" did not mean the same thing it does today. These men were profoundly Christian and wanted to rediscover the sources of their Christian culture. Reuchlin was one of them. He was considered the best Greek scholar in Germany, and believed it important to study Jewish commentaries to better understand the

Old Testament. It is ironic that the Dominican Inquisitor of Cologne accused him of heresy because of his desire to learn from Jewish literature. That was contrary to the spirit of St. Dominic.

A second great humanist scholar was Erasmus of Rotterdam. He wrote and traveled widely, using satire and humor to criticize the corruption and hypocrisy in the Church. However, his greatest work was the publication in 1516 of a new edition of the Greek New Testament, for which he used the best scholarship available at the time. Luther, among others, would use it. However, Erasmus was not willing to go as far as Luther. He once said he was not born to be a martyr. Others later observed that Erasmus laid the egg that Luther hatched.

Cardinal Ximenes de Cisneros was a third important figure. He sponsored the establishment of the University of Alcala de Henares near Madrid. Late in the fifteenth century, he brought scholars there to study the Scriptures in various languages and produce the Complutensian Polyglot which included six translations of the Scriptures. His theology was medieval; he did not seek theological reform as Luther and Calvin would do later. However, he wanted administrative and moral reform and more biblical studies. Students went to his university to study the Scriptures. Some of them began to arrive at theological positions more Protestant than Catholic in nature, but most remained in the Roman Catholic Church. Alcala was another indication of the growing desire to study the Scriptures.

Jacques Lefèvre in southern France was perhaps the most remarkable biblical scholar of the time. He insisted on returning to historical-grammatical exegesis of the New Testament. It is important to realize that the primary method of medieval exegesis was allegorical. That meant that one basically read into the text whatever meaning he already had, and then found it there. Luther accused the allegorical exegetes of making Scripture a "nose of wax" that could be twisted into any shape they wanted.

An example of one allegorical approach to the exegesis of a well-known passage was an interpretation of the parable of the Good Samaritan.

The parable is an answer to a man's question: "Who is my neighbor?" Jesus' answer was, "Don't ask, 'Who is my neighbor?' Be a neighbor to the person in need." He used a Samaritan, who is outside the pale, as far as Jews were concerned, as the hero of the story. Jesus' point, of course, was to care for any person in need.

Using the allegorical method, medieval exegetes taught that in the parable the traveler represented the human race, set upon by thieves, beaten, and left half dead by the side of the road. That was the fall. The priest and Levite represented the law and the prophets who were powerless to help. The Samaritan represented Jesus, who put oil in his wounds (the Holy Spirit), took the man to the inn (the Church) and put him in the care of the innkeeper (the Pope). He gave coins to the innkeeper (the sacraments) and promised to return (the second coming).

This is a good example of the way in which the allegorical method tragically robbed Scripture of the power to speak for itself. Lefèvre's honesty and courage was seen in his insistence that scholars needed to return to the Greek text and allow it to speak for itself.

He went further. In 1512, he translated and published his commentaries on the letters of St. Paul. Later, we find his commentary on Romans in Luther's library, with Luther's handwritten notes in the margin. Lefevre had a number of students to whom he said, "God will reform his church according to the Scriptures." He believed it would happen soon. Among his students were a future bishop, who attempted reform within the Roman Church, an early Protestant martyr, and William Farel, the Reformer of Geneva.

Piety

There were also groups seeking a deeper, more authentic piety. One was called the "Brethren of the Common Life." It included houses for men as well as women. The group was established because of the ministry of Gerhard Groote (1340–1384), who became the most popular preacher in Holland. The adherents lived a semi-monastic life but did not take permanent vows. They focused on study, prayer, and teaching. Thomas à Kempis, who wrote the much-loved devotional book *The Imitation of Christ,* was a member of the group. Their communities spread widely in Germany and the Netherlands.

Others had a similar emphasis on spirituality. One group called itself the "Friends of God" and spread in Germany, Switzerland, and the Netherlands. One of their leaders was Wesel Gansfort, a friend of Thomas à Kempis. Gansfort placed the authority of the Bible above that of popes or councils. He said God alone could forgive sins, and that we are saved by faith. He minimized the importance of the Church, the hierarchy, and confession. He criticized indulgences. His works were not published until after the Reformation had begun.

The Rise of Nation States

Great changes were also taking place on the political level. The nation state was emerging in the midst of economic and social changes. This reminds us again that as the shape of society changes, the shape of the Church will often need to be changed. It is a constant reminder to us that we are never simply to repeat the past.

From one standpoint we can see the Protestant Reformation as the recontextualization of the Christian faith, a reshaping of the Church far more suitable for the new Europe that was emerging. If Luther had been born in the twelfth or thirteenth century he could not have succeeded in initiating a movement of reform. He could only have done it in the sixteenth century.

Among the political changes taking place was the rise of nationalism. There was a growing feeling among many that they were not just Saxons (a part of Germany) but Germans; not primarily from Normandy or Brittany, but from France. Part of this process was the increasing use of the vernacular languages. Latin was still the language of scholars, who could communicate with each other all across Europe. But with the Reformation, there soon came literature in the vernacular languages. This was a manifestation of the growing sense of nationalism.

Between 1450 and 1500, there was great growth of royal power and national consciousness. By 1500, three nations—England, France, and Spain— were each unified under a monarchy. France had not been unified since the days of Charles the Great. Spain had never been a unified nation but now, with the marriage of Ferdinand and Isabella, and the expulsion of the last of the Moors in 1492, Spain was unified under the crown and the Catholic Church. England was unified as well. Germany was very different. It was still divided into a number of different political units ruled by various members of the nobility. That would be an important factor in the survival of Luther and the movement he initiated.

Technology

Finally, there was a very important development in technology in this period: the invention of moveable type and the printing press. This made it much easier to spread ideas. It is estimated that in 1450 there were fifteen thousand books in Europe. By 1500, the number had increased to nine million!

Chapter Fourteen

Luther, Calvin, and the Reformation

Introduction

The Protestant Reformation can be analyzed from a number of different perspectives: social, political, economic, ecclesiastical, and theological. All these analyses are helpful. However, as missiologists we can also see the movement as the re-contextualization of the Christian faith in the new emerging Europe of the sixteenth century. We have already noted that as the shape of society changes, the shape of the Church often needs to change. That happened to some degree in sixteenth-century Western Europe.

Some of the characteristics of contextualization involve a new understanding of the Gospel, or at least an emphasis on new aspects of the Faith that seem more relevant to people in their new context. Often new church structures are created that are more suitable to the new situation. The Church is governed differently. Often laypersons have a greater role in governing and leading the Church. New methods of communication and music are developed. There is adaptation to the culture of the people to whom the Gospel is addressed. We often see such developments in missionary situations. We also see them in the Reformation.

All of these changes took place, to varying degrees, in the different movements that constituted the Protestant Reformation. One of Luther's first achievements was the translation of the mass from Latin into German. Calvin's *Institutes* was the first major literary work to be written in French.

Luther's translation of the Bible helped to standardize the German language. Now, the liturgy and preaching were in the languages spoken by the people, the Bible was translated, and theological works were being written, not in Latin, but in the vernacular languages. This happened not only in Germany, but also in the various Scandinavian countries as Lutheranism moved north.

Church government changed radically, not in Lutheranism and Anglicanism, but among Calvinists and Anabaptists. The hierarchical system of pope, bishop, and priests, with a passive laity, seemed to fit well in medieval culture. It was the reflection of a similar structure in the state, with emperor, prince, magistrate, and people.

The emergence of any form of democracy was still far off, except in Geneva where the city was now ruled by a series of councils composed of adult male citizens. However, clearly, the emerging middle class was not satisfied with the older hierarchical order. It was no coincidence that Calvinism spread rapidly among the middle class in France and elsewhere. A new form of church government emerged in Calvinism that included lay elders. The laity played an even more important role in the growing Anabaptist movements.

Along with new church structures and government, we find a new understanding of the Gospel, and a more personal and less institutional theology. The older theology focused on obedience to the Church, which promised to bring salvation to the individual through its sacraments. These sacraments were believed to be essential to salvation, and could only be administered by priests of the Roman Church. Thus, if a person were reasonably loyal to that church, he or she would eventually achieve salvation, even though first it would be necessary to pass through a long period in purgatory.

In the older theology, the focus was primarily on what the institutional church and the individual did. Luther changed the focus to what God had done in Jesus Christ, with the assurance that we humans could simply trust in his grace for our salvation, rather than trusting in anything we or the Church could do. The newer theology was much more personal. I can trust this God who has come to me in Christ, who offers me his grace as a gift, and only asks that I embrace that gift. The Church was still essential, but its role was different. The Church was to proclaim and teach the Good News, and to be the community of believers and care for them. The laity had a more active role in worship. New music was composed and congregational singing was introduced. No longer was it only the monks who sang.

Thus, in the Reformation we find new theological understanding, new forms of worship, a reshaping of the structure and government of the Church, an increased role for the laity, and a positive view of the vernacular cultures and languages. All of these are characteristics of contextualization.

Above all, the Protestant Reformation involved a rediscovery of truth—of the biblical Gospel. Tragically, that had been obscured by medieval theology and ritual. A personal understanding of the biblical message was much more relevant to the emerging culture.

I once heard a lecture on the Reformation by a well-known missiologist. In his lecture, he spoke of anthropological, sociological, and cultural change, but did not once mention any theological factors. I was horrified, because if the Reformation was not about theology, the authority of Scripture, and the rediscovery of the Gospel, it was not a valid movement. Theology was essential in the Reformation, but I believe it is helpful to examine it in terms of contextualization.

We need to recognize that every renewal movement, Catholic or Protestant, Pentecostal or Anglican, runs the danger of losing its vitality and direction after two or three generations and perhaps sooner. The first generation must make a difficult decision to go against the grain of its church or society when entering the new movement. It often involves a turn of 180 degrees. The second, third, and subsequent generations are born into the movement, and continuing to be a part of it often means simply following the line of least resistance. Thus, often the form is maintained, but much of the life ebbs away. For Luther, faith meant belief in correct doctrine but, above all, it meant personal trust in God and his promises. A century later, Lutheran theologians in their struggle against Catholics and even Calvinists, defined faith simply as "belief in correct doctrine." This was a betrayal both of Luther's experience and understanding.

This can and indeed does happen to every movement of the Holy Spirit. It was said of the New England Puritans that they moved from their concern for holiness to the desire for respectability! A Christian friend once said to me, "For a long time I was in the Church, and I had the words without the music, but then I heard the music." Every generation needs to hear again the music of the Gospel, so that it becomes personal. Luther would agree that we are saved, not by correct theology, important as that is, but by personal trust in Jesus Christ. Remember, the purpose of theology is to guide us to the feet of Jesus.

I was once lecturing in a night course for laypersons in the Brazilian seminary where I taught. Many of the people in the course had only seen the worst of the Roman Catholic Church before hearing the Gospel in a Protestant fellowship. Thus, their impression of Catholicism was very negative. We were going through the medieval period, and I described the life and ministry of St. Francis. A dear brother raised his hand and said, "But, Professor, was St. Francis saved?" I took the question seriously, and replied, "Of course, none of us can ever fully judge whether another person is saved or not, but I would certainly be willing to take chances with St. Francis."

He replied, "But, Professor, he was an idolater. He prayed to the Virgin Mary."

I said, "That's right; but he loved Jesus." Certainly, St. Francis trusted Jesus profoundly.

This is the issue: Are we saved by correct theology, or are we saved by trusting Jesus Christ? We may be strongly Protestant in our theology (and I am), but it is not our correct theology that saves us; it is our trust in Jesus Christ. There are probably those with less theological knowledge than I have, but who have more trust and love for Jesus Christ. And perhaps there are those who have more sophisticated theology than I, but have less trust in Jesus Christ. The purpose of theology is to aid us in our thinking about God as we attempt to understand his ways, but, above all, it is to guide us to Jesus and help us to follow him.

Luther

Since this is not a course in church history, we will only take a short time on Luther and Calvin. Each one merits far more study. We will examine their lives and ministries briefly and look at their effect on mission.

Luther was born in 1483. His father was a peasant who had become a miner. This indicates some upward social and economic mobility, and Hans Luther was ambitious for his son. We will see the same ambition in Calvin's father. Germany was divided into a number of different political units, each with its ruler, and each unit needed one or more lawyers. Thus, unless the family was well connected, the study of law provided the best way to move up socially and economically.

Martin Luther went to the University of Erfurt in 1501, received the M.A. degree in 1505, and prepared to study law. As the story is told, when he was on his journey, lightning struck nearby and he fell to the ground, stunned. When he awoke, he exclaimed, "St. Ann, I will be a monk!" What was behind that statement? Luther had been raised in a home of traditional medieval piety. One of his childhood memories was of a prince who had become a begging monk, wandering from house to house, emaciated, and clad in rags. He was consid-

ered a very holy man. Luther had been raised with the theological assumption that the way to be certain of salvation was to enter the monastic life of prayer, devotion, and an ascetic life style. His decision must have been the result of a long spiritual struggle. A good friend had just died suddenly.

So Luther gave away his law books and entered the Augustinian monastery in Erfurt to seek his salvation. It represented the best of medieval monasticism, with a rigid rule and a strong emphasis on teaching. Two years later, he was ordained a priest. The following year he was sent to the University of Wittenberg. Frederick, the Elector of Saxony, one of the most powerful German rulers, and a pious Catholic, had recently established it. Luther received the Bachelor of Theology degree in 1509 and was awarded his doctorate in 1512. As a doctor of theology, he had the responsibility to preach in the city church and teach in the university. He took these responsibilities very seriously.

He was sent on a pilgrimage to Rome between 1510 and 1511, traveling on foot, over the Alps, from Germany to the seat of the papacy. He was terribly disillusioned by what he found there—the scandalous stories of corruption among priests and the hierarchy alike. In 1515, Luther was appointed as district vicar of eleven monasteries. All of this indicates that he was soon recognized as a brilliant and remarkable young leader.

The following analysis and quote come from a fine book by Heinrich Boehmer, a German scholar. The title in German is "The Young Luther." It was published in English with the title "Road to Reformation."

> Even as Luther's gifts were recognized and his responsibilities increased, his spiritual dilemma deepened. He had no sense of peace with God, and his sense of sinfulness grew. His dilemma focused on two theological terms: one was grace, the other was justice/righteousness. He had been taught that a person only receives God's grace after he or she has done all that was possible to deserve that grace. Men who wanted to bring reform to the Church, who wanted a church that lived according to high moral and ethical standards, espoused this doc-

trine. Therefore, they stressed the human responsibility to live according to the Gospel. The intention was good, but the concept tragically betrayed the Gospel. It placed the initiative for salvation on the person, not on God. It reversed the Gospel in making God respond to human initiative. It put the believer in a crippling spiritual dilemma with no way out, because no one can ever assert that he or she has done "all that is possible to deserve God's grace." In addition, it was a negation of the biblical understanding of grace. In his spiritual struggle, Luther constantly went to confession, sometimes more than once a day. He fasted and prayed and even whipped himself, but still had no peace. He later wrote that he found himself hating this God who demanded that he love him, but made it impossible to do so! His confessor, an older monk, said, "Brother Martin, God is not angry with you, you are angry with God." Luther was too rigorously honest to accept the easy solutions offered to him.

The second concern was his understanding of justice/righteousness. As he studied the Psalms from 1513 to 1515, he kept finding the phrase, "In your justice Oh Lord, deliver me!" The problem was the definition of the word "justice." If "justice" means receiving that which I deserve, God's justice will never deliver me; it can only condemn me. Luther was puzzled by the phrase, which he found throughout the Psalms. Finally, he turned to Paul's Letter to the Romans, knowing that it, too, spoke of the justice/ righteousness of God. Boehmer writes:

> In connection with this turn of expression, which appeared so frequently in the Psalms and the Pauline epistles, Luther was accustomed to think of the judicial righteousness of God that, in the feeling of his own unworthiness, he feared so greatly. It was for this reason that he actually hated the word *righteousness*. He fairly fled from it. In fact, up to this time he could never bring himself to study Paul's epistle to the Romans carefully, because the idea of the righteousness of God played such a large role in it. Nevertheless, he had a vague feeling that perhaps this idea could have a different sense in the language of the Bible than it had in the language of the philosophers, and he felt a strange urge to make up his mind about it. He therefore turned to the famous passage in Romans 1:16–17, in which the Gospel is charac-

terized as "the saving power of God for all who believe, because in it the righteousness of God is revealed from faith to faith."

> But at first, a study of this passage only made his heart grow heavier and the darkness deeper. "Thus the Gospel too," he said to himself, "is only the revelation of the punitive righteousness of God, only a means of further torturing and tormenting men who are already fearfully burdened with original sin and the Ten Commandments." And just as so often before he pondered this, there now arose up in him a feeling of passionate hatred for this cruel God who always requires love, love, and yet actually makes it impossible for His creatures to love Him.

> So he raged in his little room in the Tower of the Black Cloister with a wounded and confused spirit, reading that passage in St. Paul, thirsting with the most ardent desire to know what the Apostle really meant, until finally, after days and nights of thinking, he hit upon the idea of examining the context more carefully. The righteousness of God is revealed in the Gospel; the just shall live by faith. Therefore, he concluded, what is meant here is not the punitive righteousness of God, but rather the forgiving righteousness of God, by which in his mercy he makes us just. As it is written, the just shall live by faith.

> Then, in his words, "It seemed to me as if I were born anew, that I had entered into the open gates of Paradise. The whole Bible suddenly took on a new aspect for me. I ran through it as much as I had it in my memory and gathered together a great number of similar expressions as 'work of God,' that is, that which God works in us; 'power of God,' that is, the power through which he makes us powerful; 'wisdom of God,' that is, the wisdom through which he makes us wise. As much as I had heretofore hated the word 'righteousness of God,' so much the more dear and sweet it was to me now. And that passage of St. Paul became for me in very truth the gate to Paradise" (Heinrich Boehmer, *Road to Reformation*, J. Doberstein and T. Tappert, translators, [Philadelphia: Muhlenberg Press, 1946], 110).

That was his great theological discovery.

So Luther experienced a radical change in his understanding. One writer described it as a "Copernican Revolution" in theology. That is, the primary focus changed from the action and initiative of the human being to the initiative and action of God. Theology was transformed from human-centered to God-centered. The change in Luther's thinking involved a rediscovery of the biblical understanding of God's grace, which is offered to us freely, with no merit on our part. Luther also came to a new understanding of the righteousness of God. It is a gift to us that we receive by faith. This completely changed Luther's theological paradigm.

He said, "Salvation is a new relationship with God, based on trust in the divine promises, not in our own merit." The redeemed man is still a sinner, but fully forgiven. The sum of the Gospel, the Good News, is that we can absolutely trust God and depend on his word for the forgiveness of our sins.

We are not sure what year he arrived at this understanding. We only know that in 1517, Johan Tetzel, a Dominican monk, arrived in the adjacent state just across the river and began to sell indulgences. As we mentioned earlier, a plenary indulgence promised that the one who purchased it, or the one for whom it was bought, would have all of his or her temporal penalties for sins forgiven and be released immediately from purgatory. The medieval concept was that while Jesus had paid the eternal penalties for our sins, each person had to pay the temporal penalties, either by doing sufficient penance in this life, or by spending time in purgatory after death. In medieval thought, this normally meant thousands of years spent in the flames of purgatory. The Church also taught that the Pope had power to transfer the excess merit acquired by the saints to the account of normal sinners, and thus forgive part or all of the time they would spend in purgatory. According to Georges Barrois, the typical medieval Catholic feared purgatory much more than hell.

A reasonably obedient son or daughter of the Church, would avoid hell, but the belief was that everyone would spend time in purgatory. Luther's prince, Frederick the Elector, had collected 'relics' from all over Europe. If one venerated them all, it was supposed to reduce his or her time in

purgatory by over twenty thousand years! "Relics" were very important in medieval piety. They might include alleged pieces of the true cross, bones of various saints, vials of milk from the breast of the Virgin Mary, or pieces of the crown of thorns.

Thus, the promise of release from purgatory was an offer one could not refuse! And now Tetzel, a powerful salesman, appeared selling indulgences. His sales pitch was, "The moment the coin clinks in the box, the soul of your loved one flies from purgatory to heaven!" (The German had it, "When the coin "clinked" the soul "sprinked.")

This happened because Albrecht of Brandenberg, who was a layman and too young to be a bishop, wanted to become Archbishop of Mainz, Archbishop of Magdeburg, and also administer the bishopric of Halberstadt. Of course, this violated canon law. Nevertheless, the pope consented after Albrecht paid a significant amount of money. Albrecht had borrowed the money from the Fuggers Banking house, and needed to repay it. It was agreed that the necessary funds would be raised through the sale of indulgences. Half of the funds would go to repay Albrecht's debt; the other half would go to finance the building of the Basilica of St. Peter in Rome. You now know, when you see the magnificent architecture of St. Peter's, that some of the money to build it was raised through the sale of indulgences that triggered the Protestant Reformation.

Frederick would not allow this huckster Tetzel to sell indulgences in his own territory, but it was easy for the people to cross the river to where Tetzel was at work. Luther found that his parishioners were crossing the river and returning with pieces of paper indicating they had purchased indulgences.

He was enraged! This practice negated everything he had come to believe about the Gospel. Remember, it was his responsibility to teach the people faithfully. Therefore, to encourage theological debate on the issues, he wrote his ninety-five theses. They are not very radical or inflammatory. Among other things, Luther asserted that the true Christian does not flee from the discipline of God, since God intends it for his or her own good. He also suggested that if the Pope had power to release poor souls from purgatory, he should do so without charging money—an observation embarrassing to the papacy! Luther wrote the theses in Latin and posted them on the door of the church in Wittenberg which was the normal way to invite academic debate. Soon someone translated it into German and it began to circulate widely. It was like throwing a match into dry grass. There was already widespread resentment over the high taxes that Germans paid to Rome. Now Luther began to challenge the entire theological basis of the Roman Church.

One monk wrote to him and said, "Brother Martin, you are right, but go to your cell and pray, 'God, be merciful to me, a sinner,' because you will not live very long." Tetzel said, "I will have this heretic burned within two weeks." Few people expected Luther to survive. However, in the providence of God, and because of the historical context, his movement grew.

At first, Luther thought even the Pope would support him. After all, Luther knew far more about Catholic doctrine than did the Pontiff. Pope Leo X was a member of the notorious Medici family, well known for its corruption. He is reputed to have said, "God has given us the papacy; now let us enjoy it."

Luther was soon called a "Saxon Huss." At first, he denied it, saying that Huss was a heretic. However, as Luther read Huss, he concluded the so-called heretic had been right.

In 1520, Luther wrote three famous treatises. One was called "To the Christian Nobility of the German Nation." In it, he depicted three walls by which the papacy had buttressed its power, and now he began to tear them down. The first wall was the claim that spiritual power was superior to temporal power. Since all believers are priests, that claim was invalid. This also overthrew the second claim that only the pope could interpret Scripture. In affirming that the temporal authorities, not just the pope, could call a council to reform the Church, he tore down the third wall. Luther laid down a program for reform that included allowing clerical

marriage, forbidding the Mendicant orders from begging, closing the brothels, and greatly reducing taxation and church offices. Luther said that all believers are called to be priests. It was a nationalistic document in which he called for the leaders of Germany to organize a council to reform the Church. He said, "We need to rise up against the exploitation of Rome." That document was written and widely circulated in German.

The second document, written in Latin, was on "The Babylonian Captivity of the Church." He said that the real Babylonian Captivity of the Church was not the papacy in Avignon. It was the teaching of the Church regarding the sacraments. The sole value of a sacrament, Luther wrote, is its witness to the divine promise; it points to the God-given pledge of union with Christ and the forgiveness of sins. It strengthens faith. And there are only two sacraments: baptism and the Lord's Supper. He said that pilgrimages and works of merit were man-made substitutes for the forgiveness of sins freely promised to us by faith. He also doubted transubstantiation and rejected the doctrine that the Supper is a sacrifice to God. He said the other Roman sacraments had no basis in Scripture.

The third document was "On Christian Liberty." Here Luther presented the paradox of the Christian life. "A Christian man is the most free lord of all, and subject to none. A Christian man is the most dutiful servant of all, and subject to every one." He is free because he is justified by faith, not under the works of the law, and is in a new personal relationship with Christ. He is a servant because he is bound by love to live according to the will of God and serve his neighbor. Therefore, for Luther the essence of the Gospel is the forgiveness of sins that comes through faith. It is nothing less than a vital, personal, transforming relationship with Christ.

Thus, by 1520, Luther had arrived at his basic theological concepts which were the heart of the biblical message.

In 1521, Luther, the peasant's son, was summoned to Worms, to recant or defend his ideas before the most powerful rulers of church and state in Europe. He was guaranteed a safe conduct, but knew that Huss had been given a similar promise when he went to Constance, where he was burned at the stake! At Worms, Luther refused to recant unless either Scripture or clear reason convinced him. There he proclaimed, "I cannot do otherwise. Here I stand. God help me. Amen." It was certainly one of the great moments in history.

The movement spread rapidly, but as it did so, it followed the medieval pattern in which it was assumed that everyone in a given territory or state would follow the same religion. There was no concept of religious pluralism at the time. It was assumed there could be no political or social unity without religious unity. The Prince, not the people, decided whether a given territory would remain Roman Catholic or become Lutheran. Some princes made their decision out of deep religious conviction and others for political reasons. The people conformed or fled; that was true for both Lutherans and Catholics. Through that process, territories in Germany became Lutheran or remained Roman Catholic. A few areas also became Calvinist.

In his early writings, Luther seemed to advocate a church of true believers: a gathered community. He showed some ambivalence about whether a state church should be established. The problem was that the Christendom model of the Church, in which each person was baptized and consequently a church member, contradicted the basic concept that we are justified only by our personal faith. But Luther was a very conservative person. He saw some of his followers carry his ideas much further than he wished. He observed the Anabaptists and feared that such movements would destroy the fabric of society. Partly for these reasons and partly out of political necessity, Luther finally endorsed the idea that the prince would determine the religion of the people. So the Lutheran state church was established in many territories of Germany. The state would appoint the bishops, and all the people would be baptized. It continued the Christendom model that had existed for nearly twelve centuries.

At first, the Catholic princes expected to crush the Protestant Reformation by use of force; however, the Turks were advancing into Western Europe and were at the gates of Vienna. In order to defeat them, the more powerful Catholic states needed an alliance with the Protestants in the struggle. Thus, from a human perspective, the attack of the Turkish Empire rescued the Protestant Reformation!

Some scholars have accused Luther and Calvin of having no missionary vision and have affirmed the missionary activity of the Anabaptists. That view is incorrect. Lutheran missionaries to the Scandinavian countries followed the older medieval Christendom pattern of mission. They won the rulers to the new faith, and the Church was reformed following the Lutheran model. We will see that Calvinists followed the Christendom model in some places but also formed gathered churches in France and elsewhere. The Anabaptists formed gathered churches of adult converts out of the established churches. That is, their understanding of the Church and its relationship to the broader society determined their missionary methodology.

Most Lutheran missionaries were Luther's former students. They took the movement to Denmark, Norway, Sweden, and Finland. One of the greatest was Johannes Bugenhagen, a former monk, who established a national Lutheran Church in Denmark. There is evidence that the King asked Luther to send missionaries to Norway as well. At that time Norway was under Danish rule. Since Lutheranism appeared to be a vehicle of Danish domination, the Reformation progressed more slowly there, but came eventually.

Remember that in the eleventh century, Celtic missionaries from England had evangelized Scandinavia. Their churches were now national churches, only loosely tied to Rome. Eventually, all of the Scandinavian nations—Denmark, Sweden, Norway, and Finland—became Lutheran.

Gustavus Vasa was King of Sweden from 1523to 1560. With his chief advisor, he inaugurated a program of reforms based on the authority of Scripture and public ownership of church property under royal management. The Roman Church owned a third or more of the arable land in Western Europe at the beginning of the sixteenth century. This meant that land was off the tax roles, and it made the Church the most powerful economic force in society. Thus, the reformation of the Church inevitably involved politics and economics. If the Church was to be reformed, who would get its land? There was great economic motive for powerful nobles who hoped to take church lands. In Scotland John Knox wanted to take the Church land and make it the basis of public education, but the nobles took most of it. Knox, like many other reformers, was concerned about social, educational, and economic issues along with theology and church structure. The issues could not be separated.

Sweden had greater success in bringing about a degree of social reform. Reforming the Church meant reforming society to some extent. There, Olavus Petri, who had studied with Luther in Wittenberg, preached widely. He and the King's advisor, Andreas, were responsible for the translation of the New Testament into Swedish. It was the first literary work published in that language. The Reformation stimulated a great output of evangelical writing in Swedish, and those works became the foundation of modern Swedish literature.

We see this pattern elsewhere: first, the translation of the New Testament, followed by other literature, much of it evangelical, in the vernacular languages. The leader of the Reformation in Finland was Archbishop Agricola. He is considered the father of the written Finnish language. He too, had studied with Luther in Wittenberg. We see the same pattern: he translated the New Testament, which was published in 1548, and other literature followed.

Thus, Lutheran missionaries went cross-culturally to the countries in northern Europe, but they followed the older, medieval, Christendom model. They won the rulers, who then led changes in the Church. This of course did not mean that most of the people understood or even embraced the new theological ideas. However, it did bring the opportunity for church leaders to teach the people and restructure the Church. That took place with varying degrees of success in different places. As we will see, a century later, Pietism carried the Reformation a step further.

Luther was a very complex figure. One can quote him on both sides of many issues, depending on his mood at the time when he spoke. His collected works and his "table talk" make up a large library. He could blast the Jews or Turks one time and speak of the need to convert them at others. At times, he supported the peasants' need for better conditions, but denounced their rebellion. His overriding concern was the reformation of the Church and the proclamation of the Gospel. He fought against anything that seemed to threaten that goal, and his zeal oftentimes made him intemperate. Nevertheless, we must recognize his greatness as a Christian, a theologian, and a reformer. In addition, through his superb translation of the Bible, he gave the Germans a common language.

Calvin

Before we examine the life of John Calvin, I will make an important assertion. The more freedom men and women have to discover and use their gifts in ministry, and the more they are encouraged to do so, the more effective the Church will be both in evangelism and in ministries of compassion and social transformation. There are examples of this all through history: in early Calvinism, in the early Anabaptist movement, and in renewal movements in general. Later, we will see this especially in evangelical revivals.

This is one of the most important reasons for the success of Pentecostalism. At its best, it encourages people to discover and use their gifts in ministry. Up to now, gifts in the movement have been focused primarily on ministries within the Church and not so much on the broader society. However, there are signs of positive change in some areas. In Central America, for example, a Pentecostal movement that has established good primary schools for thousands of children seeks to use that to change its society. (cf. Peterson, Douglas, *Not by Might nor by Power, A Pentecostal Theology of Social Concern in Latin America*. Oxford, Regnum, 1996) It is important to understand that while many of the gifts of the Spirit are to be used within the Church, others are to be used to express God's concern for the societies in which we live. In some of the Reformation churches, in Calvinism, Puritanism, and Pietism at their best, we see these two aspects combined. Often we tend to focus only on one or the other.

Now we will go to Geneva. In 1536, the Protestant Reformation had been spreading for nineteen years. Huldreich Zwingli had led Zurich to adopt its ideas. There were a number of other reformers in central Europe. One of those was William Farel, who as we saw earlier had studied with Jacques Lefèvre. Farel, a fiery evangelist, arrived in Geneva during this period of turmoil and held public meetings expounding Protestant ideas. For a number of years, Geneva had struggled to overthrow the domination of the Dukes of Savoy and the bishops whom they appointed. A vigorous, more democratic political tradition was developing, with various councils governing the city, culminating in a General Assembly of adult male citizens. The cities allied with Geneva in the struggle were Protestant. Thus, in 1536, more for political than religious reasons, the General Assembly of Geneva decided to adopt the Reformation, declaring its determination "to live by this holy Evangelical law and word of God." It was a great opportunity to begin anew. But what would it mean to be "reformed"? That was still undefined. Geneva was a city of ten thousand people, almost all with a very low understanding of the Christian faith and life. The issue was how to implement the declaration "to live by this holy and Evangelical law and word of God."

Now we leave Geneva for a time, and turn to John Calvin. He was born on July 10, 1509 in Noyon, northeast of Paris. His father was secretary to the local bishop. Although his father was a commoner, he had good relationships with the bishop and the nobility. Believing that his son had good prospects for advancement in the Church, he sent him off at the age of fourteen, to study for the priesthood at the University of Paris.

Calvin accompanied the sons of some local members of the nobility, and he received two benefices from the Bishop. A benefice was the income from property that people had donated to the Church.

The benefices meant that John could be economically independent. If he were ordained as a priest by the time he was twenty-five years old, he would continue to receive that income all his life. It is important to remember that.

After some time, Calvin's father lost favor with the bishop, meaning that young John's prospects for advancement in the Church were greatly diminished. So his father sent Calvin to Orleans to study law. One of his professors there was a secret Lutheran. We do not know how much influence the professor had on Calvin, if any. When his father died, Calvin, still economically independent, returned to Paris. His goal now was to study the classics, to become a humanist scholar. In 1532, he published his first book, *A Commentary on Seneca's Treatise on Clemency*. As far as we know, he showed little interest in religion at that time. However, the ideas of Luther and others were being discussed, and many expressed the desire for reform. In 1529, Louis de Berquin, one of Lefèvre's former students, was burned at the stake for his Protestant ideas. For some months in 1533 and early 1534 Calvin lived in the house of Etienne de la Forge, a Waldensian cloth merchant. After Calvin left, la Forge was martyred. We can only guess the content of their conversations!

Unlike Luther, Calvin was a very private person and gave us almost no details about his conversion. In one of his works, he spoke only of a "sudden conversion." But we do know that shortly before his twenty-fifth birthday in 1534, he visited the aged Lefèvre and, after the visit, returned to Noyon and surrendered his benefices. This clearly marked a radical change in the direction of his life and faith. He rejected ordination as a priest and gave up his income from the Church. We know little about where he lived in the following two years. In 1536, the first edition of his book, *The Institutes of the Christian Religion,* appeared. It was published under an assumed name. The work expounded Calvin's understanding of the historic Christian faith and leaned heavily on the early church fathers. Calvin wrote it for two reasons: to instruct the growing French Protestant movement and to show the king (Calvin addressed a preface to him) that Protestants were not subversive and that they believed what the earliest church fathers had taught and believed.

By now, Calvin was in correspondence with various people for whom he had become a spiritual counselor. One was the Duchess of Ferrara in northern Italy. Returning to France from a visit to her, Calvin had to stop overnight in Geneva. It was shortly after the city had declared it would be Protestant. Farel heard that Calvin was in town, knew he was the author of *The Institutes*, and went to the inn to find him. There he insisted that Calvin remain in the city and help give leadership to the new movement. Calvin was very reluctant, apparently preferring a life of scholarship to church leadership. Nevertheless, Farel is reported to have said, "If you do not stay, God will surely judge you!" As Calvin later wrote, "God thrust me into the fire!"

Calvin never occupied a position other than as one of the pastors of Geneva. However, because of the force of his intellect and personality, he became the dominant person in the movement. Indeed, in the first reference to him in the city records, his name was not yet known—he was simply, "that Frenchman."

Calvin and Farel ministered together in Geneva for a time before they clashed with the city council over the issue of how the Lord's Supper should be administered, and who should make the decision. Calvin insisted secular authorities should not make any decision about liturgy. Consequently, the two men were expelled from Geneva, and Calvin went to Strassburg, where he was pastor of a congregation of five hundred French Protestant refugees. There he learned to enjoy their singing and love the pastorate. He married, but his wife soon died. Later, when someone taunted him because he had no sons, he replied that he had many spiritual children.

Meanwhile, the situation in Geneva worsened and fell into chaos. The city leaders sent a delegation to Strassburg, begging Calvin to return. He did so most reluctantly. As he said, he went back weeping, only because he felt the strong call of God.

One of the greatest achievements of Calvinism was the creation of church governance that included laymen as well as pastors. The result was a church structure that could travel and exist in places where the government was unfriendly. Calvinistic churches did not depend on the sanction of the secular government to exist. Their cells were formed in Roman Catholic Holland when it was dominated by Spain. They were formed in France, even though the King favored Roman Catholicism. The form of government that included laymen helped Calvinism to grow among Puritans in England and Presbyterians in Scotland.

That method of governance was able to operate independently of the secular state in a way that Lutherans and Roman Catholics found more difficult. The growth of the house churches in China, Ethiopia, Cuba, and elsewhere in recent decades has shown, in a powerful way, the importance of church structures that value lay leadership! Thus, the act of bringing the laity into the leadership of the Church was one of its most important aspects of Calvinism. It helped the movement survive under persecution and grow in areas where the government was hostile.

Soon Geneva counted around thirteen thousand citizens and seven thousand refugees. It became an influential center as many came to study there. Because of its strong focus on education and because of the skills of many refugees who fled to Geneva from persecution in other places, the city prospered economically.

Calvin was not the rigid, legalistic person that many people have painted him to be. He had many friends. It is remarkable how many highly placed friends he had at the University of Paris. Obviously, they were attracted to this brilliant young man. John Knox told that one time he went to Calvin's house on a Sunday afternoon and found him bowling on the lawn. That changes our image of a strict legalist regarding Sabbath observance.

However, it is important to examine the story of Calvin's involvement in the burning of Miguel Servetus. Servetus was an arrogant Spanish genius: perhaps the first to discover the circulation of the blood. As a theological heretic, he had been captured by Roman Catholic powers and condemned to death, but escaped. He had been in correspondence with Calvin for some time and now went to Geneva, hoping to take leadership and have Calvin expelled. The authorities put him on trial and Calvin testified against him. Calvin could have simply sent him back to the Roman Catholic territory, where he would have been burned. However, Calvin was never a man to shirk from what he perceived to be his duty. He believed that Servetus, who put souls in danger of eternal loss, should be executed. He wanted a more merciful death for Servetus, but the secular authorities burned him.

This was a period in which many people were executed for crimes we would consider petty today. Many of the crimes were religious. Of course we repudiate any persecution for religious reasons, but I believe it is important to note that even though Servetus was executed in Geneva, there were hundreds of victims of the Spanish Inquisition. Years later, a monument was erected in Geneva with an inscription that read, "We, the loyal spiritual children of John Calvin, erect this monument of expiation [that is, repentance] for the burning of Servetus." We are always called to recognize our mistakes and sins of the past and repent. In addition, it does appear that even though Protestants were not blameless in the sixteenth century, they recognized much earlier than did the Roman Catholic Church that such action was contradictory to the Scriptures and Christian discipleship.

Education was an important factor in Calvinism and Geneva. In 1536, the same year it adopted the Reformation, the city established compulsory education for every child. As far as we know, this was the first such law in history. Later Puritans in New England also established compulsory education. In contrast, Roman Catholic Portugal did not do so until 1954, and even then, the Archbishop was against the law! Calvin also established the Academy that became the University of Geneva. In a building alongside the St. Pierre cathedral, he lectured on theology and biblical studies to students who came from other areas. John Knox, and many who fled from England during the reign of

"Bloody Mary" (Mary Tudor, Queen of England) from 1553 to 1558, studied with Calvin.

Calvin's influence also spread through his writings. The last edition of *The Institutes,* greatly expanded, was published in 1559. He trained over 160 pastors, whom he sent as missionaries to France, where many were martyred. Eventually, France became one-third Protestant before much of the Church was destroyed by persecution. Calvinist missionaries were also sent to the Low Countries (that is, Holland and Belgium), to Hungary, and to Poland. Therefore, it is not correct to assert that Calvin had no missionary concern; to the contrary, he was active in preparing and sending missionaries to other European countries.

Perhaps because of different personalities, or perhaps because Calvin was in the second generation of reformers, he was more aggressive than Luther was in mission. The French Huguenot mission to Brazil from 1555 to 1558 was the first Protestant missionary effort outside of Europe. Sponsored by French Calvinists with the approval of Calvin, they landed on an island in the Bay of Guanabara. Rio de Janeiro is now built on the edge of that bay. They tried to establish a Calvinist colony and reach out from there. Eventually, the Portuguese killed some of the leaders and sent the rest back to France in a leaky ship.

Protestantism, an Evaluation

Now we want to examine the Protestant movement through missiological eyes. The genius of Protestantism at its best was the freedom it gave to the creativity of the Holy Spirit, and the human personality guided by the Spirit, to break out in new forms of the Church and new methods of sharing the Gospel. People in the sixteenth century were certainly searching for a form of faith commensurate with their changing society—with the rising middle class, cities, and commerce—but the Roman Church was unwilling to recognize that.

There is no doubt Protestantism has led to great diversity of expression of the Christian faith, and the possibility of contextualization in ways that often the Roman Catholic Church has not permitted. Of course, this can become very divisive, which Protestants must recognize. How do we encourage the legitimate diversity of expressions of faith and at the same time affirm our unity with the whole Body of Christ? Protestants have often been rightly accused of being divisive and dividing repeatedly, often for no reason. The Baptists have a saying in Brazil: "Baptists fight like cats and always have kittens!" (Kittens refer to churches.) Protestantism at its best has been free to try new methods, and follow new visions, because of its less centralized control. That has been more true of Protestants than of the Roman Church.

The doctrine of the priesthood of all believers has encouraged this at times. We must be honest and recognize that in the classical Protestant churches, the doctrine of the priesthood of all believers has often remained a paper doctrine. It has not been put into practice because we, too, have fallen into clericalism.

There are also dangers in Protestantism: excessive individualism, lack of appreciation of the history of the whole Church, and lack of appreciation of the different ways in which God has worked through history.

Often we seem to believe that the way we worship, train our leaders, and formulate our faith is the definitive word, and that churches that we help to establish should be replicas of our own. For example, can Lutheran missionaries in Indonesia allow Lutheran Christians, or people who became Christians in Indonesia through Lutheran witness, to do the same kind of contextualization in twenty-first century Indonesia that Germans did in sixteenth century Europe? Or are they expected simply to repeat the forms of earlier Lutheranism? These issues arise repeatedly. If John Calvin found himself leading a movement in a city in the interior of Brazil today, would he structure the Church, its government, worship, and theology just as he did in sixteenth-century Geneva? How would he prepare pastors? I suspect he would do some things differently while continuing to affirm the same basic faith.

We must recognize that some Protestants can become as sectarian and intolerant as Roman Catholics and have often done so. Protestantism can also become just as culture-bound. I have heard about missionaries in Nigeria who told the Nigerians they could not use drums in worship because drums were pagan. Then some missionaries got the idea of starting a movement similar to Boy Scouts, and they wanted to use drums as they marched. What would they do? They had already said African drums were pagan. They decided to use old gasoline drums and tie rubber over the head and use them as drums. Apparently, an American drum was acceptable, but an African drum was pagan! There is often danger of judging certain instruments or practices according to how they might appear in our own culture without asking what that practice might mean in the receptor culture. We Protestants have often done so.

The Roman Catholic Church has tended to superimpose the Roman structure and ritual on older cultures and religions and absorb many elements of those older cultures and religions. This has often led to serious syncretism. In Latin America, the pre-Colombian and African gods and goddesses were often baptized with the names of Catholic saints. In the minds and practice of many Catholics, the focus has been on the favorite saints, especially the Virgin Mary, with little attention to Jesus Christ. Therefore, the Roman Church has often stressed too much continuity between the older religion and culture and the Christian faith.

Protestants have often gone to the opposite extreme and stressed discontinuity between the Gospel and non-Western cultures. We have superimposed Western forms and culture on non-Western cultures, believing these Western forms were inherently Christian. Consequently, pre-Christian forms have not been used in the Church. This issue is still with us. The Old Testament took over the sacrificial system and many other forms from surrounding pagan peoples. However, the Old Testament poured new meaning into those forms.

Sometimes we Protestants have fallen into a new kind of religious syncretism, confusing the Christian life with the "American Dream." This is the teaching that if you become a Christian, you will become prosperous. Of course, this is both tragic and unbiblical. First, it is a false promise. Even worse, it distorts the Gospel and makes it primarily a servant of our own selfishness. I do not think Peter and Paul became very wealthy as they served Christ—quite the contrary.

However, it is still true that at its best, Protestantism gives flexibility to discover new forms of the Church and encourage lay leadership. As the Church worldwide is being reshaped significantly in many cultures today, this is increasingly important.

The Reformers and Missions

Some have asserted that the sixteenth-century Protestant Reformers were not concerned about mission beyond their own territories. This accusation is valid to some extent.

Luther is accused of not showing concern for mission, yet he wrote about the need to win the Jews and even the Turks. This was at a time when the Turks were attacking Western Europe, and there was danger they might conquer Vienna. They were enemies.

The picture of Reformers and Christian mission is more positive than some critics have alleged. Some have said the Anabaptists engaged in great missionary activity while the Lutherans, Calvinists, and Anglicans had no mission interest. This is not correct.

The Lutherans followed the older medieval pattern of mission, seeking to win the prince, with the understanding that the people would follow. They followed that pattern in various German territories and in Scandinavia.

Calvinists went two ways. There were some people movements in areas of western Germany and central Europe. However, Calvin also trained a large number of pastors in Geneva, many of whom were refugees from the Low Countries, England, Scotland, France, and elsewhere. He trained them and sent them back to their countries as missionaries. The Calvinist Church emerged in Holland as a very powerful force in the rebellion against Spain. It began as a struggle for religious freedom and became a successful fight for independence. The Calvinist movement at one time included a third

of the population of France. There were also Calvinist churches in Hungary, Poland, and, as we have noted, parts of Germany. John Knox, the Reformer of Scotland, studied with Calvin in Geneva. The Puritan movement that began within the Church of England was greatly influenced by Calvinism. In addition, as we noted earlier, Calvin had a minor role in sending missionaries to Brazil in 1555.

Thus, there were Calvinists in Hungary, Poland, and parts of Germany. The Puritan movement in England was partly at least, an attempt at a Calvinist reformation within the Church of England. John Knox, who was trained by Calvin in Geneva, led the reformation in Scotland. So Calvinism was missionary in a different way from both Lutheranism and the Anabaptists.

On the other hand, the Anabaptists were active in mission within their own communities and territories. Their goal was to win adult converts (whether Roman Catholic, Lutheran, or Calvinist) who would become part of their gathered communities, separate from the Christendom model of the Church. For Anabaptists, none of those churches was valid. Thus, their understanding of the nature of the Church and the Christian life led them to seek adult converts from both Roman Catholic and Protestant state churches.

So, it is not correct to say that Luther and Calvin had no concern for mission. But we must ask why we do not see more missionary activity among sixteenth- and seventeenth-century Protestants.

One reason was theological, and represented a tragically incomplete understanding of the Church. Traditional Protestant ecclesiology defined the true Church as existing where the "Word is rightly preached and the sacraments properly observed." The Reformers were referring, of course, to the Word and sacraments as they understood them biblically, and were defining the Church against Roman Catholicism. The Reformers' definition was good as far as it went, but was incomplete, lacking a missionary dimension.

In the second century, we already find the statement that there should be "one holy catholic apostolic church." At least three of those four words have great missionary implications. If the Church is to be catholic (universal), obviously it must be missionary, or it cannot become universal. The fundamental meaning of "holy" is "set aside for a purpose," and that purpose is mission to the nations. As we noted earlier, the word "apostle" means the same in Greek that the word "missionary," does in Latin: one who is sent out with a mission, or purpose. Therefore, if the Church is to be apostolic, it must be apostolic both in doctrine and in practice. An apostolic church is a church sent out into the world. So if the Church is to be "one, holy, catholic, and apostolic," it must be missionary!

The Reformers wanted to recapture the apostolicity of the Church in doctrine, but in their definition of the true Church, they forgot the other half of apostolicity—its "sentness." I believe this problem of inadequate ecclesiology is still with us. Even the curriculum in a typical theological seminary illustrates this problem, by either the complete absence of or peripheral nature of any course on mission.

Indeed, some sixteenth-century Roman Catholic leaders criticized the Protestants, saying, "You are not a true church, because you're not missionary." Whatever disagreements we would have with the sixteenth-century Roman Catholic Church, it engaged in mission far more than the Protestants of that era. Our theologians and biblical scholars need to define our ecclesiology in terms that put mission in the center of the purpose of the Church. Emil Bruner, a Swiss theologian, once stated, "The Church exists in mission as the fire exists in burning."

There were other reasons for the lack of Protestant missionary activity in the sixteenth century. We must realize that for years, Protestants were fighting military and political battles for their very survival. For several decades, it appeared that the movement in Europe (which Protestants saw as their primary mission field) would be crushed. By the time its survival was ensured, the Protestant territories were exhausted militarily, economically, and spiritually. In some areas, a third of the population had been killed.

In addition, the Protestant nations were not maritime powers at the time. In the late fifteenth cen-

tury and throughout the sixteenth century, the only European powers able to expand overseas were Spain and Portugal. It was later that the Protestant nations, the Dutch and English, expanded overseas. However, tragically, by that time, much of the Protestant movement had lost its vitality with the advent of Protestant scholasticism.

Seventeenth-century Protestant theology, especially Lutheran, engaged in fierce theological battles. Its focus was on correct doctrine. Luther had insisted that faith consisted of belief in the truth, correct doctrine, and personal trust. 'Fiducia' is the Latin word for faith, meaning personal trust. Most Lutheran theologians a century later defined faith simply as belief in correct doctrines. The element of personal trust had died out to a significant degree. This rather sterile, scholastic view of faith did not inspire people to a high standard of the Christian life, let alone to mission. This concern for the Christian life and mission would come later with Pietism.

Winter pointed out the final reason we do not see more missionary activity among Protestants in the sixteenth and seventeenth centuries. The Protestant churches rejected monasticism for theological reasons. Luther had a bad experience with monasticism—with its tendency toward a theology of salvation by good works instead of faith. So he became very negative toward the movement. He did not force monks or nuns to leave monasteries or convents in Lutheran territories, but gave them the option of doing so.

Yet, as we have seen, for at least twelve centuries nearly all missionaries had come from the monastic movement. While some monasteries were rich and corrupt, others were missionary communities. The dissolution of monasteries and convents in Protestant territories effectively destroyed the only mission structures that existed at the time. There was nothing to take the place of those monastic structures until the rise of the Protestant missionary movement two centuries later.

As we speak of the dissolution of the monasteries and convents, it is worth telling the story of how Luther got his wife. Luther was a very good monk. He had no particular urge to marry. Every indication is that he observed his vows of celibacy and was a very moral person. As the Reformation progressed, and men and women were allowed to leave the monasteries and convents, a serious problem arose: what to do with the former nuns? Often, they could not return to their families. There was no adequate place for single women in that society. It was necessary to find husbands for them and that became one of Luther's pastoral duties. One former nun, Katherine von Bora, was especially headstrong and rejected the men whom Luther suggested. The story is that finally, in exasperation, he said, "Well then, whom will you marry?" She replied, "I would only marry Dr. von Armstadt, or you." Luther decided that he liked the idea, and they were married. It was a great love story!

His marriage and family life brought out some of the most winsome aspects of Luther's life and ministry. He wrote children's catechisms and songs for children. It is a very beautiful story, even though it did not begin as a Hollywood romance!

Chapter Fifteen

The "Radical" Reformation:
The Anabaptists

Devotional

I am going to read one of the greatest and hardest passages in the Gospels. It is found in Luke and repeated in slightly different words in Matthew and Mark. It comes immediately after the disciples confessed Jesus as the Christ, the Son of God. He told them he would be rejected, put to death, and rise from the dead. Then He said to them all, "If anyone would come after me, he must deny himself and take up his cross daily and follow me. For whoever wants to save his life will lose it, but whoever loses his life for me will save it." (Luke 9:23–24 NIV)

When I was in seminary, I wanted to prepare a sermon on this passage. After working on it for a while, I decided I could not do it. I was not ready. I am not sure I would be ready today, many years later. I am not sure any of us is ever ready to prepare a message on that passage. It is one of the hardest sayings in the New Testament. Perhaps it is one we need to live more than we preach about. Perhaps we can only preach about it only after we have lived it.

Throughout this course, we frequently study the lives of people who have lived that passage, who have known what it means to take up their cross to follow the Crucified One, wherever that might lead them, whatever the circumstances might be. If we get down to the bedrock issue, this is what mission is all about.

Mission is about understanding culture, people groups, and theological and missiological issues.

However, important as these things are, they are never enough. Above all other factors, mission is about denying the right to be the lord of our own lives. It is about taking up a cross and following Jesus wherever he leads us.

I suggest we keep that in mind as we study, and let that passage continue to drive us constantly to the point where we want, above all else, to be Jesus' people, following wherever he leads, even though following Him may lead to a cross.

Let's pray together.

> Father, as we come to you today, we ask that you to work in our lives so that we are led closer and closer to you, to follow the one who did not count it something to be grasped to be equal with the Father, but who emptied himself, became a human person, and was willing to go to death, even death on the cross. Help us to follow him more and more closely, as he leads us into mission. We pray in His name. Amen.

Introduction

Now we will examine the "Radical Reformation," or the Anabaptist movement. Both terms are important. "Radical" means "going to the root of things." In 1962, George Williams of Harvard Divinity School published a book with the title, *The Radical Reformation*. It is a massive encyclopedic work on all of the so-called left-wing movements of the sixteenth century. It was a period when there were literally hundreds, maybe thousands, of different religious movements that broke off from the medieval Church and sought new forms of Christian faith. When the old monolithic structure began to break up, new attempts to define the faith and the true Church were almost endless.

The term "Radical Reformation" included everything except the Lutheran, Calvinist, and Anglican movements, the three major branches of the so-called "Classical Reformation." Those in many movements felt that because Luther and Calvin had not gone far enough in reforming the Church, they had to go back to the "root of things" in the New Testament.

Some of these groups were not orthodox in belief. A few rejected the divinity of Christ and were Unitarian in theology. Some believed the Holy Spirit spoke directly to them and put that word above Scripture. They became very subjective and often fell into strange doctrines and practices. Others were very socially and politically radical. Some encouraged the Peasants' Revolt and became militaristic. We will not deal with those groups.

We will focus on the groups usually called the "Evangelical Anabaptists." While there were various communities that fit that category, their primary representatives today are the Mennonites, not the Baptists. (The Baptists emerged later. As far as we can tell from the historical data, the modern Baptist movement emerged as the left wing of Puritanism in seventeenth-century England, not from the sixteenth-century Anabaptist groups.)

The term Anabaptist meant "re-baptizer." Their opponents called them thus because they baptized only adult converts to their cause and rejected the validity of infant baptism. Of course, they did not consider themselves to be re-baptizers; they saw themselves only as baptizers.

Tensions within Lutheranism and Calvinism

The sixteenth century was a time of great religious, social, and political ferment: the most radical new idea was justification by faith. Luther and Calvin both experienced tension in their thought and practice. They retained a medieval view of Christendom in which everyone in a given territory should belong to the state-sanctioned church. Yet they recognized that not everyone who was a part of the Church, had personal, justifying faith. That is where the tension arose. Luther's first motivation was to bring proper biblical understanding of the gospel back to the Church. He did not want to start a new church. Calvin was part of the second generation of the Reformation. He started his ministry in Geneva nineteen years after Luther posted his Theses. By that time, it was clear now that a separate Protestant church existed and that the Roman Church was resisting any theological or structural reform. Calvin's first goal was to instruct the Church theologically. Then he was forced into leadership in the city of Geneva which had just decided to be reformed. That meant he had to give pastoral as well as theological leadership through writing and preaching and teaching.

Some have the impression that Luther believed in salvation through faith and that Calvin stressed good works. Not at all. Calvin and Luther differed very little theologically. Some believe that while Calvin believed in predestination, Luther did not. That too is incorrect. Luther believed just as strongly in predestination and election as Calvin did. Justification by faith is as important for Calvin as it is for Luther. However, Calvin put more stress on the Christian life and the need for discipline in the Church.

But there were tensions in the Reformation of Luther and Calvin. Both continued to advocate the medieval ideal that all people in a given territory would be church members. They believed strongly in the corporate nature of the Church. In the sixteenth century, being a Christian was not understood simply as an individual issue; each person was seen as part of the broader community, and that community was to be Christian. For most Protestants who practice the baptism of infants, the act is recognition that God calls a person, from his or her birth, into the body of Christ, into the Christian community. My purpose is not to argue for that theological point of view, although I agree with it, but to explain it to those who come from different traditions. It is based primarily on the Old Testament concept of the covenant. For example, in Presbyterian churches, in baptism, the phrase "child of the covenant" is used.

So Luther and Calvin agreed with the Christendom model that had been in effect in Europe for nearly 1300 years. At times Luther talked about a believers' church, a gathered group of true believers. He probably opted for state or territorial churches primarily because of the political context in which he lived. However, he knew that not everybody in the state church was a converted person.

As we have seen, the primary doctrine of the Reformation was justification by faith, meaning personal faith. But it is clearly not consistent with a territorial church that includes all the people in a given area. We can never say everyone in a given territory has justifying or saving faith. So Luther and Calvin spoke of the "visible" and the "invisible" Church. The "visible" Church includes everyone who is baptized into the churchly structure; the "invisible" Church is comprised of those who truly have justifying faith. That was their theological solution.

So while Calvin and Luther recognized that not all the baptized were among the elect and that the Church was sinful and imperfect, both wanted a close relationship between church and state. They believed the state was ordained by God and should be honored by the Church. However, both men, especially Calvin, believed the Church should be more independent of the state than did Luther. Again, this was in part due to their different contexts.

Calvin carried the issue further. He believed that a high standard of morality should be enforced by both church and state, even though not everyone was among the elect. That led to tension in Geneva. There was a party of Libertines in the city who wanted a much freer sexual lifestyle. Naturally, Calvin was very much against this. The issue was, to what extent should the state and church attempt to impose a Christian life style on non-believers? Of course, this issue is still with us in Western pluralistic societies in our post-Christendom era. As we will see, the question was best solved later in Lutheranism and Anglicanism by the formation of small, committed groups of believers who sought to take the Christian life more seriously than did their nominal Christian neighbors. Those movements were Puritanism and Pietism.

The situation faced by Luther and Calvin was not too different from that faced by some of us who have been pastors of large older churches. Among the members, we have seen some very committed believers who obviously had a deep personal faith in Jesus Christ and wanted to serve him. However, in nearly every church there are also those who have been raised in the Church and professed their faith at some point, but do not exhibit a strong personal faith. There are others—perhaps second or third generation believers—who are members of the Church, but whose personal faith is questionable. So the dynamics of most local churches are really quite similar to the situation that Luther and Calvin confronted, even though we do not live with a legally established Christendom model of the Church and society.

In South Africa, at the time of these lectures, one of the major issues for Christians and church leaders was to change the theology of a government and a church that perceived themselves as Christian and yet supported apartheid. Theologians such as David Bosch and Nico Smith have worked on that issue, even though they were rejected by the leaders of their church.

When we call for personal faith in Jesus Christ, we insist that faith is meant to lead believers into a journey of discipleship. And discipleship should include personal conduct, ministries of compassion to those in need, and the desire to transform our societies so they reflect more fully the values of the Kingdom of God. Often we have not done very well in the third of these emphases.

The Anabaptists: A More Radical Approach

The Anabaptists had a different solution to these tensions. While there were many forms of the movement, its primary characteristic was its belief that the true Church was composed only of adult believers who should be baptized on their own personal confession of faith. Equally important was the use of Scripture, especially the New Testament, as their authority. Their goal was to return to New Testament Christianity. They rejected traditions and practices that had evolved since the age of the Apostles.

Thus, they believed Luther and Calvin did not go far enough in reforming the Church. Luther was more conservative toward change. As he looked at various church practices and traditions, his principle was, "Anything not expressly forbidden in Scripture is acceptable." Calvin was more radical. His principle was, "We can only accept and do that which is expressly allowed in Scripture." The Anabaptists went much further in rejecting medieval churchly tradition. They believed the only true Church was a gathered community of adult, baptized believers. They believed the Church, far from being identical with the community at large, was not only separate from it, but also countercultural in many respects.

It was logical that the Anabaptists rejected infant baptism. Other traditions saw the Church and state as two aspects of one community, even though they recognized not everyone in the state had saving faith. Nevertheless, they believed the Church should be coterminous with the state. They saw society as a sacral unit with two sides, church and state, in a positive, mutually supportive relationship. From that standpoint, it was a great sin to tear asunder the fabric of that sacral unit. The Anabaptists, on the other hand, had a radically different view of both church and state. The Church was to be a separate, gathered community of adult believers. Their children would be part of the community, but not full members until they professed their own personal faith. The state was completely separate from the Church and was perceived as neutral or even hostile to the Christian life.

Therefore, the Anabaptists had little to do with the state, and withdrew into separate communities where it was possible. Of course, they only baptized adults. At first they baptized by pouring water on the head; later, they practiced immersion. The mode of baptism—aspersion or immersion—was not an issue at the beginning.

They took the New Testament very literally and attempted to follow the Sermon on the Mount. They would not go to war; nor take oaths. Some groups practiced what we would call today "charismatic phenomena and prophecies." These occurred among the common people, especially in the countryside. In some areas, there were Anabaptist people movements, even though that may appear to be a contradiction in terms. Some groups sent out many missionaries. Some were untrained lay men and women. Others were very well educated, some with graduate degrees in theology. Thus, the movement went clear across the spectrum in terms of educational preparation and social and intellectual life.

The Anabaptists insisted on a high standard of morality. They believed just as strongly as Luther or Calvin that we are justified by faith; but they insisted that saving faith must always lead to a life of high moral standards and good works. Luther and Calvin had also insisted that saving faith must lead to a transformed life—"faith active in love" was Luther's way of affirming it. The difference was more a matter of emphasis. It was easier to insist on a high standard of the Christian life and discipline in a separate, gathered community than in a territorial church. The difference here was not so much in the theology that saving faith should lead to good works but in the understanding of the Church. If everyone were a member of the Church, many would not follow a very high moral standard. Church discipline was difficult and rare in the territorial churches. However, the Anabaptists, by forming gathered communities, could insist on a high level of morality and use discipline to exclude those who did not adhere to their standards. Nevertheless, because they put such a focus on a high moral standard and on good works, some Lutherans or Calvinists accused them of believing in salvation by works and not by faith.

In a sense, then, these Anabaptist communities were the sixteenth century Protestant equivalent of the monastery. They were, in a sense, the "second decision" people, the spiritual athletes, the people who wanted to take the Christian faith and life very seriously and live it to the hilt. They were people who wanted to discover what it meant to take up their cross daily and follow Jesus. Many of them did so, even when it meant death. Thus, in some ways, they were analogous to the early monastic communities. But they married and did not follow an extremely ascetic life style. However they did believe in simplicity.

The Anabaptists often were persecuted as subversives. Society was considered a sacral unit where everyone was a part of both church and state. If one group separated itself from the Church and, by implication, from the society, that act was seen as tearing apart the fabric of society and, thus, was subversive. This is still an issue in many mission situations. For example, in Chiapas state in Mexico, when Protestants refuse to participate in folk-Catholic festivals that involve veneration of favorite saints, use of alcohol, and other practices that go against their beliefs, they are accused of tearing apart their communities.

Anabaptists were looked upon as subversive for a second reason. A radical group went to the city of Munster near the Dutch German border in 1534, and identified itself with the Anabaptists. Others flocked to join them. They proclaimed the city to be the New Jerusalem, and drove out all who did not agree with them. They established polygamy, instituted community of goods, and killed opponents. Catholics and Lutherans fought against them, conquered the city, and killed the leaders. The event was a catastrophe for Anabaptism in Germany. However, the events in Munster were really a betrayal of the movement's principles and practice.

This introduces you to the Anabaptists. Now we will examine their history.

Anabaptist Beginnings in Zürich

Go back to the sixteenth century a few years after Luther had posted his ninety-five theses.

Many new ideas are being advocated. The most important concepts are justification by faith, the authority of Scripture, now much more available in the vernacular languages, and the priesthood of all believers. Many are rejecting the older medieval church and advocating new ideas about theology and church structure. Luther was not the only leader. There were many others, but none except Huldreich Zwingli approached him in ability and stature.

Whereas Luther was more of a medieval man, a monk who became a reformer, his contemporary, Zwingli, had studied under a number of humanists and could be characterized as a Christian humanist. In 1519, he was appointed the priest in Zurich, and began to read the works of Luther. Zwingli was unwilling to admit any debt to Luther, and the personalities and experience of the two men were very different. From 1522 to 1525, through a series of acts by city leaders and public debates led by Zwingli, Zurich adopted the Reformation. Zwingli taught that only that which the Scriptures commands or for which clear authorization can be found within its pages, is binding or allowable in the Church.

Zwingli worked with the city government to reform the Church. In a debate in 1523, he advocated the immediate abolition of images and the mass. The civic leaders did not allow him to go that far. However, other, younger leaders in the city were much more impatient for church reform. Among them were Conrad Grebel and Felix Manz, both from prominent families. Two issues arose among them. The first issue was, "What should be the role of the government in reforming the Church?" It is important to understand the historical context for this question. Luther was protected by Frederick the Elector of Saxony, who was a strong Roman Catholic. Frederick the Elector did not understand what Luther was about, but he was proud of his university and its professors, and consequently refused to hand Luther over to those who wished to eliminate him. It is ironic that a Roman Catholic prince in Saxony protected Luther. Without that protection of the state, Luther would have been martyred immediately. Calvin, of course, had the cooperation of a city-state that had declared itself to be Reformed. Zwingli was working with the government of a city that had also declared itself to be Reformed. However, "Reformed" still had to be defined! So what would happen when the religious reformer, following the Scriptures, wanted to go further than the civic government allowed? Who should make the decision? Was the government an adequate instrument in Church reform? In addition, if Scripture and the government seemed to disagree on a specific issue, which should be obeyed?

The second, more specific, issue was infant baptism. As Grebel, Manz, and others read the Bible, they concluded that there was no warrant for it. They were not the only ones. Balthasar Hubmaier, who had a doctorate in theology and was pastor in nearby Waldshut, came to reject infant baptism and discussed the question with Zwingli. Now priests in two nearby villages stopped baptizing infants.

Grebel wrote to Luther, Karlstadt, and Müntzer, all reformers, asking for counsel. The basic argument of Grebel and Manz was that if the Word of God was their only authority, the government could not be a proper instrument of church reform. They received no reply. On January 17, 1525, the two men publicly debated Zwingli on the question of infant baptism. The following day the city authorities ordered all parents to have their children baptized and demanded that Grebel and Manz stop arguing against the practice. This decision appeared to them to contradict directly the Word of God. So, on January 21, a small group met in a home and, after prayer, ignoring their infant baptism, Grebel baptized George Blaurock, who then baptized the others. This implied the rejection of the validity of infant baptism and the affirmation of believers' baptism alone.

Spread, Consolidation, Persecution

The group of baptized adults formed a believers' church, some were ordained, and the movement began to spread rapidly in rural Zürich, Basel,

and St. Gall. By the middle of 1525, there were Anabaptist groups in most areas of Switzerland. Hübmaier baptized three hundred followers in Waldshut by Easter. He had to flee, and went to Moravia where thousands were baptized. (We wonder if the response there was at least partly a carryover from the Hussite movement a century earlier.) The movement spread from German-speaking Switzerland to Austria, southeast Germany, Strassburg, and into the Netherlands. Often, fifteenth century movements that sought a deeper spiritual life had prepared the way. There were many who spread the message: some were scholars and some were very common people—merchants, traders and others—without much formal education. Apparently, it was a genuine people's movement.

Zwingli continued to lead the reformation in Zurich, and was eventually killed in battle. He differed from Luther especially on the question of the presence of Christ in the Eucharist, but he also differed strongly with the Anabaptists.

Persecution soon began. In 1527, Manz was martyred in Zurich by drowning. Grebel escaped the same fate by dying of the plague. A number of others were martyred in Lutheran and Roman Catholic areas. Tragically, drowning was considered an appropriate way of martyring Anabaptists, who by this time practiced immersion. The basic accusation against the Anabaptists was "sedition against the state": they were seen as tearing its unity asunder, a civil crime. The Anabaptist movement consolidated, but there was danger of disintegration, because there was no centralized structure and no central leaders. However, in February, 1527, at Schleitheim, on the German-Swiss border, a group of Anabaptists met and adopted seven principles, known as the Schleitheim Articles.

The first three Articles spoke of church membership, baptism, the Lord's Supper, discipline, and the ban. The movement held a very high standard of discipline: those who did not live in a manner consistent with the Anabaptist understanding of the Christian lifestyle, would be banned—expelled from the community. The other Schleitheim articles focused on separation from the world, leadership standards based on I Timothy for the pastor, and church-state relations. They would not engage in violence, nor accept the protection of the government, and they would not take any oaths. They had a very simple creed. It was so simple that an uneducated person could understand it, propagate it, and, if necessary, die for it. Most of those who met at Schleitheim were martyred within a few months or years.

The Mennonites

The most prominent Anabaptist movement that continues to this day is known as the Mennonites. The name "Mennonite" came from Menno Simons, a Roman Catholic priest in Holland. After studying the Bible and the ideas of the Reformation, he became convinced that the Reformation was indeed correct, but that Luther and Calvin were wrong on the question of baptism. The fall of the city of Münster in 1535 in some ways left the Anabaptist movement in ruins because of the violation of so many Anabaptist principles by the leaders there. Immediately after the fall of the city, Simons was baptized and joined the movement. This very heroic man began an itinerant ministry that took him over wide areas of Northern Europe.

He lived as a fugitive and outlaw in the Netherlands, in Germany, and often went to Denmark, where a Lutheran nobleman protected him. He often stayed with him in safety before returning to his itinerant ministry. He spent the rest of his life visiting isolated Anabaptist groups, teaching, preaching, evangelizing, and writing. He organized congregations; he wrote much of their theology, and became the most outstanding leader of the movement in the Netherlands and northern Germany. In time, the Mennonite Church took its name from him.

The Mennonite Church still exists in Holland, apparently as a small group without much vitality. Later, Mennonites were invited to Prussia by

Frederick the Great to help develop agriculture, and were given exemption from military service. Others went to Russia under similar conditions. From Russia some came to Canada and, eventually, the United States. There are also Mennonite communities in Brazil and Paraguay. Along the way, they divided into a number of different groups.

It is interesting to note that some of the Russian-German Mennonites who have returned to Germany have expressed concern about the corrosive effects of secularism in Germany, not wanting to raise their children in that environment. Some have wanted to return to Russia where the movement has been persecuted for decades, believing that there it would be easier to keep separate from the broader society.

I once met a Mennonite missionary in Brazil who was from Kansas. He said, "My family can trace its pilgrimage from Kansas back to Canada to Russia to Prussia to Holland." All the way back!

The Mennonites raise an interesting question for all Christians. What does it mean to be separate from the world? What relationship should the Church, and Christians, have with the world? Does it mean that we should not be involved in politics, or commerce, or developing technology? Does it mean we should dress differently? Or is separation from the world primarily a matter of having different goals, values, and lifestyles? At one extreme we have the Amish, who retain a lifestyle of an earlier century and remain very isolated from those they call "the English." They have their own unique dress, drive buggies drawn by horses, and only marry within the group. They cannot use automobiles, and do not allow telephones in the homes, although some can use a public phone or have one in the barn for work. Their religion seems to focus primarily on their lifestyle. There seem to be many rules about what is permitted and what is not. But the great majority of Mennonites today live like most of their contemporaries, except that often they focus on lives of simplicity and are pacifists. Their witness for peace has been impressive.

To what extent were the Anabaptists missionary? Certainly more than the Lutherans, and probably more than the Calvinists. However, the difference was not as great as some have suggested. Luther and Calvin worked with a Christendom model of the Church and society, as we have seen. The Anabaptists rejected that model. Thus, mission for Lutherans and Calvinists consisted primarily of winning the political leaders and changing the theology and structure of the existing Church. However, Calvinist missionaries went to hostile areas such as France and Holland where, under persecution, they planted their communities in the midst of Roman Catholic dominated areas. The Anabaptists, with their understanding of the Church as gathered communities of adult believers, had a different understanding of mission. Their mission was to win whomever they could—Catholic, Lutheran, or Calvinist—to their understanding of the Christian life, to adult commitment and baptism, and to their gathered Christian communities. To the Anabaptists, all of Europe was a mission field. In many areas the Anabaptists became popular movements among the common people and like the early Methodists and later the Pentecostals, spread the faith by the laity, not just by the ordained leaders.

Lutherans or Calvinists would call this "proselytism," but Anabaptists would call it "evangelism": bringing people to genuine faith. Therefore, the Anabaptist missionary movement came out of a different view of the Church and its relationship to the state, a different view of the Christian life and, consequently, a different view of mission. They were no more cross-cultural than the Calvinists or Lutherans because they did not move beyond Europe.

Thus, our view of the Church will have a great impact on our understanding of mission. Often Evangelicals have not adequately thought through their understanding of the Church. But that understanding of ecclesiology will determine both the goals and methodology of mission to a significant extent. We do believe strongly in the Church. We believe that people are not genuinely evangelized until they are part of a body of believers. What that body of believers should look like, how it should govern itself, what its relationship should be to other groups of believers—these are important questions we must consider if we are to remain faithful today.

An important part of our life-long theological and missiological pilgrimage will be to discover a genuinely biblical view of the Church and our place in it. That, of course, was an important part of the struggle in the sixteenth century.

Understanding of the Church and Missionary Outreach

As we have seen in comparing the Anabaptists and Lutherans, our definition of the Church and the Christian life will largely determine our understanding of mission. We see that a more personal understanding of faith in the early Church moved to a primarily institutional understanding after the fourth century. When Franciscans and Dominicans went to Nestorians, they believed the Nestorians were outside of the Christian faith and the Kingdom of God because they were outside of the true Church. Their theology, and that of the Roman Catholic Church until the Second Vatican Council, was that outside of the Church of Rome there was no salvation. In that view, it is no exaggeration to say that the personal faith and theology of a person was irrelevant if he or she was not a member of the Roman Church. As we have seen, Lutherans and Calvinists in sixteenth-century Europe saw their mission primarily as reforming the theology, worship, and structure of the Church, with the hope that through a Reformed church, people would come to vital personal faith. Anabaptists understood their mission as winning those whom they perceived as nominal Christians to genuine personal faith. I do not believe the goals of Lutherans, Calvinists, and Anabaptists were different, but their methods were.

I had to face that issue as a Protestant missionary in the largest Roman Catholic country in the world. While ninety-five percent of the population said they were Catholics at that time, less than ten percent went to church even once a year. Thus, I understood my mission as evangelizing people who, even though they called themselves Catholic, demonstrated little or no understanding of the Gospel or commitment to Jesus Christ.

Chapter Sixteen

The Catholic Reformation and Mission

Devotional

I will quote two passages that have been very important to me. I hope they will be important to you, also. The first is from Exodus chapter 19. The Exodus was the defining event in the formation of the ancient people of God, Israel. In it, they were liberated, received their identity, and at Sinai were given directions about how they should live. The New Testament writers saw the cross and resurrection as the new Exodus: the greater Exodus of the new People of God that would eventually include men and women from every race, language, and culture. In the cross and resurrection, the new People of God are liberated from sin and death, and receive direction for the future. Now listen to God speaking to the people:

> Now if you will obey me and keep my covenant, you will be my own people. The whole earth is mine, but you will be my chosen people, a people dedicated to me alone, and you will serve me as priests. (Exod. 19:5–6 GNT.)

In 1 Peter 2, the Apostle picks up on that Exodus theme:

> But you are the chosen people, a royal priesthood, a holy nation, God's special possession, that you may declare the praises of Him who called you out of darkness into his wonderful light. Once you were not a people, but now you are the people of God. Once you had not received mercy, but now you have received mercy. (1 Pet. 2:9–10 NIV)

If the ancient people of God were constituted primarily (but never exclusively) by race (the Jews), the new people of God are constituted not by race, culture, or language, but by one fact alone: that Jesus Christ has died and risen again and that we have heard his call and responded to him by faith. The New Testament message universalized the People of God, not in the sense of universal salvation, but in the sense that men and women of every race, language, and culture are called to become part of this new People. It follows that the purpose of this new People of God is to proclaim the marvelous works of him who called us out of darkness into his marvelous light. This shows the primary purpose of the Church!

The ancient People of God were to be a kingdom of priests. A priest is one who stands with one hand in the hand of God and the other in the hands of the people. A priest was to be a link between God and the people; the word for "priest" in Latin is *Pontifex* (bridge builder). We are to be a kingdom of priests. The missionary implications of this concept are powerful.

I encourage you to continue to reread the Scriptures, both Old and New Testaments, with the following question in mind: What does the passage tell us about our mission to the world, our understanding of the nature of the Christian life, and the purpose of the Church? Part of the Good News, as Luke shows us in the closing chapter of his Gospel, is not simply that Jesus Christ came, died on the cross, and rose from the dead, but that this message of forgiveness and reconciliation will be proclaimed to all nations, all *ethne*! In a fragmented world, where we build many racial, cultural, ideological, political, and national barriers, Jesus Christ came to destroy those barriers and call us into his body, to be his agents of reconciliation in the world. Our task, then, is to continue to proclaim the Good News out to all the cultural, geographical, racial, and national edges, until people of every race, language, and culture are included in the People of God. This is to be the controlling concept of our lives.

Let us pray together.

> Father, again we know that you have called us to be part of this expanding, multicultural, multilingual, multiracial People of God. We pray that you help us to keep balance. On the one hand, deep gratitude for the call to be a part of this people; on the other hand, our recognition that there are many yet to be called, and that you give us the privilege and responsibility of continuing to push out the edges, to be your instruments, part of what you are doing in the world to include more and more people in your Kingdom. Continue to stretch each one of us, to increase our vision. Draw us closer to yourself and guide us as we seek to be faithful. We ask this in the name of Jesus Christ. Amen.

Introduction

The best book available on pre-Vatican II Roman Catholicism is *The Riddle of Roman Catholicism*, by Jaroslav Pelikan (New York: Abingdon, 1969). Now we will examine the Catholic Reformation and missionary movement in the sixteenth century. The rest of this course will focus on Protestant missionary movement. The first half of this book focused on the early and medieval church. This is important because most Protestants know little about some important movements of the Spirit that took place in those periods. However, most or all of us are heirs of the Protestant Reformation or later movements of renewal that originated within Reformation churches.

Many historians speak of the Catholic "Counter-Reformation." This term is not completely correct; it suggests that the Reformation in the Roman Catholic Church came only as a reaction against Protestantism. That is not correct. There were a number of movements seeking reform in the Roman Catholic Church long before Luther. But for the most part, the reforms they sought were administrative, moral, and spiritual, but not theological. There were movements of prayer seeking a deeper spiritual life in Spain and Italy, along with Bible study groups in France and Italy. Unfortunately, the papacy and hierarchy remained unaffected by them. However, after the Protestant movement, and primarily in response to it, there was a movement in the Catholic Church that we call the "Catholic Reformation." The term "Counter-Reformation" is used to emphasize its negative response to Protestantism, but it is correct to use the term "Catholic Reformation" because it included administrative, moral, and educational reforms.

Characteristics

As we have noted, the Catholic Reformation did not include theological reform. It reaffirmed—in fact, narrowed—the theological focus of the medieval church.

Dr. Georges Barrois, a former Dominican priest and professor at Princeton Theological Seminary, described that "narrowing" process. In the medieval church, he said, the limits of acceptable theology were wide. One might hold some ideas that we would consider biblical, and quite different from traditional Roman Catholic sacramentalism. The most important issue was loyalty to the Church and papacy. There was some theological flexibility as long as one was loyal.

However, in the sixteenth century, he said, in reaction to Protestantism, the Church greatly narrowed the limits of acceptable doctrine. Some in the Roman Church had already advocated many of the ideas that Luther and others espoused, perhaps with some danger, but those who advocated such ideas remained in the Church. Now, after Luther, the Church did not broaden and accept some Protestant ideas. Rather, it reacted against the Protestant movement by narrowing and denying any possibility of justification by faith alone. The Church insisted that one could only be justified by faith plus good works. It reaffirmed the necessity and validity of the seven sacraments, the primacy of the papacy and the hierarchy, and anathematized any taint of Protestant. This took place primarily at the Council of Trent, which met from 1545 to 1563.The Council was Rome's primary response to the Protestant Reformation. The Roman Church continued in a very reactionary mode against Protestantism until the middle of the twentieth century.

In 1854, the dogma of the immaculate conception of the Virgin Mary was promulgated, and in 1864 came the Syllabus of Error.The first declared that to be a good Roman Catholic, one had to believe that the Virgin Mary was conceived without original sin. The Syllabus of Errors was not quite in the category of absolute dogma, but it rejected modern concepts of the separation of church and state, religious freedom, universal education, and even democratic government. Then from 1869 to 1870 came the first Vatican Council. It proclaimed the infallibility of the pope when he spoke *ex catedra* (from his chair) on matters of faith and morals.

Pope John XXIII came as a great surprise. He was expected to be a caretaker Pope, making little change. He surprised almost everyone when he convened the Second Vatican Council (1962–1965). His goal was to begin a process of opening up the Church to the modern era, and, to some extent, to other Christian churches, including Protestants.

The council invited Protestant observers and even requested their counsel on some issues. It initiated a process that continues today, but not without setbacks. Vatican II did not change any doctrines of the Church, but it changed its posture and direction. For example, for the first time, it endorsed Bible societies. It now referred to Protestants as "separated brethren." Some believe it diminished the focus on Mary and the use of images.

When I was doing doctoral study in Princeton Theological Seminary in 1965, Hans Kung, a well-known Roman Catholic theologian, came to lecture there. It was the first time, as far as I

know, that a Roman Catholic had been invited to do so. One of my professors told an interesting story. In his doctoral dissertation, Kung had compared the doctrine of justification in the Council of Trent and in the work of Karl Barth, the great Protestant theologian. Kung's conclusion: the two were teaching the same doctrine of justification by faith. Kung sent a copy of his dissertation to Barth, who read it and then replied, "My dear Hans Kung, you have understood my thought on justification by faith. However, if Trent taught the same thing back in the sixteenth century, why hasn't anyone discovered it until now?"

That was a way of saying that the Roman Catholic Church can change, and does change. Not all of the change is necessarily good. Yet certainly, that church is very different today—what can be believed and practiced is very different—from the Church of fifty years ago. There are still very great differences in faith and practice between Roman Catholics and evangelical Protestants, but we are seeing some positive change today and it is important for us to be aware of it.

However, the Roman Catholic Church is in a crisis in Latin America. Evangelical Protestantism, primarily Pentecostalism, has been growing rapidly and continues to grow at twice the rate of population growth. Only a small minority of the population can be considered "practicing" Catholics. In Brazil, the Church is distributing the Bible for the first time, and the Charismatic movement has been growing in some areas. However, the hierarchy has not been able to end the decline in the Roman Church. An American Jesuit wrote in 1968, "We Roman Catholics came and 'Christianized' the people. But the continent still needs to be converted to Christ. We need to learn from the Pentecostals."(Klaiber, Jeffrey, "Pentecostal Breakthrough," *America*, CXXII4 Jan 31, 1970, p.99)

Not all Roman Catholics would agree with him, but it was a remarkable statement.

To a significant extent, the Roman Church is in the process of redefining itself. That will take a long time, but it is happening. How far it will go, we cannot say. However, it is significant that recently, the Lutheran World Federation and the Roman Catholic Church have agreed on a statement of justification by faith.

We return to the Catholic Reformation. As I indicated, it became doctrinally narrower and rejected any Protestant tendencies. It began to advocate biblical studies, but only for the scholars whom the Church trusted, not for the masses.

The Inquisition was strengthened and reorganized in 1542. There was administrative and moral reform. The immorality and corruption among the hierarchy and clergy decreased. The Catholic Reformation also brought educational reform and more preaching.

Two Main Instruments

The first instrument of the Catholic Reformation was the Council of Trent, which met from 1545 to 1563. Luther had asked for a Council of the Church, but by the time the Council was convened, it was under the domination of the papacy and the Jesuits.

The Jesuits and the renewed Dominican and Franciscan orders was the other main instrument of reform. They brought better preaching, education, and mission to the Church. By medieval standards, the papacy was renewed. During the Renaissance, some popes had led armies, fathered illegitimate children, and in general exploited their office for personal gain. That changed. After Trent, most popes lived lives consistently with their ideals of piety.

Renewed Papacy

Administration was improved, which meant the papacy was stronger. There was a greater focus on piety, but there was no compromise with Reformation theology. Trent clearly rejected any Protestant doctrines. The concept of Scripture alone as authority was rejected. Authority was lodged both in Scripture and tradition. But the Roman Church alone had the right to interpret Scripture. Justification was not by faith alone; it was by faith and good works. The seven medieval sacraments were again defined in the medieval way: *ex opera operato.* That is, the Church taught that grace came

almost automatically (and exclusively) through the sacraments unless the recipient purposely resisted that grace. The sacraments were baptism, confirmation, mass, confession, ordination, matrimony, and extreme unction. With the exception of baptism under extreme circumstances, the sacraments could only be administered by a priest who had been ordained by a bishop who was subordinate to the Pope and thus stood in what was believed to be apostolic succession. This meant that for all practical purposes, saving grace could only come to a person through the Roman Church.

The Emerging New World

However, a new world was emerging. If a visitor from Mars came to earth slightly before the end of the fifteenth century and looked over its civilizations and peoples, there's no way he or she could have predicted that very soon, Western European culture, with its rather small population and area, would suddenly burst out of its bounds geographically, and begin to dominate the world militarily, economically, politically, and culturally for several centuries. Nevertheless, it began to happen just before the end of the fifteenth century.

Europe Bursting Its Bounds

European influence was expanding far beyond its boundaries. For nearly a thousand years, Islam had been stronger militarily and culturally. Chinese civilization was higher in many respects. Now the world was moving into a period when European technology and culture would become dominant.

Today that period has ended. Globalization is the key word now. None of us understands all that this means for technology, commerce, political and social developments, and mission. But clearly, we have entered a new era. And I believe this new era has far more positive aspects for Christian mission than negative.

New Factors

The Church had to face a number of new factors. When we come to the end of a historical era and experience great change, we must always ask, "What does this mean for Christian mission, for the way we carry out the mission?" These are issues we need to struggle with all our lives. First, let us look at new factors in the world.

As the Church moved outside of Europe, it had to face the challenge of the great religious systems of the Far East, India, and the Muslim world. (Many of our contemporary missiological issues begin to emerge.) First, the Church needed to think through its attitude toward tribal peoples. Should their cultures be destroyed, and the people often almost destroyed in the process? That often happened when European culture, which considered itself "civilized," was imposed on so-called "primitive" peoples. Should these cultures be preserved as they were, eliminated, or transformed in some respects? In addition, how should such decisions be made, and by whom? Were there elements in receptor cultures that should have been incorporated into the Church's practice and communication of the Christian faith? These questions would arise as European culture and church spread to new areas, and of course they are still with us today.

The Church as Part of European Culture
Earlier I spoke of a friend who told me that when his grandfather became the first Christian in his tribe, he had to give up his Kenyan name and dress and adopt a European name and dress, because European names and dress were "Christian." That reflected a common attitude.

European culture was considered "Christian," and thus Christian faith was identified with European "civilization." Most Europeans did not distinguish between their faith and their culture. The reasoning, perhaps implicitly, went like this: "We are Christian; our culture is Christian; therefore, the way we do things is Christian. If you become a Christian, you will dress and worship like we do." This mindset represented Acts 15 in reverse. Many who are from the non-Western world can probably tell some painful stories about such assumptions.

Reversing the situation of the first three centuries, the Church now saw itself as going from the powerful to the powerless—from a superior, "Christian" culture, to those that were inferior. Paul certainly did not see himself that way as he

went from Jerusalem to Rome. While Paul certainly believed in the superiority of Jewish culture over Roman paganism, he knew he was going from a small provincial city, seen as a backwash by the Empire, to the very center of that Empire. He went to proclaim the message of the Creator God who had become a man, a servant, and gone to a cross. The process of going from a powerless culture to one that saw itself as all-powerful certainly fit the message of Jesus Christ, who, being in the form of God, emptied himself and went to the cross! Now, as Europeans took the Christian faith to Asia, Latin America, and later, Africa, the missionaries went as men and women coming from powerful cultures and states, to those who were seen as powerless. We need to ask how that distorted the Gospel message.

Soon questions about indigenous church leadership would arise. How soon could a man from a tribal group become a pastor, and could only men be pastors or priests? How soon could newly established churches become autonomous? Two centuries passed before the Spaniards and Portuguese began to ordain any indigenous Latin American peoples to the clergy or allow them to enter the monasteries. The clergy were all European for the first two centuries. It was not until 1794, three centuries after the arrival of the Spanish, that the first man who had no European blood was ordained as a priest. That is one reason the Catholic Church is so weak in Latin America. One criterion of whether or not a church is genuinely indigenous is that it provides its own leadership. By that criterion the Roman Church has never become fully indigenous in Latin America. It still suffers from a great shortage of priests, and many who are there come from Europe. In addition, there was never a sufficient number of priests from Portugal and Spain during the colonial era.

When the need for indigenous church leadership was recognized, another question arose. What would be the requirements for ordination? Would a church leader need a completely European-style theological education? What relationship would the indigenous pastors or priests have to the missionaries? (Missionaries remained in control of the Catholic Church in Latin America for a long time.) And what relationship should the Church in Latin America have to the mother church in Spain, Portugal, or Rome? What forms of worship and structures of theology were permissible?

A whole host of new questions arose when the Roman Catholic missionaries took their message from Europe to Asia or Latin America. Their typical mode of operation was to reproduce the structures they knew at home: the theologies, the methods of selecting and training clergy, the style of worship. That was the natural mode of operation for the early Roman Catholic missionaries to Latin America, as it would be for Protestants who came later.

The movie "Mission," which depicts the early Jesuit mission in Paraguay and Southern Brazil, is very powerful. We see some indigenization there, but not very much. The Jesuit missionaries were admirable in many ways, but the movie shows tribal people worshipping in Latin in the jungles of Paraguay, using European musical instruments. The movie raises important missiological issues. How much of the structure, worship, and theology of the new church should be imported from Europe? How much should arise out of the cultural context?

A third point was that now the Church went as part of the general movement of western European culture to Asia, Africa, and Latin America. That had its advantages. It provided the missionaries with transportation and a degree of protection. But it had disadvantages. For one thing, the missionary often had to battle on two fronts: he had to struggle against the paganism of the European nominal Christians who were there, and he had to battle against the paganism of the people to whom he went. The paganism of the nominal Christians was probably a harder problem to deal with than that of the receptor people.

How would they deal with the temptation of the missionary to rely on Western governments for protection? That would become a big issue, especially in China. Then, there was the identification of the missionary, and therefore the Christian faith, with Western culture. How closely would both the missionaries and the people to whom they went identify the Christian faith with that culture?

Fortunately, today we are moving into an era when many people will no longer see Christianity primarily as a Western religion. Africans, Asians, and Latin Americans increasingly take the Gospel to unreached peoples. New, non-Western forms of the Church are emerging. However, when the missionary movement from Europe and North America began, there was a close identification between Western culture and Christian faith. This was ironic because, of course, Jesus was born in Asia and visited Africa, but never Europe (and certainly not North America). Yet he would come to be seen as a European or North American figure in many cultures because of the missionaries. I am not criticizing the missionaries; what other options did they have? It is easy for us, speaking from the safe vantage point of history, to say that they should have been more sensitive to non-Western cultures, but we must be careful not to judge them too harshly. To a significant extent, they were prisoners of their own culture and historical context, just as we are. However, even if we wish to criticize them on some issues, we must also recognize their great heroism. Most went out, knowing they would never see their homelands or families again.

The "Discoveries"

Late in the fifteenth century, Europe moved into the period of the "discoveries," when Europeans began to cross oceans and eventually circumnavigate the globe. Sagres is a town on the south Portuguese coast. There lie the ruins of the School of Navigation founded by Prince Henry the Navigator, in the fifteenth century. If you visit the beautiful church at Batalha, on the main highway north of Lisbon, you may see his tomb.

Henry was a devout Christian—almost a monastic figure. He never married. He had great interest in the science of navigation. In the fifteenth century, he founded his School of Navigation, brought the best students of navigation there, and developed new techniques and instruments. Great explorers studied there: Vasco da Gama, Pedro Cabral, Christopher Columbus, and Magellan.

Henry's encouragement of the study of navigation had a major impact on world history. He was motivated by four factors. First, he had a scientific frame of mind. Second, he wanted to extend the influence of the Portuguese royal house. Above all, however, the explorations may be understood as a continuation of the Crusades. Islam had defeated the Christians in their frontal attack, but the explorations were an attempt to outflank Islam by sailing around Africa and discovering another route to the fabled riches of the Indies. Fourth, they would seek to Christianize the peoples in the areas they reached.

Do you remember how schoolbooks, at least those in the West, pictured the ships of Columbus and the other explorers with crosses on their sails? As Latin Americans have observed, they were going "for gold and souls," in that order. Normally monks and priests were on board the ships. If you visit Salvador, Bahia, one of the oldest cities in Brazil, you will see a large mural depicting the arrival of Cabral in 1500. The mural shows the Portuguese priests, soldiers, and sailors celebrating mass immediately after arriving, with the indigenous people watching.

So a major goal of the explorations done by the Spanish and Portuguese was to outflank Islam, both religiously and economically. The Roman Catholic missions were carried out in that context. This helps us understand many of the problems of church and state in Latin America even today. Many of the current issues in Latin America have their roots in the colonization by Spain and Portugal in the sixteenth century.

Loyola, 1491-1556, and the Jesuits

As we have seen, the Roman Catholic missionary movement accompanied the explorations. The last Moorish rulers were defeated and expelled from Iberia in 1492, the year that Columbus sailed. Both countries, Portugal and Spain, were unified around the Roman Catholic faith. In the perception of the people and their leaders, to be truly Spanish or Portuguese was to be Catholic! That was one reason for the great burst of Roman Catholic missions. Another reason was the leadership of one of the greatest figures in the history of the Roman Church: Ignatius Loyola. He was a Basque from the part of northern Spain that is still trying to be independent today. He was a soldier, wounded in a siege at Pamplona, and could no longer follow his chosen profession. During a time of isolation, prayer, and meditation in a monastery, he went through a period of spiritual conflict somewhat similar to that of Luther. However, he came to a very different solution. Luther was led to reexamine the Scriptures, arrive at a new understanding of the Gospel, and break with Rome. Loyola, however, moved in the opposite direction, and was led to great devotion to the papacy. He adopted a disciplined spiritual life, and established an organization with the strongest spiritual discipline of any Roman Catholic order. His order, the Society of Jesus (the Jesuits), would be completely devoted to the pope.

Loyola read *The Imitation of Christ* by Thomas a Kempis along with other works. He made a complete confession to a priest, gave away his clothes, took a vow of chastity and poverty, and began to live a very ascetic life. He fasted, prayed, cared for the sick, and begged for his food. As he did so, he worked out his spiritual exercises. They have been compared to military discipline adapted to the spiritual life.

Loyola went to Palestine hoping to be a missionary to the Muslims. He was sent back. He then went to Alcalá and began to preach to the poor. The hierarchy was suspicious, did not trust him, and put him in jail. He was forbidden to preach for three years.

Again we note that out of the three greatest Roman Catholic missionary orders, laymen established two. Loyola was a layman when he founded the Jesuits. Francis was a layman when he established the Franciscans. We always need to remember this when new mission groups arise, often led by men and women with few if any ecclesiastical or academic credentials.

Despite rejection and prison, Loyola remained a loyal son of the Church. Finally, he went to the University of Paris, where he studied from 1528 to 1535. He was a contemporary of John Calvin there, but probably they never met. There he gathered a nucleus of young men around him. Francis Xavier was among them. In 1534, the year of Calvin's conversion, Loyola and his six companions formed the Society of Jesus. They took vows and determined they would go to the Holy Land as missionaries, or wherever the pope might send them. Xavier told other students in Paris, "Give up your small ambitions and come with me to Asia!"

Six years later, the pope approved the society as an order, an army of the Church. This was their vow: to be "obedient to the pope for the good of souls and the propagation of the faith" in whatever countries he might wish to send them, "whether to Turks or other infidels, to India, to lands of heretics, schismatics [that meant Protestants], or faithful Christians" (Kenneth S. Latourette, *A History of Christianity* [San Francisco: Harper-San Francisco, 1975 Revised Edition], 847). It was a great missionary vision! We disagree with the Jesuits on a number of issues, but must recognize their great missionary vision from the very beginning. They simply put themselves at the disposal of the head of the Church, as they understood it, to go anywhere and do anything as missionaries.

Some Protestants might wonder whether the Jesuits, who were very dedicated to a narrow stream of belief of the Roman Catholic Church, planted a believing church in the places they went. As a matter of fact, they did. Hundreds of thousands of Roman Catholic Christians remained faithful in Japan in the midst of terrible persecution. They were faithful to their understanding of the Christian faith. We are not judging at this point how biblical they were; we are looking at the missionary dynamics here. It is interesting that a strong evangelical like Herbert Kane, who served with the China Inland Mission in China and taught at Trinity Evangelical Divinity School, spoke of the Jesuit St. Francis Xavier in very glowing terms as a man who loved Christ and was a great missionary.

I am not advocating the Jesuits' theology of mission here, but I do want us to understand the dynamics involved. They were a group of men who believed passionately in the Gospel and the Church as they understood them. Protestants have some important theological differences with the Jesuits. Yet the Jesuits were willing, because of their faith, to put themselves at the disposal of the Church, to go wherever the Church might send them, whatever that might cost, and to do so in the service of Christ, as they understand him. I find that very impressive.

Therefore, even though we feel some ambivalence about Roman Catholic missions, we want to examine them briefly in this chapter. There are important lessons to be learned from some of the best Jesuit missionaries. Some of them dealt with important missiological issues two centuries before Protestants faced them.

Also, changes in the relationship between Protestants and Roman Catholics are taking place today. A Catholic friend who was sympathetic to Protestantism once told me, "I will believe the Roman Catholic Church has really gone a long way toward reformation when it reverses the excommunication of Luther." Some day that will happen. Incidentally, up until the 1920s, Roman Catholic writers depicted Luther as a bad monk who rebelled against the true Church because he wanted to marry. He was always seen in a very negative light. But in the 1920s a German priest, Joseph Lortz, wrote a new book on Luther, *Das Reformation in Deutschland* (The Reformation in Germany), in which he depicted Luther as a sincere man—misguided, in the opinion of Lortz, but still a sincere Christian. Thus, over the last fifty years, the view of Luther in Roman Catholic circles has been changing. As I mentioned earlier, recently the Lutheran World Federation and the Roman Catholic Church have agreed on a statement that we are justified by faith. I can only see this as a reversal of Trent.

Every movement should be understood and evaluated according to its original vision and values, when it shows its greatest vitality. Tragically, in every movement we see the tendency to run down, lose vitality, and even turn its back on its original vision. This has happened to genuine movements of the Spirit in various Protestant groups, also. We saw the Dominicans eventually reversed their original vision and used the sword and fire against "heretics." However, we also will see that Puritanism, originally a renewal movement in Anglicanism, eventually became more concerned with respectability and prosperity than with renewal. In addition, the YMCA, instrumental in initiating the greatest missionary movement in nineteenth-century America, eventually lost almost all of its Christian character. We want to understand and evaluate movements according to their original vision and values, to discover what we have to learn, in their times of greatness as well as their decline. When we look at the early Jesuits, Franciscans, and Dominicans, we see a high level of spiritual discipline and devotion, coupled with deep commitment to mission. We can all profit from these examples!

Specific Mission Fields

Francis Xavier

Now we will look at some of the specific missions of the Jesuits and other Roman Catholics, beginning in the sixteenth century. The man who would be known as St. Francis Xavier went to Asia, where he spent the rest of his life.

Xavier went first to Goa on the Coromandel Coast of India. He described his methodology:

> On Sundays I assemble all the people, men and women, young and old, and get them to repeat the prayers in their language. They take much pleasure in doing so, and come to the meetings gladly ... I give out the First Commandment, which they repeat, and then we all say together, Jesus Christ, Son of God, grant us grace to love thee above all things. When we have asked for this grace, we recite the Pater Noster [the Lord's Prayer] together, and then cry with one accord, 'Holy Mary, mother of Jesus Christ, obtain for us grace from thy Son to enable us to keep the First Commandment.' Next we say an Ave Maria, and proceed in the same manner through each of the remaining nine Commandments.

> And just as we say twelve Paters and Aves in honour of the twelve articles of the Creed, so we say ten Paters and Aves in honour of the ten Commandments, asking God to give us grace to keep them well (Stephen Neill, *A History of Christian Missions* [New York: Penguin Books, 1969], 150).

We might not agree with much of his theology and methodology. Yet Xavier did leave behind him a rather strong Roman Catholic community in India, which continues to this day.

Later, Xavier went to Japan and was part of a group that established a Roman Catholic Church that grew to number three hundred thousand people. Later it was terribly persecuted: thousands of Japanese Catholics were martyred, along with many missionary priests. The Catholic Church was nearly destroyed in Japan, but it did continue underground until modern times. Xavier died, hoping to go into China. He was a man of great vision. The greatest clue to his heart can be seen in a hymn he wrote:

> My God, I love Thee, not because I hope for heaven thereby,
>
> Nor yet because those who love Thee not must die eternally,
>
> Thou, O my Jesus Thou didst me upon the cross embrace,
>
> For me didst bear the nails and spear and manifold disgrace,
>
> Then why, O blessed Jesus Christ, Should I not love Thee well,
>
> Not for the hope of winning heaven or of escaping hell,
>
> Even so I love Thee and will love, and in thy praise will sing,
>
> Solely because Thou are my God and my eternal King (Fred Bock, ed., *Hymns for the Family of God* [Nashville: Paragon Press, 1976], 509).

China

One of the greatest Jesuit missionaries was Matteo Ricci, an Italian who went to China in 1583. This was the third attempt to plant the Church in China. The first attempt, by the Nestorians, was in the early seventh century. In the thirteenth century, Franciscans arrived. In the sixteenth century, Matteo Ricci arrived.

It was very difficult for a European to get permission even to enter the nation. China considered its people and culture superior to all others, not without some reason. Ricci was a genius, and made it his task to learn the Chinese language and classics as well as any Chinese scholar. He also learned to make clocks and maps, so that he would be useful. He spent ten years in the imperial capital, and won respect for his message because he showed such great respect for Chinese culture and traditions. He succeeded in leaving a strong nucleus of Chinese Roman Catholic Christians and some Christian literature in Chinese.

An extremely important missiological issue arose with Ricci: what name to use for God in the Chinese language? This is almost always a critical missiological issue in a new culture.

For example, is it legitimate to call God "Allah"? Arab Christians called God "Allah" before Mohammed did so. Where did the Greek New Testament get its word for God? Right out of Greek paganism! *Theos*. It is not a specifically Christian term. Where did the Old Testament get its names for God? *Elohim*. Yahweh probably was new with the Hebrews, but *Elohim* and *Adonai* were not. They were used in the surrounding religions. My point is that in both the Old and New Testaments, as well as throughout history, the People of God have adopted the names for God used in the surrounding cultures, but then poured new meaning into them. Whatever name we use for God, we believe that God has ultimately defined himself for us in the Incarnation, in Jesus Christ.

When we go into a new culture, we must decide what word is going to be used for God. This is often a very critical and difficult issue. Our Korean brothers and sisters tell us that many feel that one reason for the success of Protestant churches in Korea is that they chose the right name for God.

Ricci got into a struggle with other Roman Catholic orders, and finally with Rome, over the issue. The struggle was whether to use T'ien Chu (Lord of Heaven), Shang-Ti (the King Above), or simply T'ien (heaven). We do not need to go further into the matter, except to say that Ricci faced a very critical missiological issue. The problem for Ricci was that Rome made the decision instead of allowing the Chinese Catholics to do so. That was very prejudicial to the Church in China.

Let me give you another contemporary example as told by a Muslim convert from Bangladesh. In Bangladesh, there exists a small church in which the believers come from a Hindu background rather than from the majority Muslim population. The Bible translation was done for Christians of Hindu background, and therefore used Hindu terminology for God. However, a Muslim reading Hindu terminology for God sees polytheism, because Hinduism is very polytheistic, whereas Islam is rigidly monotheistic. Therefore, the translation of the Christian Bible that used Hindu terminology for God was very offensive to Muslims, and ran the danger of distorting the Christian message to them.

The Bible Society recently did a new translation of the Injil, the New Testament, using Muslim terminology for God and Islamic-style calligraphy on the cover. My friend said it became a best-seller! He said, "I have seen Muslims buy it, hug it to their breast, kiss it, and begin reading it, because it used Islamic terminology for God." Our Bible translator friends deal with these issues. We run across this issue with Matteo Ricci in China. He struggled with Rome over it, and lost his battle. That, of course, raises the question as to who should make such decisions: the outsiders or the insiders.

There are many languages, and many of them are small and close together. Therefore, when translators are trying to find a word to be used for God, there might be three choices. One is to use an indigenous term, which may have so many pagan connotations that it cannot be transferred. Another is to bring a foreign term from outside, from English or Pidgin English for example. The third is to borrow a term from a neighboring language, which the people in this group may be aware of, but which does not hold the problematic connotations of an indigenous term. These are some of the choices that Bible translators often face. It appears that all three of them have been used at different times.

Ricci got involved in a second issue: ancestor veneration. This is another critical missiological issue, especially in Asia and Africa. Ancestor veneration is a way of affirming and expressing the solidarity of the family and giving thanks for one's ancestors. We in the West are far too individualistic, but our brothers and sisters in many other cultures have a strong sense of family through the generations. Here is the issue: are they worshipping their ancestors, or simply showing their respect and gratitude for them? Is it legitimate for a Christian to participate in the veneration of ancestors, which, in some cases, appears to be worship? Is the veneration of ancestors not legitimate? How does one decide? Moreover, who should decide?

This is a very critical issue, one that needs to be considered with a great deal of care. I believe that ultimately, this and similar issues can only be decided by the Christian community in the local culture. Indigenous believers must study the Scriptures to understand the revelation of God, and then think through the meaning of such acts in their culture. An outsider, a missionary, can give orientation, because he or she will probably have a greater understanding of the history of the Church and the way such issues have been dealt with elsewhere. The expatriate missionary, whether from the West or a non-Western culture, can help in understanding the broader questions. Nevertheless, I believe that the Christian community in that context must make the ultimate decisions.

A third issue that Ricci confronted was the question about how Confucius should be viewed by Chinese Christians. Was he a religious leader, or simply a philosopher they could see as someone with useful views?

A large part of our journey to spiritual maturity and to more effectiveness lies in discovering the right questions to ask, and in encouraging others to ask them. We should always be asking questions of ourselves, of God, of the Scriptures, and of our culture as we attempt to shape our lives and the Church in accordance with God's will.

Latin America

Latin America presents a very mixed picture of Roman Catholic missions, much of it not very attractive. Roman Catholic missions were not entirely negative: the Jesuits and some others whom we will mention, sought to protect the indigenous people from the colonists. In general, however, the picture is bleak. The *conquistadores* (conquerors) and priests came in the ships together. They were after gold and souls. There are many horror stories about how gold was more important than souls, even for the priests. They came with mixed motives.

A Brazilian author, Viana Moog, wrote a significant book some years ago. The title in Portuguese is "Bandeirantes ou Pioneiros." *Bandeirante* (flagbearer) referred to the Portuguese who went into the interior of Brazil, carrying their flag. Their goal was to find easily removable riches, which they would take back to Portugal. The *pioneiro* was one who went to settle and build a new community. Moog's thesis was that the goal of the Spanish and Portuguese conquerors in Latin America was not primarily to form new communities, but to exploit the land and its people, then return to Europe with their riches. He said that the first to be called "Brazilians" were not those who settled in the new land, but those who returned to Portugal with the wealth they had accumulated in the Brazilian colony. Moog contrasts them with the Puritans in North America, whose goal was to build a "city set on a hill" that would seek to glorify God and be an example to the world. I do not want to idealize the settlers in North America. However, Moog, a Brazilian, points out two very different attitudes toward the new land.

His thesis is that the goal of acquiring riches resulted in the attitude that the land and its people were there to be exploited by the colonists and much of the Church. There were exceptions to this, but in general, that was the attitude, which is still at the root of many problems today.

Another problem was that a decaying medieval feudalism, which existed in Spain and Portugal, was transferred to Latin America. There were huge land holdings in Latin America, with power concentrated in the hands of a relatively few people who were usually appointed by the European kings. The power base was established very quickly in the hands of a relatively small number of people who have never been willing to give up that power. This is a root of the current struggles in Central America.

There were also mass baptisms. People were baptized very quickly, with very little understanding even of the medieval Roman Catholic faith, let alone of a more biblical faith.

In many cases, the indigenous people, erroneously called "Indians" because the explorers thought they had discovered a new way to India, were forced to live in communities called *reducciones*, or *encomiendas*. The landowner had the rights not only over the land, but also over the indigenous people who lived there. It was a form of slavery. However, some of the religious communities, especially the Jesuit, as we see in the movie *Mission*, took much better care of the indigenous peoples. This provoked the hostility of both the colonists and the other Roman Catholic orders, and was one reason the Pope dissolved the Jesuit order. It was later reestablished.

In general, the colonization and "Christianization" of Latin America in the sixteenth century was a tragic tale of economic and sexual exploitation. Indigenous people died by the thousands, sometimes by the sword, more often by disease and overwork.

One early Franciscan missionary in Mexico wrote in 1529, "I and the brother who was with me baptized in this province of Mexico upwards of 200,000 people—so many, in fact, that I cannot give an accurate estimate of the number. Of-

ten we baptized in a single day 14,000 people, sometimes 10,000, sometimes 8,000."

Remember that sacramental theology says if you are baptized into the proper ecclesiastical institution and are reasonably obedient to that Church, you will go to heaven. With this theology, we can understand why mass baptisms were the rule.

The attitude toward the indigenous people was normally extremely negative. Some argued about whether they had souls. Some theologians believed, following Aristotle, that certain races were created to be slaves. That was a very convenient doctrine. Listen to what one sixteenth-century historian wrote about them.

> They are naturally lazy and vicious, melancholic, cowardly, and in general a lying, shiftless people. Their marriages are not a sacrament but a sacrilege. They are idolatrous, libidinous, and commit sodomy. Their chief desire is to eat, drink, worship heathen idols, and commit bestial obscenities. (Quoted in Neill, *A History of Christian Missions*, 146).

That tragic racist viewpoint of course helped justify the mistreatment of the people. On the other hand, two great Spanish missionaries demonstrated a radically different attitude. One was Antonio de Montesinos, a Dominican. In 1511, he preached a sermon on the text, "I am a voice crying in the wilderness." Listen to his words about the sins of the Europeans:

> Tell me; by what right or justice do you keep these Indians in such cruel and horrible servitude? Why do you keep them so oppressed and weary, not giving them enough to eat nor taking care of them in their illnesses? For with the excessive work you demand of them, they fall ill and die, or rather you kill them with your desire to extract and acquire gold every day. Are these not men? Have they not rational souls? Are you not bound to love them as you love yourselves? Be certain that in such a state as this, you can no more be saved than the Moors or Turks. (ibid., 170).

That was a very courageous sermon!

Bartolome de Las Casas arrived in the new world as a typical priest, not very concerned about the people, but experienced a radical conversion. He became the champion of the indigenous peoples. He may be too idealistic about them, and a bit patronizing, but listen to what he said:

> God created these simple people without evil and without guile. They are most obedient and faithful to their natural lords, and to the Christians whom they serve. They are most submissive, patient, peaceful, and virtuous. Nor are they quarrelsome, rancorous, querulous, or vengeful. They neither possess nor desire to possess worldly wealth. Surely, these people would be the most blessed in the world if only they worshipped the true God (Neill, 171).

Las Casas debated others who said some people were born to be slaves. There is no denying that he was patronizing, and his comments suggest that he held feelings of racist superiority. Nevertheless, he recognized what was happening to the indigenous peoples was wrong. He worked for years to try to achieve better treatment for them, with only partial success.

Of course, as a North American Protestant I must recognize the beam in my own eye before being too quick to criticize the speck in the eye of the Roman Catholic Church in Latin America. After all, many or even most Protestants in North America supported slavery! Judgment should always begin with ourselves!

One of the great weaknesses of the Roman Catholic Church in Latin America today is the high level of religious syncretism. In most cases, there exists a thin veneer of traditional Catholicism over a huge substructure of folk religion. In Brazil today, a large number of people practice spiritism, which is similar to Haitian voodoo. For the great majority of the people, certainly among the poor in the interior, religion is focused on a few saints, with a favorite manifestation of the Virgin Mary as the primary functional deity. Most follow a non-institutionalized Catholicism, which has little or no connection with the Church.

The traditional saying in much of Latin America is that most men only go to church three times in their lives, and they are taken there all three times.

They are taken there to be baptized, to be married, and to be buried. My experience in the interior of Brazil indicated that increasingly the poor are not having their children baptized because they cannot or will not pay for the sacrament. In addition, since the only legal marriage in Brazil is the civil act, people often do not marry in the Church, again for financial reasons. Moreover, in the interior of Brazil I saw few funerals proceeding from the Church. The general feeling of alienation from the Catholic Church is very common among the poor in Brazil. That seems to vary from country to country in Latin America. One result is that in general, the Evangelical churches, mainly Pentecostal, have grown from fifty thousand in 1900 to around seventy million in Latin America today, and continue to grow about twice as rapidly as the population.

Another negative aspect of the Roman Catholic Church in Latin America was the great scarcity of priests. There were almost no indigenous priests in Latin America for two centuries. Only Europeans could enter monastic orders or be ordained to the priesthood. A few mixed-race *mestizos* (part European, part indigenous) were ordained, but it was not until 1794 that three priests who had no European blood were ordained in Lima, Peru. As far as we know, they were the first indigenous priests ordained in Latin America.

The question of celibacy was also an obstacle. The Church taught that celibacy was essential for the clergy, and that it was a higher spiritual state that all clergy should observe. It generally was not observed, just as in the medieval church. The issue of celibacy was especially weighty in a culture that seemed to believe a man was not fully a man unless he was married and had a family. That created a very serious problem. I am not saying no priests observed their vow of celibacy. However, in most Latin American countries, the majority of people do not believe that most priests remain celibate. I knew a Presbyterian elder in Aquidauana, Mato Grosso. His grandfather had been a priest. This Presbyterian elder said, "My grandfather was an honorable man, because he had one wife and one family, and he was faithful."

Such factors led to a great scarcity of priests. A book written by a French priest in the 1930s said that the most urgent problem in Brazil was the lack of priests. Since then, the problem has only gotten worse.

John Considine, a Roman Catholic priest, published his book *Call for Forty Thousand* in the 1940s. He estimated it would take that number of priests to fill the void in Latin America. At the time, there was one active priest for approximately every nine hundred to one thousand Catholics in the United States. However, in Brazil, today there is one priest for every fifteen to eighteen thousand Catholics, and many of those priests are foreign. As far as we can tell, with the population growth and the decline in the number of priests, the problem is getting worse.

I will note one other critical issue: up until the middle of the twentieth century, the Roman Catholic Church in Latin America was always seen as the ecclesiastical bulwark of the status quo. It was heavily identified with the powerful in societies in which there was great disparity between rich and poor; the Church was seen as allied with the great landholders, the military, and absolutist governments.

Then, in 1968, at the Conference of Roman Catholic Bishops of Latin America in Medellín, Colombia, the focus began to shift. We can take that date as the birth of liberation theology. Whatever one may think of many of the theological and ideological aspects of liberation theology, it meant that the Roman Catholic leadership for much of Latin America made a radical shift. They said, "We must not be identified with the status quo in society; we must be identified with the poor."

That led to some important changes in some areas of Roman Catholic thought. While it called to Church to focus more on the problems of injustice and the poor, it was seriously flawed as it used Marxism as its tool of social and economic analysis. It has also led to the perception on the part of more powerful people that the Church has betrayed them. And it created great turmoil and radical divisions within the Latin America Church. It did not succeed in winning the poor, and Pope John Paul II has led the Church in a more conservative direction in appointing new bishops.

India and de Nobili

Another significant Jesuit missionary was de Nobili in India, early in the seventeenth century. He anticipated some of the observations that McGavran made much later in taking homogeneous cultural units seriously. He discovered that the relatively small church there was identified with the lower castes. A Brahmin, a high caste person, would not associate with the Church at all. Therefore, de Nobili became a Brahmin culturally, lived as a Brahmin, and cut himself off from contact with the existing Catholic Church to avoid contamination in Brahmin eyes. He taught that converts did not have to break their caste rules unless these rules involved idolatry. Certainly, he believed that later on there would be unity in the Church, but he felt that as an evangelistic strategy, he had to identify totally with that cultural group in order to win them. There was much more involved in his identification with Indian culture, but that was one of the main aspects—that he studied Indian culture and identified with it in order to win Brahmins to Catholicism. He became an "insider" to a significant extent.

This question of homogeneous units is still controversial today. Do we encourage churches to separate themselves in terms of caste or other social categories? How far should we carry that? De Nobili got into some trouble in Rome, and his methods were eventually rejected, but this missiological issue is still with us today.

New Structures

Governments of Spain and Portugal sponsored and supervised Roman Catholic missions in the sixteenth and seventeenth century. Most missionaries were Jesuits, Dominicans, or Franciscans. That meant divided loyalties on the part of the missionaries. Were they primarily agents of the Church or of their governments? The governments financed the voyages, furnished the ships, and encouraged or ordered priests to go and take possession of these new lands in the name of the king and the Church, which were considered two sides of one coin. Even in Roman Catholic circles, this would raise the question, is the government an adequate agency for sending missionaries and supervising the Church in these countries?

In order to maintain their power, the governments of Spain and Portugal had the authority to appoint bishops in Latin America and in other territories. It was not in their interests to appoint too many bishops, because they might get too powerful and work against the interests of the crown. On the other hand, it was in the Church's best interest to appoint more bishops, to have more pastoral supervision and more priests. Thus, there was tension between the Catholic governments and churches.

There was also great rivalry between the various orders. Some of the infighting among Franciscans, Jesuits, and Dominicans was very destructive. In 1622, the pope created the Sacred Congregation for the Propagation of the Faith. This brought some positive change in Catholic missions. More research was done on the various mission fields and their peoples, and the first secretary of the 'Propaganda,' Francisco Ingoli, took a much more positive attitude toward indigenous cultures. He began to see the need for more indigenous monks, priests, and eventually bishops.

Then, in 1663, as the Roman Catholic center in Europe shifted more to France, the Society for Foreign Missions was inaugurated in Paris and a seminary was established to train Roman Catholic missionaries. France became the main Roman Catholic sending nation, and remained so to the time of the French Revolution.

We will end our brief survey of Roman Catholic missions, except to mention Catholic missions in North America. There were French Jesuits in the heartland of what is now the United States. Some suffered terrible persecution.

Father Junipero Serra, a Franciscan, began work in Mexico and moved with his colleagues up the California coast. These Franciscan missionaries started all of the missions up the California coast in the eighteenth century. Many of the towns and cities in California are named for them: Los Angeles, San Fernando, San Gabriel, San Diego, San Francisco, Santa Barbara, San Luis Obispo, and others. Those Franciscan missionaries had a tremendous influence on the early history of this part of the United States.

It is quite amazing to see how these Roman Catholic missionaries not only went to Latin America, but also to various places in North America and many parts of Asia. We must recognize that they did so two centuries before Protestants went from Germany to India.

Chapter Seventeen

Puritanism and Pietism

Introduction

Now we will begin to examine four movements that began in the seventeenth century, and gained momentum in the eighteenth. They motivated and initiated the Protestant missions that will be our focus for the rest of the book.

Some have used the term, "God's vanguards." Mellis spoke of "committed communities." You may have other words to describe them, but nearly always, we see that an individual or small group that has read the Scriptures more profoundly, listened to God more intently, and sought to obey him more faithfully, has initiated mission movements. They have been the pioneers who moved beyond the narrow, ingrown attitudes of their cultures and churches to follow God's vision for the world. In turn they have led others into mission. We have already encountered some of these people, and we will discover more.

Continue to ask yourself, "Why are some people used by God to make new breakthroughs, while most sit back only to watch?" What are the characteristics of the men and women whom God uses to make new breakthroughs? Dick Hillis went to China under the China Inland Mission before World War II. He saw thousands come to Christ, and trained pastors, but then it appeared that his ministry was over. The Communists expelled him. However, when he returned to the United States, his concern for mission did not wane. Influenced by Billy Graham and others, he went to Taiwan. His ministry evolved into an organization that works in effective ministries with churches in over twenty countries.

It is important to ask why some men and women develop vision that continues to expand. Often God uses them in an extraordinary way. I am convinced it is the result of the way they listen to God in Scripture and prayer, and their willingness to obey him, no matter how strange their ideas appear to their contemporaries. But they not only listen to God, they look out at the world and see needs and possibilities to which most are indifferent or blind. I cannot think of a single new missionary breakthrough in history that did not look impossible at the beginning. Go back and examine history. We look at the mission pioneers, put them on pedestals, and rightly see them as great men and women, yet their contemporaries often dismissed them as dreamers or hopeless fanatics.

Now we will begin to look at four movements led by creative minorities—"God's vanguards." They became the launching pad for the Protestant churches' world missionary movement. The four are Puritanism, Pietism, Moravianism, and the Evangelical revivals of the eighteenth century. The latter included the Wesleyan movement but were much broader in scope. We examine the first two in this chapter.

It is important to emphasize that these were movements of minorities. Many of us are a part of a minority in our own churches and even missions, as we attempt to push out the edges of understanding and obedience to God. When we take such a position, we often feel very lonely. This is typical of visionaries and pioneers.

These four movements had a number of characteristics in common. To a significant extent, they were a continuation of the basic thrust of the Reformation. The most erudite theologian I ever knew was Dr. Otto Piper at Princeton. In the 1930s he was dismissed from his university teaching post by Hitler, and had to leave Germany. He was a very learned yet humble, godly man—a great combination! In a context where many disparaged the Pietist movement, Piper said it was a continuation of the basic impulse that brought the Reformation. It did not represent the Reformation as going astray; on the contrary, it recovered an essential emphasis in Luther that the German Lutheran Church had largely forgotten in the seventeenth century. That was the focus on faith as personal trust and, as a result, a Christian life that led to "faith active in love."

In addition, these movements within the classical Reformation churches—Anglican, Lutheran, and Calvinist, led them to embrace some aspects of the Anabaptist movement that had been rejected in the sixteenth century. Like the Anabaptists they put a greater focus on piety and discipleship, and mission to the world grew out of these emphases.

They also had a great impact on modern concepts of society and the development of the ideas of religious freedom, human rights, and the rise of democracy. John Locke, the philosopher who espoused such ideas in *The Social Contract*, had great influence on English, and indirectly on American culture. He was not a Puritan, but he was influenced by Puritanism. These movements also influenced the educational systems in Germany, England, and the United States.

The four movements arose in different places and denominational situations, but they shared a number of important values. They arose in contexts where everyone was a "Christian," and belonged to an established church. However, with rare exceptions, many did not demonstrate a concern to live as serious disciples. Thus, two emphases of these movements were the importance of conversion and the desire to live an authentic Christian life. Of course, those had been major Anabaptist emphases.

They also focused on the personal use of Scripture. All Protestants accepted Scripture as the only rule of faith, and the source of theology but these movements went further. Was Scripture only the source of theology for the theologians, or was it the Word through which God speaks to us here and now? Could the written Word of God become a personal Word to me? These groups taught their adherents to use the Bible much more personally.

Another important focus, in varying degrees, was on the ministry of laypersons. An important Reformation doctrine was the "priesthood of every believer," but it was a doctrine that, for the most part, had remained on paper. As we will see, the recognition of the gifts of every believer is an essential characteristic of renewal movements. This became a focus, in different ways, in each of these four groups.

Finally, each one soon developed a strong sense of mission. For them, mission included evangelism and ministries of compassion and outreach to the marginalized in their own societies. Then they initiated mission to other continents. In addition, the evangelical revivals led to significant movements of social transformation.

It is helpful to analyze these movements in terms of the key theses of this book. They include theological breakthroughs, or theological rediscoveries; the role of key leaders; new patterns of selecting and training leaders; spiritual dynamics; the importance of understanding historical contexts; and the creation of new mission structures. Puritanism, Pietism, Moravianism, and the eighteenth-century Evangelical revivals all illustrated these theses in diverse ways. Furthermore, I believe all four fit the criteria for renewal movements. We will see that one remained within the established church while the other three left it, partly of their own will, and partly because they were forced to leave.

Puritanism

With these issues in mind, let us look briefly at Puritanism. An excellent book on Puritanism is J. I. Packer's *A Quest for Godliness* (Wheaton, IL: Crossroads Books, 1990). We have not examined the Anglican Reformation in England, but we will outline it here. In 1534, Henry VIII declared that the Church of England was separate from the Church of Rome, and declared himself the head of the Church. He was not interested in either theological or spiritual reform, but he wanted to divorce his wife Catherine, and the Pope would not allow him to do so. Catherine was the aunt of Charles V of Spain, and at the time, the Pope was his prisoner. Naturally, he did not want to offend Charles. Otherwise, he would have granted Henry the divorce as a routine favor.

Therefore, Henry declared the Anglican Church to be separate from Rome. From one perspective, the English Reformation was simply a political act. However, we need to realize that there were men (and, I am sure, some women, who do not appear much in history at this point) at Cambridge and other places, reading Luther and the Scriptures and hoping for genuine reform. The legacy of Wycliffe and the Lollards must have been a factor as well. Thus, there were two streams contributing to the Anglican Reformation: one purely political and the other deeply spiritual and theological.

After Henry died, his son Edward succeeded him. Edward was a young boy and his advisors who were more Protestant in sympathies, moved the Church somewhat in that direction. Edward died in 1553, and Mary, the daughter of Henry and Catherine, came to the throne. Since the Pope had been the protector of her mother, she was ardently Catholic and reestablished Catholicism. At lease three hundred Protestants were burned during her five-year reign, which lasted until 1558. She would be known in history as "Bloody Mary."

During those five years, many English Protestants fled to the European continent, where they studied with Lutherans in Frankfort, Martin Bucer in Strassburg, and John Calvin in Geneva. Naturally, when they returned to England, they brought back the new theological currents they had studied.

In 1558, Elizabeth I came to the throne and ruled until 1603. She was in a precarious situation as a woman on the throne, with some claiming she was an illegitimate daughter of Henry. She was one of the great women of history. Her major concern was to consolidate her authority and unify the nation. England's greatest enemy was Spain. The Spanish Armada, a vast fleet, came in 1588 expecting to re-conquer England for Catholicism. It was defeated by a combination of British seamanship and a storm. The English believed that to be providential.

Therefore, we can understand why Elizabeth wanted a church that would unify the nation. She chose a middle way: not Catholic, but not too Protestant. Many of the church leaders who had studied on the continent now returned and occupied various positions in the Church and universities. Many hoped to move the Church of England in a direction they believed to be more reformed, and more biblical. They wanted to "purify" the Church according to their understanding, and consequently were called "Puritans."

The Goals of Puritanism

When Henry declared the Church of England separate from Rome, he did not make any changes in its structure, theology, or practice. A few changes were made in the Book of Prayer under Edward, but the medieval hierarchical structure continued. The bishops were from the nobility, there was great disparity between ordinary priests and the bishops, and many priests did not live in their parishes. Some were political appointees who did little or no pastoral work. Most had little theological training. Thus, one of the first Puritan principles was that all pastors or priests were equal to each other. Such a radical idea, coming from Calvinism, would abolish the hierarchical system. A second goal was to have a well-trained, godly pastor resident in every parish. The Puritans wanted pastors who would faithfully expound the Scriptures, and thus were strong advocates of education.

In addition, they protested against the use of certain vestments—the special garments the priests used in the mass—because they saw it as a violation of the priesthood of all believers. They protested against the use of wedding rings, saying it implied marriage to be a sacrament. They believed that baptism and the Eucharist, or Lord's Supper, were the only biblical sacraments. However, they held a high view of marriage. They did not believe sex was evil; on the contrary, they wrote some very beautiful love literature. One Puritan wrote that a wife was not a necessary evil, she was a necessary good! Another wrote of his wife as a companion and wise counselor. They believed that sex was a gift of God to be enjoyed in the context of a man and woman who were committed to each other in marriage for life. On one side, they were criticized by Roman Catholics who advocated celibacy for the clergy, and at the other extreme, by libertines!

They protested against the act of kneeling at the Eucharist because it implied the adoration of the host and the doctrine of transubstantiation (the dogma that in the Mass, the bread and wine literally became the body and blood of Jesus Christ). It is always important to ask what meaning lies behind certain symbols and acts. For example, later on, the Quakers broke off from the Puritan movement. A Quaker man would not take off his hat to anyone. Some of us were raised in cultures where men wore hats and it was considered polite to tip one's hat to a woman. Were the Quakers simply rude? No, of course not! In their culture, a man tipped his hat to a person of a higher social class. By refusing to do so, the Quakers were proclaiming that all persons are equal—a profoundly biblical concept! It is always important to understand the meaning of a gesture in its context. Otherwise, we run the risk of serious misunderstanding.

To summarize, the Puritans wanted a church with well-trained pastors who would expound the Scriptures faithfully, leading to a church and nation of men and women who were converted and reflected that reality in private and public life. They advocated a greater role for laymen in governing the Church and advocated small group meetings called "conventicles" for greater biblical study.

Persecution and Controversy

The Puritans were not separatists; they wanted to reform the entire Church of England. However, there was persecution by the government and controversy within the movement. Eventually the Puritans fragmented. Some remained in the Anglican Church; others became Presbyterians, then Congregationalists, Baptists, and Quakers.

Presbyterians advocated an established church governed by pastors and elders, Congregationalists advocated the independence of every local congregation, and Baptists insisted on the autonomy of each local church and the baptism by immersion of adult believers. The Quakers rejected the celebrations of the sacraments, ordained clergy and preaching, and called church buildings "steeple houses." They also gave a greater role to women in the Church and would eventually become pioneers in the anti-slavery movement.

After the death of Elizabeth in 1603, James I came from Scotland to assume the English throne. Son of a Catholic mother but raised as a Presbyterian, he quickly adopted Anglicanism. When a delegation of Presbyterians met him, hoping he would adopt their form of church government, his reply was "Presbytery agrees with monarchy as well as God agrees with the devil." He wanted no part of a church government with lay participation! He was responsible for the King James translation of the Bible in 1611. Under his son, Charles I, controversy increased. Heavy taxation and insistence on the divine right of kings led to alienation among country landowners, parliament, and Puritans on one hand, and the King, nobility, and bishops on the other. Revolution came in 1642, led by Oliver Cromwell, an ardent Congregationalist. The revolution was successful and Charles was executed. Cromwell proclaimed religious toleration for all except Catholics, and allowed Jews to return to England. During this period, Puritans established a number of schools for poor children.

After Cromwell died, the crown was restored to Charles II and Puritans were again persecuted. A number of laws were passed against them greatly restricting their activities. During that period, John Bunyan, a Baptist Puritan, wrote *Pilgrim's Progress* while imprisoned in the Bedford jail because he refused to stop preaching. Charles was secretly received into the Roman Catholic Church before he died and was succeeded by his son, James II, who was openly Catholic.

Fearing the religious absolution of Catholicism, English authorities brought William of Orange from Holland and his wife, Mary, to the throne in 1688. Mary was the daughter of James II, who was deposed. It was essentially a bloodless revolution. It is important to note that Calvinist Holland was an island of religious liberty. The following year, Parliament passed the Act of Toleration, which gave religious liberty to all except Unitarians and Roman Catholics. This act could be considered the beginning of concern for human rights, since religious liberty also implied freedom of speech and assembly. (In the middle of the following century, Presbyterians in the English colony in North America went to England to argue successfully that the Act applied to the colony, as well. Religious toleration in England and North America would have positive implications for the evangelical revivals and the development of the missionary movement.) Some Roman Catholics continued to practice their faith secretly in England, and priests came from abroad to serve them. A number were martyred. There was still fear of Catholicism because of the terrible persecution of French Protestants, especially the St. Bartholomew's Day massacre in 1685.

Puritans wrote a great deal of devotional and theological literature, certainly the best produced in England at the time. Their literature would influence Philip Spener, the leader of German Pietism.

Puritan Missionaries in the New World

Some Puritans, expelled from England, went first to Holland and then to New England. Some, but not all, were ardently missionary. John Eliot, who arrived in Massachusetts in 1631, evangelized the Algonquin "Indians" and translated the Bible into their language. It was the first Bible printed in North America. In addition, three generations of the Mayhew family evangelized "Indians" on Martha's Vineyard off the coast of New England. Each ministry saw over 3000 converts. Puritan theology would also have an important influence on the early North American missionary movement.

Pietism

Puritanism can be considered a truncated renewal movement, cut off by persecution. However, it influenced Pietism, which spread widely in Germany and the Scandinavian countries. The Moravians, part of whose roots lay in Pietism, became the major catalyst of Protestant missions. Pietist and Moravian missionaries went to Asia, Africa, and the West Indies long before Carey sailed to India in 1793. Carey is rightly called the father of the Protestant missionary movement because of the unique role he played in stimulating the formation of mission agencies, but during the eighteenth century, long before Carey, over fifty German Pietists went to India, and Moravians went to over a dozen countries.

Aftermath of the Thirty Years' War

By the middle of the seventeenth century, much of Germany had been devastated. The Thirty Years' War, the last gasp of the wars of the Reformation, ended in 1650. Germany was exhausted, much of it in ruins. Economic and political life was at a low level. At least a third of the population had been destroyed. Spiritual life, for the most part, was dismal.

Lutheran Orthodoxy

Lutheran orthodoxy was engaged in a series of theological battles, both within Lutheranism and against the Calvinists. The focus was on correct doctrine as defined by the Lutheran confessions. These had been elevated almost to the level of Scripture. Faith for Luther included belief in correct doctrine plus personal trust in Jesus Christ. Now theologians reduced the definition of faith simply to "belief in correct doctrine." The Christian life was understood as quite passive: one went to church, took the sacraments, and believed correct dogma. Some Lutherans taught baptismal regeneration. According to Spener's critique, most sermons focused on obscure points of doctrine that were neither understood nor relevant to the common people. Thus, Lutheranism was very different from what Luther had envisioned. It had become a rather external, dogmatic religion with little vitality.

The Pietist Movement

Puritanism had a number of leaders, but one man initiated the movement: Philip Spener, who lived from 1631 to 1705. He was born and raised in Strassburg, where both Lutheran and Reformed influences were important. Martin Bucer, the sixteenth-century reformer of the city, represented a theological bridge between the great reformers. He also encouraged the formation of small groups for fellowship and study. Raised in that environment, Spener read Lutheran theological works and also those of some of the greatest Puritans. Among them was Bayley's work, *The Practice of Piety*, which focused on the deeper Christian life. He also visited Geneva, where Calvinism was still concerned about the inner Christian life. There was a movement in Holland at the time called "Precisionism" that also sought personal piety. Another important influence was an earlier seventeenth-century work by Johannes Arndt, *True Christianity*. Arndt returned to Luther's focus on faith as personal trust and the Christian life as relationship with God.

In 1666, having completed his doctorate, Spener became the pastor in Frankfort. He found that the Christian life of most of his parishioners was dismal. Everyone was a member of the state church, and he was not permitted to discipline anyone. He initiated better catechetical instruction for the youth, and invited those who were serious about growing in their faith to come to his home one evening each week. There they would study the Scriptures, discuss the sermon, and pray for each other. His goal, of course, was to deepen the spiritual life of the participants. He was not a rebel against the Church, its structures, or theology. He simply added a new structure to encourage spiritual growth. He called his groups a "Collegia Pietatis" (College of Piety). They were

not a college in the institutional sense. They followed the model used earlier by Bucer in Strassburg, and by the Puritan conventicles. They were simply groups who came together informally to study the Scriptures, pray, discuss the sermon, and deepen the spiritual life. They included men and women of very different social classes. They were criticized because at times servants sat around the same table with members of the nobility. This was in a culture where at times a pastor could not use the same water to baptize the child of a commoner and a noble!

In 1675, Spener wrote a small book as an introduction to a new edition of Arndt's work. He called it *Pia Desideria* (Pious Desires). In it, he outlined his program for reform of the Church. (I reference here the English translation by Theodore G. Tappert [Philadelphia: Fortress Press, 1964]). Spener said many of the evils came from government interference in the life of the Church. Members of the nobility, who often were not sincere Christians, appointed pastors. It is important to note that both early Anabaptists and Calvin protested government interference in the Church. Spener said that many of the clergy now saw themselves simply as functionaries of the government. Thus, their primary role was to please those who appointed them. This can still happen. A few years ago, I had a student from Ethiopia, who had migrated to Sweden, where he studied and was ordained in the state church. He told me that just before his group was to be ordained, the bishop called them together and said, "If any of you have not yet been baptized, you must do so before being ordained." This seemed to indicate that they were primarily state functionaries rather than men called by God to ministry. In addition to the problem of government interference in the life of the Church, Spener criticized theological controversies that had little relevance to the Christian life. Other problems were the immorality and drunkenness of the people.

As a solution, he proposed the formation of small fellowship groups in each church for Bible reading, prayer, and mutual encouragement. In other words, he wanted the Church to encourage the priesthood of every believer. He said, "Christianity is more a life than a system of doctrine." This was a critical point. Often Pietists were accused of ignoring theology or even of being heretical. That was not correct. They were orthodox in their theology but believed that correct teaching was not enough by itself. Orthopraxis, the living of the life with Christ, was important as well. After all, that was the purpose of orthodoxy. In addition, for Pietists, Scripture was more important than the Lutheran creeds. To their critics this seemed to indicate theological laxity.

Spener also called for better training of the clergy. He insisted that no one should be a pastor unless he had been converted. He called for preaching designed to build the Christian life of the people. He stressed the importance of the new birth and a Christian lifestyle as a result. He advocated moderation in food and drink and taught that Christians should not be involved in the theater or in playing cards. This may appear legalistic, and at times, it became so. However, in this context the theater often involved immorality, and cards were for gambling. At times Pietism insisted on a particular order of the experiences one should have in the process of conversion, which was also a kind of legalism. Yet as we have seen, there was far more to Pietism than avoiding certain amusements.

The primary emphases in the movement were the need for personal conversion, the desire to live an authentic Christian life in the midst of a nominally Christian culture, the personal study of Scripture, koinonia, and group prayer. Pietism, like Puritanism, encouraged the laity to read the Bible, finding in it God's word to each person, as well as doctrine for the theologians. As we will see, the movement developed a strong sense of mission, both within its own society and beyond it to Asia.

Unlike many renewal movements, the Pietists for the most part did not separate from the broader Church. They remained within the Lutheran Church, working to lead its people to a more authentic Christian life by encouraging small fellowship groups. They formed a "church within the church." In a sense they were like the early Anabaptists, seeking to form committed communities, except that their groups remained inside the traditional churches. Their model is relevant to many today who live in cultures or even churches that perceive themselves as Christian but constantly violate basic Christian concepts. The "Bible Belt" in the United States during the struggle for civil rights is one example. Tragically, most of the Church supported racial discrimination. South Africa, with its official establishment of apartheid, was another. In both cases, there were small groups of followers of Jesus, black and white, who courageously spoke out against the churches and cultures they loved. We are all aware of Martin Luther King, Jr. in the United States. We may not know that the great missiologist David Bosch was one of a small group who told his church in South Africa that it must declare apartheid a heresy. They and others were ostracized and persecuted, but eventually prevailed. Since renewal must always have its ethical as well as spiritual aspects, such struggles are inevitable.

It is also important to note that while Puritanism and Pietism continued a strong emphasis on the role of the pastor and the importance of his preparation, they also encouraged greater lay activity. The ministry of laypersons would expand greatly in the Moravian and Methodist movements, as we will see.

Pietism spread across much of Germany and into Norway, Denmark and, to some degree, Sweden. It played an important role in organizing and consolidating Lutheran churches among colonists in North America. Wherever it went, it encouraged better catechetical instruction of the youth and in many places established schools for the poor.

Some of the fine hymns we sing came out of German Pietism. It is always interesting to go through the hymnal and look at the dates when hymns were written. We find that very often, the great hymns come out of periods of renewal. In fact, I think we could even make this a criterion for a genuine renewal movement. Most genuine renewal movements lead believers to sing, and often to sing new, different music that identifies with the culture more than did the older music. This is certainly true among our black brothers and sisters in the United States and among charismatic movements.

The late nineteenth-century revivals were characterized by music. Of course, one of the greatest examples in history was the Wesleyan movement. Charles Wesley was perhaps the greatest hymn writer who ever lived. The evangelical revivals within the Anglican Church that led to the founding of the Church Missionary Society and the Anti-Slavery Movement also produced great hymns.

A. H. Francke in Halle

The second great Pietist leader was August Hermann Francke. In 1687, while writing a sermon on John 3:16, he experienced conversion! Apparently, his sermon spoke to him when he realized he had never come to personal terms with the reality of the new birth. He spent time with Spener and became his successor as the leader of the Pietist movement. In 1691, he went to the newly established University of Halle in East Germany.

Francke stayed there until his death in 1727. He taught in the university, which became a center for the training of Pietist pastors. He also served as pastor in a nearby town.

For many people today, the term "Pietist" implies a piety that focuses only on one's own spiritual life, with little or no regard for society. This was not true of early Pietism—quite the contrary. Sattler's fine book on Francke is entitled *God's Glory, Neighbor's Good* (Chicago, Covenant Press, 1982) That expresses well the Pietist understanding of the Christian life. Francke put that into practice to a remarkable degree. Education was not available to many at the time, and he established a school for the poor. When he died, it enrolled twenty-two hundred children. He founded an orphanage that numbered 134 children. He also started an organization to publish and distribute the Bible inexpensively among the people. This led to more widespread study of the Scriptures. At the University of Halle, the Instituto Judaicum was established to prepare men to share the

Gospel among the Jews. It continued until the Nazi era.

Remarkably, Francke supported all of these enterprises by faith. We know of George Mueller of Bristol and his famous orphanage, supported by faith. When J. Hudson Taylor established the China Inland Mission, he adopted the same policy. So the influence of Francke continues today through its successor organization, the Overseas Missionary Fellowship.

Other Pietist Leaders

Halle became the most important center of Pietism. The first Protestant student mission movement arose there. Thousands of Pietist pastors were trained in Halle under the influence of Francke. Bengel, one of the greatest German exegetes, was a Pietist. He showed his love of Scripture in his exegesis. Henry Muhlenberg, the father of American Lutheranism, was a Pietist who went from Halle to North America. He traveled widely, visiting Lutheran settlers, organizing churches, and providing pastors for them. Muhlenberg College is named for him.

Danish Halle Mission, 1706

In this period of history, European Protestant nations were forming colonies in Asia and elsewhere. Normally they provided chaplains for their own citizens in the colonies, but showed no concern for mission to the indigenous people. That of course indicated a tragic misunderstanding of the Gospel. However, in 1706, King Frederick of Denmark was persuaded by his Pietist chaplain to send missionaries to the indigenous people in his colony in Tranquiebar, southern India. Two young men from Halle, Heinrich Plütschau and Bartholomew Ziegenbalg, volunteered to go. The German Lutheran Church refused to ordain them, but the Danish church did so, no doubt under pressure from the King.

Almost a century earlier, Baron von Welz, an Austrian Lutheran, had begged the Lutheran Church in Europe to send missionaries to other areas. He was considered a fanatic and accused of wanting to throw pearls before swine! Von Welz said, "We have so many theological students in

Europe; shouldn't we be sending some of them to the rest of the world? We have so many resources; shouldn't we be sharing the Gospel with the rest of the world?" Von Welz sought, unsuccessfully, to be ordained by the Lutheran church. Eventually he was ordained by an independent group and went to Suriname on the north coast of South America, where he died. In some ways he was a tragic figure, but in other ways a John the Baptist, a forerunner.

When Ziegenbalg and Plütschau arrived in South India, they experienced hostility and harassment from the Europeans there who wanted chaplains for themselves but no missionaries for the local people. Missionaries have often been caught in that kind of struggle. They certainly are not perfect, but in many cases where Westerners wished to exploit non-Western people, the missionaries received at least as much enmity from the Western nominal Christians as they did from the non-Christian peoples. This was the case in Hawaii and a number of areas in Africa. We need to recognize this aspect of history.

Not even the Danish chaplains welcomed the two missionaries. Plütschau returned after a few years, but Ziegenbalg remained until his death in 1719. In those thirteen years, his achievements were remarkable. He learned the Tamil language and completed the translation of the New Testament in 1714. When he died, he had translated the Old Testament as far as the book of Ruth. He believed that the Word of God must be available in the language of the people. He also believed that the Church and the school must go together. Christians needed to learn to read so they could read the Word of God. So Christian children would be educated, girls along with boys. That was a radical step in eighteenth-century India! He also established an industrial school to aid the economy.

He believed that the preaching of the Gospel must be based on the knowledge of the mind of the people. Today we would speak of their "culture and worldview." He studied and wrote on Hindu religious beliefs. As a Pietist, his aim was personal conversion of the people, and he wanted to organize an Indian church with its own ministry. When he died, he left behind a church of about 350 people. He had also begun to prepare an Indian pastor for ordination.

Ziegenbalg visited Europe from 1714 to 1716, where the king of Denmark received him. There were a number of important results from his visit. The Royal College of Missions was established in Copenhagen. Other Pietist missionaries to India and a number of Moravians would study there. He visited the University of Halle and had a powerful influence on a number of students, especially a young man named Nicholas von Zinzendorf.

The Order of the Mustard Seed, the first Protestant student mission band, was formed at Halle as a result. Zinzendorf was its leader. Members of the group pledged to work for the renewal of the Church and to take the Gospel to unreached areas of the world. Ziegenbalg also visited England, seeking to arouse the interest of British Christians in his mission. He was granted an audience with the King, who had a Pietist chaplain, and received the cooperation of the Anglican Society for the Propagation of Christian Knowledge (SPCK). The group had been formed at the turn of the century to work primarily with English colonists.

Between fifty and sixty missionaries were sent to India by the Danish Halle mission during the century. The greatest of these after Ziegenbalg was Christian Friedrich Schwartz. He remained in India over fifty years, never returning to Europe, and was loved and respected by Hindus and Muslims both powerful and the humble. When I was in Mumbai (Bombay) in 1989, I met a young seminarian whose ancestress had been a little Hindu girl, married to an older man who had died. She was to be burned alive with the body of her husband, as was the custom, when her brother stole her away in the middle of the night and took her to Schwartz, who cared for her. She became a Christian, and now in the late twentieth century her descendent was studying to be a pastor!

At the end of the century, the work of the Danish Halle Mission was turned over to the Anglicans.

This was probably due to growing English influence in India.

The Order of the Mustard Seed introduces us to the importance of student movements in missions. We have already noted the importance of students who studied with Wycliffe at Oxford and took his ideas back to Bohemia and to Huss. We have seen the role of the Franciscans, Dominicans, and especially Jesuits in the University of Paris and elsewhere. We find Luther at Wittenberg and see his students take the Lutheran Reformation to the Scandinavian countries. Calvin in Geneva became a convinced Protestant Christian at the University of Paris about the same time Loyola was forming the first Jesuit band. Now we see the Order of the Mustard Seed at Halle. Later we will learn of the Haystack Prayer Meeting at Williams College in 1806. That group was instrumental in forming the first North American mission board four years later. The Student Volunteer Movement began in 1886. It motivated over twenty thousand young men and women to go out from North America and Europe to the world beyond. Such movements continue.

Today student interest in mission is not limited to North America and Europe. Now there are growing, vital student movements in Asia, Latin America, and Africa. This is an extremely important development. Student mission movements have played a key role in the world mission of Christ in the past and will continue to do so in the future.

Chapter Eighteen

Moravians, Methodists, and Mission

Devotional

This hymn captures the spirit of one of the movements we will examine in this chapter: the early Wesleyan movement. It is "O for a Thousand Tongues," and it is reported to have been written by Charles Wesley on the first anniversary of his conversion. He said, "If I had a thousand tongues I would use them all to praise my Lord." It expresses both the vitality and the missionary vision of the movement. This is the last verse of the hymn:

> Glory to God and praise and love
> Be ever given
> By saints below and saints above
> The church in earth and heaven.

That is marvelous! Often we Protestants do not have enough sense of the Church Triumphant: the Church in heaven composed of the saints who have gone on before us. We see that in this verse.

There are several dimensions in this hymn. There is praise—the cry of gratitude to God for conversion and salvation. There is the missionary dimension—"spread through all the earth abroad the honors of Thy Name." Then in this last verse, there is "glory to God" and "saints below and saints above, the church in earth and heaven." There is a magnificent sense of the Church as well as personal redemption. The hymns of Wesley combine marvelous music and theology as few others do.

Introduction

Now we will examine two movements that failed to remain in the existing churches. But even though they became separate movements, they brought a measure of renewal to the broader Church. That was especially true of the Methodists, but also to some extent of the Moravians. Whether a renewal movement will remain in the broader Church or separate from it is always a critical question. Since such movements always seem to arise on the periphery of the traditional institution, they run two dangers. One is that church leaders will see the movement as a threat to the status quo, and thus reject it. The other is that renewal leaders will fail to care about the broader Church and will leave voluntarily, often with a self-righteous attitude.

Most existing Protestant churches and mission movements began in renewal. At times, they have remained in the existing Church, but not without controversy. The East African Revival is an example. Others began in a major denomination but were rejected. I have already mentioned the Christian and Missionary Alliance. Its founder, A. B. Simpson, was a Presbyterian minister who formed two interdenominational "alliances." One sought a deeper Christian life; the other focused on mission. Because there was no space for him in his own denomination, his movement eventually became a new denomination. Pentecostals exhibited a different dynamic. Because their earliest leaders were so far from the "mainstream" of the traditional churches, and because of their emphasis on certain charismata, or gifts of the Spirit, there was never any possibility they would be accepted by the existing "mainline" churches. We must recognize the diversity of movements of renewal. Pentecostalism became the most dynamic missionary movement of the twentieth century.

Howard Snyder has suggested that ideally, a renewal movement has the following characteristics. Since no movement is perfect, none exhibits all of these characteristics completely. However, here is a good template by which to evaluate a movement.

- It "rediscovers" a forgotten or neglected aspect of the Gospel (a "theological breakthrough").

- It uses some kind of small group structure: a church within the Church. Thus, it keeps a link with the larger Church.

- It is committed to the unity, vitality, and wholeness of the larger Church.

- It is oriented toward mission beyond itself.

- It is conscious of being a distinct covenant-based community.

- It provides the context for the rise, training, and exercise of new forms of ministry and leadership. Thus, it is flexible in forms of ministry and leadership selection and training.

- Its members remain in close contact with society, especially the poor.

- It maintains a balanced emphasis on the Word and Spirit as the basis of authority.

Now we will examine both their dynamics and the influence of two movements. A question that always arises for those who seek renewal, is how to deal with the broader church that resists such efforts. Should they remain in the larger church and continue to work within it, or should they leave and form a "pure church?" The problem with a "pure church" is that it will never be 'pure,' and will become institutionalized after a generation or two, and exhibit the same problems the founders reacted against in the parent body.

I am not suggesting there are easy solutions to this question. We believe in both unity and mission, but

historically we recognize there has often been tension between them. We can even see this in the case of the mission of Paul and Barnabas to the Gentiles, and the tension it created with the Jerusalem church. That was resolved in the "Council of Jerusalem" in Acts 15, but there is evidence the tension continued in the second century between the bishops, who represented unity, and the itinerant evangelists, who represented mission. Dr. Samuel Moffett has observed that very often mission movements have spun off on their own and have not contributed to unity. On the other hand, movements that have focused on unity have often forgotten about mission. We who believe in both unity and mission must always recognize this dilemma.

Sometimes the question is decided for a movement, as it was for Wesley. He had no intention or desire to leave the Anglican Church. Indeed, he considered himself a loyal priest of that church to the end of his life. However, because of the need to have pastors who would baptize and serve the Lord's Supper to his converts, Wesley ordained his preachers. That constituted a de facto separation from Anglicanism, although Wesley refused to recognize it as such.

Zinzendorf

Now we turn to one of the most remarkable mission leaders in history, Nicolaus Ludwig von Zinzendorf. He was born in 1700 into a family of the landed nobility. The family was influenced by Pietism. His father's friend, Philip Spener, was his godfather. His Pietist grandmother, who read her Bible in the original languages, raised him. Early in life, Nicolaus developed a deep personal devotion to Jesus Christ.

It is said that one day he was contemplating a painting of Christ on the cross. Written underneath were the words, "All this I have done for thee; what hast thou done for me?" The motto of his life became "I have but one passion; it is he and he alone." Few people in history have lived out that passion as fully as he did.

He studied at the University of Halle as a teenager. (Younger boys went to university at that time). He was somewhat repelled by the legalistic rigor, but appreciated the zeal. When Ziegenbalg visited Halle in 1714, he helped form the Society of the Grain of Mustard Seed, the first Protestant student mission society.

Zinzendorf studied law at Wittenberg, and at the age of twenty-one settled down on his estate near Dresden and began the life of a court official. He married and was apparently destined to a life of wealth, comfort, stability, and prestige.

Germany was still a semi-feudal society in which many people lived on the land of the nobles, who appointed pastors for their people. Zinzendorf was concerned with what he called "heart religion"—a warm, personal faith—and appointed a Pietist pastor for his people.

Origin of the Moravians

Then, in 1722, a small group appeared on Zinzendorf's estate. They had come from Moravia, part of what is now the Czech Republic. They were a small remnant of the Unitas Fratrum, the spiritual descendents of John Huss, and probably of Peter Waldo. The group had survived as an underground church through the sixteenth and seventeenth centuries, despite persecution. Their great seventeenth-century bishop, Johan Comenius, had been a refugee during the Thirty Years War, but gave effective leadership to his flock. Knowing of Zinzendorf's Pietist sympathies, the group asked for permission to settle on his land. He agreed, and they called their community Herrnhut (The Lord's Watch.)

Others joined them, coming from various theological backgrounds: Hussites, Lutherans, Calvinists, and even Roman Catholics. The great diversity of the group made it difficult to establish any sense of unity. One issue was the question of whether or not the community should become part of the state Lutheran Church. Eventually, Christian David, the leader of the original group, was alienated from the community. He and others who had come from Moravia were impatient with the formalism of Lutheran practices in confession and communion. Various theological currents were swirling around, including differences between Calvinism and Lutheranism, and even one person who espoused Unitarianism.

Beginning in 1725, Zinzendorf began to work toward reconciliation of the various elements. In February 1725, Rothe, the pastor, followed Zinzendorf's suggestion and appointed laypersons to various ministries. Recognizing that it was an apostolic practice (Romans 12:4–8), Zinzendorf wrote, "In order that the work might proceed... and especially that revived Herrnhut might be kept in pure apostolic ways, Mr. Rothe accepted helpers from among the loyal souls of the congregation for exhortation, for observance of the work (overseers), for service and for alms-giving, for visiting the sick, and particularly for the guidance of souls." (Douglas Rights, *The Story of the Thirteenth of August, 1727* [Winston Salem, N.C.: The Moravian Archives, 1994], 10.) Both women and men were appointed for these ministries. Soon another crisis came, and in January 1727, a nearby pastor wrote, "In Herrnhut it looks as if the devil will turn everything upside down." (ibid., 24.)

Zinzendorf was tireless as he worked for unity and reconciliation. In May, twelve elders were appointed, and Christian David, who had been alienated from the community, was among them. There was a growing sense of revival and unity. They decided to have Bible conferences instead of the usual song and prayer services, and David proposed they study the letters of John, which spoke so strongly on love and unity. Zinzendorf was away on a journey for three weeks beginning July 22. When he returned, he told the people about the history and discipline of their spiritual ancestors, the Bohemian and Moravian Brethren. He had discovered more of their heritage while reading the works of Comenius. The people were amazed to discover they had been led to the same emphases their earlier bishop had taught. They held night watches for prayer in which Zinzendorf participated. On August 12, Zinzendorf visited each house in Herrnhut, "to examine the people lovingly and send them to the communion on the morrow."

On August 13 the "Moravian Pentecost" occurred. It is considered the birthday of the Moravian Church. They prayed they would be fruitful and not violate their fidelity to Christ or their common love, "that not one soul should be led astray from the blood and cross theology on which our salvation depended." Zinzendorf described their humble attitude before the Lord:

> All the people who were together in Herrnhut on August 13, 1727, were quite dissatisfied with themselves…Each was conscious that he was not worth anything, and in this consciousness they all came before the Savior. Therefore, they were certain that He, the Man of Sorrows, would be their Patron and Priest, and would transform all their tears to oil of joy. (ibid., 24).

Zinzendorf made confession in the name of the whole congregation, absolution followed, and they took the Lord's Supper. Apparently, there were no special manifestations of the Holy Spirit, but there was a profound sense of his presence and power. Christian David and another member of the group were visiting an orphanage in another town and at the same hour had a strong impulse to pray. They knew something unique had happened. Zinzendorf wrote, "At that communion, which was in name and deed a real love feast, the Lord let a spirit come upon us, of which we had formerly known nothing." He said that until that day, he and the others "had come to help," but "now they had to let the Holy Spirit work." After this experience they instituted a twenty-four-hour prayer watch that lasted one hundred years. Two people prayed every hour, around the clock every day, and almost immediately they developed a remarkable missionary vision.

The Moravian Church as a Mission Structure

They became a remarkable, deeply committed community. They never numbered more than a few hundred in Herrnhut, and yet they became one of the most creative and zealous Christian movements in history. Zinzendorf, who became their bishop, developed his ideal that they would be a body of soldiers of Christ ready to advance Christ's cause at home and abroad as God led them. Lay leadership was very important. People were chosen as elders and teachers, not according to their social rank or formal education, but their gifts. Leonard Dober, a potter, was known to be an especially gifted Bible teacher. Members of the nobility as well as commoners listened to his teaching.

In many ways, they were like a Protestant monastic movement, except for the fact that they married. They followed spiritual disciplines with daily prayer and worship. Each person was part of a small group for mutual encouragement, single men with single men, married women with married women, etc. Marriage choices were regulated; people were told whom to marry. Children were separated from their parents at quite an early age, seeing them only at meals. They were a community separate from the world, with a high level of spiritual discipline, ready to go anywhere to spread the Gospel.

In 1732, they sent their first missionaries to the West Indies. Some said they were willing to sell themselves into slavery if it was the only way they could go there to minister to black African slaves. Fortunately, this was not necessary. However, they did incur the wrath of the Dutch plantation owners when they evangelized the slaves. On one occasion, the missionaries were put in prison, and used the opportunity to preach to several hundred slaves through the prison bars! Many were converted. Half of the missionaries and their families died from disease. They went to some of the most difficult areas of the world: to South Africa, where a Moravian baptized the first Black African there and the Dutch expelled him; to Labrador, where the whole group perished. Moravians went to Greenland in 1733. Other areas of mission were Egypt, Central America, Alaska, Guiana, and Suriname. In 1735, Spangenberg, of whom we will hear later, went to Georgia on the southeast coast of what is now the United States. There he met a young Anglican clergyman named John Wesley. It was reported that in a period of twenty-eight years, the Moravians sent missionaries to twenty-eight countries. One of every thirteen or so persons in the community went elsewhere as missionaries. In keeping with their theological focus on the atonement for sin on the cross, they went out to gain "souls for the Lamb."

Normally they farmed or engaged in trade, so they were self-supporting communities. Obviously, they were not supported from Germany. They stressed conversion more than the planting of the Church. Perhaps that was one of their weaknesses. They worked with Native Americans in North America and had hundreds, even thousands, of converts whom they attempted to protect from other European settlers. In some cases, Moravian missionaries and Native American converts were killed in the wars between hostile tribes and settlers.

The testimony of Tschoop, a Native American chief, converted through the ministry of the Moravian Henry Rauch in 1740 shows both the spirit and the focus of Moravian missions.

> Brethren, I have been a heathen and have grown old among the heathen. Therefore, I know how the heathen think. Once a preacher came and began to explain that there was a God. We answered, 'Doest thou think us to be ignorant as not to know that? Go back to the place from whence you came. Then again, another preacher came and began to teach us and to say, 'You must not steal, nor lie, nor get drunk,' etc. We answered, 'Thou fool, doest thou think that we don't know that? Learn thyself first and then teach the people to whom thou belongest, to leave off these things. For who steals, or lies, or is more drunken that thine own people?' And thus we dismissed him.
>
> After some time brother Christian Henry Rauch came into my hut and sat down by me. He spoke to me nearly as follows. 'I come to you in the name of the Lord of Heaven and earth. He sends me to let you know that he will make you happy and deliver you from the misery in which you lie at present. To this end, he became a man, gave his life a ransom for many, and shed his blood for him,' etc. When he had finished his discourse, he lay down upon a board, fatigued by the journey, and fell into a sound sleep.

> I then thought, what kind of man is this? There he lies and sleeps. I might kill him and throw him out in to the wood, and who would regard it? But this gave him no concern. However, I could not forget his words. They constantly recurred to my mind. Even when I was asleep, I dreamed of that blood which Christ shed for me. I found this to be something different from what I had ever heard, and I interpreted Christian Henry's words to the other Indians. Thus, through the grace of God, an awakening took place amongst us. I say therefore, brethren, preach Christ our Saviour and His sufferings and death, if you would have your words gain entrance among the heathen. (T. A. Hamilton, *A History of the Missions of the Moravian Church* [Bethlehem, Pennsylvania: Times Publishing Company, 1901], 24–25.)

The Moravians did not leave large churches behind, for the most part, although there are some Moravian churches in the eastern part of the United States. Their greater influence was on the larger Christian community. Zinzendorf was very ecumenical; he wanted to bring Christians together and work for renewal. That had been one of the goals of the Order of the Mustard Seed at Halle. He was not interested in making other Christians into Moravians, although some suspected him of doing so. In North America he worked among German settlers, seeking to bring scattered Christians together, regardless of denomination, into worshipping, witnessing, serving communities.

Zinzendorf was eventually banished from Saxony, his state in Germany. He traveled widely, working in western Germany, in the Baltic provinces, in the West Indies, and in London. In December 1741, he arrived in New York and went to Pennsylvania, where he and a small group of Moravians founded the town of Bethlehem on Christmas Eve that year. Today a Moravian college and seminary are located there. Now the Moravians are a small denomination in the United States, and have lost most of their missionary vision. However, there are strong Moravian communities in other countries, the result of their earlier missionary zeal.

Moravians showed great respect for other cultures and encouraged indigenous music. On some occasions, they held multicultural celebrations in Herrnhut, with converts from various nations participating. They also used music to teach children to read, using some of the ideas of Comenius, who had been a pioneer in pedagogical theory.

In 1760 Zinzendorf died in Herrnhut, a poor man, By that time the little Moravian community had sent out 226 missionaries. One example of his greatness may be seen in an incident in one of his voyages. As a nobleman, he had the only relatively comfortable cabin on board, with the other passengers in extremely difficult accommodations down in the hold of the ship. When he learned that a Jewish couple was among the passengers and that the wife was ill, he gave up his cabin to them and stayed below in the hold! He had spent all of his fortune, his life, and his energy on mission—one of the great missionary pioneers in history! He was great not so much for what he accomplished, although he and his people did accomplish a great deal. His greatness lay even more in the scope of his vision and the effect he and his followers had on the emerging evangelical movement. He felt God's heartbeat for the world, and believed that followers of Christ should be ready to go anywhere and accept any sacrifice to take the Good News to the world. Few have shared that vision as well; none has done it better.

Chain of Influence

Zinzendorf and the Moravians became a major catalyst of Protestant missions. Carey and the founders of other mission societies spoke of their example. However, their greatest impact probably came through their influence on John Wesley. His heritage is remarkable. It includes the Methodist churches around the world, and other groups that came from it. They include the Nazarene Church, the Salvation Army, the Holiness movement, and the Pentecostal tradition. The Salvation Army was one of the first Christian groups to affirm the leadership of women. Evangeline Booth was an early leader and, more recently, Eva Burroughs

served as its worldwide commander, the second woman to occupy this post.

As we will see, the Wesleyan movement was an important part of the broader wave of the eighteenth-century evangelical revivals in England and North America. The revivals motivated the formation of the first Protestant missionary societies, including Carey's Baptist society, the interdenominational London Missionary Society, the Anglican Church Missionary Society, and the British and Foreign Bible Society. They also triggered significant movements of social reform including the anti-slavery movement.

It is important to see these networks and discover how much can be traced back (not exclusively but to a significant degree) to Wesley and his colleagues. Then we remember that Wesley was profoundly influenced by the Moravians. We want to continue to trace these streams back to their sources, which at times were forced underground. It helps us understand some of the ways in which God has worked. This encourages us to be faithful. We will not always see, and in fact normally we will not see, the fruits of all of our labors. However, we can trust that God uses any person who is faithful in ways that will never be seen, at least while we are alive. Often the fruits of a person's ministry will only be seen decades or even generations later. This is an important lesson from history.

England in the Early 18th Century

Early in the eighteenth-century England, Puritanism had declined and lost its fire. The theology of the Anglican Church was rationalistic. It was a time of spiritual lethargy among both Anglicans and dissenters. There was little or no outreach to the poor, who existed in terrible conditions. The drawings of contemporary English cartoonists depicted widespread drunkenness and brutality among the poor. A person could be executed for any number of petty crimes, and hangings were public spectacles. The poor, who comprised a majority of the people, had little or no meaningful contact with the Church. The inflexibility of the

Anglican structure made it difficult to establish new churches as people came into the growing cities from the countryside. Thus, most of the poor were alienated from the Church both geographically and culturally. The industrial revolution was on its way and would bring great changes to English society.

Yet there were signs of renewal—the underground streams we have mentioned earlier. In 1728 William Law, an Anglican clergyman, wrote *A Serious Call to the Devout and Holy Life,* a great devotional book. Early in the century, Isaac Watts, dissatisfied with the poor quality of congregational singing, began to write new hymns. One was "When I Survey the Wondrous Cross," considered by many to be the greatest hymn in the English language. Moreover, long before Carey sailed to India, Watts wrote the great missionary hymn "Jesus Shall Reign Where'er the Sun." In addition, there were a number of religious societies similar to Pietist groups that met for prayer, scripture reading, and communion. Anthony Horneck, who had known Spener in Germany, initiated those societies. They became a mini-renewal movement. Besides following devotional rules, the members visited the poor in their homes and helped some to become established in a trade. They also helped prisoners to be freed and supported poor scholars in the university. There were a hundred of them in London in 1700. Samuel Wesley, father of John and Charles, established such a society in his parish in 1702. Along with the reading of Scripture and devotional exercises, its purposes included the establishment of schools for the poor, the dissemination of devotional literature, and the care of the sick.

Two laymen, the Erskine brothers, were instrumental in an awakening in Scotland early in the eighteenth century. They had to preach in the fields because the churches would not hold the crowds. There were more Praying Societies, as they were called, in Scotland.

The Wesleys

Susanna Wesley was the twenty-fifth child of a Puritan pastor. Apparently, she received great interests in theology and spirituality from him. She was a remarkable woman, and obviously had a major impact on her children, especially John and Charles.

She married Samuel Wesley, an Anglican priest, and gave birth to nineteen children, eleven of whom lived beyond infancy. John was the fifteenth and Charles, the eighteenth. At one point, the house caught on fire and when they counted the children, they discovered that one was missing, still in the house—this was young John, whom they rescued. Later, as an evangelist, he often referred to himself as a "brand snatched from the burning." John told in his journal that on one occasion, when his father was in London for an extended stay, Susanna found a book in the study. She called it "the memoirs of the Danish missionaries," presumably Ziegenbalg and Plutschau. She was so impressed by their ministry that, as she put it, she could think of nothing else for days.

> I was never, I think, more affected with anything…I could not forgo spending a good part of the evening praising and adoring the Divine Goodness for inspiring those good men with such an ardent zeal for His glory.…For several days I could think or speak of little else. At last it came into my mind; though I am not a man nor a minister of the Gospel…if I were inspired with a true zeal for His glory and did really desire the salvation of souls, I might do somewhat more than I do.…I resolved to begin with my own children. (J. Whitehead, *The Life of the Rev. Mr. John Wesley, M.A.* [New York: United States Book Company, n d], 39).

She decided that although she was "only a woman," she could do more for her Lord. She began family prayers with her children and servants. She invited the neighbors to come on Sunday evenings when she would read sermons to them, and soon two hundred were in attendance. Her husband, when he heard of it, was against the practice. She disregarded his wishes and continued. She also resolved to spend an hour each week with each child still at home, instructing and encouraging them all in their faith. Later, when the movement initiated by her son John was growing beyond his capacity to take care of all the needs, Susanna referred to one of his lay leaders and said, "That layman can preach as well as you can." As a result, Wesley began to appoint lay preachers. Later they would be ordained.

John went to Oxford in 1720. He was chosen a Fellow and ordained a deacon in 1725 and a priest in 1728. He spent three years as assistant to his father from 1726 to 1729 before returning to Oxford. Arriving there, he found that his brother, Charles, and several others had formed a group to help each other in their studies but also to pursue the Christian life. John became their leader. They were called "The Holy Club," and, because of their focus on spiritual discipline, were also called "Methodists." The members spent an hour each morning and evening in private prayer. At nine, twelve, and three o'clock, they recited a prayer. They examined themselves closely watching for signs of grace. They read the Bible frequently and spent an hour each day in meditation. They fasted twice a week and received the sacraments every Sunday. They read devotional books such as William Law's *A Serious Call to a Devout and Holy Life* (published that year), and Thomas a Kempis' *Imitation of Christ*. Theirs was a high Anglo-Catholic piety. Soon George Whitefield, son of a tavern keeper and thus of a lower social class, joined them.

In 1735, the Wesley brothers sailed to Georgia, a new colony in North America, as missionaries of the Anglican Society for the Propagation of the Gospel in Foreign Parts. They hoped to minister to "Indians" as well as colonists. John wrote in his journal that he went to Georgia with the hope of saving his soul.

On their way to Georgia, during a terrible storm at sea, the main sail was split and water poured into the ship.

> A terrible screaming began among the English. The Germans [Moravians] calmly sung on. I asked one of them afterward, 'Was you not afraid?' He answered, 'I thank God, no.' I asked, 'But were not your women and children afraid?' He replied mildly,' No, our women and children are not afraid to die. (P. L. Parker, ed., *The Heart of John Wesley's Journal* [New York: Revell, nd], 7).

As another writer noted,

> A third positive development for Wesley in his Georgia experience was the acquaintance he formed with the Moravians, who taught him, by example and precept, that faith should be fearless and that it can be buoyant. It was no accident that when he returned to England he made immediate contact with the Moravians there (Albert C. Outler, ed., *John Wesley* [New York: Oxford University Press, 1964], 13).

The brothers worked hard in Georgia but were unsuccessful. They appeared judgmental and legalistic to the colonists. In Georgia, John met August Spangenberg, a Moravian leader, who asked him,

> 'Do you know Jesus Christ?'
>
> I paused, and said, 'I know he is the Saviour of the world.'
>
> 'True,' replied he, 'but do you know He has saved you?'
>
> I answered, 'I hope he has died to save me.'
>
> He only added, 'Do you know yourself?"
>
> I said, 'I do.'
>
> But I fear they were vain words (Parker, *Wesley's Journal*, 8).

Charles returned to England in 1736 and John returned in 1738, in spiritual turmoil, feeling he was a failure. At this point, the Wesley brothers certainly believed the Gospel and were zealous Christians as they understood the Faith. John studied his Greek New Testament and in 1735, while still at Oxford, had preached a sermon that he later said included all the principles he taught in later years. These included salvation from all sin and the importance of loving God with an undivided heart. However, apparently he still lacked the assurance that God's grace and salvation had come to him.

After he returned to England, John wrote,

> I went to America to convert the Indians, but Oh, who shall convert me? Who...will deliver me from this evil heart of mischief? I have a fair summer religion. I can talk well...while no danger is near, but let death look me in the face and my spirit is troubled. Nor can I say, 'To die is gain' (ibid., 19).

Remembering the Moravians they had met on their mission to Georgia, they spoke with Peter Boehler, a member of that group who was in London. He told them of the importance of self-surrender, instantaneous conversion, and joy in the assurance of salvation.

In February, Boehler wrote to Zinzendorf about John Wesley, 'He knew he did not properly believe on the Saviour and was willing to be taught.' In March, John wrote, 'I was, on Sunday the 5th, clearly convinced of unbelief, and of the want of that faith whereby along we are saved' (Howard Snyder, *The Radical Wesley* [Downers Grove: InterVarsity Press, 1980], 25.)

On May 21, 1738, Charles had an experience of such assurance and peace. Three days later, John went "very unwillingly," as he put it, to a meeting of a religious society on Aldersgate Street, where the leader read Luther's Preface to his Commentary on Romans. John recorded in his journal,

> About a quarter before nine, while he (Luther) was describing the change which God works in the heart through faith in Christ, I felt my heart strangely warmed. I felt I did trust in Christ, Christ alone, for salvation; and an assurance was given me that he had taken away my sins, even mine, and saved me from the law of sin and death. (ibid., 26.)

After the Aldersgate experience, John read Jonathan Edwards' "Surprising narrative of the conversions lately wrought in and about the town of North Hampton in New England...and it struck Wesley with great force." (Outler, *Wesley*, 15.)

Seeking to learn from the Moravians, John went to Germany and visited Zinzendorf. He was critical of some features of the movement but also favorably impressed with the strong sense of koinonia and the small group structure.

Ministry and Development

John Wesley came back and began preaching actively in Anglican churches and in the praying societies. Soon pulpits were closed to him because of his enthusiasm. "Enthusiasm" was a bad word in those days. George Whitefield had already had

pulpits closed to him and was now preaching in the fields. Whitefield said, "I don't care where I preach, as long as I preach." This was very hard for Wesley to, since, as he said, I scarcely believed anyone could be saved outside the four walls of an Anglican Church. He was finally persuaded by Whitefield to preach in the fields and in the streets. As he put it, " I resolved to become vile!"

We know Wesley as one who preached anywhere—in the streets, and in the fields. He was very slight of stature. Mobs often beat him and he was almost killed, but he kept going. He had one of the most remarkable evangelistic careers in the history of the Church. A comment written about Whitefield gives insight into his message, and applies to Wesley as well. An English aristocrat protested against his preaching, saying, "It is monstrous to be told you have a heart as sinful as the common wretches that crawl on the earth." But Whitefield told of the response of the coal miners to his preaching. "The white gutters made by their tears...ran down their black cheeks." The Good News to the poor was not always seen that way by the privileged. (Review of the book by Alan Jacobs, *Original Sin, A Cultural History*. Harperone, 2008, in *Christianity Today*, July 2008, vol 52, no.7, p. 54)

George Hunter, former dean of the School of Evangelism and Mission at Asbury Seminary, makes an interesting point in his book, *To Spread the Power: Church Growth in the Wesleyan Spirit* (Nashville, Abingdon, 1987). He said that Wesley did not consider people converted when they were simply awakened in his meetings. He felt that conversion did not take place until a person had begun the journey of Christian discipleship in the context of a small group.

There is an important lesson here. Some kinds of evangelists apparently believe that if people raise their hand or go forward in a meeting, they have been converted, no matter what happened later. We know how ineffective that often is.

Wesley was not just a great preacher/evangelist, he was a great organizer. Indeed, although everyone would agree that Whitefield was a greater preacher than Wesley was, the results that White-field left behind were far less because he did not enfold the people into worshiping, nurturing communities. However, Whitefield was a major voice in the Great Awakening in North America, where majority of the converts joined Presbyterian, Congregationalist, and Baptist churches.

Wesley began to preach outdoors and then to organize Methodist classes for nurture of the new believers. He had no desire to leave the Church of England. Following the precedent of the praying societies, he began to organize similar groups for new converts. Normally the poor would not feel at home in the existing churches, nor would they be nurtured or challenged to discipleship. Soon he appointed a lay leader of each class to nurture, to lead, and to exercise discipline, in a sense. A number of classes made up a 'society,' that would correspond to a local church. Society "tickets" (renewed every three months) were given to full members, and others were received on trial. Each member of a class of twelve paid a penny a week, and the leader had the responsibility of spiritual oversight and mutual help. Thus, the classes had three primary functions: the nurture of new believers, stewardship, and leadership training. There were other discipleship groups for the class leaders. Some of them would become lay preachers.

The clergy were largely unsympathetic. If Wesley was to find more preachers as the movement grew, he had to use laymen from his small groups. The organization grew into circuits, and eventually Wesley appointed superintendents. Since the Anglican Church could not and would not meet the needs of the new converts, in a sense, Wesley had to create new structures of the church for his movement.

As an Anglican, Wesley believed that only ordained clergy should baptize and serve the Lord's Supper. Of course, the Anglican Church would not ordain Wesley's lay preachers, hence, his dilemma. Finally, in 1784, Wesley began to ordain his lay preachers as presbyters, or pastors. He also ordained two superintendents for North America: Francis Asbury and Thomas Coke.

Even then, Wesley did not see this as a break with the established Church of England even though in reality, it was. He died at the age of eighty-eight in1791, active in ministry almost to the end. He continued to consider himself a loyal Anglican clergyman, even though his movement by that time had clearly separated from the traditional church.

Wesley believed in a holistic ministry. While he traveled on horseback he wrote books on various subjects to help guide his converts in their daily lives. The Methodist movement at its best has been concerned not only with conversion and salvation, but also with social transformation.

He was repelled by the rigid Calvinism of his day, which he saw among some of the Puritan churches. He became more of an Arminian in his theology, and rejected predestination. This led to a more socially active form of the faith, which at times has tended to run into a kind of liberalism without moorings.

Wesley also believed theoretically in perfection. He believed that the Christian in the process of sanctification could reach the point of perfection where one no longer willfully sinned. Most would see that as a less-than-Biblical understanding of sin. Wesley would not say that he had achieved perfection, but some later Methodists would. It is still a doctrine in the Nazarene Church. There was a great deal of focus on a second blessing and sanctification. The problem is that the idea of perfection implies a rather superficial view of the pervasiveness of human sin.

But Wesley was one of the great men of Christian history. As you read his Journal, you see at times healings, power encounter, and phenomena we would today call "charismatic" in style. It was a very impressive renewal movement.

The day after his eighty-first birthday, he wrote "I am as strong at eighty-one as I was at twenty-one, but abundantly more healthy." He preached on Monday evening. On Tuesday, he wrote, "I preached in the street at Scotter, to a large and deeply attentive congregation. It was a solemn and comfortable season. In the evening, I read prayers and preached in Owatone church, and again in the morning, Wednesday, 30. In the evening I preached at Epworth. In the residue of the week, I preached morning and evening in the neighboring towns." (Parker, *Wesley's Journal*, 455.) This was his schedule, several times a day, traveling, until he was a very old man! When asked what he would do if he knew he would die the next day, he replied, "And when I would finish doing what I have scheduled to do, I would say my prayers and I would go to bed, and I would meet my Lord." In other words, up to the day he died, he was doing what he believed that God had called him to do.

It is impressive to look at streams of spiritual life through out history. First we see the influence of the Moravians and Pietists in Wesley's life. Then we look at the Methodist Church and other groups that find their roots there: the Nazarenes, Free Methodists, Wesleyan Methodists, the Salvation Army, the Holiness and Pentecostal movements—all profoundly influenced by this one man.

Influence on the Anglican Church

In large part because of Wesley's influence, an evangelical movement grew up among Anglicans. It would have worldwide influence. Its leaders remained in the Anglican Church. They included John Newton (the former slave trader who wrote "Amazing Grace"), Augustus Toplady (who wrote the hymn "Rock of Ages"), William Wilberforce (who was primarily responsible for the abolition of slavery in the British Empire), and John and Henry Venn (who became mission leaders).

Clapham is a suburb of London, and during that period was an enclave of wealthy and influential people. John Venn was their rector. He had been influenced by Charles Simeon at Trinity Church, Cambridge. Simeon was another great evangelical leader in Anglicanism. Out of Clapham came a number of significant movements. One was the Church Missionary Society (CMS), established in 1799. It has been the greatest of the Anglican missionary societies. The East African Revival came primarily out of its ministry. Max Warren, who was quoted earlier, was one of its greatest leaders.

A second was the movement to abolish slavery, led by William Wilberforce. He was a brilliant, gifted, and ambitious young parliamentarian. He hoped to be Prime Minister someday, and his gifts and influence made that a possibility. But his conversion to evangelical Christianity changed his direction. As he thought about the Christian faith and looked at his own society, he became convinced that slavery was a terrible sin against God and against people. He used all of his resources in fighting the slavery movement. He was virtually on his deathbed when the slave trade, and eventually slavery, were abolished in the British Empire. That was the beginning of the end of slavery, at least in the Western world.

A number of other social projects were advocated by the Clapham group, focusing on prison reform and better care for the poor.

Many do not realize how often we see this model in various missionary movements. The focus on evangelism has often led to ministries of compassion, and in turn, to the concern for broader social transformation. Carey's ministry in India followed the same order. While the Wesleyan movement and the Clapham group are probably the best known example of that wholistic model, there are many others.

The Great Awakening in North America

As this evangelical movement spread into the Church in Scotland, the Church divided into the 'evangelicals' and the moderates, who advocated the status quo. One of the evangelical leaders was John Witherspoon.

The Awakenings on the Atlantic coast of North America antedated the Wesleyan Awakenings in England. They were led by Presbyterians William and Gilbert Tennent in New Jersey, and Jonathan Edwards in New England. George Whitefield traveled up and down the coast and participated.

Because they needed an institution closer to home, and were not satisfied with the colleges in New England and Scotland, Presbyterians started the College of New Jersey to train pastors. They brought Witherspoon from Scotland to lead the college. Later it would be known as Princeton.

He was the only clergyman who signed the Declaration of Independence of the United States. Richard Stockton, an elder of the Presbyterian church in Princeton, and Witherspoon, his pastor, were two signers of that historic document.

Witherspoon specialized in what we call "political science" today. James Madison, who would be known as the Father of the American Constitution, studied an extra year with Witherspoon. Many believe that he had a profound effect on the American Constitution through Madison.

Thus we see that at their best, movements of renewal were concerned about the poor, the dispossessed and the alienated. As they went beyond their concern personal salvation alone, they had a profound effect on many areas of history.

Chapter Nineteen

William Carey and the Emergence of Protestant Mission Structures

Introduction

We have now looked at four movements: Puritanism, Pietism, Moravianism, and the Evangelical Awakenings. The latter included, but was not limited to, Methodism. The Protestant missionary societies were formed as a result of the 'Awakening,' first in the British Isles and then in North America. They led to what Latourette called "The Great Century of Missions."

As we have seen, the four movements were related to each other, and although they took place in different areas and espoused different forms of the Church, they had similar emphases. They stressed the necessity of conversion and the importance of an authentic Christian lifestyle in the midst of nominally Christian societies. They applied Scripture to life, stressed the atonement on the cross, gave a greater role to the laity, emphasized evangelism and mission, engaged in ministries of compassion and education, and hoped to lead their societies to live more in accordance with the values of the Gospel. The formation of small groups for mutual encouragement and nurture was important as well.

They understood the task of the Church differently from their Lutheran, Anglican, and Reformed traditions. Instead of focusing inwardly only on the care of church members, these movements, in various ways, focused outward, seeking to evangelize nominal Christians in their own cultures and non-Christians in the world beyond. Contemporary Evangelicals, in various ways, are heirs of these movements. They formed "the launching pad" of the Protestant world mission movement.

Missions before Carey

There were various attempts at mission before William Carey. We have already looked briefly at Baron Von Welz, an Austrian. In 1664, he called for the Church in Europe to take the Gospel to the rest of the world: He said,

> Is it right that we hold the gospel in our hands and do not extend it? We have many students of theology. We should encourage them to labor in places where the Gospel is not heard. We spend so much on ourselves and so little on others.

He was called a fanatic, and denied ordination by the Lutheran Church. A visionary, he suggested the formation of a missionary training school. Finally, he gave up his title, was ordained by an independent body, and went to Dutch Guyana in South America, where he died.

Puritan and Other Cross-Cultural Missions in America

We have mentioned John Eliot, a Puritan from Cambridge University, who arrived in Massachusetts in 1631 and became pastor of a congregation in Roxbury. He also began to evangelize the Algonquins, a Native American tribe. He learned their language and translated the Bible into their language. As far as we know, it was the first Bible published in North America. He gathered three thousand converts into "praying villages" where he did his best to protect them from the exploitation of other colonists. The news of Eliot's success reached England, and "The New England Society" was formed to support his work. Parliament and Cromwell approved it in 1649.

Three generations of the Mayhew family worked on Martha's Vineyard, an island off the coast of Massachusetts. They had thirty-six hundred Native American converts and ordained two Native American pastors. This was remarkable at a time when most Europeans considered indigenous races inferior.

John Campanius, a Swedish Lutheran, evangelized Native Americans along the Delaware River in the mid-seventeenth century. Some of his "Praying Villages," as they were called, were caught in the wars between the settlers and hostile tribes.

There were other attempts to evangelize Native Americans in the seventeenth century.

Later we will speak of the life and ministry of David Brainerd, who worked in central New Jersey near what is now the town of Cranberry, from 1744 until 1747.

Anglican Societies

Thomas Bray, an Englishman, who had visited North America briefly, established the Society for the Propagation of Christian Knowledge (SPCK) in 1699, and the Society for the Propagation of the Gospel in Foreign Parts (SPG) in 1701. The goal of these societies was to minister to Englishmen in other lands and preach to non-Christians. Their primary concern was to supply Anglican priests and Christian literature to English colonists. However, they also ministered to others, including slaves, and aided the Pietist mission in India. The Wesley brothers went to Georgia under the auspices of the SPG.

Moravians

Moravians worked in various areas in what are now the states of New York and Pennsylvania. During the French and Indian War against the British, nine Moravian missionaries out of a community of fifteen, and many of the Christian Native Americans, were killed. Often European settlers persecuted the Moravians and their converts. One community of Moravians and Native American converts eventually moved further inland to Ohio to avoid the violence.

Thus, we see that Puritans, Lutheran Pietists, Moravians, and Anglicans who were influenced by these movements were engaging in mission in North America well before Carey, and even before Ziegenbalg and Plütschau sailed for India. Sometimes we fail to see the many streams of thought and movement that flow, sometimes underground and sometimes in clear sight, before a great person like Carey catches our attention and inaugurates a new era. Such figures are important, but we cannot ignore the many forerunners who are sometimes forgotten. Such a more complete understanding of history will encourage us in our own ministries. We can be sure that the Holy Spirit does not "waste" any faithful ministry, whether or not the world notices it.

Carey and the Baptist Society

Despite these earlier initiatives, William Carey is rightly called the "Father of the Protestant Missionary Movement." The term is correct, not because he was the first Protestant missionary, but because of the unique role he played.

Carey's Background

Carey was a Baptist lay preacher and part-time schoolteacher who supported himself as a cobbler; that is, he mended shoes. Yet this man, who was largely self-taught and supported himself and his family at a humble profession, was one of the most brilliant and gifted linguists in history. He was also an incredibly persevering and dedicated servant of Christ. Converted in the evangelical awakening in eighteenth-century England, he was greatly influenced by the works of Jonathan Edwards and David Brainerd, and by the example of the Moravians. He was a Baptist but was influenced by the Wesleyan movement. He participated in the "concerts of prayer" that had been encouraged on both sides of the Atlantic by Edwards. Apparently, Carey was not considered a very good preacher. His first two attempts to be ordained in his "Particular Baptist" group failed. He succeeded the third time.

As Carey worked at his cobbler's bench, he began to dream. The British had now become a maritime power, and Captain Cook, the English explorer, had been "discovering" new islands in the South Pacific. As word of his "discoveries" came back to England, Carey's world expanded. He had heavy family responsibilities, but yet he began to believe that God was calling him to go to places where people had never heard the Gospel.

As we have seen, there was already considerable missionary activity on a small scale, but the movement had not yet taken off. We can think of a plane beginning to move down the runway, but not yet at the takeoff point. To continue that analogy, we can say it began to move down the runway in the 1631 with Eliot, gained momentum with Ziegenbalg and Plütschau in 1706, and still more with the Moravians in 1732. Then, with Carey, the wheels of our plane cleared the runway and it began to gain altitude.

Carey taught himself Hebrew, Greek, and Latin. He preached, taught school, and mended shoes to support his family. He dreamed, studied, and prayed. In 1792, he published a small book with the title, *An Enquiry into the Obligation of Christians to Use Means for the Conversion of the Heathen*. A friend furnished the funds for its publication. The modest little book was destined to have great influence.

We need to understand the term "Use Means" in the title of Carey's book. Many Christians theoretically believed that non-Christians should hear the Gospel and come to Christ; the question was, how should that happen? Most of the Church was indifferent to the question. Some, including Carey's "Particular Baptists," had adopted a rigid Calvinism that taught that God would do it in his own way, apparently without the use of human means or structures. As we mentioned before, the story has often been told (whether true or apocryphal) that when Carey suggested the formation of a mission society, an older pastor responded, "Young man, sit down! When God chooses to convert the heathen, he will do it without the likes of you or

me." Such rigid hyper-Calvinism, which did not represent Calvin himself, was one problem Carey faced. There was another. Some theologians taught that the Apostles had offered the Gospel to the whole world, but that the rest of the world had rejected it. Therefore, they reasoned, the Church had no more missionary obligation.

Obligation to Convert the "Heathen"

Carey cut through these theological rationalizations when he wrote his *Enquiry*. The phrase "use means" meant "form a mission society": a structured, committed community of men (and eventually women) who knew that their call was to take the Gospel to other areas of the world. In Carey's concept, not only those who went were part of the missionary society, but also those who stayed home and gave support. Whether they went or stayed, their concern was to carry the Gospel to the world. Building on the commercial ventures of the day, Carey's Baptist Society adopted a structure similar to these companies, except that their purpose was different.

Carey's missionary society was a significant new step. The Danish King had sponsored the Pietist mission to India. The Moravians were a missionary community. The SPG and the SPCK were directed mainly at Englishmen. Now Carey's society was directed specifically to non-Christians, and the purpose of the structure was to support and direct the mission.

Carey's *Enquiry* was divided into four parts. Part One examined the theological question, "Is the Great Commission binding upon people of our time?" He demolished the argument that said it was directed only to a certain period of history. Obviously, the answer was "yes." The Great Commission was binding on Christians of every period of history.

Part Two examined history. He reviewed previous attempts to convert the non-Christian world, and showed a remarkable knowledge of the history of the Church up to that point. He examined its history from Acts to Constantine. He knew about Ulfilas' mission to the Goths, the mission to England, and the Celts. He spoke of the Spanish and Portuguese missions, of which he had a very low opinion. (He saw them as trying to force "popery" on the people.) He wrote of Wycliffe, Huss, Luther, Calvin, John Eliot, and David Brainerd. He wrote of Ziegenbalg and Plütschau, and the Moravians. He knew that Wesley had sent two men to the West Indies.

Part Three consisted of an estimate of the world's population, the number of adherents of different religions, and an estimate of the number of Christians, including those of various churches. Carey's research and knowledge were remarkable when we realize how difficult it must have been for him to access sources. His research and writing were powerful.

One of the theses of this book is that communication of ideas, or "information distribution," has often played a key role in stimulating new movements. We have seen how important this was in the life of Huss, who read the writings of Wycliffe. Carey is another example. Among the books that influenced him was *The Journal of David Brainerd.* The young American, converted in the Great Awakening in New England, had lived sacrificially while ministering to Native Americans in New Jersey. Becoming ill with tuberculosis, he died in the home of Jonathan Edwards, whose daughter he was planning to marry. As he died, he gave Edwards his journal and said, "Use this for the glory of God." That was a great Puritan phrase!

Edwards published *The Journal of the Late Reverend Mr. David Brainerd* in the hope that it would indeed be used for the glory of God. It was read on both sides of the Atlantic, and it had an impact on Carey. Edward's writings on revival and his call for concerts of prayer for revival and mission were also important. The work of the Moravians was still another influence. Later, we will see how students in North America at Williams College and Andover Seminary read about Carey and were motivated to begin the American missionary movement. It is important to write and share ideas!

The Formation of the Baptist Society for the Propagation of the Gospel

In the last section of his *Enquiry,* Carey insisted that the time had come to form a mission structure. That same year, 1792, with the support of a group of Baptist pastors and laymen, "The Baptist Society for the Propagation of the Gospel Among the Heathen" was formed. Carey was not narrowly denominational, but his only support came from a group of Baptists. The original contribution was thirteen pounds, ten shillings, and six pence, roughly equal to sixty-five dollars today—not a great beginning, but of course a far greater sum then than it would be now. Before sailing to India, he preached on Isaiah 54:2,3. "Enlarge the place of your tent...lengthen your cords...for you will spread out to the right and to the left." (NIV) In his sermon he said, "Attempt great things for God; expect great things from God." Note the order. His theology was clear. He only dared to attempt great things for God because he knew that God was already working in advance of his arrival. It is God who calls us and takes us into mission, and he is there long before we arrive.

The British East India Company was strongly opposed to any mission to India. In 1793, its representative in Parliament proclaimed,

> The sending out of missionaries into our Eastern possessions is the maddest, most extravagant, most costly, most indefensible project that has ever been suggested by a moonstruck fanatic. Such a scheme is pernicious, imprudent, useless, harmful, dangerous, profitless, fantastic. It strikes against all reason and sound policy; it brings the peace and safety of our possessions to peril. (George, Timothy, *Faithful Witness. The Life and Mission of William Carey,* Birmingham, Alabama, New Hope: 1991, p. 1)

Carey and his colleagues were called

> apostates from the loom and anvil, ...renegades from the lowest handicraft employments, ... venders of a coarse theology who had crawled forth from the holes and caverns of their original destination. (*ibid.*)

Carey's wife was strongly against the venture, but finally was persuaded to go. Her unwillingness turned to resentment and grief when one of the children died, and she eventually lost her mind and died. That was the tragic side of Carey's life and ministry.

Hostility in India

As we have seen, the British East India Company, which dominated India at that time, was very hostile to Carey and any Christian mission to Asia. Carey was not allowed to embark on one of its ships, but sailed on a Danish vessel. Missions have often been accused of being the religious side of colonialism, and that accusation is partially true. However, we must also remember that often the colonists expressed great hostility to missionaries, fearing they would interfere with their profits and the exploitation of the indigenous peoples.

It is important for us to recognize both the courage and some of the failings of the earliest missionaries. They were children of their time and often believed their culture and even their race to be superior to others. Nevertheless, we must recognize their commitment and, in the long run, their effectiveness. Most went to far places of the world, knowing they would never see their families or homeland again. Often, six months after a missionary group of two or three families arrived at their destination, half had died of disease. This was especially true in East and West Africa. The first American missionary to die was Harriet Newell. She died at the age of nineteen, in 1813, before reaching her destination.

We see incredible heroism on the part of both wives and husbands. Robert Morrison was the pioneer Protestant missionary to China. His wife had to return to England for reasons of health, and he died alone in China. While it was not true of Carey, in most cases, husband and wife made their decisions together, suffered together, often buried their children, and continued in mission even after a spouse died. We will see another example of that kind of love and sacrifice in the case of Adoniram and Ann Judson.

Carey's Work

As we noted, Carey encountered the hostility of the East India Company and was not allowed to remain in territory under its control. Under great hardship, the Careys went to live in Serampore, a Danish colony. It is ironic that eventually Carey supported himself and much of the ministry by working for the East India Company.

In 1804, Carey and his associates formed a "brotherhood" in Serampore, sharing their possessions and living in community. Their covenant contained eleven statements of purpose:

To set an infinite value on men's souls.

To acquaint ourselves with the snares which hold the minds of the people.

To abstain from whatever deepens India's prejudice against the gospel.

To watch for every chance of doing the people good.

To preach 'Christ crucified' as the grand means of conversion.

To esteem and treat Indians as our equals.

To guard and build up the 'hosts that may be gathered.'

To cultivate their spiritual gifts, ever pressing upon them their missionary obligation, since Indians only can win India for Christ.

To labor unceasingly in Bible translation.

To be instant in the nurture of personal religion.

To give ourselves without reserve to the Cause (*ibid*, p 123).

The scope of Carey's ministry was extraordinary. He was an evangelist, but worked for seven years before baptizing his first convert. By 1810, the number had grown to three hundred. After he witnessed the rite of *suttee*, in which a young widow was burned alive with the body of her husband, he campaigned against the practice. He also worked to end infanticide. While the East India Company did not want to interfere with such practices, Carey succeeded in arousing evangelical sentiment in England and, with the support of Hindu reformers, suttee was prohibited. As an educator, Carey established Serampore College. He also initiated agricultural research, having been an amateur botanist back in England. However, Carey would be known especially as a Bible translator. He began to study Indian languages—first Bengalese and Sanskrit. With his colleagues, John Clark Marshman and William Ward, he translated and printed six complete Bibles, twenty-four New Testaments, and ten parts of Scripture into various Indian languages. The broad scope of the ministry of this man, who had little formal education, is simply astounding. It included evangelism, education, translation, social work, and agricultural research. Beyond that, he became a great stimulus to missionary efforts by others in England, Scotland, on the Continent, and in North America!

After some years, the original leaders of the Baptist Missionary Society were succeeded by a new generation that did not enjoy the same personal relationship with Carey, nor did he have their confidence. They did not understand or agree with some of Carey's policies, and eventually the society he had established broke with him and demanded that he turn over all of the territory and buildings that he had built. They were against the establishment of the College, and that was the only property they allowed him to keep. Carey's concept of mission was much broader than theirs. This event pointed to an issue that has often arisen in the missionary movement: the need for freedom by those on the field in contrast to the need for control by those at home. We have seen it in the case of the Jerusalem church and the Antioch mission, and between Matteo Ricci in Peking and Rome, for example.

While teaching a class in a church in New England, I was once asked if those missionaries went out to "change the cultures" of the people to which they went. I replied, "Yes, often they do." That is never the primary goal. Yet when Carey saw young widows being burned alive, he sincerely believed that aspect of Indian culture should be changed. Scottish Presbyterians in Kenya fought to end the practice of female circumcision, and one was killed for her efforts. Foot binding in China was another issue, and so was the possibility and desirability of educating girls. The main issue here is not whether or not the Gospel (and missionaries) should attempt to change a culture. We recognize that at times missionaries have made serious mistakes in attempting to do so. At the same time, we must all agree that every culture needs to be changed

in significant ways by the Gospel, that, of course, includes mine. The questions to be asked are, what aspects of each culture should be changed, who should make the decisions, and through what process? While expatriates may often play a role, as Carey did, ultimately only those inside a culture can bring significant change.

The Explosion of Mission Societies

With Carey, the Protestant missionary movement gained great momentum as the next century began. Latourette called it "The Great Century of Missions." We define that "Great Century" as the period from 1792 to 1914 when World War I broke out and changed the face of the world. In other words, the great century of missions lasted about a century and a quarter.

In Britain

A number of other societies were now established. Presbyterians, Congregationalists, and some evangelical Anglicans established the London Missionary Society (LMS) in 1795. This was initiated by a letter from William Carey to John Garland urging him and others to form such a society. Many of the great names in missions were associated with it: the LMS sent Robert Moffat and David Livingstone to Africa, Robert Morrison to China, and John Williams to the South Seas. A Scottish society was formed in Edinburgh and Glasgow the following year. The Church Missionary Society (CMS), the greatest of the Anglican Societies, was formed in 1799.

These societies were not sponsored by their churches. Some were denominational (Baptists and Anglicans) and some were multi-denominational (LMS), but none was established by an official church body. All of them arose on the periphery of their church structures and were governed by groups of clergy and laymen. Often church leaders expressed opposition and antagonism to these mission initiatives. Fifty years passed before the Anglican bishops recognized the validity of the CMS. Yet today we can see that most of the growth of the Anglican Church in Africa, where it outnumbers its mother church in England many times over, is the result of the work of the CMS.

The SPG enlarged its foreign mission work at this time. The Wesleyans formed their society in 1813, which took over existing work. The Methodists had already sent missionaries to Africa and West Indies.

The interdenominational Religious Tract Society was formed in 1799 to produce literature for various missions, and then the British and Foreign Bible Society in 1804. Its purpose was to print and make the Scriptures available around the world. Other international Bible societies would be its descendents. In these societies, evangelical Anglicans and dissenters (that is, Presbyterians, Congregationalists, Baptists, and Methodists) cooperated. Thus, the first ecumenical cooperation originated with awakenings and the missionary movement.

On the Continent

A number of mission societies were formed on the European continent: in the Netherlands in 1796, in Basel, Switzerland, in 1815, and in Berlin in 1824. So after Carey, there was a great explosion of missionary societies in England, Scotland, on the Continent, and eventually in North America. Growing numbers of young men and women from Europe and North America went to Asia and Africa, and eventually to Latin America, to share the Gospel as they understood it and to establish the Church.

In Europe, all of the early mission societies were formed on the periphery of the Church, whether it was a church established by the State, or a dissenting body. At times, some European churches would ordain a person for mission work, but did not consider that ordination valid in Europe. Think about the implications of that! Did it imply that missionaries were second-class pastors and that believers in the new churches were inferior in some way?

There are three Lutheran mission societies in Norway, none of them sponsored by the established church. All of them arose in renewal movements led by laypersons on the periphery of the official church. They have received their support from people in the Church; have their boards constituted by pastors, lay men, and women of the Church; receive their personnel from the Church; contribute to the establishment of the Church in other cultures; but are not officially seen as part of the Church structure in Norway. Clearly, that reflects a very inadequate ecclesiology.

Up to the latter third of the nineteenth century in the United States, denominational mission societies were the norm. But a group of students had stimulated the formation of the first American mission board, The American Board of Commissioners for Foreign Mission. It was established by clergy of the Congregational and Presbyterian churches, but the initiative came from the students. But in a wave of denominationalism, by mid-nineteenth century, almost all of the mission structures in the United States were denominationally sponsored and administered. The largest were the Congregationalist, Presbyterian, Baptist, and Methodist boards. However, that pattern has been changing rapidly in the United States since the middle of the twentieth century. The Southern Baptists and Assemblies of God have very strong denominational mission agencies, and so do the smaller evangelical groups, but the older "mainline" denominations (those churches that came out of the Protestant Reformation or subsequent seventeenth- and eighteenth-century movements, Congregationalist, Baptist, and Methodist churches) have radically reduced their mission efforts. At the beginning of the twentieth century, approximately seventy-five percent of all American missionaries served under boards of the "mainline" denominations. Today that number has fallen to about five per cent. In some cases (e.g., the Congregational American Board of Commissioners for Foreign Missions), they have ceased to exist. To put it another way, in the 1920s, there were about thirteen thousand North American career missionaries. About eleven thousand served under denominationally sponsored boards. Today there are about forty thousand career North American missionaries, but the number serving under the older denominational boards is less than two thousand.

There are a number of reasons for this decline, but two stand out. One is theological: some church leaders apparently are not convinced of the need for world evangelization. A second reason is structural: a number of older denominations have merged their mission structures into other entities, where mission has become a low priority. It is a great tragedy.

Along with the growth among Southern Baptists, Assemblies of God, and other evangelical denominations, we have seen significant increase in the number and creativity of multi-denominational groups. Youth With a Mission (YWAM), Operation Mobilization (OM), Wycliffe Bible Translators (WBT), Pioneers, Frontiers, and many others are examples. Many evangelical young people from the older "mainline" churches are serving in them. At the same time, the number of missionaries from various Charismatic groups has grown. Thus, the movement that began to grow so rapidly with Carey continues today, even as older structures decline and die, and new ones take their place. The new groups often demonstrate new vision and methodology. However, the most important development today, as we shall see, is the internationalization of the missionary movement. We will examine that in a later chapter.

Chapter Twenty

The Beginning of Mission in America

Devotional

Paul traveled on to Derbe and Lystra, where a Christian named Timothy lived. His mother, who was also a Christian, was Jewish, but his father was a Greek. All the believers in Lystra and Iconium spoke well of him. Paul wanted to take Timothy along with them, so he circumcised him. He did so because all the Jews who lived in those places knew that Timothy's father was Greek. As they went through the towns, they delivered to the believers the rules decided upon by the apostles and elders in Jerusalem, and they told them to obey those rules. So the churches were made stronger in the faith and grew in numbers every day. (Acts 16:1–5 GNT)

This opening paragraph of Acts 16 illustrates several relevant principles of missiology. The question arises, was Paul contradicting his own principles when he had Timothy circumcised before adding him to his missionary team? Second, what was the strategic importance of Timothy?

Timothy was a "bridge person." The apostle Paul, and indeed the entire early Church, came out of a mindset that the people of God were identified by and limited to those who observed the Jewish Law. That law was the clear boundary, the wall, between the people of God and those who were not God's people. However, Paul and his colleagues were proclaiming a new message. The Law was no longer the determining issue. One became a child of God by accepting God's gift of salvation by grace simply through faith in Jesus Christ. It is the message that Luther and many others would rediscover, and that Wesley would reaffirm in his own experience. It was the basic message that has always been central in movements of renewal.

Paul and Silas went across Asia Minor proclaiming this message: God has broken down the barrier between Jew and Gentile, between those who were the people of God because they observed the Law and those who did not. God has broken down the barriers of race, ethnicity, tradition, and ethical or religious performance. The only requirement to become part of the people of God is to have faith in Jesus Christ. Now Paul chose Timothy, to be part of his missionary team. Timothy was uniquely qualified to serve as a bridge person between the Jewish and Gentile communities because he was half-Jewish and half-Greek. Thus, when Paul and Silas proclaimed that God had broken down the barrier between Jew and Gentile, they not only proclaimed it verbally, they modeled that reality in the composition of their apostolic team.

A good illustration of this recently may be seen in the ministry of African Enterprise in South Africa. In that context of apartheid, racial oppression and violence, the AE teams have made it a point to include Black and White evangelists together, on the same platform, as they proclaim the Good News that God has broken down racial barriers in Jesus Christ. They not only proclaim the message verbally; they model it.

Thus, we can see the importance of choosing Timothy to be part of that apostolic team. Later on, at the end of the chapter, as they moved across into Macedonia, Luke, a Gentile, was added to the apostolic team. Whether Paul planned this or the Holy Spirit led him that way, or a combination of the two, we can see the importance of this step. It is similar to having a multi-national, multi-racial, multi-cultural team communicate the Gospel in many parts of our fragmented world today, where the Christian faith is still thought by some to be a "white man's religion."

But why was Timothy circumcised? Wasn't this a violation of Paul's own principle that the believer did not have to observe the Law? I believe he did it as a matter of accommodation to make Timothy, the bridge person, acceptable to the Jews. They would have been scandalized to know that Timothy, son of a Jewish woman, had not been circumcised. That would have appeared to be a total rejection of his heritage and the Old Testament covenant. However, the message of Paul and his team was not the rejection of the Old Covenant, but its fulfillment in Jesus Christ. Circumcision had no relevance to Timothy's salvation, but it was essential to make him more acceptable to the Jewish community.

An analogy today might be a situation in which a missionary among Muslims, whether of the same or a different culture, adopted a Muslim style of worship instead of a Western Christian style. This might involve sitting on the floor in worship and bowing one's head to the ground in prayer as a Muslim does, instead of standing or sitting as many Christians do.

The third issue in this story is the process by which Timothy was trained. A basic thesis of this course is that we see the Holy Spirit lead his people into new methods of selecting and training leadership wherever we see renewal movements breaking out, and usually in mission movements. Usually these methods are more "grassroots" and less elitist than traditional methods. That is, leaders are chosen for their demonstrated gifts and trained in context, instead of being selected for their formal educational qualifications.

As far as we know, Timothy had no formal training. He was simply a young believer. Paul saw the potential in him, took him along, and trained him in an apprenticeship system. Later on we will discover from Paul's letters that Timothy became a very valued colleague in ministry.

This is an example of looking at a familiar passage through missiological eyes to discover important lessons for our own ministries. Acts 16 has a number of important lessons.

Let us pray together.

> Lord, we thank you that you have so much to teach us through your written Word, as we look at it through the eyes of our experience in other cultures. We thank you for your servant Paul, your servant Timothy, and what we have to learn from them: the issues they faced and how they met them, the clear leading of the Spirit in their lives, and their responsiveness to the leading of the Spirit. And we pray that you would continue to work in our lives, that we might be ever more sensitive to these kinds of issues, and at the same time more sensitive in listening to the Spirit as he leads us in our own contexts. Now guide us as we continue to think and study together. In Christ's name. Amen.

Introduction

We will now examine the beginning of overseas mission from the United States. Sometimes we think churches in the United States were similar to their parent churches in Europe. But there were many differences.

We might look at the Atlantic Ocean as a huge sieve that only allowed certain types of people to pass through. It was dangerous and expensive to cross the ocean. What kinds of people did so, and what motivated them? Most came for religious, economic, or political reasons, or perhaps a combination of all three. While some parts of the world today may look upon the United States as a bastion of conservatism, in the seventeenth and eighteenth centuries it was a leader in radical political, economic, and religious thought. Religious radicals who left Europe and came to the United States helped shape the Church here.

Some wanted to worship differently or were seeking more freedom. Many were looking primarily for economic opportunity. However, the people who came for specifically religious reasons were considered radicals. They included Quakers, Puritans, Methodists, and Baptists.

Almost all those who came for economic reasons were nominal Christians. Theoretically, everyone who came from Europe was a "Christian," except for a small handful of Jews. Perhaps 99 percent of those who came were church members in Europe, but only about 6.9 percent became church members in America. In other words, the majority of the immigrants left their faith and church relationships in Europe.

Another difference from Europe was the great variety of churches in North America. In Europe, for the most part, geography determined your church. For example, if you lived in one part of Germany, you were Lutheran; if in another area, you were Roman Catholic. If you were from Scotland or Northern Ireland, you were Presbyterian. If you were from England, you were probably Anglican, unless you came from one of the more radical groups that had come from the Puritan movement. These included Presbyterians, Congregationalists, Baptists, and Quakers. Therefore, England was an exception, and a significant number of these more radical groups immigrated to the new world.

So the religious uniformity that existed in Europe broke down in North America. Even though Anglicans were dominant in Virginia and Congregationalists in New England, in general there was a great diversity of churches in the colonies. Anglicans, Presbyterians, Congregationalists, Quakers, Baptists, and Methodists might exist almost side by side. The concept of "denomination" arose. In most parts of Europe there was simply "the Church." It might have been Lutheran, Roman Catholic, Presbyterian, or Reformed, but it was simply "the Church" where it existed. In most cases, it was the only church in its area. Now, in America, there were various churches side by side. The word "denomination" implied that the particular body was simply one way of "denominating" or defining the Church. It did not imply that the group represented the totality of the Church in that place. Soon, each "denomination," no longer able to rely on the State, had to organize itself to carry on its work and churches of the same tradition cooperated with one another. The first three functions of the denominational structures were to define their theology, train and validate ministry, and engage in mission.

A high percentage of the people in Europe still worshipped in their churches. When they came to America, often there was no church of their tradition within reach. Frequently, their faith was not very vital. There was great need for men like Muhlenberg, a Lutheran Pietist, who worked to gather Lutheran settlers in Pennsylvania into churches and provide pastors for them.

Even in Puritan areas where the Congregationalists formed the dominant church, the majority of the population were not members, even though the majority might attend in some communities. Soon there were Anglican and Baptist churches in New England, but most of the people were not church members. Only a minority of the immigrants to New England was Puritan, and as the years went on, many of the descendents of the Puritans drifted away from the Church. As one writer put it, New England Puritanism shifted its focus from "holiness to respectability." In addition, standards for church membership were high. A person was required to tell of a specific conversion experience in order to be accepted for membership, and many could not do so. Consequently, in the North American colonies only 6.9 percent of the population held church membership.

Therefore, the situation was very different from that in Europe. Baltimore, Maryland, was predominantly Roman Catholic; Pennsylvania was predominantly Quaker, Lutheran, and Presbyterian; New Jersey was predominantly Presbyterian and Dutch Reformed. While those were the dominant churches in their areas, the situation was not analogous to that of Europe, where almost everyone was a member of the Church.

In addition to the European denominations that came across the Atlantic, new, indigenous denominations arose in North America. Methodism arose in the United States soon after it did in England, and grew to be the largest Protestant group in the nation. The Baptists soon outnumbered their English brethren. In addition, a completely new denomination (even though they do not like the term), the Disciples of Christ, arose on the American frontier.

This new context meant that the Church in North America was challenged to develop new techniques for evangelizing or re-evangelizing the nominal Christian masses outside the Church. Many leaders believed there was danger of the new nation becoming totally pagan, and feared the Church might disappear. Revivalism and new patterns of leadership selection were part of the response that would be extremely important in American Christianity.

We will see new, more flexible structures of church leadership arising in North America. Those groups most flexible in their methods of selecting and training leaders and structuring the Church grew most rapidly. It was clear to many that traditional European methods were not adequate for the new frontier. This was a missiological issue for North American churches, just as it is for those who go into new cultures to evangelize and plant churches.

An additional factor was the presence of a frontier in North America. For many, that meant free land further west, even though it ignored the rights of the Native Americans. The "Go West, Young Man!" mentality implied opportunity and openness to new ideas. Historians have written about the presence of a frontier in North America and the effect it had on the American mentality. Without doubt, the frontier spirit had its effect on the churches.

So we can understand revivalism, new methods of selecting and training leaders, and more flexible church structures as attempts to contextualize the Christian mission in North America. To be faithful and effective in North America, the churches that came from Europe had to change. Simply to repeat the European patterns would have meant failure.

As we examine mission movements throughout history, normally we see four necessary factors. The first is a theology of mission. Our theology will tell us what we are about, and what our goals are. Theology might lead us to focus on evangelism and church planting, or on ministries of compassion and social change. If both are included, and they should be, our theology will help us understand the relationship between the two. The second essential factor is the spiritual dynamic. After all, what motivates men and women to leave their comfort zone and to go out in response to the call of God, to places where they might confront danger, disease, and hostility? Only a strong impulse of the Holy Spirit! This is why mission movements have normally come from either corporate or personal renewal, or both. The third essential factor is a mission structure that sends and supports the missionary. And the fourth is leadership that communicates the vision. I am not saying that all of these have been present in every mission movement, but normally they are. They do not necessarily come in that order. Often a movement has begun, motivated by a spiritual dynamic, with the theological reflection coming later; at times men and women have gone to a new field in response to the call of the Spirit, and later a mission structure has been created to support them. Nevertheless, the first three factors are necessary for a healthy movement, and usually we will find the fourth as well. We will see how that developed in North America.

Developing a Theology of Mission

The Puritans were the most active and creative English-speaking theologians of their day. They made a significant contribution to missionary thought in the eighteenth century. It is important to note that we always operate, consciously or unconsciously, from a specific theology of mission. That theology may be implicit or explicit, but it shapes our motivation and action whether we realize it or not.

A Theology of Partnership with God

First, Puritan theology taught that we are called to be partners with God in redemption. Christians are called to be participants with God in his plan for history. When the Puritans came to New England, they believed God had given them a twofold task. They believed they had been called to "establish a new Zion in the wilderness." They saw themselves as participating in a new Exodus. The Atlantic Ocean was the Red Sea; Europe was Egypt; New England was the Promised Land. That powerful analogy gave them direction and sustained them. They were bearers of the New Covenant, although not to the exclusion of other Christians, they believed they were inaugurating a new era in history.

They saw the Church and state in Europe as decadent, were convinced that God had called them to shake off the dust of the old world from their feet, come to this new land, and build "a city set on a hill." This city would be a light to the world and a demonstration of what a people committed to God and obedient to his covenant could be and do. They wanted to be an example to the world. Their goal was not without some arrogance, but they aimed high in seeking to be obedient to God. They were not perfect, but they did accomplish a great deal as they established their communities and founded colleges.

The early Puritans also came to convert the "Indians." Some (John Eliot, the Mayhews, and others) did so. However, as the generations went by, others simply exploited the Native Americans. Nevertheless, the earliest Puritans did believe in evangelization of the indigenous people.

The Glory of God as the Primary Motive

Secondly, as good Calvinists, the glory of God was the Puritans' primary motive. The Westminster Catechism, a Puritan document, began by asking the question, "What is the chief end of man?" The answer was, "To glorify God and enjoy him forever." A marvelous statement! "Enjoying God" gives a very different impression from the idea many have of the Christian faith.

What does "glorifying God" mean? The best definition I know came from Dr. Otto Piper at Princeton. He said that to glorify God means to live in such a way that the reality of who God is, his character and beauty, may be seen even in our flawed human lives. God is glorified when he is lifted up in his splendor. For the Puritans, God was glorified when his kingdom was advanced. That concept obviously had great missionary implications. Thus, for the Puritans, the glory of God was the first motive of mission. Love for Jesus Christ and compassion for the lost were also important, but they were secondary.

The Potential of Humankind in Redemption

Thirdly, the Puritans saw all men and women as persons with great potential. They recognized of course, that all were sinners, but they believed that in redemption, all men and women had enormous potential.

Jedidiah Morse was a New England Congregationalist pastor. He served on the board of Andover Seminary and the American Board of Commissioners for Foreign Missions. (He was also the father of Samuel F. B. Morse, who invented the telegraph.) At that time, most Americans, including the faculty at Harvard, saw the Native Americans as second- or third-class people with little potential. However, early in the nineteenth century, Morse wrote, "The Indian has the same potential that any other person has. When redeemed by the blood of Christ, the Indian has the potential to advance as much in civilization and spiritual things as any white person."

That may not seem startling to us today but it was a radical affirmation two centuries ago! It came from Morse's Calvinistic theology, that knew men and women were sinners, but also had a high view of their potential when redeemed. The missionary implications of this concept are clear.

Doctrine of the Church

Fourthly, the Puritans had a high view of the Church. They believed it existed under the cross, an army in warfare against Satan and evil. Baptism meant that one entered that army and took part in the struggle. It was a pilgrim church, never totally at home in this world. John Bunyan's *Pilgrim's Progress*, probably the most translated book in the world after the Bible, came out of Puritanism. He was a Baptist Puritan. His view of life as a pilgrimage, a struggle against temptation, against the attacks of the devil, characterized the Puritan view of life.

Thus, they understood their mission was not simply to call for individual conversions, but to plant the Church throughout the world. The Church loomed large in their theology.

One defect in some evangelical theologies in the past has been an inadequate view of the Church. The Church is the Body of Christ, and planting and nurturing the Church is essential. However, we agree with the Puritans that it should be a converted church! John Eliot, the Puritan who worked to establish a Native American church, not only planted several such churches; he advocated the ordination of Native American pastors. He felt that "an Englishman who was raw in the language" would be a hindrance to the "Indian" church, and he wanted to see "Indian" pastors. It was a remarkable viewpoint in the eighteenth century. And we have seen that the Mayhews ordained two Native American pastors on Martha's Vineyard.

Eschatology

Fifth, the Puritans also had an interesting eschatology. They believed there were three periods in the history of the Church. The first was the apostolic period, when theoretically—this was fiction, but they believed it—the Gospel had been offered to the whole world. How this was done is a bit mysterious. This is one reason there was not more missionary vision. It was a convenient doctrine to excuse the lack of missionary vision in the Church.

The second period, they believed, began with the manifestation of the Antichrist and persecution. They identified the Antichrist with the pope, and identified the time of persecution with the Reformation.

They believed that history was moving into the third period, when the Church would go to the Gentiles (i.e., non-Western peoples). It would expand to the ends of the earth, and people of every race and language would eventually come to Christ. They believed they were at the end of the second period and beginning to move into the third.

The Purpose of Election

Finally, the doctrine of election was important in their theology. At times, the doctrine has led to complacency or even a feeling of spiritual superiority. But that is a caricature of the Calvinistic doctrine of election, and is not how the Puritans viewed it. For the Puritans, election was always for a purpose, for obedience to God, to be his servants.

In addition, the Puritans believed God chose which nations should hear the Gospel at certain times in history, but they believed that every nation would eventually hear the Christian message and that some of its people would be converted.

Some believed the day had arrived when the New England "Indian" nations would hear and respond to the Gospel. The missiological implications of that idea are clear.

The Dynamic: The Great Awakening

It requires a great jolt of spiritual energy to motivate people to leave their places of comfort and security, family and friends, to go far away to places and people who appear different, dangerous, and even hostile. Such energy has nearly always come from movements of renewal or revival. The Great Awakening in North America in the middle of the eighteenth century, followed by a second awakening at the turn of the century, provided the motivation for mission on this side of the Atlantic as it had in Britain.

Over a century after the Puritans arrived in New England, their descendents had lost much of their zeal. They had settled down, many had prospered, and the newer generations were often respectable church members—but most of the fire had gone out of the movement.

Solomon Stoddard

Solomon Stoddard was pastor of the Congregational Church in North Hampton, Massachusetts. He was greatly concerned about the need for a spiritual awakening. He also advocated the evangelization of the Native Americans even though at times they were hostile and attacked the colonists. He wrote an exposition of Matthew 28, insisting that it applied to the Church of his day. In that sense, he anticipated Carey's view. A few years before his death, Stoddard's grandson, who had recently graduated from Yale, became his assistant and was destined to succeed him as pastor. His name was Jonathan Edwards.

Cotton Mather

Cotton Mather, another Puritan leader, had a growing vision for mission. He engaged in correspondence with Francke in Halle, Ziegenbalg in India, and the Anglican court chaplain in England. That was remarkable at a time when denominational barriers were very high. An American Congregationalist, two German Lutherans, and an English Anglican focused together on world mission, a rare example of early ecumenism, the result of a common missionary vision.

Mather also introduced the thinking of continental Pietism to America. Puritanism had been one of the influences that resulted in Pietism, and now Pietism began to influence Puritanism in New England.

Mather was concerned for church union as well as world evangelization. Eschatology was important. His view of history demanded action: he saw God calling us to obedience. He believed the missionary expansion of the Church would be an integral part of the events that would immediately precede the consummation of history, the Second Coming. In his writings Mather expressed concern for "Indians," Black slaves, Jews, and Spanish Americans. He wrote widely, and his works were circulated both in North America and across the Atlantic. He was a voice calling the Church to a much greater vision.

Jonathan Edwards and the Great Awakening

The Great Awakening began in the Raritan River Valley of central New Jersey. There, a Dutch Reformed pastor, Theodore Frelinghuysen, was pastor of several scattered congregations. A movement similar to Pietism had influenced him. The Dutch Reformed churches were very formal, and reacted against Frelinghuysen's preaching of a more personal Gospel and his call for conversion. In 1725 and 1726, a revival arose in some of the churches, but not without a reaction by traditionalists against the pastor. Then Frelinghuysen allowed a young Presbyterian, Gilbert Tennent, to use his church buildings to preach in English to colonists who spoke that language. Some of the Dutch colonists felt the Gospel should only be preached in Dutch.

Tennent's father, William, had come to North America from Northern Ireland, where he had been influenced by Puritan and Pietist ideas. He was concerned about the difficulty of sending pastoral candidates to New England or Europe, and was dissatisfied with the quality of spiritual life in the older institutions. Therefore, he established a small school in Pennsylvania, derisively called a "log college." There he trained nearly twenty young pastors, including his four sons. They proclaimed with great conviction the necessity of a deep inward transformation instead of mere outward performance of religious duties. They also went to settlers who lived a great distance from the organized churches. Clearly, because of the great distances involved, and the relatively few churches with pastors, the system of small parishes common in Europe was not viable in the North American colonies. The revivalists also advocated higher standards for the clergy. Some of those who came from Europe were unworthy men.

Conflict arose which led to schism among New Jersey Presbyterians in 1741 when the dominant group refused to ordain any more Log College men and expelled the revivalists. When the two sides came back together in 1758, the revivalists had increased their number of pastors from twenty-two to seventy-three, with even greater growth in the number of churches. The anti-revival group had declined from twenty-seven to twenty-three pastors. Tennent's log college was eventually reestablished as the College of New Jersey, and later moved to Princeton. It continued its original goal, to train pastors for the revival!

A similar movement broke out in Northampton, Massachusetts in 1734, when Jonathan Edwards preached a series of sermons on justification by faith. There were many conversions, and an awakening began. Shortly afterwards, Edwards published his classic *A Faithful Narrative of the Surprising Work of God in the Conversion of Many Hundred Souls*. It circulated on both sides of the Atlantic and stimulated further revivals. The movement subsided in 1735, but began again in 1739 and spread across New England and then up and down the east coast of North America.

Before Carey, Edwards advocated the use of means or missionary structures. He called for concerts of prayer, and they were influential on both sides of the Atlantic. Edwards saw revivals as signs of a new age that was coming, and in 1744, a group of ministers in Scotland called on the churches to join in public prayer for the coming of the millennium. Edwards wrote a book to encourage it.

George Whitefield, who had been part of the "Holy Club" at Oxford, crossed the Atlantic and preached to great multitudes. Considered the greatest English-speaking preacher of his day, this Anglican became a close friend of Tennent the Presbyterian and Edwards the Congregationalist. Most Anglicans in the colonies would have nothing to do with the revivals, but the majority of Congregationalists and Presbyterians supported them and received thousands of new church members. In New England, some lay preachers left the Congregational churches and became Baptists.

Because of the Awakening, the churches grew significantly and a number of educational institutions were established.

Two delightful stories are told about Whitefield. Benjamin Franklin, who was a deist and not a Christian, admired Whitefield greatly. It was said Whitefield preached out of doors to crowds as large as thirty thousand. Franklin had a scientific mind, and in one of the outdoor meetings, paced off the distance within which he could still hear Whitefield's voice. Then he determined the area of a semicircle with that radius and calculated that fifty thousand people could stand in that area and hear Whitefield preach outdoors.

The other story about Whitefield illustrates his ecumenical spirit at a time of great religious rivalry. In one of his sermons, he imagined Father Abraham in heaven. He called out to Abraham, "Whom do you have in heaven? Do you have Anglicans?" "No!" came the answer. "Do you have Presbyterians?" "No!" came the answer. "Do you have Baptists?" "No!" "Congregationalists? "No." Then whom do you have in heaven?" "We have none here except those who have been washed in the blood of the Lamb," was the reply!

Then the Revolutionary War came, and the movement died down. It re-emerged after the war and would give birth to the North American missionary movement.

David Brainerd

By 1740, Protestants in New England had supported missions among Native Americans for one hundred years, but no one caught public imagination the way David Brainerd did.

He was a student at Yale during the revival, and when some of the faculty were unsympathetic to the movement, he remarked that a certain professor had no more religion in him than the leg of his chair. For that remark, he was expelled from the college.

He became a missionary to the Native Americans near Cranberry, New Jersey, in the central part of the state. He saw a number of conversions, but lived in very difficult circumstances and was exposed to harsh weather. After three years he contracted tuberculosis, and went back to die in the home of Jonathan Edwards. He was engaged to Edwards' daughter. When he died, he gave his papers to Edwards, asking that they be used for the glory of God.

Edwards published *An Account of the Life of the Late Reverend Mr. David Brainerd,* writing in the preface that Brainerd's concern was the glory of God. Since God would be glorified primarily by the conversion of the heathen, Brainerd had become a missionary. Brainerd's journal circulated on both sides of the Atlantic and has had a powerful influence up to the present.

The Second Great Awakening

The Revolutionary War, which freed the North American colonies from England, began in 1776. At this time, there was a period of religious decline in the United States, and Deism became fashionable in the colleges. Some felt there was little future for the Church. In 1795, Timothy Dwight, the grandson of Edwards, became president of Yale. He began to teach systematic theology to every student, and the power of his thought and life began to have an effect. In 1802, one-third of the students in the college professed conversion, and numbers of them entered the ministry. There were also revivals in other colleges, and later the movement moved across the southern part of the United States to the western frontier.

We see the theological foundation laid by the Puritans, the dynamic of renewal in the work of the Holy Spirit through the lives of Tennent, Edwards, Whitefield, Dwight, and others. It was a great marriage of solid theological thinking, with a deep concern for spiritual renewal and the work of the Holy Spirit. Clearly both are needed, one without the other results in a stunted or deformed movement.

Samuel Hopkins was one of the most important spiritual heirs of Edwards. Hopkins had lived with him as a young pastor. He exerted great influence both on the early missionary movement and the anti-slavery campaign. His theology taught that the greatest goal of the Christian should be disinterested benevolence—seeking to do good for another without any gain to oneself. That had an interesting, two-pronged effect in American life and culture.

Hopkins taught the concept of disinterested benevolence in his church in Newport, Rhode Island, where he had slave traders in his congregation. He said, "Disinterested benevolence means that we are willing to go anywhere to serve and glorify God and to serve people. We should be willing to do things that will be against our own economic self-interest, if it's right." Several left the slave trade as a result. We wish that the whole Church had agreed with Hopkins, but that did not happen. Slavery was abolished quite early in

New England, partly because of the influence of Hopkins and others, and partly because it was not as important to the economy as it was in the South. Among the plaques at Yale Divinity School honoring their greatest graduates are one for David Brainerd, and another for Hopkins.

The Mission Structures

Now the first American foreign mission structure emerged, built on the foundation of theology and the Awakenings.

Missionary Societies among Native Americans

There were many groups concerned with missions on a small, sporadic scale on the American frontier. In many states, there were small mission societies of Congregationalists, Moravians, Lutherans, Quakers, Presbyterians, Methodists, and Anglicans, mostly directed toward Native Americans and some among settlers on the American frontier. There were a number of these by the end of the eighteenth century.

Denominational Stirrings

Presbyterians began to organize early in the nineteenth century. In 1803, the Presbyterian General Assembly formed the Standing Committee on Missions. It hoped to engage in missions on the frontier to settlements, Native Americans, and Blacks. It was a small beginning.

The Mission Becomes Global

The key person in the beginning of American foreign missions was Samuel F. B. Mills. He was a missiological entrepreneur—a person who had vision that far exceeded that of his contemporaries. Like others we have observed in history, his vision resulted in new mission structures.

We would like to know more about Mills' mother. She was married to a Congregationalist clergyman, and dedicated her son to missions before he was born! That was before Carey sailed for India. In 1806, Mills was a student at Williams College, and he and a small group of students held prayer meetings seeking revival in the college. They normally gathered in a field behind the main college building. One day they were caught in a rainstorm and took refuge under a haystack. As they prayed there, they pledged themselves to world evangelization. Four years later, they were students at Andover Seminary where another young man, Adoniram Judson, joined them. Judson was the son of a Congregationalist pastor, but while in college at Brown, he had imbibed the skepticism and deism of the day, and become an unbeliever. On a journey shortly after finishing college, he arrived at an inn and asked for a room. The innkeeper said he had only one, but it would be unpleasant since a young man was dying in the room next to it. Having no other choice, he took the room, and was awakened during the night by the groans and screams of the dying man. The next day, knowing the man had died, the innkeeper said to Judson, "You might have known him. He went to the same college you did." When Judson heard his name, he was shocked to discover it was the friend who had been instrumental in leading him to abandon his Christian faith. This was a powerful motivation for Judson to return to faith and attend seminary.

As the Haystack group studied at Andover Seminary, Judson joined them and they continued to pray about missions. In 1810, with the encouragement of their professors, they went to the church leaders in New England and asked them to form a mission board, adding that they were ready to go overseas.

The nation was young. It was small, with few resources. The church leaders were reluctant, but in response to the students they formed the first American mission board, the American Board of Commissioners for Foreign Missions (ABCFM) in 1810. Two of them, Judson and Luther Rice, became Baptists on board ship. Judson, unable to remain in India, went to Burma where he had a very impressive ministry. Rice returned to the United States where he persuaded the Baptists to form their own board in 1814.

Only men were considered "missionaries" in that chauvinistic era, but the Board encouraged them to marry before sailing. It was not an easy task to find wives for them. Judson contacted an attrac-

tive, godly young woman, Ann Hasseltine, who somewhat reluctantly replied that she was willing to marry him and go to India if her parents consented. Judson's letter to her father is worth citing.

> I have now to ask whether you can consent to part with your daughter early next spring, to see her no more in this world…her subjection to the sufferings and hardships of missionary life…to the dangers of the ocean…the fatal influence of the southern climate of India, to every kind of want and distress, to degradation, insult, persecution, and perhaps a violent death…all this for the sake of Him who left His heavenly home and died for her and for you, for the sake of perishing immortal souls, for the sake of Zion and the glory of God…in the hope of meeting your daughter in the world of glory, with the crown of righteousness, brightened with the acclamations of praise which shall redound to her Saviour from heathens saved, through her means, from eternal woe and despair? (Courtney Anderson, *To the Golden Shore: The Life of Adoniram Judson* [Valley Forge: Judson Press, 1987], 83).

Ann went, gave birth to three children—all of whom died in infancy—and saved her husband's life and his New Testament translation while he was imprisoned under brutal conditions. She finally died in Burma. After her death, Judson married the widow of a missionary colleague, and after she died, he married a third time. He lost two wives and three children in Burma. His case was not unusual.

By 1817, the American Board had missionaries in Bombay, Ceylon (Sri Lanka), and among the Cherokee Indians in the United States. A Foreign Mission School for training was established in New England. The ABCFM was predominately Congregationalist, but the Presbyterian and Reformed churches cooperated with it until their denominational boards were established later.

Mills never became a missionary, even though that was his goal. He initiated a number of other mission organizations that focused on the American frontier and slaves in the south. He died in his mid-thirties, but stands out as one of the key people in the history of North American missions.

One footnote to American mission history: while Judson and his colleagues are considered the first American foreign missionaries, that is not correct. Nineteen years before Judson sailed, the Black Baptists of Savannah, Georgia, sent out two former slaves as evangelists and church planters. David George went to Nova Scotia and then to Sierra Leone, where he planted the first Baptist church in West Africa. George Lisle went to Jamaica. These two former slaves were the first two missionaries to go overseas from the United States. As we study history, it is always important to dig beneath the surface and ask new questions, recognizing that all too often, the contribution of men and women who did not come from the dominant group are ignored or forgotten.

Chapter Twenty-One

The American Frontier:
New Patterns of Leadership

Introduction

This topic has important lessons for mission in new cultures. It may seem to be a diversion from the history of the missionary movement, but the lessons to be learned are relevant to our concerns.

Church membership in the new nation of the United States was a small part of the population, even after the Revolutionary War and the revivals. Most of the immigrants pouring in from Europe had left their faith and church relationships behind in Europe. Most came for economic reasons, seeking opportunity and free land. The population of this small nation was beginning to move west. Politically, socially, and religiously, nearly everything was in a fluid state in the first decades of independence. The new nation had created political structures never previously seen in history, and there was openness in general to new ideas in religion as well as politics. That was especially true in the populations that moved west.

Some of those who first reached the eastern seaboard of North America were from the nobility and had wealth. They included William Penn, who had large landholdings in Pennsylvania. Anglican Virginia had an aristocratic social and economic structure, and little new land was available. However, there was land in the west for those who could go there—hence the great westward movement.

In 1790, the population of the new nation was four million. Only five percent lived beyond the Allegheny Mountains; the rest lived up and down the east coast. In 1800, the territory of Indiana, west of the mountains, counted only five thousand people of European descent. In the year 1816 alone, 42,000 new settlers came, and the population of the territory was 63,800. Similar population growth was typical of other new territories and states to the west. Great numbers of people were arriving from Europe and pouring across the mountains seeking land and opportunity. As we examine the changing population patterns in the United States during that period, they remind us of the importance of demographic studies in mission work today. It suggests we look at the rapid urbanization in most of the world as many people from rural areas flock to the burgeoning cities. That is the opposite of population movements in early nineteenth-century America.

By 1820, there were twelve new states in the United States, and ten were west of the Allegheny Mountains. Church leaders spoke of the importance of evangelizing the frontier and planting churches and schools there. Otherwise, they were fearful of what they termed "a new barbarianism." They expressed fear that the nation would become almost totally pagan with little influence by the churches. They clearly saw that the future of the American churches would depend on how well they moved to the frontier.

In this fluid situation, most people were open to new ideas and loyalties as, above all, they sought new opportunities to determine their economic and political destinies in a manner not possible in the older European cultures. It was clear that those churches that adapted themselves most rapidly to the frontier context and were most effective in evangelizing people on the frontier would grow the most and exert the greatest impact on their societies.

Earlier I mentioned an important missiological issue I discovered in my study of Presbyterianism in Brazil. The Presbyterians in the United States had been much too slow in moving west to the American frontier, as we will see. The Baptists and Methodists moved much more rapidly and were far more flexible in methodology and structures. Not wishing to repeat their mistakes on the American frontier, when Presbyterians went to Brazil, they moved west, and left the coastal cities behind. The problem was that in Brazil, the people were moving east, to the cities. For example, when Philip Landes, a son of missionaries, already fluent in Portuguese, joined the mission in 1916, there was a question as to where he should serve. One possibility was the growing city of São Paulo, with a population of five hundred thousand at the time, but only two Presbyterian churches and pastors. The other was Cuiaba, capital of Mato Grosso, a state twice as big as Texas, with a total population smaller than that of São Paulo. The mission sent him to Cuiaba, where he had an effective ministry. However, we wonder if his gifts would not have been put to greater use in the urban center. Today greater São Paulo has a population of over twenty million.

Presbyterians and Congregationalists

We see the importance of studying demographics from the example above. Where are the people going? In this case, in the United States after the Revolutionary War, the people were rapidly moving west. Before the Revolutionary War, Congregationalists were the largest church and Presbyterians were next, followed by Baptists, and Anglicans. Methodists were arriving from England and would begin to grow after the war.

The Presbyterians, an Early Advantage

At the end of the war, the Presbyterians were the best situated. Many Scotch-Irish Presbyterian immigrants were arriving. They were Scots who had moved to Northern Ireland and then come to the United States. Others came from Scotland. They settled primarily in the middle colonies, New Jersey and Pennsylvania. Some went further south and then moved west. In the Presbyterian system, the presbytery is the regional body of churches located in a geographical area. The synod is a larger body made up of a number of presbyteries. Both presbyteries and synods in the east sent pastors to work on the frontier for short periods of time. This system was not very satisfactory. Travel was difficult and time-consuming. It meant that either the pastor was away from his church for a long time, and was on the frontier only a short time, only to disappear and return later.

In 1785, there were twelve Presbyterian congregations in the new territory of Kentucky. They constituted the largest church in the territory. By 1820, the population of the territory had grown to 560,000, and 46,730 were church members. Among them, twenty-seven hundred were Presbyterians and one thousand were Cumberland Presbyterians. The Cumberland group had split off from the parent body primarily because they wanted different methods of choosing and training pastors. However, by that date, the Baptists and Methodists each numbered around twenty-one thousand. The total number of Presbyterians, who had arrived first and thus had a great advantage, was only thirty-seven hundred, far less than the Baptists and Methodists.

What happened? This history has important lessons for us, especially when we are engaged in mission in new cultures and situations. My basic thesis is that the greater flexibility in selecting and training pastors and evangelists, and forming churches, was the primary factor in the different rates of growth. The more rigid Calvinistic theology of Presbyterians in contrast to the Arminianism of the Methodists was an additional factor. But that was not as important because, as we will see, Presbyterians were leaders in the frontier revivals along with the others.

Education and the Log Colleges

Coming from the Puritan and Reformed traditions, Presbyterians and Congregationalists put great stress on education. Remember, one goal of the Puritans was to have as resident in every parish a well-trained pastor who could expound the Scriptures. However, when there seemed to be a conflict between the two sides of that ideal, education was given priority over the goal of a pastor resident in every parish. Thus, they made a great contribution to education. In many places on the frontier, they started informal institutions modeled on Tennent's "Log College." Some turned out very effective pastors.

So in general, Presbyterians and Congregationalists focused on higher education. A man could not become a pastor until he had studied the biblical languages, along with traditional philosophy and theology. Thus, it was a long process to become a pastor. This led to an inadequate number of ordained men, and in Presbyterian and Congregational churches, typically only those who were ordained could preach. It is also possible that formal theological training tended to isolate these pastors from the thought patterns of the frontiersmen.

The Issue of How Pastors are to be Prepared

My thesis is that our patterns of selecting and training leadership are extremely important in enabling the Church to evangelize effectively, to grow, and to make a major impact on society. This is a key issue today in many areas of the world: sub-Saharan Africa and many areas of Latin America and Asia, where churches are growing rapidly. It is also an issue among the poor in urban areas in the West.

Churches in many areas are outgrowing their capacity to select and train pastors using traditional institutional methods. That method typically selected bright young men (still men in most places), sent them away to school for an extended period, and then sent them back as pastors. There is no way this system can ever prepare enough leadership for growing churches! This would be true even if it worked perfectly, but it does not. All too often, those who come from the countryside to spend years of study in an institution in the city find it difficult to return and identify with the people from whom they came. The question of how leaders are chosen and trained is one of the most critical issues in missions today. That is why I take this American frontier situation as a paradigm from which we may learn.

In the Presbyterian pattern, a young man had to finish his course in a college or university and then either spend some years in an apprenticeship with a pastor or attend seminary. Andover was the first North American seminary, established in 1808, and Princeton the second, in 1812. Increasingly, the pattern among the more established churches was to send a young man to college and then seminary before he could become a pastor. This involved seven years of formal education, and greatly limited the number of candidates.

The pastor usually served two or three churches, and perhaps spent a few weeks each year on a preaching tour in the new territories. To make ends meet, he often taught school as well. Presbyterians and Congregationalists made a great contribution to education, establishing primary schools and colleges, but their contribution to evangelization was not as great.

The initiative in forming a new church on the frontier normally came from Presbyterian laymen after they moved west. They contacted a presbytery in the east, asking to have a pastor sent. Often a long period passed before a pastor could be found who was willing to go and the congregation could support him. Thus, several years often passed between the formation of a Presbyterian congregation and the calling of a resident pastor.

At the same time, laymen gave some leadership in the Presbyterian and Congregational churches, but they were not encouraged to preach. Thus, the system of requiring ordained clergy, trained in colleges and seminaries, did not allow for rapid expansion.

Early Presbyterians in Brazil were different, to some extent. In the early days, some of the northeastern states had only one Presbyterian pastor for the whole state. He normally resided in the capital and was pastor of the Church there. He usually had a number of congregations throughout the interior of the state, often established through the heroic witness of laymen. The pastor might visit them once or twice a year.

The rest of the time, laymen led the congregations and often evangelized their friends and neighbors. They conducted worship, the men preached, and both men and women led Sunday schools. But they could not baptize new believers or serve the Lord's Supper. Only an ordained, seminary-trained person could do that. I often wondered if that was the biblical pattern!

Roland Allen, the great Anglican missiologist and father of much of modern missiology, asserted that in the New Testament any Christian group could celebrate the Lord's Supper and baptize new believers, but only especially chosen people could preach. (Roland Allen, *The Spontaneous Expansion of the Church and the Causes which Hinder It* [World Dominion Press, 1927], 175). We have reversed this in most of the modern missionary movement. In some situations, anyone can preach, but only

ordained people can celebrate the Lord's Supper or baptize.

We always need to ask, "Do the structures and methods of selecting and training leaders contribute to the growth of the Church and its impact on the world, or do they hinder it?" Then we must ask what alternatives we might explore.

Even so, Presbyterians experienced significant growth on the frontier, much of it coming from Scotch-Irish immigration. Congregationalists, the largest church before the War for Independence, fell far behind. Their requirements for ordination were the same as those for Presbyterians, but they did not benefit from immigration across the Atlantic. Often, when Presbyterian and Congregationalist settlers went west, they organized their churches together and then voted on their affiliation. In most cases, such churches opted to become Presbyterian.

Baptist Expansion in the South

There were Baptists in Anglican Virginia before the Revolutionary War but Anglicanism was established. The government would not allow a non-Anglican to preach without a license. As a matter of principle, the Baptists refused to ask permission of anybody—church or state—to preach. At times they went to jail. That brought them great sympathy among the common people, and led to growth. The Southern Baptists, not yet separate from those in the North, received a strong impulse from the Great Awakening in New England. A number of laymen who were converted in the Awakening felt called to preach, but were denied the opportunity in the Congregational churches. Some of them became Baptists, went to North Carolina and Virginia, and began to move across into Kentucky and Tennessee.

Baptists and the Poor

Baptists appealed primarily to the poor, while Presbyterians and Congregationalists were usually middle-class. Attracted by free land on the frontier, the poor rapidly moved west. They were also attracted by the greater degree of democracy there and the greater freedom from social constraints that existed in the more aristocratic east.

The Whole Church Often Migrated

Often an entire Baptist community migrated—a local church on the march. At times, they met other groups moving in the same direction, preached to them, and invited them to be baptized and join their group. Most were already nominal Christians and were attracted to the Baptist message that emphasized the importance of personal decision and conversion. Thus, at times, the Baptist churches grew as they journeyed west!

I saw an interesting parallel to this in Brazil. The state of Ceará is in the northeast and the state of Mato Grosso is located in the interior, further south and west. Terrible drought and poverty exist in the interior of Ceará. For years, there has been migration from that area, down the coast to Rio and São Paulo, and from there, west to Mato Grosso. When I was a pastor in Corumbá, Mato Grosso, five kilometers from the Brazil–Bolivian border, the two fastest growing churches in town were the Assemblies of God and the Presbyterian church. The pastor of the Assemblies of God had led group of his church members, fleeing from intolerable conditions in Ceará, all the way to Corumbá, a journey of twenty-five hundred miles. He was their Moses! His church members were very loyal to him. Their situation was not different from some of those early Baptist churches on the American frontier.

Farmer-Preacher Leadership

As we have seen, the Baptists preached along the way. Others joined them, and they baptized new converts in creeks. They were something of a people movement as they went along. The pattern of leadership in the Baptist movement was especially significant. The preacher was one of the people. He was a farmer-preacher and supported himself by farming, just as the others did. At times, the people paid him in kind with some of their crops or animals. That released him from some of the farm work so he could devote more

time to preaching and traveling to other areas to evangelize. But he was one of the people who supported himself, and was chosen to be the pastor because he exhibited gifts and zeal. It is clear that this was a different method of selecting and training leaders, and well suited to the frontier context. It made a great contribution to the rapid growth of the Church.

William Warren Sweet, the Methodist historian, wrote of a Baptist named Taylor, a native of Virginia. Of Anglican background, he was converted under the preaching of William Marshall. (Marshall was a Baptist farmer-preacher, and an uncle of the future Chief Justice of the United States.) Taylor married a Baptist woman in 1782, and the next year set out for Kentucky. The trip down the Ohio on a flatboat and through the wilderness on horseback took three months.

> [Taylor] settled in Woodward County, where he, with other Baptist preachers in the settlement, formed the Clear Creek Baptist Church, which he served for nine years as pastor. At the same time, he, with his sons and slaves, [we wish that was not there, but it is] cleared a large farm, and he became a man of importance in the whole region. He helped form seven other Baptist churches in Kentucky as well as others in western Virginia, North Carolina and Tennessee. It was his lifelong custom to set out from his home in the latter part of the summer and visit eight or ten Baptist Associations, and throughout the year he always found places to preach every Sabbath. All this labor was formed of his own volition and without compensation or overhead direction. (William Warren Sweet, *The Story of Religion in America* [New York: Harper, 1950], 216).

Democratic Structure

Such an account was not unique to John Taylor. He was a prototype of the fearless, self-reliant farmer-preachers who planted Baptist churches throughout the length and breadth of the new West. They were highly individualistic, and yet were part of a community. Usually a church had more than one pastor, although one of them might be given overall responsibility for the congregation. Local churches came together with others to ordain those who were called to preach. The Baptist pastors typically supported themselves and their families, preaching several times during the week. Then during the off-season, when there was little work to do on their farms, they traveled to other places to evangelize and establish new Baptist churches. It was a very interesting model of leadership selection.

Therefore, where the Presbyterian congregation waited until it could support, find, and call a Presbyterian minister who had been trained in college and seminary, the Baptist farmer-preacher went with his people. When they arrived in their new surroundings, there was no delay in establishing the Church with its pastor; nor was there any social or cultural gap between the pastor and the people. The local congregation was a church-on-the-move—a type of mission structure as it moved. Of course, it was not cross-cultural.

I do not mean to idealize the Baptist method. Pastors were not well-trained in theology or Scripture. They often showed prejudice against pastors who had formal education, and it appears that such a system made it easier for the churches to conform to their surrounding slave-holding culture. On the other hand, there is no evidence that the Presbyterians, who presumably had better theological education, were any more prophetic in speaking out against slavery.

Methodists on the Frontier

The Methodists were even more effective in evangelization than were the Baptists. They came from the same social class, but their structure and pattern of ministry were very different. The Baptists were totally democratic and individualistic. John Wesley, who was an authoritarian leader, appointed Francis Asbury and Thomas Coke as superintendents for North America. Asbury, understanding the American temperament, knew they should not accept such a position until the

American Methodist lay preachers had chosen them. In 1784, they were elected bishops of the American Methodist Church. Wesley did not approve of the term "bishop," but it remained in use in American Methodism.

Ministerial Pattern

The Methodist pattern of ministry was flexible and effective. A young man who showed gifts of exhortation and preaching could move from being a class leader, become a lay preacher, and eventually a circuit rider and ordained pastor. There were no social or educational barriers to any level of ministry if he demonstrated the gifts and zeal.

Methodist work was organized into "circuits." The ordained preachers itinerated, serving circuits of different sizes. In a new territory, the circuit might take four to five weeks to cover by horseback. In older, established regions, the churches were closer together and the circuit was more compact.

The first thing a Methodist preacher did when he went to a new territory was to preach and where there were conversions, establish classes. Because he appointed class leaders among the new converts, laymen began to move into leadership immediately. Thus, a new convert who showed some degree of maturity and zeal was given leadership responsibilities with little or no delay. There were probably twenty to thirty classes in the average circuit.

The Methodist preacher did not confine his preaching to Sundays or Wednesdays. He preached every day, wherever he found people. He might preach anywhere, in a half-finished log cabin, if the people were there, or in a tavern, or under a tree. In other words, he was not looking for Methodists; he was looking for people who might be converts! Wesley's goal was that the Methodist preachers be well educated. He prescribed a very healthy reading goal for them. Thus the method of training pastors was different.

The Presbyterian pastor often came looking for Presbyterians. The Baptist pastor-farmer evangelized along the way and sometimes baptized new members in the streams as they moved west. The Methodists went wherever there were people and sought to convert them and bring them into the Methodist Church! They all had different approaches to ministry, and to selecting and training leaders.

The key issue for early Baptists and Methodists was that any promising young man who could speak was encouraged to exercise his gifts and become a lay preacher. You will notice that both Baptists and Methodists used laymen. In other words, they applied the old Lutheran doctrine of the priesthood of all believers to a much greater extent than most other Protestant churches had done. In both groups, the pastors were very close culturally to the people they evangelized.

Message of Free Will, Free Grace

The theology of the Methodists was also well-fitted to the frontier mentality. Its Arminian theology focused on free will. To people on the frontier, moving west, hoping to determine their economic and political destinies, the Methodist message was that they could also determine their spiritual destiny. It said, "If you want to become a follower of Christ, you can do so. There are no obstacles to becoming a believer except the obstacles in your own mind and will." The message was a direct challenge to the individual. The Methodist message was in contrast to that of the Presbyterians, who tended to speak in more abstract, less personal theological terms.

Hierarchical Structure

Presbyterians had a represented democracy—a kind of republican system. Baptists theoretically had a pure democracy. Methodists used a hierarchical system. This may indicate there is no clear correlation between structure and the growth of the Church. In this case, in the period from 1785 to 1850 the Methodists with their hierarchical structure grew twice as large as the purely democratic structure of the Baptists, and four times as large as the Presbyterians.

Asbury was responsible to administer the Methodist Church in the United States. He appointed the preachers and traveled extensively across the mountains. He wrote in his journal that he found the preachers "indifferently clad, with emaciated bodies." They did not need a pension system at that time, because few lived long enough. It is worth noting that the Bishop received the same salary as the humblest circuit rider.

Growth

Methodist growth was impressive. In 1800, the Western Conference, including all Methodists west of the Allegheny Mountains, showed 2,622 white and 179 black members, organized in nine circuits. Twelve years later, the number had grown to 29,083 white and 1,648 black members, in sixty-nine circuits. By 1830, there were 158,000 white, 15,000 black, and 2,000 Native American members. By 1850, the Methodist Church, which had been the smallest at the beginning of our period sixty-five years earlier, had 1,324,000 members; the Baptists had grown to number 815,000; the Presbyterians, 467,000; and the Congregationalists, 197,000. Lutherans, who were primarily an immigrant church, counted 163,000 members, while Disciples of Christ, a new movement that arose on the frontier primarily from Presbyterians and Baptists, numbered 118,000. The Anglicans, now called "Episcopalians," had 90,000 members. Thus, we can see that while Presbyterians and Congregationalists made the largest contribution to education on the frontier, they did not succeed in evangelism and church growth as much as Baptists and Methodists.

Church		1850 Members
Methodist (smallest in 1776)	1st	1,324,000
Baptists (3rd in 1776)	2nd	815,000
Presbyterians (2nd in 1776)	3rd	467,000
Congregationalists (1st in 1776)	4th	197,000
Lutherans	5th	163,000
Disciples	6th	118,000
Episcopalians (4th in 1776)	7th	90,000

Frontier Revivals

While revivals in the East took a more sedate form, camp meetings, a form appropriate to the frontier, became an indigenized form of evangelism. After the settlers had worked hard for most of the year, a period of rest and socializing was needed. Evangelists and others began to hold camp meetings, and people came from long distances. Camp meetings were both social and religious events. Many saw friends whom they had not seen for a year. Normally many preachers participated, and often there were conversions.

Even secular historians have recognized the positive role of the meetings. They were not very orderly, but they had a significant impact on the growth of the Church. Early Presbyterian missionaries in Korea brought thousands together for Bible study that lasted for several weeks during the time of year work in the fields was light— another example of finding appropriate ways to minister within the context.

One of the most outstanding leaders of the frontier camp meetings was James McGready, a Presbyterian of Scotch-Irish heritage. It was said he was so ugly he attracted attention. As often happened in such movements, the Presbyterians initiated it and then became uncomfortable with the disorder, leaving Methodists and Baptists to assume leadership.

The Cane-Ridge Meeting took place in Kentucky in 1801. The crowd was estimated to number between ten and twenty-five thousand people. This was amazing when we consider the size of the population! One eyewitness wrote:

> I attended with 18 Presbyterian ministers; and Baptists and Methodist preachers, I do not know how many; all being either preaching or exhorting the distressed with more harmony than could be expected. The governor of our State was with us and encouraging the work. The number of people computed from 10, to 21,000 and the communicants [those who took the Lord's Supper] 828. The whole people were serious, all the conversation was of a religious nature, or calling in question the divinity of the work. Great numbers were on the ground

> from Friday until the Thursday following, night and day, without intermission, engaged in some religious act of worship. [That does not mean they were lying on the ground; that means they were there.] They were commonly collected in small circles of 10 or 12, close adjoining another circle and all engaged in singing Watts' or Hart's hymns; and then a minister steps upon a stump or log, and begins an exhortation or sermon, when, as many as can hear collect around him. On the Sabbath I saw above 100 candles burning and I saw 100 persons at once on the ground crying for mercy, of all ages from 8 to 60 years…When a person is struck down he is carried by others out of the congregation, when some minister converses with and prays for him; afterwards a few gather around and sing a hymn suitable to the case. The whole number brought to the ground, under convictions, was about 1,000, not less. The sensible, the weak, etc., learned and unlearned, the rich and poor, are subjects of it. (from a letter of the Rev. John Evans Finley, a Presbyterian minister in Kentucky, Sept. 20, 1801, published in the *New York Missionary Magazine*, 1802; reprinted in Sweet, Religion in America, 228-229).

Camp meetings continued on the American frontier throughout much of the nineteenth century. As time passed, they were used especially by the emerging Holiness movement and thus became one of the roots of Pentecostalism. Indeed, the Azusa Street meetings that launched Pentecostalism into the world can be seen as a continuation of the camp meetings. Willis Banks, a Presbyterian lay evangelist in the southern part of the state of São Paulo in Brazil, used a similar technique very effectively early in the twentieth century. He was a descendent of Americans who had migrated to Brazil after the Civil War. We do not know if he got the idea from the experience on the American frontier, but he used it very effectively. In addition, he encouraged education, brick making, constructed the first pit silo in the area, and taught better nutrition. It is interesting to note that the Presbyterians never ordained him. If he had been a Baptist or Pentecostal, no doubt he would have been ordained. We must ask if that would have enhanced his ministry.

There is evidence of power encounter, healings, and "glossolalia" (tongues) in the camp meetings. It is difficult to discover the frequency of these phenomena, because most of those who wrote about them were quite skeptical or embarrassed by them.

The Role of Voluntary Societies

Historians have used the term "voluntary societies" to refer to a number of organizations that arose primarily in England and the United States as a result of the evangelical revivals. As the name implies, they were not sponsored by any official church or government body, but, rather, by groups of clergy and laymen, often at lay initiative. The early mission structures fit into this category, but there were many others established for a variety of purposes, both religious and social.

The voluntary societies usually included men from different denominational backgrounds. They might have disagreed on issues of theology and church structure, but they agreed on the essentials of the evangelical faith. This made it possible for them to work together on important issues facing their society. Among these were the anti-slavery and temperance movements, and the need for educational facilities on the frontier. They also produced and distributed Bibles and other literature. The American Bible Society, the American Tract Society, and the Sunday School Union were all voluntary societies. The American Home Mission Society had as its goal "A Bible for every family in the Missouri River valley, a Sunday school in every neighborhood, and a pastor in every locality." The American Education Society worked to train pastors and missionaries and give funds to seminary students. Because they bypassed the cumbersome church bureaucracies, they were more flexible, had greater freedom of action, and were able to include people from a variety of churches. They were a very effective model of Christian mission in the broader society.

A number of such societies resulted from the ministry of Charles Finney, the Presbyterian lawyer who was called to become an evangelist. Among his converts were two wealthy New York businessmen, Arthur and Lewis Tappan. (You can still purchase Tappan stoves today). The Tappan brothers became leaders in the anti-slavery movement and gave heavily to establish Oberlin College, the first to admit women as well as men. The first woman to be ordained in the United States was a graduate of Oberlin.

These voluntary societies, organized on the periphery of the churches, had a significant ministry for two centuries. Many, but not all, had a missionary focus, while others focused on issues in society. The great number of new, multi-denominational mission structures today continues their heritage.

The churches began to react against them, insisting on greater denominational control. Presbyterians had cooperated with the ABCFM almost since its inception, but in 1837, the Presbyterian General Assembly said, "The Presbyterian Church is a missionary society and every member is a member of that society." It ended its cooperation with the ABCFM, and formed the Presbyterian Board of Foreign Missions. A division also took place between the so-called "New School" and "Old School" Presbyterians, cutting the denomination into two roughly equal parts. The New School was supportive of revivalism and was strongly against slavery. The Old School took the opposite position on those two issues. The New School continued to support the ABCFM although that board eventually became the mission arm only of the Congregational churches.

There were some theological issues in the decision of the Presbyterian Church, but the desire to exert denominational control was the main reason. It also reflected the common view that ministry carried on outside the denominational structures was not quite legitimate. This idea involves a refusal to recognize much of mission history.

Today, the American missionary movement has come full circle. It began with a group of students whose initiative resulted in the formation of a multi-denominational mission board. However, for most of the nineteenth and early twentieth centuries, denominational boards predominated.

They included Congregationalist (ABCFM), Presbyterian, Baptist, and Methodist societies. At the beginning of the twentieth century, seventy-five percent of American missionaries served under the older denominational boards. Today, only five percent do so. The great majority serve under either multi-denominational agencies or the newer, conservative evangelical churches.

We note that Methodists, Presbyterians, and Baptists all divided into their northern and southern branches over the issues of slavery in the Civil War. Presbyterians and Methodists eventually reunited. However, the Southern Baptist convention has remained separate from the Northern (American) Baptist convention. Today, the Southern Baptist International Mission Board has approximately four thousand career missionaries and is the largest denominational agency. The number of Northern, or American Baptist missionaries has declined greatly.

Chapter Twenty-Two

The Dynamics of Renewal Movements

Devotional

We want to examine the characteristics of renewal movements because of the close link between renewal and mission throughout history.

Immediately following Pentecost, Acts 2 says:

> They devoted themselves to the apostles' teaching and to fellowship, to the breaking of bread and to prayer. Everyone was filled with awe at the many wonders and signs performed by the apostles. All the believers were together and had everything in common. They sold property and possessions to give to anyone who had need. Every day they continued to meet together in the temple courts. They broke bread in their homes and ate together with glad and sincere hearts, praising God and enjoying the favor of all the people. And the Lord added daily to their number those who were being saved. (Acts 2:42-47, NIV)

This was not a renewal movement, because it happened at the birth of the Church. Everything was new. The Gospel, the community, the lifestyle, were all new. There was freshness and vitality. This describes what has often happened in renewal movements as the Church, through the power of the Holy Spirit, has been called back to its first love and given new vitality.

The elements we see are intense *koinonia* (the sharing of life and sometimes even possessions), the study of the Word, that is, the apostles' teachings, deep intense prayer, a strong sense of communion and love for each other, and a deep desire to listen to God's voice and be obedient to Him. These are typical characteristics of movements of renewal.

I suggest that sometimes in our writing about revival (or renewal; I'm using the two terms interchangeably here), such movements have been portrayed as though they were almost perfect—as though there were no ragged edges, no corrupting influences, either within or without. We must be careful in our expectations, because no movement is perfect. The Holy Spirit works in and through flawed men and women, and thus every work of the Spirit will be less than perfect, messy at the edges, and sometimes at the center. We want to avoid the unrealistic expectation that when revival comes everything will be perfect and everyone in it completely obedient.

The early Church was not perfect, as we see in reading the Book of Acts. In the early Church, we find the story of Ananias and Sapphira, who cheated, lied to God and the community, and were struck down by the Spirit of God. That is a very harsh story, and yet it is a reminder to us that along with the genuine work of the Spirit, there will always be imitations. It is also a reminder to us that we should not attempt to deceive God, especially in the midst of intense spiritual activities.

There were bizarre episodes in the Great Awakening in New England. For example, James Davenport, an advocate of the Awakening, began to burn books, and stated that he could look into the face of a person and tell if he or she was converted. He brought the movement into discredit and later repented, but did a lot of damage. Critics seized on his actions to dismiss all of the great contributions of the Awakening. My point is this: if we are involved in any movement of the Spirit, we should not be surprised when the enemy counterattacks and we are disappointed by some actions of our colleagues and ourselves. It has happened before. Hudson Taylor once said that every time there was an advance in his mission in China, there came a counterattack by the adversary. We should be realistic, expect this, and not be taken by surprise.

I want to bring out from this passage in Acts that in whatever context and group we work, we are called to pray and strive for this same level of fellowship, sharing, and responsiveness to the Word of God. Evangelism is shown not as a special program, but as a natural outcome of the quality of the life of the community and the power of the Holy Spirit in the community.

This is not to say that evangelism should not be and is not intentional. After describing the vitality of the group and the work of the Spirit, including miracles, the passage says, "Every day the Lord added to the group those that were being saved." It is depicted as an on-going process. The Christian community was the primary evangelist. That does not leave out the importance of individual witness, but it says that when the Christian community genuinely reflects the power of God, evangelism happens naturally. People are drawn to faith simply because of what they observe in the Christian community.

Let us pray together.

> Father, we thank you again that you have called us, not to nominal Christianity, but to a vital exciting relationship with you, with our brothers and sisters in the faith, that leads us into a vital relationship with the world around us.
>
> We dare to pray that you will continue to draw each one of us to seek renewal in the groups, churches, and missions with which we work. Let there be seen in us a lifestyle that experi-

ences the on-going presence and power of the Holy Spirit, that demonstrates deep love and sharing, that shows to the world the reality of your presence and power in our lives. We pray for these things wherever we are and wherever we work. Now guide us as we study together. In Christ's name. Amen.

Introduction

We have often said that mission normally comes out of renewal movements. Therefore, if we are interested in mission, we must be interested in renewal. Many of the movements or groups with which we are associated have come out of an experience of renewal. Such an experience does not always produce mission, but if it does not produce mission, it soon stagnates and becomes truncated. I believe that to be true both theologically and historically.

Another way of putting it is this: no matter what experiences a person or group has, if it does not lead to mission, we must ask if it can be called "renewal." The Holy Spirit comforts, empowers, and equips believers. His empowering and equipping are primarily to carry out the will of God throughout history, both in the Church and in the world. Therefore, the two are inextricably connected. Any experience of renewal that does not lead to mission is incomplete at best.

The late Dr. J. Edwin Orr wrote extensively on revival. He focused on the phenomena of Acts 1 and 2. Here we see a corporate prayer of dependence on the Holy Spirit, followed by the Spirit's work, which reenergizes and empowers the Church to preach, teach, and minister. Then this revival reaches outside the Church in evangelism and healing social ministries, which eventually lead to large numbers of conversions, both inside and outside the Church. That is a very good picture of revival, and defines it well.

We have examined a number of earlier movements. One of the most interesting series of revivals occurred in various parts of the world in the first few years of the twentieth century. First came the Welsh revival in 1904, then the Pentecostal/

Charismatic movement in 1906, and the Korean revival that began among a few missionaries in 1903 and reached its peak in1907. It also spread to Northeast India, South Africa, Brazil, and Chile around 1910. It is interesting how this series of renewal/revival movements spread, usually with connections between them. In many cases, news of revival in one place became a stimulus to similar movements elsewhere.

We saw the same thing happen in the eighteenth century with Edwards, Whitefield, Wesley, Tennent, Frelinghuysen, and others on both sides of the Atlantic. We saw three streams flow together to form the evangelical revivals of the eighteenth century. They were, of course, Puritanism, Pietism, and Moravianism. Then the Holiness movement developed out of Methodism, primarily in North America, and from that emerged Pentecostalism. Since 1906, the broader evangelical movement and Pentecostalism have remained separate, but today there is a tendency for the two to move closer together without becoming identical. It is clear that those two movements are in the forefront of Christian mission today. We must recognize that the Pentecostal/Charismatic movement is the most rapidly growing branch of the worldwide Christian Church today.

The best theological analysis of renewal I have seen comes from the book *Dynamics of Spiritual Life: An Evangelical Theology of Renewal* by Richard Lovelace of Gordon Conwell Seminary (Downers Grove: InterVarsity Press, 1979).

Lovelace first examined the Old Testament renewal movements under Josiah and Hezekiah. He theorized that there is a relationship between reformation of doctrine, reformation of structure, and spiritual revitalization. He saw this as a complex but important relationship.

Lovelace's basic thesis is that renewal comes first from awakened spiritual interest, as we noted with Luther. However, he suggests that spiritual renewal does not continue very long without continual reformation in both structure and theology. When a group undergoes some spiritual renewal and individuals are drawn closer to

Christ, resulting in a much deeper spiritual life, the movement usually needs to make some theological and even structural reforms in the Church. Otherwise it becomes truncated, stagnated. In other words, proper structure and theology can never bring renewal, but bad structure and bad theology can cut the nerve of such a movement. The reason is clear: when the Holy Spirit does a new thing, he always seems to move beyond the structural and sometimes the theological boundaries the existing Church has established. We have seen this clearly in Moravianism and Methodism, for example. It will become even more clear in Pentecostalism.

Bad theology and excessively rigid structures can hinder or even prevent renewal by creating obstacles. Structures that are excessively clerical and do not encourage lay men and women to express their faith, hinder renewal. Theologies that are not clear on issues of Christology and salvation by grace through faith, and theologies that are legalistic, can also hinder and cut the nerve of revival.

A fundamental thesis of Lovelace is that when renewal comes, it will challenge existing structures and even theologies with the need for change. However, structures and theology in traditional churches are very hard to change, and that always becomes a major problem. It is a problem for many from both the non-Western and Western world.

Finney reacted against the excessive Calvinism of the old Princeton theology of his time. Ashbel Green was a great Presbyterian leader, and President of Princeton College. Finney told in his memoirs how he counseled a man in Philadelphia in one of his campaigns. The man had wasted his life, and now wanted to become a Christian. As a young college student, he had gone to Green and asked, "What should I do to become a Christian?" Green responded, "Go and pray. If God chooses to awaken you, he will do so." That expressed Green's extreme Calvinism. The young man did not experience any kind of awakening, and so lived most of his life without any Christian faith.

Although Green was a great and godly Christian, his Calvinism was overdone. Instead of encouraging the young man by saying, "God accepts you as you are, trust him," it appears that Green's exaggerated Calvinist theology blocked the man's spiritual progress. Apparently, the ultra-Calvinists of Princeton went too far in cutting the nerve of personal responsibility, and thus hindered a personal response to the Gospel.

Finney reacted against that. He was an attorney when he was converted. His pastor encouraged him to go to Princeton, but he refused because of his negative impression of Princeton's theology. In his Arminianism, Finney went to the other extreme with his focus on free will. "You can do it if you will; it all depends on you," he said. That theology would eventually become social gospel liberalism, and in turn would cut the nerve of evangelism. However, during his own lifetime, Finney kept evangelism and social action in healthy balance. Finney himself always believed evangelism to be the priority, some of his converts (the Tappan brothers, for example), became leaders in the anti-slavery movement, and believed that to be the priority at the time.

We can look at Calvinism and Arminianism in the thought of Jonathan Edwards and Charles Finney. Edwards wrote of a "Surprising work of God" in describing the awakening in Northampton. Finney wrote that if we do all the right things, God will send revival. How do we resolve the dilemma between God's sovereignty and the free will of humankind? First, we recognize that God comes to us when we are "dead in trespasses and sins," and calls us to himself. Therefore, we can completely depend on him. This is the point of Calvinism: God takes the initiative. On the other hand, we recognize that we have the responsibility to respond to the gracious initiatives of God. We hold the Calvinism/Arminianism paradox in tension, and can use it to understand the dynamics of renewal, as well. We are to pray and seek renewal, both personal and corporate, but when it comes, we recognize it to be a gracious gift of the sovereign God.

As for the relationship between evangelism and social action in renewal movements, we can see many historical examples where renewal has led to significant social action. A strong biblical theology of the Kingdom of God provides the best model for that relationship.

Precondition

Lovelace described what he calls three "preconditions," four "primary" elements, and five "secondary" elements of renewal. As we examine this, we may remember illustrations from history or even our own experience.

Precondition #1: Knowing God and Knowing Ourselves

The first precondition for genuine renewal is to know God and know ourselves—to see ourselves in the light of the nature of God. We see this precondition present in Luther, the Puritans, the Pietists, and the first Great Awakening.

Edwards, for example, focused his attention on the Holiness of God. Who is God? What is he like? When we begin to see God as he is, then we look at ourselves in a new light. We think of Isaiah's experience in the temple in chapter 6. Young Isaiah, who no doubt had been in the temple many times, entered it in a time of national political crisis. King Uzziah had died. It was the end of a long period of peace and prosperity, with an uncertain future. There were storm clouds on the horizon.

As Isaiah entered the temple and worshipped, he saw the Lord, high and lifted up, surrounded by heavenly beings. He saw the glory and the majesty of God as he had never seen it never before. As a result, he saw himself and his people with new depth and realism. His response was, "Woe is me! I am a man of unclean lips. I dwell in the midst of a people of unclean lips."

A vision of the nature of God: His greatness, power, and holiness, is the first step leading to renewal. The lack of emphasis on the character of God may be the greatest problem in contemporary evangelical theology in North America. We have a very human-centered theology.

Precondition #2: Seeing the Depth of Sin

The old Puritan goal of seeking to glorify God is largely absent from North American evangelicalism. I suspect genuine renewal will come when we begin again to see the transcendence and greatness of God in the midst of a very human-centered, secular society. We will receive a new vision of God, his holiness, and his purpose for the world. The new vision of God led Isaiah to see the depth of his own sin and that of his community. This new understanding defined sin, not simply as isolated acts, but, using Lovelace's phrase, as "a network of compulsive attitudes, beliefs, and behaviors deeply rooted in our alienation from God" (ibid., p. 88). That is a profound definition!

Precondition #3: Discovering Our Conformity to the World

The third precondition follows logically. After we have seen the holiness and purpose of God with much greater clarity, and then taken a new look at ourselves, we look at ourselves in relationship to the world differently. Immediately, we discover how much we are conformed to this world. Indeed, if we read many Christian books, we get the impression that our goals, as evangelical Christians, are not very different from the goals of most people in our society. The message seems to be that the gospel simply helps us to achieve those goals more successfully!

Remember Romans 12: "Do not be conformed to this world." J. B. Phillips translates it beautifully in his "Letters to Young Churches:" "Don't let the world squeeze you into its own mold." If we take a deep look at some of the great men and women of God who have made breakthroughs in history, we will see how hard they resisted being squeezed into the world's mold, and how persistently they tried to let God remold and transform them. That transformation involved ambitions, goals, lifestyles, relationships, and use of their gifts and resources.

When J. Hudson Taylor was a young medical student in London, he deliberately lived in poverty-stricken, difficult surroundings, even though it was not an economic necessity for him. He came from a middle-class family. Because he knew he would live in very difficult circumstances in China, he wanted to get used to living in poverty. That was one way in which he resisted being conformed to this world.

Primary Elements of Continual Renewal

Element #1: Rediscovery of Justification by Faith

Lovelace suggested that the first primary element of continuous renewal is the recognition of justification by faith. Here we see the influence of Luther, Calvin, Edwards, Wesley, and others. The fact that Jesus died on the cross for my sin is the heart of the gospel. It answers the problem of my own guilt, bondage, and alienation from God and others, because of sin. How many sermons have you heard on justification by faith lately—sermons that focused on the work of Christ on the cross? Could it be that we often let that emphasis slip away, assuming that everyone understands and believes it? The point is that we need to appropriate the justifying work of Christ in our lives constantly, recognizing that everything we are before God depends on his justifying grace through Christ.

Very subtly we often fall into the trap, with one part of our mind, anyway, of assuming that God accepts us because we are pretty good people, because we are being sanctified, because we are good believers, perhaps even because we are committed to mission or ministry. The attitude always comes in through the back door, leading us to feel, at least in part, that we are accepted by God because of our fine qualities or activities. That leads us away from focusing constantly on the fact that we are justified by God through Christ, just as much as the greatest sinner, and that we need God's grace just as much as the dying thief.

Lovelace put it this way:

> In order for a pure and lasting work of renewal to happen, multitudes in the church must be led to build their lives on this foundation: that our new life is a sheer gift of God through Jesus Christ, and to be led to an awareness of God's holiness, the depths of our own sin, and the sufficiency of Christ's atoning work, for our acceptance by God. (ibid., p. 101).

That needs to be reaffirmed every day.

Primary Element #2: Sanctification

To avoid falling into "cheap grace," to use Dietrich Bonhoeffer's term, the next step is our commitment to sanctification. The great word "sanctification" is not used much in many churches today. It refers to the process of being made holy. However, like so many great biblical words, we have frequently trivialized the term. What does sanctification mean? Does it primarily mean being good?

There were many fine things about the church in which I was raised. However, if the word "sanctification" was used at all, it was trivialized into avoiding certain kinds of destructive conduct, or "being a good boy." It had lost much of the force of the biblical word, which, we have just said, means being made holy. The root meaning of "holy" is not simply "morally good and correct," but is "separated for a purpose."

Thus, first of all, sanctification involves being separated for God's purpose in the world. The ethical and lifestyle aspects we normally associate with the word are simply logical consequences of recognizing that we are separated to be God's persons and to work for his purpose in the world. "Cheap grace," which entails no commitment to living our lives in terms of God's purpose, is illegitimate. We cannot separate a justifying faith and repentance from the goals and choices that really make up our lives.

The Puritans told us, "We cannot be in union with half a Christ." That is, we cannot be in union with the Christ who died on the cross for us, without being in union with the Christ who said, "Follow me." No conversion is complete that does not deal with the issue of sanctification. We are born again, or recreated, for new life.

The process of sanctification is to be a lifelong process. In Lovelace's words, "It involves the breaking up of every area of conformity to the world's patterns, and increasing transformation of our lives by the Holy Spirit's renewing work." This reminds us again of Romans 12:1–2, one of the great passages in the New Testament.

Primary Element #3: The Indwelling Holy Spirit

The third aspect of continuous renewal is the reality of the indwelling Holy Spirit. Lovelace does not define the indwelling or baptism of the Holy Spirit in terms of a particular type of experience—for example, speaking in tongues. In my judgment, sometimes it is accompanied by tongues, and sometimes it is not. I recognize that there are differences of opinion on that question. However, I believe all will agree that the filling of the Holy Spirit has two primary purposes: to bring power for service and to result in growth in sanctification. The two are connected.

I do not think God is primarily concerned with creating beautiful, shiny new Christians who never get scratched. That would be like buying a new car and storing it safely in the garage where it will not get dented. I believe that the person who is filled with the Holy Spirit and following his leading will often get bruised and battered. He or she may not always be the kind of person who can get up at every prayer meeting and give a triumphant testimony of how great things are. Such people always intimidate me.

I believe that if we are attempting to follow the guidance of the Holy Spirit, and, indeed, if we are filled with the Spirit, he will lead us into places where we will often suffer, and be battered, beaten, and bruised. After all, the Holy Spirit leads us as we follow the One who was crucified! The Spirit-filled life does not normally look very easy or "triumphant" in the sense that we feel we are always on top of things.

I believe that normally, renewal brings the discovery that the supernatural gifts of the Holy Spirit are available today. They are not limited to a particular era such as the apostolic age. Some theologies teach that certain gifts ceased after the apostolic age. The old Princeton theology took that position, and so does Dispensationalism. Calvin and Luther reacted against the excessive credulity and many tales of miracles in the Middle Ages. Their goal was to bring the Church back to the Scriptures. In their overreaction, perhaps they failed to recognize that the Holy Spirit still does surprising things today. They also reacted against some of the radical movements of the day that said, "We follow the Holy Spirit! We are not bound by the Scriptures, because the Spirit speaks to us directly." The Reformers responded, "Not so! Any time the Spirit speaks, he speaks in accordance with the Scriptures." Thus, in their denial of some gifts of the Spirit, Luther and Calvin were attempting to protect a key doctrine of the Reformation: *Sola Scriptura*.

The late David Hubbard, President of Fuller Seminary for thirty years, was a fine biblical scholar. I once heard him say, "There is not a shred of exegetical evidence for the view that certain gifts ceased with the end of the apostolic era." I would add that there is no historical evidence for that position either. But even as we speak of gifts such as prophecies and "tongues," we remember that less spectacular gifts like teaching, administration, and giving, are also given by the Spirit.

My hope is that along with appreciation for the normal activities of the Spirit in the life of the Church, we will be open to the extraordinary and unusual acts of the Spirit that do not fit our usual categories.

Thus, renewal movements usually come to a new realization that the Holy Spirit is "alive and well" and has not exhausted all his creativity. He still has new things to do, and he might even do them through us. The new openness to the Spirit in much of the Church today is very healthy. At the same time, we must recognize that the grace and the fruit of the Holy Spirit are to be sought much more than the spectacular gifts. Lovelace

wrote that the eager seeking after wonders can be a work of the flesh.

If we constantly want God to do something spectacular, we have to ask why. While we remain open to the spectacular and the extraordinary work of God, we must not forget that the fruits of the Spirit are love, joy, peace, etc. We are called to embody those in our lives and in the life of the Church. In these days, love, joy, and peace may be the greatest miracles of all! To summarize, the work of the Spirit is always designed to lead us to be obedient to God in every level of our lives.

Primary Element #4:
Authority in Spiritual Conflict

The fourth element in renewal is authority in spiritual conflict. We read about principalities and powers in the New Testament. For some more liberal theologians, principalities and powers refer to political, social, and economic structures that keep people in oppression. They refer to structural evil. For others, they are personal demonic forces that attack people. Certainly, personal evil often embodies itself in political, social, and economic structures that dehumanize people. In my judgment, we should never limit our understanding of principalities and powers either to the personal or the corporate. I believe there is ample evidence that they are both.

Scriptures show us examples of personal demonic activity, and many of our students have encountered that in their ministries. On the other hand, we can see evil institutionalized in political, economic, and social structures of every society. They often oppress people because of race, social class, caste, or other factors.

Lovelace's fourth point about continuous renewal is that we are given authority in spiritual conflict. There are three major traditional theories about the cross and resurrection of Jesus. The first is the substitutionary theory of the atonement. Anselm formulated this doctrine in the eleventh century, but I believe it is derived from the New Testament. The heart of it is simply "Jesus died on the cross for my sins."

There is a second picture of the atonement. We can see the atonement as a courtroom, where the judge has placed the penalty on himself. Thirdly, we can also see the cross and resurrection as a cosmic battlefield, where God in Christ went into battle against all the forces of evil, sin, death and hell, and defeated them. That is also a legitimate New Testament picture of the atonement, and, according to some scholars, was Luther's primary understanding of the event. We can understand that since he was involved in the spiritual and political battles of the Reformation.

We affirm the validity of all three understandings of the work of Christ. They are complementary. But when we see the cross and resurrection as the ultimate battle in history over sin, death, and evil, and we believe that Jesus Christ has triumphed, it gives us confidence to move into the battle against all forces of evil, whether they are personal, social, or structural. Structural evil certainly involves anything that threatens to destroy human life including disease such as malaria or AIDS. We move into the battle with confidence that God is going to bring the victory: maybe during our lifetime, maybe not, but with confidence in the final victory. Renewal brings new authority in spiritual conflict.

The picture of conflict was prominent in the preaching of George Whitefield and the writings of John Bunyan. It was an essential conceptual tool in Jonathan Edwards' writings about the Great Awakening. John Nevius was a pioneer Presbyterian missionary in China in the latter part of the nineteenth century. He had studied under Hodge and Warfield at Princeton, who both denied any miraculous activity on the part of God today. He experienced a paradigm shift in China, where he saw a great deal of demonic activity and wrote about it.

Nevius is especially familiar to Koreans, because at a retreat for the Presbyterian missionaries in Korea in 1890, he shared some radical ideas about missionary practice that his own mission in China had rejected. The Korea missionaries accepted his ideas and followed what was called "The Nevius Plan." No church was to have a pastor until it supported him, nor a building until the local believers constructed it. There was also a strong focus on Bible study. The Plan was one of the reasons for the strength and growth of the Korean church.

"Secondary" Elements of Renewal

To conclude Lovelace's analysis, we will describe what he terms the "secondary elements of renewal." I do not think they should be called "secondary," because I believe any genuine renewal movement will include them.

Orientation Toward Mission

The first "secondary" element of renewal is orientation toward mission. If the Holy Spirit has genuinely renewed us, we begin to look beyond ourselves at the world and attempt to relate the work of Christ to the rest of the world. We begin to follow the Holy Spirit, using the authority he gives against the powers of darkness. This takes us back to our thesis that any genuine renewal movement must lead us outside of ourselves, and that will involve mission, however it might be defined in the context. Remember Isaiah 6:1-8. After the prophet's new experience of God, the recognition of his sinfulness, and the cleansing from sin, he overheard God saying, "Whom shall I send, who will go for us?" And he answered, "Here am I, send me."

I believe some of us are called to focus primarily on the Church where we are, calling it to renewal, while others are called to go elsewhere, to take the Gospel across cultural and geographical barriers. It is a matter of our personal call. But it is clear from both Scripture and history that renewal and mission are closely related.

Dependent Prayer

Prayer is a natural outgrowth of renewal. It is possible because we are united to Christ. We are impressed anew with the fact that we have been received in his righteousness and are indwelt with the Holy Spirit. Prayer is necessary because we are engaged in a mission against spiritual forces. The struggle does not take place simply on a human level. Prayer is necessary because the battle is also on a spiritual level.

If you read the unedited biographies of great men and women of God, you realize that things were not always easy for them. Sometimes they fell into terrible depression, a state that has been called "the dark night of the soul." However, that did not mean they were any less indwelt by the Holy Spirit.

Prayer, then, is possible because we are united with Christ. It is necessary because we are engaged in a spiritual battle.

Koinonia

Koinonia, or fellowship, grows out of our common life in Christ. We see it in the earliest Christian communities in the Book of Acts.

Martin Luther suggested the formation of small groups of committed believers, but did not follow through on the idea. Martin Bucer, the reformer of Strassburg, on the French-German frontier organized small groups. So did the Pietists. (It is possible the Puritans and Pietists got the idea from Bucer.)

As we have seen, most renewal movements have incorporated small groups for koinonia into their structure; the Methodist classes, the Moravian bands, Puritan conventicles, and Pietist groups are examples. However, even where such groups were not part of the formal structure, meetings for intense prayer and fellowship have been important. Out of such groups, spiritual power, encouragement, and new initiatives in ministry have often come.

Theological Integration

Theological integration involves the modification or reconstruction of our theology in order to incorporate new experiences and insights that have come from new movement of the Spirit. They must always be tested to make sure they are consistent with Scripture, of course. Our theological systems are always formed in specific historical contexts, and deal with the most important issues of that time. Often they do not address issues that arise in other situations. Thus there is often the need to reconstruct our theology so it

will reflect more fully the breadth of Christian life and experience. It must be based on Scripture, but now include the elements in our experience that our traditional theology has ignored.

For example, we might take a new look at the statement of faith or particular creeds of our church or mission. A few years ago, I chaired a committee to rewrite the Statement of Faith of the Latin America Mission. It is a fine mission, but its statement of faith reflected the fundamentalist/modernist controversy, and spoke of salvation primarily in individualistic terms. It spoke of the atoning work of Christ exclusively in terms of individual salvation and forgiveness. Even though the Mission was active in a number of social ministries, there was little about the cultural mandate in the Statement of Faith. The pastor of the largest church in Caracas, Venezuela, a charismatic church, was also a member of the committee. Recognizing two important issues in Latin America today, poverty and spiritual power, we included affirmations sections in the new Statement that dealt with them. We included language from the Lausanne Covenant about the need for ministries of compassion. We also included biblical material that spoke of Christ defeating the principalities and powers.

Other examples of the need to integrate ignored biblical concepts in theology (and structure as well) will include the affirmation of the role of the ministry of the laity and the recognition of the gifts of the Spirit poured out on all believers. As we have seen, that is a key issue in almost all renewal movements, but often, traditional church structures give little place to the ministry of the laity.

Disenculturation

"Disenculturation" is not a term we normally use. It refers to a process in which we become loosened or detached, in a sense, from our own culture. This is possible only when we rely fully on Christ for our justification and sanctification. All of us come to our Christian Faith in a specific cultural context. And we are sorely tempted to identify our faith with our culture, in effect, to perform a marriage of the two. That, of course, makes it nearly impossible to stand outside our culture and judge it in light of the Gospel. It also makes it difficult to move into another culture with a positive attitude and communicate the Gospel in a relevant manner.

The process of disenculturation, as I understand it, has two sides to it. We begin to take a new look at our own culture—the things we have taken for granted within it that are clearly contrary to the will of God and unbiblical. For many North Americans, this would mean rejecting our assumptions about materialism and the belief that the highest goal of the Christian life is to fulfill the American dream: to make more money, have a bigger house, and buy a better car. That has become a common aspect of our American evangelical ethos! Other issues in our North American culture we need to address would include racism, a sense of cultural superiority, and economic injustice.

An important emphasis at Fuller Theological Seminary is to value every culture and seek to communicate the Gospel in a manner that exemplifies that respect. We believe strongly that people should come to know and follow Christ in the context of their own cultures. On the other hand, we also recognize that every culture is in need of constant transformation if we are to reflect more completely the reality of the Kingdom of God. We are called to hold these two sides in creative tension. Disenculturation will lead us to re-examine our culture through the lens of the Kingdom of God. That will lead us to work to embody the values of the Kingdom, not only in our personal lives, but also in our society. We can readily see how this process has often led to ministries of compassion for the marginalized, and social transformation.

There is another side of disenculturation. As we grow more in the Christian life, we realize with greater passion that our primary citizenship is in the Kingdom of God and not in our nation or culture. We realize that we do not have to live within our own cultural context in order to have an authentic life. Authentic life depends on our relationship with God through Jesus Christ, not on our cultural context. This understanding frees us to respond to the Spirit in obedience and go to people who are different culturally, racially, nationally, and geographically from ourselves. The implications for mission are powerful. It will also mean that our primary community is not defined by our culture, but by our citizenship in the Kingdom of God.

A final remark: the revival in Korea early in the twentieth century began primarily in reconciliation between the missionaries and some of the early Korean Christian leaders. There were some feelings of superiority on the part of the missionaries and, naturally, resentment on the part of the Koreans. As that was confessed and broken down, it became the trigger of revival. I once talked to Harold Voekel, a great Presbyterian missionary in Korea. He said that as far as he knew, there were no manifestations of tongues or the miraculous in the movement. I did hear from another Korean missionary that there were many healings in the early days in Korea, but as far as he knew, no manifestation of tongues.

This does not mean that tongues have not played a role in other kinds of renewal movements. I believe it does mean that we should never dictate to the Holy Spirit just what characteristics a renewal movement should have in a particular context.

The trigger of the East Africa Revival apparently was similar to that in Korea. The English Anglicans, good people, came, perhaps unconsciously, with feelings of European white superiority. After all, they felt they had made great sacrifices to live in Africa, in circumstances that appeared to them to be difficult. However, the African brothers and sisters saw attitudes of superiority and racism there. When these attitudes were broken down between some English and African workers, it was a major factor in bringing the revival. Perhaps such reconciliation might be a critical element in sparking other renewal movements as well.

To conclude, while the circumstances and contexts will differ, the Holy Spirit is especially concerned with breaking down all barriers between believers so they will reflect more fully our reconciliation with God. Often that has been the critical spark in bringing renewal.

Chapter Twenty-Three

The Second Burst of New Mission Structures

Introduction

In the last third of the nineteenth century we find a much greater acceptance of Christian mission. But the movement that had begun with Carey in 1792 was still quite small. Near the end of the 19th century, less than a thousand Americans served overseas.

It was a period of growing confidence and optimism in the West, a time of progress and new inventions—the telephone, for instance. (The automobile and airplane were just around the corner.)

This helps us understand the optimism and sense that Western civilization was progressing more than any other in human history. New inventions would make life easier, and communication and transportation took great leaps forward. The feeling was that progress was inevitable, and that it would come through European and American culture and institutions.

It was also assumed that the western European and North American culture, which produced this progress, was Christian. That was true in a limited sense. Sociologist Rodney Stark has argued persuasively that Christian faith, because of the value it gave to human reason, made it possible for modern science and technology to develop. At the same time, we must recognize that despite Christian influence, Western culture was far from Christian in any profound sense.

Isaac Watts wrote his great hymn "Jesus shall reign, where e'er the sun does his successive journeys run" long before Carey sailed to India. However, we are embarrassed by the verse in that hymn that says, "Western empires own their Lord, while savage tribes attend His Word." The British, one of those Western empires that "owned their Lord," was engaged in the slave trade and would soon force opium on China. The British were not the only ones. The Arabs were heavily involved in the slave trade, and so were the Americans. There was a blind and too-easy assumption that Western culture was both Christian and superior, and that all other cultures should become like it.

The concept of the "white man's burden" in colonialism, the view that Westerners should help to civilize other people, reflected a combination of idealism and naïveté, cynicism and exploitation. We should not view colonialism in a completely negative light. There were some very noble people involved in the movement who genuinely tried to help people. Nevertheless, in reading the literature of the period we find the assumption that western Europeans and North Americans were destined to be leaders and show others the way to "Christian civilization."

These were some of the underlying assumptions of the age that accompanied the theological underpinnings of the missionary movement. We must recognize them and be honest about them, and recognize that some of the reactions against the missionary movement, especially in China, are the result of such attitudes.

To understand the context of the last third of the nineteenth century, we need to list some of the key political and intellectual developments.

Darwinism

Darwin's *Origin of Species* was published in 1859, launching the idea of evolution. Evolution could easily become the concept of "automatic progress"—the idea that things are getting better and better all the time. It fit well with the era's excitement about innovations in science and technology. Automatic progress became a secularized version of Christian eschatology. Some of the more liberal theologians rejected the hope that God would bring in his Kingdom and shifted to the concept that we would bring in the Kingdom of God through our own efforts, motivated by our Christian faith. This would be one of the important ideas of the more radical Social Gospel advocates. Marxism could be seen as a kind of violently secularized form of Christian eschatology.

Darwinism, of course, also cast doubts on the Christian view of creation and even on the concept of God. While many theologians attempted to reconcile evolution and creation, in its more extreme form, Darwinism was atheistic.

Higher Criticism of Scripture

Higher critical views of the Scripture were launched around 1860. Scholars in Germany began to analyze the Scriptures using the tools of literary criticism. While many insights from higher criticism helped Christians to understand and interpret the various books of the Bible more accurately, the more radical critics tended to undermine biblical authority and thus challenge basic theological doctrines.

The End of the Papal States

The Papal States had included the middle third of Italy for over a thousand years. They ended in 1870, Italy became a unified nation, and the papacy was confined to the Vatican State. That political defeat pushed the Roman Catholic Church into an even more defensive posture that lasted nearly a century.

Britain Accepts Responsibility to Rule India

During this period, the British government accepted responsibility to rule and administer In-

dia. Previously, the East India Company was dominant, but now Queen Victoria assumed the task. It was an improvement over the East India Company. One stipulation was, "There shall be religious toleration in India." It was one of many cases in which missionaries were given greater scope for work because of political decisions made in Europe. Obviously, that had both its positive and negative aspects.

The Opium Wars: An Open Door in China

A new door opened to the interior of China. England went to war against China twice over questions of trade. Among the issues was England's insistence on forcing the opium trade on China. As a result, treaties that met England's demands were signed in 1842 and 1858. The last one gave Westerners permission to travel in the interior for the first time. It also stipulated that Christianity would be tolerated, and missionaries and Chinese Christians would be protected. Naturally, this created great bitterness among many Chinese and led even more to the association of Christian faith with Western imperialism, the sword, and the opium trade. This perception would last over a century.

Some missionaries welcomed the treaties and saw them as the hand of God. Others were embarrassed by them, understanding that their negative effects outweighed the positives. For some Chinese, Christianity was identified with the worst kind of colonialism and imposition of foreign powers.

The Second Evangelical Awakening

The second Evangelical Awakening in the United States was largely a lay movement. It began in a prayer meeting of businessmen in 1858. Soon it spread across the United States. Dwight L. Moody, an ambitious young businessman in Chicago, was caught up in it and became its best-known evangelist. The movement crossed the Atlantic to England.

A new surge of missionary interest resulted and gave rise to the Student Volunteer Movement.

Roman Catholic Missionaries Enter Japan

In 1858, a Catholic priest entered Japan, the first missionary there in the modern period. Japan had remained closed to any outside influence until Commodore Perry, an American naval officer, sailed with his ships into the Bay of Tokyo and succeeded in opening the nation to Western influence.

David Livingstone

In 1857, David Livingstone published his missionary travels and researches in Africa. That stimulated mission interest among students, and the Universities' Mission to Central Africa was initiated.

In this context we will look at two movements, both important in themselves, but also symbolic of even broader trends. One is the China Inland Mission and the other, the Student Volunteer Movement.

The China Inland Mission

Alfred James Broomhall published seven volumes entitled *Hudson Taylor and China's Open Century* (London: Hodder & Stoughton, 1984) on the life of J. Hudson Taylor. The Broomhalls have long been involved in the China Inland Mission. It is the most thorough study of Taylor's life and times, an incredible piece of work. A one-volume work by Dr. and Mrs. Howard Taylor entitled *Hudson Taylor and the China Inland Mission* (London: The China Inland Press, 1918) is also helpful.

Taylor's great-grandfather had been a "scoffer at religion," but was converted through the preaching of John Wesley. Taylor's father was a lay leader in a Methodist church, and he was raised in a strong Christian home.

However, he had grown away from the faith and was moving ahead in business. One day, when his mother was away and praying for her son, she had a strong conviction that he had returned to faith. That same day, Taylor had entered his father's study and began reading a book whose message struck home to him. He committed himself to Christ and very soon, to mission.

He decided he would become a medical doctor and go to China. Medical studies were much less formal at that time, and he studied with various physicians. He made it a point to live in difficult circumstances in London, believing that would help prepare him for life in China. The woman he wanted to marry would not go to China with him. He fell in love with another. She, too, refused him, so he went to China as a single man in 1854. Serving under a mission society that was not always responsible in supporting him, he exhibited great perseverance, eager to penetrate the interior of China. However, the Chinese government did not allow it, and even if it had been permitted, the danger and hardships would have been great. Taylor returned to England in 1860, discouraged but still committed to China. He spent twelve hours each day working on a revision of the Chinese New Testament and improving his medical skills while he prayed about the next step in his life and mission.

He compiled more information on China and discovered that the number of Protestant missionaries there had decreased from 115 to 91 in the previous year. He noted that China had half of the non-Christians in the world. He also noted that there was only one Protestant missionary in China for each number of people equivalent to the population of Scotland. Taylor said the fact that each person had an immortal soul and needed to know Christ constituted a missionary call. No other call was necessary.

One weekend in 1865, he went to Brighton, a resort city on the ocean, south of London. On Sunday morning when he was in church, he felt such a burden for China that he left and went to the beach all alone. There he had a profound experience alone with God and came to the conclusion that God was calling him to the interior of China. He went to the bank and opened an account in the name of the China Inland Mission (CIM), even though he had no mission and only ten pounds (fifty dollars). He began to pray that God would give him two missionaries for each of the twenty-four provinces in the interior of China. His survey of the nation told him that even in the six provinces where there was mission work, 185 million were out of reach of the Gospel, while there were 200 million in the other provinces. He began to call for volunteers. No special educational qualifications were necessary, and they could come from any denomination. The missionaries would be supported by faith. Taylor followed the principles of George Müller, who believed that he should never ask for money, but only pray and depend on God to bring in whatever was necessary. The CIM was the prototype of the faith mission. Many missions that call themselves faith missions today should not use that term, because the missionary must raise his or her support before going to the field. I do not criticize that practice. However, the CIM has never solicited funds. It still follows the practice of praying that God will send the necessary resources.

The CIM became the first of a new wave of interdenominational faith missions, and accepted members from different traditions. It included Anglicans, Presbyterians, Methodists, Baptists, and Brethren. It soon became international, with personnel and support from many countries. Today it has personnel from at least twenty-six countries. When China expelled missionaries in 1951, the CIM changed its name to Overseas Missionary Fellowship (OMF) and now works throughout Southeast Asia. With the growing openness in China, the Mission now has a significant number of men and women who work there as professionals in education and health care, among other things.

Following the faith principle, missionaries did not receive a guaranteed salary. They had to trust God for their needs, and the Mission refused to go into debt, spending only whatever came in. The practice of the Mission was to keep three months salary on hand and use it as the basis of their spending for the following three months. There was no personal solicitation for funds, and no collections were taken at their meetings, but they did make their needs known.

The missionaries were to conform as closely as possible to the living conditions and dress of the Chinese. That was a time when Westerners assumed that their culture was Christian. Taylor deliberately turned his back on some aspects of his culture and adopted Chinese dress and hairstyle. He was greatly criticized by the other European missionaries. They considered him a fanatic and

counseled Maria, who became his wife, against the marriage!

Victorian England was a man's world, but Taylor found that many single women applied for missionary service along with married couples. The first group of volunteers included seven single women and eight couples. Therefore, at a time when it was not considered proper for women to be unaccompanied by a man, he "manned" mission stations in the interior with either married couples or a pair of single women. The women as well as the men preached in the streets, evangelized, and established churches. They did everything that men would do. One does not know how much influence this had later on the growth of the Chinese church. We do know that today in the Chinese house churches, three-fourths of the leaders are women, in a culture that traditionally has not given women a high place. It is a very interesting phenomenon.

Another unique aspect of the CIM was that the director of the Mission was to be in China, not England. There was to be no direction by remote control. This kept the leaders in much closer touch with personnel and issues on the field. It helped avoid a frequent source of tension that has arisen when administrators in Europe or the United States showed inadequate understanding of issues on the field.

At first, the main purpose of the mission was not to win converts, but to diffuse the knowledge of the gospel throughout China as soon as possible. That policy soon changed, and church planting became the goal. However, despite Taylor's own medical training, the Mission did not emphasize educational or medical work.

The CIM grew rapidly, numbering nearly seven hundred missionaries in China in 1900. When the Boxer Rebellion came at the turn of the century, the CIM suffered greatly, losing more of its personnel to death than did any other mission. They were in the interior, and thus much more vulnerable. But when the European powers forced the Chinese government to pay indemnity to the missionary societies for their loss of life and property, the CIM refused to accept any compensation. The Presbyterians accepted indemnity but kept the funds in China, reinvesting them in their ministries there.

By 1900 there were 1500 Protestant missionaries in China with a half million adherents in the churches. The CIM, which counted almost half of the Protestant missionaries in China, also stimulated others to focus more on China. It soon counted more missionaries and investment of financial resources than any other country in the world. Thus, China was the greatest focus of Western Protestant missionary effort in the first half of the twentieth century. In a later chapter we will look at the history of mission in China in the twentieth century.

Brief Overview of the Eras of Mission

Before we move to the student movements, we will briefly examine a helpful schematic of the eras of mission devised by Ralph Winter. The key person in the first era, beginning in 1792, was William Carey, for reasons that are obvious, even though, as we have seen, missionaries had gone from Europe to Asia much earlier. The second era began with Hudson Taylor and the China Inland Mission in 1865. The third era began in 1934 with Cameron Townsend. Student mission movements arose at approximately the same time as each new era, providing an important source of personnel. These were the Haystack Prayer Meeting in 1806, the Student Volunteer Movement in 1886, and the mission meetings of Inter-Varsity Christian Fellowship, which began in Toronto in 1946 and moved to Urbana, Illinois, in 1948.

Winter noted that in the first era, missionaries went primarily to the coastal areas, and in the second, to the interior of various nations and continents. Along with the CIM, groups like the Sudan Interior Mission and the African Inland Mission were established. Both of these categories were geographical. With Cameron Townsend and later with Donald McGavran, the focus shifted to culture and "people groups," with the concept of "bypassed" or "hidden" peoples introduced. As mentioned earlier, when Townsend was selling Bibles in Spanish in Guatemala, he found that half of the population spoke little or no Spanish, their languages were various Mayan dialects. The discovery led him to establish Wycliffe Bible Translators.

I suggest we add a fourth era: that of the burgeoning urban centers of the world. They are important in Europe and North America, but even more so in Latin America (Sao Paulo and Mexico City), Asia, (Seoul, Jakarta, Shanghai, Mumbai) and Africa (Lagos). Both categories, geography and culture, are relevant to the cities. They are growing rapidly in the Majority world and all, with the possible exception of those in Japan and Korea, contain a hundred or more different language groups. I believe they constitute the greatest missionary challenge in the new century. It is estimated that at least two billion poor people live in the great cities of the world. New mission structures are being formed by young men and women who chose to go and live among them in incarnational ministries. But much more is needed.

This schematic is helpful.

Date	Person	Mission Society	Focus	Student Movement
1792	Wm .Carey	BMS	Coastlands	Haystack Prayer Meeting
1865	J. H. Taylor	CIM	Interior areas	SVM
1934	C. Townsend	WBT	Hidden peoples	Urbana, IVCF
1980	R. Bakke/ Viv Grigg	Servants	The cities	Urbana, International Student Movements

Student Movements

Student movements have been important in mission since the establishment of the Dominicans in the thirteenth century. While students in the formal sense did not form the Celtic and Nestorian movements since there were no universities at the time, both were primarily led by young people.

We remember Calvin's ministry at the academy in Geneva, where he trained over 160 pastors whom he sent as missionaries to France, the Low Countries, Hungary, and Poland. Lutheranism was taken to the Scandinavian countries by Luther's former students. Plutschau and Ziegenbalg went from the University of Halle to India, and when the latter visited Halle in 1713, Zinzendorf and others formed the Order of the Mustard Seed. We have spoken of the "Holy Club" at Oxford, where the Wesley brothers and Whitefield were involved. Charles Simeon was converted in 1782 at Cambridge and exercised his entire ministry at Holy Trinity Church in Cambridge until he died in 1836. Henry Martyn, one of the great early missionaries, and others, came out of Simeon's ministry. The Cambridge Christian Union, another result of his ministry, was the predecessor of InterVarsity Christian Fellowship.

We remember the "Haystack Prayer Meeting" at Williams College in 1806, where the American missionary movement began. D. L. Moody held evangelistic meetings at Cambridge in 1882. He was a layman, an American with little formal education and poor grammar, speaking at one of the most prestigious universities in England. At first the students laughed at him. However, a combination of the prayers of many and the power of Moody's message brought many students to faith in Christ. Seven of the most prominent students were converted, among them, C. T. Studd. The seven volunteered to go to China with the CIM and were known as "the Cambridge Seven."

The Society of the Brethren

One result of the Haystack Prayer Meeting at Williams College, and the leadership of Samuel Mills, was the formation of the Society of Brethren, whose goal was to stimulate missionary interest. Established in 1808, two years later it moved to Andover, the first graduate seminary in the United States. Over a sixty-year period, 527 students at Andover became members; half of them became missionaries overseas.

The Society of Inquiry

As part of the same movement, "Societies of Inquiry on the Subject of Missions" were established at a number of colleges and seminaries across the eastern United States. They were influential in stirring up churches, as well as seminary and college students, to greater missionary vision. We can consider these two societies as one growing stream of emphasis on mission.

The Young Men's Christian Association

A second stream was the Young Men's Christian Association (YMCA). George Williams established the YMCA in 1844 to work with young men who came from the countryside to London and other cities. It was very evangelical, with a focus on Bible study and evangelism. In 1851, it came to North America and grew rapidly. In 1877, Luther Wishard became secretary of the YMCA. His focus was on college students. He put great emphasis on personal prayer and Bible study, and soon began to focus on foreign missions. He was committed to mission and made a personal pilgrimage to the site of the Haystack Prayer Meeting. There he knelt in the snow and committed himself to the missionary cause.

The Princeton Foreign Missionary Fellowship

The third stream was the Princeton Foreign Missionary Fellowship. Royal Wilder, a member of the Society of Brethren at Andover in the 1840s, had served in India for thirty years. Because of poor health, he returned to the United States and lived in Princeton where he edited *The Missionary Review of the World*, the primary missionary publication in the country.

Wilder had a son, Robert, and daughter, Grace. Robert became a student in Princeton College in 1881. In 1883, he and two others heard Adoniram Judson Gordon speak on the Holy Spirit. They returned to Princeton, resolved to pray and work for renewal in the college and to stir up missionary interest. Grace had graduated from Mount Holyoke College, where she had worked to stimulate mission interest. The college had been established earlier to train women as missionaries. She had an intense life of prayer.

Now Robert Wilder invited other students to meet for prayer and discussion about missions. They formed the Princeton Foreign Missionary Fellowship. Their constitution said:

> The object of this Society shall be the cultivation of a missionary spirit among the students of the College, the information of its members in all subjects of missionary interest, and especially the leading of men to consecrate themselves to foreign missions work....Any student of the College who is a professing Christian may become a member by subscribing to the following covenant: 'We, the undersigned, declare ourselves willing and desirous, God permitting, to go to the unevangelized portions of the world. (Timothy C. Wallstrom, *The Creation of a Student Movement to Evangelize the World* [Pasadena: William Carey International University Press, 1980], 35.)

The group met daily at noon and for an extended period on Sunday afternoons. They prayed and discussed the needs of the missionary movement. While they met in the parlor, Robert's sister Grace, prayed alone for them in another room. During the 1885–86 school year, brother and sister met regularly to pray for a widespread missionary movement in the colleges and universities of America. They asked that ultimately one thousand volunteers might be secured to labor in foreign fields. Their prayers were answered twenty times over!

As we examine mission movements, it is important to look at the kind of people who were behind them. We note here that nearly all of those who stimulated the Student Volunteer Movement were laymen.

Other Streams
We should note two other streams. One was Dwight L. Moody, the lay evangelist. The other was Arthur Tappan Pierson. Pierson was a gifted Presbyterian pastor, a graduate of Princeton Seminary, who had occupied prestigious pulpits, but his great passion was world mission. He was given the name "Arthur Tappan" because his father had worked for Tappan, the businessman who had been converted under the ministry of Charles Finney. As we noted earlier, the Tappan brothers were leaders in the anti-slavery movement and helped establish Oberlin College, the first co-educational college in the United States.

The Mt. Hermon Student Conference
In 1885, Luther Wishard persuaded Moody to hold a monthlong student conference at Mount Hermon, Massachusetts the following year. The focus was to be Bible study. Robert Wilder had just graduated from college and attended the conference. John R. Mott was a student at Cornell University and a leader in the YMCA there. He also went. Grace Wilder stayed home and prayed. It is reported the Wilders made a covenant to pray for one hundred missionary volunteers at that meeting.

The conference continued throughout the month of July, with 251 students present. The emphasis was on the Bible and music as two important agencies to reach the world. There was no formal missionary emphasis during the first two weeks, but Wilder and a group were praying. On July 16, Pierson gave an address on God's providence in modern missions, with the simple motto: "All should go, and go to all." This was catchy and easy to grasp.

A week later, on July 24, the students persuaded Moody to let them present the spiritual needs of the nations. Various students did a study of different nations, presented their needs, and then went to prayer. Wilder circulated the Princeton declaration and students began to sign it. As they went into the closing prayer meeting of the conference, ninety-nine had signed the declaration, then one more person signed, making it exactly one hundred. It was very dramatic!

The Student Volunteer Movement
Two traveling secretaries, Wilder and John Forman (a Princeton friend of Wilder), began to itinerate

and visited one hundred and sixty-two colleges and seminaries during the following year. During that period, 2106 students signed the pledge, including 500 women. Among them were Samuel Zwemer and Robert E. Speer, two of the greatest American mission leaders in the first half of the century. However, movements cannot continue very long without structure. Therefore, in 1888, the YMCA, under Wishard's leadership, organized the Student Volunteer Movement for Foreign Missions (SVM) under its auspices. It adopted as its slogan, "The evangelization of the world in this generation." John Mott became its General Secretary. (Later, he would turn down a job offer from a company at $100,000 a year. Do you know how much $100,000 would have been in the early 1900s? He wept as he said, "Do you think I would leave serving Christ to make $100,000 a year?") The SVM began to hold conventions every four years, the first in 1891. That year, 551 students attended from 151 educational institutions. By that time, there were 6,200 volunteers from 352 institutions, with 321 having sailed as missionaries.

Its fivefold purpose was as follows:

> ...to lead students to a thorough consideration of the claims of foreign missions upon them personally as a lifework; to foster this purpose by guiding students who become volunteers in their study and activity for missions until they come under the immediate direction of the Mission Boards; to unite all volunteers in a common, organized, aggressive movement; to secure a sufficient number of well-qualified volunteers to meet the demands of the various Mission Boards; and to create and maintain an intelligent, sympathetic and active interest in foreign missions on the part of students who are to remain at home in order to ensure the strong backing of the missionary enterprise by their advocacy, their gifts and their prayers. (John R. Mott, *Five Decades and a Forward View* [New York, Harper Brothers, 1939], 8).

It was estimated that between five and seven persons committed to mission were needed at home for every one who went overseas. In a twenty-five-year period, beginning in 1890, the number of American missionaries rose from less than one thousand to over nine thousand. By 1945, when the movement was largely over, 20,500 student volunteers had sailed, primarily from North America, with some from Europe.

The Student Volunteer Movement declined rather rapidly after World War I. The 1920 convention was the largest to date, with 6,890 students in attendance. However, disillusioned by World War I, many began to challenge the validity of evangelization by the West. There were only 2,783 new volunteers that year, and in 1938 there were only 25. It is interesting to note that young Donald McGavran, son and grandson of missionaries to India, was present with his fiancé, Mary. He was determined not to become a missionary, but at the conference he spoke and prayed with Wilder, and resolved to go to India!

Apparently, several factors led to the demise of the SVM. First, there was great theological confusion after World War I. The SVM related positively to both the older mainline denominations—Presbyterians, Anglicans, Baptists, Congregationalists, Methodists—and to some of the faith missions, like the China Inland Mission. Mainline denominations and faith missions were theologically much closer to each other at the time. But as the social gospel movement grew, accompanied by the development of liberal theology, the Movement's focus on world evangelization blurred. Social concerns had always been an important aspect of missionary activity, but evangelism had always been the priority. Now, growing theological liberalism began to question the authority of Scripture, the need of salvation from sin, and, consequently, the uniqueness of Jesus Christ. This, of course, led to doubts about the importance or even legitimacy of evangelization.

Secondly, up to World War I, it was assumed that Western culture was Christian. The West was Christendom. That was the perception both in the Western and non-Western worlds. That assumption was shattered at one blow by one of the most stupid and tragic wars in history. There was no reason for World War I. It was a quarrel between dynasties in Europe. It was brutal. Because the technology of warfare had advanced so much, millions died for no reason at all. Could this be Christian civilization? Suddenly the confidence of the West and Western Christians about their faith and their "Christian civilization" was shattered. Many students to feel they needed to get their own house in order before talking about missions.

A third reason was a shift in the leadership of the SVM. As Mott grew older, his interests expanded. He led the International Missionary Council and World Christian Student Movement, and turned leadership of the SVM over to others. The second generation of leadership was not nearly as gifted or focused as Mott.

Missionary education in the churches, often stimulated by the SVM, declined. The YMCA began to lose its evangelical theological foundation. By the 1940s, the SVM had all but disappeared. The Student Christian Movement, established by Mott as an outgrowth of the SVM, also declined and nearly disappeared by the late 1950s.

The Student Foreign Missions Fellowship
A small student conference held in Ben Lippen, North Carolina, in 1936 expressed concern over the decline in mission interest by students. Two years later, the Student Foreign Missions Fellowship was formed. By October 1941, it had thirty-six chapters with over twenty-six hundred members in the United States. In 1939, the Inter-Varsity Christian Fellowship entered the United States through Canada. The Student Foreign Missions Fellowship and Inter-Varsity merged in 1945, after World War II. They held their first international Student Conference on Missions in Toronto in 1946, with 575 students present. In 1948, the conference was moved to Urbana, Illinois, and it has been held every three years since then, with up to twenty thousand in attendance.

Now, of course, there are student mission movements in many countries as both the Church and the missionary movement have grown in Asia, and increasingly, in Latin America, and Africa. Just like the missionary movement, the student mission movement is now international. These new student groups have much to learn, both from the positive and negative aspects of the Student Volunteer Movement.

Chapter Twenty-Four

Women in Mission

Introduction

I want to read a few verses from Acts 18:

> After this, Paul left Athens and went on to Corinth. There he met a Jew named Aquila, born in Pontius, who had recently come from Italy with his wife Priscilla… (Acts 18:1–2a GNT)

We know that Paul stayed and worked with them, earning his living as they did, making tents. Continuing:

> Paul stayed on with the believers in Corinth for many days, then left them and sailed off with Priscilla and Aquila for Syria….They arrived in Ephesus, where Paul left Priscilla and Aquila. He went into the synagogue and held discussions with the Jews. (Acts 18:18a,19 GNT)

Later on in the same chapter, it says:

> At that time a Jew named Apollos, who had been born in Alexandria, came to Ephesus. He was an eloquent speaker and had a thorough knowledge of the Scriptures. He had been instructed in the Way of the Lord, and with great enthusiasm he proclaimed and taught correctly the facts about Jesus. However, he knew only the baptism of John. He began to speak boldly in the synagogue. When Priscilla and Aquila heard him, they took him home with them and explained more correctly [the Word or] the way of God. (Acts 18:24–26 GNT)

We want to look at Priscilla and Aquila. Often in the history of the Church, men have taken a few Scripture passages that seemed to impose restrictions on the ministries of women, and focused on those, but ignored the practice of the New Testament Church. Yet it is clear that women were greatly involved in ministry in the early Church. In Romans 16, Paul speaks of several women in very positive terms as co-workers. There he uses technical terms for ministry to describe women.

However, the case of Priscilla and Aquila is especially interesting. When they were first introduced, Aquila was mentioned first because he was a man; that was the way you identified a family. The next three times they are mentioned, her name is first. In our culture, the woman's name is often mentioned first as a matter of courtesy. However, in that context, it probably indicated she was the more prominent and active person in their joint ministry.

Although Priscilla is mentioned first three out of the five times the couple is mentioned in the New Testament, the translators of the King James version of the Bible put Aquila first all five times, reversing the order of the Greek three times! This indicates a male bias.

One of the growing edges for most, if not all, of us, is the need is to appreciate more fully the gifts that God has given to every follower of Christ. Men and women of every culture, tend to look on some people as being more gifted for ministry than others. Perhaps it is because of social status, formal education, race, gender, social class, or other reasons. However, history teaches us that the Holy Spirit delights in surprising us by working through unexpected people and methods. Think of the diversity of some of those we have already studied in this course: Francis of Assisi, Peter Waldo, and Carey. Wycliffe and Luther had doctorates in theology, the others had very little formal education, and had no status in the established Church of their day. It is profitable to examine history from this perspective and see how God has taken the "nobodies," those whom most believed to be incapable of ministry, and used them. Today we will see that many of them were women. In addition, they have come from every continent!

Ruth Tucker's book *Guardians of the Great Commission: The Story of Women in Modern Missions* (Grand Rapids: Academic Books, 1988) has a number of stories of women of various countries and cultures who have been used greatly by God.

My fundamental thesis in this chapter is that whatever we believe about the role of women in ministry, we can all agree that the Holy Spirit is leading the Church to the recognition today that every believer is gifted for ministry. The Church is most effective in outreach and in making an impact on society when it encourages all of God's people, men and women, to discover and use their gifts in ministry.

This is a simple thesis, but has been forgotten so often in the history of the Church. It is obvious that at least fifty percent or more of the gifts of the Spirit reside in women. For this reason, we want to encourage women as well as men to use those gifts. It is clear there are both theological and historical reasons for doing so.

When we begin to look beyond the histories that were written by men (usually white men), we will discover the remarkable ways in which God has used women as well as men who were not of European descent. Our goal is to encourage the whole Church to recognize the gifts of every believer, male and female, Western and non-Western.

Now we will look at another example of a fundamental thesis of our study. So often in history, God has raised up small groups on the periphery,

ignored at first, to start a new missionary effort. They have often encountered indifference and faced great odds against their projects. Perhaps they were people of no status, or their interest was directed toward neglected groups. We will see this as we examine the role of women in mission.

Beginnings: Women in Support of Mission

R. Pierce Beaver wrote the first significant work on women in mission—*American Protestant Women in Mission* (Grand Rapids: Eerdmans, 1968). Dana Robert, who wrote *American Women in Mission* (Macon, Ga.: Mercer University Press, 1996), and Ruth Tucker, the author of *Guardians of the Great Commission* (Grand Rapids: Zondervan, 1988), have done additional research and writing on the subject. Beaver added an interesting subtitle to the second edition of his work: he called it *A History of the First Feminist Movement in North America*. He made another important observation. Speaking of the women's missionary effort directed primarily toward women and children in the non-Western world, he wrote, "No other form of American intervention overseas has made a more powerful cultural impact than this work for women and children" (Beaver, *American Protestant Women*, p. 9).

In the preface to the second edition, he wrote,

> It began as the first feminist movement in North America and stimulated the rise of various other streams in the nineteenth-century struggle for women's rights and freedom. Now after its decline it is no longer a great creative force within society at large, but it still has impact within the churches, and the forces it set in motion will work for the liberation of women in Asia and Africa. The present struggle for women's full rights in the churches, focusing on ordination and parity in pastoral appointments, has probably deflected from churchwomen's interest in world mission. Yet that mission remains a tremendous challenge to American women. (ibid., 11).

The first recorded phase of women's involvement found them in support of mission. Mary Webb, is one of the many forgotten heroines of the faith. She lived in Boston, and in 1800 gathered fourteen women, Baptists and Congregationalists, and formed "The Boston Female Society for Missionary Purposes." Each member would pay annual dues of two dollars, a considerable sum at that time. It is of special interest to note that Mary Webb was an invalid, confined to a wheelchair. Yet she started a small movement that would grow greatly. Two years later, another woman, Mrs. Simpkins, organized a Cent Society for the same purpose. Each woman gave a penny a week.

The early missionary societies were all made up of men. They not only supported the missionary work; they determined policies. It was assumed that it was neither proper nor possible for women to serve in that capacity.

Wars have an interesting way of changing things. Women began to play a greater role in American society during the Revolutionary War. They became more independent and showed their abilities in taking on new tasks of necessity when there were few men around. We note that Mary Webb's society antedated the formation of the first American foreign missionary society by ten years! The ABCFM was established in 1810. The American missionary movement had not yet begun when Mary Webb and Mrs. Simpkins founded their societies. But the function of the women's groups was still limited to prayer and fundraising.

Then Mrs. Hannah Stillman, the wife of a pastor, took a new step. She and a few others established the "Boston Female Asylum for Orphan Girls." That was thought to be beyond "female duty." Females were to stay home and take care of their husbands and children, and be silent—certainly not to venture out in establishing organizations for social uplift! Nevertheless, some of these courageous women did so. They kept pushing out the edges.

The early women's societies raised funds and sent them to existing mission agencies—some to Serampore to help William Carey. The total raised during the first seven years of these women's

groups was over three thousand dollars, a substantial amount at that time. After 1810, the American women raised money for the American mission societies.

It is important to note that the small groups of women had vision and ventured out beyond that which was considered proper for them. Most had no independent income and, if they were married, received money from their husbands only to run their households. They set aside a bit of that to give to missions. However, with their prayers and vision, they launched a movement.

The first legacy that the ABCFM received came from a domestic servant, Sally Thomas, who left her life savings of $345.38. That was amazing! It must have represented her savings over many years. The first large bequest of thirty thousand dollars, also came from a woman. We would need to multiply that many times to get the equivalent in our currency today.

The men did not know what to think about the activities of the women. They were glad to accept the money and prayers, but that was as far as they wanted it to go. Listen to this sermon preached by a pastor, Walter Harris, to the Female Cent Society of Bedford, New Hampshire, in 1814. (There were now various "Cent Societies.")

> Though God has made known, that it is his will that females should not be public teachers of religion, nor take an active part in the government of his church on earth; yet much may be done by them to assist and forward the preaching of the Gospel, and the propagation of religious knowledge in the world; and thus promote the Redeemer's interest. Above all they can persevere in prayer for the success of the gospel and the enlargement of the church, for blessing on the work of ministers and missionaries. They can encourage and strengthen ministers. They instruct children and youth in religion and morality. ...They can contribute of their worldly substance for preaching, Bible distribution, and the like. (ibid., 30).

Another New Hampshire, pastor, Ethan Smith, spoke to the ladies of the Cent Society in his area. He approved of not only private prayer but also group prayer by women. He said with approval, "Lately females have been uniting to pray for the church, ministers, the missionary cause, the salvation of the heathen and destitute, and for the gift of the Holy Spirit" (ibid., 31). He went a bit further than most others did at that point.

However, it was still a struggle. Some criticized the women. They were not sure it was proper for females to meet together for prayer without a man to lead and supervise them. But the movement continued.

We have mentioned Ashbel Green, who was pastor of the Presbyterian Church in Princeton and President of the College. He still maintained traditional limitations on women, but was open to some expansion of their ministries. He agreed that unmarried women might serve as missionaries if they were under the protection of men. This was not without reason, because nearly all missionaries at the time were going to cultures where there was no place for a single woman who was not a member of a household led by a man.

The issue soon came up with Adoniram Judson. When Mrs. White, a widow, volunteered to go to Burma and aid a missionary couple in their ministry, he raised a serious question. What to do with her? Burmese society understood a single woman to be under a man's authority either as a ward or a concubine. Obviously, if she was a ward under his protection, a wealthy Burmese who wanted to marry an American woman could come to him and offer money to do so. In other words, she would be seen as a chattel to be traded, and it would have been very difficult for Judson to say "no." On the other hand, if he kept her in his household as a single woman, the Burmese would naturally conclude that she was a second wife or a concubine, thus negating the Christian view of marriage. Therefore, the reluctance of missionary men to accept single women was not entirely due to archaic views on the place of women. Fortunately, when Mrs. White arrived in Calcutta, she met and married an English missionary whose wife had died.

By 1820, women were generally conceded the right to organize themselves for fundraising, prayer, and mission education for themselves and their children. However, they got little support from denominational offices.

Many of us have seen the remarkable role of women in supporting and encouraging missions in local churches. Earlier in the twentieth century, women's groups in most churches focused on missions, and were called "women's missionary societies." None of us can fully appreciate the great influence that women have had in missionary education. Today that focus is in sharp decline in the American churches as leaders in the women's movements have stressed other issues. While some of them are important, it is tragic that most women's groups in the 'mainline' churches have lost their focus on world mission.

Women As Missionaries

The second phase began shortly after the first. At first women went only as wives of missionaries. All the early missionaries who went out from the United States were encouraged to marry, but only the men were considered to be "missionaries." Their wives were considered "assistant missionaries," yet many accomplished remarkable things, and as their letters home were published in the missionary magazines, they stimulated great interest. Some of the best-known women in North America early in the nineteenth century were missionary wives.

Ann Hasseltine Judson was one. Scores of books have been written about her. She was very heroic. She married Adoniram Judson a week before they sailed; they had their honeymoon on the ship. When the East India Company refused to allow them to stay in India, they went to Burma. When England and Burma were at war, Adoniram was imprisoned under horrible circumstances and almost died. While he was in prison, she protected his translation of the Bible, took him food and drink, nursed him, and kept him alive. All three of her children died in infancy, and she eventually died as well. Her letters and story made a powerful impression on women as well as men in the United States.

While the missionary wives believed their primary role was to support their husbands and educate their children, they soon saw the great needs of women and children in the societies where they served. This often led them to engage in ministries that would have been denied to them at home. There was some historical precedent: the Moravian wives had shared ministry with their husbands as they worked in various parts of the world. However, that was not common in American society.

Yet the vision was expanding, even for the first missionary wives. Listen to the farewell sermon preached to the brides of two of the first ABCFM missionaries who sailed. The speaker spoke of their ministry, not that of their husbands:

> It will be your business, my dear children, to teach these women, to whom your husbands can have but little or no access. Go then, and do all in your power, to enlighten their minds, and bring them to the knowledge of the truth.... Teach them to realize that they are not an inferior race of creatures; but stand upon a par with men. Teach them that they have immortal souls; and are no longer to burn themselves, in the same fire, with the bodies of their departed husbands. Go, bring them from their cloisters into the assemblies of the saints. Teach them to accept Christ as their Savior, and to enjoy the privileges of the children of God. (Beaver, *American Protestant Women*, 51–52).

This was a positive vision for their ministries. That sturdy Calvinism was not without its defects, but at its best, it recognized that, when redeemed, all people had the same potential as children of God, regardless of race or gender.

Many of the missionary wives died young. There was the tragic case of Harriet Newell, one of the first Americans to sail. In 1813, she and her husband were ordered out of Calcutta ten days after they arrived, even though she was ill. They went to the Isle of France nearby, where she died at the age of nineteen. Others lost their husbands and remarried. After her husband died, Sarah Boardman, a Baptist missionary in Burma, became the second wife of Judson. He outlived her and married a third time. These women were sources of inspiration to the women at home. Many had strong personalities, made sacrifices, and had effective ministries.

Single Women Pioneers

The third phase saw single women missionaries. Married women could not take care of all the needs. Most believed their families to be their primary responsibility, and that was natural. Because their husbands usually worked in very difficult circumstances, the support and companionship of their wives was essential, and of course the converse was true. The women gave birth to the children and cared for them often in contexts where there was danger from disease. So mutual support was necessary. However, in most cultures the ministry of men to women was greatly limited. Only women could enter into significant contact with other women. Thus, even though it was foreign to much of Western culture, the ministry of single women was necessary and would be very fruitful. Eventually nearly a third of all Protestant missionaries would be single women. Many demonstrated great heroism, some made an intentional sacrifice of marriage and home, feeling called by God to do so.

We have already mentioned Charlotte White, the first single woman missionary from the United States. Since she had already been under the protection of a man and was going to pay her own way, the Baptist board accepted her to go to Burma. And we understand why Judson was opposed to the idea. Now we turn to the story of Betsy Stockton, the first single woman (who had not been married) missionary from the United States. She had been a slave, born to the Stockton family who lived in the Stockton mansion in Princeton, New Jersey. Richard Stockton, an earlier member of the family, had signed the Declaration of Independence. Her owners encouraged her to use their library and learn to read. When the Stockton daughter married Ashbel Green, pastor of the church and the president of Princeton College, Betsy was a wedding gift to the couple. They promptly freed her.

This young woman, a former slave, became a missionary to the Hawaiian Islands under the ABCFM. She served there a few years, teaching school, and eventually returned to the United States. She opened a school for black children in Philadelphia, and was one of the founding members of the Witherspoon Presbyterian Church in Princeton. A wonderful story!

Another single woman, Cynthia Farrar, sailed to India in 1827, served thirty-four years, and opened a school for girls as well as boys. Remember, that was in a culture where it was not considered either possible or desirable to educate girls. Most Hindu fathers bitterly opposed education for their daughters. She opened several schools, to show the value of women and to witness to the Gospel. Eleanor Macomber, the third single woman sent by the Baptists to Burma, had a remarkable career as an evangelist in dangerous areas. Her ministry might have been more effective than that of a man because she was a woman and perceived as powerless. She died at the age of thirty-nine. Eliza Agnew went to Ceylon (Sri Lanka) in 1839, and remained there until she died in 1883 at the age of seventy-six. Over six hundred of her students became Christians.

Lucy Sheppard went to Africa with her husband, William. They were African Americans, and recruited four single African American women to serve in the Congo with them. One of them, Althea Brown, married another missionary. She reduced one language to writing and prepared a dictionary and grammar for it. At the same time, she directed day schools, Sunday schools, women and children's work, and a home for girls. She also produced hymnals and schoolbooks. She and her husband translated and printed the Bible in a local language. She died of malaria in 1937.

There were woman physicians. Clara Swain went to India in 1869, and was the first of many. She trained the first female physicians and nurses in India.

Up to 1860, the American Board had appointed 567 men and 691 women. So at least 124 women were single, but only 30 of them served overseas. The others served in the United States. Other

Black, as well as White, women went to Africa and to Asia as missionaries during this period.

Women's Mission Boards

The fourth phase began before mid-century, when women's mission boards were formed. In 1834, David Abeel of the Reformed Church persuaded women in London to organize "The Female Agency for Christian Education in China and Other Countries." He said China could use all the teachers the women could find. Then, in 1847, Methodist women in Baltimore organized the Ladies' China Missionary Society. Two years later, having raised five thousand dollars, they sent three young women to China. The first focus of these women's boards was women and children in other countries. In 1861, Sara Doremus of the Reformed Church in New York took the lead in organizing the Women's Union Missionary Society (WUMS). Within ten years, it had workers in China, Syria, Greece, Japan, Burma, and India. After twenty years, it had 101 workers in twelve countries. The Zenana Mission that focused on women was organized in England in 1852. It later became the Bible and Medical Missionary Fellowship, merged with the WUMS in 1976, and is now known as INTERSERVE.

We began by seeing small groups of women who collected money for mission societies. Then we found them gathering to pray and educate themselves and their children about mission. They also began to educate the Church about its missionary task. A new step came when mission boards began to send out single women as well as missionary wives. Now we have come to another stage, where the women, impatient with the men and their foot-dragging on women's issues, organized their own mission boards. The sequence is interesting!

In 1860, there were five major U.S. boards and four minor ones. By 1900, there were ninety-four sending boards and forty-three support agencies: forty-one of these agencies were women's boards! Ruth Tucker found in her research that at least forty mission societies were run and supported by women in the last half of the century. In part, this was due to the fact that so many young men had been killed during the Civil War resulting in more opportunity for women to take leadership. That was before the faith mission movement began.

Tucker wrote that a number of missiological texts grew out of the thinking and administration of these women, but have disappeared from our consideration. She suspects the reason is the societies themselves were slowly absorbed into the male-dominated denominational agencies, and men eventually replaced the women.

That often happened to mission structures in the older "mainline" churches. Now those structures have been absorbed into the larger church structure where denominational maintenance has taken precedence, and mission has been de-emphasized. Thus much of the focus on women and their contribution has been lost.

What were some of the factors in this growth of women's boards? Co-education: the first higher educational institution in the U.S. that included both men and women was Oberlin College, where Finney had a strong role. Finney was instrumental in its establishment and then became its second president. The Tappan brothers, converted through the ministry of Finney, were its most important financial contributors.

Oberlin College was a center of evangelism, the anti-slavery movement, and women's rights—an interesting combination. Unfortunately we do not put those three things together very often today. That indicates a tragic bifurcation in much of American Christianity, where evangelicals typically support struggles against certain kinds of social ills, but not others. Our concern for evangelism should lead us to advocate human rights for every person, encouraging everyone to develop his or her complete potential as a child of God. This is not some wild-eyed radical proposal, it is biblical, and we need to realize it.

Another factor was the recognition of teaching as an appropriate profession for women, in the United States as well as overseas. A third factor was the activity of women in the movement to abolish slavery. Women were taking a more active role in society in a number of ways.

Mission and Culture Change

This brings us one of the dilemmas of missiology. First, we believe every culture is valid in providing a context in which people live and function. Every culture has important values that relate to how people live together. Thus, it is important to affirm the values of each culture, whether it is Asian, African, or Western. We should never give the impression that people must be ripped out of their cultural context and become something else in order to become authentic followers of Jesus Christ.

The second point is that God does not want to leave any culture as it is. In other words, every culture needs to be transformed by the Spirit, by the Word of God. One of our tasks as Christians, in whatever culture we live, is to work toward its transformation so that it will be more in accordance with the will of God.

It is easy to look back and see historical examples of cultural practices that needed to end. Slavery was one problem. Get rid of slavery! Suttee (sati) in India was another. It is easy to see widow burning was not in accordance with the will of God. However, what about the caste system, or class systems that keep some people from developing their full potential? What about systems in which women have no rights? Moreover, there are more subtle issues in every culture, and usually those who are within a cultural context need outsiders to point them out to us.

I think we would all agree that God wants to transform cultures, even as we accept them as a starting point. The difficult question is how: what is the process?

I believe we all agree that God wants every society—don't even use the word culture—every society to be constantly transformed, so that it moves toward conformity to his purpose. Certainly, part of God's purpose is that every individual be encouraged to develop his or her full potential as a human being and as his son or daughter. There are several questions to consider in this process. What is the role of the outsider to that culture and the insiders in it? What are the roles of the Word of God and the Church? These are extremely complicated questions.

Missionaries have had to deal with this issue. In 1877, a conference of missionaries in China decided that Bible women (evangelists) would not be selected for training unless they had no young children, and had their husband's permission. A modern feminist might object to that stipulation, but I believe the decision showed sensitivity to the cultural context.

We might think that those nineteenth century missionaries were impervious or insensitive to such issues. At some points they were, just as we are. But actually many were very sophisticated in trying to deal with those questions. Many secular people do not realize that Christian missionaries have often been the best friends that women had in Asia and Africa. They worked against many practices that degraded women, as we have seen. Among them were female genital mutilation in Africa, foot binding in China, suttee and infanticide in India, and the lack of education for girls in many places.

Examples from among the Many Great Women in Mission

A Southern Baptist woman named Charlotte "Lottie" Moon went to Shantung, China, in 1873. She trained other missionaries, itinerated as an evangelist, and wrote extremely well to Baptists at home, expanding their vision. During a famine in 1912, she shared what she had with starving people and appealed for more help from her board. Very ill because of her self-sacrifice, she died on her way to the United States to recuperate. Each year her denomination, the Southern Baptist Church, takes its Lottie Moon offering to support missions. Today it amounts to over one hundred million dollars annually.

The China Inland Mission used a number of single women as evangelists. German missiologists criticized the practice, but Hudson Taylor required married catechists to accompany them on their journeys. In 1882, the Mission had fifty-six married couples and ninety-five single women.

Mary Slessor went to Calabar, now part of Nigeria, in 1886. She broke her engagement to another missionary because his health made it impossible for him to accompany her into the interior where there was danger from disease. Mary evangelized, made peace between warring chiefs, saved twins from being killed and, overall, had a courageous and effective ministry.

Malla Moe served with the Scandinavian Alliance Mission (TEAM) in South Africa. Her pulpit was more often a stone under the open sky than a table in a chapel. She wore plain dresses and her sermons were simple. She really served as a bishop, overseeing the work of her converts. But when she visited her native Norway, she was not allowed to speak in the State church because women were to keep silent there!

Ida Scudder, daughter and granddaughter of medical missionaries, was born in India in 1870. Believing she would never become a missionary, she visited her parents in India after two years of college. One night, three men came to her father's home, asking her to assist their wives who were having difficulty in childbirth. One was a Muslim and two were high caste Hindus. She suggested her father go, since he was a physician and she was not. However, the men refused to allow a man to see their wives. The next day, she learned that all three women had died. That constituted her call to go to medical school and return to India, where she established a medical center in Vellore. That became one of the great medical centers in India, with the cooperation of many Christian groups. It includes a hospital, medical and nursing schools, and rural clinics.

The great number of non-Western women in mission and Christian ministry deserves much more space, but I will mention just a few. When the first Protestant missionaries entered Korea in 1884 and 1885, a woman had status primarily as the daughter of her father, the wife of her husband, and the mother of her eldest son. Women had an important role in Shamanistic religion, but not elsewhere. However, shortly after the middle of the twentieth century, Dr. Helen Kim was President of Ehwa Women's University and a leader, not only in education, but also in evangelism. She was honored by becoming the first Korean ambassador to the United Nations.

Pandita Ramabai was a brilliant Indian woman, well educated in the Hindu classics by her father. She became a Christian in England and returned to India where she had an extensive ministry with young widows and orphans. Many of them would have become temple prostitutes were it not for her ministry. There is ample evidence of miraculous activity in her ministry.

Bible women in India and the Middle East were effective evangelists. Today we know that between two-thirds and three fourths of the house church leaders in China are women.

Ministries of women have included evangelism, medicine, education at every level, orphanages, leprosariums, and the training of women physicians and nurses. Some conservative groups that deny the validity of the ministry of women need

to rediscover their historical forbears. Fredrik Franson, the founder of The Evangelical Alliance Mission (TEAM), C. T. Studd, founder of WEC, and others put single women in charge of mission stations in remote areas. Studd wrote,

> Single women go on long evangelizing treks among the villages where there is a shortage of men. In one district, a single woman missionary led the worst cannibal in the region, who was reputed to have a hundred men inside him, to Christ. Two of the most thriving stations with congregations from 500 to as many as 1500, are 'manned' by single women only. In some places where there have been only two workers, they have sacrificed human companionship in order the one may go further a field and evangelize a new area. (Ruth A. Tucker and Walter L. Liefield, *Daughters of the Church* [Grand Rapids, Michigan: Zondervan, 1987], 309).

Thus, we cannot study the history of Christian mission with integrity unless we seek to discover the essential role of women. Equally, we cannot be advocates of mission without encouraging women as well as men to use their gifts of ministry.

Chapter Twenty-Five

Edinburgh 1910
and the Ecumenical Movement

Introduction

The Edinburgh Conference of 1910 was a landmark event. It was the largest conference held specifically to study the missionary movement and its critical issues up to that time. It was also the beginning of the "ecumenical movement." For some, *ecumenical* is a good word; for others, it is a bad word. For many, it refers only to the World Council of Churches. However, the word, which comes from the Greek word *oikos* (household) is an ancient term. Its best definition, adopted at the Manila conference of the Lausanne Committee in 1989, means "the whole church taking the whole Gospel to the whole world." Of course, we all aspire to that goal. But first, some history.

By the end of the nineteenth century, a theological bifurcation or division was occurring in the American Church. The theological consensus with which the missionary movement had worked for over a century was breaking down. It began a bit earlier in Europe. There were several factors. Darwinism led some to believe in automatic progress and thus identified sin primarily with the lack of education and proper social institutions. Higher criticism of the Scriptures was a second factor. While it often aided in understanding the context and message of the Bible, in its more radical form it seemed to deny biblical authority. The growth of industrialization and often the poverty and injustice in Western economic systems led to the rise of the "social gospel." Although up to the middle of the century revival-

ism had often been in the forefront of social reform, a shift took place. The division began as some began to focus exclusively on social concerns and ignore the need for personal salvation from sin.

Soon there was a fundamentalist reaction. Liberalism tended to doubt or minimize the center of the faith (the incarnation, the cross, the resurrection, the indwelling of the Holy Spirit, Christ's second coming, and the authority of Scripture) and focus only on the application of faith to society. It was guilty of a kind of reductionism, focusing only on hoped-for results in society. Yet fundamentalism began to focus only on salvation and feel that any kind of concern for society was a betrayal of the Gospel. It also reduced the Gospel to less than its fullness, but it did hold on to the center. Some traditions seemed to fear that if they began to talk about the application of the Gospel to society, they were in danger of betraying the faith.

This led to a "life boat" mentality of evangelism among some. The concept was that the world and everybody in it was going to hell. The ship was sinking, and the task of the Church was to get as many people as possible "into the lifeboat." Even the great D. L. Moody likened the concern for social action to the desire to polish the doorknobs on a sinking ship.

These polarities are perhaps an over-simplification of tendencies in the Church at the end of the nineteenth century, yet they do portray the issues. Of course, these differences would have their effect on the missionary movement.

Student Volunteer Movement (SVM)

The Student Volunteer Movement arose in this context. It was very evangelical, to begin with, but it grew up in contact with a broad spectrum of the Church and mission. The mission societies (except for the ABCFM) were still quite united theologically at the end of the nineteenth century. For example, men and women who were members of the Student Volunteer Movement went out under the older "mainline" missions: Presbyterians, Methodists, etc., as well as the China Inland Mission. The great faith missions as well as the older denominational missions received personnel who came through the SVM. However, after World War I the SVM moved in a more liberal theological direction and soon lost its effectiveness.

The Social Gospel and Evangelism

A number of questions were being raised by the end of the nineteenth century. One was the relationship of Christian mission to social reform. Since Ziegenbalg and Carey, missionaries had assumed that Christian faith would bring changes to the receptor societies. However, that left a number of questions unanswered. What kind of changes? By what process? Moreover, should missionaries work directly to attempt to bring changes, or should they trust that the leaven of the Gospel would bring the desired changes gradually? What should be the relationship of Christian faith to the nationalism arising in a number of places? In addition, how "Western" should the new churches and their adherents look?

Some missionaries believed in attempting to transform the cultures to which they were sent by establishing Western-styled educational institutions where future leaders would study. The hope was that this "civilizing" or "westernizing" influence would bring conversion from the top down. Others believed strongly in the necessity of personal conversion, hoping that converted people would gradually transform their societies. This raised the question about which values in each culture should be preserved as compatible with Christian faith. In China, for example, some early Christians, especially students, were not nearly as concerned about personal salvation as they were about how the Christian faith could transform their nation and help build a better society. These are all legitimate questions for us as Christians. Some North American Christians need to ask deeper questions about the impact of our faith on our society and be much more sympathetic when some of our brothers and sisters from other cultures ask these questions in their cultures.

What do Western Christians say about a country where many people claim to have personal salvation but show little concern for terrible issues like apartheid, racism, or great economic inequality? These questions must be asked. The evangelical Church is again beginning to ask them. Many evangelicals are recovering their early conviction that social change is an implication of the Gospel. Some missionaries and national church leaders are beginning to feel that social change is not just an implication of the Gospel; it is part of the Gospel.

A second major issue faced by the missionary movement was the division of the Church into many denominations. Increasingly that was seen as a scandal in many areas. What meaning did Western denominational divisions have in Hindu India or a Muslim country, for example? Did it make sense to be a Southern Baptist in Northern India, or a Missouri Synod Lutheran instead of another kind of Lutheran in Tanzania? We can multiply examples. Most church divisions arose in Europe in the sixteenth century or later in North America, but had no relevance to mission in India or China in the twentieth. In some ways, the renewal movements that gave rise to Protestant missions were the most ecumenical arms of the Church and a number of the great mission societies were interdenominational. Even so, they could not help but export European and American church divisions to other parts of the world. The widespread perception was that such divisions greatly hindered the missionary effort.

As the twentieth century dawned, mission leaders began to look at these issues.

Edinburgh 1910

Antecedents

One of the great landmarks in the missionary movement was the Mission Conference held in Edinburgh, Scotland, in 1910. John R. Mott served as its chairman. He had attended the conference in 1886 where the SVM began, and became its traveling secretary when it was organized two years later. Mott was a man of great ability, vision, and energy. He eventually served as the leader of the International Missionary Council, established as a result of Edinburgh. He was one of the architects of the World Council of Churches, and helped organize national Christian councils in a number of countries. He played a key role in the organization of the World Student Christian Federation. A remarkable man, Mott was deeply committed to Jesus Christ. He remained a Methodist layman, and was clearly evangelical in his personal faith.

Before 1910, a series of mission conferences were held in England and North America. They were primarily inspirational. Over two hundred thousand people attended all the meetings of the Ecumenical Mission conference in New York in 1900. President McKinley, a Methodist, former President Benjamin Harrison, a Presbyterian, and future President Theodore Roosevelt, an Episcopalian, all spoke. That indicates something about the Protestant ethos of American society at the time. Groups such as the German Protestant Mission Society and the Foreign Mission Conference of North America had been organized to discuss subjects of mutual concern, seeking greater cooperation.

Student groups were important in furnishing leadership to movements of cooperation. They included the YMCA, the Student Christian Movement, the Student Volunteer Movement, and the World Student Christian Federation. Mott was deeply involved in all of them. They were the streams that led to the Edinburgh conference. The same movements contributed much of the leadership to the ecumenical movement.

Characteristics

There were twelve hundred delegates at Edinburgh sent by their mission boards or independent mission agencies. Note that at Edinburgh both denominational and multi-denominational mission structures were present. This would not be true of some of the later ecumenical gatherings when mission structures were increasingly eliminated. Edinburgh was a working body. Much research was done on the progress of Christianity around the world and sent to the delegates for study before the meeting. The purpose was to form a global strategy of world mission.

They were people of vision. Perhaps they were too optimistic, but on the other hand, we can never be too hopeful. They limited their focus to the non-Christian world. This was a great offense to Latin American Protestants, because the organizers of the Conference defined Catholic Latin America as a part of the Christian world. They did so to insure the participation of the continental Lutherans and English Anglicans who would not have attended otherwise.

Thus, Latin American Protestants were excluded because some Europeans did not consider Latin America a mission field. That was a serious affront to them. The greatest Protestant leader in Latin America at that time was Alvaro Reis, pastor of the First Presbyterian Church of Rio de Janeiro, the largest Protestant church in Latin America. The Presbyterian Board took him to Edinburgh as an observer.

The Brazilian church newspaper from that period, "O Puritano" (The Puritan) published Reis's letters from Edinburgh, which were read in Presbyterian homes in Brazil. The perception that Protestant churches in Latin America were somehow illegitimate was offensive, and did not help the Brazilians look favorably on the ecumenical movement later on. The American mission boards who worked in Latin America held a second conference in Panama in 1916 on Christian work in Latin America. That was a kind of Latin American Edinburgh.

Otherwise Edinburgh was very inclusive. Those in attendance ranged from Anglo-Catholics (high Anglicans) to Quakers. There were Lutherans, and leaders from the China Inland Mission, people from mainline churches and faith missions. A broad spectrum! Unfortunately, all the delegates (except for seventeen Asians) were Westerners. The organizers wanted many more Asians in the delegations, but did not get them. A continuing committee of thirty people was established to continue to work toward greater cooperation; three of its members were Asians. There were also regional conferences afterwards, primarily in Asia, but elsewhere as well.

Achievements

There was a focus on prayer: prayer on all continents beforehand, prayer at the beginning of each day, and a half hour of prayer at midday. These were praying Christians, seeking to formulate a strategy for world mission. They were optimistic. They did not yet realize the depth of the problems of colonialism or western arrogance. Azariah, the first Indian Anglican bishop and one of the seventeen Asians, asked that "the Gospel be conveyed in a fellowship of missionaries and nationals in a spirit of equality, not in a spirit of condescending love."

The word "ecumenical" at that point referred to the worldwide character of the missionary task and the need to see it as a totality. It did not refer to any particular movement or organization. However, Edinburgh did form a continuation committee, designed to work toward greater cooperation and unity.

Four years later, World War I broke out. It was a terrible shock to the world, and to the European nations that looked on themselves as Christian. It caused a loss of confidence in European culture, leading many to ask serious questions about their faith and its relationship to that culture. Non-Europeans who had looked upon Europeans and North Americans as Christians began to ask some of the same questions.

The formation of the International Missionary Council (IMC), which had been contemplated at Edinburgh, was delayed until 1921. Mott was instrumental in its formation. The goal of the IMC was to help to coordinate missionary work around the world, not to tell missions what to do. It sought ways to encourage greater cooperation in various fields. In the Philippines, South India, China, and Japan, the IMC encouraged church unions. Some were more successful than others.

The IMC held meetings that brought together Christian leaders from all over the world. The first took place in Jerusalem in 1928, and the second in Madras, India, in 1938. Participants considered the various issues facing the missionary movement, and increasingly participants came from non-Western churches and missions. Eventually half came from Asia, Africa, and Latin America. Some of the most international gatherings ever held in history up to that time were these first meetings of the IMC. Where else in the world would you find Asians, Africans, Latin Americans, and Pacific Islanders meeting with Europeans and North Americans in a spirit of equality, to discuss issues and to learn from each other? That was a major achievement of the IMC.

A second stream, the Life and Work Movement, began in Stockholm in 1925. With some roots in Edinburgh, it was more concerned about Christian social witness. World War I was only a few years in the background. What could the churches say to the world about war, revolution, and now, communism? Bishop Brent, an American Episcopal bishop in the Philippines, said, "The world is too strong for a divided church. We must cooperate. We must speak together in one voice if we are to have an impact." At the second meeting of Life and Work, the group had to consider the new totalitarianisms arising in Europe: Hitler, Mussolini, and Franco.

A third movement soon developed. The first focused on missions, the second on ethics, and now a third focused on theology. It was known as Faith and Order. Three different streams: the International Missionary Council on mission, the Life and Work Movement on social concerns, and now Faith and Order on theology. Faith and Order held meetings in 1927 and 1937. They involved church leaders from the older established denominations, but no Pentecostals, who were still a small, ignored sect, and no one from the Holiness tradition except the Methodists who had grown away from that tradition. Although the more conservative "faith missions" continued to be involved in the IMC, those in the other two movements came from the older churches with roots either in the Protestant Reformation or subsequent movements that included Methodists, Congregationalists, and some Baptists.

The World Council of Churches

In 1941, two of these groups—Life and Work, and Faith and Order—resolved to form a World Council of Churches. However, World War II intervened. After the war, in 1948 in Amsterdam, the World Council of Churches (WCC) was formed. The stated goal was not to be a super-church, but to be a council of churches that would speak to each other and to the world. The WCC consisted of 147 different denominations from forty-four countries. In an official statement, it defined itself as "a fellowship of churches which confess the Lord Jesus Christ as God and Saviour according to the Scriptures." In a statement in 2005, the phrase was added, "and therefore seek to fulfill their common calling to the glory of the one God, Father, Son, and Holy Spirit." No Latin American churches were represented at the beginning. At its first meeting the member churches still were so divided they had to celebrate communion in four different worship services, because some would not celebrate communion with the others. The goal in the minds of many of the founders was greater unity so that the world might believe. John 17:21–23 was a key text.

In 1961, the IMC merged with the WCC and became the Division of Overseas Mission and Evangelism of the World Council.

Two great men held different views on the issue of the merger. One was Dr. John MacKay, President of Princeton Seminary. MacKay had spent his missionary career in Latin America and was passionately in love with Jesus Christ and deeply committed to mission. He often said, "The church that is not committed to mission is not truly the church!" He was one of the architects of the World Council of Churches. He also had great respect

for the Pentecostal movement. MacKay was chair of the International Missionary Council, and believed that its merger with the WCC would put mission at the heart of the World Council. It turned out his position was naïve in its failure to recognize the need for specifically focused mission structures. Max Warren, the Secretary of the Anglican Church Missionary Society, spoke against the merger. We are already familiar with his view that we will always need separate, focused, voluntary missionary structures to maintain the missionary cause and the vitality of the church.

The merger took place in 1961, but it failed to put mission at the heart of the WCC. Warren was right, and MacKay, one of my theological heroes, was wrong. With the merger, the IMC now became the Division of Mission and Evangelism of the WCC. It resulted in less unity in the missionary movement because some conservative missions that were members of the IMC, did not want to be associated with the WCC. Even more serious was the drift of the WCC away from the focus on world evangelization toward social, political, and economic concerns. Certainly theological erosion lay behind that drift. The Uppsala meeting of the WCC in 1968 seems to have been a turning point. Its focus almost exclusively on political and social concerns brought forth Donald McGavran's challenge, "Will Uppsala Betray the Two Billion?" He was referring to the estimated two billion people in the world at that time who had never heard the Gospel.

Since that time, there have been some shifts in WCC emphases, but in general it has lost any strong focus on world evangelization. The 2006 meeting in Brazil stressed compassion for the poor, peace, justice, the responsibility to preserve the integrity of creation, violence against women and children, the need for drinkable water, HIV/AIDS, and violence and terrorism. One listened in vain for a call to world evangelization.

At the same time, one writer recognized that the churches that formed the WCC are largely in decline, while those outside of it are often those churches growing dramatically and shaping the future of Christianity in the world, especially outside of North America and Europe. They have kept their distance from the WCC. They include, among others, Latin American Pentecostalism. At the 2006 WCC meeting in Brazil, Dr. Norberto Saracco, a Pentecostal leader from Argentina, addressed the Council. He suggested that the WCC's "way of doing ecumenism has gone as far as it can," and called for openness to the ecumenism of the future. For him that meant recognition of evangelicals and Pentecostals and pointing to the centrality of Jesus Christ.

The "Evangelical Ecumenical Movement"

A second ecumenical stream began with the Lausanne Committee on World Evangelization (LCWE) in 1974. This movement focused primarily on world evangelization and included evangelical leaders from the older "mainline" denominations as well as Pentecostals, newer evangelical groups, and mission structures. Thus, it was more broadly representative of the worldwide missionary movement and many of the growing churches. The Lausanne Covenant, written primarily by John Stott and adopted in 1974, is a fine, well-balanced theological statement that we can all study and follow with profit.

On the other hand, the World Council of Churches continued to represent the older churches or denominations simply by the nature in which it was formed. Its membership is made up of churches; separate mission structures have no place in it. That is, it correctly assumed that the Church is always called to mission, but saw no role for any mission structures separate from the traditional churches. Thus, while it is more liberal theologically and politically, it is more conservative in its suspicion of new movements, including multi-denominational mission agencies. While some have hoped for greater dialogue and understanding between the WCC and the evangelical ecumenical movement, this has not happened to any significant extent.

Three important meetings were held in 1980. The Division of World Mission and Evangelism of the WCC met in Melbourne, Australia. The theme

was "Thy Kingdom Come," and it focused on God's creation and the hope of changing society.

Two weeks later the Lausanne Committee met in Pattaya, Thailand. There the theme was "How Shall They Hear?" Thus, while Melbourne focused on the transformation of society, Pattaya stressed the necessity of world evangelization. In its discussions and documents, Pattaya rejected any definition of mission that sought to put social action on an equal level with evangelism. Three months later the World Consultation on Frontier Missions was held in Edinburgh focusing as the name implies on frontier mission and frontier peoples. It intentionally commemorated the 70th anniversary of Edinburgh 1910.

However, in 1982 a meeting of forty evangelicals, half from the majority world, was held in Grand Rapids, Michigan, to discuss further the relationship of evangelism and social action in mission. Its statement, again written primarily by John Stott, reflects a fine balance. It insists that the concern for human needs and social transformation must always go hand-in-hand with evangelism. Sometimes ministries of compassion will antedate, and sometimes they will follow; sometimes they will accompany evangelism, but the two cannot be separated.

The Lausanne Committee held other congresses in Manila in 1989 and Bangkok in 2005. Other evangelical movements urging greater cooperation have included the AD 2000 movement that ended in 2000, as its name implied. However, networks and partnerships are continuing to develop as new forms of the Church and mission emerge. There have been some attempts at greater dialogue between the WCC and the evangelical and Pentecostal streams of church and mission, and it is to be hoped that they will continue. Certainly, the evangelical and Pentecostal streams need the historical perspective that the older churches can bring. On the other hand, without a return to a focus on the centrality of Jesus Christ and the priority of world evangelization, the World Council will continue to decline.

To conclude, there are both theological and structural differences between the two streams. The theological issue has to do with the centrality of Jesus Christ and the urgency of the communication of the Gospel to every people as the priority. It also involves the relationship of evangelism, ministries of compassion, and social transformation. A related question is the way in which social transformation should take place. Should the tools of analysis follow a more Marxist or a more free market methodology? The second issue is structural. Must the Church be defined primarily or exclusively as the traditional denominational structures we have known in the West, coming out of a Christendom model, with mission structures simply an arm of those churches? Or will there be recognition of the new models of church and mission that are emerging in various parts of the world today? It appears obvious that any effective ecumenism must deal with these questions.

Chapter Twenty-Six

Survey of Modern Missions:
Asia

Theological, Missiological, Ethical, and Cultural Issues in Acts 15

From a missiological perspective, Acts 15 is a key passage. Its importance for the missionary movement, then and now, can scarcely be overemphasized. It tells how Paul and Barnabas returned after their successful missionary journey across Asia Minor and reported how the Gentiles had turned to God. This news brought great joy to all the believers. When they arrived in Jerusalem, they were welcomed by the Church, the apostles, and the elders, to whom they told all that God had done through them.

However, some of the believers who belonged to the party of the Pharisees stood up and said, "The Gentiles must be circumcised and told to obey the law of Moses." So they met together to consider the matter. Peter was the spokesman, and even though he was not always consistent on this issue, this time he gave the decision.

> And God, who knows the thoughts of everyone, showed his approval of the Gentiles by giving the Holy Spirit to them, just as he had to us. He made no difference between us and them; he forgave their sins because they believed. So then, why do you now want to put God to the test by laying a load on the backs of the believers which neither our ancestors nor we ourselves were able to carry? No! We believe and are saved by the grace of the Lord Jesus, just as they are. (Acts 15:8-11 GNT)

There are four issues here. The first is theological. Are the Gentiles, or anybody else for that matter, saved by faith plus something else (in this case, the works of the law)? Often the Church, in one way or another, has attempted to add something else to faith alone; for example, being part of the correct institution, living a particular lifestyle, or even dressing in a certain manner. Or are we all saved by the grace of God alone, received by faith alone? The Church rightly replied, "Both Gentiles and Jews are saved by faith alone." Luther later put it in these terms: *"Sola fide, and sola gratia."*

The second issue is missiological. This issue is more subtle, and most commentators do not catch it. Was it necessary for Gentile believers to adopt Jewish culture in order to be authentic followers of Jesus, the Jewish Messiah, or could they remain in their Gentile cultural context? If so, what aspects of Gentile culture had to be given up, changed, or transformed in order for one to be authentic Christian disciples?

This issue is always with us in one form or another. In 1973, after returning from seventeen years as a missionary in Brazil and Portugal, I became pastor of a downtown Presbyterian church that was very conservative both theologically and methodologically. Some of those fine people did not understand the difference between theological and methodological orthodoxy. To be honest, for some, if they had to choose, methodological orthodoxy was more important (and easier to recognize) than theological orthodoxy!

My predecessor was able to break through that situation, but not without some difficulty. We had a strong college group that developed a marvelous folk singing group. The songs they sang were excellent: very biblical. Nevertheless, the first time they introduced guitars into the sanctuary, the roof almost fell in! It was very hard for the Church to accept that. The congregation got over it, fortunately, and we learned to use different styles of music and worship. I might add that a few weeks after we arrived, two other mainline churches, one of which had once numbered two thousand members, closed, and their buildings were torn down. First Presbyterian continues to be a thriving congregation in the middle of the city, and has become the center for a number of downtown ministries. Of course, worship style was only one of many factors in that process. But that is another story.

The next issue treated in Acts 15 was ethical. The Gentile believers are specifically told to avoid fornication because that problem was so prevalent in Greco-Roman culture, just as it is in ours. There were, of course, other Christian ethical issues that could have been addressed, but the early Church pointed out sexual morality as one of the significant issues for followers of Jesus Christ.

The fourth issue was cultural. It was a matter of sensitivity to brothers and sisters of a different culture. Gentile believers should avoid practices that would be offensive to Jewish believers. For all of us there are times we can choose not to do something because, although it may be consistent with our discipleship as followers of Christ, it may be offensive to believers of other cultures. One example today would be choosing not to eat pork in a context where there are believers with a Muslim background.

I bring up the issues found in this passage specifically because we will now begin a brief overview of the modern Protestant mission movement over the last century and a half. One issue that arises constantly is this: How much should the new Church on the "mission field" look like the Church back home? For example, Ludwig Nom-menson, a great German missionary, planted the Church among the Batak people in Sumatra, Indonesia. How much should that church look like Nommenson's church in Europe? How much should the Church in Shantung, China, where the China Inland Mission sent its Anglican missionaries, look like the Anglican Church in England, in style of worship and methods of selecting and training leaders? That has been an ongoing issue in missiology, and will continue to be critical wherever the Gospel breaks across barriers.

As early believers took the gospel from Jerusalem, taking the message from a Jewish context into Gentile culture, they faced this question: How should the Church be shaped in its new contexts? What should the Christian life look like? How should leaders be selected and trained? We see critical missiological questions through history, whether in Acts, in the England of John Wesley, among Dalits ("untouchables") in India today, or in American urban ghettos.

Let us pray together:

> Father, again we thank you that you have called us to the most exciting adventure and the most significant task in human history. We know how unworthy and unfit we are. Yet we know that if we die, you raise us, fill us, channel your Spirit through us—very inadequate instruments—and use us for your glory. We thank you that you have done this with many generations of women and men who have simply attempted to be faithful to you and sensitive to the people to whom they went. We pray that will continue through us today. In Christ's name. Amen.

Introduction

We have studied the historical background of the Protestant missionary movement and examined the renewal movements out of which it came. Puritanism, Pietism, Moravianism, and the evangelical revivals of the eighteenth century formed the "launching pad" of Protestant missions.

These movements defined the Christian faith and life somewhat differently from the Christendom model of their traditional churches. In Christendom, everyone was considered a Christian. The focus in the Church was much more institutional, sacramental, and liturgical. In many cases, there was little emphasis on the importance of personal conversion and the call to serious discipleship. These four movements sought to shape the Christian life differently from their nominal Christian societies, following the Scriptures as they understood them. They often utilized small face-to-face groups to encourage serious discipleship, and in different ways they began to move forward both in social action and mission. The modern missionary movement came out of them.

Assumptions of Early Missionaries

Missionaries always go out with a set of assumptions, whether they recognize them explicitly or not. What were some of the theological convictions the missionaries from Europe and the United States, took to Asia, Africa, Latin America, and Oceania? Some of them were that all persons were sinful; that redemption was possible for those of every race, language, and culture, through Jesus Christ; that personal conversion was essential; and that conversion should lead to a changed life style, the planting of churches, and eventually, the transformation of their societies. They also believed that they represented a more progressive culture that was, to some degree, Christian, and believed that other cultures were evolving in the direction of Western culture. Obviously, they were often naïve in that respect. On the other hand, among the Westerners who went to Asia and Africa in the nineteenth century, the missionaries were far more sensitive and sympathetic to those cultures than were the other Westerners there.

A second assumption was that Western education would lead to more receptivity to the Gospel and positive social change. They also believed that Western medical work—clinics and hospitals—was a logical expression of Christian compassion.

Their attitude toward other religions was usually quite negative. Some, later on, began to see Christ as completing the hopes of other religions, but most missionaries stressed discontinuity between Christian faith and the existing religions.

Most early missionaries did not see much of value in the local cultures. Their descriptions of those cultures were sordid, but not entirely false. The missionaries rightly condemned *suttee* and infanticide in India, foot binding in China, female genital mutilation in Africa, and the mistreatment of women. However, they often failed to see the positive community values in many non-Western cultures.

Many missions were reluctant to ordain local people quickly, partly because they believed that a minister had to have a high level of education, and partly because of feelings of cultural and racial superiority that might have been covert and not fully recognized. This was a critical issue.

Some had a strong colonizing attitude. They wanted to transplant their culture along with their theology. They often believed Western culture and Christian faith went together, so that when people of other cultures became Christians, they would look very much like New England Christians. The Church in the mission field should look much like the Church back home, not only liturgically and theologically, but also, in some cases, architecturally. They assumed that leadership styles in the receptor cultures should be similar to that of their home cultures and churches.

They assumed the primary way of presenting the gospel was through the spoken word. Remember, they came out of the Protestant Reformation. In their reaction against medieval pageantry, which often included much that was syncretistic and pagan, the Reformers went overboard in their emphasis on the spoken word. We all agree the spoken word is very important. However, often there was a failure to recognize that in many cultures, indeed in most, the traditional form of Protestant sermons may not be the most effective way of communicating.

Denominational divisions were taken overseas. Carey, however, did not want to start a specifically "Baptist" missionary society. He wanted to start a Christian missionary society. However, only the Baptists supported him. You see his dilemma. We should not think all of these early missionaries were necessarily denominationally narrow. However, ultimately, the denominations were transplanted.

I mentioned earlier the quote from Jedadiah Morse about the Native Americans in the United States. He went far beyond the so-called liberal thinkers at Harvard in saying that the "Indian," when converted, had all the potential that anyone of European descent had. That understanding would also apply to people in Africa, people in Asia, or people anywhere in the world. It was embedded in the Biblical concept that each person was created in the image of God, whether one's theology was Calvinist or Arminian. We cannot say the Puritans always lived out all the implications of their theology, any more than we do. However, the concept was there, and at times, it was carried out in some remarkable ways.

Consider the role of women. Certainly, the missionaries were initially no more progressive in that respect than their contemporaries back home. However, when they got to their mission fields and often saw the mistreatment of women on one hand, and the remarkable ministries of Western female missionaries on the other, many of them changed their views.

We hold certain theological beliefs very strongly and do not always see all of our assumptions. However, as we continue to try to follow the Holy Spirit, He leads us further in recognizing the incredible potential and gifts of every person, regardless of race or gender. That is, as we follow the Spirit beyond our familiar contexts, He leads us to discover new implications of the Gospel. We see many examples of it in history.

The Goal of Missions

What was the goal of the missionary movement? Was it to make individual converts? The earliest missionary movement had a much more churchly attitude. We mentioned Ziegenbalg and Plütschau, who wanted to form a church of converted men and women and their families and train leadership in India. The first American missionaries, heirs of the Puritans, also had a strong sense of

the Church. Some (the early China Inland Mission, for example) at first sought only individual conversions. However, that soon changed, and most early Protestant mission groups wanted to plant the Church.

Furthermore, they wanted it to be indigenous. But what did that mean? The classic formulation in the nineteenth century came from two men, Henry Venn and Rufus Anderson. Venn was the secretary of the Anglican CMS in England. He was the son of John Venn, who had been rector in the parish where both the CMS and the anti-slavery movement had begun—the so-called "Clapham sect." The other was Rufus Anderson, secretary of the ABCFM.

As far as we know, they arrived at their conclusion independently. They said the goal of missions should be the formation of churches that were self-governing, self-supporting, and self-propagating. This was the first attempt to define a genuinely "indigenous" church. Today we recognize it is not a complete or adequate definition of indigeneity. We know that a church may be very Western in its forms and still meet those criteria. However, that early definition was a start.

In 1932, a committee known as the Laymen's Foreign Missions Enquiry was sent to Asia and Africa to study the missionary enterprise. W. E. Hocking, a professor of philosophy at Harvard, led the group. Its report, entitled "Rethinking Missions," included many helpful observations and recommendations, especially about the need for greater cooperation. However, the heart of the report suggested that the role of the missionary was to seek the best in every religion and to cooperate with each one in social reform and the purification of religious expression. The aim should not be conversion, but greater cooperation in the emergence of a world fellowship. There were strong reactions against the report, led by Robert E. Speer of the Presbyterian board, among others. The report indicated the growing current of theological liberalism and a breakdown in the theological consensus that had guided the movement in the previous century. The ABCFM, the oldest American board, was the only one to send a copy of the report with its approval, to its missionaries.

Missions in Three Asian Countries

Now we will look at three countries in Asia and note that different issues arose in each one. No two mission fields are identical, and missionaries and national leaders have had to face very different questions in their contexts.

China

China shows that we cannot separate colonialism and imperialism from the missionary movement. We have already examined briefly the history of the Nestorians, Franciscans, and Jesuits in China. The first Protestant, Robert Morrison, arrived in 1807. The British East India Company would not allow him to go on one of its ships, so he sailed on an American vessel. The story is that when the ship's captain learned that his passenger was going as a missionary, he asked, "So, Mr. Morrison, do you expect to make an impact on the great Chinese Empire?" Morrison replied, "No sir, but I expect God will!" It is important to realize that at the time, foreigners were not allowed to live in China except for limited areas in a few coastal cities. It was forbidden on pain of death to teach the language to a foreigner. The complex and even ironic nature of the relationship between missions and imperialism was seen in the fact that eventually Morrison had to earn his living by working as a translator for the East India Company.

I remember going to Canton (now Guangzhau) in 1982 with Dr. Arthur Glasser. It was my first trip into China and his first trip back after having been expelled thirty years earlier. As we went up the Pearl River on the boat from Hong Kong, he said, "In one of those warehouses along the river, Morrison labored for years to translate the New Testament into Chinese." That was a dramatic moment! I will never forget it. It turned out that the warehouse where Morrison had worked had burned down, but just the idea of his working in such a place was impressive.

Morrison sat across the table from a Chinese Roman Catholic Christian, who, at the risk of his life, taught Chinese to the Protestant missionary. They kept a pair of shoes on the table between them, so if anyone came in they could claim to be involved in a commercial transaction. That is how Morrison learned Chinese and began translating the New Testament.

He had to work for the East India Company if he was to remain in China. Then the first Opium War (1839–1842) came. Opium was not the primary reason, it was only the occasion of the war. The British claimed that the true cause was the conceited arrogance of the Chinese government, its utter contempt for treaty obligations entered into, the outrageous restrictions placed upon commerce, and the insulting and intolerable treatment of foreigners.

Be that as it may, the British forced China to initiate trade (including that of opium) and open five treaty ports to European residents. Then the second Opium War (1856–1860) came. The treaty ending that war ceded Hong Kong to England in a long-term lease, to end in 1997. The treaty also stipulated that missionaries should have the right to travel freely and propagate their faith, and that Chinese Christians be protected. There were other aspects to the treaties. England was far more concerned with trade. The clause about missionaries and Christians was included no doubt because England considered itself a Christian nation at that time and Evangelicals had significant political influence.

That was a bitter pill for the Chinese to swallow. The impression that missionaries were forced on them by the European powers brought a great disadvantage to Christian missions in China. Some missionaries were sensitive to Chinese feelings, but there was not much they could do about it. However, most saw this as the hand of God in opening up China.

History is full of such dilemmas, resulting in mixed feelings. What would you have done, if you had been a missionary in China at that time? Sometimes early missionaries faced such dilemmas with sensitivity; sometimes they did not.

The China Inland Mission had missionaries resident in all but three provinces by 1882. Its policy at first was the widest possible diffusion of the Gospel, rather than church planting. Some missions (Presbyterians, for example) hired evangelists and Bible women to evangelize the common people, who lived in great poverty. Some hoped to permeate the nation with "Christian" ideals and institutions in order to win influential people.

Their hope was to evangelize China in that manner. A number of lower schools and universities were established, along with hospitals.

China was in the process of great change at the end of the nineteenth century. The Manchu dynasty was collapsing. The Boxer Rebellion occurred in 1900, based largely on resentment over the presence of foreigners (or "foreign devils," as they were called). The dowager empress declared that the people should kill all foreigners. Protestant missions lost a total of 180 adults and children, martyred by the rebellion. A larger number of Chinese Christians were killed. The China Inland Mission, more vulnerable because its personnel were in the interior, lost the greatest number. The Roman Catholics lost a smaller number of missionaries than the Protestants, but they lost a considerable number of Chinese Christians.

Despite this, by the end of the century there were fifteen hundred Protestant missionaries, including wives, in China, and a Protestant community of about five hundred thousand. That included eighty thousand communicants (people who had arrived at the point of baptism and confession of faith). We do not have complete statistics, but by 1914, there were 5,462 Protestant missionaries and about 250,000 communicant members of the Church. This means there were probably two or three times that number in the Protestant community. Roman Catholics had twenty-five hundred missionaries. They would all have been single. Their community numbered about one and-a-half million, but they counted children as well as adults. Neither Christian community was very big, given the total population of China.

After the Boxer Rebellion, the European powers forced China to pay reparation for lives and property lost. The China Inland Mission refused to accept any kind of payment from the Chinese government. The American mission societies sent the money received back to China to invest in institutions, schools, etc. The European powers demanded compensation.

During the 1920s, a strongly nationalistic, anti-foreign movement occurred. The Versailles Treaty after World War I had ignored the interests of China and there was great resentment, especially among the students. That led to an anti-Christian movement as well. In that context, we see the beginning of Chinese indigenous churches: the "Jesus Family" and the well-known "Little Flock" of Watchman Nee. The latter became one of the major streams contributing to the house church movement under the Communist regime. Most of the older "mainline" denominations merged into the Church of Christ in China.

There was great suffering in the 1930s, especially from the Japanese invasion during World War II; thousands and thousands were killed very brutally, particularly in the Nanjing Massacre. It was reported that three hundred thousand civilians were slaughtered there. Chinese Christians suffered along with the rest of the population. Whole villages, churches, and families trekked for hundreds of miles to get away from the invaders. There were many stories of great heroism.

China was the greatest mission field of the Protestant churches. There were about fifty-five hundred missionaries there in 1914, and the number continued to grow, although there was some decline in the 1930s with the Depression.

When the Communist movement triumphed in 1949, China counted approximately 750 thousand Protestant church members and three million Roman Catholics. Within two years, nearly all missionaries were forced to leave, the churches suffered growing pressure to renounce any foreign connection, and its leaders were often persecuted and removed. The government soon took over Christian institutions, and churches were closed.

That development, along with the independence of scores of former European colonies in Africa and Asia, led to great pessimism about the future of the missionary movement. The widespread perception was that it was over. When the International Missionary Council met in 1952, its theme was "Missions Under the Cross." Missions would exist, but they would do so under great persecution and danger. Max Warren, the leader of the CMS, said, "We must be prepared to see the end of the missionary movement as we have known it." In addition to the perception that the movement was over, the view often expressed was that Christian missions had been a tragic failure. This sentiment dominated the thinking of the "mainline" or conciliar churches during the period. The more conservative faith missions did not share this feeling, but were not always open to the important lessons to be learned from China.

Eric Fife and Arthur Glasser authored one of the best books of the period—*The Crisis in Missions* (1960). Glasser went far beyond most evangelicals in raising key issues. In humility, he wanted to hear God speak to the Church through the apparent defeat in China. He said missionaries should reject paternalism and strongly encourage national leadership. He affirmed the necessity of communicating the core of the Gospel, criticizing liberals for their one-sided social gospel. However, he also scolded evangelicals for failing to teach the "whole counsel of God contained in the Scripture," for erecting a false antithesis between the material and spiritual worlds, and for failing to transmit the deeply rooted social concerns of both the Old and New Testaments. He called for a more positive approach to Chinese culture. He concluded by criticizing missionaries for their naïveté about Western imperialism, but still expressed confidence in the sovereignty of God working in China and its Church.

The Cultural Revolution in China began in the 1960s. It was forbidden to be a Christian or to possess a Bible. All churches were closed. In the West we believed the Church had ceased to exist in China, except perhaps in a few tiny, scattered groups.

Now we know otherwise. The perseverance, heroism, and faithfulness by Chinese believers is one of the most remarkable stories in history. It is also an amazing example of the power of the Holy Spirit!

It is difficult to determine the number of believers in China at this time. The latest statistics suggest from sixty to one hundred million Christians in the nation. They include sixteen million in the open "Three-Self, " government-recognized churches, around fifteen million Roman Catholics, and estimates that range widely from thirty to seventy million in the house fellowships. There is some overlap between the Three-Self and house fellowships, since some of the latter are registered with the government. However, the majority are not, because they distrust both the government and the Three-Self organization. The picture is complex. There are at least twelve recognized Three-Self seminaries and an uncounted number of underground institutions of the house fellowships. There can be no doubt of great vitality in both branches of Protestantism in China, although neither stream is without problems. It is interesting to note that the "Three-Self Church" took its name from Venn and Anderson's nineteenth-century "self-supporting, self-governing, and self-propagating" concept.

Remarkably, in 1983 the government allowed the Amity Foundation to begin publishing Bibles in China. To date, over fifty million Bibles have been published, some in tribal languages. Its new presses allow it to publish up to six million each year.

The Roman Catholic Church has grown, but not as dramatically as the Protestants have. There seem to be two primary reasons for this.

First, the Roman Catholic Church teaches that the Church can only be present where there is a priest to give the sacraments, and only a bishop consecrated by Rome can ordain a priest. That understanding makes it impossible for Catholics to have a true church function without the presence of a priest. It is different for Protestants, who believe that any group of believers led by a layperson constitutes the Church.

Secondly, this foreign allegiance, essential in Roman Catholic theology, is not acceptable to the

Chinese government. Bishops who have insisted on recognition of the Pope as the head of the Church have been imprisoned. Of course, allegiance to a foreign power outside of China is not an issue for Protestants. In addition, the Protestant understanding of what constitutes "the Church" brings the possibility of much greater flexibility in forming new churches and leading them.

It is clear that there has been remarkable growth of the Church in China in these last decades. It is significant that two-thirds to three-fourths of the leaders are women in a culture that has not traditionally honored women's leadership.

The Church has grown after a time of great disillusionment in society: disillusionment with the Cultural Revolution, with Mao Tse Tung, and with Marxism. Many Christians remained faithful through persecution, and as they emerged—often from prison—their faith was so strong it was almost transparent. We can compare these believers to people carrying buckets of cold, clear water through a desert surrounded by thirsty people.

Another aspect of the Church's growth in China has been the obvious work of the Holy Spirit in signs and wonders. There have been many stories of unusual, miraculous activity of the Holy Spirit—the kind of things we see in the book of Acts. While it is possible that there have been some exaggerations, I do not doubt the validity of many such stories.

The Church in China considers itself post-denominational, and I believe this is accurate. I hope it can remain that way. However, that does not mean there are no divisions. As we have seen, most house churches remain separate from the Three-Self Church, and the government persecutes some of them. In addition, there are various networks within the house church movement. Some, such as the "shouters," have lapsed into fanaticism. One of the great needs is for appropriate training models for the house church leaders. There are numerous underground seminaries.

The "Back to Jerusalem Movement" initiated by the Chinese church (house churches) is another important development. It is a vision for the Chinese church to preach the Gospel and establish fellowships of believers to all regions and people groups between China and Jerusalem. While there is much we cannot know about the Church in China now, we can say without doubt the growth of the Church in that nation over the last half century is one of the most remarkable stories of Christian mission in history. Just when most believed the mission had failed, it became clear that the Holy Spirit was working in and through the lives of Chinese believers far more than any could have imagined.

Korea

Each nation is unique, and the history of mission in each one is different. That fact should make us go to each situation with the attitude of a "learner," not only of the language and culture, but of the historical context. A convergence of factors in Korea's unique history resulted in a remarkably strong church and missionary movement. In 1783, a Korean government official contacted a French Roman Catholic missionary in Beijing, China. He had studied Roman Catholic books and asked for baptism. He returned to Korea and won converts there. Priests entered Korea from China and baptized around ninety others over a period. Despite sporadic persecutions, the church grew, but finally, in 1864, the fear of French imperialism led to the death of thousands of Korean Catholics.

In the 1870s, two Scottish Presbyterian missionaries, John Ross and John McIntyre, worked across the Korean border in Manchuria, China. A small group of Koreans became Christians through their witness, returned to Korea, and established churches before any Protestant missionaries entered the country.

Up until that time, Korea was known as "the hermit nation" and attempted to remain isolated from Western influences. However, with growing Japanese power Korea began to open to the West, and after a treaty in 1882 an American embassy was opened in Seoul. In 1884, Dr. Horace Allen, a Presbyterian physician, became part of the staff of the Embassy. After he saved the life of a member of the royal family who had been wounded in an assassination attempt, permission was given for American missionaries to enter. In 1885, two ordained men—Horace Underwood, a Presbyterian, and H. G. Appenzeller, a Methodist—entered the country. There are now fourth generation Underwoods still serving in Korea in various capacities.

There were a number of factors in the growth of the Korean church. First was the interaction with Japanese imperialism. The Japanese defeated the Russians and began rapidly to dominate Korea. In 1910, Japan formally annexed Korea, and from then until 1945 attempted to suppress and destroy Korean culture and any sense of nationalism. The geography of the area shows us that Korea is sandwiched between China and Japan, two great powers. Much of Korean history has involved the struggle for survival, culturally and nationally, against these two powers.

The American missionaries in Korea did not represent colonialism. Their situation was very different from those in China, India, and Africa. As they encouraged education for the common people, girls as well as boys, they were soon seen as allies of Korean nationalism. In 1919, when thirty-three men courageously signed a call for independence from Japan, sixteen of them were Christians, even though Christians numbered less than one percent of the population at the time. The fact that almost one-half of the men who signed the call for independence were Christians reflected well upon the Church.

A second important aspect of growth in the Korean church was the Nevius Plan. John Nevius, a missionary to China, was invited to lead a retreat for Presbyterian missionaries in Korea in 1890. Through his experience in China, he had formulated principles that went beyond those of Venn and Anderson. While his mission in China rejected his concepts, the Presbyterians in Korea embraced them. The plan included five basic principles:

1. Each Christian should abide in the calling in which he was found, support himself by his own work, and be a witness for Christ by life and word where he was.

2. Church methods and machinery should be developed only in so far as the Korean Church was able to take responsibility for its work.

3. The Church itself should call out for full-time work those who seemed best qualified for it and whom the Church was able to support.

4. Church buildings were to be built in native style by the Christians themselves from their own resources.

5. Great stress was laid on periods of intensive Bible teaching to equip believers for witness.

Hundreds of such sessions, for men and women, were soon held every year. In the agricultural economy they met during the periods when the fields lay fallow. In addition, there was a strong focus on prayer.

A third remarkable factor in the growth of the Korean church was the Hangul alphabet. Created in the fifteenth century by King Sejong, it was far simpler than the Chinese and Japanese ideograms, and made it much easier for Koreans to learn to read. The Bible was soon translated, and literacy was encouraged by the missionaries. That encouraged intensive Bible study by many believers. The Hangul alphabet was disdained by the elites, who said it was so simple, "even a woman could learn to read." But it became a powerful tool in evangelism and education of the common people.

A fourth factor was the revival movement that began in 1903 and peaked in 1907. It began in a small group of missionaries led by Dr. R. A. Hardie, a physician who had become an evangelist. From them it spread to a group of Korean leaders, and by 1906 a number of Korean men took leadership. There was confession of sin and restitution. Men, women, and students journeyed to the countryside to share the Gospel. Thousands were converted. Early morning and all-night prayer meetings were initiated. One of the most critical issues that triggered the revivals was the reconciliation between missionaries and Korean leaders. This included the recognition on the part of some missionaries that they had feelings of racial and national superiority, and confession of this as sin. Reconciliation came with Korean leaders, who naturally resented those attitudes. God seemed to use that process uniquely in revitalizing and giving a tremendous spurt of growth to the Korean church. I might also add, however, that this Korean revival was also part of a general wave of revivals taking place in Wales, in the United States, and elsewhere at the time. There was some interaction between the various movements.

In the 1930s, the Korean church faced the "shrine issue." As the Japanese became more and more dominant, they began to require every school child, and eventually every person, to pay obeisance at Shinto shrines. The question arose: was this simply a civil act, showing allegiance to the Japanese state, or was it a religious act, showing worship to the Japanese gods? Great pressure was put on church leaders and other Christians! Mission schools were closed if they did not encourage people to do obeisance. Some people were imprisoned.

Some church leaders interpreted it as a civil rather than a religious act. That was the official position of the Methodist mission. The Presbyterian mission saw it as a religious act and refused to do it. A number of Presbyterian leaders went to jail. We admire the heroism of those who, in my judgment, stood up for the faith, but recognize the great difficulty. After World War II, when the Japanese finally left, this issue brought turmoil to the Church. Those who had not participated in worship at the shrines felt that those who had done so could not be in leadership. That was one of the issues that led to divisions in the church.

There were large churches in Korea before World War II. The city of Pyongyang, which is now the capital of North Korea, had five Presbyterian churches, all with over a thousand members. It was the most Protestant city in Asia. The majority of Christians before 1945 were in the North.

After World War II, Korea was divided. The North rapidly became hard-line communist. Many Christian leaders were executed, and others fled to the South. Then the Korean War broke out in 1950, with great tragedy, loss, and hardship.

As we know, after the war there was remarkable growth. Now at least twenty-five percent of the South Korean people are professing Christians!

Seoul is a city with many churches. Many are small, but it is also known for its "mega churches." Many are filled two or three times each Sunday. The best known is the Full Gospel Central Church, which is said to have 750 thousand members. Young Nak Presbyterian Church has about fifty thousand members. Each of these has spawned others. The Young Nak Church, for example, was established in 1946 or 1947 by a group of twenty refugees from the North who had come across the border. When they arrived in Seoul, they sat in a circle, took off their packs, each one took out the Bible, and formed the Church. They had just built a huge stone church in Seoul in 1950 when the war broke out. Bombs fell all around it, but did not touch the building!

While Presbyterians are the largest group in Korea, there are also strong Methodist, Holiness, and Pentecostal groups along with others. The most recent estimate is that the Koreans have now sent between fifteen and sixteen thousand cross-cultural missionaries around the world, working in around 170 countries.

Many observers now believe the Korean church must face its need for renewal. Growth has leveled off and perhaps stagnated. It has suffered many divisions; indeed, the very competitiveness in the culture has often become a negative factor. Often the Church has not spoken out clearly against social injustice and corruption in its society, especially during military authoritarian governments. Shamanism continues to be an issue. To some observers it appears that traditional shamanism, in which the goal is to manipulate the spirits for one's benefit, is still a strong factor in much of Korean Christianity.

Nevertheless, even with these questions, there can be no doubt that the Holy Spirit has worked in an extraordinary manner in Korea since those first missionaries arrived in 1884 and 1885.

Burma (Myanmar)

Adoniram and Ann Judson arrived in Burma in 1813, having been refused entry into India by the

British East India Company. Adoniram learned the language of the dominant Burmese people and began to translate the Scriptures. In Rangoon, he preached in a Burmese *zyat* (a type of dwelling where a religious figure might teach), but it was five years before he baptized his first convert. In 1824, he moved to the capital, Ava, but when the Anglo-Burmese war broke out, he was imprisoned for twenty-one months in the worst of conditions. His wife, Ann, was allowed to visit him, and kept him alive. After he was released, she died. All three of their children died in infancy.

The breakthrough came through one of the most unlikely evangelists in history! The Karen tribespeople were terribly oppressed by the dominant group. One Karen, Ko Tha Byu, had been a criminal and had killed numerous people. Converted through Judson, he became a flaming evangelist to his own people back in the mountains, and thousands of Karens became Christians.

The Karens had some remarkable traditions that seem to have prepared them to receive the Gospel. They believed in a creator God and had the story of a fall in which they had lost his favor. They also believed that in the past they had a sacred book their fathers had lost. When evangelists came, telling them the Good News of Jesus, they responded in multitudes. By 1850, the Karen Christian community numbered thirty thousand.

The Karens soon began to evangelize other tribes: Chins, Ka-Chins, Ruangs, and others. Most Christians in the country are from the tribal groups and there has been little growth among the dominant group.

With independence from the British Empire, Burma expelled missionaries in the 1960s and later changed its name to Myanmar. The Church has continued to grow, with Baptists still the largest denomination. While there has been a decline into nominalism and legalism in some areas, renewal movements have also occurred. The nation's most serious problem now is the extremely repressive military government. It has left the democratically elected President under house arrest, killed many of the tribal people, and been a disaster for the economy. Myanmar currently has one of the worst governments in the world, with little prospect of change. There is serious military repression of the tribal peoples.

Chapter Twenty-Seven

Survey of Modern Missions:
Oceania, the Middle East, and North Africa

Devotional

I will read the last few verses in Acts 15. This was after Paul and Barnabas had made their first missionary journey, reported back to the Church, and were preparing to go out again.

> Some time later Paul said to Barnabas, "Let us go back and visit our brothers in every town where we preached the word of the Lord, and let us find out how they are getting along." Barnabas wanted to take John Mark with them, but Paul did not think it was right to take him, because he had not stayed with them to the end of their mission, but had turned back and left them in Pamphylia. There was a sharp argument, and they separated. Barnabas took Mark and sailed off for Cyprus, while Paul chose Silas and left, commended by the believers to the Lord's grace. He went through Syria and Cilicia, strengthening the churches." (Acts 15:36–41 GNT)

Barnabas was always the person who encouraged others. When Saul was distrusted by the Church in Jerusalem, Barnabas found him and brought him to Antioch, where he soon became part of the leadership. The first missionary team included Barnabas, Saul, and Mark, with Barnabas as the leader. However, Mark apparently turned back, probably out of fear. When they prepared to go again, Barnabas, typical of his personality and understanding of ministry, wanted to help the one who had failed, give him a second chance and take him along. Paul, who was probably more task-oriented than person-oriented, said, "No! He failed once. We cannot risk taking Mark

again, after his failure the first time." So they had a sharp disagreement. They separated, but God used this division between Paul and Barnabas to form two missionary teams where previously there had been one.

I suggest that sometimes in the providence of God different people have different functions in the life of an individual and his or her growth in discipleship. Paul and Barnabas exercised different functions in the life of Mark. One needed to hold him accountable, and Paul did so. It was a very serious thing to abandon the task as Mark had done. It is possible that Paul was too harsh. Barnabas, on the other hand, frequently stood by the person who was suspect or rejected, encouraged him or her, and eventually launched the person into ministry. He had encouraged the Gentile church in Antioch, he had encouraged Saul/Paul, and now he did so with Mark. We can look at this in terms of the law/grace dichotomy. Paul, in a sense, represented the law here, and Barnabas represented grace. We all need both in our lives, and in our ministries. We all live in this law/grace continuum. We need to be held accountable to live up to the standards that God has set for us, even as we recognize our frequent failure and our need of God's grace that picks us up, forgives us, and sends us on our way again.

Here is the proof that God was working in Mark's life through Paul as well as Barnabas. Tradition tells us that Mark later accompanied Peter and that the Gospel of Mark is probably based on the preaching of Peter. We know that later, in his second letter to Timothy, Paul sent for Mark, implying reconciliation and recognition of Mark's ministry. Therefore, while we usually make Barnabas the hero of the story, because of his role in encouraging Mark, we need to recognize the function of Paul as well. We can see how through these different personalities and emphases, God somehow brought significant growth, maturity, and ministry out of Mark's failure. This gives hope to all of us.

One of Latourette's fundamental theses is that the Church of Jesus Christ is always attempting to penetrate culture and not only convert individuals, but transform that culture—and has succeeded to some degree through the centuries. At the same time, the culture constantly attempts to penetrate the Church and make the Church its captive. Historically it often appears to be a standoff, with some wins and some losses on both sides.

It is helpful to analyze various movements from this perspective. For example, the early Pentecostal movement was countercultural in some very significant ways. First, it elevated the status of women as no other Christian body did at that time. They were the poor, people without status. They were not thinking in theoretical terms about human rights. They simply recognized the Holy Spirit had gifted women as well as men. Consequently, there were a number of women in leadership early in the movement. However, this has decreased.

But the traditional barriers that our society erects between people—barriers of status, race, educational class, social status—were largely eliminated in the early Pentecostal movement. It was interracial. A black leader ministered to whites, for example. Thus, the early Pentecostal movement was countercultural as it turned its back on some of the norms of North American society. The culture said that one had to have education and perhaps money to achieve status, but the early Pentecostal movement affirmed that the gifts of God, salvation, and ministry were the important things. But then in 1914 the Assemblies of God was organized as white denomination, with little

or no place for Blacks in leadership. Only recently was there public repentance for its racism.

Another historical example can be found in Methodism. Wesley was adamantly against slavery and would not allow a slaveholder to exercise leadership in the early Methodist movement. His last letter went to Wilberforce, encouraging him in his anti-slavery campaign. Nevertheless, a few decades later, Methodist leaders in the United States were slaveholders.

In other words, when the Holy Spirit brings renewal to his church, it becomes countercultural to some degree, following the norms of the Kingdom of God instead of those of society. However, there is always danger of reversing that process as the Church conforms again to its surrounding culture.

Let us pray together.

> Father, again we thank and praise you that you continue to teach us through your Word. We look at Barnabas and Paul and their gifts and ministries; we look at Mark, who was a failure at one point. We can identify with that, and we thank you that in your grace you lifted him up and made him a useful person in your Kingdom. We look at people who have fallen into grievous sin and error today and pray for them. We pray for the Church, for the witness of the gospel. We pray that somehow the Church of Jesus Christ might communicate the gospel with integrity, proclaim that we are called to a life consistent with your purpose for human persons, and at the same time communicate that when we fail, there is grace and forgiveness to restore and renew us. So we pray for faithfulness and understanding—we pray for our own particular parts of the body of Christ, and we pray for the body of Christ worldwide, that the witness of Jesus Christ would be bright and strong and clear. We ask this in his name. Amen.

Oceania

We will now continue our survey of modern missions, focusing briefly primarily on Oceania, Africa and the Middle East.

The London Missionary Society (LMS)

You will recall that the voyages of Captain Cook, the English explorer, helped to trigger the interest of Carey in world mission. In 1795, the LMS was established by a group of Presbyterians, Congregationalists, and evangelical Anglicans. As we know, it was one of three great societies initiated in England in the 1790's. All three were a result of the wave of evangelical revivals earlier in the century.

The LMS sent its first missionaries to the South Pacific. The peoples of the islands appeared to live in beautiful places, but the culture involved cannibalism, almost incessant wars, and other practices that were tragic and destructive. One writer said that cannibalism had been elevated into a national cult. The man who had eaten the greatest number of human beings was highest in the social order. They sometimes marked these achievements by memorial stones. One great chief had 872 stones set up to mark his prowess! One of the first missionaries to set foot on Fiji, according to Stephen Neill, began his missionary career by gathering and burying the heads, hands, and feet of eighty victims who had been cooked and eaten. This is not to say that it was an unrelieved picture of terror, but clearly, there was great brutality and suffering. Some writers have portrayed the peoples to whom Western missionaries went in very idyllic terms, as though the missionaries had destroyed a superior kind of romanticized culture. That was not true. In addition, many early missionaries to the South Seas islands suffered great hardships and confronted danger, and some lost their lives.

Tahiti, Tonga

Among the first group of missionaries in Tahiti, three were killed and eaten and one "went native" by rejecting his faith and living with native women. Others left. By 1800, after five years of missionary service, only seven missionaries were left out of the original group of thirty or forty. It was very discouraging.

Then, in 1812, the King of Tahiti rejected idols and requested baptism. That happened in Tonga as well. There had been little progress until the chief asked for baptism. The chief had great power in these tribal societies. It is analogous to the history of Christianity in early medieval Europe,

as the tribes came west from Asia. We remember that Clovis, king of the Franks, was baptized with three thousand of his soldiers in 496. In both cases, we see "people movements," although the level of Christian faith and life in these islands seems to have been much higher than that of some of those barbarian tribes in sixth century Europe. In both instances, a people movement was probably the only way conversions could take place, because these were societies in which the group, not the individual, made important decisions. The leaders represented the group and usually consulted others when important decisions were to be made.

A friend who had worked in Papua New Guinea said that if you go into a tribal situation there and tell people they must make a personal, individual decision for Christ, you are saying it is not important. The group makes important decisions. This is still true of a number of cultures today. For example, some caste leaders in India are now seeking Christian leaders, affirming that they want to become followers of Jesus, along with their people. This can have remarkable and very positive long-term consequences for the Church and nation if handled sensitively.

It required a great paradigm shift for Western missionaries to accept people movements. They had all come out of movements that emphasized the necessity of personal conversion out of nominal Christianity. It is to their credit that often they were able to move away from Western individualism.

John Williams was probably the greatest of the LMS missionaries. Arriving in 1817, he soon realized it was not possible to place European missionaries on all the islands. He chose recent converts, gave them some training, and sent them out. His goal was to have at least one teacher/evangelist on every island. It was a great vision. The majority of these men were faithful and effective, even though they had little training. Some were martyred and a few abandoned the work, but most were effective, and the faith spread.

We see another principle here. These early missionaries went out from England with assumptions of their own cultural superiority and no opportunity to study anthropology, which did not yet exist as a social science. Yet they did recognize positive aspects in the receptor culture and realized the importance of recruiting indigenous leadership very early. Some of the earliest missionaries were more progressive than others who went out later, at the end of the century. For all the greatness of the SVM, the missionaries who came out of that movement often seemed to believe that no one could be in church leadership until he had a western style education. That was logical since the SVM had flourished in the colleges, universities, and seminaries in the United States. But it probably resulted in slower growth of the Church in some areas. One of the most critical issues in growing churches around the world today is that of leadership selection and training. In many areas where the Church is growing rapidly among the poorest of the poor, it is clear that our traditional institutional model of training leaders is inadequate. A variety of models for men and women already in active ministry, appropriate to their needs and situations, is necessary.

The early missionaries went into cultures very different from their own. They confronted unexpected issues, and groped for principles to guide them. They certainly made mistakes, but we cannot doubt that the Holy Spirit led them to a remarkable degree. This is one reason why we study history. We do not want simply to ask what happened. Rather, what did these early missionaries discover that is profitable for us? How can we learn from what they did wrong as well as what they did correctly?

Samoa, Fiji

Methodists went to Samoa. The work was very slow until revival came. Latourette mentions power encounter as an important aspect in some areas of the South Pacific. For example, in his *History of the Expansion of Christianity*, volume 5, pg. 223, we find this,

> The victories of Christians in warfare furthered the change of faith, for by the test of combat the Christian God had been proved more powerful than the old deities." That may not be a method of missions that we would agree with

today. "Indeed, on at least one occasion, victorious Christians gave the vanquished pagans the choice of death or conversion.

That is what Charles the Great had done in France in the ninth century. In addition, one chief embraced Christianity because in a time of drought, the prayers of non-Christian priests failed to bring relief, but rain fell copiously during the Christian service on Sunday. The healings of diseases after prayers by missionaries and Christian teachers won some. A priest of the old cult ascribed his conversion to a dream in which his pagan god bowed before the Christian God.

Such methods are not normal for many of us, but we should not disdain them. One thing we are learning today is to be more open to the various ways in which the Spirit of God has worked in history, and, indeed, still works today. The research of Dr. J. Dudley Woodberry indicates that for half of the Muslims who are coming to Christ today, some kind of "power encounter"—a dream, vision, or healing—has been a significant factor in their pilgrimage. This tells us we should never limit the work of the Spirit of God to the ways we have known.

Hawaii & the ABCFM

The American Board of Commissioners for Foreign Missions sent missionaries to Hawaii early in the nineteenth century. James Michener in his book, *Hawaii*, painted a much-distorted picture of them. They were New England Calvinist Puritans and they, no doubt, went with assumptions that their culture was superior to others.

However, it is clear that the only westerners in Hawaii (and many other places) who were there not to exploit the people but to work for their welfare were the missionaries. Other Westerners who bitterly criticized the missionaries—traders, sailors, politicians, and slave traders—were there to exploit the people in some way. On one occasion, the American consul in Honolulu wrote to his creditors in Boston, telling them he could soon pay what he owed them if they could only "get rid of the missionaries." Apparently, missionaries had insisted on fair prices for the goods he was buying from the Hawaiians. On other occasions, the missionaries aided the Hawaiian leaders in protecting their women from the sexual exploitation by the crews of the ships that came to the islands.

The major focus of the missionaries was the conversion of men and women to Christ and church planting. They also worked to end infanticide and other destructive practices. After a few decades, the islands were dotted, not only with churches, but also with schools in which Hawaiian teachers taught Hawaiian children. Missionaries devised a system of writing using Roman characters and translated the Bible and other works. Eventually they published 153 different works and thirteen magazines in the local language. It is also unfortunately true that some of the children of the early missionaries remained in the islands, bought land, went into business, and became wealthy. This has reflected negatively on the Hawaiian mission.

The process in which a "higher" or more powerful culture enters into contact with a traditional tribal culture has usually been destructive for the latter. We can all think of many tragic examples, including the treatment of Native Americans in the United States. Wycliffe Bible translators have been accused unfairly of destroying people's culture. Some ardent nationalists in Latin America have criticized them bitterly, accusing them of destroying the indigenous cultures. Behind this accusation lies the assumption that these cultures are ideal and static. Of course, the reality is that they are changing, especially today, and as they are exposed to the outside world, they will be much more seriously damaged and destroyed. I saw that with the Caiua people in southern Mato Grosso in Brazil. There, various Brazilian Protestant churches worked in mission among the people. They had a farm, a tuberculosis sanitarium, school, church, and sawmill. Even then, the people were not prepared to face life in the nearby city. If they went there to get jobs, the girls were often sexually exploited, and some men ended up in alcoholism. It was a very tragic situation.

Dr. Millie Larson of Wycliffe wrote a marvelous book that shows a mission approach sensitive to indigenous culture. The book, Treasure in Clay Pots, describes a genuinely wholistic ministry. She went into an Amazon tribe and worked with them in every way to help them maintain their own culture even as they dealt with the dominant Latino culture.

Lamin Sanneh, who now occupies Latourette's former chair at Yale, wrote one of the most important books in this debate. His thesis in *Translating the Message: The Missionary Impact on Culture* is that the Christian mission throughout history has been a culture-affirming, not a culture-denying, movement. The fact that Christians have reduced numerous languages to writing in order to translate the Bible has been the most important factor in this process. The fact that Sanneh is a West African convert from Islam gives great weight to his argument.

We all need to learn much more about how to deal with other cultures with compassion and integrity, respecting their validity and values and helping them cope with the onslaught of modernity, or "civilization."

The Middle East and North Africa

The Middle East and North Africa have been one of the most difficult areas for Christian mission. The earliest groups that went were Presbyterians and Congregationalists from the United States and Anglicans from England. They saw very few Muslims come to faith in Christ. However, there were ancient churches there—the Nestorian Church (now called the Assyrian Church) in Iran and Iraq, the Coptic Church in Egypt, and others in Lebanon and Armenia. The ancient Orthodox Church was dominant in much of Ethiopia. Neill is quite critical of the interaction of American missionaries with these ancient churches. As an Anglican, he has great respect for them.

The early American missionaries wanted to work with these ancient churches, and encourage both study of the Bible and renewal toward what they considered a more biblical faith. However, as Scriptures were introduced and people came alive in their faith, they were usually rejected by the ancient churches, and new Protestant denominations were formed. That was not the original goal of the early missionaries.

Turkey and Armenia

During much of its history, Armenia was dominated by neighboring nations, among them Turkey and Russia. Nevertheless, it maintained a strong sense of cultural identity, much of it centered on the Armenian Apostolic Church. When American missionaries entered the area, the traditional church resisted their emphases and, consequently, evangelical denominations, usually Congregationalist or Presbyterian, were formed. Then, early in the twentieth century, Turkey carried out a terrible genocide against the Armenians, beginning with the best educated. A million and a half were killed.

Today, after decades of Communist rule, Armenia is once more an independent nation, but very poor. There is a small but growing renewal movement in the Apostolic Church, led by a Fuller Seminary graduate, Dr. Petros Malaykan, an evangelical seeking to work within the ancient Church.

This raises a significant issue. What should be the approach of expatriate missionaries in an area where a traditional church exists but seems to exhibit little spiritual vitality or openness to change and renewal? Evangelicals face it in Europe, in both Protestant and Catholic areas. It has been a major issue in Russia with the Orthodox Church. Evangelicals have faced it in Ethiopia, where the dominant Orthodox Church seems to have little understanding of New Testament faith or outreach to Muslims. There the evangelical movement has grown to number over fourteen million.

Yet in some areas, there are renewal movements in the traditional churches. Dr. Glasser has written in favor of American missionaries in Europe working with the existing churches. Others have followed the pattern of planting American-style denominations that are normally regarded as "sects" by Europeans. Still others are seeking to plant new "emerging" churches. Some may be called to different modes of ministry. These are issues we need to consider as we increasingly move into a post-Christendom era in the West. Perhaps that question will be better addressed by others. It is reported that the pastors of the largest churches in Kiev, London, and Paris are Nigerians!

Egypt, the Coptic Church, and Protestants

Egypt, which spoke Coptic before Arabic became its language, was the one country in North Africa where a significant church survived after the invasion of Islam. Today that Coptic Church numbers around six million within the country, despite centuries of its people being treated as second-class citizens. When the early Presbyterian missionaries arrived, the ancient Church rejected their emphases and, as a result, the Coptic Evangelical Church was organized. It now numbers 150 thousand members and is the largest Protestant church in North Africa and the Middle East. I had a friend at Princeton in 1952 who was the pastor of a large congregation of that denomination. He criticized the ancient Church because, he said, they worship in a language no one understands and there is little genuine understanding of the Gospel and Christian life. He felt justified in being a Protestant in that situation and he has had a very effective ministry through the years.

On the other hand, a few years ago I met Bishop Markos of the Coptic Church of Egypt. He clearly loves Jesus Christ and as a teenager was involved in starting Sunday schools in the villages. He became a medical missionary to Ethiopia and now works in Nairobi with some of the "African Initiated" churches. The oldest and youngest churches in Africa working together—how are we to put these two things together? I am not sure, but I think we need to be very sensitive to both the existence of older churches and the possibility of renewal within them. My own bias is that we always seek the unity of the body of Christ and work with existing churches if we can. However, we may have to work on the edges. We must believe that the Holy Spirit can bring new life to older churches, but we have seen that renewal will usually begin on the periphery through unexpected leaders and movements.

The American missions in the Middle East and Egypt started educational institutions. They hoped they would be a positive influence in society. The American University in Beirut is an example. They also established medical work. Lest we be too critical of that approach, we must remember that in many cases the only way the missionaries could function in the society was to establish institutions that would be perceived as useful. They hoped to use them for Christian witness. Unfortunately, these universities have slowly become secularized and in some cases, have little Christian influence.

The goal of the missionaries was to reach Muslims. As they met people of the ancient churches, they believed that if those churches were renewed along more Protestant lines, they would become channels of God's grace to reach the Muslim population. It did not work that way. Often the few converts from Islam could not find a place in the existing churches, nor would most churches accept and trust them.

Because Islam is rigorously monotheistic, it takes great offense at any statue or even picture that might be considered a representation of God. Thus, often Muslims interpreted some practices of the ancient churches as polytheistic and even pagan. That included the icons and images used as aids to worship in the Eastern Church. Orthodox Christians do not worship icons, but that theological distinction is not understood by most outsiders. Thus, to a Muslim who has become a believer in Christ, much of the worship in either the older Orthodox churches or newer Protestant churches appears strange and unfamiliar. That helps us understand the focus today on "Muslim background believer" fellowships that are more contextualized.

Sometimes it is easy for us to misinterpret or misunderstand the dilemmas the early missionaries faced. But it is always important to try to understand their context. We may or may not agree with their decisions and strategies. That is not the point. But we must attempt to understand the issues they were facing.

Let me mention two great names among many who worked in the Muslim world.

Zwemer and Harrison

Samuel Zwemer became known as the "Apostle to Islam." He came out of the Student Volunteer Movement at the end of the nineteenth century, and spent his entire ministry focusing on mission to Islam. My colleague, Dr. Woodberry, received his call to mission to Muslims when he heard him speak. Zwemer went to Bahrain under the Reformed Church of America, and lived, wrote, and labored for decades in the Middle East before teaching missions at Princeton in the later years of his life. At the International Missionary Meeting in India in 1938, Paul Harrison, his colleague, said that in fifty years they had five converts. We need to honor such people. Often we are caught up in the excitement of seeing rapid growth of the Church in some areas. We need to realize that there are people whose mission is not to reap, not even to sow, and not even to plow the field, but, as one put it, to take the stones away from the field so that others can plow, then sow, and then reap. Some are called to that kind of ministry.

Of course, in the last few years the entire world has become much aware of Islam. Until quite recently, there were only a few sporadic attempts by Franciscans and Dominicans to reach Muslims. The proportion of missionary resources and personnel devoted to them has been very small, especially in proportion to those going to other parts of the world. Cultural and political barriers, colonialism, frequent warfare, the Crusades, and perceptions of Christianity as identified with Western society have all had negative effects on mission to Muslims. A positive element today is the desire to be much more culturally sensitive as we approach them. In the midst of turmoil and very real conflict, we are seeing some positive developments. One authority has asserted that more Muslims are becoming followers of Jesus (they are often unwilling to call themselves "Christians") than ever before in history. Obviously, the number is still not large and the situation calls Christians to humility and self-examination as we approach this challenge.

Chapter Twenty-Eight

Survey of Modern Missions:
Africa

Introduction

An appropriate Biblical metaphor for much of nineteenth-century mission is the grain of wheat that falls into the ground and dies in order to bring forth fruit (John 12). We see an example in the early Basel (Swiss) mission in Ghana. In the first twelve years of the mission, there were eight missionary graves and only one survivor!

Andrew Walls suggests that we imagine the following groups: a small group of Jews who worshipped Jesus as Messiah in first-century Jerusalem; Egyptian monks in the desert two centuries later; Waldensian believers meeting secretly in homes in twelfth-century Italy; early Pentecostals in Azusa Street in Los Angeles; a Korean megachurch in twenty-first century Seoul; a group of Masai worshipping under a tree in Kenya; a house fellowship in China led by a lay women; or an American suburban congregation. We could add many others.

Culturally and even theologically, these groups will be very different. They have only one characteristic in common: all seek to worship God through Jesus Christ and be his disciples. I believe this is the only essential characteristic to be part of the universal Church, the Body of Christ. This understanding will help us look beyond the structures and cultural forms we value and through which we have come to faith, and begin to discover the great variety of forms in which the People of God have gathered and worshipped

throughout history. It will also help us be open to the new forms of the Church the Holy Spirit seems to be creating today.

In his book *The Missionary Movement in Christian History* Walls identified two principles that are always important in mission. The first is "the indigenous principle." This suggests we should respect each person's cultural identity and social relationships. Everyone should be able to hear the Gospel in a context where he or she feels "at home," where there is a sense of belonging. No person should be ripped out of his or her cultural and social context in order to follow Christ. This is very similar to what McGavran called the "homogenous unit principle," that people should be able to become followers of Christ without crossing great cultural barriers.

Walls's second principle is equally important. He calls it "the pilgrim principle," and in many ways it is similar to Lovelace's concept of "disenculturation." The "pilgrim principle" recognizes that God in Christ receives us as we are. However, as we begin to be transformed into citizens of God's Kingdom, we will increasingly find ourselves to be out of step with our culture and society, since none is totally in accord with his will. This is a universalizing principle and is somewhat paradoxical. While the believer continues to live within his or her old culture and relationships, he or she, now changed by Christ, has a completely new set of relationships with other members of the family of faith. Every Christian has a dual citizenship: as a member of his or her society, and as a member of a worldwide community of citizens of the Kingdom of God. One important indication of growth toward maturity is the ability to love, worship with, and learn from brothers and sisters in Christ from cultures and races different than our own.

All too often Christians have not understood this and have continued to define their primary identity in terms of their particular racial, ethnic, or national group instead of seeing themselves as members of the universal Body of Christ. This has led to "tribal Christianity," resulting in racism, tribalism, caste divisions, social and economic distinctions, and even apartheid in the Church. One feature of renewal movements, as Lovelace points out in his concept of "disenculturation," is that such attitudes are overcome to a significant extent. All of us are called o a lifelong pilgrimage as we become citizens of the Kingdom of God instead of simply citizens of our culture. We do not stop loving and appreciating the traditions in which we first came to faith, but we also come to love and appreciate the great diversity of ways in which others worship and express their Christian discipleship.

This is a long introduction to our brief look at Christian missions in Africa. The factors I have mentioned are important everywhere through history, but perhaps especially so in Africa.

Beginnings by Africans and African Americans

A group of African Americans who had become Christians either while working as slaves, serving in the British army, or as immigrants to Nova Scotia after American independence, formed the first Protestant church in tropical Africa. A group numbering eleven hundred arrived in Sierra Leone in 1792, marching ashore singing hymns of Watts and entering their "promised land." They settled on land purchased for them by members of the "Clapham Sect" in England. Over a sixty-year period, the community grew to fifty thousand and supplied one hundred ordained men

for the Church Missionary Society in addition to numerous catechists and other mission workers.

In Uganda, many of the Ganda people became Christians through the Anglican mission. A number of them worked as evangelists far from their home areas, where they learned other languages, evangelized other people groups, and planted churches. They were cross-cultural missionaries just as much as the Europeans who came.

A survey in one area of Nigeria indicated that Christians who moved to new areas often spread the Gospel. Such Christians might have been court clerks, railroad workers, tailors, or traders. When they arrived at their new places of residence, they began family prayers, stopped working on Sundays, and sang hymns instead. As local people became interested in their faith, a church was started. In most cases, the role of the missionary was to come afterwards, in response to a request from the community.

The Missionaries
Some Generalizations on the Most Difficult Issues

1. Disease and death: Often, six months after a group of two or three families arrived in Africa, two-thirds of them had died. Nevertheless, knowing the risks, they continued to go.

2. Relationships with the chiefs: Some chiefs were very brutal and killed their subjects over the slightest pretext; others accepted the Gospel and opened the door to movements.

3. Some local customs: polygamy, the practice of killing twins in some cultures, witchcraft, and syncretism were all difficult issues to address.

4. The relationship with European colonists: Often the missionary was caught in the middle between colonialism and his concern for the welfare of the indigenous people. At times missionaries were not critical enough of colonialism. However, at other times they called attention to its abuses. Early in the twentieth century, two American Presbyterians in Congo, one white and one black, published an article

entitled, "Twentieth-Century Slavery," exposing the cruel treatment of Congolese rubber workers by the Belgian government. It caused an international incident and resulted in a slight improvement in the treatment of the Africans. (Sholoff, Stanley, "Presbyterians and Belgian Congo Exploitation," *Journal of Presbyterian History*, v 47, p. 192)

5. The relationship between evangelism and other ministries such as education, medical work, and agricultural development: How were the scarce resources to be most effectively used?

6. The identification of Christian faith with Western civilization: The danger in the minds of many was that to be truly Christian meant looking western.

South Africa

Three primary groups were in play in South Africa: the Dutch, the English, and the Black tribes. Tragically, the Dutch Calvinists adopted a theology that said, "The destiny of the whites is to rule the blacks." A Moravian, George Schmidt, arrived in 1737 and baptized the first black convert. The Dutch expelled him in 1744.

In 1799, John T. Vandenkemp arrived, sent by the London Missionary Society. He defended the rights of the Black people and thus was in conflict with European colonists. He and some of his colleagues married black women, which seemed scandalous at the time. Along with the conflict with European colonists, Vandenkemp had to struggle with issues of tribal rivalries among the Africans.

John Phillip, another LMS missionary, arrived in 1820. He too worked for the rights of the black people, fought slavery, and worked for peace between warring tribes. He also attempted to put pressure on the government in England through evangelical influence there, to secure greater rights for the Blacks. That brought him into conflict with Boers (the Dutch).

A fourth significant figure was Robert Moffatt, also of the LMS. He brought new agricultural methods and introduced irrigation. He learned the unwritten Twasana language and translated

the Scriptures. This led to revival and growth of the Church. However, he was very patriarchal in his attitude toward the Africans.

The best-known missionary of the nineteenth century was Moffatt's son-in-law, David Livingstone. Before one of his long journeys, he wrote,

> I place no value on anything I have or may possess except in relation to the Kingdom of Christ. If anything will advance the interests of the Kingdom, it shall be given away or kept only as by giving or keeping it I shall most promote the glory of him to whom I owe all my hopes in time and eternity. (Neill, p. 314)

Livingstone had two goals in his travels: to end the slave trade, and to open Africa to commerce. He believed that commerce would bring alternatives to the slave trade by opening up new economic possibilities to the Africans and would also result in the spread of the Christian faith. It is important to note that Arabs, Black tribes, and Europeans all cooperated in the trade. There was guilt all around.

We are all aware of the tragic history of apartheid in South Africa. In general, it had the support of the Afrikans Reformed Church. However, in 1982, I spent an afternoon with Dr. and Mrs. David Bosch and three other pastors of that church. That year they were part of a group of seventy-one Afrikans clergy who had sent a letter saying the Church must declare apartheid a heresy. At the time of my visit, they were ignored and ostracized. Now we are aware of the eventual defeat of the terrible system of apartheid and the subsequent change in government. Despite the work of many missionaries in the past, it now appears there is much the Church there needs to do to gain any degree of credibility.

Uganda and the Baganda People

The Baganda were an isolated people with an effective social system under the leadership of their chief, Mutesa. He was brutal, often executed his subjects, and was said to have "a larger collection of wives than any human being of whom we have record."

There were rivalries among the older African way of life, Islam, Anglican Christianity, and Roman Catholics. After civil war, the British established a protectorate in Uganda and divided the area into Protestant (Anglican) and Roman Catholic spheres of influence.

The first Anglican baptism took place in 1882. Two years later, Mutesa died and was succeeded by his eighteen-year-old son, Mwanga. At this time, Anglican bishop James Hannington attempted to enter Uganda from the east through the territory of traditional enemies of the Baganda, and was killed by order of Mwanga. When young converts refused to submit to the sodomy of the king, three were roasted to death slowly, thirty-two others were burned to death, then more were martyred. Finally, Mwanga was banished, a railroad was built from the coast, and large people movements to Christian faith began.

The Baganda showed great evangelistic zeal. They took the Gospel to three other people groups who were their traditional enemies. One evangelist learned a pygmy language and translated the Scriptures into it.

Bishop Alfred Tucker, who served from 1893 to 1911 in Uganda, saw great movements of people and sought to build a church in which Africans and Europeans were equals. Most missionaries opposed him, believing that Europeans should remain in positions of leadership.

African Leaders

William Wade Harris was one of several African evangelists who had unique calls to ministry and effectively spread indigenous forms of the Christian faith. Born in 1860 in a traditional village in Liberia, he came under Methodist and Anglican influence. Around 1910 he believed the angel Gabriel visited him and told him he was to be a prophet of the last times. He should abandon "civilized" clothing, don a white robe, destroy fetishes, and preach Christian baptism. The context was one of political and military strife between African and African, and European and African.

We cannot doubt that the Holy Spirit anointed Harris in a powerful manner. He went out preaching that Christ must reign and that he was his prophet. He was convinced that Christ would return soon and establish his kingdom of peace. Harris took his marching orders from Matthew 28:18-20. A politician wrote of him, "You come to him with a heart full of bitterness and when he is finished with you all the bitterness is gone out of your soul. Why? He calls on the living God. He calms, under God, the troubled soul. He casts out strife, he allays bitterness. He brings joy and lightness of soul to the despairing…He attaches no importance to himself…He is the soul of humility" (David Shenk, "The Legacy of William Wade Harris," *International Bulletin of Missionary Research* 10, no. 4 [October 1986]: 170–176.)

He went up and down the Liberian coast preaching repentance and baptism, dressed in white, a staff with a cross in one hand, a Bible and baptismal bowl in the other. He attacked the local spiritual powers and often entered into contests with their practitioners, and was victorious in such contests. Village people often brought their fetishes to be burned and when they came for baptism, he taught them the Ten Commandments, the Lord's Prayer, and the Apostles' Creed. Then he instructed them to build chapels and appoint twelve apostles to govern the local church.

Remarkable healings and wonders attended his ministry. Sometimes those who opposed him died suddenly. One British administrator said he could hardly believe the moral transformation in the villages. Harris denounced the use of alcohol but accepted polygamy. He was imprisoned three times and died in total poverty in 1929 at the age of seventy.

His impact was exceptional. His ministry was inter-tribal. He broke strongly with African religions. Fetishes, some taboos, and certain practices against women were abolished. He also encouraged education.

A number of Protestant and Roman Catholic churches reaped thousands of members because of his ministry, even though many more could not become church members because of their polygamy. A "Harris church" exists today in Ivory Coast with twenty thousand members holding seven weekly services in three languages.

Clearly, the major question in his ministry was power, so important in the African context and traditional religions in general.

Samuel Crowther

In 1864, the CMS consecrated Samuel Crowther, a former slave, as the first non-European bishop of the Anglican Church in Africa. He was sent to eastern Nigeria to develop the work without European help or support. He had been away from Nigeria for years, and was sent to a people different from his own, and never learned their language. He saw himself as a "Black Englishman." Thus, although the mission had good intentions and Crowther was a good man, he was not very successful. After he died, the diocese was in disorder and a European bishop with African assistants replaced him.

We can see Crowther's appointment as an attempt at indigenous leadership that was badly flawed, showing a tragic lack of understanding of the African cultures.

Growth and Current Trends and Issues

1. The East African revival began in the 1930s with a very positive effect on the growth of the Church and vital Christian life. It was one of the factors that have led to an estimated 350 million Christians in sub-Sahara Africa by the end of the twentieth century. Similar to the Korean revival, it was triggered in part, at least, by reconciliation and mutual recognition of the gifts of both European and African believers.

2. Tribalism continues to be a major issue in Africa, and at times has led to tragic results. Christians carried out the genocide in Rwanda in part, at least, against fellow believers of another tribe. Tribalism is a problem still to be adequately addressed in both Church and political life.

3. The most rapidly growing form of Christian faith in Africa is taking place in the African-initiated, indigenous churches. One estimate is that there are at least six thousand different "denominations." These churches are culturally much more African in styles of leadership and worship. Some churches continue to accept polygamy, and theologically they range from historically orthodox to very syncretistic.

4. Some have described the African church as "a mile wide and an inch deep," but this is unfair. The African churches have many excellent leaders and theological thinkers. The churches are growing and remain faithful in the midst of poverty, warfare, and political corruption. Africa counts a growing number of fine theological seminaries and universities. But still today the Church is often characterized by a mixture of traditional beliefs mixed with Christian faith that often leads to involvement with witchcraft. This needs to be addressed by a deeper understanding of African culture and the power dimension of biblical faith.

5. Another major issue in Africa today is aggressive Wahhabist Islam. Much of African Islam has been quite nominal and tolerant. However, the more rigid, intolerant version is growing, financed by Saudi oil money. There has been growing persecution of Christians in northern Nigeria, for example, and scores of churches have been burned. On the positive side, we are seeing some conversions from Islam to Christ.

6. The scourge of HIV/AIDS is tragic and calls for action in a variety of ways. Obviously one issue is the importance of a Christian standard of sexual conduct. Of equal importance is the need to care for the millions of victims of AIDS, most of them children.

Thus, Africa, once known as the graveyard of missionaries, continues to be problematic. On the one hand, the Church has grown to be very large. On the other hand, it is the continent where poverty, warfare, and political corruption seem to be endemic. Certainly, it challenges the worldwide Church to work for a transformation of its societies that will include economic development and political integrity along with evangelism and theological education.

Chapter Twenty-Nine

Survey of Modern Missions:
Latin America

Introduction

Iberian Roman Catholicism was brought to Latin America by the Spanish and Portuguese conquerors in the sixteenth century. Those two nations, having recently expelled the last of the Moors, were united around a nationalistic, intolerant form of Catholic faith. That faith was rapidly imposed on the indigenous and later the slave populations en masse. At times priests baptized thousands in one day. However, there was little or no instruction in the essentials of the Christian faith.

A second problem was the lack of an adequate number of priests. And in addition, most of those who went to the new world were unworthy, despite some outstanding exceptions. The kings controlled the Church and deliberately kept the number of bishops at an inadequate level. Since only a bishop could ordain a priest, that, along with other factors, meant that the number of priests was always far from the ideal. For example, it was reported that in 1907, there was only one priest for every fifteen thousand people. Some parishes had no pastor for twelve years. (P.E. Pierson, *A Younger Church in Search of Maturity* [San Antonio, Trinity University Press, 1974], 4). There is no indication that the situation has changed. Even today, many priests in Latin America are foreign. Thus, the Latin American Catholic Church has never produced anywhere near an adequate number of priests. Because of the Catholic understanding of ordination and the priesthood, which is essential to administer the sacraments, the role of the laity is severely limited.

A third factor was religious syncretism. The Catholicism that was brought to Latin America already focused primarily on the Virgin Mary and the saints. Syncretism grew when first the indigenous populations and then the slaves, primarily in Brazil and the Caribbean, brought their traditional deities into the mix. Forced to accept Catholicism, their deities were simply baptized as Catholic saints and continued to be venerated or worshipped in their new guise. This led to religious practices such as spiritism in Brazil and Voodoo in Haiti.

The primary focus of piety for most has been a favorite manifestation of the Virgin Mary along with a few favorite saints. John MacKay, in his book *The Other Spanish Christ* (New York: Macmillan, 1933), pointed out that Jesus Christ has usually been depicted in three ways in Iberian art: as a helpless baby in the arms of his mother, a dead figure on the cross, or a judge with sword in hand coming at the end of history. None of the three seems to attract allegiance. On the other hand, Mary is seen as the sentimental mother, the dispenser of grace—but grace that often does not seem to call for repentance.

The result can be seen in the following observation made by a Brazilian writer (Thales de Azevedo, "Catolicismo no Brasil" in *Vozes*, Petropolis, LXIII, 2 [Feb 1919], 117–124). There were

> three principal types of Catholics in Brazil: a
> tiny minority who knew and believed at least

a minimum of doctrine and were faithful in religious duties; a much larger group of nominal Catholics; and, finally, the 'Brazilian' or folk Catholics, stigmatized by the bishops and denounced by the priests. Although the categories overlapped, the great majority of the population, especially the lower middle class and the poor, belonged to the third group. Their non-institutional religion, centered in the 'festas' and private devotion to the Virgin and saints, had almost no contact with the clergy (Pierson, *Younger Church*, 13).

Thus, a very low percentage of the people, perhaps ten percent, may be considered practicing Catholics, which some define as going to Mass and confession once a year.

That figure is typical of Brazil. It might be lower in the most secularized nations (Uruguay, for example), and possibly higher in some others, such as Mexico.

The close relationship between Church and state has been another important issue. A close alliance existed between the two for four and a half centuries. Despite the protests of a few, the Catholic Church upheld the status quo in a close alliance with the powerful—the landowners, and the military. That changed with the Conference of the Latin American bishops held in Medellin, Colombia, in 1968. Influenced by the concepts of liberation theology, the bishops declared a "preferential option for the poor." The best-known Latin American theologians and many bishops and priests (but not all) followed this orientation. The movement did not seem to bring positive social or economic changes, nor did it win greater allegiance of the poor. It did alienate many of the middle-class and the more wealthy groups. Thus, Latin American nations continue to exhibit some of the greatest disparity in the world between rich and poor, with luxurious mansions and apartments very close to urban slums in cities such as Rio de Janeiro.

On the other hand, there have been two other movements along with liberation theology: the "base communities" and charismatic renewal. The "base communities," which grew greatly during the 1980s, focused to some extent on Bible studies for the laity, but especially on mobilizing people for specific social projects. Perhaps because they were dominated by the priests and were not truly lay movements, they have decreased greatly in number and influence. Charismatic movements have grown in a number of localities, often depending on the favor of the local priest or bishop. Some have combined a focus on the work of the Holy Spirit with continued devotion to Mary. At times they have broken away from the Roman Catholic Church and become independent groups.

For four and a half centuries, Protestants were condemned, almost without exception. The Protestant versions of the Bible were said to be false. A significant shift took place with Vatican II. For the first time, Protestants were recognized as Christians—"separated brethren"—and Bible societies were endorsed. Eventually, the Brazilian bishops put their imprimatur on the version of the Bible used by the Brazilian Bible Society and began to distribute it.

Vatican II also encouraged greater movement toward a focus on Jesus Christ and less on Mary and the saints. However, it is doubtful that this brought much change to the popular religion of the masses. Pope John Paul II reversed that process, appointed more conservative bishops, and encouraged traditional popular religion.

During most of its history, Latin America has not enjoyed religious liberty. The Roman Catholic Church was established and subsidized by the various states, and often Protestantism was forbidden and persecuted. Religious liberty came to Brazil before the end of the nineteenth century. However, there was no freedom of worship in Colombia until after the middle of the twentieth century.

Yet to some extent, popular Catholicism served as a preparation for the evangelical faith. It brought a concept of God, of human sin and the need for forgiveness, and the hope of a God (or the saints) who would be active in lives here and now. Thus in some ways, both popular and institutional Catholicism promised something that it rarely produced: an experience of forgiveness and peace with God, and confidence that the Holy Spirit was active to help and guide the lives of believers.

The First Phase: Older "Mainline" Churches and Their Missions

Although colporteurs of the Bible Society had arrived earlier, permanent work was initiated in Brazil by Presbyterians, Baptists, and Methodists shortly after the middle of the nineteenth century. Robert Kalley, a Scottish Presbyterian physician, arrived in 1855 and established a Congregational church. He was followed by Ashbel Green Simonton, an American Presbyterian, who arrived in 1859. Baptists and Methodists from the United States soon followed. Because of a relatively liberal government, religious freedom, and extensive itineration by the early missionary evangelists, these churches grew quite rapidly.

The critical issue of control over theological education and leadership training soon arose among Presbyterians. The American Missions and their supporting boards refused to give up control over theological education. Resentment by some of the most able Brazilian leaders led to schism in 1903. The question of Masonry was a secondary issue but emerged on the surface of the dispute. Some of the earliest missionaries had been Masons and the movement had worked for greater religious liberty in the nation. However, the movement was clearly deistic in its philosophy.

A related question was the role of educational institutions established by the missions. Was their primary goal to prepare Protestant youth for leadership in the churches, to evangelize non-Protestant students, or to introduce American culture and educational methods into Brazil? While these questions did not lead to schism in most cases, they would be recurring problems in the various Protestant missions. For example, while Baptists emphasized evangelism and church growth, Methodists established a number of fine educational institutions. But the Baptists grew much more rapidly, and eventually established a number of seminaries to train pastors.

Another major issue for Protestants in Latin America was the relationship to the Roman Catholic Church. While some mission leaders in the United States favored a conciliatory approach, that was not possible in Latin America. As nominal Roman Catholics embraced the Protestant message, they often discovered a new life of freedom from destructive lifestyles of their past. This often led to healthier family life and upward social mobility. At the same time, Roman Catholic leaders, almost without exception, denounced and at times persecuted them. The first ordained Brazilian Protestant pastor, Jose Manoel da Conceicao, was a former priest—an irenic, St. Francis-like character—He was totally rejected by his former church. Hence, almost without exception, Catholics and Protestants looked on each other as adversaries and enemies of the true faith. After the Edinburgh Conference of 1910, from which Latin American Protestants were excluded, the American Boards called for a conference on Christian work in Latin America, to be held in Panama in 1916. The nature of Catholic-Protestant animosity was demonstrated when American mission executives suggested that Roman Catholics be invited. Prominent Latin American Protestants replied that they would not attend if Roman Catholics were invited. And the Bishop of Panama threatened to excommunicate any Catholics who attended! If Protestant-Catholic relationships in the United States were at a twentieth-century level, they were still at a sixteenth-century level in Latin America.

Before the end of the nineteenth century, Presbyterians, invited by a liberal President, entered Guatemala and established a school. The Central American Mission, from a dispensationalist background, followed. It soon became important to recognize the existence of non-Spanish speaking indigenous groups that constituted a majority of the population. The Spanish-speaking Ladinos were economically, culturally, and politically dominant, and the law required that all education be conducted in Spanish.

Paul Burgess, a Presbyterian missionary who had done graduate study in Europe, insisted on ministering to the indigenous peoples and eventually established a pastoral training institution using one of the Mayan languages. At times he was jailed for that. Burgess also collaborated with Cameron Townsend, a Presbyterian layman who worked with the Central American Mission, to establish Wycliffe Bible Translators.

Thus, by the beginning of the twentieth century, American denominational boards and some of the newer, conservative, multi-denominational "faith missions" had established work in a number of Latin American countries. However, in most cases, growth was slow.

The Second Phase: Pentecostals, 1910

Three streams of Pentecostalism arrived in Latin America around the same time. One originated in Chile from the Methodist mission there; another in Brazil, led by Swedish Baptists; and the other, also in Brazil, led by an Italian former Presbyterian.

Chile

Willis Hoover, a Methodist missionary in Chile, heard of the Pentecostal movement in Los Angeles and India. He was seeking a deeper spiritual life and a return to the dynamism of early Methodism. Pentecostal-type manifestations began to break out in his church and it grew rapidly. When his bishop ordered him to return to the United States, Hoover refused and left the Methodist mission. This was the origin of the movement in Chile that has grown, in its many branches, to number close to fifteen percent of the population. The Methodist Church in the nation remains very small.

Brazil and the Assemblies of God

In 1910, two Swedish Baptists, Daniel Berg and Gunnar Wingren, who had been caught up in the Pentecostal movement in the United States, arrived in Belem, Brazil, at the mouth of the Amazon River. They went in response to a prophecy they had received but they knew no one, and had no visible means of support in the new country. They found a Baptist congregation, worshipped there, and, after learning the language, began to share their experience and doctrine. The Church divided, but most accompanied them. That was the beginning of the Assemblies of God in Brazil.

Their methodology was similar to that of the early Methodists in some ways. As laymen (and they were always men in Brazil) showed their gifts, they were sent out up the Amazon River, and down the coast, to plant congregations. In the cities, growth was rapid but it was decades before the older Protestant groups accepted them as Christians. They had great appeal, especially to the poor, who were flocking to the cities from the hinterland. In their new surroundings, many found a sense of community in the Pentecostal congregations. Healings were often claimed, and no doubt some of the claims were legitimate. Unlike the situation in the more historic churches, there was little or no social distance between leaders and people. As soon as a person became part of a congregation, he or she was given a task to perform and made to feel significant.

With many divisions into various regional groups, and not without friction, the Assemblies have grown to number around twelve million members in Brazil, and have also been the source of several other groups.

There can be no doubt that this movement has led millions of Brazilians into an authentic Christian life. Often it has tended to become legalistic, seeing sin only in terms of specific prohibited acts—drinking, smoking, and sex outside of marriage—without seeing its broader personal and societal dimensions. Some pastors have become extremely authoritarian, and the issue of pastoral succession is often a serious problem. In addition, the "health, wealth, and prosperity" gospel has invaded from the United States.

In the 1950s, the Assemblies began to open Bible schools to give more formal training to pastors. By the 1970s, they began to open seminaries. One of the best seminaries in Brazil at the present, with high academic standards, is the South American Theological Seminary in Londrina. Most of the faculty are Presbyterians but over half of its students are currently Pentecostals. While this is very desirable, it raises an important question: Will the movement continue to accept pastors who come from the poor? If it does not, will that gradually change the nature of the Church as it distances itself increasingly from the poor and marginalized? In other words, will it follow the example of Methodism?

The Christian Congregation in Brazil

Luigi Francesconi had migrated from Italy to Chicago, where, for a time, he was a member of an Italian Presbyterian church. He worked with other Christian groups and was influenced by Pentecostalism. In 1910, he arrived in São Paulo, Brazil, and began to worship at a Presbyterian Church in a heavily Italian section of the city. There, the Christian Congregation of Brazil (CCB) was formed. During its first two or three decades, it grew primarily among Italian immigrants, including some businessmen.

Much more sectarian than other Pentecostal groups, the CCB relates to other Christian groups only through the Brazilian Bible Society. It has no pastors. Similar to the Plymouth Brethren, the preaching is done by the elders. I once attended a service at the mother church in Brás where men sat on one side, women on the other. Two aspects of the service were especially impressive. One was the enthusiastic music. The other was the testimonies. One after another, men on one side, women on the other, told how God had met a particular need in their lives. There was a very real sense that God was alive and working today!

The group uses its offerings, which are considerable, to build large "temples" for worship. It is much less legalistic regarding dress and the use of alcohol than are most other Pentecostals. It probably numbers around a million and a half members in Brazil and has now spread to surrounding countries, Portugal, and the United States.

While these are the oldest Pentecostal churches in Latin America, today there are so many others that one cannot keep track of them. Some, like the Foursquare Church, are related to churches in the United States; most are not.

It is also worth noting that the Seventh Day Adventist Church numbers over a million in Brazil and is now larger than its mother church in the United States.

The Third Phase: Conservative Evangelicals

The Latin America Mission (LAM) arrived in 1921, established by Harry and Susan Strachan as the Latin American Evangelistic Crusade. They had originally gone to Argentina as members of a conservative group from which they launched their movement. Establishing their headquarters in Costa Rica, the mission took several steps uncommon among the more conservative groups. It encouraged greater contextualization, with greater acceptance of Latin music. It worked to mobilize all evangelicals in evangelistic campaigns called "Evangelism in Depth." It initiated a number of social ministries, including a fine hospital as well as a seminary. In 1971, the mission formed local boards (unusual at the time) to direct each of its specific ministries, and assigned its missionaries to work under their direction. In some cases, those ministries flourished; others failed or followed a theological direction very different from the mission.

Wycliffe Bible Translators has, of course, worked with scores of indigenous groups in Mexico, Brazil, and elsewhere. Working also as the Summer Institute of Linguistics, they have reduced scores of languages to writing and translated the Scriptures.

In addition, a number of other groups have focused on work with indigenous groups. The South American Indian Mission worked in Brazil. "Friends" (Evangelical Quakers), and others have worked with Aymaras and Quechuas in the high Andes. The mission of the Reformed Church of America has seen great growth among indigenous groups in Chiapas, Mexico.

The New "Post-Denominational" Churches

In recent decades many new churches have developed. Most have emerged out of the older Pentecostal groups but developed new characteristics. Some focus almost exclusively on signs, wonders, and healings; some are more middle class; a few are more wholistic. A number of the largest are cell-based churches in which every member is to be in a cell. They have been growing. The largest is the Charismatic Mission of Bogotá, Colombia. It is said to bring fifty thousand together for worship celebration. There are others, numbering from five thousand to ten thousand members.

All of these churches, as far as we can tell, are charismatic in the sense that they believe in all of the gifts, but most do not stress glossolalia (tongues) as classic Pentecostals do. Normally they have leaders who are charismatic both in the popular sense that they are strong, visionary men, and in the biblical sense that they have a special call from God. While these factors give the leaders great power, when they are no longer on the scene their would-be successors often encounter great difficulties. Some at times fall into dubious theology or ethics.

We will look at two interesting and very different examples. The first is the Las Acacias Church in Caracas, Venezuela. Samuel Olson, the pastor, is the son of Assemblies of God missionaries. He holds degrees from Johns Hopkins University and Princeton Theological Seminary. The church numbers around five thousand members and includes government officials and professional people, as well as the poor from the urban slums. Its ministries range from job training programs to prayers for healing and exorcisms. The church has also established a multi-denominational seminary. It is very wholistic both in its theology and ministry.

At the opposite extreme is the Universal Church of the Kingdom of God (IUR in Portuguese) led by its bishop, Edir Macedo. Its message is clear and simple: If you come to the IUR, Jesus will solve your problem, whether it is illness, poverty, lack of a job, or even demon possession. Estimates of its membership range from two to four million, and it has spread to other countries, including the United States, where it holds services in Spanish. It puts great stress on money, expecting adherents to contribute two tithes, and if local pastors do not produce enough offerings, they are dismissed. Bishop Macedo lives outside of Brazil, at times in the United States, and at times elsewhere. The church owns a number of newspapers and television channels in Brazil.

The IUR has been very controversial in Brazil, and evangelical leaders have varied opinions about it. Often its leaders have been unduly offensive, and at times it has adopted some customs of folk Catholicism. Most would agree that its Christology and understanding of the Gospel are orthodox, but lament the superficiality of its message and understanding of discipleship. One study focused on the group's marketing techniques. No study has been done, as far as we know, on the retention of its members. I had a friend, a very fine and effective pastor in Brazil, who told me of a woman who worked in his family's home. The family witnessed to her and attempted to win her to faith without success. However, he said, she did come to Christ in the Universal Church.

Statistics of Growth

It is difficult to keep up with the statistics of growth, but in general the evangelical movement, primarily Pentecostal and charismatic, is growing about twice as rapidly as the population throughout Latin America as a whole.

It is reported that there are one hundred thousand new believers in Rio de Janeiro each year, but that cannot be verified. However, there is no doubt that new churches, usually Pentecostal, spring up constantly. Often upward social mobility is a result. The story of Benedita da Silva is impressive. Raised in great poverty with little formal education, she was converted in an Assembly of God church. She became active in the labor movement, was elected to the federal congress, and became the first woman of African descent to become a member of the Federal Cabinet.

Chile and Brazil, along with Central America, have the highest percentage of evangelicals. Evangelicals in Brazil are said to number between sixteen and twenty percent of the population in Brazil, and eighteen percent in Central America. Guatemala reports over twenty-five percent. At the other end of the spectrum, Uruguay, Paraguay, and Venezuela are said to number only two to five percent evangelicals. Recent statistics indicate that Latin America as a whole is now twelve per cent evangelical and that the movement is growing at the rate of 5.7 per cent per year, compared with population growth of 2.5 percent annually. In most cases 75% of evangelicals are Pentecostals.

Major Issues for the Evangelical Movement

With rare exceptions, all Protestant churches in Latin America are evangelical and even fundamentalist in their theology. They have focused strongly on evangelism. However, often there has been little stress on growth in discipleship. In general, the Christian life has been defined in terms of church participation and avoidance of certain destructive behaviors: smoking, drinking, and sexual misconduct. But Latin America exhibits one of the greatest disparities between rich and poor in the world. Political life has been characterized by corruption. The approach of the Christian left, inspired by Liberation Theology, has not been productive. However, when conservative Protestants have been elected to public office many have failed to approach their duties in terms of their faith, and have simply been loyal to their political parties. At times some congregations, especially Pentecostals, have agreed to vote for a candidate if he promised gifts or privileges to them. Thus, there is a great need for Protestants to think deeply about their faith and discover how to apply it, not only to personal morality, but also to social and economic issues. Certainly a growing number of local churches are beginning to minister to poor and marginalized people. Much more needs to be done.

A second major question is the relationship to the Roman Catholic Church. Historically, Catholics and Protestants have gone their own way, usually ignoring each other. At times friendships have developed between some leaders in the two groups, but these have been rare. There are situations where local Protestant congregations can join forces with Catholics in seeking to solve local problems, using community efforts to do so. These might involve putting pressure on authorities to provide better health care, sanitation, and educational facilities, for example. The post-Vatican II context has opened up new possibilities for that kind of cooperation.

When we realize that in 1900 evangelicals numbered no more than fifty thousand in Latin America, and were usually found among the poorest groups, it is extraordinary to contemplate the size, growth, and constituency of the movement today. The very size and prestige of the movement brings great new possibilities for continued growth and influence in society. However, it also brings the temptations of nominalism and growing conformity to the surrounding culture.

Chapter Thirty

Pentecostalism and Mission

Introduction

Pentecostalism has been the most rapidly growing Christian movement of the twentieth century. It has also played a major role in reshaping many churches outside of its own orbit. Often it has been untidy or even messy. Frequently it has lapsed into legalism and, at times, triumphalism. However, we can have no doubt that it has stimulated the Church worldwide to recover a focus on the ongoing work of the Holy Spirit and at times, rediscover the gifts of all believers. First, we will examine its background, and then look briefly at its missionary expansion throughout the world. Some believe that if we put together all Christians who can be classified as Pentecostal and/or charismatic—including charismatics in the Roman Catholic Church, the older denominations, the African independent churches, and the house fellowships in China—it constitutes the largest branch of practicing Christians in the world today. The various Pentecostal groups and newer charismatic churches together are certainly larger than any Protestant denomination.

Historical Background

Four helpful books on Pentecostalism are these: Donald W. Dayton, *Theological Roots of Pentecostalism* (Metuchen, New Jersey: Scarecrow Press, 1987); L. Grant McClung, Jr., ed., *Azusa Street and Beyond: Pentecostal Missions and Church Growth in the Twentieth Century* (South Plainfield, New Jersey: Bridge Publications, 1986);

Cecil M. Robeck, *The Azusa Street Mission and Revival: The Birth of the Global Pentecostal Movement* (Nashville: Nelson Reference & Electronic, 2006), and Miller, D. and Yamamori, T. *Global Pentecostalism*, Berkeley: University of California Press, 2007.

Methodism was important in the development of the Pentecostal movement. Wesley was a fine theologian. He knew the church fathers; he read Luther and Calvin, but did not agree with them completely. In his desire for converts to lead an authentic Christian life, he developed the doctrine of perfectionism. That is, he believed that a Christian could arrive at the point where he or she no longer willfully sinned. Wesley did not consider himself to have arrived at that. However, later movements that emerged out of the Wesleyan tradition put more stress on the possibility of perfectionism and encouraged people to seek an experience that would enable them to reach this state.

Then as Methodism became more respectable and lost some of its original focus on "scriptural holiness," a new movement developed from its roots. Appropriately, it was called the "Holiness Movement." It developed principally in the United States and England. Some women were prominent in its leadership. It focused on a deeper and more consistent life with God. The Keswick Conference in England was a major center. The various holiness groups focused on a "second blessing," which had some roots in Methodism. They believed a Christian could and should undergo a second crisis experience in which he or she would receive the Holy Spirit more fully than at conversion. That would lead to a new level of holiness or sanctification in one's life. At the beginning, the holiness groups did not teach the importance of a specific experience that would lead to such a state. The Nazarene denomination continues to believe strongly in a second blessing, but does not associate it with tongues—in fact, the denomination is strongly against that experience.

The revival movements led by Charles Finney were another factor in the development of Pentecostalism. Finney was a Presbyterian lawyer who had a very powerful experience of the presence of God when he received his call to preach. He rejected the older Calvinist theology of Hodge and Warfield at Princeton because he believed it cut the nerve of evangelism. Finney became the greatest evangelist of the first half of nineteenth-century America. He emphasized the ability of the human will to respond to the gospel, different from the older Calvinism that tended to minimize the importance of the human will.

In his concern for evangelism, Finney and his colleagues stressed the use of "means," or specific techniques, to encourage people to make decisions for Christ. His understanding of holiness led to a strong concern for the problems of society, especially the issue of slavery. The role of women in ministry was also important. Antoinette Brown Blackwell, the first woman to be ordained in the United States, came from Oberlin College, which Finney and Mahan were instrumental in founding. The Temperance movement was another focus.

So we see that four issues in the early holiness movement were education, women's rights, the abolition of slavery, and temperance. Asa Mahan, the first president of Oberlin, believed that the baptism of the Holy Spirit would empower Christians to begin to solve such issues. Thus, much of the earliest holiness movement focused outward on social issues, not merely on questions of personal conduct.

Azusa Street, 1906

Charles Parham, who had established a small Bible college in Topeka, Kansas, began to teach that "speaking in tongues," or *glossalalia*, was the essential evidence of the baptism of the Holy Spirit. During the night of December 31, 1900, while his students were praying for that experience, a young woman received the gift. A few years later, Parham was teaching a similar group in Texas. An African-American preacher, William Seymour, attended his classes. Because of racism he was forced to sit outside of the room and listen through the window. Seymour had very little formal education and had lost the sight in one eye. In 1906, he was invited to speak in a holiness church in Los Angeles, led by Nelly Terry, an African American woman. When he preached on Acts 4 and affirmed, "Anyone who does not speak in tongues has not received the baptism," he was told to leave. He began services in a house, and on April 9, 1906, several received the gift. The crowds grew, and they moved to a former Methodist church, then used as livery stable, on Azusa Street in East Los Angeles.

The meetings there, which continued every night for three years, are considered the beginning of the Pentecostal movement. There were many manifestations including "tongues, prophecies, people being slain in the Spirit, strange utterances, and healings." The newspapers and churches ridiculed the movement.

> Breathing strange utterances and mouthing a creed which it would seem no sane mortal could understand, the newest religious sect has started in Los Angeles. Meetings are held in a tumble-down shack on Azusa Street, near San Pedro Street, and the devotees of the weird doctrine practice the most fanatical rites, preach the wildest theories, and work themselves into a state of mad excitement in their peculiar zeal. (Los Angeles Times, page 1, 1906. Quoted in L. Grant McClung, Jr., ed., *Azusa Street and Beyond: Pentecostal Missions and Church Growth in the Twentieth Century* [South Plainfield, New Jersey: Bridge Publications, 1986], 3).

In a sense, it was a continuation of the revivalism of the American frontier, now occurring among the poor and dispossessed, on the new frontier. Along with African Americans, immigrants from Latin America, Asia, and elsewhere were present. A few well-educated people were involved, as well. In the beginning, the Pentecostal movement was interracial, and women played a prominent role, both of which made it very countercultural at the time. In fact, of all the socio-religious movements in the United States at that time, the Pentecostal movement gave the greatest scope for the gifts of women. Soon there were nine Pentecostal churches in Los Angeles, but not all were on good terms with the others.

The movement was missionary from the beginning. Pentecostals believed Christ would return very soon and felt compelled to reach as many as possible with the message of His salvation before He did so. In addition, some believed that the gift of tongues meant they would be able to speak the languages of the people to whom they went without studying them, simply through the work of the Holy Spirit. Before the end of 1906, they began to go to the "regions beyond."

> Whole families volunteered for the missionary task, sold their possessions, and started for the field. They demonstrated a passion to get to the ends of the earth for their Lord. No sacrifice seemed too great so that the Gospel might be proclaimed and the coming of the Lord be hastened. (Horace McCracken quoted in ibid., 10).

Early Pentecostal Success

Differences between various groups soon emerged. The Assemblies of God, formed in 1914, is the best known. It had two hundred missionaries on the field the year it was established. Virtually all of them had been members of other groups and were expelled because of their Pentecostal type experience. Hoover, who established the Pentecostal movement in Chile, was one of the best known. However the Assemblies soon rejected the early racial inclusiveness, and became a white denomination for most of the century. The Church of God in Christ became predominantly black. The predominately white Church of God, Cleveland, was the third major group. There were others. The

Foursquare Church emerged in the 1930s from the ministry of Aimee Semple McPherson.

A key feature of Pentecostal theology was that subsequent to conversion, one should have a definite experience of sanctification. In classical Pentecostal theology, this was the baptism of the Holy Spirit validated by the experience of "speaking in tongues." Thus, "tongues" became the essential sign of the baptism of the Holy Spirit in classical Pentecostal theology. That continues to be the official doctrine of the Assemblies of God. However, there is a serious question about what proportion of its members now has that experience.

Jack Hayford, the most prominent Foursquare leader, has said he does not believe the experience of "tongues" is essential, but that he does believe that believers should seek a definite experience, usually called a "baptism" or "infilling" of the Holy Spirit, subsequent to conversion. In some cases, the experience may come at the same time as conversion. This classical Pentecostal doctrine is somewhat different from charismatic beliefs in some of the older denominations. "Charismatics" in the older denominations affirm those gifts that have received prominence in the Pentecostal movement, but their theology does not always identify the gift of tongues with the baptism of the Holy Spirit.

We can look at Pentecostalism in many different ways: as a social movement of the marginalized, as renewal in the Church, in terms of its theological rediscoveries, and as a mission movement. Indeed, it is all of those. Grant McClung in his book, *Azusa Street and Beyond*, points out that among the characteristics of early Pentecostalism was the conviction that the power and presence of God are to be experienced today. God is not simply a far-off god of the past or future, but present and active in human life today. Hence, the attraction of the movement consisted of a powerful individual spiritual experience. The stress is not on any system of doctrine. Arminians and Calvinists found themselves on the same platforms. Teachers with different views on holiness and eschatology were conscious of a new fundamental unity in the Spirit.

People of diverse church traditions were involved: Episcopalians, Methodists, Brethren, Salvation Army members, men, and women from almost every section of the Church. It demonstrated an early ecumenism. Participants felt their unity lay in the Spirit, not in a particular doctrine of the Church, or even in a particular theology. Their unity lay in the Spirit and emphasized a second work of grace.

There were a number of causes for the initial success of the movement:

1. In its attitude toward the ongoing miraculous activity of God, the Church in North America was divided into three groups at the time. Princeton orthodoxy denied any miraculous activity of God after the age of the apostles. Dispensationalism taught the same cessationalist view. Growing liberalism tended to deny miraculous activity at any time. And yet, almost all traditional cultures and religions, especially among the poor, sought the intervention of God or the spirits in human life, especially in times of crisis. Thus, Pentecostalism arose in a world conditioned to expect the supernatural, even though most organized religion had no place for it. Today, we see that much of the Church in the West, having learned from both Pentecostalism and our brothers and sisters in the Majority world, has been moving back to the recognition that God is still active in human life today. That, of course, is the biblical world view, and prior to the enlightenment, it was the expectation of Christians.

2. Early Pentecostalism emphasized experience rather than doctrine or church government.

3. It saw itself as a revitalization movement within the Christian Church. Early Pentecostals did not see themselves as starting a new denomination or being divisive. At first, they wished to speak to nominal Christians and lethargic believers rather than to the un-

converted. When we looked at the Cluniac movement in the tenth century and Pietism in the seventeenth, we discovered that both focused first on personal renewal, then on the renewal of the Church. After that they hoped to move out into the world beyond, both in mission and social change. Pentecostalism moved very rapidly into world evangelization, but nearly a century would pass before many Pentecostals began to work for social change beyond their own communities.

4. For most of the twentieth century, the movement appealed to the lower strata of American society. Most early Pentecostals were people with little or no professional, educational, or social status.

5. Similar to John Wesley, but different from the traditional churches, they took the initiative and went to people wherever they might be, rather than waiting for people to come to them. They often preached out of doors, on street corners.

6. Mass meetings were important in creating a sense of belonging to a larger community. That was important, for example, to the newly arrived poor in Latin American cities. They had come from areas where they belonged a community, but now in the cities they were part of an anonymous mass. They often found a new community in Pentecostal churches.

7. The early movement used newspapers and periodicals effectively to disseminate its message.

8. Early Pentecostalism drew people of all classes, but especially the poor. There was no discrimination. In the early Azusa Street meetings, nearly anyone could speak who felt led to do so.

9. The emphasis on divine healing was important.

10. The movement gave its adherents a strong sense of belonging. Normally, new believers were immediately given a job to do. They might pass out tracts in a street meeting, play an instrument, or even give their testimonies.

11. The early adherents had the conviction that God had raised them up for a unique mission at a special time in history.

12. There was a great spirit of sacrifice. Some of the early Pentecostals sold everything and went to other countries, knowing little about the peoples to whom they were going. Usually they had little or no means of support. However, they believed God had called them. In some cases, Brazil, for example, rapidly growing churches were established; in others, the missionaries died or returned home very soon.

13. A primary goal was to establish indigenous churches.

14. Similar to the early Methodists, the leaders came from the "grassroots," chosen and recognized because of their gifts and effectiveness in ministry rather than their educational or social status. Similar to the early Baptist and Methodist preachers on the American frontier, there was little social distance between pastor and people.

The Early Spread of Pentecostalism
Europe
Pentecostalism spread to Europe early on through a Norwegian Methodist minister, T. B. Barratt, who was of Celtic background. He introduced the movement to Norway. From there it spread to Finland and Sweden, then to Switzerland, Germany, England, and eventually to Italy.

It is interesting that Pentecostalism has grown far more in countries of Roman Catholic than Protestant background. The worldview of traditional Latin American Catholicism believes the Virgin Mary, the saints, and even spirits to be extremely active. Indeed, traditional piety focuses on seeking their intervention in the problems of life. Thus, Pentecostalism, with its focus on the active participation of God in human life here and now to help us in our daily crises, spoke to that worldview. There are at least four times as many members of the Assemblies of God in Brazil (AOG) as in the United States. And adherents of the AOG

in Brazil probably constitute only half of the Pentecostals in that nation! The Foursquare Church, with 10,700 churches and congregations, is also larger in Brazil than in the United States.

Among the European countries, it has grown most in Italy. Giacomo Lombardi, converted in the United States, introduced Pentecostalism there when he returned in 1908. By 1929, it counted 134 churches. Now it numbers 350 thousand members and is the largest non-Catholic church in the nation. It has grown especially in Sicily, a center of poverty. The greater freedom given to women and the challenge to patriarchal culture seem to have been factors in its growth. Pentecostalism has also been significant in Sweden, led by Levi Petrus. The Assemblies of God in Brazil has roots both in the United States and in Sweden, but the latter has been more important in its life.

Latin America: Brazil
The story of Pentecostalism in Brazil is very important. Part of the story was already told in the chapter on Latin America; other details are important because they give us much of the ethos of the movement in its early days.

Two Swedish Baptist laymen in South Bend, Indiana, Gunnar Vingren and Daniel Berg, were caught up in the new movement. They believed they received a prophecy that God was telling them to go to Pará. Not knowing where it was, they went to a library, looked it up, and found it was a state on the south bank of the Amazon River in northern Brazil. They had no money, but made their way to New York, hoping to go further. On a street in the city, they met an acquaintance who said, "I was just on my way to mail this to you in Indiana but I didn't expect to meet you here." He gave them an envelope with some money. It was enough for a one-way passage to Belém, at the mouth of the Amazon!

Arriving in Belém, not knowing what the next step would be, they sat in a park where they met a young Brazilian who spoke English. He was a Presbyterian and guided them to a small Baptist church. The missionary who led the Church traveled frequently.

Vingren and Berg began to worship there and soon learned some Portuguese. When they began to share their Pentecostal doctrines in the Baptist church, it divided and the missionary ordered them to leave. We have two contrasting versions of this event. The first is from Vingren and Berg. Berg said:

> One evening the local preacher appeared in our simple premises. When he opened the door, a wave of song and prayer struck him. We got up and invited him to take part in our improvised service. He refused and declared that it was now time to make a decision. He said that a short time before he had discovered that people had dared to engage in a discussion of doctrines, something that had never happened before. He accused us of sowing doubt and unrest and of being separatists.
>
> Vingren got up and declared that we did not desire any division. On the contrary, we wanted unity among everyone. If only everyone had the experience of the baptism of the Spirit, we would never be divided. On the contrary, we would then be more than brothers, like a family.
>
> The local preacher spoke again. The discussion was open. He said that the Bible did indeed speak about the baptism of the Spirit and also said that Jesus healed the sick. But that was in those days. He said that it would be absurd if educated people of our time believed that such things could happen today. We had to be realistic—he continued—and not waste time with dreams and false prophecies. Nowadays we had knowledge to know what to do with it. "If you do not mend your ways and recognize your error, it is my duty to inform all the Baptist congregations and to warn them about your false doctrine.

The other account comes from a Brazilian Baptist:

> In April 1911, two Swedish missionaries, Gunnar Vingren and Daniel Berg, landed in Belém. They called themselves Baptists…They immediately went to Nelson, their fellow-countryman, to find shelter with him. They were offered the cellar of the church; they put up there and learnt the language in order to be able to help Nelson in the work of evangelization. The good missionary [Nelson] then made one of his numerous journeys into the state of Piaui and left those

> two behind in the church, in the sweet hope that even though they could not speak [Portuguese], they would be able to continue the work. After a short while, however, these (so-called) Baptists began to quiver and shriek in a meeting. Soon Brazilians imitated them. What had happened? What kind of a new religion was this, people asked. They replied that it was the baptism of the Spirit. The speaking with tongues and the cackling made the services frightful. Nelson was away, and the work of the congregation was under the supervision of a young man without any experience…The whole church was infected, because so many people were already talking in this so-called speaking with tongues, with the exception of the deacons, whom this development did not escape. The evangelist called a meeting of the congregation with the help of the organist, declared the Pentecostals, who were already in the majority, to go outside and…excommunicated those who had falsified sound doctrine…

Thus, the Pentecostal movement was launched in northern Brazil. It moved up the Amazon River and down the Atlantic coast. Most of the population of Brazil even today is concentrated in the coastal cities, and the Pentecostals jumped south from one coastal city to another, and from there, to the interior.

The two Swedes arrived in 1910; the division occurred in 1911, and the Pentecostals began to grow. In 1930, they had 13,000 members; by 1940, 400,000 members; by 1960, 960,000 members. By 1967 they had grown to 1,400,000. The Assemblies of God in Brazil now numbers around twelve million believers. If we add the Foursquare Church, the Christian Congregation of Brazil, the Brasil Para Cristo (Brazil for Christ) Church, and a number of other newer Pentecostal movements in, the total is probably at least between twenty and twenty-five million in the nation. This is a conservative estimate.

There are nearly two million Baptists in Brazil. The major group rejects "charismatic" manifestations, and a smaller "renewed" group accepts them. It is a strong church, making a fine contribution in many ways, but it is not nearly as large as the Assemblies of God.

The Christian Congregation of Brazil was established by Luigi Francesconi, an Italian of Waldensian background who had come to the United States and was one of the founders of the Italian Presbyterian Church in Chicago. He was caught up in the charismatic movement and went to São Paulo in 1910. He began to live and worship in the Brás Presbyterian Church, one of three Presbyterian congregations in the city at the time. It was located in an area where many Italian immigrants lived.

Francesconi began to teach his doctrines, and the church split. He also apparently had some influence in a Roman Catholic community. Out of this grew the Christian Congregation (Congregação Cristã do Brasil—CCB)—a very different kind of Pentecostal church. It has now spread to some adjacent countries, and has a few congregations in the United States. Perhaps because of the Waldensian background, the movement exhibits a stronger sense of social service than other Pentecostals. However, the social service focuses primarily on the church's own members.

The Christian Congregation of Brazil probably has around one-and-a-half million members in Brazil. It does not cooperate with any other Christian ministry except for the Brazilian Bible Society. The CCB builds very large church buildings that attract large congregations.

I once attended a worship service in the mother church in Brás. Similar to the system among the Plymouth Brethren, the elders sat in the front and when one felt led by the Spirit, he got up and preached. The preacher was not selected ahead of time, and no one was trained in any formal sense. The preaching was not very striking. However, the sense of worship, the music, the joy, and the testimonies were impressive. The major part of the service came when people were asked to give their testimonies. There were two microphones on the platform with men on one side and women on the other. They lined up and spoke, one after another.

The testimonies almost all focused on how God had met some significant need or answered prayer.

They were very specific: some spoke of an illness or other problem that was solved. One man had lost his place of business; his lease had run out and he had to find a new place in a good area with decent rent or he was out of business. He prayed and God helped him find a satisfactory location. Another person was traveling to visit relatives and wanted to share his faith and lead these people to Christ, and had done so. That was the nature of the testimonies. They were real and current, telling that God is active here and now in the lives of ordinary people.

If a testimony got a bit negative and the speaker began to criticize someone, the person who was running the PA system simply turned off the power from the microphone. The person soon realized that he or she was talking to the empty air and sat down.

We have already mentioned Pentecostalism in Chile. In recent years, the movement has grown rapidly in Central America as well. Thus, it is no exaggeration to assert that in a number of Latin American nations, there are more practicing Protestants/evangelicals than there are Roman Catholics if the same criteria of "practicing" are used. We can generalize by asserting that three-fourths of all Protestants in Latin America are Pentecostals and/or charismatics.

South Africa

The Pentecostal movement in South Africa has some interesting roots. Andrew Murray was a Dutch Reformed pastor, and a Calvinist heavily influenced by the Holiness Movement. He sought the baptism of the Holy Spirit and took part in revivals in the nineteenth century.

John Alexander Dowie was a second major influence. Born in Edinburgh in 1847, he became a Congregationalist preacher and an evangelist in Australia, and then went to the United States. He began to pray for the sick and founded the town of Zion, Illinois, which became headquarters for the movement he led. (He fell into some aberrations and errors later in his life. This has happened more than once to some Pentecostal leaders, as well as others. We are all in danger of forgetting that we are very human sinners, and need the counsel and help of others.)

In 1908, a group went from Zion to South Africa and founded the Apostolic Faith Mission, which has become one of the largest Pentecostal churches in that nation. David du Plessis, who died recently, was the best-known Pentecostal leader from South Africa. He was, I believe, the most ecumenical Christian of his generation. As a Pentecostal he came to the United States, in the 1940s began to contact the Vatican and the World Council of Churches. He said, "We do not agree theologically on many issues," and made it clear that he would not give up his Pentecostal beliefs and practice. "But," he said, "these are brothers and sisters in Christ; we need to get to know each other and find ways of affirming each other." He was defrocked by the Assemblies of God in the United States, but later finally accepted back.

David and his wife chose to spend the last years of their lives in Pasadena and donate their house and papers to Fuller Seminary. They felt that Fuller would be the place where their twin concerns for Pentecostal spirituality and broad ecumenism would be honored.

When the David du Plessis Center for the Study of Christian Spirituality was inaugurated some years ago, Father Kilian McDonnell, a leader in the Roman Catholic charismatic movement, was the preacher. His sermon centered on Jesus Christ. The participation of a Roman Catholic priest in founding a center named for a Pentecostal perhaps symbolized a new unity, not of structure, but of the Holy Spirit.

There are other movements in South Africa. While none is typical, the one started by Nicholas Bhengu is interesting. He is the son of a Lutheran pastor. In his spiritual and ideological journey, he became a communist, then a Jehovah's Witness, and finally was converted in a Full Gospel church. He returned to the Lutheran Church, but it rejected his experience of sanctification. He approached some white Salvation Army leaders, but was rejected because of his race. (What would William Booth have thought of that?)

Finally, the Assemblies of God in South Africa ordained him.

Bhengu now has his own movement. He is not a traditional Pentecostal; he does not stress "tongues." Rather, he focuses strongly on healing the sick, on Jesus as Redeemer, on the struggle against ancestor worship (an important issue in many parts of Africa), and on baptism in water. He has a negative view of many of the African independent churches, which he feels are not sufficiently Christian.

Other Pentecostal movements are constantly arising in Africa and elsewhere. The Deeper Life Church, which began as a Bible study led by a university professor of mathematics, Dr. William Kimuyu, has spread throughout the nation and to surrounding countries. Its mother church in Lagos, Nigeria, is said to attract over sixty thousand worshippers each Sunday. The Redeemed Christian Church of God, also Nigerian, is said to bring half a million persons to a monthly all-night prayer meeting.

Most observers report that most of the house churches in China are Pentecostal in style and theology.

The most rapidly growing churches in some parts of Asia, including Thailand, Singapore, and Malaysia, are Pentecostal. Although most Christians in Korea are Presbyterians, the largest individual congregation is the Full Gospel Central Church, which claims 750 thousand members.

Contemporary Growth in Latin America

Pentecostalism continues to grow in Latin America. But the growth of the older churches in that tradition seems to have slowed, while newer groups are springing up.

The Jotabeche Church in Chile came out of the work of the American Methodist missionary, Willis Hoover. After he led his church into charismatic manifestations, the Methodist Church divided. The mother church remained very small, but now about fourteen percent of the population is Pentecostal; other Protestants represent perhaps one percent of the population. Today, in most Latin American countries, Pentecostals constitute the largest Protestant groups. If we use the same criteria for "practicing," in terms of church attendance and involvement, there are probably more practicing Pentecostals in Chile, Brazil, and probably a number of other nations, than there are practicing Roman Catholics.

Characteristics

What are some of the unique characteristics of Pentecostal churches and missions today?

1. A literal biblicism: The Pentecostals take the Bible very literally. There is no doubt about the truth of every aspect of Scripture. If this leads to naïveté at times, it can also lead to courageous steps of faith like that of Vingren and Berg, who went to Brazil based on a prophecy.

2. An experiential Christianity: Pentecostals focus on the personality and power of the Holy Spirit. Paul Hiebert has written about the concept of the "excluded middle." A simplified understanding of this concept divides mission concerns into three levels. At the top, we find the great questions of life regarding meaning and purpose. Western evangelical theology has done well in addressing those questions. The bottom level addresses technology: educational, agricultural, and medical. Western missions have made a great contribution at that level. The "middle zone" has to do with the daily crises of life that often have to do with survival in traditional cultures: questions such as, will my wife have sons to take care of me in my old age? Will there be rains so my fields will produce? Will I recover from my illness? If we look at Scripture, we see that the vast majority of miracles had to do with these kinds of issues, including those of Jesus.

The Bible shows us how God has often intervened miraculously in human life at crisis points. The need for divine aid has been the major focus of traditional religions. Pentecostalism recovered that emphasis, which had been forgotten to a significant extent by most Western churches.

Charles Kraft has pointed out that most traditional religions focus more on power than on truth. Furthermore he asserts that Jesus demonstrated his power in order to lead people to the truth, and then, ultimately, to allegiance to him. Thus, prayer for the sick has been an important aspect of Pentecostal life with the faith that God still heals today.

3. A strong Christology: Pentecostals have no doubt at all about who Jesus is. Some have been accused of holding to a Unitarianism of the Holy Spirit. This is not accurate. Classical Pentecostalism has always held a high Christology, even though at times it may have exaggerated the role of the Holy Spirit and certain of His gifts. The overemphasis on the Holy Spirit has been a counterbalance to the lack of focus on his role in much of traditional Protestantism.

4. An urgent missiology: In the early days, Pentecostal missionaries went all over the world, usually on their own, often strictly by faith as we saw in the case of Vingren and Berg. They were called "missionaries of the one-way ticket" for two reasons: most had only enough money for a one-way ticket, and they believed the Lord would return soon so there was no need to plan for the future. Some ended up disillusioned and came home, defeated. Some accomplished amazing things. They had interesting methodologies. In Brazil, for example, the Foursquare Church began with the National Evangelization Crusade. They normally entered a city where there might already be existing Protestant churches, erected a tent, and preached. They advertised healing services. And people came! If you advertise a healing service in the interior of Brazil, often thousands will come. Frequently they were accused of being fakes and charlatans by the existing churches, and often there were exaggerated claims. Yet there conversions of people who would not have entered the existing churches. In a few weeks, the missionaries would leave a group of believers behind. Sometimes those groups would evolve into strong churches; sometimes they would not. However, their urgent missiology took them out to the people. There is evidence that this traditional methodology of the Foursquare

Church is no longer effective in the changing Brazilian society.

5. A belief in supernatural recruitment: Many of the early Pentecostal missionaries went as a response to a direct word from the Lord. They believed that God had spoken to them and told them to go somewhere. Vingren and Berg are good examples, and a church of twelve million came from their faithfulness. When I was in Pattaya, Thailand, in 1980, a veteran Assemblies of God pastor there said that the Assemblies of God in Brazil had fifty-five thousand *obreiros* (workers)—ordained deacons, elders or pastors—at the time. The number must be twice that today. That is about equal to the number of members that the Methodist Church of Brazil has after nearly a century and a half of missionary activity.

6. A tendency towards legalism and sectarianism. We must recognize that often Pentecostals become legalistic in their understanding of the Christian life and judgmental toward other believers. The Pentecostal pastor in Corumba, Brazil, where I worked, was once asked if Presbyterians and Baptists were his brothers. He replied, "Well, maybe they are cousins." However, along with such attitudes we recognize great vitality and dedication. There can be no doubt that this movement has been instrumental in winning millions of the poor of the world to a vital and living faith in Jesus Christ. Pentecostals have communicated the gospel of hope, salvation, and new life to millions who would never be reached by more traditional churches.

7. A lay movement: Similar to the early Methodists, leadership came from the common people. Anyone (but in most cultures only men) who demonstrated gifts and zeal in ministry could become an elder and eventually a pastor. Formal education or the lack thereof was not the issue; gifts and zeal were necessary. Laypersons were expected to participate loudly and enthusiastically in worship, witness, and service. Early in the movement, women played a prominent role. However, their role has decreased in the United States and they were rarely encouraged to use their gifts in Latin America. Nearly half of the early missionaries of the American Assemblies of God were single women. That has decreased to only five percent today. Pentecostal women in South India have had a powerful ministry, but often it has not been recognized by their male counterparts.

8. An emphasis on music and worship: The enthusiastic music and sense of joy and vitality are often the most impressive aspect of Pentecostal worship. Often the sermon has great zeal, but not great content. I was once invited to preach at an anniversary service in a large Assembly of God congregation in the city of Cabo, in Pernambuco, Brazil. The city was built on a hill surrounded by sugar cane plantations as far as one could see. Throughout the area, there were many small Pentecostal congregations. The people walked miles to attend this special service. Most of them were dressed in white. When I arrived, the church was packed with six or seven hundred in attendance. The service had been going on for some time before I arrived. The musical groups stand out in my memory. One group after another came up to play and sing. The performers were gaunt young men, probably with little education—workers in the sugar plantations. They played home-made instruments and sang songs they had written. They were very simple. It was not great music, but it was biblical and it was theirs! The truth and joy were communicated in an idiom that the people could understand. The other thing that stands out in my memory is that after the service, the pastor took me to a room in back of the church where items were available for members in special need, including simple medical supplies and baby clothes.

9. A church of the poor and the dispossessed: While this is changing in the West, Pentecostalism in many parts of the world is still a church of the poor. The issue of "redemption and lift," or upward social mobility, is important and must be faced.

10. An urban movement: Early Pentecostalism arose in cities in the United States and jumped from city to city in Brazil. From the cities, it moved to the countryside. One significant factor in its growth seems to have been the ways in which it ministered to the needs of recent immigrants who had come from the countryside to the urban centers.

11. A focus on church planting and stewardship: These have both been important emphases in the Pentecostal Church.

Pentecostals and Social Change

As a church of the poor, focused primarily on personal salvation and a new lifestyle, Pentecostals have traditionally been indifferent to and even suspicious of programs of social reform. Their focus has been on the 'saving of souls.' They have often instituted programs to help their own people, but have shown little interest in political programs. Much of that indifference in Latin America comes from the disillusionment from the many political figures who have made promises that never materialized.

David Martin, the English sociologist of religion, in his book Tongues of Fire suggests that now, after nearly a century, Pentecostalism might begin follow the trajectory of earlier movements such as Puritanism and the evangelical revivals, and begin to show a stronger social concern. An interesting move in that direction may be seen in the book by Douglas Peterson, Not by Might nor by Power. The author outlined a social ethic for Pentecostals and described a program of primary education in Central America sponsored by the Assemblies of God. It seeks to not only help the thousands of children involved, but also eventually change their societies. The recent book by Miller and Yamamori, *Global Pentecostalism*, describes an impressive number of social ministries.

Contributions and Potential Problems

Among the contributions Pentecostalism has made to the larger Church, a rediscovery of the active role of the Holy Spirit, and the understanding that God is active in human life here and now, are primary. A second contribution is the rediscovery of the gifts of every believer. We have already seen that this is normally a characteristic of renewal movements. Pentecostalism is no exception.

Another factor is the importance of Christian experience. Someone characterized early Pentecostalism as "Christianity on tiptoe": that is, faith that expects God to come in power and do new things in the lives of his people.

Other elements include a sense of joy and praise in worship, and the urgent sense of mission that has taken Pentecostals all over the world, especially to the poor and marginalized, telling them the Good News that they are called to become sons and daughters of God through Jesus Christ.

However, there are dangers in this and every new movement. At the beginning, Pentecostalism was quite counter-cultural in terms of its interracial character (in the United States, at least). But it quickly began to conform to the surrounding culture, and separated white and black believers. In addition, the opportunities for women in ministry decreased greatly.

There is also the danger of too great a focus on experience. At times, Pentecostalism runs the risk of making experience an end in itself, failing to recognize that the purpose of any experience given by God is to lead us into more faithful discipleship. In addition, there is the second danger of falling into a new "legalism of experience": that is, classifying believers according to the kinds of experiences they have had.

The growing institutionalization of the movement and the authoritarianism of many of its leaders is another concern. At times leaders have not been accountable to others and have fallen into grievous sin. This can happen to anyone who feels that his or her experience or prominence puts him or her above the law.

Currently in the United States and at times in Latin America, the "health and wealth" prosperity gospel seeks to make God a means to an end—

the comfort of believers—instead of calling men and women to take up a cross and follow Jesus.

To summarize, I see the following tendencies in most renewal movements throughout history:

1. They begin with a powerful rediscovery of grace, but after a time often move to legalism. We see this in Puritanism as well as Pentecostalism.

2. They begin with an ecumenical spirit, welcoming all believers, but move toward sectarianism that excludes those who are not part of the movement.

3. They begin with the poor, but after a period of upward social mobility aided and stimulated by the movement, become a respectable middle class, out of touch with the poor.

4. They often begin with leaders from the common people, who are chosen because of the recognition of their gifts, but evolve to the point where only those with some level of formal training can be in leadership. We rejoice in the growth of Pentecostal scholarship and excellent theological institutions. However, it raises a question regarding the openness to Pentecostal leadership that arises from the periphery and the poor, who have always brought unique gifts to the Body of Christ.

Statistics

In 1985, Peter Wagner wrote an article for the *Dictionary of Pentecostal and Charismatic Movements*. Much of our statistical data is from his work.

In 1985, David Barrett estimated there were 168,800,000 Pentecostal or Charismatic Christians in the world. He included fifty million Roman Catholic charismatics in this estimate. Most thought his figure was too high. However, Barrett only included ten million Chinese, and many believed that number was too low.

Wagner believed there were around 178,000,000 Christians at that time who considered themselves Pentecostals or charismatics. He included those in African Independent Churches, charismatics in mainline denominations, and in the Roman Catholic Church, as well as Pentecostals. These statistics are not anywhere near precise, but Wagner's point is well taken: that this is the highest rate of growth of any non-military, non-political movement in human history! That is, it is the highest growth rate of any purely voluntary movement.

In 1945, as far as we can tell, there were seven million Pentecostals in the world. In 1955, that had grown to twelve million; in 1965 to twenty-five million; in 1975 to fifty-five million; and in 1985, according to Wagner's estimate, to 178 million. This is remarkable growth, even allowing for some imprecision, possible exaggeration, and data that we simply do not have. This includes probably forty million in China.

Estimates of Pentecostals and Charismatics (in Millions)

1945	1955	1965	1975	1985
7	12	25	55	178

Today we estimate there are between 350 and 400 million Pentecostals and charismatics in the world. This includes most of the house churches in China and most of the new "post-denominational" churches. Clearly, these statistics are imprecise. However, there can be no doubt that they represent the most rapidly growing branch of Christian faith in the world today and indicate lessons we can all learn. To be honest, we must recognize that a significant percentage, but by no means the majority of members of Pentecostal churches, were previously identified with more traditional churches.

Chapter Thirty-One

Our Changing Era in Mission

Introduction

The period since World War II has seen unprecedented changes in the political, economic, technological, religious, and social life of the world. We now live in a post-Western, post-colonial, and post-ideological era. In the West, we also live in a post-Christendom world. In addition, In addition, most Christians we live in a post-denominational period. Therefore, it is a great understatement to say that the historical context in which we engage in mission has changed radically. Our new context brings changed assumptions about the Christian mission.

Until recently, mission went primarily, but never totally, from "the West to the Rest." The West, of course, considered its culture and institutions to be Christian. In European nations there were state-supported, established churches, whether Roman Catholic, Lutheran, Anglican, or Reformed. There was no established church in the United States, but the nation perceived itself to be a Protestant nation. This was illustrated when, at the 1900 Protestant missionary conference held in New York, the President of the United States, along with a former and future President, were speakers.

Furthermore, with some exceptions, mission was carried out by the older denominations that had either come out of the sixteenth-century Reformation or subsequent renewal movements (Methodists, Baptists, Congregationalists). Most missionaries before World War II went either to European colonies or to China. Then, from 1945 to 1989, the Cold War was the dominant political reality, with the world divided into the Communist, non-Communist, and non-aligned blocks. This left the non-aligned world struggling between the two. An additional change in our context, especially since 2001, has been the emergence of resurgent, militant Islam, financed by oil money. In part, this is a reaction against Western influence, secularization, and the perceived loss of traditional values.

While we can never predict how these changes in our context will affect the way we carry out mission, there is no doubt they will open up many new possibilities for the creativity of the Spirit, often through unexpected men and women, and often from the periphery of the established churches. The new context will require new approaches to mission.

The Retreat (?) of the West

The Political Retreat; the End of Colonialism

After 1945, movements for national independence began in the European colonies in Asia and Africa. Within twenty years, scores of former colonies became independent nations. India and Burma (now Myanmar) asked Western missionaries to leave. Other new nations, especially in Africa, were headed by men who had studied in mission-established schools. In some cases, they rebelled against the Christian faith and what they perceived as religious colonialism. At times there were prolonged military struggles before independence came. Angola, Mozambique, and Guinea-Bissau, Portuguese colonies in Africa, were the last to gain independence in 1974.

After 1989, the Eastern European nations that had existed as part of the Soviet empire were freed from its domination. At the same time, a number of nominally Muslim nations, along with Armenia, which was historically Christian, became independent. Several Asian nations became economic powers, among them Japan, South Korea, Taiwan, Singapore, and more recently, China and India. In some of these (Korea, Singapore, China, and now India), the Church has grown rapidly.

Some nations have thrown off Western economic and cultural domination. Cuba and China are examples. However, China, technically Marxist, and the West, especially the United States, are now in a mutually dependent economic relationship. This has made it possible for Christians from the West, as well as South Korea, to live and minister again in China.

Economic Changes

Along with the desire for self-determination in every nation, there is the paradox of a global, increasingly interdependent economy. Multi-national corporations are important and even essential in the global economy. Capital flows in every directions. Japanese and now Korean automobile companies are building plants in the United States. The computers we buy are often manufactured in China with parts made in a number of other countries. Luxury cars (such as Mercedes and BMWs) are assembled in Bangkok for export to other parts of Asia. Today no nation can expect to make economic progress unless it becomes part of this worldwide economy. I am not suggesting that globalization is all positive. There are negative consequences as well, as heavily subsidized agricultural products from the West undercut farmers in Asia, Africa, and Latin America. However, globalization has brought greater prosperity to many in India and China, for example. The hope is that the gains will outstrip its negative aspects. But there can be no

doubt that globalization is here to stay. We must ask what it means for Christian mission.

One result of this global economy is the ease of travel and residence in almost any nation on earth if one has the necessary business and/or technical skills. It has never been as easy for a Christian believer to travel to and live in another part of the world as it is today. In many cases, he or she cannot be called a missionary, but the possibilities of travel and residence in unreached areas are almost without limit.

The rapid growth in technology has revolutionized communication. Email is now almost universally used. CDs can be taken into a "closed" country and used to print instructional materials. Satellite television is beamed to North Africa and Iran with Christian programming. However, this is a two-way street, as militant Islamic programs go into Europe, the United States, and elsewhere.

The insatiable appetite for oil that exists in great quantities primarily in the Muslim-dominated areas continues to be a factor in economic and political life.

The Spread of Western Culture

Much of Western culture, spread through movies, television, etc., is destructive of values that many hold dear. Since in many parts of the world the West is perceived as Christian, these aspects of western culture often reflect very negatively on the Christian faith. This makes it even more important that we seek to be culturally sensitive as we attempt to communicate the Faith.

Nearly all nations are Multi-Ethnic today. African and Asian nations include many different language and cultural groups, often hostile to each other. For example, Indonesia counts 585 languages spoken by its citizens. Donald McGavran said that India speaks 1,600 different languages and uses at least twelve different alphabets. All African nations south of the Sahara include many different tribal groups, often in conflict with each other.

Korea and Japan are the most significant exceptions to this phenomenon, but with the increasing number of immigrants from other Asian nations, they are becoming more diverse. Men, and increasingly women, go to those two nations from the Philippines, Pakistan, and elsewhere, seeking work. Some Christian leaders in the Philippines are attempting to prepare Filipino believers to become tent-making missionaries wherever they take jobs. In Saudi Arabia, some have been persecuted and perhaps even killed for such activity.

Immigration from Asia, Africa, and Latin America to the United States and Western European nations has led to rapid growth of nontraditional populations there and is changing the character of those nations. Those from Latin America are nominally Roman Catholic, but it is estimated that at least fifteen per cent of the Hispanic immigrants in the United States today are Pentecostals. Among Asians in the United States, relatively few are Christians except for the Koreans, where a majority professes Christ. Many of the Africans are also Christians. There are large and growing numbers of Muslims, especially in Europe, where they do not assimilate well into the traditional cultures.

When we add to the mix the growing secularism in Europe and the United States, it is clear that we live in a new missionary situation. The reality is that we are called to be engaged in cross-cultural mission in every part of the world.

These changes have led to increasing tension between traditionalists and secularists in many countries over such issues as sexuality, roles in the family, freedom of speech, and lifestyles. It is becoming more and more difficult to find points of unity in the midst of these struggles. All of these are relevant to our Christian mission.

Missions after World War II

Optimism

In 1942, the Anglican Archbishop, William Temple, said that the "great new fact of our time" was the existence of the Christian Church in nearly every nation on earth. In many places it consisted of a tiny minority, sometimes composed only of expatriates. In five or six nations (Nepal, for

example), there was no church as far as anyone knew. Nevertheless, Temple said, for the first time in history, the Church existed in nearly every nation on earth. This statement reflected optimism even in the midst of war.

After 1945, with the triumph of England and the United States over Germany and Japan, optimism grew. General MacArthur, who ruled Japan for the Allies, called for Christian missionaries to go to that nation. The hope was that Japan would become Christian. Of course, that did not happen.

Men who had served in the U.S. Army and Navy had their horizons greatly expanded as they served overseas. Returning home with an expanded view of the world and its needs, many volunteered for missionary service and several established new organizations. These men established 150 new mission agencies in five years. Greater Europe Mission and Mission Aviation Fellowship are examples.

Pessimism

The optimism soon turned to pessimism when Communism triumphed in China in 1949. Soon Christian institutions were seized, church leaders persecuted and imprisoned, missionaries expelled, and eventually, all churches closed. Even the possession of a Bible was a crime. China had been the greatest of all mission fields, and now, because the Church apparently had disappeared there, the validity of the entire missionary movement was called into question. In addition, the series of independence movements in the former European colonies in Africa and Asia led to the belief that when independence came, missionaries would have to leave and the churches would collapse. When some missionaries were brutally treated and others killed, it added to the pessimism. In 1964, the cover of *Time* magazine pictured Paul Carlson, a missionary physician from the Covenant Church, who was martyred in the Congo. Some missionary women, Protestant and Catholic, were raped.

The secular press seemed to be happy to proclaim the end of the missionary movement, and some of the more liberal Christian organizations suggested that if mission were valid at all, it should focus on social, economic, and political issues.

Back to Optimism

Even as secularists and many church leaders proclaimed the end of the missionary movement, two voices took the opposite view.

Donald McGavran traveled from India to Kenya and across Africa in 1954. He discovered that the African churches were growing, and predicted that the number of Christians in the continent would total three hundred million by the end of the century. He began to say to all who would listen, "We are at the sunrise, not the sunset, of missions." He told me that when he wrote an article giving his conclusions, no one would publish it! However, the work by Ralph Winter, *The 25 Unbelievable Years* (William Carey Library, 1969), underscored this unusual optimism.

In *Christianity in a Revolutionary Age* (New York: Harper, 1958), Latourette asserted that the Christian faith was now more widespread than any religion in history and was continuing to grow. Furthermore, he said, this growth was achieved less through government support and direction than at any time since Constantine. In addition, the faith was becoming more deeply rooted among more different peoples than at any previous time. Moreover, it was having a wider effect on peoples outside Europe than any other religion had ever had.

Latourette also wrote that Christians were coming together in a global fellowship embracing Europeans and non-Europeans as never before. He was referring to the World Council of Churches. Today the WCC is increasingly on the margin of world evangelization, and most of the growing churches are not included in its membership. However, the new "evangelical ecumenism" symbolized by the Lausanne movement and others has become a mission-oriented worldwide fellowship.

The Lausanne Movement

This movement, which began in 1974, has been the primary, but not the only representative of the "new evangelical ecumenism." Billy Graham was instrumental in calling for the Berlin Congress on Evangelism, held in 1966. It was primarily moti-

vational and inspirational in nature. The Lausanne Congress went more deeply into substantive theological and missiological issues. In a key address, Ralph Winter presented the "unreached peoples" concept. It introduced the thought of Donald MacGavran and the Fuller School of World Mission and represented a major shift in mission thinking for many. It changed the focus in mission from geography to culture, from "foreign" to "cross-cultural" mission. Of course the concept was not totally new, but the address was important in advancing missiological thought.

The second major achievement was the Lausanne Covenant, written primarily by John Stott. The document clearly stated evangelical convictions about the Gospel and the mission of the Church, and included a strong biblical balance between evangelism and social concerns. Nearly all evangelical Christians could unite around the statement.

The third achievement was the establishment of the Lausanne Committee for World Evangelization (LCWE). The LCWE did not intend to become an evangelical alternative to the WCC. Rather, it sought to work with smaller national or regional groups to stimulate world evangelization. Subsequent meetings were held in Thailand in 1980, in Manila, in 1989, and again in Thailand 2004.

For a number of years, up to 2000, the AD2000 movement, led by Luis Bush of Argentina, sought to see churches planted in every people group by that year. While it did not succeed in its goal, it was a further stimulus to evangelization. Other international and regional meetings focusing on evangelization have been held during the last few decades.

We have already discussed some of the growth of the Church around the world in previous chapters. According to David Barrett, Africa was three percent Christian in 1900, twenty-eight percent Christian in 1970, and forty-six percent Christian in 2000. In Latin America, the evangelical movement is growing twice as rapidly as the population. The remarkable growth of the Church in China is well known. Not as well known is the growth among other groups such as the 'Dalits' ("untouchables") in India.

Hence it is now recognized that two-thirds of all active Christians in the world now live in Asia, Africa, and Latin America. That compares with ten percent in 1900, and one percent in 1800.

Critical Issues

There are a number of critical issues to be faced if the growing churches around the world (and in the West) are to be healthy, vital fellowships, effective both in evangelization and in bringing transformation to their cultures.

One of the greatest needs is to encourage growth toward maturity in the Christian life. Many movements have emphasized evangelism without an equal concern for growth in discipleship. Admittedly, this is a difficult challenge. Often resources and personnel are scarce. A major problem is that the Gospel has often been presented as the gift of personal salvation without the corresponding call to discipleship. Clearly, something was tragically wrong when many Christians were involved in carrying out the genocide in Rwanda, and when HIV/AIDS is a scourge among Christians as well as non-believers in Africa.

A second major issue is the need for appropriate methods of selecting and training leaders. Traditional institutional methods should continue to be part of the mix, but obviously they are not adequate by themselves. One estimate is that there are over three million functional pastors in the world who have no formal biblical or theological training. Many have no book except the Bible. Some are even illiterate. However, many of them are doing the cutting edge work of evangelism among the poor and marginalized. Short-term intensive courses, extension programs, and other models must be used. They need to be appropriate to the context. If growing churches are led by men and women with little or no biblical understanding except a few salvation passages, there are the dangers of superficial discipleship, legalism, authoritarianism, and a quick lapse into nominalism.

A third question is our unity as members of the Body of Christ. How are we to manifest that unity? Jesus' prayer in John 17 was that his followers would be one so that the world might believe. This has been a favorite passage of the conciliar ecumenical movement, which, unfortunately, now shows little interest in world evangelization. However, evangelicals have often ignored this call for unity by our Lord. Yet there is growing evidence that where the Gospel is communicated by partnerships of believers from different mission groups, denominational traditions, and cultures, we see greater effectiveness.

Another issue is the nature and process of indigenization. The nineteenth-century definition of Venn and Anderson—"self-supporting, self-governing, and self-propagating"—was a beginning, but far from adequate. It had nothing to say about styles of worship, music, which theological and social issues the Gospel should address, or leadership styles. Sometimes missionaries have established a church in a new people group, with the goal of helping it to become indigenous. However, Alan Tippet said that churches can and should be born indigenous. This is a significant challenge.

There are many other issues to be addressed beyond evangelism. They include the relationship of the Church to social issues within and outside of its fellowship. These include poverty, HIV/AIDS and its victims, ethnic rivalries and tribalism, racism, and the oppression of women and minority groups that still exists in many cultures.

Certainly we must understand that the Gospel manifests a concern for the poorest of the poor and the marginalized, the kind of people to whom Jesus especially reached out.

Churches in every culture need to discover how they are called to be involved in change on both the personal, and, eventually, on the societal level.

To summarize, the last fifty or sixty years have seen a radically changed world, the context in which we are called to mission. Many of the older patterns are no longer relevant or even possible. On the other hand, the Church has grown enormously in the former "mission fields" since 1945. We are seeing new personnel as well as new approaches to mission today. The Christian mission remains the same, but our context is very different from that of Ziegenbalg, Carey, or Hudson Taylor. That fact calls us to sensitivity to each culture, hard thinking, and openness to the creativity of the Holy Spirit.

Chapter Thirty-Two

New Personnel in Mission

Introduction

We have already looked at the great changes in our historical context after 1945, and the second major shift in 1989 with the end of the Soviet Union and Communism in Europe.

Significant changes also occurred in the older "mainline" churches after the middle of the twentieth century. Tragically, those changes led to a great decline in their involvement in world mission. The first change was theological, as creeping universalism began to undercut the sense of urgency about evangelization. An examination of the documents produced for the various WCC meetings indicated the growing focus on social, political, and economic issues. That was often reflected in the policies of the member churches. A second factor was structural. Denominational boards that had been focused on world mission were often absorbed into broader agencies in which mission was only one of a number of agendas. Many of the earlier leaders of denominational boards—Robert E. Speer, the Presbyterian, for example—had been involved in the Student Volunteer Movement. Often their successors were church officials with little or no understanding of, or commitment to, mission. Some denominations formed "program agencies" in which mission was only one program among many. In addition, many or most of the leaders of the older denominations continued to be affected by the post-1949 pessimism. They failed to see the new possibilities in mission and the growth in non-traditional churches around the world.

As we have already noted, another important development has been the rapid growth of the Pentecostal/charismatic movement in the last sixty years. Indications are that the movement continues to grow.

It is impossible to keep up with the numbers, but there is little doubt that more new mission structures have arisen in the United States in the last sixty years than any comparable period in history. And an equal or greater number has been created in the Majority world.

The most remarkable development has been the growth of churches in Asia, Africa, and Latin America. At the same time they have become independent from the Western mission agencies that originally established them. As long as Western missionaries were dominant, it was easier to believe that the word "missionary" necessarily meant an expatriate, a westerner. However, with independence they often began to realize that every church was called to mission beyond its geographical and cultural boundaries.

Because of these factors, a massive change has taken place in the churches, agencies, and personnel involved in world mission.

Statistics and Trends

John R. Mott of the SVM called for fifty thousand missionaries in 1900. However, by 1915, the number sent from the United States was less than ninety-five hundred. At that time seventy-five per cent of the American missionaries were sent by agencies of the older "mainline" churches. Those churches had roots primarily in the Protestant Reformation modified by Pietism, and the evangelical revivals. They included, of course, Methodists and Baptists. But by the end of the twentieth century, only five percent of American missionaries were sent by the more traditional, "mainline" denominations.

The statistics for the second half of the twentieth century tell the story.

nominations and formed new mission boards. The Presbyterian Church of America (PCA) separated from the Presbyterian Church, USA (PCUSA) in the 1970s. The three Presbyterian groups that make up the present PCUSA had approximately 2700 missionaries in the 1920s, but that number has now fallen to less than 200. The much smaller PCA currently has 461. The American Baptist Board, formed in 1814 to support the Judsons in Burma, now has about 120 missionaries. The Conservative Baptist Mission Society, now known as World Venture, which split off in the early 1940s, now has around 480

Denomination	1918	1935	1952	1968	1980	1996
"Mainline" Missions	8900	7400	8800	8700	4000	2600
Seventh Day Adventists	700	1200	1100	1500	1000	700
Interdenominational Foreign Mission Association[1]	800	900	3000	5700	5800	5700
Evangelical Foreign Missions Association[2]	400	1700	2100	6800	8400	10.800
Independent or unaffiliated[3]	-	900	3600	11,600	16,400	23,800
Total	10.800	12,100	11.600	34,300	35,600	43,600

[1]Conservative groups, not including Pentecostals or charismatics

[2] Evangelicals including Pentecostals. Established in 1945. The earlier figures include agencies that became members after it was organized.

[3]Includes Southern Baptists and newer Charismatic groups.

(Paul E. Pierson, "The Rise of Christian Mission & Relief Agencies," The Influence of Faith, Abrams and Eliot, eds. [New York: Rowman & Littlefield], 160.

The shift has been dramatic. Even though a significant number of missionaries still come from the older churches, most no longer serve under their own denominational structures. Reasons are the lack of opportunity, theological differences, or the perception that the newer agencies are more creative and accepting of new initiatives and methodologies. It is clear that now, the great majority of personnel come from Evangelicals within the older denominations, the Southern Baptists, the newer evangelical groups, and Pentecostals and charismatics.

In a number of cases, new, more conservative groups have separated from their parent de-

(Statistics from John A. Siewert and Dotsey Welliver, eds. Mission Handbook, U.S. and Canadian Christian ministries Overseas, 2001-2003, 18th ed. Wheaton, Ill. Evangelism and Missions Information Service, 2000).

Other examples could be cited, but the trend is clear. The more liberal groups are sending fewer and fewer personnel overseas. The first American mission board, the ABCFM, became the sending agency of the United Church of Christ, formerly the Congregational churches. Eventually it merged with the mission board of the Disciples of Christ. The last Mission Handbook indicated that the combined boards supported fifteen career missionaries overseas.

The short-term mission phenomenon has grown so much that no one can keep up with the statistics. "Short-term" can mean anything from a week to a year. Participants may build houses, teach English in China or Vietnam, or offer medical services. Alternatively, they may simply observe ministries of partner institutions in order to gain a greater understanding of their ministries. Short-term missions have both positive and negative aspects. They can easily become religious tourism, but, if well managed, can be a significant growing experience for the participants and their churches. There are many cases where such experiences have led churches as well as individuals to deeper commitment, broader vision, and significant partnerships with churches and institutions overseas.

New Movements from the West

Scores, if not hundreds, of new mission agencies have been established since 1945. Some are small and may not survive, while others are growing rapidly. Some examples follow.

Pioneers was established in 1982 as "a sending agency of evangelical tradition engaged in church planting, evangelism, and mobilization for mission." In 1996, it had 220 career personnel overseas. Today it numbers one thousand, coming from twenty different countries and serving in over fifty nations. It is both multi-denominational and multi-cultural. This is a positive and growing pattern.

Campus Crusade for Christ was established in 1951. By 1996, it had 665 persons serving in 137 countries. Navigators, established in the 1940s, works especially among students. Youth With a Mission, established in the 1960s, sends out over one hundred thousand short-term missionaries each year and now numbers around six thousand career personnel. Over half are non-Western. Operation Mobilization operates in a similar manner.

Other mission agencies have often spun off new structures, usually with their blessing, to focus on specific ministries. OC International (formerly Overseas Crusades) is the parent of the "Discipling a Whole Nation" movement as well as Harvest Evangelism. The Latin America Mission gave birth to Christ for the City, a growing mission focusing on cities, first in Latin America and now elsewhere.

Local churches also act as sending agencies. New movements often send missionaries to plant their style of churches in other nations. The Vineyard is one example. Many independent charismatic churches are doing the same.

Thus, it is clear that a massive shift has taken place in the American missionary movement during the twentieth century, especially since 1945. The shift represented a theological change, from an earlier broad-based evangelicalism that began to move toward theological liberalism, to groups that were conservative evangelical, Pentecostal or charismatic, and even fundamentalist. Among the implications of the change was a greater focus on church planting and less on the establishment of institutions such as schools and hospitals. The newer movements may show a greater understanding of indigenization. However, there is also the danger of focusing on personal salvation alone with a failure to seek to understand the implications of the gospel for the various cultures.

Cross-Cultural Missions from Asia, Africa, and Latin America

Early Non-Western Cross-Cultural Mission
We begin with a theological perspective. Every church is called to mission, both within its own culture and beyond it. Throughout this book, we have assumed that mission involved taking the Gospel beyond one's own culture or geographical area. We have also assumed that mission focused first on communicating the Good News of Jesus Christ, calling men and women to believe in him and become his disciples, and be gathered in worshipping, nurturing, witnessing, serving communities called churches. Those churches should not look the same in every culture. We also recognize that in some situations, verbal proclamation may not be the first step. The goal, whether through

ministries of compassion or the spoken word, is always to bring people to faith in Christ.

With this perspective in mind, we can assert that no church is genuinely indigenous until it becomes missional: that is, until it engages in mission in one form or another.

We recognize that cross-cultural mission from areas other than the West is not entirely new. Latourette called the nineteenth-century spread of Christianity among the Pacific islanders one of the most spectacular events in church history. Our missionary biographies tell of a number of Western missionaries who were killed and sometimes eaten by cannibals. However, they do not tell the stories of the much greater number of Melanesians who gave their lives in a similar fashion. In the 1820s, they began to sail in their long canoes to distant islands to spread the Gospel. Often they suffered terribly. Some were martyred, but they went with great heroism and effectiveness.

A chapel in the Pacific Theological College in Fiji is dedicated to those missionaries. It represents over a thousand men who, with their wives, went to other islands as missionaries. The Methodist Church of Fiji sent 269 couples; the Congregational Church of Samoa send 209; 197 went from the Cook Islands; 139 went from the Solomons. Men from Tonga, who had previously gone on voyages of plunder, now went with the Gospel!

In 1833, the Karens in Burma began to send evangelists to other tribal groups. The evangelists had to learn new languages. They went to Chins and Kachins, who then went to Rawangs in the north. When the Presbyterian Church of Korea ordained its first seven pastors in 1907, one was sent to Cheju Island as a missionary. Within a few years, Koreans were ministering in China and Siberia as well. In 1910, the Brazilian Presbyterians sent a missionary to their mother country, Portugal. These are only a few examples of early non-Western mission.

Contemporary Non-Western Cross-Cultural Mission

However, the great new fact of our time is the explosive growth of cross-cultural mission com-

ing out of Asia, Africa, and Latin America. Three research projects done at Fuller are of interest. The first, done in 1972, concluded that there were thirty-four hundred non-Western cross-cultural missionaries at work in the world. The second, in 1980, estimated the number to be thirteen thousand (L. Keyes, *The Last Age of Mission* [Pasadena: William Carey Library, 1983], 65). The third, in 1988, found the number had grown to 35,924 (L. Pate, *From Every People* [Monrovia, California: MARC, 1989], 17). Today it is almost impossible to do the research necessary to come up with a firm number. The situation is changing so much that any research soon becomes outdated, but the number is large and growing. Dr. Ki Ho Park of Fuller Seminary faculty asserts that the Korean churches have deployed at least sixteen thousand missionaries around the world, serving in as many as 150 countries. In 2002 the Secretary of the India Mission Association in said that from 1972 to 1999 the number of Indian cross-cultural missionaries increased from 543 to 20,000; the number of mission agencies from twenty-six to three hundred. The number of both is still growing. Most of them work within India, ministering to peoples of different languages and cultures. Some also work in other nations. Many go from south India to the north, while the Nagas and Mizos in northeastern India have sent a large number of evangelists to other parts of the country and into adjacent nations, as well. A number of Indian Christians also work in Bible translation. Now there is a complete Bible in fifty-three Indian languages, and New Testaments in an additional forty-two (from a personal conversation with P. E. Pierson).

The definition of "crosscultural mission" is not always precise. We are not speaking only of those who leave their countries of origin and go to another. The word "mission" in this context means crossing a significant cultural and/or linguistic barrier, but not necessarily a geographical one, in order to communicate the Gospel.

I do not think it an exaggeration to assert that the total number of non-Western cross-cultural missionaries at work today exceeds 125,000.

One model consists of cross-cultural mission within the mission society's own nation. The Friends Missionary Prayer Band (FMPB) in India is an example. The group emerged out of a vital church in Madras over forty years ago. The pastor was Dr. Sam Kamaleson, who later became a Vice President of World Vision. Believers came together to pray for each other, but also began to pray for the evangelization of their nation. As they formed into bands for prayer, they began to seek God's guidance. He led them to individuals within the groups who volunteered to go to other areas of the country to evangelize. Those who stayed behind committed themselves to support their missionary financially and by prayer. The movement spread to other churches and grew. The prayer bands were organized into a loose confederation so there was some accountability.

Thus, everyone in the prayer band was committed to fulfilling the task, whether he or she stayed home, prayed, and gave, or went out as a missionary. All were committed to the same task. Their goal was to send workers to unreached areas of India. They identified 220 "headquarter" cities in other areas of India, and adopted the goal of placing at least two workers in each one. By the end of the century, the FMPB counted 611 missionaries working in 187 fields in twenty states with 165 people groups. They had planted 3312 churches. The total number of believers was 214 thousand.

The group has remained totally Indian and refused to accept funding from outside the nation. This has avoided any dependency on the West and blunted any accusation that its work is an imposition of a foreign religion on Indians.

The Indian Evangelical Mission (IEM) is somewhat similar. People of various denominations within India support the workers. Funds and prayer support come from individuals, families, and local churches that remain in close contact with the workers. While the large denominations (the Church of South India and the Church of North India) do not support them officially, many local churches and believers do. Currently, the IEM has over 150 supporting churches in ad-

dition to prayer bands, and counts nearly three hundred missionaries. Converts are formed into churches and affiliated with whatever denomination is strong in the area.

The IEM receives financial support from Indian Christians overseas, but their gifts are used only for special projects and capital expenditures. The Mission has sent five couples outside of India, who work in Thailand with OMF, in the Middle East with INTERSERVE, and minister to Tamils in England.

A common pattern consists of denominational mission boards that send workers outside their own country: for example, Brazilian Baptists work in Bolivia, Brazilian Presbyterians in Paraguay, and Korean Presbyterians in many countries. Along with the denominational agencies, there is a growing number of multi-denominational agencies. They are probably the most rapidly growing mission groups.

Many Western-based societies are now multinational. Among them are Wycliffe and OMF (the former China Inland Mission, which now has a man of Chinese descent as its President). At least half of the personnel of Christ for the City are Latin American.

In some cases, Western and non-Western agencies cooperate. The Evangelical Missionary Society (EMS) of Nigeria was organized by the Evangelical Church of West Africa (ECWA). The church came out of the missionary work of SIM, formerly the Sudan Interior Mission. The EMS supports over six hundred missionaries, mainly among unreached peoples of Nigeria but also in adjacent countries. SIM cooperates financially with EMS in some special projects, but the ongoing work, recruitment, and training are all supported by the Nigerian church.

There is a growing tentmaker movement from a number of countries. The Filipino and Ethiopian churches, among others, are encouraging this form of mission. When Christians go as workers from impoverished countries to the Middle East, there are special opportunities for this kind of mission. However, it is not without danger.

New patterns of mission are constantly being created, or old patterns rediscovered. Missionaries from Nigeria and other African nations are planting churches in Europe and the United States. It is said that Nigerians pastor the largest churches in London, Paris, and Kiev. They often begin with other African immigrants and then reach out to the more traditional populations.

Another recent development is the "Back to Jerusalem" movement of some of the house church networks in China. The goal is ambitious, but there can be little doubt that a large number of Chinese Christians will venture west through central Asia to share the Gospel, undoubtedly in situations of great danger.

In 1987, over twenty-seven hundred delegates met in São Paulo, Brazil. Most were from Latin America, Hispanic North America, Spain, and Portugal, with observers from thirty-three countries. For the first time in history Latin American and Hispanic churches met on their own initiative to discuss the fulfillment of the Great Commission. It initiated an ongoing process and offices were established in Quito and São Paulo, seeking to mobilize one thousand Latin American churches for mission.

An Analysis of the Positive and Negative Aspects of New Movements

I believe we can say without doubt that the Christian message is now being communicated by more men and women coming from more diverse racial, cultural, and national groups than any other message in history. In addition, it is being heard by more diverse racial and cultural groups than any other. The importance of this can scarcely be overestimated. While this has many positive aspects, there are concerns as well.

The Positive Contributions of the New Movements

1. Obviously, there is a great advantage in the sheer numbers involved. Over the last fifty years, the total Christian missionary force has probably quadrupled. It has grown more rapidly, proportionately, than the world population.

2. The internationalization of the faith works against the perception that Christianity is "Western." We can understand this perception. The modern missionary movement went from Europe and North America to the rest of the world. It accompanied Western colonialism, and at times colonial governments supported its institutions. The churches assumed the Western cultural forms brought by the missionaries. Today, while many non-Western Christians continue to worship and structure their churches using Western forms, we are moving into an era when both churches and missions are more free to discover new forms more suited to their cultures. None of us can fully foresee what this will mean, but there are already some interesting examples of contextualization taking place in Asia and Africa.

3. In many cases, non-Western missionaries will encounter lower cultural and political barriers. An Asian in India, for example, will not be perceived as one associated with colonialism. There is evidence that Latin Americans are more accepted in Islamic culture than Europeans or Americans.

4. Missionaries from Asia and Africa do not come from cultures that historically have been Christian. They are accustomed to living in pluralistic societies and recognize that the Church is always in a missionary situation.

5. The theology of non-Western churches, with rare exceptions, is solidly evangelical. Often they show greater spiritual vitality and evangelistic zeal. In many cases, their prayer life is deeper and they expect God to work with power.

6. Often, but not always, their lifestyle is closer to that of the people to whom they go. Often, because of necessity, they live much closer to the economic level of the people.

7. In some cases they are more free to experiment with new patterns of church life and mission.

Possible Negative Factors

1. One danger is the feeling on the part of some that because they are not from the West, they

will automatically avoid the mistakes of earlier missionaries. Thus, they can fall into the error of thinking they do not need to learn from the past. For example, there is evidence that some Korean missionaries have forgotten the lessons of the Nevius Plan, which was important in building the strength of the early Korean church. The concept was that no church would have buildings, leaderships, or structures until they could support them. Thus, it was a genuinely indigenous church from the very beginning. However, with the great prosperity in Korea today, some Korean missionaries seem to be taking in significant funds and building institutions that the local believers are unable to support.

2. At times the newer groups become fiercely competitive, seeking to affirm their validity, and failing to cooperate with existing churches or missions.

3. In many cases, the missionaries do not receive adequate training. This can often lead to ineffectiveness and disillusionment.

4. Financial support is often inadequate. Missionaries are sent with great enthusiasm, but adequate support does not continue. Too many return home too soon, due to inadequate support and inadequate training.

5. Non-Western missionaries can be just as culture-bound as earlier Westerners were. Brazilian Baptists in Bolivia were once accused of "acting like North Americans." Dr. Ki Ho Park observed that Koreans in the Philippines expected Filipino believers to do everything the Korean way.

In conclusion, these newer movements tend to put greater focus on evangelism and less on medical and educational institutions. This is probably the result of their understanding of the missionary task as well as the changing needs in many areas. However, as time goes by and churches grow, there is evidence that the concern for social needs will grow along with the focus on evangelism.

Many of the newer missions are more charismatic, that is, more open to power encounter and the unusual works of the Holy Spirit. This attitude is much closer to the worldview of most of the unreached peoples in the world.

Finally, they should prove to be more open to greater flexibility in methods of leadership selection and training in keeping with the gifts of their laypersons.

I believe it is no exaggeration to say that we have entered the most creative and productive period of mission in history. This is not to ignore the problems, obstacles, and dangers. There will be defeats and disappointments. But there can be no doubt that the worldwide church and missionary movement is growing as never before.

Chapter Thirty-Three

New Places and Patterns in Mission

Introduction

I have spoken earlier of two "ecumenical" movements today. We use the term here as defined by the 1989 Manila Congress of the Lausanne Committee: "The whole Church taking the whole Gospel to the whole world." This is a goal to which we all aspire. Note that this definition does not speak primarily of the structure of mission, but rather its goal. This is important to keep in mind. Structures exist to move us toward the achievement of goals, but all too often, the maintenance of structures becomes an end in itself, while the goal is forgotten.

The two major ecumenical streams in the world today are the World Council of Churches and the Lausanne Committee for World Evangelization (LCWE). The WCC is composed, for the most part, of the older denominations of Europe and the United States plus the Orthodox family of churches. Roman Catholics are observers but not members. A number of churches from Asia and Africa are also members. In recent years, the WCC has focused primarily on social, economic, and political issues. Often it has been criticized for taking a leftist stance on such questions. Theologically, it deals primarily with sixteenth-century issues: the doctrine of the Church, its ministry, and the sacraments. An important question for some is whether Lutherans, Reformed, and Anglicans can all take Communion together. For Anglicans and Orthodox, church structure and the understanding of the priesthood are believed to be essential aspects of the true Church. Such issues are not seen as relevant by the great majority of growing churches in the world.

The second stream, symbolized but not limited to the LCWE, is based on certain theological assumptions held in common. They include the historical emphases of the evangelical movements that gave birth to the modern missionary movement: the authority of Scripture, a high Christology, the necessity of conversion and the importance of the Christian life, justification by faith alone, the role of the Holy Spirit, the importance of evangelism and mission, and the understanding that the Church is central in God's work in history. This stream is much more pragmatic and flexible on issues of leadership, church structure, and the sacrament, but more conservative theologically.

The evangelical stream is more task-oriented. That is, its major focus is world evangelization: the desire that people of every race, language, and culture have an opportunity to hear and respond to the Gospel in culturally relevant ways.

The Manila conference of the LCWE in 1989 was perhaps the most representative Christian gathering yet seen. Men and women from 150 nations came together. They came from the older "mainline" churches, newer evangelical denominations in the West, and churches established by the older faith missions (such as the evangelical church of West Africa, established by SIM). There were classical Pentecostals, and newer charismatic groups. One emotional moment came when fifty or sixty men and women from the Soviet Union came in one evening. They had been delayed, but arrived in the middle of the conference. Their entrance was a powerful symbol of our changing world. As they entered four thousand men and women stood, cheered, and wept for joy!

The AD2000 movement was seen by some as the functional successor of the LCWE. However, as its name implied, it ceased to exist in 2000, but not without some accomplishments. Two men from the West, then a Chinese pastor (Leighton Ford, Tom Houston, and Thomas Wang) were the primary leaders of LCWE. Luis Bush from Argentina led AD2000. That is symbolic of some of the changes in the world Christian movement.

A good example of the goals of the evangelical stream can be seen in the statement of the AD2000 meeting in Panama, 1996:

> We, the participants of this meeting of leaders of different denominations, representing diverse parts of the Body of Christ, being conscious of the Great Commission, declare…We came to Panama with the profound conviction that the Holy Spirit is directing His church in this juncture of history to unite our energies to accelerate the fulfillment of the proclamation of the Gospel to all peoples, tribes, languages, and nations of the world. And here, having prayed together, shared in fellowship… and having heard about the efforts to network, the desire for unity…we believe the Holy Spirit is guiding us…to act as one body, expressed in many forms through the denominations and other Christian organizations.

> We…declare our commitment to establish 'a church for every people and the gospel for every person by the year 2000,' to fulfill this objective we call on every component of the Body of Christ to freely give our hands, hearts, minds, and souls in the great cause of Jesus Christ and to pray for and cooperate with others to present the gospel to the unreached, while respecting each other's doctrinal convictions.

> We will encourage our denominations and fellowships:

> 1. To prioritize focus on peoples who do not have access to the Gospel, most of whom are located in the area known as the 10/40 window.

> 2. To call our people to pray, acknowledging prayer as the central strategy.

> 3. To encourage churches to take part in national initiatives, to cooperate with the AD2000 movement networks where they exist, and to encourage the development of national initiatives where they do not exist.

> 4. To establish intercontinental fellowship links in order to share resources, ministries, strategies, objectives, and goals to avoid duplication of efforts and facilitate the acceleration of the remaining task.

> 5. To search for ways to accelerate the missionary efforts from our denominations…and the recruitment of a new missionary force directed toward the unreached.

> 6. To establish bridges of constant communication in order to support each other as one body in our common goal to fulfill the Great Commission.

> 7. We make this commitment for the greater glory of our Savior Jesus Christ and for the extension of His Kingdom among the millions who have not yet heard the Gospel.

After decades in which many conservative evangelical groups have often ignored each other, this statement indicates a new hope for greater unity of focus and cooperation. Historically, movements of structural unity have not produced a greater focus on mission. Indeed, the opposite has often been the case. But conservative evangelical groups have all too often gone their own ways, working in isolation from other Christian groups. The new evangelical ecumenism represented by the LCWE and AD2000 points in a new and positive direction. Even though the AD2000 movement did not achieve its goal, it did stimulate greater missionary effort.

Examples of New Places in Mission

The comparison of the context for mission before and after 1989 is striking. We can consider only a few of the new areas now open to various forms of Christian mission.

Russia and the Commonwealth of Independent States (formerly the Soviet Union)

Russia again has defined itself as Orthodox. After 1989, a large number of people returned to the Orthodox Church. But to an evangelical, it is clear that Russian Orthodoxy is seriously in need of renewal. The Scripture and liturgy are in Old Church Slavonic, and attempts to put them in modern Russian have been met with resistance by the leadership. Priests who are more evangelical, who favor religious liberty, and who have tried forming small groups have met resistance. Orthodoxy is strongly identified with Russian nationalism, but the Church was very subservient to the Communist regime.

Baptist and Pentecostal churches have existed in Russia for decades, but many have a "ghetto mentality" and have great difficulty reaching and accepting secularized people from outside of their own traditions.

Some new churches have been established, many by Koreans. They have also started seminaries. One major issue is how these new churches might seek to relate positively to the older Baptist and Pentecostal churches, and, with much more difficulty, to the Orthodox Church and culture. Since the Orthodox Church considers itself to be the only true church, this presents a great problem. It is important to know that the Russian Church considers Moscow "the third Rome." Underlying that concept is the belief that Rome (Italy) was the first center of the Church, Constantinople, the second, and, with the fall of that city, Moscow became the center of the universal Church. Added to this is the fact that the Orthodox Church, unlike the Roman Church, has never had to confront anything like the Protestant Reformation.

The former Soviet republics such as Uzbekistan and Kazakhstan have nominally Muslim majorities, and often Christians face restrictions within them. One issue for missionaries is whether to concentrate on the Russian-speaking or the traditional indigenous populations in these countries. There are opportunities for evangelism and church planting, but it appears they should be post-denominational, open to all the gifts, and must take power encounter seriously.

I knew of one team in Kazakhstan composed of personnel from Pioneers from England and the United States, charismatic Baptists from Singapore, and a couple from the very conservative Presbyterian Church of America. The team has had trouble maintaining its unity.

A number of Koreans are working in this area of the world. One Korean missionary reported in 2003 that his church in Almaty, Kazakhstan had grown to six thousand people in attendance, with 950 cell groups over a twelve-year period. The Church included both local Russians and Kazakhs. The Alpha course has been an essential part of its methodology. As people, many of them university students, come to faith, they establish deep relationships with both Christians and non-Christians, and fit into home cell groups. Lay leaders have penetrated into their workplaces and opened Alpha courses where they lived. The Church plans to send church planting teams in both directions along the silk route.

The largest church in the Ukraine numbers 25,000 and is located in Kiev. The pastor is a Nigerian and the church has given leadership in social issues. During the last national election, when it appeared that forces of reaction would frustrate the popular vote for a more democratic candidate, members of the church lined the streets, demanding an honest election. The effectiveness of their protest brought great prestige to the church.

Eastern Europe

Post-Communist societies are characterized by a lack of trust. The previous system taught people never to trust anyone. There are strong evangelical churches in some areas: the Baptists in Romania, for example. There are also traditional Reformed and Lutheran churches with good theology but often rigid structures. The Orthodox churches are dominant and often exhibit a strong sense of ethnic and nationalist identity. Most see themselves as the only true church.

How are we to engage in mission in such a context? I observed an excellent example in Novi Sad, Serbia, when I visited Dr. and Mrs. Dimitri Popadic. They had served previously in both Serbia and Macedonia, where they planted several churches. While in Macedonia, Dimitri, a Pentecostal, had formed a friendship with the local Orthodox Archbishop as they worked together in the Bible Society. After finishing his Ph. D. at Fuller, Dimitri and his wife Cveta went to Novi Sad, where they were asked to re-open a former Baptist Bible college. They accepted, with the stipulation that it become multi-denominational and eventually offer a Master's degree. When I visited, the school had over two hundred students from seventeen denominations, most of whom studied by extension. It was the largest Protestant theological institution in Serbia, and reached out to the Roma people (often referred to as "gypsies") as well as the majority population. On Sunday we worshipped in an Orthodox church in Belgrade, whose priest was Dean of the Orthodox seminary. Afterwards, we spent two hours in conversation with him and some of his people and then were hosted at lunch. I asked Dimitri about the content of the liturgy, and he replied that it was very biblical, rehearsing the history of salvation. This was a unique experience in ecumenical relationships. A Pentecostal couple took us to meet and worship with an Orthodox leader! Because we were outsiders, Dimitri felt it was easier to take such a step.

There are two lessons here. We find a model of leadership training that is multi-denominational and flexible, with both residential and extension students. And we see that friendship must be the first step toward better relationships between Protestants and Orthodox.

Western Cities

Western cities are increasingly multi-ethnic. Almost every large Western city has over one hundred different language-ethnic groups in its population. Some of the newer groups have many Christians among them, and immediately start churches. Others come from cultures where there are few Christians or even none. Thus, mission in these cities requires careful research. For example, it was recently reported that in Boston, while many of the older traditional churches have been dying, there are many new congregations among immigrant groups. The same is true in New York City. In some cases, multi-ethnic churches are being formed, but most focus on a particular group.

A significant development is the number of African missionaries going to Europe and the United States, often planting their own indigenous churches. The Redeemed Church of Christ from Nigeria is ardently missionary, and is planting churches in a number of nations.

An important issue we must face in the West is the push toward religious relativism in our pluralistic and secularized societies. We affirm the positive value of religious liberty, but religious relativism and the 'post-modern' mindset looks on the evangelical desire for conversion to Christ as intolerant and arrogant. We are called to humility and sensitivity even as we continue to call men and women of every *ethne* to follow Christ.

Nominal Christians or "Post-Christian" People in the Secular West

When he returned from India to England, Leslie Newbigin found that it was harder to talk about the Gospel with an ordinary Englishman than with a person in India. He said that the secular West might be the most difficult mission field in the world! George Hunter speaks of people with "no Christian memory." They have little or no knowledge of the Christian faith. They may think they know what the Gospel is, and believe they have tried and rejected it. However, in reality, usually they have turned their backs on some tragic distortion of the Christian message. This too, calls for new forms of mission.

The Muslim World

This, of course, is a vast subject and the focus of much attention, especially since September 11, 2001. However, I want to mention some important developments.

Islamic fundamentalism is growing. There are a number of reasons for this. One seems to be the perception that it is the destiny of Islam in its strictest form to rule the world, and that the West is the major obstacle to that goal. Then there is a legitimate reaction against what is perceived, often correctly, as the decadence of Western culture, which, for most Muslims, is seen as Christian. Arab oil money finances much of Islam's expansion. The conflict between Israelis and Palestinians, in which the United States and much of the West has supported Israel, is another source of hostility.

However, according to Dr. Woodberry, more Muslims have come to Christ in the last few decades than ever before. The number is still not large, but there are significant movements that should not be publicized. We hear of the growth of underground groups of Muslim background believers (MBB's) scattered across North Africa and especially in Iran. A few decades ago there were almost no Christians in Algeria, now there are at least 60,000, perhaps more, primarily among the Berbers. The growing movement toward contextualization in Muslim evangelization is important. This involves, among other things, the use of theological terminology that makes sense to a Muslim, forms of worship, and leadership selection and training.

Western missionaries will continue to have a role in the Muslim world. Great sensitivity is required, and some areas will be much more open than will others. I know a young American who spent a year with Kurds in northern Iraq. He was very well accepted, and often invited into their homes.

Another recent example is relief work in the areas of Pakistan devastated by the recent earthquakes, done by volunteers of the mission "Frontiers." Clearly, their goal is evangelism, but ministries of compassion may well be the first and essential step. Dr. Woodberry has done research on seven hundred people who have been converted from Islam to Christ. In every one, friendship played an essential role. In half of the cases, some kind of power encounter—a dream, a vision, a healing—also played a role.

New Concepts in Mission
Unreached Peoples
The concept "unreached peoples" was popularized by Ralph Winter at Lausanne in 1974. It is a very useful category, easy to popularize and communicate, but not always easy to define. Its great strength is in recognizing the importance of taking each culture seriously. However at times it may fail to recognize that cultures are constantly changing. Dr. Marvin Mayers, former Dean at Biola University, said that if we wish to reach a certain people group in Guatemala, we must go to two different places. The first is located in a region in the north of that country; the other is in a certain barrio of East Los Angeles! But we may be sure that after a

few years the immigrants to Los Angeles are quite different from their relatives in Guatemala.

The 10/40 Window
A more recent focus of mission interest is the so-called "10/40 window." It is defined as the area that lies between 10 and 40 degrees north of the equator. It includes most of China, India, Thailand, Malaysia, Pakistan, Iran, Arabia, and North Africa. It includes ninety-five percent of the world's people who are out of reach of any meaningful Gospel witness. It is now the focus of prayer and new attempts in mission. However, while the 10/40 window is a useful concept, it must be recognized that the Church has been growing rapidly in China, and that there are new movements growing among Dalits in India. And we must recognize that at least 30% of the unreached people groups are outside of the 10/40 window.

New Patterns in Mission
Partnerships
Three books have been published on the subject of partnerships in mission. They are *Kingdom Partnerships for Synergy in Missions*, edited by William Taylor, *Partners in the Gospel: The Strategic Role of Partnership in World Evangelization*, edited by James H. Kraakevik and Dorsey Welliver, and *Well Connected*, by Phill Butler.

The basic concept is that various groups from different denominations, mission agencies, and/or countries will cooperate in their focus on a particular unreached people group. Each one will bring its particular gifts and areas of expertise. The assumption in the hypothetical example we will cite below is that resident missionaries are not permitted in the process. Personal witness (either by tentmakers or students who have visited specifically for that purpose) is a part of this strategic partnering, along with the witness of other visiting teams, literature, broadcasting, community development, medical work, and Scripture translation. The goal is to bring people to Christ, disciple new believers, and eventually plant the Church.

Ahmed, who lived in a North African country, was seeking the meaning of life and began to listen to a Christian radio program that offered a Bible correspondence course. He wrote, requested the course, and studied it. Then he was put in contact with a Christian worker—a tentmaker—who led him to Christ. Running his shop and caring for his family, Ahmed attended a night Bible course in another town and became part of a growing church fellowship.

In order for all of this to occur in Ahmed's life, five agencies coordinated their efforts over several years. The broadcaster gave his name to the agency that furnished the Bible correspondence course, who in turn referred him to the tentmaking missionary. The 'tentmaker' put Ahmed in contact with Bible teachers, who in turn led him to a group of national believers. None of the agencies could have achieved the desired result alone, by partnering they were used to help start a small church.

Non-Residential Missionaries

The key book on this subject is *The Non-Residential Missionary* (Monrovia, CA: MARC, 1990) by David Garrison. The definition of a "non-residential missionary" is "a full-time professional career foreign missionary who is matched up with a single unevangelized population segment for purposes of concentrating on priorities of initial evangelization and eliminating gaps and duplications with other agencies." The missionary lives outside the target area and, from this non-residential base, networks with all other concerned Christians, local and non-local, to do the following:

1. Do research on the situation of the group, becoming an expert on that people for purposes of evangelization and ministry.

2. Become fluent in the group's primary language.

3. Draw up and help implement a wide range of evangelizing ministry options directed toward that group, advocating its evangelization with other agencies.

4. Report regularly to a home office to monitor progress and receive assistance as needed.

5. Relate to resource networks such as The World Evangelization Database of the Southern Baptist Convention.

6. Relate as part of a global team to other non-residential missionaries assigned to different groups.

Thus, there are three essential characteristics. He or she operates from a non-residential base,

builds networks with all Christians with a similar concern, and takes responsibility for the evangelization of a single, predominately unevangelized population segment. Obviously this kind of mission requires great vision and perseverance. It operates on the theological assumption that God is already at work among that people and that it is His will to bring a number to faith in Christ.

The Prayer Focus

Millions are being mobilized for prayer for the unreached as never before. It is important to note that an important source of the modern missionary movement were the "concerts of prayer" advocated by Jonathan Edwards and others in the seventeenth and eighteenth centuries. They had a powerful influence on William Carey.

The movement seems to be growing stronger on all continents. There are prayer movements in Nepal, India, and Kenya, as well as in the West. I will give some examples. The South Korean churches have established the goal of one hundred thousand people praying daily for North Korea. A crowd of fifty thousand has prayed around the Parliament House in Canberra, Australia. In Rochester, New York, a march for Jesus was reported in the newspaper. It quoted a psychiatrist and member of a Full Gospel Church who said they prayed for a "commitment to fair business practices; liberation for the poor and needy and those trapped in addictions; comfort and shelter for the homeless; productive lives and healthy relationships for prisoners after they are freed from jail; better education, integrity, discipline, and honor in our institutions; the overcoming of violence with compassion; the replacement of murder and death with life;…justice, mercy, and humility in government; unbiased reporting with a desire to know and tell the truth in the press; and, of course, salvation for all."

The scope and holistic nature of that particular prayer walk is impressive and reflects a Kingdom of God understanding of our task.

In summary, we live in a period of great creativity that involves new forms of mission. We have cited only a few. Others, such as marketplace ministries and business development for mission, are also emerging.

Chapter Thirty-Four

The New Churches

Introduction

The Church has changed its forms and even its theological emphases many times throughout history. Acts 15 tells us of the first major change: when the Church was freed from Jewish culture into which it was born, and allowed to move into the Gentile world, where it grew rapidly. This change was not just theological—from "salvation by faith plus the law" to "faith alone"—it was also cultural.

Today we may be entering a similar shift. It appears that the Church is being freed from its traditional Western forms, and beginning to discover new, more indigenous forms of worship, leadership, and church life. This is true in the West as well as the rest of the world. One book to consult on new Western forms of the Church is *Emerging Churches: Creating Christian Community in Postmodern Cultures* by Eddie Gibbs and Ryan K. Bolger.

Sometimes new forms of the Church have been rejected as heretical or schismatic by older bodies. Examples are the churches of the Protestant Reformation, Methodism, and Pentecostalism. At times, the new forms have been heretical: for example, Mormonism, or the Iglesia Ni Christo in the Philippines. At times, heretical churches have returned to theological orthodoxy: for example, the fourth-century Arian churches and the contemporary Worldwide Church of God. At other times, orthodox groups have left the historic faith. Unitarians and some liberal Protestants are examples.

At times, new church forms do not involve new theology, but they use new styles of worship, leadership, structure, and cultural adaptation. Often they are the result of dynamic spiritual movements. Sometimes the old wineskins became incapable of containing the new wine. It is important to note that often some believers confuse "methodological orthodoxy" with "theological orthodoxy," and at times do not seem to know the difference!

In all of these cases, certain issues must be faced. How are the newer groups to be evaluated? How should other Christians relate to them? This is complicated by the fact that often the newer churches are not interested in relating to the traditional denominations. Will it even be possible for mature believers from more traditional groups to work with some of the newer churches and bring a historical perspective that may help them avoid some of the errors of the past? These are all important questions as we enter the twenty-first century.

My thesis is that we are seeing greater changes in the shape of the worldwide Church than at any time at least since the sixteenth century, and perhaps more so. This change is taking place first in Africa, then in Asia and Latin America, then North America. I believe it will come last of all in Europe because of the strong cultural traditions that identify most Western Europeans with certain churches, but often without a living faith.

Some of the older churches still struggle with sixteenth-century issues in working out their relationships. A few years ago, Dr. Jane Dempsey

Douglas, President of the World Alliance of Reformed Churches, was asked about the purpose of conversations between Reformed, Anglican, and Lutheran theologians. She said that the goal was for Christians to be able to take the Lord's Supper together. Her statement reflected different views of ministry and church leadership: Who ordains a person, who should be ordained, and what does ordination mean? For a high Anglican, only a priest ordained by a bishop in the 'apostolic succession' can celebrate the Eucharist, or Lord's Supper. Some Lutherans will take the bread and wine only with other Christians who hold their view of the presence of Christ in the sacrament. Thus, the conversations about celebrating the sacrament together reflected an attempt to overcome different views of the ministry and the presence of Christ in the Eucharist. But that would not be an issue for the great majority of evangelicals today. Most of us would be pleased to sit together with brothers and sisters of different traditions and take the bread and wine together, as long as we all confessed Jesus Christ as Lord and Savior. We would agree that he is genuinely present without attempting to define the nature of his presence. In addition, for most of us, it would not matter much who broke the bread and served the wine.

To be fair, many of these older churches are struggling with major social and economic issues: poverty, political oppression, disparity between rich and poor, and ecology. At the same time, one cannot avoid the impression that some of these same churches show little concern for world evangelization and appear to be weak on Christology and soteriology.

As we have seen earlier, the new "evangelical ecumenism" is task-oriented, seeing world evangelization as its priority. It works off a theological consensus: a high Christology, the authority of Scripture, the necessity of conversion, the importance of the Church, etc. Certainly, Evangelicals need to broaden its concern for social, economic, and ecological issues without losing their focus on evangelization.

Different Forms of Worship and Leadership within Theologically Orthodox Churches
Characteristics

Most theologically orthodox churches that use different forms of worship and leadership, are open to all the gifts of the Holy Spirit. This reflects the positive influence of Pentecostalism, and worldviews that are different from our Western, post-enlightenment understanding of reality. Thus, they are more open to the unusual, miraculous work of God and can generally be classified as "charismatic."

Such churches are power-oriented. Most have arisen in cultures where power is an essential religious category. Most, if not all, traditional religions are focused on power, and power is obviously an important aspect of biblical faith. However, power was generally ignored and even eliminated as a valid category in post-enlightenment Protestantism. At times, that was formalized in theological systems that taught the miraculous gifts had ceased after the apostolic era. Benjamin Breckinridge (B. B.) Warfield, the primary theologian of nineteenth-century Calvinistic orthodoxy, said that God had not performed one miracle since the days of Peter and Paul. Fundamentalist Dispensationalism took the same position. The newer churches reject this view and recognize that the Holy Spirit is still active, often in the crises of daily life. Paul Hiebert's concept of "the excluded middle" is important here.

These new churches normally use different patterns of leadership selection and training. Often they reject traditional Western-type institutions, preferring to train their own leaders in context. Often, as time goes by, their own structures become more institutionalized and seek academic respectability and accreditation. The Assemblies of God institutions are a good example.

Usually such movements are sectarian at the beginning, and consider other churches "dead" or worse. Thus, positive relationships prove to be difficult, but they can be developed over time.

They normally have strong "charismatic," authoritarian leaders. Often a crisis comes when the founding leader is no longer able to continue because of age, death, or perhaps even scandal. There is always the danger, where leaders are not accountable to others, of falling to temptations of greed or sex.

Of course, a major feature is worship that is more contextualized, freer, and more praise-oriented. Original music that speaks more clearly to the concerns of worshippers is often composed and used.

Examples

Pastor Joseph Wongsak established the Hope of Bangkok Church in Thailand. He earned a Ph.D. in economics in Australia, where he became a charismatic Christian. He then returned to Thailand, where he teaches at the University of Bangkok, and established the Church. It holds twenty-four worship services each week in its center and extension centers in Bangkok, and counts several thousand members. By the end of the twentieth century, it had planted 480 churches in Thailand, 6 in Malaysia, and 26 others in fifteen different nations, including the United States.

The movement enjoys good relationships with other "post-denominational" charismatics, but not with most traditional evangelicals. Pastor Wongsak seeks to be "salt and light" in society, and has written books on economics, sociology, and politics. He also writes columns in newspapers and has relationships with political leaders. The movement is remarkable in that it has grown in a Buddhist culture in which traditional churches have grown very slowly.

Dr. Kimuyi, the founder of The Deeper Life Church in Nigeria, was a professor of the theory of mathematics when he became a charismatic Christian. He initiated a Bible study in his home that grew into The Deeper Life Church. While I do not have current statistics, in 1990 it numbered around sixty thousand worshippers in the central church in Lagos, and had planted churches in many areas of Nigeria.

When I worshipped there, I found the service to be very orderly, using traditional church music and English as the main language. Worshipers were arranged in sections like spokes in a wheel, with different language groups in each one. The message was translated for each group. In general, this movement has not enjoyed positive relationships with others in Nigeria, but there are indications that this is beginning to change. Another indigenous movement in Nigeria is the Redeemed Christian church. While more research needs to be done, it is reported that its monthly all-night prayer meeting draws five hundred thousand people. It is planting churches in a number of other countries, including the United States, where it is said to have two hundred congregations.

I have already mentioned the Universal Church of the Kingdom of God (IURD in Portuguese) in Brazil, established in 1977. According to an article published in 1996, it numbered four and a half million members in Brazil with churches in forty other countries. It owned the fifth largest television network in the country and published a weekly newspaper with nearly one million circulation. It also published daily newspapers in several localities and had dozens of radio stations.

One analysis by a sociologist believed that marketing was the key to its growth. There is a great focus on the "money of God," and the church was reported to receive 960 million dollars in offerings annually. The pastors receive some theological training in their local churches, but there is no formal preparation. Each pastor must report the effectiveness of his work each week, showing the number of people in the meetings and the size of the offerings.

There are two inflexible rules: absolute loyalty to Bishop Edir Macedo, the founder and leader, and respect for the "money of God." Pastors who are not productive are dismissed. The message of the church focuses on the help that Jesus brings to solve the problems in our lives. There are many testimonies of healings, finding jobs, and even exorcisms. The church claims that when a person enters it, his or her problems will be solved. The message is, "Stop suffering; in the IURD, a miracle awaits you."

The church has entered politics, and elected six federal congressmen in 1994. It has elected others to state and local offices. Recent polls showed that its prestige had fallen to a very low level. Its theology is orthodox but superficial, and the opinion of other evangelicals in Brazil is mixed.

The Graman Prachin Mandal movement among the Dalits is a rapidly growing movement among the most oppressed people in India. The word *Dalit* in Hindi means "ground-down people." They are also called "untouchables," and it is believed that they were not created by the gods, and are inferior to all other humans and even to animals. They cannot worship in the Hindi temples, because the gods will not accept them. They must perform the most menial tasks, and often women are required to carry human waste in baskets to prepare fertilizer for the fields. Normally their children cannot study in the village schools. It is considered both impossible and undesirable for them to learn. They must accept whatever they can get by begging. In addition, Dalit women are, of course, considered inferior to men.

Philip Prasad, son of a Dalit pastor, established the movement. Through a series of circumstances that can only be considered miraculous, he was able to study in the village school, go on to a boarding high school, to college, and then to an American seminary. After some years of ministry among poor minorities in the United States, he was led to return home and began to preach to his own people. When asked if this Jesus was a foreign god, he began to examine his own culture. He noted that in Hindu thought, an Avatar was a god who became incarnate for a specific purpose, always among the upper castes. As he read Luke chapter 4 in the Hindi New Testament, he noted that the text said that Jesus came to "the Dalits." He began to preach that Jesus was the "Dalit Avatar," the God who had become incarnate as one of them, the oppressed Dalits. This radically changed the perception of who Jesus was and is. The people refer to themselves as "Dalit Avataris," followers of the Dalit Avatar, Jesus Christ. They do not use the normal Hindi term for church: rather, they call it a mandal (a

circle), which implies a protected place where the people can gather safely. The other two terms in the name of the group are *graman* (rural) and *prachin* (elder), to refer to their locale and system of government.

Since men could not minister to women in the Dalit culture, Philip began to appoint "pastor couples" as pastors. After a few months of training, each couple serves twelve village congregations each week, traveling on bicycles to visit them. They follow a prescribed liturgy and teaching. Because traditionally no one would accept anything from a Dalit, the people are taught that an essential part of the new life is to give an offering to God through the church, no matter how small.

They have contextualized worship in many ways, among them music and the marriage ceremony. Believing that inner transformation should lead to social change, there is a strong focus on education for every child, girls as well as boys. Many go on to secondary school and even university. In addition, half of the elders are women. While the terminology used is often different from the traditional churches in India, the statement of faith follows historic Christianity.

Since its beginning in 1984, over one and a half million people have been baptized, with 125 thousand added each year. Normally it takes five years to form a new presbytery that will number several thousand believers in a number of pastoral circuits. Presbyterians in the United States furnish twenty-five thousand dollars per year for five years to finance a new presbytery, and after that, it is self-supporting. Funds from the United States are also being used to build schools and other training centers. However, the leaders insist that the movement will continue to grow, albeit more slowly, without subsidies from outside.

We are becoming aware of other rapidly growing movements among Dalits in India, but research is lacking.

Some of these groups may be described as "insider movements." This term is increasingly being used to refer to movements of people who come to Christ but do not leave their traditional cultures. In some Muslim contexts, they call themselves "followers of Isa" (Jesus, in the Koran) and continue to worship Islamic-style, affirming Isa as Messiah in their prayers. This may be a manifestation of the shift from Western to non-Western models of the Church, as significant as the shift from the Jewish to Gentile church in the first century.

Culturally African Churches

These churches merit an entire book since they seem to be the most rapidly growing segment of the Church in Africa.

Characteristics and Examples

They affirm African culture in worship and leadership to a much greater degree than the mission-organized churches, and include much more use of African music and dancing in worship. Often their adherents use specific dress than identifies them as church members. They often include traditional African religious practices to different degrees. At times that includes sacrifices. Some church members adopt traditional African cultural practices such as polygamy.

Examples are the Zionist Church in South Africa and the Kimbanguist Church in Congo and adjacent countries. This family of churches, divided into at least six thousand different "denominations," probably has as many adherents as all other churches in Africa combined.

Newly Contextualized Churches

Many of these newly contextualized churches continue to be a part of traditional denominations but are post-denominational in ethos. Others have left their denominations, still others have always been independent.

Characteristics

Characteristics of these churches include an emphasis on praise music, casual dress, and a strong focus on prayer and expectancy. Sermons are longer, with a focus on teaching. (No twenty-minute homilies!) They use contemporary language and affirm all of the gifts. Some are very holistic in their ministries, with programs to care for the poor and marginalized. Often those who seem to be the rejects of society find a place in them.

Examples

The Congregational Church of Bento Ribeiro in Rio de Janeiro, Brazil grew from twenty members to thirty-five hundred in twenty years, and now has around twenty-one hundred adherents. During this period, it has planted twenty other churches and twenty-nine unorganized congregations that will become churches. It trains and sends missionaries to other parts of Brazil. Both senior pastors had successful careers—one as an officer in the Brazilian Air Force, and the other as an architect—before entering the ministry. The church has also established two schools for poor children and one house for men and one for women who are escaping from drug addiction.

The congregation is part of the Congregational Churches of Brazil, established when a Scottish physician, Robert Kalley, arrived there in 1855. It is a very conservative denomination and has not grown much. When Pastor Amaury, the former Air Force officer, became its pastor and initiated a new style of worship and outreach, other church leaders opposed him.

When I preached there, several aspects of the church impressed me. First, the large sanctuary was still unfinished: rough concrete risers, no walls, and a roof that did not extend over the entire congregation. Apparently, the leaders felt the priority was to continue their outreach ministries before finishing the building. Secondly, when people were invited up for prayer, a large number came and the pastors prayed for them. Obviously, they believe in prayer and give it priority. Thirdly, there was a sense of joy and vitality in worship. Sensing that joy, neighbors who were not believers began to come.

I have already described Las Acacias Church in Caracas, Venezuela, similar in many ways to the Bento Ribeiro Church.

Obviously one characteristic of all of these new churches is the quality of their leadership. In some cases, the leaders have formal theological training; in some, they came from professional life into ministry with no formal theological education. All of the leaders are apparently men of vision that goes beyond that of most of their contemporaries. Perhaps they would suggest that Westerners consider a different method of choosing and training leadership for the church.

Heretical Movements

Some groups that clearly fall outside the definition of historic Christian faith have grown rapidly. We need to look at their characteristics and perhaps learn from them.

Characteristics

Heretical movements usually exhibit a strong sense of community, more so than the surrounding society. They often feel isolated from the dominant society, and their primary identity is as a member of the group. Often they have a strong sense of social concern for their own people, but not for those outside. High commitment, strong discipline, and stewardship are required. Expectations of commitment are high. They usually emphasize certain aspects of the historic faith while neglecting, distorting, or rejecting others. Often a characteristic of a heresy is the tendency to overemphasize one or more aspects of the faith while neglecting others that we consider essential.

Often they adhere to some authority along with the Bible (for example, the Book of Mormon), a distorted translation of Scripture (as do the Jehovah's Witnesses), or a prophet who has given an authoritative interpretation of Scripture.

Examples

Among the examples of heretical movements are Mormons (the Church of Jesus Christ of Latter Day Saints), Jehovah's Witnesses (which originated in the United States), and the Iglesia Ni Christo in the Philippines. Mormons may be seen as an over-contextualization of Biblical faith in the United States, with Native Americans as the older chosen people and Mormons as the new People of God, with their own exodus (the

journey to Utah, the new Promised Land) and a new Moses (Brigham Young).

The Iglesia Ni Christo in the Philippines was established by a leader who had participated in a number of Protestant mission churches, rejected them, and formed his own movement. The group holds to an Arian Christology. That is, it teaches that Jesus was more than man, but less than God—a figure halfway in between. They construct elaborate buildings, all with the same architecture, and adherents are expected to be highly committed. Like the Universal Church of the Kingdom of God and the Mormons, this group often seeks political power.

Criteria for Evaluation

With so many new forms of the Church evolving today, we need to think about criteria with which to evaluate them. Most will agree that church structure or worship styles are not the most important criteria unless they clearly violate biblical norms. I suggest we all think carefully about this issue.

The first essential criterion must be the authority of Scripture, free to interpret itself, unfettered by any extra-biblical source or tradition.

Christology is of equal importance. Who is Jesus Christ? What did he accomplish in the cross and resurrection?

Soteriology is a third issue. How do we men and women receive the benefits of the work of Jesus Christ? Is the message of salvation by grace alone, received by faith, clear?

The importance of the Church—the worshipping, witnessing, serving community—is also essential. It may assume different forms, but the community of believers is essential.

The role of the Holy Spirit and the freedom of every believer to seek to be led by the Spirit, and not subject to authoritarian control, are also essential.

You may want to add to or modify these criteria. As we see a multiplicity of new forms of the Church emerge in our era, it will become more and more important to follow the example of Barnabas. When he went to Antioch and "saw what the grace of God had done in the gentile church, he was glad and encouraged them to remain true to the Lord with all their hearts," because "he was a good man and full of the Holy Spirit."

Chapter Thirty-Five

Issues for the Future:
Urbanization and the Poor

Devotional

As we conclude this survey of the Christian missionary movement, I want to begin with the words of the great hymn by Isaac Watts, "When I survey the Wondrous Cross." It is important to note that he also wrote the hymn, "Jesus shall reign wher'er the sun does his successive journeys run," three-fourths of a century before Carey sailed. An amazing vision! But I want to read the first and last verses of "When I Survey the Wondrous Cross." It has been rightly called the greatest hymn in the English language.

When I survey the wondrous cross on which the Prince of glory died,

My richest gain I count but loss, and pour contempt on all my pride.

Were the whole realm of nature mine, that were a present far too small,

Love so amazing, so divine demands my soul, my life, my all.

Let us pray together:

Father, we are mindful of the cross. We want to come back to that cross over and over again, and all that the incarnation, the cross, and the resurrection mean to us, and to humankind—how they point to your agenda for history. We pray that all of our study, our reading, lectures, conversations, thinking, might point us clearly toward your agenda for history. That people of every race, tribe, culture, and language might come to know, worship, love, and serve the One

who died on the cross for our sins, who rose from the dead to conquer death and evil and give us new life. We thank you for the privilege of being your people, and being called to participate in your mission throughout history and throughout the world. We pray in the name that is above every name, Jesus Christ our Lord. Amen.

Introduction

In this last chapter, I want to examine some of the most important issues we will face in the coming decades. The first is urbanization. The growth of cities around the world, but especially in Asia, Africa, and Latin America, is simply staggering. But culture change in the urban centers is even more striking. Some have said that by 2006 the middle class would live mainly in urban, rather than rural areas, and that while languages would differ between countries, the inhabitants of the cities would otherwise resemble each other. The differences between the inhabitants of the city and the countryside in a given nation are predicted to be greater than the differences between city dwellers of different nations. Perhaps this is an overstatement, but it gives us food for thought. A World Vision publication, "Together," estimated that by the year 2000, one-fourth of the world's population would live in squatter settlements in the cities of Asia, Africa, and Latin America.

Thus I believe the greatest missionary challenge for the Church in the coming decades will be the growing cities on every continent, where we see almost obscene affluence alongside desperate poverty. Spiritual, social, economic, and political issues are all involved. Certainly the People of God are called to express compassion and work for change in this world even as we proclaim the Good News of eternal life.

The Growth of the Cities

Examples

I will give only a few illustrations, but there are many more. São Paulo, Brazil, was just approaching a population of three million when I arrived there in 1956. Today the entire metropolitan area has a population of over twenty million. Mexico City was recently increasing its population by nine hundred thousand each year, and today numbers over thirty million.

Lagos, Nigeria, had about six hundred thousand people thirty-five years ago. Today we cannot be sure of its population, but it probably approaches ten million. We could add examples of other cities in Asia and Africa, but the point is clear. The world is rapidly urbanizing. In some nations, twenty-five percent of the entire population lives in the capital. That is true of Argentina and South Korea. Today half of the world's people live in burgeoning urban areas, and most of the growing cities are in Asia, Africa, and Latin America.

Projection to 2025

According to National Geographic, by the year 2025 non-Western cities will hold four billion people. Half of them will be desperately poor. Today there are at least ten cities in the world with more than ten million people each. In most situations, the churches are unprepared for these challenges.

Roger Greenway suggested that, at the beginning of the twentieth century, thirteen percent of the world's population lived in cities, and eighty-seven percent lived in small-town or rural settings. Today that thirteen percent has grown to at least fifty percent. Some put it higher, but again there is some variation in defining cities. We remember the great population growth during the twentieth century, and must recognize that this growth will probably continue.

Some of the reasons for such growth are economic and cultural. In many countries, a push-pull effect takes people to the cities. The push consists of intolerable conditions in the countryside: less and less arable land and unwise agricultural policies designed to keep food prices down for city dwellers, making it hard for farmers to make a living. In Latin America, these problems are coupled with unjust patterns of land tenure, with large land holdings in the hands of a few people who have not used the land well. Drought and growing populations among the rural poor are additional factors. The Sahara is advancing every year across Africa. More and more land is being taken out of production, partly through the ravages of nature, and partly through deforestation and other unwise use of land. Thus, there are demographic, natural, political, economic, and social forces pushing people away from the countryside to the cities.

The "pull" effect is the lure of the city. The person who lives in the country sees a slick paper magazine, listens to the transistor radio, or now maybe has TV. He sees or hears of a glamorous life portrayed there that looks very exciting and much better than his life in the country. So, families move to the city. They go seeking jobs and better opportunities for the next generation. At their best, the cities do offer better education, health care, and economic possibilities. Nevertheless, what they find there is usually very different from their hopes. Most end up in the growing slums—shantytowns ringing major cities. This is especially true in Africa, Asia, and Latin America. However, we also see it in the Western world, in North America—not exactly in the same configuration, but it exists. This is one issue we must deal with.

Characteristics

What are some of the characteristics of cities?

First, most cities are multi-ethnic and include people speaking many different languages. It is almost impossible to keep up with the statistics, but inhabitants of Los Angeles and London probably speak 150 different languages.

São Paulo counts over 100 different languages. Indonesia has at least 586 languages spoken in the country, and at least one-fourth or one-fifth of those languages are probably spoken in Jakarta.

Seoul and Tokyo are exceptions to some degree, since both nations speak only one language. However, with increasing immigration (often illegal) of other Asians arriving to seek jobs in those prosperous economies, they, too, are becoming more multi-ethnic. People in Singapore speak a number of varieties of Chinese along with other Asian languages and English, but it is not as diverse as Jakarta. McGavran said that there are over sixteen hundred different languages spoken in India. How many of them are spoken in Calcutta or Mumbai (Bombay)?

We cannot say how many languages are used in Lagos or Nairobi. It must be a large number. I visited a church in Lagos in 1986 where the worship service was in English even though the congregation was totally Nigerian. The congregation was divided into sections where the message was translated into seven different Nigerian languages plus French.

The issue of linguistic diversity constitutes a great challenge to effective evangelization. We are speaking of mutually unintelligible languages. They may be related, like German and Dutch, or Spanish and Portuguese, but a person who speaks one cannot understand the other.

The issue is not only language; it is language and culture. This means that we have to look not just at a geographical map of a country or a city, but also at a sociological map. We all recognize that the homogeneous unit idea is dangerous. It can be used as a sanction for racism or ethnocentrism. Yet it is a useful tool as we think about the work of Jesus Christ. As we think about the Gospel, we see two poles here. At one pole, we see the unity of the body of Christ. We are all one in Christ, and we strive to find ways to express that. At the other extreme, we must respect the culture from which a person comes. If I do not respect your culture when I try to communicate the Gospel to you, implicitly I am saying that you must become like me culturally in order to become an authentic Christian. This is dehumanizing. If we cut these two poles apart either way, we distort the Gospel.

The recognition of the validity of culture is not the ultimate goal. It is a penultimate principle. The unity of the body of Christ is the ultimate. I am not putting the two on the same level. But even as we strive to manifest our unity in the Body of Christ, we must continue to give value to each culture. That is one of the lessons of Pentecost.

Let's look at this from the standpoint of strategy. I had a student who came from Hong Kong to do a Ph. D. at UCLA. He became a Christian in a Chinese church in Southern California. He was at home with the people of that church. They were his kind of people; they spoke his language. He could relate to them. I asked him, "Do you think you would have become a Christian in an Anglo church?" "Probably not," he replied. This principle is important as we think of Iranians, Thai, Burmese, Arabs, and Egyptians.

Even the forms of Spanish spoken in Nicaragua and El Salvador, Puerto Rico and Mexico are different from each other. Therefore, it is an important principle to recognize the need to hear the Gospel in terms that are meaningful linguistically and culturally.

If we go to an area of Los Angeles that is heavily Hispanic, the billboards are not in English, and they shouldn't be. As we attempt to communicate the Good News of Jesus should we not be just as sophisticated (or more so) as those who are trying to sell beer or cosmetics?

Another characteristic of the major cities is the apparent anonymity and solitude, the loneliness in the midst of the crowds. People can feel very isolated in the middle of a huge city. Often we feel far more alone in the middle of a huge mass of people than in a small village or town. Christian community is the answer the Gospel brings to that condition. However, we do not always communicate or live out that answer very well.

Along with the apparent anonymity and solitude, we discover that in most cities there are neighborhood networks. Many cities can be broken down into neighborhoods. Dr Ray Bakke suggests that we need to exegete the city. There are networks of remarkable homogeneity in many cases. For example, there are areas in Los Angeles with large concentrations of people from El Salvador or Nicaragua. Los Angeles counts around eighty thousand people from these two countries.

We could multiply examples of this. Los Angeles is said to be the second largest city of El Salvadorans, Mexicans, Guatemalans, and Filipinos in the world.

When talking about Guatemalans, we have to ask, what kind of Guatemalans? Are they Ladinos, whose first language is Spanish? Or are they indigenous groups, who speak a number of Mayan languages? We need to do this kind of analysis. This is both a challenge and an opportunity for the Church.

It is important to recognize that when people move to cities they are usually more open to change. In the previous environment, usually a small town or village, people were normally part of a rather tight network of relationships. That network of relationships, to a significant degree, dictates the person's identity making it very difficult for him to change religion. In the city, he or she is freed from the old network. At the same time, the need for new networks gives the Church an opportunity to share the Good News and invite the person into a Christian community. Often the Church will find opportunities to minister to other needs of urban newcomers.

I do not mean to idealize the Korean church, but it is a rather amazing success story. Our Korean brothers and sisters tell me that fifty to seventy-five percent of the Koreans in the United States now are professing Christians, while only about twenty-five percent are professing Christians in Korea. This either indicates that all the Korean Christians are immigrating from Korea—which is not true—or it indicates that large numbers of Koreans are finding the Korean church an entry point into North American society, a point at which they hear the Gospel and discover community. Many respond.

Another situation that may be analogous occurs among the Hispanic population. It is said that fifteen percent or more of the Hispanic immigrants in the United States are Pentecostals. That indicates that the Hispanic Pentecostal churches are functioning in some respects like the Korean churches.

A fourth aspect of life in the large city is the strong drive toward materialism and secularism. Simply stated, materialism means we want all the things, the gadgets, which our society provides. Television sets and VCRs or CD players are among them.

A recent article in the Los Angeles Times told about Cambodian refugees who were extremely disoriented in the United States. However, in the midst of their tragic disorientation, they constantly watched television and thus were bombarded with American values that disoriented them even more. It is hard for a Westerner to understand fully what impact American television had on them. The feeling thrown at viewers from every quarter of contemporary life is that if we have enough gadgets, we will be happy and fulfilled people. This is obviously not true, but there is a strong drive to acquire these gadgets, even though they may be very destructive of family life.

In some cases, upward social mobility takes place. Some immigrant families put a very high stress on education. Their children work very hard and go to university and graduate school to end up in well-paying professions. If they come from Christian families, there is danger that they will not feel at home in the church of their parents.

Secularism is the worldview that says the only things that count, or the only things that are real, are those that you can weigh and measure and touch. It is the view that if God exists, he is not relevant to our lives. So a secular person organizes his or her life as if God did not exist and there is nothing beyond this life. Even relationships are temporary. We are seeing the bankruptcy of that worldview today.

The paradox is that we are seeing a rapid growth of interest in the occult in urban societies around the world, including very secularized societies, in Europe and the United States. Santeria, similar to Brazilian spiritism or Haitian voodoo, is common in southern California. The New Age movement shows interest in the occult. An amusing illustration came from Paris recently. In one of the most secularized cities in the world, there was such an interest in astrology that some enterprising people began to use the computer to cast horoscopes. Think of the irony but also the spiritual hunger that indicates.

What does this tell us? It shows the desire to reach out beyond things we can weigh, measure, touch, and feel. It is not a very satisfactory reaching out, but nevertheless it indicates something. The New Age movement that we see in the United States, especially on the West coast, also is an indicator of this interest. People dabbling in the New Age movement and the occult are now spending millions of dollars.

For the poor in the cities, there is a struggle just to survive. Between 1955 and 1960, Maria Carolina de Jesus, a woman living in a slum in São Paulo, kept a diary. She scribbled on scraps of cardboard and paper in which she described her struggle for survival. It was translated into English and published under the title *Child of the Dark: the Diary of Carolina Maria de Jesus.* But in Portuguese, the title is *Quarto de Despejo,* which means "Garbage Room." That described how she had to live, just to survive.

It is not uncommon for people to live off the garbage of others. In large cities, someone who is fortunate enough to have a job may have to get up at four o'clock in the morning to catch a bus and travel an hour one way, then catch another bus and go half an hour another way, to get to work at seven or eight o'clock. Then the same route is repeated at the end of the day. Long hours of transportation are often required to keep a job that barely pays enough to survive, if that. Many people live in this situation. All indications are that the numbers of those who live in such situations will grow.

The breakdown of the family is often another consequence of urbanization. Absent parents, both of whom must work, means inadequate care for the children, who are often left on the streets. The use of drugs and alcohol makes the situation worse. In Northeast Brazil, when families migrate from the hinterland to the cities and the men fail to find work there, they often migrate to the more prosperous south, hoping to find jobs there, promising to send for their families when it becomes possible. All too often, they fail to do so, leaving abandoned women and children to fend for themselves. The result is growing prostitution and abandoned children.

How Does the Gospel Address the Needs of This Urbanized Population?

Obviously we can barely begin to answer the question of how the Gospel can address the needs of this urbanized population. However, we should ask what aspects of the Gospel are most apt to meet the felt needs of new immigrants to the city. The preaching of the Gospel always must be related to the needs of the people. We all agree that the greatest need is to come to faith in Christ. However, there are other needs as well that can be addressed in our ministries. So it is legitimate to ask, what are some of the aspects of the Gospel that relate to the needs of urban dwellers?

This principle is clear. The communication of the Gospel must be in a language the people can understand, and this must include respect for each culture as well as language.

What are some of the needs of people who have recently arrived in the cities that the church might address? Among them are the needs for community, for jobs, safety, legal help, medical care, nutrition, and, in the United States, English studies. Are these concerns of the Gospel? I believe they are, because they can be works of compassion that affect the well-being of people in need. Such ministries would be analogous to Christian ministries to victims of earthquakes or famines, for example.

The Church can never do everything. It must think through its priorities in the light of its understanding of the Gospel and its mission. However, the Church can do many things. At times, it can provide services such as teaching English or tutoring children, for example. On the other hand, it may act as a broker, and point people toward the services they need. In some cities in Latin America, churches have banded together to pressure city officials to provide education and healthcare in slum areas. In addition, they have continued to work together to train lay leaders and plant new churches among the urban immigrants. Such activities can become a strong witness to the reality of Jesus Christ and the Gospel. Robert Linthicum, former director of Urban Advance for World Vision, endorsed this kind of cooperation. He wrote:

> No church by itself can successfully mount a ministry to its community. If it does, that ministry will be effective only as long as the church chooses to make it a high priority and contributes its volunteers and money to the project. Unless the community feels a sense of ownership for that ministry and responsibility for it, the ministry will ultimately be ineffective.

Many people come to the city from various non-Christian religions. Often they want to be in touch with God, but do not know how to express that desire. They might not define this yearning in Christian terms yet. However, we would all agree that they need salvation.

One of the questions is how we begin. Where do you get a handle on some of these needs?

Jesus in the synagogue at Nazareth, quoting an ancient messianic passage from Isaiah, said, "The Spirit of the Lord is upon me, because he has chosen me to bring good news to the poor." (Luke 4:18a GNT) There is more than one kind of good news. Obviously, the ultimate Good News is the coming of the Messiah, the forgiveness of sins and salvation. There are other aspects of the Good News that may point to the greatest Good News. We must take all of that passage literally. Some have spiritualized it and understood it to mean only salvation from sin and reconciliation with God. I believe that is the primary, but not the only, meaning. Others have gone to the opposite extreme, believing it refers only to social and economic issues. Why not both? The Old Testament prophets included both aspects. I believe Jesus did, too.

The Gospel of John gives us a helpful theological paradigm. The miracles of Jesus, giving bread to the hungry, opening the eyes of the blind, turning the water into wine, were all called "signs." They were signs pointing to the greater work that Jesus came to do, the greater gift he came to give. Thus, a medical clinic or an English class might be signs pointing to the greater gift of salvation. The ministry of compassion is important and valid in itself, but it can also have the even greater function of a sign pointing to the greatest gift of all.

Jesus healed ten lepers, but only one returned to say thank you. I have always been grateful the story was in the gospels. I do not like it; I wish all ten had come back. It is important to note that the one who returned was a Samaritan. What were the gospel writers trying to tell us there? I believe they are saying that is still valid to heal the ten lepers even if nine, tragically, do not receive the greater gift.

We can look at the example of the Good Samaritan. When he found that person on the road, he did not ask about his spiritual, ethnic, or social status. He just helped him. Could that be a model for us? One of the comments made by non-Christians about early followers of Christ was that they loved each other and cared for others. That is a good model for us.

I want to make it clear that the proclamation of the Gospel of grace, forgiveness, and personal transformation must always be the central task, whether in the city or elsewhere. However, sharing the Gospel will involve going to where the people are, not simply waiting for them to come to our churches.

Some Models of Urban Churches

I hope we will all become students of the urban scene, no matter where we are called to serve. God is raising up new models of the Church today, especially in the urban areas.

I worship in a traditional middle class church and I enjoy it. I am thankful to worship there. However, I do not believe that is the only valid model. No doubt we need other forms of the Church in south central Los Angeles, in the ghetto and poor neighborhoods. I believe we are entering a period of history when we will see the Holy Spirit raise up a variety of new models of the Church, doing for our generation and our cities today what God used Wesley to do in eighteenth-century England.

A church that combines a large worshipping congregation with many small groups is one urban church model that combines both celebration and community. Worshippers are part of something great, with a sense of grandeur. At the same time, they are members of small groups where there is a sense of intimacy, fellowship, and growing discipleship. These house groups also become means of outreach and evangelism for neighbors who might be hesitant to enter a church but will respond to an invitation to a home. A classic example of this "cathedral plus small groups" model is the Full Gospel Central Church in Seoul, Korea. It is reported to have 750 thousand members and 350 thousand in attendance in the various services on a Sunday. It has between forty and fifty thousand small groups that meet weekly.

We see similar churches on a smaller scale in many parts of the world. I do not believe we can ever build solid Christian discipleship based on worship celebration and strong preaching alone, no matter how strong the preaching is or how exciting the worship. In smaller groups where people meet with their brothers and sisters in Christ, pray together, pray for each other, and challenge and stimulate each other, growth in discipleship comes. This is an important lesson from history.

Note that this model meets two needs of urbanized people: the desire to identify with a movement that seems larger than life, and conversely, the need for intimacy and community.

Another model, the house church, is spreading in the United States and elsewhere. A few years ago, I was taken to preach in a house church in Jakarta, Indonesia. There were about two hundred

people there, mainly Chinese Indonesians from the neighborhood. All they had to do was walk down the block to get there. They did not have to take two buses to get to a big church downtown where they felt strange. They seemed to be a homogenous group, led by a layman. Worship was informal, but it was very real. That church was one of half a dozen similar house churches in the city. It had six or seven different branches and it was growing.

It was an effective model, but of course we must ask about certain issues it will face as it continues. The most important is the question about the selection and training of leadership. In addition, there is the relation of the various churches to each other. Movements that begin as informal fellowships inevitably begin to establish some structures or they tend to disappear. That was the fate of a "no-church church" in Japan some decades ago. The movement will need to form structures that enable it to continue to expand without stifling that growth. The question of deeper nurture is another that needs to be addressed.

A third model has been used in Acapulco, Mexico, by a group of missionaries. They formed many small Bible study groups. After several were formed and a number of people came to Christ, a church was established out of them. However, the small groups were continued and they became the best way of entering the church.

Even for those of us who were raised in the Church, it is often a difficult experience to go to a church where we are strangers. It is easy to feel isolated. Think how hard it must be for a nonbeliever to go to a church where he or she feels like an outsider and does not understand much of the music and terminology. Think how much harder it must be for someone of a culture different from that of the majority. We need to find ways of lowering the barriers. Small groups with evangelistic Bible studies in homes are a good way of doing so. It is not very hard to go to somebody's home. It is ten times as difficult to go to a church, especially if that church is perceived as belonging to another religion, another people, or another class.

Mathari Valley is a densely populated slum of Nairobi, with a population estimated at one hundred thousand. Men, women, and whole families come from rural areas seeking work in the city, and live in squalor in the valley. One church had its buildings constructed just above the valley, on its edge. Here I found a large sanctuary for worship and facilities for classes teaching various skills, such as sewing, to help newcomers find employment. It seemed to be effective.

Another church was pastored by a Presbyterian who had begun work there as a layman, then attended seminary and remained as a pastor. He had established four congregations with a membership of fifteen hundred. He wrote, "When people come to urban areas they are really quite lost. They need a support system to help them adjust to urban life. It's difficult for them to establish relationships and to build new networks like the ones they knew back in their villages. That is where the church plays such an important role."

Then he told how newly arriving Christians came to his church in Mathari Valley with letters from their village pastors, and how the parish helped the newcomers find housing and jobs, welcome them with love into the fellowship, and make the painful transition less terrifying.

Viv Grigg and others are advocating the formation of communities of believers who live in an incarnational ministry among the poor. It is a growing movement that requires great sacrifice similar to some of the best of the Roman Catholic orders. I am convinced that God will call more Protestants to imitate the early Franciscans and live among the poor on a subsistence level in order to incarnate the Gospel. It may involve a call to be single for part or all of one's life in order to do so, or it may involve a call to some couples to forego having children for a time in order to minister in hard places. We must consider those kinds of choices if we are going to take seriously the mission of the cities.

Other Issues

There are a number of other issues that the Christian mission must confront in the new century, and I will only mention some of the most important.

The Decline into Nominalism and Loss of Vitality

Often the vitality of the first generation of believers is lost within a few decades. That is one of the great dilemmas of Christian history. The question of how to maintain or bring revitalization is paramount. It is certain that ongoing, more effective discipleship and better leadership are part of the solution.

The Relationship between Evangelism and Social Concerns

The relationship between evangelism and social concerns is a second issue. While I believe that evangelism must always be the primary focus of Christian mission, we know that in the purpose of God, the Gospel is designed to transform society. A biblical understanding of the Kingdom of God, emphasized by Arthur Glasser, will help us maintain the proper relationship between the two.

Here we are called to focus especially on the poor and marginalized. There are two reasons for this. Clearly, the Old Testament prophets constantly called the ancient people of God to care for the poor, the widow, the orphan, and the victims of injustice. They are close to God's heart. Moreover, Jesus himself went out of his way to seek out the leper and the beggar. The second reason is that often throughout history, the poor have been most responsive to the Good News that they are created in the image of God and called to become his sons and daughters through Jesus Christ!

Children at risk, street children, abandoned children, or runaways because of abuse must become a high priority for the Church. Usually the result of poverty, drug and alcohol abuse, and prostitution, they are abused in unspeakable ways. In addition, few if any government agencies are helping them.

The victims of HIV/AIDS are a related need. We can scarcely comprehend the magnitude of the disaster. It calls for both more faithful Christian discipleship concerning sexual practices, and compassionate care for the victims.

Theological Breakthroughs for Today

One thesis of this course is that theological break-throughs, or rediscoveries, have often contributed to or motivated new advances in mission. I am going to conclude with three that I believe are of great importance.

A Rediscovery of the Biblical Understanding of the Kingdom Of God

Jesus spoke constantly of the Kingdom. He told us to "seek first the Kingdom." Yet the Kingdom of God is curiously absent from the message of most churches, especially in the evangelical tradi-tion. The reason may lie in the struggle between fundamentalists and liberals beginning at the end of the nineteenth century. While the liberal "so-cial gospel" movement tended to secularize the Kingdom and identify it with an ideal human society in this world, changed by the values of the Gospel, fundamentalist dispensationalism pushed it safely into the future after the return of Christ, making it irrelevant to this life. Both re-duced the Kingdom to less than its biblical reality and reduced its power for us.

Two scholars who have helped the Church re-cover the understanding of the Kingdom were George E. Ladd, a New Testament scholar at Fuller, and John Bright, an Old Testament spe-cialist. Dr. Arthur Glasser focused his theology of mission around this concept.

The biblical concept of the Kingdom helps our understanding and practice of mission in a num-ber of ways. First, it reminds us that to be a fol-lower of Jesus is to be a citizen of the Kingdom, and that should shape our values and priorities in life. It brings us to a lifelong journey of discovery and obedience that takes us far beyond our con-cern for personal salvation, the free gift of God, to a life of joyful response to his grace. Secondly, because the Kingdom has entered history in Je-sus Christ, he and his power are available to his people in their lives and ministries. He is not an absent Lord! Thirdly, as citizens of the Kingdom, we not only seek to live according to its values in our personal lives but we want our societies to express its values. This will enable us to overcome the unbiblical dichotomy between evangelism and social reform.

The "Excluded Middle"

A second theological breakthrough was termed the "excluded middle" by Paul Hiebert. It is clearly related to the concept of the coming of the Kingdom of God in power and to the em-phasis on the continuing work of the Holy Spirit in Pentecostalism.

In an oversimplification of Hiebert's model, we divide life into three tiers of concern. At the top are the ultimate questions: the meaning and pur-pose of life. Western theology has often focused there. Those questions have been important in the spiritual journeys of many of us. The third tier has to do with technology: educational, medical, agricultural, etc. The modern missionary move-ment often introduced such western technologies to other cultures, to their great benefit.

The middle zone focuses on the daily crises of life, especially in traditional cultures. The issues here often have to do with survival. Illness: will I be well enough to work and support my family? Weather: will the rains come so I can plant the crops? Fertility: will my wife have sons to care for us in our old age, and will my flocks and herds re-produce? It is important to note that most or per-haps all of the biblical miracles focused on such issues of survival. However, traditional Western theology and mission has often ignored such questions. One reason for the growth of Pente-costalism is the conviction that God, through the Holy Spirit, is active in aiding us in such daily crises. Expectant prayer is an essential aspect of the Christian faith and life.

It is important to recognize that we do not seek to manipulate God. However, we do believe he still acts in our lives for his glory and for our welfare. This does not mean a "health, wealth, and prosper-ity gospel" that exempts us from pain and suffering. It might mean the opposite. Corrie Ten Boom was a Dutch woman whose family was sent to a Nazi concentration camp during World War II because they had hidden Jews. Even though she was the only family member to survive, she gave testimony to the reality and protection of God. In the horror of that camp, she was miraculously preserved. She gave testimony to that reality all over the world after the war. She is a wonderful illustration of this reality: Faithfulness will often bring suffering, but God is with us, and sometimes delivers us in the midst of the suffering.

The "excluded middle" concept means that God continues to be alive and active in human history, and in the lives of His people.

The Gifts of Ministry for Every Believer

The third important breakthrough represents an important discovery in our study of history. It is the conviction expressed in Acts 2: "I will pour out my Spirit on all people." (Acts 2:17 NIV) Old, young, men, women, even slaves! Every believer is gifted for ministry, and the primary task of leaders is to encourage each one in the employment of his or her gifts for the mission of Christ and the glory of God. That discovery has always been a major characteristic of renewal movements.

Conversely, when the Church encourages every believer to use his or her gifts in ministry, it can become a stimulus to renewal.

The People of God will always make the greatest impact on the world when the Church recognizes and affirms this reality.

We have examined nearly two thousand years of the history of Christian mission. We have seen defeats and triumphs, weakness and strength, faithfulness and failure. We have seen the lives of many heroic men and women, but we know there are an uncounted number of others, equally faithful, whose names will never appear in the history books.

I believe we have now entered the most creative and productive period in the history of the missionary movement. The needs and challenges are great. But so are the opportunities. Above all, we continue to follow the same Lord who goes before us. As Carey said, we only dare attempt great things for God because first, we expect great things from God!

Index

CPSIA information can be obtained
at www.ICGtesting.com
Printed in the USA
LVOW03s0521210118
563323LV00005B/47/P